The Wall Street Journal Special Edition
of
ECONOMICS

The Wall Street Journal is not a typical supplement to a textbook. However, it contains important information about markets and the global economy—including key statistical reports that appear regularly and predictably.

A student using *The Wall Street Journal* in conjunction with this textbook acquires a surprisingly quick and firm comprehension of the ups and downs of the American business economy in a systematic, pleasing, and nontechnical manner. The macroeconomy becomes real, not abstract. The real-life aspect of the data and applications goes a long way in supporting theoretical arguments and a student's motivation to learn them. Applications to microeconomics can be found almost daily in insightfully written articles about consumers, firms, and regulators.

Irwin and *The Wall Street Journal* have teamed up to offer an extremely useful, interesting, and timely tool for learning about the American and global economies. While each of you will have instructors that use information from *The Wall Street Journal* differently, we challenge you to discover for yourself the power and effectiveness of maintaining your own economic literacy.

How the Statistical Series Are Presented in
The Wall Street Journal

The Wall Street Journal is divided into three sections: a first section on general business news, a second section on marketing (called MarketPlace), and a third section on the financial markets (called Money & Investing). Regular updates of the monthly and quarterly statistical indicators usually appear in summary form in the second column on the first page of the first section. The news stories to which these summaries refer are almost always published on the second page of the first section. On Mondays the *Journal* publishes on this page a tabular summary (called Tracking the Economy) of all the statistics that appeared in the previous week as well as a calendar of those you can expect in the present week. The weekly and daily data you will need appear in the Money and Investing (third) section. Check the index at the top of this section's first page for location.

Listing of Statistical Series According to *The Wall Street Journal* Publication Schedule

Quarterly (Jan.–Mar., Apr.–Jun., Jul.–Sep., Oct.–Dec.)	
Day of Month Usually Published in *The Wall Street Journal*	**Series Description**
Middle of last month of quarter	Balance of payments
25th	GDP
Month after end of quarter	Productivity

Monthly	
Day of Month Usually Published in *The Wall Street Journal*	**Series Description**
1st	Leading indicators
1st week	Consumer confidence
1st week	Manufacturer's orders (nondefense capital goods)
5th, 15th, 25th	Auto sales
Monday of 2nd week	Employment
2nd week	Consumer credit
Middle of 2nd week	Retail sales
Midmonth	Inventories
Midmonth	Industrial production
Midmonth	Capacity utilization
Midmonth	Producer price index
Midmonth	Consumer price index
3rd week	Balance of trade
17th to 20th	Housing starts
3rd week	Personal income
Thursday or Friday of next-to-last week	Durable goods orders
Last week	Federal expenditures, receipts, and deficit

Weekly	
Day of Week Usually Published in *The Wall Street Journal*	**Series Description**
Monday	Bond yields (chart)
Friday	Federal Reserve data
Thursday	Short-term interest rates (chart)
Tuesday	Treasury bill auction

Daily	
	Series Description
	Foreign exchange rates
	Treasury bill rates

Alphabetical Listing of Statistical Series Published in
The Wall Street Journal

Series Description	*The Wall Street Journal* Publication Schedule
Auto sales	Every ten days
Balance of payments	Quarterly
Balance of trade	Monthly
Bond yields (chart)	Weekly
Capacity utilization	Monthly
Consumer confidence	Monthly
Consumer credit	Monthly
Consumer price index	Monthly
Durable goods orders	Monthly
Employment	Monthly
Federal expenditures, receipts, and deficit	Monthly
Federal Reserve data	Weekly
Foreign exchange rates	Daily
GDP	Quarterly
Housing starts	Monthly
Industrial production	Monthly
Inventories	Monthly
Leading indicators	Monthly
Manufacturers' orders (nondefense capital goods)	Monthly
Personal income	Monthly
Producer price index	Monthly
Productivity	Quarterly
Retail sales	Monthly
Short-term interest rates (chart)	Weekly
Treasury bill auction	Weekly
Treasury bill rates	Daily

Tracking the Economy

Economists will look to the February employment reports scheduled for release Friday for clues to future Federal Reserve action on interest rates.

"Unless there's a big change in employment, we don't expect a policy change from the Fed," says L. Douglas Lee, chief economist for County NatWest Securities USA in Washington.

Mr. Lee says he expects the unemployment rate to creep up to 6.3%, from January's 6.2%, but he doesn't see much change in the employment payroll figures. The consensus view holds that unemployment rose to 6.3%.

Looking ahead, Mr. Lee predicts unemployment will continue to climb as high as 7%, as the number of new jobs fails to keep up with growth in the labor force.

Unemployment Rises Again
Total unemployment rate in percent

Economists aren't looking for much improvement in January new home sales. But with interest rates and home prices both coming down, some expect signs of improvement to show up in February's housing data.

— *Kathryn Graven*

Statistics to be Released This Week

ECONOMIC INDICATOR	PERIOD	RELEASE DATE	PREVIOUS ACTUAL	CONSENSUS FORECAST
New Home Sales	January	March 4	−6.7%	−2.8%
Auto Sales (ann. rate)	Late February	March 5	6.0 million	6.4 million
Factory Orders	January	March 5	No change	−0.8%
Consumer Credit	January	March 7	−0.2%	+0.1%
Initial Jobless Claims	Week to Feb. 23	March 7	488,000	N.A.
Money Supply: M1	Week to Feb. 25	March 7	+$2.5 billion	No change
Money Supply: M2	Week to Feb. 25	March 7	+$6.8 billion	+$2.5 billion
Money Supply: M3	Week to Feb. 25	March 7	+$5.4 billion	+$4.0 billion
Unemployment Rate	February	March 8	6.2%	6.3%
Non-Farm Payrolls	February	March 8	−232,000	−108,000

Statistics Released Last Week

Real GNP (annual rate) 4th qtr. revised	$4.150 trillion −2.0%	**Leading Indicators Index** January	139.1 −0.4%
Durable Goods Orders January	$118.5 billion −0.7%	**Construction Spending** January (annual rate)	$396.6 billion −2.6%
Personal Income January (annual rate)	$4.719 trillion −0.5%	**Purchasing Managers' Index** (February)	38.5% +0.8
Personal Consumption January (annual rate)	$3.719 trillion −0.6%	**Farm Prices Index** February	144 −0.7%

N.A.=Not available   *Source: MMS International*

SOURCE *The Wall Street Journal*, March 4, 1991.

42-4958-01
ISBN 0-256-16256-5

Macroeconomics

THE IRWIN SERIES IN ECONOMICS

Appleyard and Field
International Economics

Baily and Friedman
Macroeconomics, Financial Markets, and the International Sector

Barron and Lynch
Economics
Third Edition

Baye/Beil
Managerial Economics and Business Strategy

Blair
Urban and Regional Economics

Bornstein
Comparative Economic Systems: Models and Cases
Seventh Edition

Brown and Moore
Readings, Issues, and Problems in Public Finance
Third Edition

Colander
Economics

Colander
Microeconomics

Colander
Macroeconomics

Denzau
Microeconomic Analysis: Markets & Dynamics

Hyman
Economics
Third Edition

Hyman
Microeconomics
Third Edition

Hyman
Macroeconomics
Third Edition

Hyman
Modern Microeconomics: Analysis and Applications
Third Edition

Katz and Rosen
Microeconomics
Second Edition

Lehmann
Real World Economic Applications: *The Wall Street Journal Workbook*
Third Edition

Lindert
International Economics
Ninth Edition

Maurice and Phillips
Economic Analysis: Theory and Application
Sixth Edition

Maurice, Thomas, and Smithson
Managerial Economics: Applied Microeconomics for Decision Making
Fourth Edition

Nadler and Hansen
Microcomputer Macroeconomics with IBM Disk

O'Sullivan
Urban Economics
Second Edition

O'Sullivan
Essentials of Urban Economics

Peterson
Principles of Economics: Micro
Eighth Edition

Peterson
Principles of Economics: Macro
Eighth Edition

Prager
Applied Microeconomics: An Intermediate Approach

Rima
Development of Economic Analysis
Fifth Edition

Roger and Daniel
Principles of Economics Software Simulation

Rosen
Public Finance
Third Edition

Schwarz and Van Dyken
Manager: Managerial Economics Software

Seo
Managerial Economics: Text, Short Cases
Seventh Edition

Sharp, Register, and Leftwich
Economics of Social Issues
Eleventh Edition

Shepherd
Public Policies toward Business
Eighth Edition

Shugart
The Organization of Industry

Slavin
Economics
Third Edition

Slavin
Microeconomics
Third Edition

Slavin
Macroeconomics
Third Edition

Streifford
Economic Perspective

Walton and Wykoff
Understanding Economics Today
Fourth Edition

Macroeconomics

Third Edition

David N. Hyman
North Carolina State University

IRWIN
Burr Ridge, Illinois
Boston, Massachusetts
Sydney, Australia

Cover image: *Inhabited Planet* by Josh Simpson of Massachusetts; courtesy of Mindscape Galleries, Evanston, IL

© RICHARD D. IRWIN, INC., 1989, 1992, and 1994

Senior sponsoring editor: Gary Nelson
Senior developmental editor: Patricia McCabe
Senior marketing manager: Ron Bloecher
Project editor: Susan Trentacosti
Production manager: Ann Cassady
Designer: Jeanne M. Rivera
Art coordinator: Mark Malloy
Photo research coordinator: Patricia A. Seefelt
Compositor: Better Graphics, Inc.
Typeface: 10/12 Times Roman
Printer: Von Hoffman Press

Library of Congress Cataloging-in-Publication Data

Hyman, David N.
    Macroeconomics / David N. Hyman.—3rd ed.
      p. cm.
    Includes index.
    ISBN 0-256-11807-8.—ISBN 0-256-15694-8 (instructor's ed.)
    1. Macroeconomics.   I. Title.
HB172.5.H96 1994
339—dc20   93–39680

Printed in the United States of America
1 2 3 4 5 6 7 8 9 0 VH 0 9 8 7 6 5 4 3

about the author

David N. Hyman is Professor of Economics at North Carolina State University where he has taught since receiving his Ph.D. in economics from Princeton University in 1969. In addition to being the author of *Economics*, Dr. Hyman is the author of widely used texts in public finance and microeconomics and is one of the most experienced textbook authors in the field of economics. Professor Hyman has taught principles of economics to large numbers of students over the past 25 years and has been the recipient of several awards for outstanding teaching. His research on economic issues has been published in respected academic journals.

Professor Hyman's broad range of professional experience outside academia gives him the breadth of knowledge required to write a comprehensive and relevant text. He was a Senior Fulbright Research Scholar in Italy in 1980 and held a CNR (National Research Council of Italy) Fellowship from 1976 to 1977 while doing research at the University of Turin in Italy. He has had considerable government experience in Washington, D.C., where he has worked as a budget analyst and has served on the staffs of the Office of the U.S. Comptroller of the Currency of the Treasury Department and the Board of Governors of the Federal Reserve System. In 1988 he was a consultant to President Reagan's Council of Economic Advisers. During this time he authored Chapter 2, "Fiscal Policy and Economic Expansion" of the *Economic Report of the President* (1989). In 1989 he was senior staff economist on President Bush's Council of Economic Advisers.

Professor Hyman is also a professional fine art photographer whose works are in the permanent collection of the Corcoran Gallery of Art in Washington, D.C. His photographs have been exhibited in many galleries and museums and have been published in art photography books and on the covers of several novels. For recreation, he enjoys the flute and working in his garden.

preface

Economics is a vital component of any student's education because an understanding of economic principles is essential for success in the modern world. The rapid evolution of global interdependence among both highly industrialized and less developed economies affects students' lives. My goal in writing this book has been to communicate the relevance of economics to everyday life by blending examples and applications with economic theory in each chapter. In this edition, I've revised to update the information, to give you the most relevant and interesting applications, and to provide analysis of emerging issues for the 21st century, including the transition to free markets in nations that formerly operated under systems of central planning.

Using the Text

This text has been designed with your learning in mind. Besides its careful and detailed unfolding of basic economic principles, the book contains a number of useful learning aids that will help improve your comprehension of the material. The introduction to each chapter is followed by a **Concept Preview** that outlines the key points you'll be exploring and that you should understand when you've finished the chapter. At the end of each major chapter section is a **Concept Check:** a series of questions that will help you test your grasp of what you've just read. Stop and respond to these questions to make sure you've acquired the background you'll need to go on to the next section. The Concept Checks will also be useful when you're reviewing material for a test. You'll notice, too, the **Concept Symbols** in the margins. These point the way to the discussions that explain chapter objectives. You'll see them again in the end-of-chapter questions—if you need to reread to answer questions, the concept symbols will help you quickly find the appropriate section(s).

Throughout each chapter, **Key Terms** are highlighted in color type and defined when introduced. These terms are defined in the margins and are also listed at the end of the chapter. The marginal definitions will be a valuable aid in building your economic vocabulary. In the back of the book you'll find all of the text's key terms in a comprehensive **Glossary.**

Learning economic theory is first-rate mental exercise—but how do we translate theory into application? In addition to the many relevant real-world examples provided throughout the text, each chapter also contains one or more boxed analyses that enlarge on and illustrate an important concept discussed in the text. Entitled **Principles in Practice,** each of these commentaries offers you a close-up view of an economic theory in action, from supply and demand to the pros and cons of trade protectionism. Some of the commentaries have a business focus and are subtitled either **Managerial Methods** or **Business Briefs.** These business-oriented features concentrate on decision making within businesses and on the competitive environment in which business firms operate. Those that carry the subtitle **Policy Perspective** apply economic principles to policy issues.

The Global Economy highlights important international trade or global economic issues to help you appreciate the increased international dimensions of the subject of economics. A global economy feature appears in almost every chapter of the text and often provides you with an opportunity to see how the theory discussed in each chapter can be applied to better understand a key international or global issue.

Inside Information highlights the sources and uses of economic information. To effectively operate in the modern world requires information. This feature helps you learn *where* to go to get economic information. You will learn the important sources of federal government data and of business-related data. This information will be useful to you for term papers and will help you later on as you move into a career as a guide to information that you will need to perform your job.

You'll encounter throughout the text a series of profiles of leading economists entitled **Economic Thinkers,** ranging from Adam Smith to Karl Marx. These profiles provide information about the subjects' major contributions to economic thought and also offer some intriguing personal sidelights. Additionally, to give you an idea of the diversity of careers available to students who choose to major in economics, we present a series of **Career Profiles** of professionals with a degree in economics.

When you read the **Prologue** to the text you will begin to see how economic issues affect you. Integrated into the text you will also find interviews with distinguished economists, including some who have been awarded Nobel Prizes, who have studied these issues in depth. As you read these **Insights on Issues** you will have a better idea about how economic policies affect you and the economy. Your instructor might use some of these interviews as a basis of class discussion.

The **Summary** at the end of each chapter enumerates the important concepts you've just learned; the **Concept Review** gives you one more check of your understanding of the chapter objectives; and the **Problems and Applications** give you the opportunity to demonstrate your understanding of these concepts in both expository and graphic form. Like the Concept Checks, these end-of-chapter features are helpful review aids.

The Study Guide

An excellent Study Guide prepared by Donald P. Maxwell of Central State University, Edmond, Oklahoma, accompanies the text. Each chapter contains learning objectives, a fill-in summary of chapter content, vocabulary exercises using key terms, and a series of activities—work with graphs, fill-in charts and tables, completion exercises, and more. These exercises are followed up by a mini-exam to check your learning and to help you prepare for taking your exams. Many of the chapters include a news item with questions to help you analyze how economic principles work in the world. Time invested with this invaluable resource will yield maximum returns for you.

Some Tips

1. Talk to Your Instructor   Your instructor is an experienced, knowledgeable professional who wants to serve as a resource for you and your classmates. If you consider this text a blueprint for the study of the relationships among economic principles, your instructor can provide the guidance you need to comprehend and connect the details of the blueprint and can serve as your interpreter as you learn the language of economics. In class and after class, ask your instructor questions. Challenge points you disagree with; request clarification of those you don't fully understand. Ask your instructor to recommend additional readings; seek his or her advice about career paths.

2. Keep Up with Current Events   People in business read a variety of publications; among them are *The Wall Street Journal, The Economist, The New York Times, U.S. News & World Report, Business Week*, and *Fortune*. Alone and in combination, these resources contain a wealth of information you'll find pertinent to your study of economics. All of these publications are available free at your library, and you should plan to become a regular reader. Their analyses, editorials, and features will bring into sharp focus the material you'll be studying, from the economics of pollution control to the cost of agricultural subsidies and government assistance to the poor. In the pages of these publications you'll be introduced to new industries and growing companies (your future job market!); to talented young entrepreneurs and corporate leaders with decades of experience; to high government officials and foreign heads of state. Reading these publications regularly gives you the chance to expand your horizons beyond the classroom and to see how the economic principles you're learning work in the real world.

3. Talk to Your Classmates Outside of Class   Discuss what you're learning and how it fits in with your curriculum and your ambitions. Their interests, family backgrounds, job experience, and career plans can be a productive resource for you. Classmates may be related to or acquainted with someone who's succeeding in a career to which you're attracted—and you may be helpful to them in the same way. Consider forming a study group for review and discussion of the material you're covering, or enhance your personal interaction skills by organizing a team to prepare a class project.

4. Consider Economics as a Major   Talk to or read about people who have degrees in economics. You'll find them in literally dozens of fields. The Career Profiles in the book show you just a few of the choices that can be made, but you'll find economics majors are succeeding as entrepreneurs, diplomats, bankers, journalists, Cabinet heads, corporate leaders, consultants, judges, and politicians.

Because economics is such a wide-ranging discipline, it's an excellent adjunct to many programs of study. If your major is business administration, political science, or international relations, a minor in economics will provide valuable insights into the contemporary social environment. If you elect to concentrate in marketing or finance, you can profitably pursue economics as a second major or a minor. A pairing of economics and journalism can help you lay the groundwork for a successful career in business communications. An undergraduate degree in economics also serves as a excellent foundation for graduate work in a variety of fields: business, law, public administration, and health, to name a few.

If you decide to become a professional economist, you almost certainly will need a graduate degree and will be pursuing career opportunities in business, teaching, research, or government. The National Association of Business Economists publishes a helpful booklet, *Careers in Business Economics,*[1] that describes the responsibilities of economists in government, insurance, banking, consulting, investments, industry, and communications. The booklet also outlines the education requirements for business economists and provides information on salaries.

5. Apply Economics in Your Life   Above all, recognize that your ''laboratory'' for economics is no less than the world you live in. In this wider environment are valuable examples that will reinforce the economics you'll be learning from this text and from your class discussion. Be in

---

[1] Copies of this booklet may be obtained from the National Association of Business Economists, 28349 Chagrin Blvd., Suite 201, Cleveland, OH 44122. Single copies are free; quantity discounts are available.

tune with these applications wherever you find them—newspapers, magazines, television and radio; or from discussions with teachers, friends, and family; or from the everyday experiences of your own life.

I think you'll find that in all your endeavors, you'll be well served by the discipline of the economic way of reasoning. It's hard to think of a situation in which you wouldn't benefit from thinking logically and weighing alternatives. Good luck as you begin your exciting adventure.

David N. Hyman

acknowledgments

It is with the utmost appreciation that I thank all those who contributed time and thought to this book. I regard them as partners in the development of this text.

I am indebted to the following reviewers of the manuscript and supplements for the first edition: Curt L. Anderson, University of Minnesota; Lloyd Dwayne Barncy, Boise State University; Philip F. Bartholomew, University of Michigan; Gil Becker, Indiana University/Purdue University; Charles R. Britton, University of Arkansas; Rick L. Chaney, St. Louis University; Howard Chernick, Hunter College; Mary E. Cookingham, Michigan State University; David Denslow, University of Florida; Loraine Donaldson, Georgia State University; Frances Durbin, University of Delaware; Gary A. Dymski, University of Southern California; Patricia J. Euzent, University of Central Florida; Donald H. Farness, Oregon State University; Irwin Feller, Pennsylvania State University; James Gerber, San Diego State University; Anthony O. Gyapong, Wayne State University; Charles M. Hill, Prairie State College; Arnold Hite, The Citadel; Dennis L. Hoffman, Arizona State University; Janet Hunt, University of Georgia; Walter L. Johnson, University of Missouri; Michael Klein, Clark University; Leonard P. Lardaro, University of Rhode Island; Robert L. Lawson, Ball State University; Charles Leathers, University of Alabama; Jane H. Lillydahl, University of Colorado; Don Maxwell, University of Central Oklahoma; Herbert C. Milikien, American River College; David Molina, North Texas State University; Margaret D. Moore, Franklin University; Michael Nieswiadomy, North Texas State University; James Price, Syracuse University; Victor H. Rieck, Miami-Dade Community College; Teresa Riley, Youngstown State University; Jaime M. Rodriguez, Edmonds Community College; Raymond Sauer, University of New Mexico; Davinder Singh, California State University; Richard N. Spivack, Bryant College; Frederick E. Tank, University of Toledo; Abigail Taubin, University of Maryland; Robert W. Thomas, Iowa State University; John Trapani, University of Texas; Abdul M. Turay, Mississippi State University; John Vahaly, University of Louisville; Mark Vaughn, Washington University; Percy O. Vera, Sinclair Community College; William V. Weber, Illinois State University; James N. Wetzel, Virginia Commonwealth University; Arthur Wright, University of Connecticut; Darrel Young, University of Texas.

Thanks to those users who filled out an initial questionnaire: Mary H. Acker, Iona College; Steven G. Allen, North Carolina State University; Irma Alonso, Florida International University; Robert T. Averitt, Smith College; Arthur A. Bayer, Babson College; Herb Beadles, Otero Junior College; Andrew Buck, Temple University; Yunhui Chen, State University of New York; Hope Corman, Rider College; Greg Delemeester, Marietta College; James L. Dietz, California State University, Fullerton; Peter Dorman, Smith College; Raymond P. H. Fishe, University of Miami; Mary Galvan, St. Xavier College; Kathie S. Gilbert, Mississippi State University; Nathan Eric Hampton, St. Cloud State University; Robert Hendricks, St. Cloud State University; Arthur Janssen, Emporia State University; Hong-Bum Kim, State University of New York, Albany; Moonsik Lee, State University of New York, Albany; Robert Lee, Babson College; John Mark Lindvall, Southern California College; Neal B. Long, Stetson University; Kevin B. Lowe, Shorter College; Daniel J. Lynch, St. Xavier College; Robert C. McMahon, University of Southern Maine; Bret McMurran, Chaffey College; John Neal, Lake-Sumter Community College; M. Reza Ramazani, St. Michael's College; Tom Riddell, Smith College; James M. Rigterink, Polk Community College; Rose Rubin, University of North Texas; Dean Schiffman, University of California, San Diego; Samuel A. Shrager, Lehman College of the City of New York; Alice Simon, Ohio Wesleyan University; J. Sondey, University of Idaho; Paul S. Taperek, South Florida Community College; H. Tuckman, Memphis State University; Katsumi Ukemori, State University of New York, Albany; R. Vaitheswaran, Coe College; Robert Von der Ohe, Rockford College; Jin Wang, Eureka College; Darwin Wassink, University of Wisconsin, Eau Claire; Dale Wheaton, University of Maine; James A. Xander, University of Central Florida.

I wish to thank the following reviewers for their detailed comments: Robert Averitt, Smith College; Colette Barr, Santa Barbara City College; Willie Belton, Georgia Institute of Technology; Ron Brandolini, Valencia Community College; Kathleen Brook, New Mexico State University; Gabriella Bucci, DePaul University; Paul Comolli, University of Kansas; James L. Dietz, California State University, Fullerton; Michael J. Gootzeit, Memphis State University; Simon Hakim, Temple University; Nathan Eric Hampton, St. Cloud State University; Thor Herts-

ix

gaard, North Dakota State University; Beth Ingram, University of Iowa; Ebrahim Karbassi-oon, Eastern Illinois University; Arthur Kartman, San Diego State University; Gary Lynch, Indiana University; Bruce McCrea, Lansing Community College; David Molina, University of North Texas; Ali Moshtagh, Eastern Illinois University; Richard Moss, Ricks College; William O'Dea, State University of New York; John Pharr, Cedar Valley College; James Rigterink, Polk Community College; Gary Rourke, Lakewood Community College; Allan G. Sleeman, Western Washington University; John Sondey, University of Idaho; Christopher R. Thomas, University of South Florida; Percy O. Vera, Sinclair Community College; Laura Wolff, Southern Illinois University.

The following focus group participants at the 1990 ASSA Convention provided excellent suggestions: James L. Dietz, California State University; Michael J. Gootzeit, Memphis State University; William P. O'Dea, State University of New York; Calvin D. Siebert, University of Iowa; Laura Wolff, Southern Illinois University.

I also express my gratitude to a panel of specialists who examined our real-world applications: Terence Alexander (international), University of California; Lewis Cain (historical), Loyola University; Phil Friedman (macroeconomic), Bentley College; Wendell McCulloch (international business), California State University; Charles E. Staley (historical) State University of New York; Michael K. Taussig (environmental), Rutgers.

The planning for the third edition included a questionnaire that was sent to instructors across the United States and in other countries where this text is used. The response rate was remarkable and provided the information I needed to fine-tune this edition. Although it is impossible to list all of you, I do want to express my appreciation for both your time and your insights.

The staff of Richard D. Irwin were helpful throughout the revision and production process for this book. Gary Nelson, sponsoring editor, provided many useful suggestions for this new edition. The late Joan Hopkins supervised the developmental process of the new edition and worked very closely with me on perfecting the various drafts of the book. Patricia McCabe completed the task for Joan and for me. Susan Trentacosti efficiently managed the editing process and Ann Cassady the production process. Jeanne Rivera provided an eye-pleasing and functional design for the book. I am grateful to all those at Irwin for the many hours of work and thought that they put into the process of producing the polished text.

My colleagues at North Carolina State University were always available to help me sound out my ideas and supply information on their areas of specialization. I also wish to heartily thank my students at North Carolina State University who always keep me on my toes and provide the inspiration for developing many of the new ideas and applications that appear in this new edition. Carolyn Smith and Janet Stern provided remarkably efficient secretarial assistance and helped me keep up with my deadlines.

Finally, I must thank my wife Linda for her support during the period I have worked on this project. She deserves a medal for her patience with a writer who has spent so many hours working on this new edition.

D. N. H.

contents

Special Features xxii

Prologue 1

I part
Introduction to Economics

1 Economics: What It's All About 8

2 Production Possibilities and Opportunity Cost 36

II part
Supply and Demand: Markets and the Price System

3 Market Transactions: Basic Supply and Demand Analysis 58

4 Using Supply and Demand Analysis 83

5 The Price System: Free Markets and the Economy 103

III part
Introduction to Macroeconomics Concepts

6 Gross Domestic Product and the Performance of the National Economy 130

7 Business Cycles, Unemployment, and Economic Growth 160

8 The Price Level and Inflation 183

IV part
Aggregate Demand/Aggregate Supply

9 Aggregate Demand and Aggregate Supply 202

10 Using Aggregate Demand–Aggregate Supply Analysis to Understand Economic Fluctuations and Growth 225

11 Keynesian Analysis of Aggregate Purchases 248

12 Keynesian Analysis of Macroeconomic Equilibrium 268

V part
Money, Financial Markets, and Macroeconomic Equilibrium

13 The Functions of Money 300

14 The Banking System 319

15 The Federal Reserve System and Its Influence on Money and Credit 343

VI part
Stabilizing the Economy

16 Stabilization of the Economy through Monetary Policy 364

17 Stabilization of the Economy through Fiscal Policy 388

18 The Federal Budget Deficit and the National Debt 414

19 Issues in Stabilization Policy: Inflation versus Unemployment and Rational Expectations 436

VII part
International Economic Issues

20 International Trade and Economic Development 458

21 The Economics of Foreign Exchange and the Balance of International Trade 492

Appendix A: Elasticity of Supply and Demand 516

Glossary G

Photo Credits C-1

Index I-1

contents

Special Features xxii

Prologue 1

The Global Economy and Your Future 1

Economic Issues for the 21st Century 2

I part

Introduction to Economics

1 Economics: What It's All About 8

Some Basic Definitions 9

The Basic Task of an Economy: Grappling
with Scarcity 9

Opportunity Cost 9

Three Basic Economic Decisions 10

Microeconomics versus Macroeconomics 11

Microeconomics 11

Macroeconomics 11

Positive Analysis versus Normative Analysis 12

Positive Analysis 12

Normative Analysis 12

principles in practice   The Economics of Drinking,
Driving, and Highway Deaths 13

Gains and Losses from Economic Policies 13

the global economy   Protectionism 14

The Economic Way of Reasoning: Models and
Marginal Analysis 15

Economic Theory and Its Models 16

Economic Variables 16

Economic Models 17

economic thinkers   Adam Smith 18

Rational Behavior 19

Marginal Analysis of Rational Behavior 20

Graphs: An Aid to Understanding Economics 23

Summary 23

Key Terms 24

Concept Review 24

Problems and Applications 24

inside information   Statistical Abstract of the
United States 25

Chapter Supplement: Graphs: A Basic Tool for
Analyzing Economic Relationships 26

2 Production Possibilities and Opportunity Cost 36

Resources, Technology, and Production
Possibilities 37

Technology 37

The Production Possibilities Curve 38

The Law of Increasing Costs 40

*Generalizing the Concepts: Peace Dividends and
a Cleaner Environment 42*

Productive Efficiency 43

principles in practice   Avoiding Waste and
Management in Production 45

Division of Labor and Productive Efficiency 46

Economic Growth: Expanding Production
Possibilities 46

Annual Growth in Available Resources 47

Improved Quality of Inputs 47

principles in practice   Personal Budgeting and
the Opportunity Cost of Choices 48

Improvements in Technology 48

Production for the Present versus Production for
the Future: A Basic Economic Choice 50

the global economy   The Gains from International
Trade 51

Scarcity and Trade-Offs 53

insights on issues   Do People in the United States

Save Enough of Their Income? Talking with Jane
Gravelle 53

Summary 53

Key Terms 54

Concept Review 54

Problems and Applications 54

II part

Supply and Demand: Markets and the Price System

3 **Market Transactions:** Basic Supply and Demand
Analysis **58**

Markets: Purposes and Functions 59

Demand 59

economic thinkers Alfred Marshall 60

*The Market Demand Curve and the Law
of Demand 60*

Changes in Relative Price 62

Changes in Quantity Demanded 62

Changes in Demand 62

Supply 66

*The Market Supply Curve and the Law
of Supply 66*

Changes in Quantity Supplied 67

Changes in Supply 68

Market Equilibrium Price and Quantity 70

Graphic Depiction of Market Equilibrium 71

Self-Equilibrating Markets 72

*The Impact of Changes in Demand on Market
Equilibrium 72*

principles in practice The Market for Medical
Services 76

the global economy The Dollar Has Its
Price Too! 77

Mastering the Art of Supply and Demand
Analysis 79

principles in practice The Stock Market 80

Summary 80

Key Terms 81

Concept Review 82

Problems and Applications 82

4 **Using Supply and Demand Analysis 83**

Prices, Scarcity, and Marketing Prospects 84

Nonscarce Goods 84

*How Demand and Supply Conditions Affect the
Success of New Products 85*

Markets for Labor and Credit 86

Labor Markets 87

*Credit Markets: The Demand for and Supply of
Loanable Funds 89*

principles in practice Operation of Labor Markets
in the United States 91

Price Ceilings: Using Supply and Demand Analysis
to Forecast Their Effects in Markets 92

Rent Control 92

*Nonprice Rationing of Shortages Resulting from
Price Ceilings 93*

principles in practice How Landlords Respond to
Rent Control 94

Price Floors: Supply and Demand Analysis of
Their Effects 95

Minimum Wages 95

Agricultural Price Supports 97

Price Controls: The Cost of Government
Intervention 98

the global economy The Transition to Free
Markets in the Former Communist Nations 99

insights on issues How Will Changes Abroad,
Especially the Movement away from Communism toward
Free Markets in Eastern Europe and the Former Soviet
Union, affect the U.S. Economy? Talking with Abram
Bergson 102

Summary 101

Key Terms 101

Concept Review 101

Problems and Applications 101

5 **The Price System:** Free Markets and
the Economy **103**

Capitalism and the Market Economy 104

Specialization and Exchange 104

principles in practice The Entrepreneurial Spirit
in American Capitalism 105

*How Production Generates Income in the
Market Economy: Circular Flow of Income
and Expenditure 106*

The Price System: How It Works 108

*How the Price System Influences What
Is Produced 108*

How the Price System Influences Production Methods 111

Who Gets the Goods and Services? 112

A Recap: The Price System in Motion 112

Some Common Defects in the Price System 112

Public Goods and Externalities 113

Externalities and Resource Use 113

principles in practice   Property Rights, Transaction Costs, and Pricing 116

Other Common Problems in a Market System 117

The Modern Mixed and Open Economy 118

Government and the Economy 118

the global economy   International Trade 120

Conclusion: Economic Activity and Economic Decisions 122

insight on issues   How Shall We Use Our Resources and Capabilities? Talking with Douglas Holtz-Eakin 123

Summary 123

Key Terms 124

Concept Review 124

Problems and Applications 125

career profile   Rhonda Williams 125

inside information   Getting Information on Financial and Commodity Markets 126

III part

Introduction to Macroeconomic Concepts

6 Gross Domestic Product and the Performance of the National Economy 130

Looking at the Economy from a Macroeconomic Perspective 131

Measuring Aggregate Output: Gross Domestic Product 131

How GDP Is Calculated 132

Intermediate Products and Value Added 132

Nominal GDP and Real GDP 134

principles in practice   The Value-Added Tax 135

Calculating Nominal and Real GDP: A Simple Example 135

How Good Is GDP as a Measure of National Well-Being? 138

The Expenditure and Income Components of GDP 139

The Expenditure Components of GDP 139

The Income Side of GDP 142

principles in practice   How the Bureau of Economic Analysis Calculates GDP Every Three Months 143

The Economy's Income Statement 144

Other Measures of Aggregate Expenditure and Income 145

The Circular Flow of Expenditure and Income: A Macroeconomic Perspective 148

Leakages and Injections of Purchasing Power and the Demand for U.S. Final Products 151

Flows of Saving and Investment in the United States: Do We Save Enough? 151

How Foreigners Helped Finance U.S. Investment between 1980 and 1991 153

the global economy   The Growing Importance of Exports and Imports for the U.S. Economy 154

insights on issues   Will Standards of Living in the United States Continue to Improve? Talking with Kenneth J. Arrow and Robert E. Litan 156

Summary 157

Key Terms 158

Concept Review 158

Problems and Applications 158

inside information   Where to Find Current Information on the Performance of the U.S. Economy 159

7 Business Cycles, Unemployment, and Economic Growth 160

Fluctuations in Real GDP: The Historical Record 161

The Business Cycle 161

Actual Fluctuations and Trend of Real GDP in the United States 163

principles in practice   What Is a Recession, and Who Can Predict When One Will Arrive? 164

Unemployment 167

The Unemployment Rate 167

Frictional, Structural, and Cyclical Unemployment 168

The Natural Rate of Unemployment and Potential Real GDP 169 principles in practice   What Influences the Natural Rate of Unemployment? 171

Cyclical Unemployment 172

How Unemployment Varies with the Business Cycle 172

The Costs of Unemployment 173

Cushioning Unemployment Costs 174

Economic Growth and Its Sources 175

The Sources of Growth 175

Improvements in Productivity 177

Saving, Investment, and Economic Growth 178

The Trade-Off between Current and Future Consumption 178

principles in practice   The Costs versus the Benefits of Economic Growth 179

Recent Trends in Investment and Productivity Growth in the United States 179

Summary 180

Key Terms 181

Concept Review 181

Problems and Applications 182

8 The Price Level and Inflation 183

The Price Level and Inflation 184

The Consumer Price Index 184

Measuring Inflation 185

Changes in the Price Level versus Changes in Relative Prices 185

principles in practice   The CPI Market Basket 186

The GDP Deflator 186

A History of the Consumer Price Level and Inflation 187

The Distortions and Costs of Price Instability 189

Real Income: Using the CPI to Deflate Nominal Income 189

Nominal Wages versus Real Wages 191

How Inflation Can Redistribute Income and Wealth from Creditors to Debtors 192

Nominal Interest Rates versus Real Interest Rates 193

How Price Instability Affects the Performance of the Economy 194

Anticipated Inflation and Economic Decisions 195

Inflationary Distortions in Saving and Investment 195

The Disastrous Effects of Hyperinflation 196

the global economy   Hyperinflation in the Computer Age 197

Summary 198

Key Terms 199

Concept Review 199

Problems and Applications 199

IV *part*

Aggregate Demand/Aggregate Supply

9 Aggregate Demand and Aggregate Supply 202

Aggregate Demand and Aggregate Supply 203

Aggregate Demand 203

Changes in Aggregate Demand 205

Influences on Aggregate Demand 205

Aggregate Supply 208

Segments of the Aggregate Supply Curve 210

Changes in Aggregate Supply 211

Macroeconomic Equilibrium 214

The Results of Unintended Inventory Changes 216

How a Decrease in Aggregate Demand Can Affect the Economy 216

Recessionary GDP Gap 217

How an Increase in Aggregate Demand Can Affect the Economy 218

How a Decrease in Aggregate Supply Can Affect the Economy 219

How an Increase in Aggregate Supply Can Affect the Economy 220

principles in practice   What Caused the Recession of 1990–1991? 221

A Recap: Economic Fluctuations and Their Causes 221

the global economy   Exports and Macroeconomic Equilibrium 222

Summary 223

Key Terms 223

Concept Review 224

Problems and Applications 224

10 Aggregate Demand-Aggregate Supply Analysis of Economic Fluctuations and Growth 225

Macroeconomic Equilibrium: The Classical Model versus the Keynesian Model 226

The Classical Model of Macroeconomic Equilibrium 226

The Classical Long-Run Aggregate Supply Curve 228

The Keynesian Model of Macroeconomic Equilibrium 230

economic thinkers   Jean Baptiste Say and "Say's Law" 230

principles in practice   How Long-Term Labor Contracts Prevent Wage Flexibility in the U.S. 232

The Great Depression: Using Aggregate Demand-Aggregate Supply Analysis to Understand What Happened 232

Why Another Great Depression Is Unlikely 234

An Overheated Economy and Stagflation 235

Wage-Price Spirals in an Overheated Economy 236

Stagflation 237

Supply-Side Shocks 237

Exchange Rates and Macroeconomic Equilibrium 238

Impact of a Higher Dollar on Aggregate Demand 239

Impact of Changes in Exchange Rates on Aggregate Supply 239

Conclusion: The Impact of Changes in Foreign Exchange Rates on Macroeconomic Equilibrium 240

Macroeconomic Equilibrium in a Growing Economy 242

Noninflationary Growth 243

principles in practice   U.S. Macroeconomic Equilibrium, 1970–1991 244

Summary 245

Key Terms 246

Concept Review 246

Problems and Applications 246

inside information   The State of the "Stats": How Accurate Are Government Economic Statistics? 247

11 Keynesian Analysis of Aggregate Purchases 248

The Consumption Function 249

Income and Consumption 249

Other Determinants of Consumption 250

Graphing the Consumption Function 251

Showing the Relationship between Income and Saving 251

Using a 45-Degree Guideline to Measure Savings 253

The Marginal Propensities to Consume and to Save 253

How Changes in Wealth Can Shift the Consumption Line 254

How a Change in Household Debt Outstanding Can Affect Current Consumption 254

The Influence of Expectations on Current Consumption 255

Investment Purchases 256

Investment Demand and the Real Interest Rate 257

Shifts in Investment Demand 258

principles in practice   Personal Consumption and Saving in the United States 259

Government Purchases and Net Exports 261

Government Purchases and the Influence of Taxes and Transfers on Spending 261

Net Exports 262

Aggregate Purchases: $C + I_P + G + NE$ 264

Summary 265

Key Terms 266

Concept Review 266

Problems and Applications 266

12 Keynesian Analysis of Macroeconomic Equilibrium 268

Aggregate Purchases and Macroeconomic Equilibrium 269

Keynesian Analysis of Macroeconomic Equilibrium 269

A Graphic Analysis 270

Conditions for Macroeconomic Equilibrium 271

Keynesian Analysis of Contractions or Recessions 272

How a Decline in Planned Investment Can Cause Equilibrium Real GDP to Fall 273

How a Decline in Consumer Spending Intentions Can Cause a Contraction or a Recession 275

economic thinkers   John Maynard Keynes 276

The Multiplier: What It Is and How It Works 277

The Respending Process 277

The Multiplier Effect and Macroeconomic Equilibrium 279

A Formula for the Multiplier 281

International Trade, the Government Sector, and
Macroeconomic Equilibrium 282

*Government Purchases, Taxes, International
Trade, and Macroeconomic Equilibrium 283*

the global economy   How a Decline in Exports or
an Increase in the Marginal Propensity to Import Can
Cause Recessionary GDP Gap 285

The Price Level, Aggregate Demand, and Inflationary Gaps Shifts of the Aggregate Purchases Line
Caused by Price Changes 286

principles in practice   The Multiplier for the Globally Integrated U.S. Economy of the 1980s 287

Deriving the Aggregate Demand Curve 288

Inflationary GDP Gaps   289

Summary 290

Key Terms 291

Concept Review 291

Problems and Applications 291

Chapter Appendix: A Complete Keynesian
Model 292

V *part*

Money, Financial Markets, and Macroeconomic Equilibrium

13 The Functions of Money 300

What Is Money, and What Are Its Functions? 301

Commodity Money 302

Fiat Money 302

principles in practice   Silver Coins in the United
States 303

Checkable Deposits as a Form of Money 304

What Money Is Not 305

Measuring the Stock of Money 305

Measuring the Money Stock: M1 306

Adding Near Money to M1: M2 306

The Demand for Money 308

Transaction Demand for Money 308

Money as an Asset 309

The Money Demand Curve 310

Changes in Money Demand 310

The Stock of Money, Money Demand, and Interest
Rates 312

*The Effect of an Increase in the Available
Money Stock 312*

*The Effect of a Decrease in the Available
Money Stock 313*

*How Shifts in Money Demand Can Affect
Interest Rates 314*

the global economy   Eurodollars 316

The Need to Understand Changes in the
Money Stock 316

Summary 317

Key Terms 317

Concept Review 318

Problems and Applications 318

inside information   Federal Reserve Bulletin 318

14 The Banking System 319

Banking 320

The Evolution of Banking 320

Fractional Reserve Banking 321

How Banks Make Loans and Create
Checkable Deposits 322

*How a Bank Accepts Deposits and
Makes Loans 322*

*Making Loans: Deposit Creation by a
Single Bank 323*

*How Checks Drawn on Newly Created Deposits
Affect an Individual Bank's Balance Sheet   324*

Multiple Expansion on the Money Stock for the
Entire Banking System 326

The Money Creation Process 327

The Reserve Multiplier 328

Deposit Contraction: The Process in Reserve 330

Bank Demand for Excess Reserves 331

The Federal Funds Market 332

principles in practice   Nonbank Financial
Intermediaries 333

principles in practice   Deposit Insurance and
Bank Failures 334

Bank Portfolio Management 334

the global economy   International Banking and
the Global Economy 337

Toward Understanding How the Money Supply
Changes 338

principles in practice   Using Balance Sheets 339

insights on issues   How Solid Is the U.S. Financial
System? Talking with Edward J. Kane 340

Summary 341

Key Terms 342
Concept Review 342
Problems and Applications 342

15 The Federal Reserve System and Its Influence on Money and Credit 343

The Federal Reserve System 344

The Federal Reserve System: How It Is Organized 344

Is the Fed Independent of Political Interference? 346

The Fed's Influence on the Monetary Base 347

Control of Required Reserve Ratios 347

Discount Policy: The Fed as Leader of Last Resort 349

How Open Market Sales of Government Securities by the Fed Affect Bank Reserves 349

How Open Market Purchases of Government Securities Affect Bank Reserves 350

principles in practice   The Fed's Open Market Operations 352

A Recap: The Operations of the Federal Open market Committee 352

Securities Prices, Interest Rates, and the Monetary Base 354

Money Supply, Money Demand, and Equilibrium Interest Rates 356

How the Fed Influences the Supply Curve of Money and the Equilibrium Interest Rate 357

the global economy   International Operations of the Fed 358

The Power of the Fed 359
Summary 359
Key Terms 360
Concept Review 360
Problems and Applications 360

inside information   Beige, Blue, and Green Books 361

part

Stablizing the Economy

16 Stabilization of the Economy through Monetary Policy 364

Stabilization and Monetary Policy 365
Money and Short-Term Macroeconomic Equilibrium 365

Short-Term Impact of Monetary Policy 366

Interest Rates and Aggregate Demand 367

Using an Expansionary Monetary Policy to Eliminate a Recessionary GDP Gap 368

principles in practice   Monetary Policy, Real Interest Rates, and the Yield Curve 370

How Effective Is Monetary Policy in Increasing Aggregate Demand? 370

Using a Contractionary Monetary Policy to Prevent the Economy from Overheating 372

principles in practice   Monetary Policy during the Great Depression 373

Money, Real GDP, Prices, and Monetary Policy 374

The Concept of Income Velocity of Circulation of Money 375

The Equation of Exchange 375

Using the Equation of Exchange to Understand Money's Role in the Economy 376

Monetary Policy: Implications of the Classical Quantity Theory 377

Monetarism 379

economic thinkers   Milton Friedman 380

Monetary Policy in the United States since 1942 381

Monetary Policy since 1990 383

the global economy   How U.S. Integration into the Modern Global Economy Has Affected Montary Policy 384

Summary 386
Key Terms 386
Concept Review 386
Problems and Applications 387

17 Stabilization of the Economy through Fiscal Policy 388

The Federal Budget and Its Impact on the Economy 389
The Federal Budget 389

How the Federal Government Budget Affects Aggregate Demand: A Quick Review 389

Using Fiscal Policy to Influence Aggregate Demand 390

How an Increase in Government Purchases Can Help Pull an Economy Out of a Recession 391

Using Tax Cuts or Government Transfers to Stimulate a Sluggish Economy 392

Equal Increases of Government Purchases and Net Taxes Are Expansionary 393

The Effects of Fiscal Policy on the Price Level 394

Contractionary Fiscal Policy 395

Problems in Effectively Implementing Fiscal Policy 396

Lags in Fiscal policy Implementation and Effects on Real GDP 397

Automatic Stabilizers and Cyclical Influences on the Budget Deficit 397

Automatic Stabilizers 398

Gauging the Impact of Fiscal Policy 399

the global economy Fiscal Policy and the Balance of International Trade 401

Supply-Side Fiscal Policies 403

How Supply-Side Fiscal Policies Can Influence Labor Markets 403

The Impact of Supply-Side Incentives to Save 404

Tax Breaks That Subsidize Investment 406

The Short-Run and Long-Run Impact of Supply-Side Policies 406

principles in practice Supply-Side Policies 407

principles in practice Clintonomics 409

insights on issues Will the U.S. Economy Be Able to Grow without High Inflation and Unemployment Rates? Talking with Lawrence Lindsey and Allan H. Meltzer 410

Summary 412

Key Terms 412

Concept Review 412

Problems and Applications 412

18 The Federal Budget Deficit and the National Debt 414

The Federal Budget Balance between Revenues and Expenditures 415

Financing Deficits: Money Creation versus Borrowing from the Public 417

The Crowding-Out Effect 418

The Deficit and Long-Term Interest Rates in the Early 1990s 420

the global economy Deficits and the Price of the Dollar 422

The National Debt 422

principles in practice The Impact of Deposit Insurance Claims on the Budget Deficit 423

Who Are the Nation's Creditors? 424

Burden of the Debt 425

Measuring the Deficit and Its Impact 426

High Employment versus the Actual Deficit 426

Other Influences on the Size of the Deficit 427

Which Deficit 427

Contingent Claims, Inflation, and the Growth of the Deficit Burden 428

Do Deficits Matter? Ricardian Equivalence and the Impact of Federal Deficits on Real Interest Rates 429

principles in practice The Social Security Trust Fund Surplus and the Federal Budget Deficit 430

Should the Federal Government Run a Surplus? 431

insights on issues Why Worry about the Federal Budget Deficit? Talking with Robert Eisner 432

Summary 433

Key Terms 434

Concept Review 434

Problems and Applications 434

career profile Nancy Shephardson 435

19 Issues in Stabilization Policy: Inflation versus Unemployment and Rational Expectations **436**

The Phillips Curve: Inflation versus Unemployment 437

Using the Phillips Curve 438

Supply-Side Shocks and the Phillips Curve for the 1970s 439

The Phillips Curve in the 1980s and 1990s 441

The Theory of Rational Expectations and the Trade-Off between Inflation and Unemployment 442

How Are Expectations Formed? 442

How Changes in Rational Expectation Can Affect the Aggregate Supply Curve 444

Inflationary Expectation and the Phillips Curve 445

economic thinkers Robert Lucas 446

The Long-Run Phillips Curve 449

Issues and Options in Stabilization Policy 450

Diagnosing the Causes of Cyclical Fluctuations in the Economy: Demand-Side Management 450

The Stabilization Policy Debate 451

A Comparison of Views: The Classical School,

*Keynesians, Monetarists, and New Classical
Economists 453*
Summary 455

Key Terms 455
Concept Review 455
Problems and Applications 456

VII part

International Economic Issues

**20 International Trade and Economic
Development 458**

International Trade 459

  The Basis for International Trade 459

principles in practice   U.S. Trade 460

  The Principle of Comparative Advantage 460

  Gains from Specialization and Trade 463

  The Mercantilist Fallacy 464

  Terms of Trade 465

  *How to Lose Comparative Advantage in
International Markets 466*

  Implications of Lagging Productivity Growth 466

Protectionism versus Free Trade 468

  *Arguments in Favor of Protecting Domestic In-
dustries from Foreign Competition 469*

  The "Cheap Labor" Fallacy 470

  Instruments of Protectionism: Tariffs 470

  Instruments of Protectionism: Import Quotas 472

  The Problem of Retaliation 473

Productivity and Trade 475

the global economy   Removing Barriers to Free
Trade 476

Economic Development 478

  The Ideas of the Classical Economists 478

  The Ideas of Karl Marx 478

  Why Were Marx's Predictions Wrong? 479

economic thinkers   Karl Marx 480

  Socialism versus Capitalism 481

  Socialism and the Command Economy 482

  *Transition from a Command Economy to a Free-
Market Economy 482*

principles in practice   Transition from Central
Planning to Free Markets in Russia, Poland, and
China 484

  Less Developed Countries 484

  *International Trade and Less
Developed Countries 486*

economic thinkers   David Ricardo 487

insights on issues   How Successfully Will U.S. Industries Face the Challenge of Competing in the Global
Economy? Talking with Rachel McCulloch 488

Summary 488
Key Terms 491
Concept Review 491
Problems and Applications 491

**21 The Economics of Foreign Exchange and the
Balance of International Trade 492**

International Trade Transactions 493

  *International Transfers of Bank Deposits Result-
ing from International Transactions 494*

  *How Foreign Trade Is Carried Out: An
Export Transaction 494*

  *How Foreign Trade Is Carried Out: An
Import Transaction 494*

Foreign Exchange Markets 496

  Equilibrium Exchange Rates 497

  *The Determinants of Foreign
Exchange Rates 498*

  Appreciation and Depreciation of Currencies 501

  The Principle of Purchasing Power Parity 502

the global economy   The ECU 503

Nominal and Real Exchange Rates 504

  *The Real Exchange Rate of the Dollar,
1973–1990 504*

International Payments and the International
Monetary System 506

The International Balance of Payments and
Balance of Trade and Foreign Saving in the
United States 508

  The Current Account 509

principles in practice   The Current Account
Deficit 510

  The Capital Account 511

Summary 513
Concept Review 514
Key Terms 514
Problems and Applications 514

career profile   Brian Gendreau 515

A **Elasticity of Supply and Demand   516**

Price Elasticity of Demand 517

How to Use Price Elasticity of Demand to Make Market Forecasts 517

Categorizing Price Elasticity of Demand as Elastic or Inelastic 518

Determinants of Price Elasticity of Demand 519

Calculating Price Elasticity of Demand from Two Points on a Demand Curve 520

How Price Elasticity Can Vary along a Demand Curve 521

Perfectly Inelastic and Perfectly Elastic Demand Curves 523

Using Price Elasticity of Demand to Forecast Changes in Total Expenditure and Total Revenue When Prices Change 525

Total Expenditure and Total Revenue 525

Predicting Changes in Total Expenditure and Revenue in Response to Price Increases 526

Price Decreases, Total Expenditures, and Total Revenue 527

principles in practice   How to Maximize Revenue 528

Other Demand Elasticity Measures 529

Income Elasticity of Demand 529

principles in practice   Empirical Estimates of Demand Elasticities 530

Cross-Elasticity of Demand 531

Price Elasticity of Supply 532

Determinants of Price Elasticity of Supply 533

Perfectly Inelastic and Perfectly Elastic Supply 534

the global economy   Import Quotas 536

Tax Shifting 537

Full Shifting 538

Partial Shifting 539

Summary 540

Key Terms 541

Concept Review 541

Problems and Applications 541

Glossary G

Photo Credits C-1

Index I-1

special features

principles in practice

1   **The Economics of Drinking, Driving, and Highway Deaths:** An Example of Positive Analysis (Policy Perspective) 13

2   **Avoiding Waste and Mismanagement in Production** (Managerial Methods) 45

     Personal Budgeting and the Opportunity Cost of Choices 48

3   **The Market for Medical Services:** How Health Insurance Increases Spending on Health Care 76

     The Stock Market: How It Works (Business Brief) 80

4   **Operation of Labor Markets in the United States** 91

     How Landlords Respond to Rent Control: The Case of New York City (Policy Perspective) 94

5   **The Entrepreneurial Spirit in American Capitalism** 105

     Property Rights, Transaction Costs, and Pricing 115

6   **The Value-Added Tax:** A New Way to Tax GDP or Its Components (Policy Perspective) 135

     How the Bureau of Economic Analysis Calculates GDP Every Three Months 143

7   **What Is a Recession, and Who Can Predict When One Will Arrive?** (Business Brief) 164

     What Influences the Natural Rate of Unemployment? 171

     The Costs versus the Benefits of Economic Growth 179

8   **The CPI Market Basket** 186

9   **What Caused the Recession of 1990–1991?** 221

10   **How Long-Term Labor Contracts Prevent Wage Flexibility in the U.S.** (Business Brief) 232

     U.S. Macroeconomic Equilibrium, 1970–1991 244

11   **Personal Consumption and Saving in the United States:** American Households Are Saving Less of Their Disposable Income 259

12   **The Multiplier for the Globally Integrated U.S. Economy of the 1990s** 287

13   **Silver Coins in the United States:** Good Money, Bad Money, and Gresham's Law 303

14   **Nonbank Financial Intermediaries** (Business Brief) 333

     Deposit Insurance and Bank Failures 334

     Using Balance Sheets: Understanding How a Depository Institution becomes Insolvent (Managerial Methods) 339

15   **The Fed's Open Market Operations:** A Visit to the Trading Desk 352

16   **Monetary Policy, Real Interest Rates, and the Yield Curve** (Business Brief) 370

     Monetary Policy during the Great Depression: How the Fed Prevented the Banking System from Recovering and Allowed the Money Supply to Decline (Policy Perspective) 373

17   **Supply-Side Policies** (Policy Perspective) 407

     Clintonomics: A New Administration Brings a Change in Fiscal Policy 793

18   **The Impact of Deposit Insurance Claims on the Budget Deficit** 423

     The Social Security Trust Fund Surplus and the Federal Budget Deficit 430

20   **U.S. Trade** 460

     Transition from Central Planning to Free Markets in Russia, Poland, and China 484

21   **The Current Account Deficit:** Why Worry about It? 510

the global economy

1   **Protectionism** 14

2   **The Gains from International Trade** 51

3   **The Dollar Has Its Price Too!** 77

4   **The Transition to Free markets in the Former Communist Nations** 99

5   **International Trade** 120

6   The Growing Importance of Exports and Imports for the U.S. Economy 154

7   Hyperinflation in the Computer Age 197

8   Exports and Macroeconomic Equilibrium 222

12   How a Decline in Exports or an Increase in the Marginal Propensity to Import Can Cause a Recessionary GDP Gap 285

13   Eurodollars 316

14   International Banking and the Global Economy 337

15   International Operations of the Fed 358

16   How U.S. Integration into the Modern Global Economy Has Affected Monetary Policy 384

17   Fiscal Policy and the Balance of International Trade 401

18   Deficits and the Price of the Dollar 422

20   Removing Barriers to Free Trade 476

21   The ECU 503

insights on issues

2   Do People in the United States Save Enough of Their Income? Talking with Jane Gravelle 53

4   How Will Changes Abroad, Especially the Movement away from Communism toward Free markets in Eastern Europe and the Former Soviet Union, Affect the U.S. Economy? Talking with Abram Bergson 102

5   How Shall We Use Our Resources and Capabilities? Talking with Douglas Holtz-Eakin 123

6   Will Standards of Living in the United States Continue to Improve? Talking with Kenneth J. Arrow and Robert E. Litan 156

14   How Solid Is the U.S. Financial System? Talking with Edward J. Kane 340

17   Will the U.S. Economy Be Able to Grow without High Inflation and Unemployment Rates? Talking with Lawrence Lindsey and Allan H. Meltzer 410

18   Why Worry about the Federal Budget Deficit? Talking with Robert Eisner 432

20   How Successfully Will U.S. Industries Face the Challenge of Competing in the Global Economy? Talking with Rachel McCulloch 488

career profile

5   Rhonda Williams 125

18   Nancy Shepherdson 435

21   Brian Gendreau 515

inside information

1   Statistical Abstract of the United States 25

5   Getting Information on Financial and Commodity Markets 126

6   Where to Find Current Information on the Performance of the U.S. Economy 159

10   The State of the "Stats": How Accurate Are Government Economic Statistics? 247

13   Federal Reserve Bulletin 318

15   Beige, Blue, and Green Books: How Monetary Authorities in the United States Compile Information to Examine Stabilization Policy 361

economic thinkers

1   Adam Smith 18

3   Alfred Marshall 60

10   Jean Baptiste Say and "Say's Law" 230

12   John Maynard Keynes 276

16   Milton Friedman 380

19   Robert Lucas 446

20   Karl Marx 480

     David Ricardo 487

Some of the "Economic Issues for the 21st Century" discussed in this Prologue are covered in the companion volume to this book entitled *Microeconomics* available from Richard D. Irwin, Inc.

Prologue

THE GLOBAL ECONOMY AND YOUR FUTURE

As we approach the year 2000, the United States is becoming more and more connected to a vast global economy it no longer dominates. Since 1960 we have become increasingly dependent on foreign suppliers to obtain such basic products as petroleum. Over the same period, U.S. businesses have looked abroad and have been selling more, opening up branches, and setting up production lines in foreign lands.

One has only to look around to be convinced of the reality of the new global economy. For example, did you know that over one third of the cars sold in the United State today are Japanese brands? Japan's prominent position in the U.S. car market may not be a surprise, but it is startling to realize that many of the Japanese cars Americans drive are produced in factories located right here in the United States. As of 1992, Japanese-owned assembly plants in the United States accounted for about one fifth of the cars produced in the nation!

Just as Japan has built factories in the United States, so have U.S. firms built production facilities abroad. For example, a major software development facility of Texas Instruments Inc. is located in Bangalore, India. This facility is linked by satellite to the company's headquarters in Dallas. Improvements in communication such as improved computers, the facsimile machine, and satellite communications make it as easy to get information from foreign locations as it is to pick up the telephone and call a coworker in the office across the street. American businesses moved aggressively in the 1980s to set up assembly lines and service facilities in foreign countries where workers were willing to accept lower wages than those paid in the United States.

Sales made by companies have also taken on a greater international dimension. For example, the Colgate-Palmolive Company, as of the beginning of the 1990s, was selling more toothpaste and toiletries outside the United States than it was selling to consumers in this country. The Hewlett-Packard Company, a major U.S. producer of electronic products, recently moved its personal computer headquarters to France because of its conviction that Europe would be the hottest market for PCs in the 1990s. As of 1990, half of Hewlett-Packard's sales of computers were accounted for by foreign buyers. Now more than ever, U.S. businesses and workers are dependent on exports to provide them with income. Americans enjoy the opportunities to purchase a multitude of goods and services from foreign producers, and we're spending larger portions of our income on imports than ever before.

U.S. businesses in 1992 sold over 12 percent of domestic production abroad—a sharp increase from previous performance. During the 1960s, only 6 percent of U.S. production was exported. Similarly, we're importing more goods and services today than we did in the past. In the 1960s, only 6 percent of total purchases in the United States were of imports. In the early 1990s, Americans were allocating 13 cents of each dollar spent on goods and services to imports. Just examine your own wardrobe and your possessions for testimony of this trend. The VCR you own was produced abroad, and it is also likely that your stereo equipment and camera were imported— and probably your shoes and sweaters as well. On the other hand, U.S.-built aircraft are proudly flown throughout the world by foreign carriers, and Russians in Moscow wait in line to taste the delights of an American Big Mac.

The world is moving toward freer exchange of goods and services and of ideas. The European Community now allows unrestricted trade and investment among its member nations. This means that European borders will no longer prevent European businesses from taking advantage of economic opportunities for profit as they arise.

Inevitably, U.S. government officials and politicians must take into account the reaction to changes in policies not only in the United States but also abroad. International financing of investment has become commonplace in the modern global economy. Fluctuations in interest rates and foreign exchange rates in the United States have dramatic repercussions throughout the world. At the same time, changes in economic conditions abroad can affect job opportunities and prosperity in the United States. Policymakers have taken steps to more closely coordinate global economic policy. The leaders of advanced industrial nations meet regularly now in an attempt to coordinate economic policies for the common good.

Globalization of production, sales, and economic policy has become a fact of life. In the 21st century, the destiny of the U.S. economy will be undeniably intertwined with that of other nations. The world is quickly becoming a global assembly line.

ECONOMIC ISSUES FOR THE 21ST CENTURY

Do you look forward to a future of prosperity? Will you be able to afford a home of your own? Will your generation live as well as or better than that of your parents?

The answers to these questions depend on how well the U.S. economy faces the challenge of providing jobs, increasing income, and solving such social problems as poverty, soaring medical costs, and environmental decay.

There are fundamental economic issued that are relevant to everyone's future. Economic analysis will help you understand why there are often conflicting views about these issues. Here are 10 that will be discussed in various parts of this text.

Issue 1: How Should We Use Our Resources and Capabilities?   What should we produce, and how should we produce it? The question of allocating productive capability to alternative uses is one of the most fundamental questions in economics. Much of economics deals with understanding how people choose to use their resources and analyzes the consequences of their choices.

Issue 2: Will Standards of Living in the United States Continue to Improve?   When income per person grows, people can afford more and better material goods and services. Growth in income per person depends on growth in production per person. Any given person's income depends on the value of that person's services. When an economy is growing, it generates more and better jobs for a growing population. As you study economics, it will become clear why some persons earn more than others. It will also become clear how investment in education, training, new production facilities, and equipment influences the development of new technologies and contributes to rising output per worker. The greater the rate of growth of production per person in the United States, the greater the growth in income per person. As income per person increases, so do living standards.

Issue 3: Do We Save Enough of Our Income?   When we save, we forgo the opportunity to use our income to consume goods and services today. Between 1974 and 1987 the United States saved less of its income than any other advanced industrial nation. While Japan was saving over 30 percent of its income and Canada, France, Germany, and the United Kingdom were saving over 20 percent of their income, the United States was saving only 15 percent of its income. Why is there so much concern about a nation's saving rate? Saving is important because it provides the funding for investments that contribute to growth of future income. A key to keeping our national living standards high is saving enough to provide the wherewithal for the investments that contribute to growth in job opportunities and income.

Issue 4: Will the Economy Be Able to Grow without High Inflation and High Unemployment Rates? For much of the 1980s, the U.S. economy expanded steadily and unemployment rates fell from a high of 9.5 percent of the labor force in 1982 to a low of 5.2 percent of the labor force in 1989. Then, in 1990, the U.S. economy stalled. Unemployment rose and job growth came to a screeching halt.

During the Great Depression of the 1930s, one out of every four workers in the United States was unemployed. Unemployment wastes a nation's greatest productive resource—its labor—and results in idle productive facilities. Some workers are more prone to unemployment than others, and the effects of unemployment are often concentrated in certain regions of the nation.

In 1980 the inflation rate, the growth rate of prices in the economy, was roaring at 12.5 percent in the United States. By 1986 inflation was a mere 1.1 percent, but by the end of the decade, in 1989, inflation had risen to 4.6 percent. As of 1992, the inflation rate fell again, to about 3 percent.

You will see that high and erratic inflation can adversely affect the way the economy functions. When inflation soars to astronomical levels of over 1,000 percent per year, as it did in Argentina and Bolivia in the 1980s, it adversely affects decisions to save and invest. Excessive inflation can induce an economic downturn and rip the social fabric of a nation. In 1989 there were street riots in Argentina because inflation was quickly eroding the purchasing power of consumer incomes.

As you study economics, you will begin to understand the causes of inflation and unemployment. You will also see how government policies can help control inflation and unemployment.

Issue 5: How Successfully Will U.S. Industries Face the Challenge of Competing in the Global Economy? The ability of our nation to provide jobs and growing income is more than ever linked to our competitive position in the rest of the world. The 1980s saw the emergence of Pacific rim nations—Japan, South Korea, Singapore, Indonesia, Malaysia, the Philippines, Taiwan, Thailand—as potent productive forces. In the 1990s the nations of Western Europe began to form a formidable new partnership that will strengthen their competitive position in the global economy. Mexico, India, Brazil, Argentina, and a host of Third World nations will emerge as major producers of goods and services. And changes in the economies of Russia and other parts of the former Soviet Union as well as those of Eastern European nations and China can also affect the United States.

To meet the challenge of increasingly competitive markets, the U.S. economy will have to keep on the cutting edge of technological advance and ensure growth in output per worker, which will keep production costs down. It will take new investments in plant and equipment to assure that U.S. industries can adequately compete in the global economy of the 21st century.

Issue 6: How Will Changes Abroad, Especially the Movement away from Communism toward Free Markets in Eastern Europe and the former Soviet Union, Affect the U.S. Economy? With the challenges of an increasingly competitive global economy will come opportunities. As incomes grow in the rest of the world, so too will the demand for U.S. products. Economic change in Western Europe is creating a vast integrated market for U.S. exports. Improved economic conditions in Eastern Europe and in the Third World will mean opportunities for U.S. businesses selling and investing abroad. Most economists believe that in the long run policies that maintain free international trade among nations will contribute to higher worldwide living standards.

As the economies of the former Soviet Union and the Eastern European nations are transformed gradually into freer marketplaces, other opportunities for foreign investment and export markets will open up for U.S. businesses. If successful, the reforms in these nations will increase their income and the productive potential of their economies. The increase in income in these nations will provide further opportunities for the United States and other nations to export goods and services.

Issue 7: What Measures Should Be Taken to Improve Environmental Quality? There is more to life than material goods and services. There is increasing concern about the effect of environmental decay throughout the world. This concern is now international as it is becoming increasing clear that pollution and destruction of environmental resources, such as rain forests, in one nation can harm the environment in other nations. But sacrifices are necessary to improve environmental quality. Measures taken to provide cleaner air and water and reduce the risks of environmental disasters such as oil spills will undoubtedly increase production costs, and this increase will, in turn, increase the prices of products people want to buy. Are we willing to trade job opportunities and reduced income today for cleaner air and preservation of natural resources tomorrow?

Issue 8: What Role Should Government Play in the Economy? Some people think that government intervenes too much in the economy, while others look to government to do more in solving the nation's problems. There are both benefits and costs from government action. Governments provide essential services that few of us can live without: roads, schooling, national defense, police and fire protection, Social Security pensions, and assistance to the poor. But the taxes and other means that governments use to finance their activities compel us to sacrifice some of our income to make these services available. Also, the taxes, regulations, and subsidy programs of governments can adversely affect incentives to use resources in ways that produce the greatest return to the nation. As you study economics, you will develop a way of thinking about government policies that will help you better evaluate their effect on you and on the nation as a whole.

Issue 9: Why Worry about the Federal Budget Deficit? Why worry about whether the federal government must borrow to finance its expenditures? After all, the federal budget has been in deficit every year since 1970 without any disastrous consequences for the economy. In fact, the latter half of the 1980s, a period of unprecedented peacetime expansion of production in the United States, was also a period in which the U.S. government ran record peacetime deficits.

Later in this book we'll discuss a key concern about the federal deficit—the fact that it constitutes negative saving by the federal government. This means that when the federal government borrows to cover its expenses, it could put upward pressure on interest rates that in turn could have adverse effects on the U.S. economy by reducing private investment.

Issue 10: How Solid Is the U.S. Financial System? The failure of a large number of savings and loan associations and commercial banks in recent years is a case for concern for everyone. Does this mean that it isn't safe to keep our money in banks? What has caused the recent rash of bank failures? Fortunately, depositors do not need to worry about losing their deposits because they are currently insured up to $100,000 by an independent government agency. Unfortunately, taxpayers (most of whom are also bank depositors) will have to foot the bill for bailing out the savings and loan associations and banks that cannot meet their deposit claims. These claims will make it more difficult for the federal government to balance its budget without increasing tax rates.

What needs to be done to make our banking system more solid and competitive? U.S. banks are facing increased competition from foreign banks in the lucrative business of financing foreign investments. An entire part of this book analyzes the way the U.S. banking system operates, showing the role that banks play in the U.S. economy. We will discuss the causes of the rash of bank failures in the late 1980s and early 1990s as well as some proposals for reducing the rate of bank failure in the United States.

The 10 issues discussed above are complex and interrelated. For example, the destruction of rain forests in Brazil can contribute to environmental decay and global warming that might adversely affect the quality of life throughout the world. Yet Brazil argues that clearing the rain forests is essential for reducing poverty in that nation. Improvements in environmental quality might come at the expense of a reduction in the improvement of material living standards. In other words, we might have to trade off material goods and services for cleaner air and water. Increased unemployment might on occasion be the price necessary to reduce rampant inflation. Unfortunately, we can rarely solve all problems in one swoop. We must be prepared to make trade-offs between objectives by looking at what we gain and what we lose when we take each course of action.

Economics will help you understand these trade-offs.

part I

Introduction to Economics

CONCEPTS

Economics and the Economy

Scarcity

Opportunity Cost

Microeconomics

Macroeconomics

Positive versus Normative Analysis

Economic Models

Marginal Analysis

Rational Behavior

Production Possibilities

Law of Increasing Costs

Productive Efficiency

Economic Growth

Ch'iu 7 Ying: *The emperor Guang Wu Fording a River*, Detail Hanging Scroll, National Gallery of Canada

1 chapter

Economics
What It's All About

When you graduate from college, will it be difficult or easy for you to find a job? How will changes in the prices of things you want to buy affect your standard of living? Will you be able to qualify for a car loan or a mortgage? What impact will federal budget deficits have on your future well-being as your tax funds are used to pay interest on the national debt? Will foreign competition deprive you of a job?

As these questions make clear, economics is about you: student, employee, consumer, and taxpayer. Economics is about the constraints you face, the choices you make, and your interdependence with others for survival.

In economics you'll study the opportunities and obstacles you will confront as you seek to make a living and to satisfy your desires for both the necessities and luxuries of life. As you learn economic principles, you'll develop a systematic way of thinking about the consequences of human behavior and the way the economy functions. You'll also gain insights into social problems and various approaches to resolving or alleviating them. The emphasis in this book is on how you can *use* economics as a practical tool to comprehend and deal responsibly with personal, business, and social issues.

☐ CONCEPT PREVIEW

After reading this chapter, you should be able to:

1. Describe the mechanism of the economy and the discipline of economics.

2. Understand the concepts of scarcity and opportunity cost.

3. Discuss major branches of economic inquiry: microeconomics, macroeconomics, positive analysis, and normative analysis.

4. Understand the concept of an economic model and its uses.

5. Explain *rational behavior* and *marginal analysis,* a method of analyzing the way we make decisions.

SOME BASIC DEFINITIONS

The economy is the mechanism through which the use of labor, land, structures, vehicles, equipment, and natural resources is organized to satisfy the desires of those who live in a society. The rules, institutions, and traditions used to coordinate economic activity differ considerably among nations, but all societies must deal with similar economic issues.

The discipline of economics is concerned with the use of available productive resources in a society to satisfy what often are conflicting desires and demands. Economics is concerned with *choices:* with evaluating and selecting among alternatives, realizing that each time we make a choice we also forgo an opportunity. One goal of this book is to help you develop an understanding of the issues of scarcity and choice within the context of the way modern economies function.

THE BASIC TASK OF AN ECONOMY: GRAPPLING WITH SCARCITY

The economy is a dynamic, constantly changing mechanism. The natural resources, workers, managers, innovators, equipment, structures, and technical know-how available to produce useful goods and services are all in some way limited. The wants we seek to satisfy, however, are seemingly unlimited. We all have biological needs for minimum amounts of food, clothing, and other basic goods—but few of us are content with minimum amounts of these items. We want amenities, comfort, and luxuries.

The fundamental economic problem is scarcity, the imbalance between our desires and the means of satisfying those desires. It is a problem faced by rich as well as poor societies—even the vast wealth of the United States is inadequate to satisfy all the desires of its people. The importance of scarcity as a unifying topic in economics is highlighted by the fact that many economists would define their discipline in the following way:

> *Economics is the study of how human beings make choices to use scarce resources as they seek to satisfy their seemingly unlimited wants.*

Opportunity Cost

When scarcity exists, we know we must sacrifice something of value to obtain more of any scarce good or service. The limited availability of resources such as land, skilled labor, structures, and equipment means that the more resources are used for one purpose, the less will be available for other purposes. The opportunity cost of choosing to use resources for one purpose is the sacrifice of the next best alternative for the use of those resources. For example, if your next best alternative to studying for an hour is an hour of swimming, then the opportunity cost of studying is the hour of swimming you sacrifice when you choose to study. If you're considering the choice between a bicycle and new stereo speakers, then the opportunity cost of choosing to buy the bike is the speakers, and vice versa.

The concept of opportunity cost is vital because opportunity cost is a measure of everything you sacrifice to attain a given objective. When you make a decision, you want to consider carefully its opportunity cost before deciding whether the gain is worth the sacrifice you must make. For example, the actual opportunity cost of attending college is more than the sacrifice of the goods and services you could buy with the sum of money, say $6,000 per year, you must give up to pay for tuition, books, and equipment. Suppose attending college requires that you devote full time

1

economy the mechanism through which the use of labor, land, structures, vehicles, equipment, and natural resources is organized to satisfy the desires of those who live in a society.

economics the study of the use of limited productive resources in a society to satisfy the unlimited desires of its members.

2

scarcity the imbalance between our desires and the means of satisfying those desires.

opportunity cost the cost of choosing to use resources for one purpose measured by the sacrifice of the next best alternative for using those resources.

to your studies so that you forgo the opportunity of a paying job. If the next best use of your time is a job that would pay $12,000 over the college year, you must add the value of this forgone opportunity to your other annual money costs of attending college.

Your actual opportunity cost of attending college is the goods and services you could have bought with the $18,000 per year you sacrifice to go to college. You can now weigh the full opportunity cost of attending college against the gains you expect from doing so. The gains include possible higher future income and improvement in the quality of your life, as well as the chance to socialize with fellow students and to participate in sports and other activities.

Three Basic Economic Decisions

The concepts of scarcity and opportunity cost are vital to understanding how the economy works. In the face of the inevitable imbalance between limited productive capability and limitless wants, the following questions need to be considered:

1. *What will be produced?* The productive potential of an economy can't be used to do everything for everybody. Decisions must be made about what to produce and how much of each item to produce with the limited resources available. These decisions are political in nature, and they involve balancing needs and wants of various groups. For example, an increase in the use of productive capacity to provide military equipment inevitably reduces the availability of consumer goods such as VCRs, microwaves, and automobiles. Choices must be made about which goods and services to make available and which to forgo.

2. *How will goods and services be produced?* There's more than one way to accomplish any given objective. For example, a certain quantity of iceberg lettuce can be produced on a large tract of land without the use of pesticides or fertilizers. However, the same amount of lettuce can be grown on less land with chemical agents. Goods and services can be produced by business firms or by government or nonprofit enterprises. Crops can be harvested by many workers using hand tools or with specialized machines and fewer workers. Textiles can be loomed and finished by hand or in automated plants where machines rather than workers perform many of the required tasks. Machines or other products (such as chemicals) can be substituted for labor or land when producing any mix of goods. Productive methods that squeeze the most out of available means allow the greatest possible material well-being from limited resources.

3. *To whom will goods and services be distributed?* Are they to be distributed equally to everyone so that each of us lives in the same type of house, eats the same amount and kinds of food, and wears the same clothes? Or are goods to be sold to those willing and able to pay? Under the latter method, people with higher incomes will enjoy more and better products and services than people with lower incomes. Will some of us be given special privileges to enjoy goods and services regardless of our ability to pay for those items? What rules will be used to decide who gets what?

The distribution of material well-being is never perfectly equal. Some people have the financial resources to enjoy great quantities of goods and services of the highest quality. Others, even in a nation with the vast productive potential of the United States, live in poverty. No society has yet discovered how to provide equally for the needs and wants of everyone while still offering the incentives that encourage high-quality production and technological innovation.

- What constitutes the economy?

- What is the discipline of economics?

- Define *scarcity* and *opportunity cost,* and explain the opportunity cost of your decision to attend college.

CONCEPT CHECK
☐

MICROECONOMICS VERSUS MACROECONOMICS

Economic analysis is divided into two main branches: microeconomics and macroeconomics. Both are important in dealing with the problem of scarcity.

Microeconomics takes a close-up view of the economy by concentrating on the choices made by individual participants in the economy such as consumers, workers, business managers, and investors. Macroeconomics looks at the economy from a broader perspective by considering its overall performance and the way various sectors of the economy relate to one another. The performance of the economy is gauged by the total value of annual production, the capacity of the economy to provide jobs, changes in the purchasing power of money, and the growth of employment and output.

Microeconomics

Microeconomics analyzes the ways individuals choose among various courses of action by weighing the benefits and costs of alternatives available to them. It emphasizes the role of prices in business and personal decisions. One of its major goals is to understand how the prices of particular goods and services are determined and how prices influence decisions. Because of its preoccupation with prices and the trading of goods and services, microeconomics is sometimes called *price theory.*

This view of economics studies the actions of individuals as they buy and sell in market transactions. As you know, some services, such as education and police protection, are provided by government agencies rather than being sold in markets. What are the advantages and disadvantages of alternatives to markets as a means of accomplishing the basic tasks of the economy? What role does government play in the economy? How do political choices influence the economy's functions and performance? You'll find that microeconomic analysis provides a useful point of view about human behavior that will give you insights into important social and political issues.

Macroeconomics

Macroeconomics examines changes in total national production and consumption, averages of the prices of broad groups of goods and services, and the employment of workers in the economy. Macroeconomists seek to explain the causes of economic fluctuations and to suggest policies that will make the fluctuations less abrupt, with the aim of preventing excessive unemployment and rapid price increases.

In macroeconomics we place special emphasis on understanding the causes of unemployment. The *unemployment rate* is the number of jobless workers who are actively looking for work or who have been laid off from a job, expressed as a percentage of the total labor force. Unemployment is often a major issue in congressional and presidential elections. In fact, the federal government is required by law to pursue policies that seek to keep unemployment from becoming too high. If such policies are to succeed, the individuals who develop them must have a keen understanding of how the economy works.

microeconomics
a branch of economic analysis that concentrates on the choices made by individual participants in the economy. Also called *price theory.*

macroeconomics
a branch of economic analysis that considers the overall performance of the economy with respect to total national production and consumption, average prices, and employment levels.

Inflation is another highly charged political issue studied in macroeconomics. *Inflation* is a general yearly increase in the average level of prices for a broad spectrum of goods and services. Inflation erodes the purchasing power of money. It can create economic instability in a nation by harming the competitiveness of firms seeking to sell products in foreign markets and by distorting economic choices as people try to unload money today that they think will be worth less tomorrow. During the late 1970s inflation was a severely disrupting influence in the U.S. economy, rising to double-digit levels along with escalating interest rates. Macroeconomics seeks to understand the causes of inflation and to help government authorities pursue policies aimed at keeping the inflation rate low and within fairly predictable bounds. Stable and predictable prices facilitate planning for the future and reduce the uncertainty associated with market transactions.

In studying aggregate production in the economy and its fluctuations, macroeconomists seek to uncover the basic influences that cause national production to increase. The key to prosperity in an economy is steady growth in national output. When growth in a nation's output exceeds growth in its population, the output per person in the economy will grow, thus improving the well-being of the population on average.

POSITIVE ANALYSIS VERSUS NORMATIVE ANALYSIS

In the field of economics we're concerned with more than understanding *how* the economy functions. We also look at ways of improving the outcomes that emerge as the economy accomplishes its tasks of producing and distributing goods and services. The operation of the economy isn't flawless, nor does it please all of us. As individuals, we differ in our opinions about the goals for which resources in the economy should be used. We also disagree about the appropriate nature and extent of government involvement in the economy, and through political channels we express our views about which groups government should help. Because we understand the concept of opportunity cost, we know that if a government action benefits one group, it inevitably imposes a cost on another group.

Positive Analysis

positive analysis a way to look at the economy that seeks to forecast the impact of changes in economic policies or conditions on observable items such as production, sales, prices, and personal incomes, then tries to determine who gains and who loses as a result of the changes.

In evaluating economic policies, we must understand the basic functioning of the economy before we can predict the impact of those policies on the economy. Positive analysis is a way to forecast the impact of changes in economic policies or conditions on observable items such as production, sales, prices, and personal incomes. It then tries to determine who gains and who loses as a result of the changes. Positive analysis makes statements of the "if . . . then" type that can be supported or refuted by empirical evidence. For example, "*If* electronics import quotas are imposed, *then* the prices of VCRs for U.S. consumers will increase." Or, "*If* the federal government deficit is reduced, *then* interest rates will fall." We can accept or reject these statements by observing whether evidence exists that changes in prices, incomes, or interest rates actually do occur as a direct result of the policy changes.

Because no one completely understands how the economy works, economists often disagree about actual cause-and-effect relationships. Such disagreements must be resolved by examining the facts, using statistical methods to test the relationships.

Normative Analysis

Positive analysis cannot be used to evaluate an outcome. For example, positive analysis of government welfare programs can look at the impact of such programs on the incentives of recipients to work and on national production, but it cannot

principles in practice

Policy Perspective: The Economics of Drinking, Driving, and Highway Deaths

An Example of Positive Analysis What does drunken driving have to do with economics? The answer is "a whole lot," according to recent positive analysis of the impact on fatal motor vehicle accidents of raising the drinking age and taxing beer.

For people in the United States between the ages of 16 and 24, automobile accidents are a leading cause of death. Evidence suggests that policies increasing the cost of obtaining alcoholic beverages also reduce highway deaths. For example, taxes on beer increase the price of beer and tend to decrease its consumption. Similarly, raising the drinking age to 21 makes it more difficult for persons under that age to obtain alcoholic beverages.

Since 1984, all 50 states have raised their minimum drinking age to 21. Positive analysis by economists of the impact of the increased drinking age has concluded that it would reduce nighttime fatal crash involvements by 13 percent.*

Most young drinkers haven't been drinking long enough to become habitual alcohol users, and they typ-ically have low incomes. Because a tax on beer will cause its price to increase, it's likely to induce young drinkers with low incomes to cut back their consumption of beer. Positive analysis of the impact of taxes on beer suggests that these too can save lives. Economists in a recent study estimated that if beer taxes in the United States had increased faster than they actually did between 1975 and 1982, over 1,000 lives of youths between the ages of 18 and 20 could have been saved annually!†

You may have your own views about the legal drinking age or increased taxes on beer. You may very well change your views in response to positive analysis of the economics of drinking and driving!

* William Du Mouchel, Allan F. Williams, and Paul Zador, "Raising the Alcohol Purchase Age: Its Effects on Fatal Motor Vehicle Crashes in Twenty-six States," *Journal of Legal Studies* 16, no. 1 (January 1987), pp. 249–66.
† Michael Grossman and Henry Saffer, "Beer Taxes, the Legal Drinking Age, and Youth Motor Vehicle Fatalities," National Bureau of Economic Research, Working Paper no. 1914, May 1986.

determine whether the programs are good or bad. To evaluate the performance of these programs, we must establish criteria or norms against which we will compare their actual outcomes.

We use normative analysis as a way to evaluate the desirability of alternative outcomes according to underlying *value judgments* about what is good or bad. A normative statement presents a point of view about what a policy *should* accomplish. For example, "Families of four with incomes below $15,000 per year should be exempted from federal income taxes." Or, "Tariffs and other restrictions that impede free international trade should be eliminated."

The normative approach used by many economists is based on an underlying value judgment that evaluates well-being in a nation only in terms of the well-being of individuals. The normative approach makes recommendations regarding *what ought to be*. It's used to *prescribe* changes in policy and the use of productive capacity in an economy as well as to evaluate performance.

normative analysis a way to evaluate the desirability of alternative outcomes according to underlying value judgments about what is good or bad.

Gains and Losses from Economic Policies
Economic policies and other changes affecting the way the economy functions usually result in gains to some groups and losses to others. In making judgments about whether an outcome is good or bad, we must weigh the gains against the losses. For example, protecting the American automobile industry from foreign competition can benefit you as an auto company owner or employee. However, as a consumer of domestic autos you can lose as a result of such protection, because the prices of cars produced by this industry are likely to be higher than they would be if foreign competition were unrestricted.

Economists don't always share the same values. In particular, they hold many different opinions about the way the success of the economy in distributing material well-being should be evaluated. Opinions about the fairness of outcomes influence the recommendations economists make about alternative policies. For example, economists often support policies recommending that tax revenues be used to provide income to the poor. However, using tax revenues in this way can have unfavorable effects on the economy by reducing productive capacity. We use positive analysis to show the effects on production and on the incomes of the poor, while we use normative analysis to make judgments about the results.

Normative analysis is used to evaluate policies and outcomes in terms of specific goals. It does, however, benefit from positive analysis. For example, even if we agree that it's good to support policies that reduce poverty, we still need to know whether a particular program designed to aid the poor *can* achieve its objective. Positive analysis can help us choose intelligently among proposed policies whose predicted outcomes are in accord with our value judgments.

🌐 *the global economy*

Protectionism

Who Gains and Who Loses? Now let's use positive analysis to examine a key issue in U.S. foreign trade policy—protection of domestic industries from foreign competition. Increased foreign competition has led to intense lobbying for protection by U.S. industries whose sales have been hurt by it. Concern about the impact of increased foreign competition on employment opportunities in manufacturing has led to still more calls to protect U.S. industries from foreign competition.

Import quotas are annual limits to the amount of goods that can be brought into a nation through international trade. *Tariffs* are taxes on imported goods designed to raise the prices of those goods to domestic consumers. Since 1947, the United States has used what is known as the "escape clause" of the international General Agreement on Tariffs and Trade (GATT) to provide temporary protection to domestic industries. Under the escape clause, industries proving to the U.S. International Trade Commission (ITC) that imports will threaten or otherwise cause serious economic injury can receive protection against those imports through import quotas or tariffs. Since 1947, more than 30 U.S. industries have applied for and received protection under the escape clause.[1]

Since 1962, the U.S. government has also provided trade adjustment assistance that cushions the impact of foreign competition on workers, businesses, and regions adversely affected by imports. Such assistance has very stringent eligibility requirements, and cash payments have been limited.

The issue of protection involves conflict between consumers and suppliers of specialized inputs, including labor, in industries whose profits and revenues are adversely affected by foreign competition. The political choice that must be made is between providing direct or indirect subsidies to these industries to keep them afloat or allowing them to go under if they can't compete. In the latter case the resources released from these industries would then have to find employment in other industries. Because the search for employment can take time, this implies increased unemployment and declines in income until the transition has been made.

---

[1] See Robert Z. Lawrence and Robert E. Litan, *Saving Free Trade* (Washington, D.C.: Brookings Institution, 1986).

The conflict between avoiding economic disloca-tion from foreign trade and protecting consumers is clear from studies of the effects of previous protec-tionist measures:

1. The Smoot-Hawley Tariff Act of 1930, which raised tariffs in the United States by about 60 per-cent, was widely credited with helping induce a worldwide depression by reducing income in foreign nations as U.S. purchases of their exports plum-meted.[2]

2. An estimate of the impact of U.S. restrictions on imports of sugar, clothing, and automobiles in 1984 indicated that these measures cost low-income consumers twice as much as they cost upper-income consumers, suggesting that trade restrictions harm the poor more than the rich.[3]

3. Import quotas for Japanese cars from 1981 through 1983 increased the prices of those cars by an estimated $1,000 per vehicle and resulted in in-creased expenditure estimated at about $2 billion by consumers of Japanese cars. The quotas also contrib-uted to a $370 per car price increase on average for American cars over the same period. The U.S. auto industry and its employees gained as a result of the quotas, while buyers of both U.S. and Japanese cars lost.[4]

4. An estimate of the impact of seven recent es-cape-clause actions found that they raised prices to such a degree as to cost consumers $340,000 per job saved.[5]

5. The combined effect of U.S. tariffs and import quotas on apparel in the late 1980s was equivalent to a whopping 46 percent tax on imported clothing! Although protection of the U.S. apparel industry saved jobs and raised the wages of textile workers, it cost us $52,000 per year to save these jobs, which paid on average less than $20,000 per year.[6]

Protectionism affects you as a consumer. The im-ported suit or dress that you would pay $200 for in the absence of protective tariffs or import quotas costs you $292 instead because of the 46 percent effective tax rate on these imported products! The benefits of protectionism to workers often fall short of its cost to consumers. Do you think we can afford protectionist policies?

- How does microeconomics differ from macro-economics?

- Explain what is meant by *positive analysis*. Give two examples of positive statements.

- Explain what is meant by *normative analysis*, and describe how it differs from *positive analy-sis*. Give two examples of normative state-ments.

CONCEPT CHECK

☐

THE ECONOMIC WAY OF REASONING: MODELS AND MARGINAL ANALYSIS

What makes you behave the way you do? Given a number of alternatives from which to choose, why do you take one course of action while your roommate or your best friend takes a completely different course?

In the discipline of economics we seek to isolate relationships of cause and effect in the economy as we study the behavior of human beings. To accomplish this objective, we gather information that will help us make generalizations about pro-duction, technology, and human behavior.

---

[2] See F. W. Taussig, *The Tariff History of the United States*, 8th ed. (New York: G. P. Putnam, 1931), pp. 490–500.

[3] Susan Hickok, "Consumer Cost of U.S. Trade Restraints," *Federal Reserve Bank of New York Quarterly Review* 10 (Summer 1985), p. 10.

[4] Robert W. Crandall, "Import Quotas and the Automobile Industry: The Cost of Protectionism," *Brookings Review* 2, no. 4 (Summer 1984), pp. 8–16.

[5] Gary Clyde Hufbauer, Diane T. Berliner, and Kimberly Ann Elliott, *Trade Protection in the United States: Thirty-one Case Studies* (Washington, D.C.: Institute for International Economics, 1980).

[6] See Congress of the United States, Congressional Budget Office, *Trade Restraints and the Competitive Status of the Textile, Apparel, and Nonrubber-Footwear Industries* (Washington, D.C.: Congress of the United States, December 1991).

A chief goal of economic analysis is to help us understand the functions of the economy and the forces influencing the choices people make under the constraints they face. Much of economic theory is based on the premise that our behavior is quite predictable. Economists often assume that we systematically pursue certain objectives, such as seeking the greatest satisfaction from our purchases or the highest profit from the sale of a product.

marginal analysis
a method economists use to study decision making; involves a systematic comparison of the benefits and costs of actions.

A method economists use to study decision making, marginal analysis, is based on the idea that it's possible for you to gain from engaging in more of an activity if the extra benefits exceed the extra costs of doing so. You'll discover that marginal analysis is more than a technique for studying decisions—it can actually guide you in decision making. In fact, you can regard marginal analysis as applied common sense because it involves a systematic comparison of the benefits and costs of actions. By studying marginal analysis, you can understand how gains are sought as you and others make business and personal choices. For example, you decide whether to take additional courses in a semester based on whether the additional benefits of doing so outweigh the additional costs. Among the benefits are the possibility of graduating earlier or having a lighter course load next semester. The costs include the dollar expense of adding courses and the extra time you'll have to spend studying instead of socializing and participating in sports or other leisure-time activities. If you have a job, your employer decided to hire you by comparing the expected benefits of doing so—the value of your services—with the cost of having you on the payroll and the time needed to train and supervise you. As you read this chapter, you'll discover how often you already use marginal analysis in your personal affairs.

Economic Theory and Its Models

Although we can observe actions and their consequences, observation and description are not sufficient to understand and, ultimately, to predict actions. We need to establish cause-and-effect relationships so we can understand the basic economic forces and the way individuals cope with the problem of scarcity. Therefore, we use theories to interpret actions and outcomes. A theory is a framework that helps us understand the relationships between cause and effect. It is a simplification of actual relationships. The purpose of theory in all scientific analysis is to *explain* the causes of phenomena we observe. To conduct economic analysis, we frequently need to make assumptions about the economic environment and human motivation. We develop economic theories to explain such important observable quantities as the production, prices, and consumption of goods and services; the employment of workers; and levels of saving and investment.

theory a framework that helps us understand relationships between cause and effect; a simplification of actual relationships.

Economic Variables

variable a quantity or dollar amount that can have more than one value.

Economic variables are quantities or dollar amounts that can have more than one value. For example, the price of an item is an economic variable representing what we must give up in exchange for each unit of that item. Price is an economic variable because it can go up or down as changes occur in the economy. The number of unemployed workers is another economic variable that fluctuates.

Just as you can't cure a disease if you don't know its cause, it's essential to understand *how* the economy works if you're interested in changing economic outcomes you consider undesirable. For example, if a goal of your economic policy is to reduce unemployment, the methods you propose will be more effective if you understand the causes of unemployment. A policy can fail miserably in achieving its objectives or can have unanticipated adverse effects if policymakers don't understand the impact of their policies on the economy. For example, economic theory can show that government policies designed to benefit consumers by controlling prices of basic goods inevitably result in shortages of those goods. If the objective of such policies is to increase the incomes of certain persons, economic theory can help policymakers consider other methods that don't result in shortages.

Economic Models

An economic model is a simplified way of expressing how some sector of the economy functions. It contains assumptions that establish relationships among economic variables. It uses logic, graphs, or mathematics to determine the consequences of the assumptions. In this way the model can make predictions about the changes in decisions affecting economic variables that result from a change in economic conditions.

A good economic model is comparable to a schematic drawing showing that when you jiggle a certain lever, you set off a series of reactions that result in the movement of certain gears. Just as the drawing fails to capture the texture and intricacy of the actual machine, so too an economic model fails to mirror the complexity of the real-life sector of the economy it seeks to explain. A model is a *tool* we can use to understand the consequences of a theory. A good model can also accurately predict changes in the economic variables it is set up to explain.

One model may seek to explain how changes in the rate of increase or decrease of the prices of goods and services affect interest rates in the economy by assuming that lenders seek to maximize the profit they make from loans. Another model may examine the way an improvement in technology that lowers the cost of producing computers affects the price of computers, assuming that businesses seek to maximize profit.

An economic model is abstract because it doesn't attempt to capture all of the relevant influences on behavior. For example, an economic model set up to explain the rates of marriage and divorce may assume that the earnings differences between males and females have an effect on marriage and divorce. The model may assume that as the gap between earnings is reduced, the gains from marriage decline. This implies that as more women pursue careers and their earning potential reaches that of men, the marriage rate will decline and the divorce rate will go up. Similarly, an assumption that sellers seek to maximize profit from the sale of their product may not capture the full complexity of business motivation. Business owners may have other goals in addition to earning profit. They may also be concerned with their public image, their sales revenue, or the dividends they pay their stockholders. However, by concentrating on only one goal, even though this is not realistic, a model can more clearly unveil basic forces of cause and effect.

Suppose we hypothesize that an increase in the availability of compact discs (CDs) over a year will lower their price. The phrase *other things being equal* or its Latin equivalent, *ceteris paribus,* is used to acknowledge that influences other than the one whose effect is being analyzed must be controlled in testing a hypothesis.

The hypothesis and the theory aren't necessarily refuted by the facts if other things *are not* equal. For example, in 1987 a number of new factories began producing compact discs. CDs became much more plentiful that year and began to outsell long-playing records. However, despite the increased abundance of the discs, their price didn't decline. Did this mean that the theory was incorrect? Before we scrap the theory, we need to determine whether *other influences* on the price of CDs changed at the same time the available supply increased. In fact, it's likely that the

economic model
a simplified way of expressing how some sector of the economy functions. Contains assumptions that establish relationships among economic variables.

ceteris paribus a Latin phrase meaning "other things being equal." Used to acknowledge that influences other than the one whose effect is being analyzed must be controlled in testing a hypothesis.

economic thinkers

Adam Smith

You don't have to have a photographic memory for dates to know that 1776 was a significant year in history. In that year the Declaration of Independence was signed in Philadelphia. Fewer people probably know that, also in that year, a Scottish professor of philosophy published a book entitled *An Inquiry into the Nature and Causes of the Wealth of Nations* (known universally as *The Wealth of Nations*). The publishing of this book represented a watershed in the development of intellectual thought on economic issues and problems. Although many of the ideas in the book weren't entirely new at the time, its author, Adam Smith, is generally credited with being the father of the discipline of economics.

Professor Smith taught moral philosophy at the University of Glasgow. His specialty was "natural theology," which sought to understand and formulate the natural laws that govern physical and social phenomena.

At the time Smith wrote his monumental work, many politicians measured the affluence of a nation in terms of the gold and silver accumulated in national treasuries. Smith pointed out that the wealth of nations was chiefly determined by people conducting their daily business rather than by the amount of gold and silver in a government treasury. He believed that the accumulation of capital equipment, such as machines and structures used by factories, was a vital determinant of wealth because it enhanced the division of labor. The thrifty Scot argued that saving was a critical means of providing the funds needed to finance the accumulation of capital.

Smith's main task in *The Wealth of Nations* was to develop a framework for understanding the mechanism through which the seemingly chaotic hubbub of daily trading actually resulted in a natural order. His background in natural theology led him to conclude that trade in unregulated markets would maximize the wealth of nations. The foundation for this belief was the no-

number of CD buyers increased as a result of increased sales of compact disc players in 1987. In addition, growth in consumer income during the year could have increased the willingness of buyers to pay for CDs. Both of these influences could have put upward pressure on the price of CDs that offset the downward pressure resulting from the increased availability of CDs.

When constructing economic models to explain the values of economic variables, economists seek to understand all the important determinants of these values. However, in concentrating on cause-and-effect relationships among particular variables, economists ignore the influence of other determinants on the values of variables by making the "other things being equal" assumption. Unlike physical scientists, who can conduct controlled laboratory experiments, economists are concerned with social relationships. In testing hypotheses, economists must therefore attempt to account for the influence of many simultaneous changes in economic conditions on data by using statistical methods. Support for hypotheses and theories from actual data is often elusive and subject to debate because in the real world other things are seldom equal. Economics is not an exact science, and for that reason there is often considerable disagreement among economists on the way to interpret data.

tion of rational behavior. The main and lasting contribution of Adam Smith was therefore the formulation of an economic interaction theory based on the view that humans carefully pursue net gains.

Smith believed that rational behavior is biologically determined and that people have an innate tendency to pursue their self-interest. Yet he concluded that in pursuing personal gains, individuals are impelled by the requirements of survival to act in the interests of society. In his eloquent statement of this principle of "enlightened self-interest," he was careful to emphasize that individuals are motivated not by altruism but by need for the cooperation of others.

The following quotes from *The Wealth of Nations* speak for themselves:*

Man has almost constant occasion for the help of his brethren, and it is in vain for him to expect it from their benevolence only. He will be more likely to prevail if he can interest their self-love in his favor, and show them that it is for their own advantage to do for him what he requires of them. (Book 1, chap. 2, p. 14)

As every individual, therefore, endeavors as much as he can to employ his capital in support of domestic industry, so as to direct that industry that its product may be of the greatest value, every individual necessarily labors to render the annual revenue of the society as great as he can . . . by directing that industry in such a manner as its produce may be of the greatest value, he intends only his own gain, and he is in this, as in many other cases, led by an invisible hand to promote an end which was no part of his intention. By pursuing his own interest he frequently promotes that of the society more effectually than when he really intends to promote it. (Book 4, chap. 2, pp. 421–23)

Smith believed that rational human beings have an inherent tendency to "truck and barter," thereby seeking out means for mutually advantageous exchanges. Another hallmark of his views was his belief that a system of unregulated markets composed of many competing sellers maximized well-being. Although he is often credited with supporting *laissez-faire*, a lack of government intervention in business affairs, he also believed governments should assure the competitiveness of markets. Smith denounced monopolies, many of which were created by governments at the time. His views on the role of government were quite complex. In general, he believed that much government intervention in markets did more harm than good.†

Smith can justly be credited with establishing economics as a separate social science. He firmly established the individual as the main object of study and provided the first attempt to systematically analyze how the economy functions.

* Page references are from Adam Smith, *An Inquiry into the Nature and Causes of the Wealth of Nations* (New York: Modern Library, 1937). This edition was edited by Edwin Cannan. The book was first published in 1776.
† For a discussion of Adam Smith's views on government, see "Adam Smith on Laissez-faire," in *Essays in Economic Thought*, ed. Joseph J. Spengler and William R. Allen (Chicago: Rand McNally, 1960).

CONCEPT CHECK ☐

- What is the purpose of economic theory?
- Give some examples of economic variables, and describe how an economic model might make assumptions that imply relationships between economic variables.
- Give an example of a hypothesis about the cause-and-effect relationship between two economic variables that can be tested. What are some of the problems involved in testing hypotheses derived from economic models?

RATIONAL BEHAVIOR

A key component of any economic model is the assumptions it makes about the way people behave. **Behavioral assumptions** establish the motivations of individuals so we can understand cause-and-effect relationships among economic variables. For example, it's typically assumed that the owners of business firms seek to maximize their annual profits from the sale of a product. Once we make this assumption, we can use a model to trace out the impact of a change in an economic variable, such as the wages paid to a firm's employees, on the quantity of a product the firm is willing to

5

behavioral assumption an assumption that establishes the motivation of persons for the purpose of understanding cause-and-effect relationships among economic variables.

sell. It's also commonly assumed that consumers act to obtain the most satisfaction possible from purchasing goods and services. We can use this assumption to examine how changes in such economic variables as the price of an item affect the quantity consumers are willing and able to purchase.

When you seek to gain by undertaking actions for which the extra benefit exceeds the associated extra cost, you're engaging in rational behavior. For example, your behavior will be considered rational if you choose to take additional courses each semester as long as the extra benefit you associate with those courses exceeds the extra cost you incur when you take them. You evaluate the benefits of actions subjectively in relation to your personal objectives. The cost of an action you take is the value you place on the sacrifice you must make to enjoy the benefits of the action. Scarcity implies that you can obtain a benefit only at the cost of forgoing an alternative opportunity. Thus, if you want to act in the dramatic society's new play and begin training for the cross-country squad and the two activities are scheduled at the same time, you decide to bask in the glow of the footlights at the cost of the chance to win glory on foot. You behave rationally when you actively pursue your self-interest, as you evaluate it, by trying to get the greatest possible well-being from the resources you have. In this case you've decided that you'll make the best (and perhaps most enjoyable) use of your resource, time, by acting instead of sprinting.

The assumption of rational behavior is a key component in many economic models. The term *rational* as used in economics implies nothing about a person's sanity. It merely supposes that each of us has certain objectives. You're regarded as rational in the economic sense if you systematically undertake actions to achieve your desired objectives. Those objectives may be good or bad from another person's point of view. For example, a burglar's objective may be to become rich by breaking into homes and stores each month. We can regard the burglar as rational if the burglar chooses the monthly number of burglaries in a way that considers both the personal benefits (such as the value of goods stolen) and the personal costs (such as tools, the value of time in its next best use, and the possibility of being caught and having to pay a penalty). Likewise, altruistic motives are entirely consistent with rational behavior. A person who is altruistic receives benefit when the person uses resources to provide material or emotional gains to others. There's nothing irrational about parents feeding and caring for their children! Parents receive benefits from these activities and consider those benefits as well as the associated costs when choosing to have children. When economists say we are rational, they neither deny the fact that we differ in our objectives, nor do they make any judgments that applaud or condemn those objectives.

Marginal Analysis of Rational Behavior

Marginal analysis is a step-by-step way of determining how people engaging in rational behavior make choices. Marginal analysis of your decision to buy compact discs would look at the benefits and costs associated with your purchase of each *extra* compact disc starting from zero. If the additional benefit you obtain from buying another CD exceeds its price, you'll be better off buying it than keeping your money to spend on something else. The dollar value you place on the satisfaction you obtain from another unit of an item is its marginal benefit. The marginal benefit of an item in dollars represents the maximum sum of money you're willing and able to give up to obtain one more unit of the item without becoming worse off or better off by doing so. The marginal cost of an item is the sacrifice you must make to obtain

---

rational behavior ways of acting that seek to gain by undertaking actions for which the extra benefit exceeds the associated extra cost.

marginal benefit the dollar value placed on the satisfaction obtained from another unit of an item.

marginal cost the sacrifice made to obtain an additional unit of an item.

each extra unit. The marginal cost of buying another CD is what you forgo to obtain it. If you choose to buy one that costs $11.99, you forgo the opportunity to use that sum to purchase another item.

The graph in Box 1 shows how the marginal benefit of an item is likely to vary as you buy more of it during the period of a month. The extra satisfaction you get from each extra unit tends to decline because you tend to tire of the item.

Suppose the price of compact discs is currently $11.99. In Box 1 this is represented by a horizontal line drawn from $11.99 on the vertical axis. This line shows that each additional disc will cost you $11.99 of expenditure on other items. The line therefore represents the marginal cost of each disc to you. Will you buy that first disc? To answer the question, you must begin using the economic way of reasoning through marginal analysis. What is the marginal benefit of the first disc? The graph indicates that it is $20. As long as the marginal benefit exceeds the marginal cost, you'll enjoy a net gain by making the purchase. In the graph the marginal benefit of $20 exceeds the marginal cost of $11.99. The net gain from exchanging your cash for the first disc will be $20 − $11.99 = $8.01. Marginal analysis therefore concludes that you'll purchase the first disc because its marginal benefit to you exceeds its marginal cost. The shaded portion of the bar *above* the price line represents the net gain of $8.01 from the first disc you buy each month.

The second bar indicates that the marginal benefit of a second disc is $16 when you've already bought one CD that month. Similarly, the marginal benefit of a third disc is $14 when you've already bought two that month. The marginal benefit of a fourth disc is $12 when you've already bought three that month. The graph indicates that the marginal benefit of a fifth disc in the month is only $10 when you've already purchased four. Similarly, the marginal benefit of the sixth and seventh discs also declines.

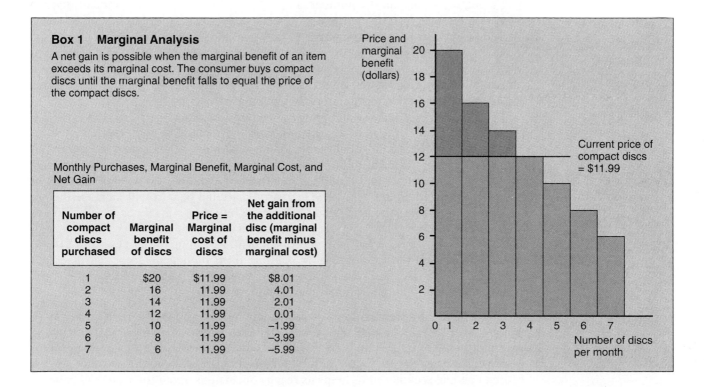

Box 1   Marginal Analysis

A net gain is possible when the marginal benefit of an item exceeds its marginal cost. The consumer buys compact discs until the marginal benefit falls to equal the price of the compact discs.

Monthly Purchases, Marginal Benefit, Marginal Cost, and Net Gain

Number of compact discs purchased	Marginal benefit of discs	Price = Marginal cost of discs	Net gain from the additional disc (marginal benefit minus marginal cost)
1	$20	$11.99	$8.01
2	16	11.99	4.01
3	14	11.99	2.01
4	12	11.99	0.01
5	10	11.99	−1.99
6	8	11.99	−3.99
7	6	11.99	−5.99

Price and marginal benefit (dollars)

Current price of compact discs = $11.99

Number of discs per month

How many discs will you buy in a month? A *rational person continues purchasing an item up to the point at which there is no additional net gain*. It's easy to see that this condition isn't met until you've bought four discs. This is because the marginal benefit of the second disc exceeds its marginal cost, as do the marginal benefits of the third and fourth discs. As shown in the table, the net gain from purchasing a second disc is $4.01 ($16 − $11.99 = $4.01). The net gain from purchasing a third disc is $2.01. However, the marginal benefit of the fourth disc is just barely above the price. You buy the fourth disc that month because you enjoy an additional net gain of 1 cent by doing so.

Why will you not buy five discs that month? Look at the graph and notice that the marginal benefit of the fifth disc is only $10. This falls short of the marginal cost of $11.99. As shown in the table, the net gain from a fifth disc per month is −$1.99. The net gain is negative because the marginal benefit of the disc falls short of its marginal cost. The negative net gain implies that purchasing that disc will make you worse off. If you're rational, you therefore buy no more than four discs per month. As shown in the table, no positive net gain is possible from purchasing more than four discs per month.

This simple economic model makes us aware of important influences on decisions to buy an item. We can reach the following conclusions from the model:

1. *The price of an item is an important influence on the amount of it that a buyer will choose to purchase.* This is because the price affects the net gain possible from buying a certain item. Each time you purchase it, you give up the opportunity to use the sum of dollars equal to the item's price to buy something else. If the price of compact discs falls, then, assuming nothing else changes, the net gains possible from buying more CDs increase. For example, suppose the price of compact discs falls to $7.99. Just substitute $7.99 for $11.99 in the third column of the table in Box 1, and you'll see the change in the numbers in the last column. When the price of discs is $7.99, you will buy six discs per month because net gains from buying a fifth and a sixth disc each month are now possible. Given all the other influences on a person's decision to buy an item, the lower the price, the greater is the net gain associated with any given amount. Lower prices allow additional net gains from additional amounts bought. Changes in the price of an item change the marginal cost of buying it and affect the amounts rational people purchase.

2. *A person's buying decision depends on the marginal benefit from purchasing an item and on the way marginal benefit varies with the amount bought.* Suppose you buy a new compact disc player that gives you much better sound than your old player. This may increase the marginal benefit you get from CDs. If the marginal benefit of each quantity purchased per month were to double, so would the height of each bar in the graph in Box 1. The increased marginal benefit will increase the net gain from each disc purchased and lead you to buy more discs per month. To see this, double the marginal benefit for each quantity in the table in Box 1 and recalculate the net gain possible for each additional disc, assuming the price is still $11.99. You will see that net gains are now possible from buying up to seven discs per month. Changes in the marginal benefit of buying an item therefore affect the quantities of the item that rational people choose to buy.

If you have mastered the logic of this simple model, you are well on your way to using the economic way of reasoning. You can see how changes that affect the marginal benefit and marginal cost of an activity (such as buying something) influence decisions to engage in that activity. You can also see how the assumption that rational people seek net gains helps us reach conclusions about the way they behave.

Rational behavior means that in deciding on any course of action, such as buying another unit of a good in a market, you compare the marginal benefit of that action with its marginal cost. As a rational person, you undertake actions as long as the marginal cost doesn't exceed the marginal benefit. By behaving in this way, you undertake all activities that provide you with additional net gains in well-being and you avoid all activities for which additional net gain would be negative.

The assumption that we are all rational decision makers relentlessly pursuing goals intended to improve our well-being has proved to be particularly fruitful in building economic models whose hypotheses are supported by facts. Not everyone agrees with this assumption. In fact, some of us don't consistently do what is in our best interest. However, the underlying assumptions of a model needn't be either realistic or without exception to be useful. Remember, the test of the usefulness of an economic model is the validity of the principles we can derive from it.

- What is rational behavior?
- Explain why you can realize a net gain from undertaking more of an activity if the marginal benefit of that activity exceeds its marginal cost.

- What can cause the marginal cost of purchasing an item to increase?

CONCEPT CHECK
□

GRAPHS: AN AID TO UNDERSTANDING ECONOMICS

If you were offered a guaranteed way to enhance your grasp of economic concepts, you'd leap at it, wouldn't you? Chapter 1 Supplement, *Graphs: A Basic Tool for Analyzing Economic Relationships*, provides a step-by-step guide to constructing, reading, and understanding graphs, a key component in the study of economics. When you've mastered the material in this supplement, you'll realize how graphs can simplify key economic relationships that might take paragraphs to explain. You'll be able to draw and label your own graphs and to interpret the graphs you'll find later in almost every chapter of this book. If you take some time now to become comfortable with graphs, you can be sure they'll serve you well throughout the course.

SUMMARY

1. Economics is concerned with the use of available productive resources to satisfy the desires and demands of people in a society.

2. The fundamental economic problem of scarcity is the imbalance between the desires of members of a society and the means of satisfying those desires.

3. The opportunity cost of choosing to use resources for one purpose is the sacrifice of the next best alternative for the use of those resources.

4. There are two main branches of economics. *Microeconomics* views the economy from the perspective of its individual participants. *Macroeconomics* considers the overall performance of the economy and the way its various sectors relate to one another.

5. *Positive analysis* seeks to predict the impact of changes in economic policy on observable items such as produc-

tion and income, then tries to determine who gains and who loses as a result of the changes. *Normative analysis* evaluates the desirability of alternative outcomes according to value judgments about what is good or bad.

6. Economic theories are designed to establish cause-and-effect relationships to help explain how economies function.

7. An economic model is a simplified way of expressing how a sector of the economy functions. Economic models can be used to develop hypotheses about the relationships among economic variables. These hypotheses represent implications of economic models that can be supported or refuted by examining facts.

8. Economic theories based on rational behavior assume that persons consider the marginal benefits and margi-

nal costs of their actions. Net gains are possible when the marginal benefit of additional activity exceeds the associated marginal cost. Rational persons seek out net gains by choosing to undertake more of an activity when its marginal benefit exceeds its marginal cost.

KEY TERMS

economy *9*

economics *9*

scarcity *9*

opportunity cost *9*

microeconomics *11*

macroeconomics *11*

positive analysis *12*

normative analysis *13*

marginal analysis *16*

theory *16*

variable *16*

economic model *17*

ceteris paribus (other things being equal) *17*

behavioral assumption *19*

rational behavior *20*

marginal benefit *20*

marginal cost *20*

CONCEPT REVIEW*

1 What functions does the U.S. economy accomplish?

2 How are the concepts of opportunity cost and scarcity related to each other?

3 Give examples of a microeconomic issue and a macroeconomic issue for which we can conduct a positive analysis.

4 What is the purpose of an economic model?

5 How can marginal analysis be used to explain rational behavior?

PROBLEMS AND APPLICATIONS

1. Suppose an economic theory sets up a model that implies that, *other things being equal,* an increase in interest rates will reduce the growth of national production. How can you test the validity of the theory? **4**

2. An economic model to explain sales of cars establishes a relationship between the price of cars and the quantity buyers are willing to purchase. A hypothesis developed from the model postulates that whenever the price of cars goes up, the quantity buyers will buy goes down. During the year consumer income increases as the price of cars goes up. The quantity of cars sold also increases. Does this mean that the theory establishing the relationship between the price of cars and the quantity consumers are willing and able to purchase is invalid? **4**

3. In what ways do economic theories and models abstract from reality? Why are unrealistic models useful? **4**

4. Give an example of a behavioral assumption in an economic model. What is the purpose of using behavioral assumptions in economic models? **4**

5. In what sense can an insane person or a criminal be regarded as engaging in rational behavior? **5**

6. A person makes decisions by habit. This person considers neither the benefits nor the costs of his or her actions. Can the person be considered rational? **5**

7. Suppose the marginal benefit to you of acquiring another suit this year is $200. If the price of suits is $250 and you are rational, will you buy one? **5**

8. You currently choose to buy two compact discs per month with your income. The current price is $14.99. Other things being equal, explain why a drop in the price of discs to $12.99 next month is likely to increase the quantity you'll buy. **5**

9. The following table shows how the marginal benefit of shoes of given quality varies with the number Jill purchases each year. As shown, the price of shoes is $29.99 per pair.

Pairs purchased per year	Marginal benefit	Price
1	$50	$29.99
2	40	29.99
3	30	29.99
4	20	29.99
5	10	29.99

---

* If you need additional help, the concept symbol refers you to the appropriate text discussion.

a. Assuming that Jill is rational and the price of shoes accurately reflects the marginal cost to her, how many pairs of shoes will Jill buy per year?

b. Suppose the price of shoes increases to $39.99 per year. Assuming that nothing else changes, how many pairs will Jill now buy? 5

10. Suppose that the marginal benefit of a pair of shoes for Joe is exactly double the marginal benefit indicated for Jill in the previous example. If the price of shoes for Joe is also $29.99 and Joe is rational, how many pairs of shoes per year will Joe buy? 5

inside information

Statistical Abstract of the United States Like it or not, statistics play a part in your daily life: you need to know facts and figures about the United States. One of the best sources of current and historical information about our economy is the *Statistical Abstract of the United States.* This serviceable "national data book" is published annually by the Bureau of the Census of the U.S. Department of Commerce.

The *Statistical Abstract* gives you 1,000 pages of facts and figures on just about everything you might want to know about the U.S. economy. It's *the* place to go when you need information in order to write papers or make economic decisions. If your job requires you to prepare reports on business conditions, be sure that you have ready access to the latest edition of this valuable volume.

You can get information about 31 broad categories from the *Statistical Abstract.* Population data include birth, life-expectancy, marriage, and divorce rates. There are statistics on expenditures for health, nutrition, and education, not to mention crime, air and water quality, parks, recreation, travel, and elections. Government spending and finance are covered in detail.

Do you want information about the labor force, employment, and earnings; income, expenditure, and wealth; prices; banking and the U.S. financial system; business enterprises; or international trade? Check the *Statistical Abstract!* Industry data span communications, science,

transportation, agriculture, manufacturing, forestry, fisheries, construction, housing, and services in the United States. You'll also find comparative international statistics.

You can use this important reference book as the first step in many research projects. Each section begins by defining the basic terms it uses and lists the primary sources of information for its figures. If the *Statistical Abstract* doesn't tell you everything you need to know, then all you have to do is check the sources from which its data came.

If you want to buy your own copy, write to

Superintendent of Documents
U.S. Government Printing Office
Washington, D.C. 20402

or telephone (202) 783-3238. In Washington, D.C., New York, and some other major cities, just go to or call one of the U.S. government bookstores run by the U.S. Government Printing Office. The book comes with a neat little bonus pamphlet, *USA Statistics in Brief.* Small enough to fit in your pocket or purse, this useful item summarizes *Statistical Abstract* data for various categories and selected years. If you don't want to buy your own copy of the *Statistical Abstract,* just go to the reference department in your school library or public library, where you can probably check the latest edition.

chapter supplement

Graphs: A Basic Tool for Analyzing Economic Relationships

Do graphs make you nervous? If so, relax—you're about to discover how helpful they'll be as you study economics.

Economists use graphs often to express relationships, such as the way the maximum possible production of one item is affected by the production of another item. Graphic analysis is a tool to aid you in learning economics and using it to reach important conclusions. Graphs show how the value of one variable changes as the value of some other variable is increased or decreased.

PLOTTING POINTS ON A SET OF AXES

A two-dimensional graph has a vertical axis along which one variable, designated in general by the symbol Y, is measured. Another variable, the X variable, is measured on the horizontal axis. As the value of X changes, so does the value of Y.

origin on a set of axes, the point designated by 0, at which variables X and Y both take on the value of zero.

The origin of the axes is the point, designated by 0, at which both X and Y take on the value of zero. The axes drawn for most economic data are at a right angle to each other, with measurement scales drawn horizontally and vertically from the origin, because most of the data used in economics are positive rather than negative. If, however, Y were to take on negative values, the vertical axis would have to be extended downward below the origin to accommodate those values. Similarly, if X were to take on negative values, the horizontal axis would have to be extended to the left of the origin to accommodate them.

The table in Box 1 shows a relationship between X and Y. The second column gives the value of Y for each value of X in the first column. The pairs of numbers on each line of the table denote a *functional relationship* between X and Y. The functional relationship implies that the value of the Y variable changes as the value of the X variable increases or decreases.

Box 1 A Curve Showing a Positive Relationship between *X* and *Y*

The curve shown is based on the data in the table below. The value of Y increases as the value of X increases, indicating a positive relationship between the two variables.

A Positive Relationship between X and Y

Value of X	Corresponding value of Y	Point on graph
1	2	A_1
2	3	A_2
3	4	A_3
4	5	A_4
5	6	A_5

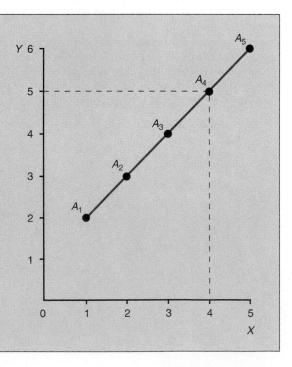

In this sense the value of *Y depends on* or is a *function of* the value of *X*. You can use the table to find the value of *Y* for each value of *X,* or vice versa.

The data from the table in Box 1 are plotted on the set of axes shown in the graph next to the table. Each line of the table has been designated with a letter *A* followed by a number to identify the points on the graph. The point A_1 corresponds to the pair of values $X = 1$, $Y = 2$. When plotted, these numbers are called the coordinates of point A_1. Similarly, when *X* is equal to 2, *Y* is equal to 3. These coordinates correspond to point A_2 on the graph. Point A_3 on the graph is the point at which *X* is equal to 3 and *Y* is equal to 4. Similarly, points A_4 and A_5 from the table are plotted on the axes and a line is drawn connecting each point. This line connecting the points corresponding to the coordinates of *X* and *Y* from the table depicts the relationship between *X* and *Y*. Such a line is called a curve even when its shape is not actually curvy. Many of the curves depicting economic relationships in this book will be straight lines.

Along the curve drawn in the graph in Box 1, there is a positive or direct relationship between *X* and *Y,* meaning that *Y increases* whenever *X increases.* For example, suppose the *Y* variable in Box 1 indicates the cost of producing each microcomputer in a factory. The *X* variable could be the number of computers produced per month. Assume that the numbers for both these variables could be estimated and the functional relationship established to draw up a table like the one in Box 1. An upward-sloping curve, as in the graph in the box (with different numbers, of course), would mean that there was a positive relationship between the unit cost of the computers and the number produced each month in the factory.

The curve drawn in any graph is used to find the value of *Y* for any possible value of *X*. For example, in the graph in Box 1, for the value of *X* equal to 4, follow the dashed line for the point on the horizontal axis corresponding to 4 *just up to the curve.* From that point, follow the dashed horizontal line from the curve to the vertical axis to find the corresponding value of *Y,* which is 5 in this case.

The data in the table of Box 2 depict a negative or inverse relationship between *X* and *Y,* showing that when the value of *X* increases, the corresponding value of *Y,* indicated in the second column, *decreases.* The graph in Box 2 plots the points that show the value of *Y* corresponding to each value of *X*. The points are labeled to correspond to the *B* letters followed by numbers in the last column of the table. The curve shows that whenever the value of *X* increases, the corresponding value of *Y* decreases.

Negative relationships between economic variables are quite common. For example, the *Y* variable may be the price of a VCR and the *X* variable may be the number of VCRs that buyers

coordinates a pair of numbers that correspond to values for variables *X* and *Y* when plotted on a set of axes.

curve a straight or curved line drawn to connect points plotted on a set of axes.

positive (direct) relationship the connection between variables that is depicted by an upward-sloping curve on a set of axes; indicates that variable *Y* increases whenever variable *X* increases.

negative (inverse) relationship the connection between variables that is depicted by a downward-sloping curve on a set of axes; indicates that variable *Y* decreases whenever variable *X* increases.

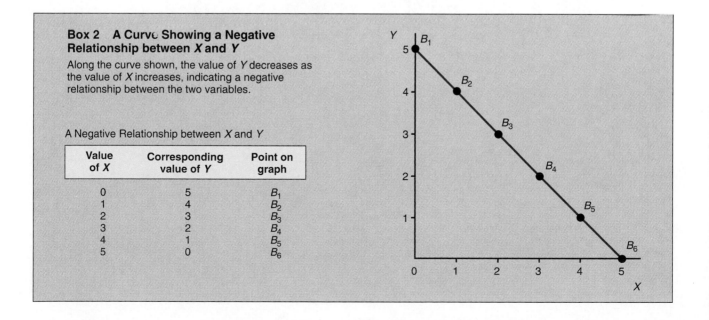

Box 2   A Curve Showing a Negative Relationship between *X* and *Y*

Along the curve shown, the value of *Y* decreases as the value of *X* increases, indicating a negative relationship between the two variables.

A Negative Relationship between *X* and *Y*

Value of *X*	Corresponding value of *Y*	Point on graph
0	5	B_1
1	4	B_2
2	3	B_3
3	2	B_4
4	1	B_5
5	0	B_6

in a market are willing and able to purchase during a certain period. A curve like the one drawn in the graph indicates that the lower the price of the VCR, the greater the number of units buyers are willing and able to buy over the given period. In other words, the graph indicates a negative relationship between the price of a VCR and the quantity buyers will purchase over a period.

THE CONCEPT OF SLOPE AND ITS USES IN ECONOMICS

slope the measurement of the rate at which the *Y* variable, on the vertical axis, rises or falls along a curve as the *X* variable, on the horizontal axis, increases.

The slope of a curve measures the rate at which the *Y* variable, on the vertical axis, rises or falls as the *X* variable, on the horizontal axis, increases. The slope of a line or curve is $\Delta Y/\Delta X$, where the Greek symbol Δ (delta) represents the amount of an increase (or decrease) in the value of each variable along the line or curve.

A curve or line that is upward sloping has positive slope. For example, along the upward-sloping line in graph **A** in Box 3, *Y increases* as *X* increases. For each one-unit increase in *X* along the line, the value of *Y* increases by two units. The slope of the line at any point is therefore $2/1 = 2$.

A curve or line that is downward sloping has negative slope. Along the downward-sloping line in graph **B,** *Y decreases* as *X* increases. For each one-unit increase in *X* along the line drawn in the graph, *Y* decreases by one unit. The slope of this line at any point is therefore $-1/1 = -1$. A downward-sloping curve has negative slope because ΔY is always negative when ΔX is positive.

A line with zero slope is, as you might expect, flat. Along the flat line in graph **C,** there is no increase in *Y* as *X* increases. It follows that $\Delta Y = 0$ for any ΔX, so that $\Delta Y/\Delta X = 0$.

The standard equation for a linear curve is

$$Y = mX + b$$

where *m* is the slope of the line and *b* is the value of *Y* that would prevail if the value of *X* were zero. The *b* of the equation represents the intercept of the line with the horizontal axis. The intercept can be either a positive or a negative number.

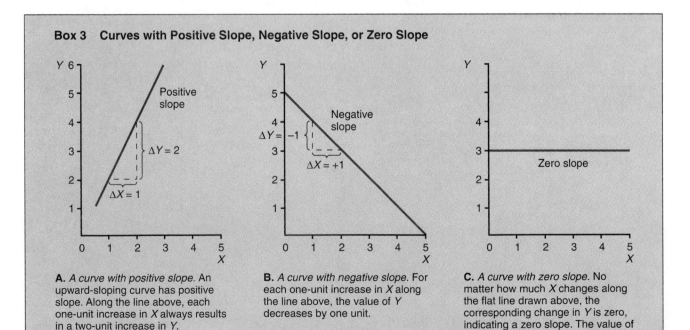

Box 3   Curves with Positive Slope, Negative Slope, or Zero Slope

A. *A curve with positive slope.* An upward-sloping curve has positive slope. Along the line above, each one-unit increase in *X* always results in a two-unit increase in *Y.*

B. *A curve with negative slope.* For each one-unit increase in *X* along the line above, the value of *Y* decreases by one unit.

C. *A curve with zero slope.* No matter how much *X* changes along the flat line drawn above, the corresponding change in *Y* is zero, indicating a zero slope. The value of *Y* is always 3 no matter what the value of *X.*

For example, the value of *m* in graph **B** would be equal to -1, while the value of *b* in the standard equation for a line would be 5. The equation corresponding to the curve drawn in graph **B** would therefore be

$$Y = 5 - x$$

This equation says that the value of *Y* is equal to 5 when *X* is zero and that each time *X* increases by one unit, the value of *Y* falls by one unit. If *X* were equal to 4, the value of *Y* would therefore be 1.

Similarly, the equation for the curve shown in graph **C** is

$$Y = 3$$

because the slope of the curve is 0 and its intercept on the *Y* axis is 3. This equation tells you that *Y* is equal to 3 no matter what the value of *X*.

Changes in Slope along a Curve

Nonlinear curves are those for which the slope changes from point to point. In Box 4, graph **A** shows a curve that has negative slope throughout but becomes steeper as *X* increases. Graph **B** shows a curve that also has negative slope throughout but whose slope becomes less negative, and therefore closer to zero, as *X* increases. When viewed from the origin, the curve in **A** has a *concave* shape, while the one in **B** has a *convex* shape.

Box 5 shows two curves, each with positive slope throughout, for which the slope changes as *X* increases. In **A** the slope of the curve increases as *X* increases. In **B** the slope of the curve decreases as *X* increases. When viewed from the origin, the curve in **A** is convex and the curve in **B** is concave.

Slope and Extreme Values of Variables

Many of the most important curves drawn in economic analysis have negative, zero, and positive slope depending on the value of the *X* variable. For example, graph **A** in Box 6 shows a curve that has positive slope at first and then, for just the value at which *X* equals 5, has zero slope. Thereafter the slope of the curve is negative because *Y* decreases as *X* increases beyond the value of 5. The point labeled *M*, at which the slope of the curve in graph **A** is just equal to zero as the slope shifts from being positive to being negative, is of great significance. The

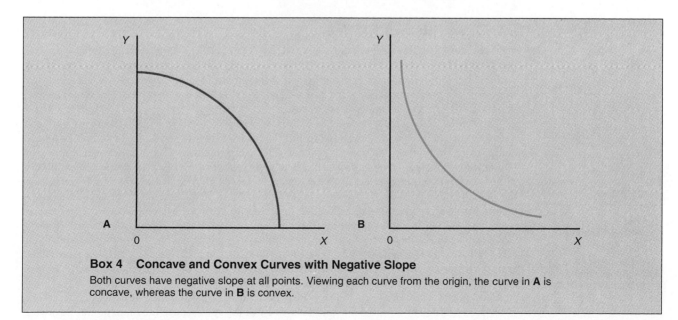

Box 4   Concave and Convex Curves with Negative Slope

Both curves have negative slope at all points. Viewing each curve from the origin, the curve in **A** is concave, whereas the curve in **B** is convex.

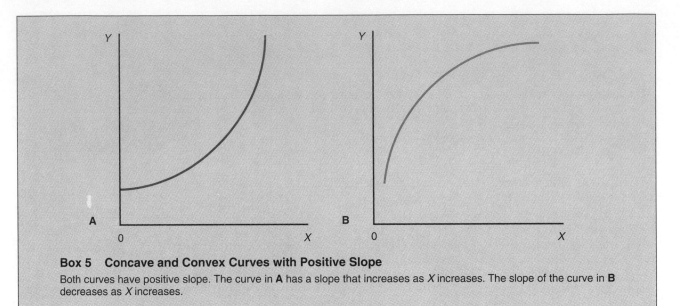

Box 5   Concave and Convex Curves with Positive Slope
Both curves have positive slope. The curve in **A** has a slope that increases as *X* increases. The slope of the curve in **B** decreases as *X* increases.

coordinates of that point give the value of *X* for which the corresponding value of *Y* is at its *maximum* value. The distinguishing feature of that point is that the slope is *zero*.

A zero slope can also indicate a minimum value of a variable. For example, in graph **B** the coordinates of point *E* give the value of *X* for which the value of *Y* is at a *minimum*. For values greater than 6, the slope is positive. When *X* equals 6, the slope just equals zero.

Be sure you understand the meaning of the concept of slope, because you'll find it very useful in economic analysis. Throughout this book we'll make assumptions about the way the slope of a curve varies as one variable is increased in value and a related variable responds. We'll use these assumptions to reach important conclusions about economic behavior and relationships.

UNITS OF MEASUREMENT

When discussing economic relationships, we need to specify units of measurement. Suppose the *Y* variable for graph **A** in Box 6 is profits. its units would be measured in dollars. The *X* variable could be number of cars sold per day by an auto dealer. The curve would therefore represent the relationship between profits and daily sales. It shows that the dealer would maximize profits by selling five cars per day.

The smoothness of a curve depends on how compact the units of measurement are along an axis and on whether it makes sense to talk about fractions of units. For example, an auto dealer can't sell half or one quarter of a car. Therefore, points on a graph between 1 and 2 or any other two integers really don't exist. In actuality, profits are likely to change substantially rather than only minutely when each car is sold. A **bar graph** shows the value of a *Y* variable as the height of a bar for each corresponding value of *X*. In Box 7 the height of each bar shows profits for each number of cars sold. The first bar shows profit when only one car per day is sold. The second bar shows how profit jumps when two cars per day are sold.

Variables that cannot vary by fractions of units are called **discrete variables.** Variables that can realistically and meaningfully take on minute fractions of values are called **continuous variables.** For example, any variable measured in dollars can be regarded as a more or less continuous variable because each dollar can be broken down into hundredths.

Economists often draw graphs of economic relationships in which actually discrete variables are regarded as continuous. Little is lost by doing so, because the main point of drawing curves is to analyze the way one variable depends on another. The curves are meant to show

bar graph a graph that shows the value of a *Y* variable as the height of a bar for each corresponding value of the *X* variable.

discrete variable a variable that cannot vary by fractions of units.

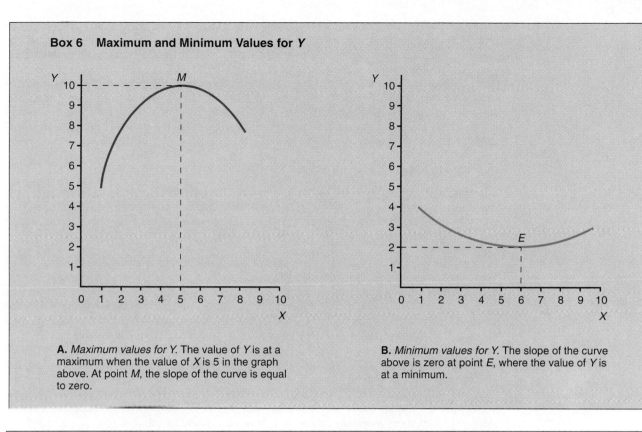

Box 6   Maximum and Minimum Values for Y

A. *Maximum values for Y.* The value of *Y* is at a maximum when the value of *X* is 5 in the graph above. At point *M*, the slope of the curve is equal to zero.

B. *Minimum values for Y.* The slope of the curve above is zero at point *E*, where the value of *Y* is at a minimum.

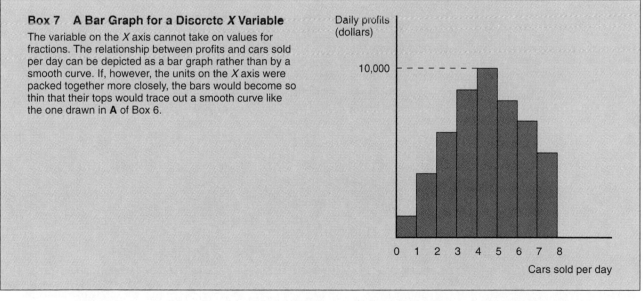

Box 7   A Bar Graph for a Discrete *X* Variable

The variable on the *X* axis cannot take on values for fractions. The relationship between profits and cars sold per day can be depicted as a bar graph rather than by a smooth curve. If, however, the units on the *X* axis were packed together more closely, the bars would become so thin that their tops would trace out a smooth curve like the one drawn in **A** of Box 6.

positive or negative relationships rather than to be realistic depictions of actual variation of the discrete units. You should also note that graphs of relationships between discrete variables can have smooth curves if the scale of measurement along the axes is very compact. For example, suppose a graph shows the relationship between profits of all automakers and number of cars sold per day. If the *X* axis depicts the variation in cars sold from zero to 8 million per year, the distance on the *X* axis between any number of cars sold and *one more*

continuous variable a variable that can realistically and meaningfully take on minute fractions of values.

car sold will be microscopic for a graph drawn on the page of a book. Similarly, the change in profits when one more car is sold will be quite small on the vertical axis when the scale of measurement is designed to accommodate millions of dollars for the millions of cars sold each year. The resulting graph of the economic relationship is therefore likely to be like the smooth curve in Box 6 rather than the bar graph in Box 7. In most of the cases in this book, smooth curves will be drawn to show economic relationships. However on occasion, when the variables are clearly discrete or the scale of measurement is not very compact between integers, bar graphs like the one in Box 7 are drawn, as was done for the graph in Box 1 of Chapter 1.

INTERSECTIONS AND TANGENCIES

The graphs used in this book are two-dimensional. This means they plot values for two variables. In many cases, however, a third variable can be introduced in a two-dimensional graph by showing how changes in its value affect the values of the two initial variables.

Intersections

intersection the point at which two curves drawn on the same set of axes cross.

In many graphs drawn to facilitate economic analysis, *two* curves are drawn on the same set of axes. The intersection of two curves is the point at which they cross. An intersection usually reveals important economic information. The graph in Box 8 shows the intersection of two curves at point *E*. The value of *X* at this point is such that the corresponding value of *Y* is the same for the relationship indicated by curve 1 and that indicated by curve 2. (In Chapters 3 through 5 you'll have lots of practice in interpreting the intersections of two curves.)

When graphs are drawn in this way, the effect of a third variable other than *X* or *Y* can be investigated. To do this, we can hypothesize the impact of the third variable, *Z*, on the relationship represented by curve 1. If the change in this variable has no effect on the relationship between *X* and *Y* depicted by the upward-sloping curve labeled curve 2, then only the downward-sloping curve will move as the value of *Z* changes. If, for example, curve 1 shifts outward as *Z* increases, there will be a new point of intersection, *E'*. The role of economic analysis would then be to interpret the new point of intersection.

Tangencies

tangency a point at which two curves just touch each other but do not intersect.

A tangency between two curves is a point at which the two curves just touch each other *but do not intersect. At a point of tangency, the slopes of two curves are equal.* Box 9 shows the tangency between a straight line and a convex curve. The slope of the convex curve varies from point to point. At the point of tangency, *T,* the slope of the convex curve is precisely

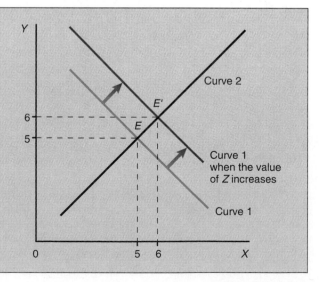

Box 8   Intersections

The intersection of curve 1 and curve 2 gives the value of *X* for which the value of *Y* is the same along both curve 1 and curve 2. Curve 1 is drawn under the assumption that the value of some third variable, *Z*, is fixed. If the value of *Z* increases, curve 1 moves to a new position and a new point of intersection, *E'*, gives the value of *X* that corresponds to the same value of *Y* along the two curves.

equal to the slope of the straight line. The straight line has a slope equal to -1 at all points. It follows that the slope of the convex curve is equal to -1 at point T. The corresponding value of X is 4. For all values of X less than 4, the slope of the convex curve is more negative than -1. For values of X greater than 4, the slope of the convex curve is less negative, that is, closer to zero, than -1.

DESCRIPTIVE GRAPHS

Most of the graphs in this book are designed to illustrate functional relationships. In many cases these graphs are not based on actual data. Their purpose may be simply to show the consequences of a positive or negative relationship and to aid in predicting the values of certain key economic variables. In other cases graphs are drawn simply to describe how actual variables vary over time without trying to interpret the trend depicted. Most *descriptive graphs* are plots of time series data. For example, the graph in Box 10 shows how unemployment in a nation fluctuates over time. This graph shows trends between 1965 and 1985, but it does not necessarily illustrate a functional relationship. Graphs like this will be drawn in the book to describe what actually happened to a variable. However, understanding what causes fluctuations like those illustrated in the Box 10 graph requires the kind of economic analysis that allows functional relations to be established. Chapter 2 shows how economists seek to establish the functional relationships that are used to obtain such insights.

time series data data that show the fluctuations in a variable over time.

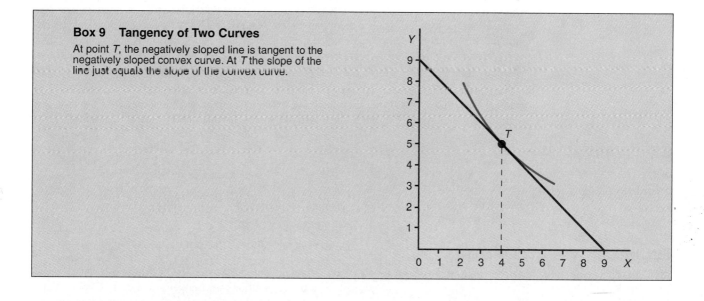

Box 9   Tangency of Two Curves

At point T, the negatively sloped line is tangent to the negatively sloped convex curve. At T the slope of the line just equals the slope of the convex curve.

Box 10   A Descriptive Graph

This graph shows the actual unemployment rate from 1965 to 1985. It does not illustrate a functional relationship between two variables.

Unemployment rate (percent)

SOME WORDS OF ADVICE

Many students have difficulty in using graphs and interpreting the relationships that curves are designed to explain. The way to avoid this difficulty yourself is to practice using graphs. You'll find it helpful to refer to this supplement whenever you have a problem with a graph. Also, a few basic points should make it easier for you to deal with the graphs you'll encounter in this book:

1. *Make sure you know the economic variables that are being graphed.* You'll have a great deal of difficulty in understanding a graph if you simply memorize the shape of the curve but forget the names or units of measurement of the economic variables!

2. *Remember that the main point of drawing a curve on a set of axes is to depict an economic relationship. Make sure that the purpose of trying to understand that relationship is clear to you.* For example, is the purpose of the graph to find the minimum value or the maximum value of an economic variable? Is the graph supposed to show how quantities purchased vary with the price of a good? Is it designed to show how unemployment fluctuates with interest rates? Is its purpose to show how the average level of prices in the economy varies with the amount of money in circulation?

3. *Always try to understand the significance of the positive or negative relationships depicted by graphs.* Practice drawing graphs yourself from the information given in the text. Make sure you label your axes and follow the common sense of the relationship the given graph is designed to illuminate.

4. *Make sure you understand how economic relationships depicted by curves change when there are changes in other variables that are not explicitly drawn on the set of axes.* For example, suppose a curve shows how consumer spending varies with income. This curve may shift if interest rates or tax rates change.

5. *Make sure you can interpret points of intersection or tangency between two curves.* These points almost always have great significance in economic analysis.

Remember that graphs represent a shortcut to reasoning. Use them as a tool. If you practice with them, you'll find that they save you a great deal of time and enable you to reach conclusions that would be much more difficult to reach with purely verbal reasoning.

KEY TERMS

origin *26*

coordinates *27*

curve *27*

positive (direct) relationship *27*

negative (inverse) relationship *27*

slope *28*

bar graph *30*

discrete variable *30*

continuous variable *31*

intersection *32*

tangency *32*

time series data *33*

PROBLEMS AND APPLICATIONS

1. The following table gives a relationship between *X* and *Y:*

Value of X	Corresponding value of Y
1	4
2	6
3	8
4	10
5	12

Plot the coordinates of *X* and *Y* on a graph, and draw a line through the points to show the relationship between the two variables.

2. Indicate whether the graph you have drawn in Problem 1 shows a positive or negative relationship between *X* and *Y*. Calculate the slope of the line you have drawn.

3. Draw up a table like the one in Problem 1 that shows a negative relationship between *X* and *Y*. Choose your numbers so that a curve with constant slope can be drawn through the coordinates. Calculate the slope of your line.

4. Weekly sales of personal computers are unaffected by the temperature of the outside air. Draw a curve that shows the absence of a relationship between temperature and sales of PCs. Let *Y* be PC sales, and let *X* be temperature What is the slope of the curve?

5. The owner of a factory producing rugby shirts can sell as many shirts as he wishes at a price of $20. The total revenue he receives is equal to the price of shirts multiplied by the number of shirts shipped. Draw a graph that shows how his monthly revenue will vary with monthly shipments of shirts. Calculate the slope

of the curve you have drawn, and interpret its meaning from an economic point of view.

6. Suppose the owner of the rugby shirt factory notices that his total costs of producing and shipping shirts from a concave curve similar to the one drawn as graph A in Box 5. His monthly profit is the difference between monthly revenue and monthly cost. Draw the cost curve on the same set of axes you used to draw the revenue curve, and then draw another curve that shows how monthly profit will vary with shirt production. Locate the point of maximum profits.

7. The following table shows how the unit cost of producing denim jackets varies with monthly output in a certain factory:

Monthly number of jackets produced	Cost per jacket
1,000	$80
2,000	70
3,000	60
4,000	70
5,000	80

Plot the points from the table and trace a curve through them. Describe the relationship between cost per denim jacket and number of jackets produced per month. What is the slope of the curve at the point at which the cost per jacket is at a minimum?

8. Draw a bar graph that shows the relationship between X and Y using the data from Problem 1.

9. The following equation describes a relationship between the price of running shoes and the quantity buyers will buy per month:

Quantity buyers will buy $= 300 - 3P$

The quantity sellers will sell is related to the price of running shoes in the following way:

Quantity sellers will sell $= 2P$

where P is the price per pair of running shoes.

Plot the graphs for the two preceding equations using the following values for P: $30, $40, $50, $60, $70, $80. Identify the value of P at which the two curves intersect, and indicate the corresponding number of pairs of running shoes that will be bought and sold.

10. A curve showing the relationship between X and Y has a slope of -2 at all points. Draw this line, and then draw a convex curve that is tangent to it. What is the slope of the convex curve at the point of tangency?

2 chapter

Production Possibilities and Opportunity Cost

Scarcity, the ever-present imbalance between desires and the ability to satisfy them, is the fundamental economic problem that households, businesses, governments, and society at large face. In this chapter we look at influences on a society's production possibilities. We use the concept of *opportunity cost* to show how choices involve sacrifices. In this way we paint a picture of the economic environment and the constraints we face daily in our personal and business lives.

We deal with the problem of scarcity and the reality of opportunity cost every time we make choices about the ways to spend our money. The greater our incomes, the wider the range of goods and services we can choose from, but the more we buy one item, the less we can buy other items. Rich or poor, each of us must face the problem of scarcity and consider the opportunity cost of our choices.

Similarly, the better endowed a nation is with productive resources, the more opportunities its citizens have. However, no matter how rich in resources a nation may be, the basic economic problem of scarcity remains. This is because all resources are in some way limited, so that in choosing to use resources for one purpose, we sacrifice the opportunity to use them for alternative purposes.

☐ CONCEPT PREVIEW

After reading this chapter, you should be able to:

1. Explain how limited available technology and scarce resources imply limited production possibilities over a period of time.

2. Show how the use of productive capacity to make more of one good or service available involves sacrificing the opportunity to make more of other items available.

3. Understand the concept of productive efficiency and discuss its significance.

4. Discuss the basic determinants of a nation's production possibilities and how these possibilities can expand over time.

5. Demonstrate that when you use income over a period to buy more of one item, you sacrifice the opportunity to buy more of some other item over the period.

6. Explain how international trade can allow citizens consumption possibilities that exceed their nation's domestic production possibilities.

RESOURCES, TECHNOLOGY, AND PRODUCTION POSSIBILITIES

Production is the process of using the services of labor and other resources to make goods and services available. (These goods and services are called *outputs*.) Economic resources are the *inputs* used in the process of production. They are divided into four broad categories:

economic resources the inputs used in the process of production.

1. **Labor** represents the services of human beings in the production of goods and services. Both physical and mental effort are included in this category. The number of workers; their general education, training, and skills; and their motivation to work are prime determinants of a nation's productive capability. The services of factory workers, truck drivers, salespeople, college professors, police officers, and physicians are all part of a nation's labor resources.

labor the physical and mental efforts of human beings in the production of goods and services.

2. **Capital** is the equipment, tools, structures, machinery, vehicles, materials, and skills created to help produce goods and services.[1] Don't confuse capital resources with financial resources. As you'll see later, firms often raise funds to acquire new capital by borrowing money or issuing new corporate stock. However, the funds acquired in this way are not an input into production. They merely represent the purchasing power needed to build or purchase new capital.

capital the equipment, tools, structures, machinery, vehicles, materials, and skills created to help produce goods and services.

3. **Natural resources** include land used as sites for structures, ports, and other facilities, as well as the natural materials that are used in crude form in production. Examples of land and other natural resources are farmland, industrial sites, deposits of minerals and petroleum, harbors, navigable rivers, sources of hydroelectric power, timber, the advantages of a region's climate, and environmental quality.

natural resources land used as sites for structures, ports, and other facilities; natural materials used in production; characteristics of an area that affect production, such as climate and environmental quality.

4. **Entrepreneurship** is the talent to develop products and processes and to organize production to make goods and services available. Entrepreneurs are innovators and risk-takers. Entrepreneurs in business seek to earn profits by satisfying the desires of consumers and by developing better and less costly ways of satisfying those desires. They undertake the tasks necessary to get the process of production started and make the decisions relating to the use of inputs.

entrepreneurship the talent to develop products and processes and to organize production of goods and services.

The United States is a very rich country in the sense that it has many natural resources, a highly skilled labor force, and a great deal of capital. Many nations lack the skilled labor force, entrepreneurial ability, and capital equipment necessary to enjoy even a fraction of the goods and services per person that we take for granted in the United States. Scarcity is therefore a matter of degree. It is, however, ever present in rich and poor nations alike, given our tendency as human beings to want more than we have.

Technology

Technology, which helps us alleviate scarcity, is the knowledge of how to produce goods and services. Improved technology can streamline production or allow more goods and services to be produced from a given quantity of economic resources. Advances in technology help us cope with the problems of scarcity by making workers, capital, and land more productive. For example, as a result of improvements in the technology of agriculture, the output of farms in the United States rose by 150 percent between 1930 and 1980, while the quantity of inputs into agriculture increased by only 7 percent. In the near future the introduction of superconducting materials will allow transmission of electricity over long distances without loss of

technology the knowledge of how to produce goods and services.

---

[1] Capital inputs can be physical or human. A portion of the labor used in production includes human capital, which represents skills acquired for the purpose of producing medical, engineering, legal, and other services. Another portion includes physical capital—machinery and tools.

energy. This means that a given amount of capital, fuel, and workers will be able to generate significantly more electricity than they can now. Development of materials that can withstand high temperatures and pressures will enable new jet engines to build more thrust using less fuel. This will allow commercial aircraft to travel faster without using more fuel per mile and without sacrificing safety.

The Production Possibilities Curve

You'll see the problem of scarcity more clearly with the aid of a simple model whose purpose is to examine the relationship between the production of goods and services and the availability and use of resources. In the analysis we make the following assumptions:

1. *The quantity and quality of economic resources available for use during the year are fixed.* There is a given amount of available labor, capital, natural resources, and entrepreneurial ability. This limits the extent to which our desires for goods and services can be satisfied during the year.

2. *There are two broad classes of outputs we can produce with available economic resources: food and clothing.* We make the assumption of only two products to simplify the analysis while showing the basic trade-offs we must consider while coping with the problem of scarcity.

3. *Some inputs are better adapted to the production of one good than to the production of the other.* A pickup truck can as easily be used to transport materials needed to produce clothing as to transport materials needed to produce food. However, a loom that's used to weave cloth is virtually useless in the production of food. The loom may be dismantled and its parts used in agricultural machinery, but it's much more productive when used to manufacture clothing. Similarly, some workers have skills that are better adapted to one use than another. Transferring a skilled tailor from clothing to food production will cause a greater loss in output of clothing than transferring a truck driver from delivering clothing to delivering food. Transferring the labor of an experienced farmer from agricultural to clothing production results in a greater loss in food output than does transferring the labor of a crop picker. The more specialized a worker, the higher the opportunity cost of transferring him or her to another type of work.

4. *Technology is fixed and does not advance during the year.* In general, advances in technology take more than one year to develop. In assuming fixed technology, we're implying that the productiveness of inputs doesn't change during the year as a result of improved knowledge or technical advances.

Given available resources, their quality, and current technology, there is a limited amount of any one good that can be produced in an economy given the output of other goods. A **production possibilities curve** shows the maximum possible output of one good that can be produced with available resources, given the output of the alternative good over a period. A production possibilities curve for food and clothing shows the maximum number of garments that can be produced each year given each possible level of food production. The curve shows the *options* available to produce various combinations of goods and services under current technology during a year, assuming the available resources are fully utilized.

production possibilities curve a curve that shows feasible combinations of two goods (or broad classes of goods) that can be produced with available resources and current technology.

Given the assumptions we just made, we can derive a production possibilities curve using hypothetical data. The table in Box 1 shows that if all resources were used to produce food during the year, the maximum possible output would be 55,000 tons that year. This corresponds to production possibility *I* in the table, for which clothing output is zero and food output is 55,000 tons. Alternatively, we might

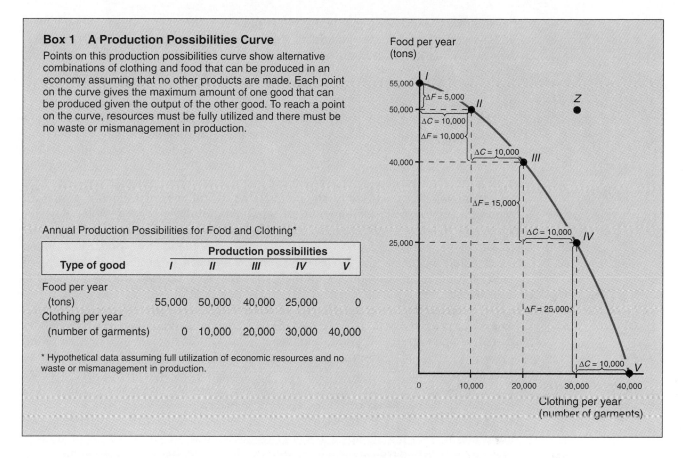

Box 1   A Production Possibilities Curve

Points on this production possibilities curve show alternative combinations of clothing and food that can be produced in an economy assuming that no other products are made. Each point on the curve gives the maximum amount of one good that can be produced given the output of the other good. To reach a point on the curve, resources must be fully utilized and there must be no waste or mismanagement in production.

Annual Production Possibilities for Food and Clothing*

Type of good	Production possibilities				
	I	II	III	IV	V
Food per year (tons)	55,000	50,000	40,000	25,000	0
Clothing per year (number of garments)	0	10,000	20,000	30,000	40,000

* Hypothetical data assuming full utilization of economic resources and no waste or mismanagement in production.

interpret production possibility *I* as implying that if food output were 55,000 tons, the maximum possible clothing output during the year would be zero. The graph in Box 1 plots this production possibility, labeled *I*, on a set of axes on which food output is measured on the vertical axis and clothing output is measured on the horizontal axis.

Now let's consider the option of producing less food and more clothing for the year. Because resources are scarce, increasing the annual output of clothing means we must sacrifice some of the annual output of food. Production possibility *II* consists of 10,000 garments and 50,000 tons of food per year. The opportunity cost of producing 10,000 garments per year is the 5,000 tons of food we must sacrifice to make that number of garments available. Production possibility *II* is labeled as point *II* in the graph.

Production possibility *III* shows the option available if 20,000 garments are produced per year. This option would require us to divert more resources away from food production and to allocate them to clothing production. If we chose this option, maximum possible food output would only be 40,000 tons per year. Notice that increasing clothing production by an additional 10,000 garments per year results in a 10,000-ton reduction in food output; this exceeds the 5,000-ton reduction that was required to produce the first 10,000 garments. The opportunity cost of the second 10,000 garments exceeds the opportunity cost of the first 10,000 garments.

This pattern of increasing opportunity cost continues as we allocate more resources away from food production and toward clothing production. At production possibility *IV,* increasing the output of clothing from 20,000 to 30,000 garments per year means we sacrifice an additional 15,000 tons of food per year. Finally, production possibility *V* shows that the output of food would fall to zero if we used our resources to produce 40,000 garments per year. The opportunity cost of increasing the production of clothing from 30,000 to 40,000 garments per year is the 25,000 tons of food we must sacrifice.

The points corresponding to production possibilities *III, IV,* and *V* are also plotted in the graph in Box 1. A smooth line has been drawn through the points corresponding to production possibilities *I* to *V.* The result is a production possibilities curve showing the maximum possible output of food for each possible output of clothing during the year, given available resources and technology. Points such as *Z,* which lie outside the area enclosed by the production possibilities curve and the two axes, represent unattainable combinations of food and clothing per year. Point *Z* corresponds to 50,000 tons of food and 30,000 garments per year. The economy lacks the resources or technology to produce the annual combinations of food and clothing represented by points like *Z.* When resources are used to produce 50,000 tons of food, the maximum amount of clothing that can be produced during the year is 10,000 garments.

All points on or within the production possibilities curve represent annual combinations of goods that can be produced. However, points *within* the area bounded by the curve and the two axes represent combinations of the two goods that correspond to *less than* the maximum possible annual production of one of the goods given the annual production of the other. Our economy might end up at a point within the area bounded by the curve and the axes if it did not utilize all the productive resources available or if resources were wasted or mismanaged.

The production possibilities curve therefore illustrates the idea of scarcity in two important ways. First, it shows that only a limited number of production possibilities exist over a year given available resources and technology. The possibilities are represented by points within and on the curve. Second, it shows that once the maximum amount of any one good is produced per year, given the output of the other good per year, additional annual production of the first good requires an annual reduction in the output of the other.

The Law of Increasing Costs

2 Box 2 shows the economy's opportunity cost for each 10,000-garment batch of clothing production. The first column of the table shows the annual output of clothing. The second column shows the increase in clothing output. The delta (Δ) shows *change in* the variable *C.* In this case *C* stands for clothing. When output increases from zero to 10,000 garments per year, the change in clothing production is $\Delta C = 10,000$. Now let's return briefly to Box 1. To obtain that increase in the output of clothing, the opportunity cost is 5,000 tons of food per year. The change in food output as the economy moves from point *I* to point *II* on the production possibilities curve is $\Delta F = 5,000$ tons, as shown in the last column of the table in Box 2. By sacrificing 5,000 tons of food per year, the economy moves from point *I* to point *II* on its production possibilities curve in Box 1.

The last column of the table in Box 2 shows how the opportunity cost of each successive batch of 10,000 garments per year increases as we allocate more resources from food to clothing production during the year. The graph plots the opportunity cost of each 10,000-garment batch of clothing per year in terms of food

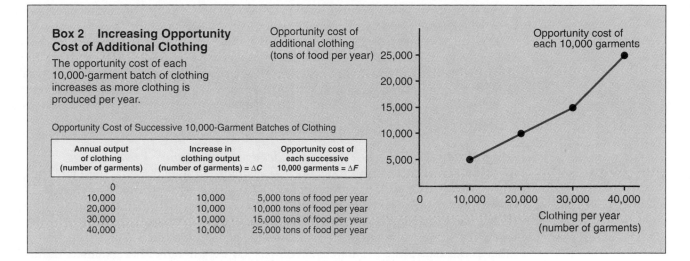

Box 2 Increasing Opportunity Cost of Additional Clothing

The opportunity cost of each 10,000-garment batch of clothing increases as more clothing is produced per year.

Opportunity Cost of Successive 10,000-Garment Batches of Clothing

Annual output of clothing (number of garments)	Increase in clothing output (number of garments) = ΔC	Opportunity cost of each successive 10,000 garments = ΔF
0		
10,000	10,000	5,000 tons of food per year
20,000	10,000	10,000 tons of food per year
30,000	10,000	15,000 tons of food per year
40,000	10,000	25,000 tons of food per year

sacrificed for each level of annual clothing production.[2] An upward-sloping curve has been fitted through the points to show how the opportunity costs of additional clothing production increase.

A basic reason that costs increase with successive units of output is the existence of specialized inputs that are more productive in a particular use. As we increase clothing production during the year, we have to sacrifice more and more food for each successive increment in the number of garments produced per year. You can see this by concentrating on the land that would have to be reallocated to build clothing factories and grow the fibers used to make cloth. At first the land least specialized for growing food can be reallocated to clothing production. As more fertile food land is transferred for successive increments in the annual production of clothing, the loss per acre transferred increases simply because the land more adapted to food production produces more food per acre than the less specialized land.

Similarly, at first the vehicles and equipment least specialized in the production of food, such as trucks and tractors, can be transferred at low opportunity cost to clothing production. However, as we produce more clothing, we must adapt more specialized agricultural machinery, such as combines, for use in clothing production. Because this type of machinery is more productive in food than in clothing production, the opportunity cost of additional clothing increases in terms of food sacrificed. Likewise, as clothing output increases, at first the workers least specialized in agricultural production are transferred to clothing production. As more and more workers are required to produce additional clothing, the more skilled and, therefore, more productive workers must be transferred out of food production. This increases the amount of food we must sacrifice to produce extra units of clothing.

The law of increasing costs states that the opportunity cost of each additional unit of output of a good over a period increases as more of that good is produced. This law is an implication of the assumption that some economic resources are more

law of increasing costs a principle stating that the opportunity cost of each additional unit of output of a good over a period increases as more of that good is produced.

---

[2] The opportunity cost of each 10,000-garment batch of clothing is the marginal cost of clothing when the units of clothing are 10,000-garment packages.

suited than others to the production of particular goods. Because this implication has been widely supported by empirical evidence, it is called a "law."

The concave shape of the production possibilities curve in Box 2 reflects the law of increasing costs. The slope of the curve at any point is $\Delta F/\Delta C$, where ΔF is the annual reduction in food output necessary for each extra garment per year. As you move from point I toward point V, the curve becomes steeper, reflecting the increase in the sacrifice of food, ΔF, required for each additional one-unit increase in clothing output.

Generalizing the Concepts: Peace Dividends and a Cleaner Environment
The economic concepts of production possibilities curve and the law of increasing costs are relevant to the world we live in. Consider the production possibilities between two broad classes of goods: military goods and all other goods. The production possibilities curve in the left panel of Box 3 shows that the more of our resources we devote to production of military goods for national defense, the less of other goods (such as cars, stereos, and housing) we will have. For example, during 1943, at the peak of World War II, the United States devoted over 40 percent of its productive resources to production of military goods and services. That year no private automobiles were produced because all automobile factories were under contract to the government to produce military vehicles. Similarly, in 1944, new consumer goods, such as housing and clothing, were very scarce, as was gasoline for private use. In 1944 the United States was at a point like A on its production possibilities curve.

As of 1992, the United States was at a point like B on its production possibilities curve, allocating only about 5 percent of production to military purchases and thus allowing considerably more resources to be used to produce other goods and services than was possible at the peak of World War II. The demise of the Soviet Union and the end of the cold war offered us the possibility of further reallocating resources from defense to nondefense uses. However, because of the law of increasing costs, the gain in additional nondefense production per unit reduction in military production is much smaller at point B than at point A, where a lot of resources were devoted to defense. Therefore, it is unreasonable to expect relatively big gains today in the capability of producing more of other goods (the "peace dividend") as the United States scales back its military purchases.

The right panel of Box 3 shows production possibilities for environmental improvement (such as cleaner air and water) and other goods and services. If the United States devotes more resources to improving environmental quality, it will move from a point like C to a point like D on the production possibilities curve. For example, the Environmental Protection Agency (EPA) could require a reduction in emission of pollutants by new cars. Because of the additional pollution control equipment required to meet the new standards, this would probably increase car prices and decrease the number of new cars consumers would be able to buy each year. Similarly, more stringent emissions standards on production facilities would raise the price of a broad array of goods and services and cause us to trade more material goods for cleaner air and water. We must therefore be prepared to give up other goods and services for improved environmental quality.

The law of increasing costs is relevant to analysis of improved environmental quality. After we have improved the environment to a certain degree by moving from a point like C to a point like D on the production possibilities curve, the cost of each unit of environmental improvement services will increase. This implies that we must

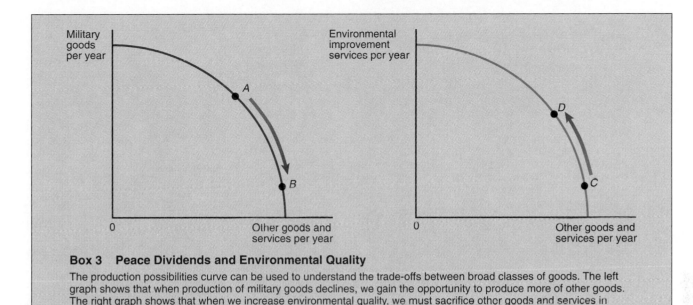

Box 3   Peace Dividends and Environmental Quality

The production possibilities curve can be used to understand the trade-offs between broad classes of goods. The left graph shows that when production of military goods declines, we gain the opportunity to produce more of other goods. The right graph shows that when we increase environmental quality, we must sacrifice other goods and services in exchange for cleaner air and water.

give up more and more items we cherish (like car driving and outdoor barbecues) for each extra unit of improvement in environmental quality.

Finally, note that there is often a period of transition in which unemployment increases when we substantially change the economy's mix of products. For example, an estimated 1 million military personnel and defense industry workers lost their jobs as a result of the cutback in military output in the early 1990s.[3] This contributed to movement to a point below those on the U.S. production possibilities curve. Similarly, as we increase the portion of our resources devoted to improving environmental quality, workers in industries that pollute excessively will also be thrown out of work and there will be a period of transition before we can return to a new point on the production possibilities curve.

- What do points on a production possibilities curve show?

- Use a production possibilities curve to show how an increase in resources devoted to producing military goods implies that annual availability of such nonmilitary goods as

housing, private automobiles, and clothing is reduced.

- What is the law of increasing costs, and how is it illustrated by the shape of a nation's production possibilities curve?

CONCEPT CHECK

☐

PRODUCTIVE EFFICIENCY

We can use the production possibilities curve to show the consequences of under-utilizing or mismanaging economic resources in a nation. For example, suppose the labor force is underutilized in production, a situation that generally occurs when the

---

[3] For a discussion of job loss from defense cutbacks, see Peter Passell, "The Peace Dividend's Collateral Damage," *The New York Times*, September 13, 1992, p. E3.

Box 4   Underutilization or Inefficient Use of Resources

Excessive underutilization of resources prevents the economy from reaching a point on its production possibilities curve. Similarly, waste or mismanagement in production results in production at a point like *R within* the production possibilities curve.

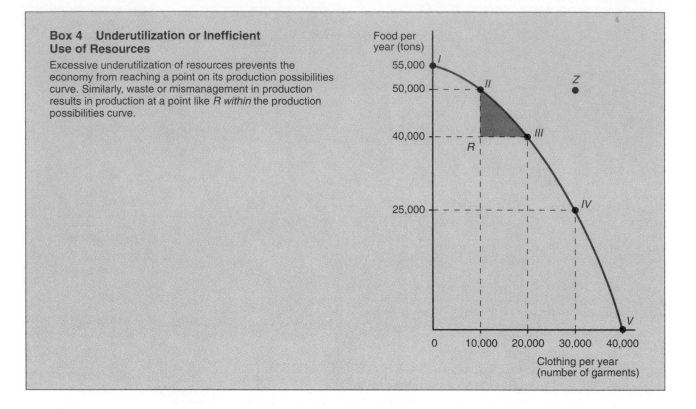

unemployment rate is excessively high. Some unemployment is normal because people who have just entered the labor force or lost their previous job take time to search for jobs. However, excessive unemployment is a matter of concern to all of us and not just to those unfortunate enough to be out of work.

Excessive unemployment or failure to fully utilize capital and natural resources implies that an economy is operating at a point *within* rather than *on* its production possibilities curve. You can see this in the graph in Box 4. If the economy were not fully utilizing its economic resources, actual annual production of food and clothing might correspond to a point like *R*. At that point we could produce more food by moving to point *II* without sacrificing any clothing each year. Alternatively, we could produce more clothing without sacrificing any food each year by moving to point *III*. If resources were not fully utilized, we could attain all combinations of the two goods within the shaded triangular area enclosed by the points *R, II,* and *III* without acquiring more resources or without an advance in technology.

Mismanagement of economic resources also causes the economy to operate within its production possibilities curve. Suppose all economic resources are being utilized in production but aren't managed so that we obtain the maximum amount of any one good given the output of other goods under existing technology. In the graph in Box 4, mismanaging resources would result in a point like *R*. As was the case for excessive unemployment, all the combinations of clothing and food represented by points within the shaded triangular area are possible without additional resources or improvement in technical know-how. Sloppy management therefore also prevents an economy from attaining production possibilities for which it has the capability.

principles in practice

Managerial Methods: Avoiding Waste and Mismanagement in Production

Whether they're making linguine or aircraft, managers of business firms continually grapple with the problem of waste and mismanagement in production. In recent years the production management techniques used by Japanese industrial firms have been highly successful in avoiding the waste of resources in production. For example, the Toyota Motor Corporation of Japan has developed a management system designed to *eliminate surplus workers from assembly line operations*. Workers on assembly lines for various products are assigned daily standardized tasks. They are instructed to leave the assembly line and report to a specific area in the factory after they have completed their daily tasks. Company managers keep records of the various assembly lines to see where there's a surplus of labor. Workers on assembly lines with surpluses are permanently reassigned to other tasks to make sure they're adequately utilized.*

Another key to the Toyota production management system is the *Kan-ban*, which is a work order sheet accompanying materials used in production. The *Kan-ban* is issued by managers to line leaders at various stages of the production process to ensure that at all times the supply of materials and parts is adequate to produce the final product. The *Kan-ban* is also used to make sure there's no surplus of materials at any time. The goal is to produce various items at any given time with the minimum required amount of materials on hand (called an *inventory*).

You can understand the goals of the Toyota system with the aid of the production possibilities curve shown in the graph. The system has three major goals:

1. *The system seeks to use resources in ways that result in the attainment of points on the production possibilities curve for each factory.* This is accomplished by making sure that available materials and labor services are utilized in ways that allow the greatest output of any one item, say a Camry sedan, given the output of any other product, say a 4 × 4 four-wheel-drive vehicle. In the graph this means avoiding points like *W* and aiming for points on the curve like *A*. This is accomplished by eliminating surplus labor and materials over any given production period. The *Kan-ban* system saves resources by preventing idle inventories, which waste material inputs, and by economizing on scarce storage space within factories. Space that would have

been allocated to inventory storage can be used for machines and equipment that can turn out more cars per year.

2. *The system seeks to attain maximum flexibility in moving from one point on the production possibilities curve such as* A *to another point such as* B. For example, if the firm suddenly receives an increase in orders for 4 × 4s and a decrease in orders for Camrys, its small-lot production techniques enable it to quickly turn out the parts to produce the 4 × 4s instead of the Camrys. Its workers can easily adapt to the new production requirements because they have been trained to be skilled in a variety of tasks.

3. *The system seeks worker input to change production techniques in ways that move the production possibilities curve outward.* Improvements in technical know-how or changes in organization suggested by workers can allow the firm to attain points that wouldn't otherwise be possible, such as *Z*. The small-lot production system contributes to rapid feedback on mistakes in production. In a small lot, in which parts are used almost immediately, worker mistakes are quickly noticed. This provides workers with incentives to work more effectively and allows improvements to be noticed almost immediately.

* For an in-depth discussion of Japanese management techniques, see Eiji Ogawa, *Modern Production Management: A Japanese Experience* (Tokyo: Asian Productivity Organization, 1984).

productive efficiency the condition attained when the maximum possible output of any one good is produced given the output of other goods.

Productive efficiency is attained when the maximum possible output of any one good, given the output of the other goods, is produced. Attainment of productive efficiency means we can't reallocate economic resources to increase the output of any good or service without decreasing the output of some other good or service. Points on a production possibilities curve represent efficient use of productive resources, because once we are on the curve, it's impossible to increase the output of one good without reducing the output of the other.

Division of Labor and Productive Efficiency

division of labor the breakdown of a larger process into particular tasks performed by workers who specialize in those tasks.

One factor that contributes to productive efficiency is **division of labor**, which is the breakdown of a larger process into particular tasks performed by workers who specialize in those tasks. By specializing, workers become more proficient at their jobs. Division of labor lets factories use mass production techniques that allow workers to produce more.

By dividing tasks, a factory obtains much more output per worker than it would obtain if each worker had to build each unit of an entire finished product alone. For example, suppose you had to build an automobile by yourself. You'd have to mold the steel; assembly the body, chassis, and motor; and do all interior assembly. You'd have to be an expert in welding, electrical wiring, painting, and upholstering. Even if you were skilled in all these operations, it might take you as long as a year to produce a finished car.

With division of labor, the numerous tasks involved would be assigned to many workers, each specializing in one task. By dividing tasks, managers can use sophisticated machinery and equipment and produce many more cars than could be produced if each worker tried to do all the tasks. Division of labor exists in a broader sense throughout the economy. People with specialized skills function as physicians, police officers, architects, musicians, and farmers.

CONCEPT CHECK
□

- Under what circumstances might an economy operate at a point within rather than on its production possibilities curve?

- What is meant by the term *productive efficiency*?

- How does division of labor increase production?

ECONOMIC GROWTH: EXPANDING PRODUCTION POSSIBILITIES

4

economic growth the expansion of production possibilities that results from increased availability and increased productivity of economic resources.

From year to year, growth in available supplies of economic resources, improvements in resource quality, and advances in technology can expand production possibilities in a society. **Economic growth** is the expansion of production possibilities that results from increased availability and increased productivity of economic resources. When economic growth occurs over time, the production possibilities curve shifts outward. This means that the economy is able to produce more of all goods. In this section we'll consider three sources of economic growth:

1. Increased quantities of economic resources.
2. Improved quality of economic resources.
3. Advances in technology.

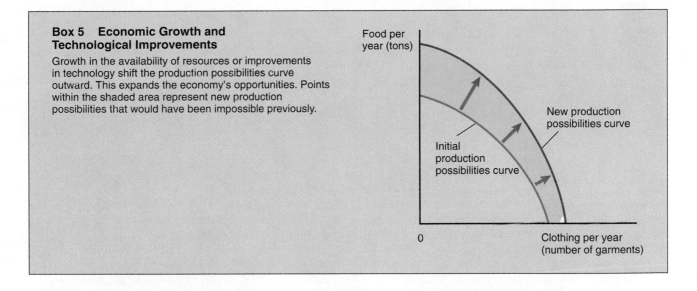

Box 5   Economic Growth and Technological Improvements

Growth in the availability of resources or improvements in technology shift the production possibilities curve outward. This expands the economy's opportunities. Points within the shaded area represent new production possibilities that would have been impossible previously.

Food per year (tons)

New production possibilities curve

Initial production possibilities curve

0

Clothing per year (number of garments)

Annual Growth in Available Resources

An increase in available economic resources allows us to produce more. Other things being equal, the more workers willing and able to work, the more capital, and the more land the greater the production possibilities. This means the production possibilities curve shifts outward in response to an increase in available economic resources, as you can see in the graph in Box 5. Production possibilities previously unattainable are now feasible. Increases in economic resources available for production therefore result in a new production possibilities curve. The shaded area in the graph represents previously unattainable combinations of food and clothing that become feasible when resources become more plentiful or their quality improves.

The availability of new capital is especially effective in pushing the production possibilities curve outward, because new capital often complements labor, land, and other natural resources. This means that additional capital tends to increase the *productivity* of available labor and land. For example, supplying workers with more and better equipment increases the *output per worker*. Similarly, using more capital per acre of farmland can be very effective in increasing the production of *food per acre*. Growth in capital is an especially important determinant of our well-being as individuals, because increases in capital per worker result in more goods per person, thereby increasing the material well-being of each of us.

By the same token, the destruction of economic resources in a nation moves the production possibilities curve inward. For example, a war destroys both human and physical resources, causing the production possibilities curve to shrink inward. A sudden decrease in the availability of a key input into production can also cause the production possibilities curve to shift inward. For example, if the United States found its fuel supplies cut in half because of difficulty in obtaining crude oil, our production possibilities curve would shift inward, making some previously attainable production possibilities no longer feasible.

Improved Quality of Inputs

Improvement in skills, education, or training of the labor force can also increase the output obtainable from any given combination of inputs. Devoting more economic

principles in practice

Personal Budgeting and the Opportunity Cost of Choices

[5]   Now that you understand the basic constraints the economy faces, let's focus on the constraints we as individuals face in satisfying our desires. Few of us have enough income to buy everything we want each month. Scarcity of both resources and time to satisfy all wants is a common personal problem. Most students have tight budgets that allow them to buy only a small portion of what they want. For example, suppose your parents give you a $100 monthly allowance that you spend entirely on gas and cassette tapes. The rest of your living expenses (such as room and board) is paid directly by your parents. In this simple example, you therefore have only two alternatives on which you're interested in spending your available income: gas and tapes.

Suppose the price of gas is $1 per gallon and tapes cost $5 each. It's now possible to derive the combinations of these two goods that you can afford with your $100 monthly income. The table shows five possible combinations of gas and tapes you can buy if you spend all of your $100 monthly income on these two items. For example, it's feasible to consume 100 gallons of gas per month. However, because gas costs $1 per gallon, you'd spend all your monthly income on gas and forgo the opportunity to buy tapes. This option, labeled C_1, is plotted on the graph. The monthly quantity of gas is measured on the vertical axis, while the monthly quantity of tapes is measured on the horizontal axis. You also have the opportunity to choose the option labeled C_5, where you'd be consuming 20 tapes per month but would have no income left to buy gas.

The options for spending your income corresponding to points C_2, C_3, and C_4 have also been plotted on the graph. The monthly *budget line* shows your opportunities to purchase two items, such as gas and tapes, if you spend all your monthly income on these two items at their current prices. With your current income and at current prices, it's possible to buy all combinations of tapes and gas on or below the budget line. Of course, if you choose a point below the line, you'll have some of your monthly income left over to save or spend on other items. If you choose a point like C_6, corresponding to 50 gallons of gas and five tapes per month, you'll be spending $50 on gas and $25 on tapes for a total monthly outlay of $75, leaving $25 to save or to spend on other items.

On the other hand, a point like C_7 is unattainable with your current monthly income given the current prices of gas and tapes. Point C_7 corresponds to 20 tapes, which would cost $100, and 50 gallons of gas, which would cost $50. This combination is infeasible because it requires a monthly expenditure of $150, which exceeds your $100 income.

The budget line therefore shows certain combinations of items that are unattainable given your limited income and the prices of the items. The shaded area represents your monthly opportunities to purchase gas and tapes. Of course, an increase in your income shifts the budget line outward given the prices of the two items. To see this, recalculate your possible consumption options when your income increases to $200 per month. A decrease in the prices of both items would shift the curve outward by increasing the quantities of the items you could buy with your $100 monthly income. To see this, recalculate the points on your budget line when the price of gas is only 50 cents per gallon and the price of tapes is $2.50. Conversely, a decrease in income or an increase in the prices of both items shifts the budget line inward. Inflation in the prices of goods

resources to education and job training in the current year pays off in the future in terms of greater production possibilities. However, those of us who pursue more education must forgo current opportunities to work full time. Recall the analysis of the opportunity cost of going to college in Chapter 1. The opportunity cost to the economy of more education is the production lost when you and others attend college rather than immediately entering the work force after high school. The loss in current output from more education is often more than made up by an increase in future output, assuming that college graduates are more productive than high school graduates.

Similarly, the quality of capital also improves as new machines that can accomplish more tasks or accomplish tasks more quickly or more accurately are introduced. Improvements in the quality of capital require advances in technology, which is the next source of economic growth we'll consider.

A Budget Line

Points on the budget line give all the combinations of two goods that can be purchased given income and the prices of the two goods, assuming that all income is spent.

Consumption*

Good	C_1	C_2	C_3	C_4	C_5
Gasoline (gallons)	100	75	50	25	0
Tapes (number)	0	5	10	15	20
Total monthly expenditure	$100	$100	$100	$100	$100

*Monthly possible consumption of gas and tapes when monthly income is $100, the price of gas is $1 per gallon, and the price of each tape is $5.

consumed decreases the opportunities available to consumers with fixed money income. This is one of the harmful effects of inflation.

So what does the budget line tell you about opportunity costs? If you move along the budget line from C_1 to C_3, each extra tape you buy will absorb $5 of your monthly income. Because the price of gas is $1 per gallon, each extra tape involves the sacrifice of 5 gallons of gas. *The opportunity cost of each extra tape is therefore always 5 gallons of gas at the current prices of these two items.*

In general, the opportunity cost of a tape or any other item depends on its price relative to the price of the item you give up. For example, if the price of tapes were $5 each and the price of gas were $1 per gallon, the opportunity cost of each tape would be 5 gallons of gas. If,

instead, the price of tapes were $10 each and the price of gas were $2 per gallon, the opportunity cost of tapes would *still* be 5 gallons of gas. This might surprise you, because the money cost of units of both items went up. However, the opportunity cost of an item depends on the *quantity* of the alternative item you forgo when you purchase more of the item you choose. When the price of gas is $2 and the price of a tape is $10, each tape you buy results in the sacrifice of 5 gallons of gas because you could have used the $10 to buy that amount of gas. Similarly, the opportunity cost of each gallon of gas is one fifth of a tape when the price of gas is $1 per gallon and the price of a tape is $5. For each 5 gallons of gas you buy each month, you sacrifice the opportunity to buy one tape.

Improvements in Technology

Like improvements in the quality of inputs, increased productive potential resulting from the development of new technologies is a very important source of economic growth. For example, technological improvements that increase the speed of computers mean that a given quantity of computers can process more information. One worker operating a more advanced computer can do the job of two or more workers. Similarly, improvements in agricultural technology mean that a given quantity of land, labor, and capital can produce more food and fiber.

As with improvements in worker skills, a cost is associated with the development of new technologies. To conduct research and development to advance technology, we must withdraw resources from production of goods for immediate consumption. By sacrificing current consumption opportunities, however, we gain future production possibilities.

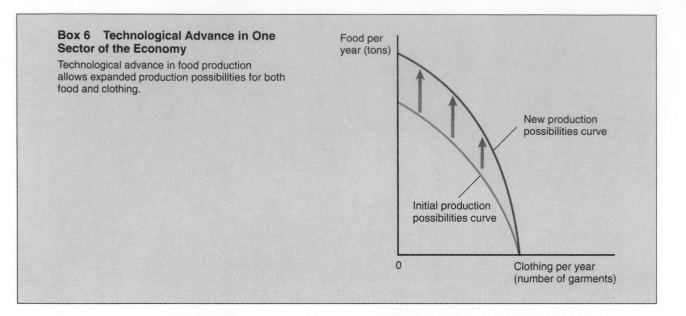

Box 6   Technological Advance in One Sector of the Economy

Technological advance in food production allows expanded production possibilities for both food and clothing.

Surprisingly, technological advances in one sector of the economy cause gains in production possibilities in other sectors as well. For example, suppose there's a technological advance in the food sector of the economy but not in the clothing sector. Improved technology in food production means that for any given quantity of food output, *more* economic resources are now available for clothing production, other things being equal. For any given quantity of food output, we can produce more clothing output than before. You can see this effect in the graph in Box 6, where the production possibilities curve moves upward, but its intercept on the clothing axis doesn't change. In other words, if we were to devote all of our resources to clothing production after the advance in technology in food production, we wouldn't be able to produce more clothing than before. However, the advance in food technology means we can devote more of our available resources to clothing production for any given amount of food produced. As a result, the maximum amount of clothing corresponding to any given amount of food output is now greater. The shaded area in the graph represents the production possibilities of both food *and* clothing gained from a technological advance in food production. In fact, improvements in agricultural technology in the United States and other nations have freed labor so it can be employed in the production of other goods and services.

PRODUCTION FOR THE PRESENT VERSUS PRODUCTION FOR THE FUTURE: A BASIC ECONOMIC CHOICE

In each economy decisions must be made about the way to allocate currently available resources between uses that provide goods for current consumption and uses that provide goods for future consumption. Education, new structures and equipment to be used in production, and research for and development of new technologies are *investments* in future production possibilities. The gain from these investments is the expansion in production possibilities they allow in the future.

Expansion of production possibilities results when workers have more and better capital (think of capital as "tools") and improved technology. Similarly, education increases workers' skills, allowing more output per worker.

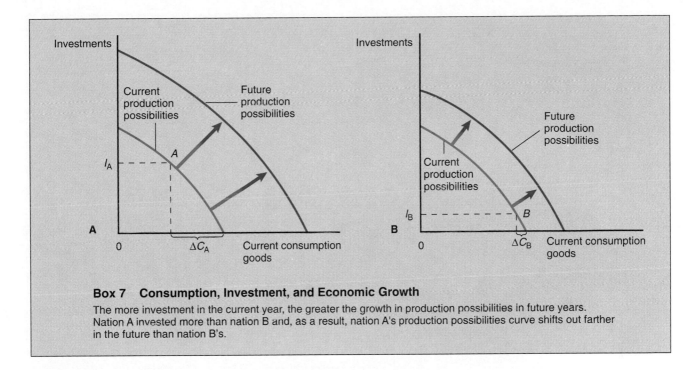

Box 7   Consumption, Investment, and Economic Growth

The more investment in the current year, the greater the growth in production possibilities in future years. Nation A invested more than nation B and, as a result, nation A's production possibilities curve shifts out farther in the future than nation B's.

The graphs in Box 7 show how future production possibilities are affected by the choice to allocate available economic resources to production of current consumption goods instead of investments. Suppose the current production possibilities for these two alternative uses of available resources are identical in the two nations. However, nation A chooses point A on its initial production possibilities curve, sacrificing ΔC_A units of consumption goods to product I_A units of investment goods. The citizens in nation B end up choosing point B on their production possibilities curve in the current year. They sacrifice a smaller amount of consumption goods, ΔC_B, which is less than ΔC_A, but produce only I_B units of investment goods, which is less than I_A. In the future, citizens of nation A are rewarded for their sacrifice of current consumption possibilities with a greater outward shift of their production possibilities curve than citizens of nation B enjoy.

In addition to deciding what to produce, how to produce it, and who will receive it, each economy must also decide what and how much it will sacrifice today to make investments that expand future production possibilities.

the global economy

The Gains from International Trade

6   The production possibilities curve can be used to show how we gain from foreign trade. Consumers gain when the United States trades with other nations to obtain goods that it can't produce itself. Less obviously, consumers also gain when the United States imports an item that it can produce itself. In general, if the opportunity cost of importing an item

is lower than the opportunity cost of producing it domestically, a nation can enjoy a net gain from international trade.

Box 8 shows the nation of Atlantica's production possibilities curve for wheat and videocassette recorders (VCRs). At any point on the curve the opportunity cost of an extra VCR is at least 1 ton of wheat, and at some points it is a lot more than 1 ton of wheat. For example, an additional 25,000 VCRs per year at point A would require that Atlantica give up

Box 8   Illustrating the Gains Possible from International Trade

The graph shows the production possibilities curve for Atlantica when Atlantica can grow wheat at lower opportunity cost (measured in terms of sacrifice of VCRs) than its trading partner, Pacifica. By specializing in wheat, Atlantica can enjoy consuming 50,000 VCRs per year and 225,000 tons of wheat per year at point *T*, which lies above its production possibilities curve. It gets to point *T* by producing 250,000 tons of wheat and exporting 25,000 tons of that to Pacifica in exchange for 50,000 VCRs.

production of 225,000 tons of wheat. Each VCR would cost an average 10 tons of wheat if the nation reallocated resources to move from point *A* to point *B*.

Atlantica is now at point *A* on its production possibilities curve, where it grows 225,000 tons of wheat and makes 25,000 VCRs per year. Wouldn't it be nice to get to point *T* where its citizens could enjoy 225,000 tons of wheat and 50,000 VCRs? Alas, that's not possible if Atlantica tries to produce both goods, since point *T* lies outside its production possibilities curve.

Suppose producers in the nation of Pacifica (where wheat costs more to produce than in Atlantica) will trade at the rate of one VCR for each half ton of wheat. Atlantica could then obtain VCRs through international trade at a much lower opportunity cost than is possible through domestic production.

Suppose now that Atlantica decides to specialize in wheat and uses all its resources to produce 250,000 tons per year at point *C*. It then exports 25,000 tons to Pacifica in exchange for VCRs. Because Pacifica is willing to trade at the rate of one-half ton of wheat for each VCR, the exported 25,000 tons of wheat buy 50,000 VCRs. By exporting 25,000 tons of wheat, Atlantica can therefore get to point *T*, where its citizens enjoy 225,000 tons of domestically grown wheat and 50,000 imported VCRs per year even though no VCRs are domestically produced.

International trade is like magic! It allows a nation's citizens to enjoy consumption possibilities (like point *T*) that go beyond its production possibilities (like point *A*).

This simple example illustrates the important *principle of comparative advantage*, which states that a nation can gain consumption possibilities by specializing in goods that it can produce domestically at lower opportunity cost than that of its trading partners. There are *mutual gains* to trading partners when they specialize in producing items for which they enjoy a comparative advantage and then engage in international trade for other goods and services. Later in this book we'll say more about the principle of comparative advantage and its implications for international trade.

■ What can cause the production possibilities curve to shift outward?

■ How can choices between consumption and investment today affect future production possibilities?

■ What is the principle of comparative advantage, and how does international trade based on this principle allow consumption possibilities that exceed a nation's production possibilities.

CONCEPT CHECK
□

SCARCITY AND TRADE-OFFS

We deal every day with the trade-offs implied by scarcity. Both production possibilities for a society and options for us as individuals to spend our available income are limited over any given period. In Chapter 1 we discussed the questions of what to produce, how to produce it, and to whom goods and services will be distributed. Now you can understand these questions better within the context of the constraints a nation faces. The problem of *what to produce* involves making decisions that eventually result in achievement of a particular production possibility. The problem of *how to produce it* affects the ability of participants in an economy to get to a point on their production possibilities curve. If efficient methods are employed to produce any given output and economic resources are fully utilized, then the maximum possible output of any one good, given the output of other goods, will be attained. Given current prices for goods and services, *who gets what is produced* depends on the way income is distributed among those of us in an economy. Naturally, the greater our income, the greater our options for consumption.

---

insights on issues

Do People in the United States Save Enough of Their Income? Talking with Jane Gravelle

Jane Gravelle was born in Sandersville, Georgia, in 1947. She holds a B.A. and an M.A. in political science from the University of Georgia and a Ph.D. in economics from George Washington University. She is an economist with the Congressional Research Service, conducting studies and writing papers on tax and investment issues for the U.S. Congress. She also has worked at the Treasury and Labor departments and has taught at Boston University. Gravelle is on the editorial board of the *National Tax Journal*.

How Is National Saving Measured? What Are Some of the Problems in Measuring It? National saving is measured as a residual. All of the country's output is measured in various ways. Then all consumption and government spending and trade are totaled. The difference between output and spending is savings. The biggest problems with measuring it is that since saving is such a small percentage of the total picture, any small error in any of the measures of output and spending leads to a large error in calculation of savings. This

is the main reason why the dollar amount of savings in this country in any given year tends to be revised upward when recalculated in later years—over time, the numbers available for the other variables tend to become more accurate.

Technically, savings is anything you produce that you don't consume. The concept is straightforward, but the measurement is tricky.

How Much Saving Is Enough? In terms of personal savings, that questaken off the budget and accumulated in a trust fund, that alone would nearly eliminate the deficit. It's all a matter of who pays for what over time. Why should we burden our children with the costs of our generation's spending?

What Are the Consequences of Low Savings Rates in the United States Relative to Other Nations? The consequence of low savings rates is a lower standard of living in the future. The rate relative to other countries, however, is essentially meaningless. A country's presence in international markets as either a buyer or a seller is influenced by the size of the aggregate economy. We buy some goods; we sell others. For example, the United States is not likely to corner the market in banana production. But ultimately it doesn't matter because we gain a comparative advantage from selling other goods and services.

If the United States borrows from another country, that alone will have no effect on savings. Sending pieces of paper around the world doesn't mean anything. But what will happen to offset that borrowing is that we wind up importing more actual, tangible goods than we export.

What Can Be Done to Increase Saving? The only thing we can do to increase saving is to reduce the federal deficit. Study after study has shown that nothing changes the behavior of individuals in this area. For example, when Social Security was started on a pay-as-you-go basis, it was expected that people would save less because they wouldn't need as much of their own money in old age. In fact, Social Security did not have an antisaving effect. That may be because before Social Security, people felt obligated to support their elderly relatives. Now that money is freed up from consumption and available to be saved.

Economists are always predicting that higher marginal tax rates will depress personal savings and that higher interest rates will reduce the investment of businesses. But when you survey people, most individuals don't know what their marginal tax rate is. And many businesspeople say they pay no attention to interest rates. If people don't even know these facts, predicting the influence of tax changes on their behavior becomes much more difficult.

tion is impossible to answer. We should leave it to individuals to make that decision for themselves. We should, however, give them enough information to work with about how long they're likely to live and how much money they're likely to need after retirement. And for people who are so poor they're living on the edge, government should use a transfer system to provide a minimal standard of living.

In terms of public savings, striving for a federal deficit close to zero would be a good idea. But much of that is simply a choice of accounting approaches. If Social Security were

SUMMARY

1. Production is the process of using economic resources to make goods and services available.

2. A production possibilities curve shows the maximum possible output of any one good that can be produced over a period of time with available economic resources and existing technology, given the output of other goods.

3. The law of increasing costs implies that the opportunity costs of extra production of any one good in any economy will increase as more and more specialized resources best suited for the production of other goods are reallocated away from their best use.

4. Not fully utilizing or mismanaging economic resources prevents the economy from achieving its full output

potential and results in attainment of a point below the production possibilities curve.

5. Increased availability of labor, capital, and natural resources, as well as improvements in technology or in worker skills, can shift a nation's production possibilities curve outward.

6. A budget line shows the combinations of goods and services a consumer with limited income can purchase over a period, given the prices of the goods and services desired. The opportunity cost of consuming more of any one good is the quantity of the next best alternative good that is sacrificed.

7. A nation can gain consumption possibilities that exceed its production possibilities by engaging in international

trade. This results when a nation specializes in goods and services that it can produce at lower opportunity cost than that of other nations and exports some of these goods and services in exchange for other items. A nation has a comparative advantage in the production of an item if it can produce it at lower opportunity cost

than that of its trading partners. There are mutual gains from international trade when trading partners specialize in the production of items for which they enjoy a comparative advantage and then engage in international trade to obtain other items.

KEY TERMS

economic resources *37*

labor *37*

capital *37*

natural resources *37*

entrepreneurship *37*

technology *37*

production possibilities curve *38*

law of increasing costs *41*

productive efficiency *46*

division of labor *46*

economic growth *46*

CONCEPT REVIEW

1. How are production possibilities influenced by technology and resource availability?

2. Explain how we would determine the opportunity cost of moving between two points on a production possibilities curve.

3. Explain why an economy that does not attain productive efficiency operates at a point below its production possibilities curve.

4. How can we use a production possibilities curve to show the impact of advances in technology and growth in resource availability on the economy?

5. Explain how the opportunity cost of consuming more of any one good or service depends both on its price and on the prices of alternative goods and services.

6. How can international trade allow us to consume combinations of goods and services that are above points on our production possibilities curve?

PROBLEMS AND APPLICATIONS

1. The United States is a rich and powerful nation with a skilled, productive labor force and a great deal of capital. Some less developed nations have few skilled workers and little capital. Why is scarcity an economic problem in rich and poor nations alike? 1

2. Make a list of the economic resources that are required to operate a restaurant. How is the number of meals per day that can be served limited by available economic resources and current technology for meal preparation and service? 1

3. The small nation whose annual production possibilities for food and clothing are illustrated in the table and graph in Box 1 receives a gift of new machines for use in clothing production and agriculture. The new machines allow the nation to produce twice as much food and clothing with the same number of workers and natural resources. Draw the new production possibilities curve for the nation, and show how the gift of capital expands its production possibilities. 1

4. Referring again to Box 1, suppose the nation receives a gift of new agricultural machinery that doubles the maximum quantity of food that can be produced for any given quantity of clothing produced. Draw the new production possibilities curve, and show why the gift expands the production possibilities of the nation to allow it to consume more food *and* clothing. Shade in the new combinations of food and clothing made possible by the gift. 1 , 4

5. A civil war erupts in the small nation whose production possibilities curve is shown in Box 1. The war results in the destruction of capital and natural resources, and causes casualties that reduce the supply of labor available for production of food and clothing. Show the impact of the war on the nation's production possibilities curve for food and clothing. 1 , 4

6. Suppose the production possibilities curve for the production of trucks and cars in a two-product factory has a constant slope equal to -2 when weekly car production is plotted on the vertical axis and weekly truck production is plotted on the horizontal axis. Draw the production possibilities curve, and explain why the law of increasing costs doesn't hold for the production of cars and trucks in the factory. 2

7. Suppose you own and run a small business. You spend 40 hours per week managing the operation. By managing the business, you forgo your next best alternative, which is working at a job for someone else that pays $10 per hour. An accountant calculates all the money costs and revenues from the business and tells you you're making a $300 profit per week. However, the accountant doesn't include the opportunity cost of your time as part of the money costs because you don't incur any cash outlay to pay for your time. Does it make sense for you to continue in business? Explain your answer. 2

8. Imagine you're the manager of a small textile factory

that has two product lines: flannel fabric and corduroy fabric. Some workers and some machines are specialized in the production of only one of these goods. The maximum amount of flannel that can be produced when 1,000 yards of corduroy are also produced is 1,500 yards per month with 10,000 labor hours per month. You can't vary the number of machines or amount of floor space in the factory. Suppose you are currently producing at an efficient level. If monthly orders drop to 1,000 yards of corduroy and 1,000 yards of flannel, what could you do to reduce costs during the month? Explain your answer using a production possibilities curve. ▣ , ▣

9. Your younger sister receives a weekly allowance of $20, which she spends entirely on movie tickets and ice-cream cones. Movies cost $4 per show and ice-cream cones are $1. Draw your sister's budget line. What is the opportunity cost of a movie? Would the opportunity cost of a movie change if the prices of movies and ice-cream cones doubled?

Show how the budget line will shift for each of the following changes. Calculate the opportunity cost of each item for each of the changes.
a. An increase in the weekly allowance to $24.
b. A decrease in the weekly allowance to $12.
c. A reduction in the price of movie admission to $2.
d. An increase in the price of ice-cream cones to $2. ▣

10. Suppose that each 35-mm camera produced in the United States involves the sacrifice of 100 pounds of beef and that in Japan each 35-mm camera produced involves the sacrifice of 50 pounds of beef. Use production possibilities curves to demonstrate how both Japan and the United States can gain from specializing in the production of one of these goods and engaging in international trade to obtain the other. ▣

part II

Supply and Demand
Markets and the Price System

CONCEPTS

Market

Demand and Quantity Demanded

Supply and Quantity Supplied

Law of Demand

Law of Supply

Changes in Demand and Supply

Shortages and Surpluses

Market Equilibrium

Price Ceilings and Floors

Nonprice Rationing

Capitalism and Free Markets

Mixed Economy

Price System

Open Economy

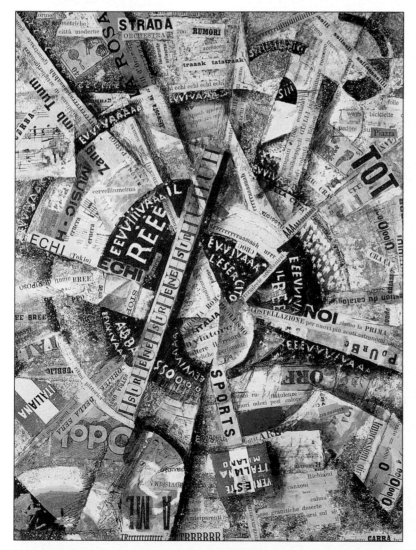

Carlo Carra, *Patriotic Celebration (Free World Paintin)*, 1914. Milan, Collection Mattioloi.
COPYRIGHT Vaga, New York/Art Resource, NY

3 *chapter*

Market Transactions
Basic Supply and Demand Analysis

No matter how independent we may be in spirit, none of us is truly self-sufficient. Think of how we rely on others for our basic needs. We go to the supermarket for food. A local power company provides our electricity. The road we drive on is built and maintained by the government and financed with taxes. Few people, even farmers, produce all the food and fiber they need to feed and clothe themselves.

Even those of us who have the skill to grow our own food, make our own clothes, build our own homes, and repair our own cars rarely, if ever, find it in our interest to be self-sufficient. Instead, we benefit from a complex division of labor and specialization in economic activities. Specialized firms and agencies provide particular goods and services to consumers, investors, and governments. In order to purchase these goods, buyers seek out sellers in markets. A market's purpose is to provide information on the goods and services sellers want to sell and buyers want to buy.

This chapter introduces you to supply and demand analysis of market transactions, which shows how prices are established by the competition among buyers for goods offered by competing sellers. Market prices play a vital role in coping with the problem of scarcity because they ration available amounts of goods and services.

□ CONCEPT PREVIEW

After reading this chapter, you should be able to:

1. Discuss the purposes and functions of markets.

2. Explain how a demand curve illustrates the law of demand and distinguish between a change in demand and a change in quantity demanded.

3. Show how a supply curve illustrates the law of supply and distinguish between a change in supply and a change in quantity supplied.

4. Describe the conditions required for market equilibrium and locate the equilibrium point on a supply and demand diagram.

5. Explain the consequences of shortages and surpluses in markets and how prices adjust in a free and unregulated competitive market to eliminate shortages or surpluses.

6. Show how changes in demand and supply affect market equilibrium.

MARKETS: PURPOSES AND FUNCTIONS

A market is an arrangement through which buyers and sellers meet or communicate in order to trade goods or services. It is a way in which buyers and sellers can do business together. For example, a local electronics store is a place that displays the range of stereos, VCRs, TVs, and compact disc players offered by various manufacturers. A flea market has both buyers and sellers: one person can offer to sell a used bicycle or car stereo and at the same time look for old records or find a couch.

Many market transactions are conducted without buyers and sellers actually meeting. For example, buyers can look through catalogs and then order merchandise by mail or telephone, without face-to-face contact with sellers. Buyers can also hire intermediaries to carry out transactions for them. For example, travel agents will check the fares of all airlines and make the best deals for their clients.

Supply and demand analysis explains how prices are established in markets through competition among buyers and sellers, and how those prices affect quantities traded. In a *competitive* or *free* market, many sellers compete for sales to many buyers who compete for available goods and services. In such a market, all those who wish to sell and all those who wish to buy can do so.

To analyze the way markets operate, you first must understand the concept of supply and demand. This concept was introduced in 1890 by British economist Alfred Marshall, who first articulated many of the principles that underlie modern microeconomic theory (see Economic Thinkers box).

DEMAND

The amount of an item buyers actually purchase in a market over a given period is influenced by a number of important determinants, such as:

1. Its price.
2. Buyers' available income.
3. Buyers' wealth (the value of assets such as stocks, bonds, homes and other real estate, and business property).
4. Expectations of future price changes.
5. The prices of alternative items.
6. Tastes or current fashions.
7. The population served by the market.

In analyzing the behavior of buyers in markets, we concentrate on the effect of each of these determinants, one at a time. We pay special attention to the relationship between the price of an item and the quantities buyers purchase. The quantity demanded of an item is the amount that buyers are willing and able to purchase over a period at a certain price, *given all other influences on their decision to buy*.

Demand is a relationship between the price of an item and the quantity demanded. The term *demand* as used in economics is not a fixed number. It signifies how the quantity buyers purchase varies with price, assuming that *all other influences on the amount buyers buy other than the price of the item* are held fixed. For example, the demand for cars over a year indicates how the annual quantity demanded varies as the price of cars changes, *other things being equal*. The other things held constant are all influences on the decision to buy *other than* the price of cars, such as income available for spending, wealth, or consumer preferences. Similarly, the demand for subway rides in a city isolates the relationship between the price of a ride and the number of rides demanded over a given period.

market an arrangement through which buyers and sellers meet or communicate in order to trade goods or services.

supply and demand analysis a theory that explains how prices are established in markets through competition among buyers and sellers, and how those prices affect quantities traded.

quantity demanded the amount of an item that buyers are willing and able to purchase over a period at a certain price, given all other influences on their decision to buy.

demand a relationship between the price of an item and the quantity demanded.

economic thinkers

Alfred Marshall

Alfred Marshall was born in London in 1842. Despite intense pressure from his ambitious father, Marshall declined a theological scholarship to Oxford and instead worked toward a master's degree in mathematics at Cambridge. His decision to study mathematics instead of theology may have given the world one of its most brilliant and influential economists. After receiving his degree in 1865, he remained at Cambridge to teach mathematics, and it was then that he began to study economics seriously.

Because Marshall admired the classical economic writers, such as Adam Smith and David Ricardo, he initially concentrated on using his knowledge of mathematical principles to reinforce the tenets of the classical school. His first effort was to translate into mathematical equations the text of John Stuart Mill's *Principles*. As Marshall's ideas gained acceptance, his influence grew. In 1885 he was appointed to the Chair of Political Economy at Cambridge, a position he retained for nearly 25 years.

In his ground-breaking *Principles of Economics*, published in 1890, Marshall set forth many of the principles that underlie contemporary microeconomic theory. Through his teachings and writings Marshall influenced many of the leading economists of succeeding generations. More than a century after its publication, his *Principles* text still has much to offer an economics student. As you study supply and demand, elasticity, equilibrium, the short run, and the long run, reflect on the astonishing fact that each of these concepts was originally popularized by Alfred Marshall.

The Market Demand Curve and the Law of Demand

2

demand schedule a table that shows how an item's quantity demanded would vary with price, other things being equal.

A **demand schedule** is a table that shows how an item's quantity demanded would vary with price, other things being equal. The table in Box 1 shows a hypothetical demand schedule for grade A eggs sold per week in a local farmers' market. The first column of the table shows possible prices per dozen eggs. The quantity demanded, shown in the second column, represents the weekly amount of eggs that buyers are willing and able to purchase at each price. The schedule is based on the assumption that there's no change in any other demand influence except price. The schedule shows a number of possible outcomes in the market. The actual quantity purchased over the period depends on the price of eggs, given all the other determinants of the amount buyers will buy.

The data in the hypothetical demand schedule indicate an inverse relationship between price and quantity demanded. When price goes down, the quantity demanded goes up. For example, at a price of $2 per dozen, the quantity of eggs demanded per week is only 1,000 dozen. At a price of $1.50 per dozen, buyers would demand 3,000 dozen eggs per week.

law of demand the principle stating that, in general, other things being equal, the lower the price of a good, the greater the quantity of that good buyers will purchase over a given period.

The **law of demand** states that, in general, other things being equal, the lower the price of a good, the greater the quantity of that good buyers will purchase over a given period. Conversely, the law implies that buyers will purchase less of a good over any given period if its price increases while nothing else changes. The law is relevant to all goods and services, not just grade A eggs. For example, the lower the price of subway rides, other things being equal, the greater the quantity demanded. Lower prices make goods more attractive to us as consumers and increase our

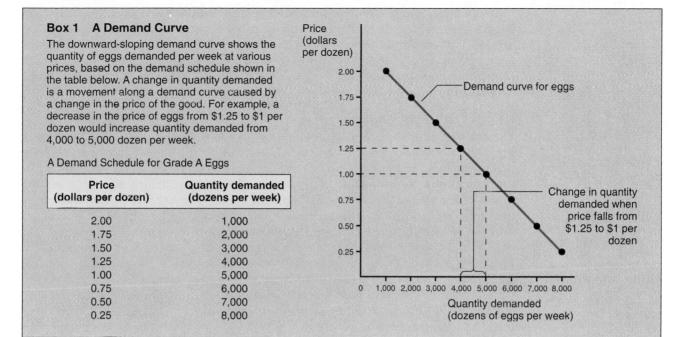

Box 1   A Demand Curve

The downward-sloping demand curve shows the quantity of eggs demanded per week at various prices, based on the demand schedule shown in the table below. A change in quantity demanded is a movement along a demand curve caused by a change in the price of the good. For example, a decrease in the price of eggs from $1.25 to $1 per dozen would increase quantity demanded from 4,000 to 5,000 dozen per week.

A Demand Schedule for Grade A Eggs

Price (dollars per dozen)	Quantity demanded (dozens per week)
2.00	1,000
1.75	2,000
1.50	3,000
1.25	4,000
1.00	5,000
0.75	6,000
0.50	7,000
0.25	8,000

willingness to buy. To see this, just visit a store that's running a sale and watch how much more quickly goods leave the shelf!

The law of demand can be derived as an implication of an economic model based on rational behavior; it is also generally supported by empirical evidence. Other things being equal, lower prices induce us to buy more of an item over a period because we enjoy additional net gains that weren't possible at the higher prices.

Examine your own behavior as a buyer to convince yourself that the law of demand is quite reasonable. If you're like most people, you buy more recordings, more clothing, and more of most items over any given period when their prices decline and nothing else changes. When the prices of these items rise, you tend to buy less of them. If the price of a movie increased from $4 to $8, you'd probably attend movies less often and look for other forms of entertainment. Other consumers like you behave the same way.

A **demand curve** is a graph of the data comprised by a demand schedule. The graph in Box 1 shows the weekly demand curve for eggs by plotting the data from the table. Price is represented by points on the vertical axis, while quantity demanded is represented by points on the horizontal axis. To see how the curve is plotted, look at the demand schedule. Note that if the price of grade A eggs is $1 per dozen, the quantity demanded is 5,000 dozen per week. A horizontal line drawn from the point corresponding to $1 on the price axis intersects the demand curve at the point that corresponds to 5,000 dozen eggs per week on the horizontal axis.

The downward slope of the demand curve reflects the law of demand. It's also useful to interpret points on a demand curve as indicating how the willingness of buyers to pay varies with the quantity of an item actually available in a market over a period of time. The demand curve indicates that the smaller the amount of eggs offered for sale each month, the more buyers are willing to pay. Conversely, the greater the amount of eggs available, the less buyers are willing to pay.

demand curve a graph that shows how quantity demanded varies with the price of a good.

You can see the relationship between quantity available and price by examining your own experience in markets. If you've ever bought a car, you know that during periods in which car dealers have few cars in stock, buyers are willing to pay higher prices. This is because buyers who are willing and able to pay the price for cars compete with one another for those available. They are willing to pay more rather than lose the opportunity to buy to a competing buyer.

Changes in Relative Price

change in relative price an increase or decrease in the price of a good relative to the average change in the prices of all goods.

The price of an item is usually measured as a sum of money. However, the money price of an item isn't always the best indication of what we must give up to obtain a unit of the item, because the purchasing power of money can change over time. For example, when an average of the prices of all the goods available in an economy increases by 5 percent over a year, each dollar will buy on average a smaller *quantity* of goods. This means that the purchasing power of the dollar is less.

A **change in relative price** of a good is an increase or decrease in the price of that good relative to the average change in the prices of all goods. The relative price of a good may not always change when its money price changes. For example, suppose an average of the money prices of all goods goes up by 7 percent over a year. If the money price of cars also goes up by that amount, the relative price of cars will be unchanged. If college tuition increases by 10 percent over the same year, its relative price will have risen because its money price has increased by a percentage that exceeds the average. Similarly, if the money price of VCRs increases by only 3 percent, the relative price of VCRs will have fallen over the year even though the money price has gone up.

When the purchasing power of money is not constant, changes in relative prices of goods measure changes in the opportunity cost of a purchase better than changes in money prices. Strictly speaking, the law of demand expresses a relationship between changes in the *relative price* of a good and resulting changes in the quantities demanded.

Changes in Quantity Demanded

change in quantity demanded a change in the amount of a good buyers are willing and able to buy in response to a change in the price of a good.

In general, the demand curve is *downward sloping*. The negative slope reflects the inverse relationship between price and quantity demanded according to the law of demand. Although the demand curve in Box 1 has been drawn as a straight line, it could also be curvilinear. Along the demand curve, quantity demanded increases as the price of the good decreases. A **change in quantity demanded** is a change in the amount of a good buyers are willing and able to buy in response to a change in the price of the good. *A change in quantity demanded is represented by a movement along a given demand curve caused by an increase or decrease in the price of the good.*

For example, for the demand curve depicted in Box 1, an increase in the price of eggs from $1 to $1.25 per dozen would result in a decrease in weekly quantity demanded from 5,000 dozen to 4,000 dozen. The 1,000-dozen decline in the quantity buyers are willing to purchase as the price of eggs increases is called a *decrease in quantity demanded*. Similarly, if the price declined from $1 to $0.75 per dozen, there would be an *increase in quantity demanded* from 5,000 dozen to 6,000 dozen per week.

Changes in Demand

As we observed earlier, the relationship between the price of a good and the quantity of the good demanded over a given period also depends on such influences as income available for spending, wealth, prices of related goods, expectations of future prices,

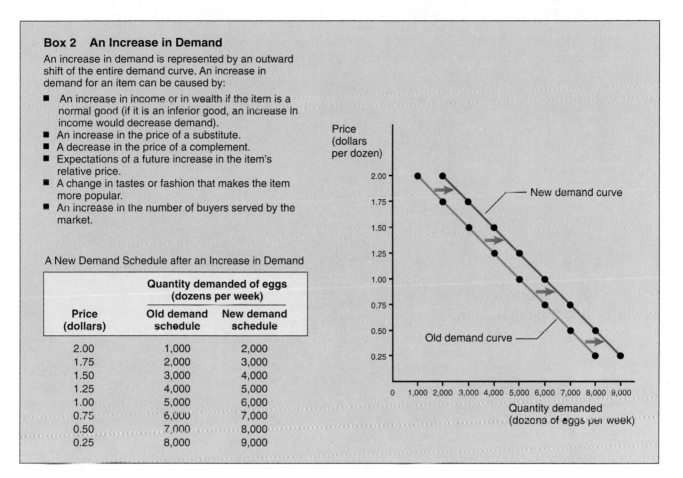

Box 2 An Increase in Demand

An increase in demand is represented by an outward shift of the entire demand curve. An increase in demand for an item can be caused by:

- An increase in income or in wealth if the item is a normal good (if it is an inferior good, an increase in income would decrease demand).
- An increase in the price of a substitute.
- A decrease in the price of a complement.
- Expectations of a future increase in the item's relative price.
- A change in tastes or fashion that makes the item more popular.
- An increase in the number of buyers served by the market.

A New Demand Schedule after an Increase in Demand

	Quantity demanded of eggs (dozens per week)	
Price (dollars)	Old demand schedule	New demand schedule
2.00	1,000	2,000
1.75	2,000	3,000
1.50	3,000	4,000
1.25	4,000	5,000
1.00	5,000	6,000
0.75	6,000	7,000
0.50	7,000	8,000
0.25	8,000	9,000

consumer preferences, and the number of buyers in the market. The quantity of a good that consumers are willing and able to buy at any given price changes if any one of these influences changes. A change in demand is a change in the relationship between the price of a good and the quantity demanded caused by a change in something other than the price of the good.

A change in demand implies a movement of an entire demand curve for a good. A new demand schedule must be drawn up, because the quantity demanded by consumers *at each price* changes. *(Be careful not to confuse a change in demand with a change in quantity demanded. A change in demand is a response to a change in a demand influence other than the price of the good, while a change in quantity demanded is a response to a change in a good's own price.)*

The table in Box 2 shows not only the old demand schedule but a new demand schedule resulting from an increase in demand. You'll notice that the quantity demanded in the new schedule is greater than the quantity demanded in the old schedule at *each possible price*. The graph uses the data in the adjacent table to plot the new demand curve on the same set of axes as the old demand curve. The increase in demand is represented by a shift *outward* of the demand curve.

The graph in Box 3 illustrates a decrease in demand as an inward shift of the entire demand curve. At each possible price, the quantity demanded by consumers declines. Note that the new demand curve need not be parallel to the old demand curve.

change in demand a change in the relationship between the price of a good and the quantity demanded caused by a change in something other than the price of the good.

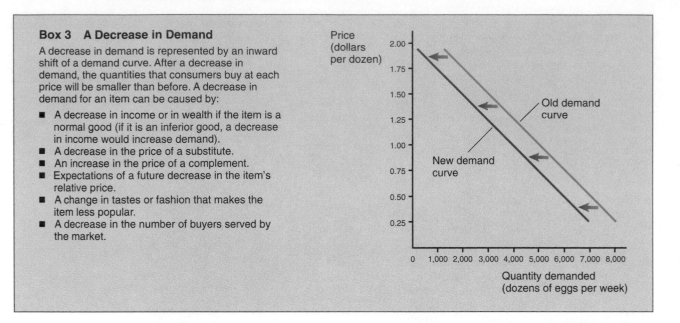

Box 3   A Decrease in Demand

A decrease in demand is represented by an inward shift of a demand curve. After a decrease in demand, the quantities that consumers buy at each price will be smaller than before. A decrease in demand for an item can be caused by:

- A decrease in income or in wealth if the item is a normal good (if it is an inferior good, a decrease in income would increase demand).
- A decrease in the price of a substitute.
- An increase in the price of a complement.
- Expectations of a future decrease in the item's relative price.
- A change in tastes or fashion that makes the item less popular.
- A decrease in the number of buyers served by the market.

Using logic and observation, we can make hypotheses about the possible impact of changes in various influences on the demand for a good:

1. *Changes in consumer income.* An increase in available income increases the *ability* of consumers to buy an item. Increases in income tend to increase the demand for most goods, while decreases in income tend to decrease the demand for most goods.

Although the demand for most goods increases as income goes up, there are some exceptions. The demand for less expensive cuts of meat, low-quality clothing, and secondhand furniture declines for many people as their income goes up. Goods whose demand declines as income increases are called *inferior goods*. Goods whose demand increases when income goes up are called *normal goods*.

2. *Changes in wealth.* Wealth is the net accumulated savings in a nation. Wealth includes such assets as real estate, stocks and bonds, money in the bank, and other financial assets such as mutual funds. Declines in real-estate values and in the values of stocks in 1990 caused a decrease in wealth that made many people cut back on spending and reduced the demand for such goods as new homes, furniture, and cars.

Some goods are relatively insensitive to wealth changes. Demand for bathroom tissue, for example, is unlikely to be affected by changes in wealth. The demand for other goods may actually increase in response to a decline in wealth. For example, people whose wealth declines may increase their demand for cars in the mid-price range because they can no longer afford luxury cars.

3. *Changes in the prices of other goods.* Our willingness to buy a particular item also depends on the prices of related items. Alternatives, items that serve a purpose similar to that of a given item, are substitutes for that item. An increase in the price of bagels is likely to increase the demand for English muffins because you can substitute English muffins for bagels at breakfast. Conversely, a decrease in the price of bagels may decrease the demand for English muffins. Similarly, an increase in the price of off-campus housing near your school may increase the demand for dormitory rooms.

substitutes goods that serve a purpose similar to that of a given item.

The demand for a good can also be influenced by a change in the price of its complements. Complements are goods whose use together enhances the satisfaction a consumer obtains from each of them. For example, a decrease in the price of compact disc recordings is likely to increase the demand for compact disc players because these two goods complement each other. Similarly, if the price of gas goes up significantly, the demand for cars may go down, because cars and gas are complements.

complements goods whose use together enhances the satisfaction a consumer obtains from each of them.

4. *Changes in expectations of future prices.* The demand for an item also depends on expectations buyers have about future events. In particular, if you as a buyer expect the price of an item to increase next week, you're likely to buy more of the item this week. If an item can be stored, as is the case for shampoo or socks, you'll increase your demand and stock up. Expectations of future price increases therefore tend to shift current demand curves outward. By the same token, expectations of price declines for an item tend to decrease current demand. If you expect the price of personal computers to decline next month, you'll be less willing to buy a PC this month. The expectation of a price decline therefore tends to decrease current demand and shift the demand curve for the product inward.

5. *Changes in tastes or fashion.* The general appeal of an item to buyers can change from time to time. If your taste for an item changes, your demand for it may decrease because you're less willing to buy it at any price. For example, the demand for long-playing records has decreased in recent years as you and other buyers have been attracted by the superior sound quality of CDs. You're also well aware of the influence of fashion on the demand for clothing. As styles change, you become more reluctant to buy certain items no matter how low the price. Even at a price of only 25 cents, you're not likely to buy a pair of plaid polyester pants, unless you're planning to attend a costume party.

6. *Changes in the number of buyers served by the market.* The total quantity of any item demanded at any price also depends on the *number* of buyers interested in buying the item at that price. Higher population tends to be associated with increases in demand for goods. The number of buyers can also change when buyers in foreign countries become willing and able to purchase an item. For example, if Europeans become more willing and able to buy American cars, the demand for them will increase, other things being equal. A breakdown of trade barriers allowing U.S. firms to sell more beef in Japan will increase the demand for U.S. beef. An increase in the number of buyers in a market tends to increase demand, shifting the demand curve outward. A decrease in the number of buyers in a market tends to decrease the demand for a good, shifting the demand curve inward.

In addition to the influences we've just examined, the demand for particular goods can be influenced by weather, demographic trends, or government subsidies or taxes. For example, a cold winter can increase the demand for sleds and warm clothing. An increase in the proportion of Americans over the age of 65 has been increasing the demand for retirement residences and nursing homes.

- What is the purpose of a market?
- Explain how a demand curve illustrates the law of demand. What influences the demand for a good?

- What is the distinction between changes in quantity of a good demanded and changes in demand for a good? Indicate what can cause changes in demand for a good and what can cause changes in quantity of a good demanded.

CONCEPT CHECK
◻

SUPPLY

The quantity of a good or service sellers are willing to sell in a market is affected by a number of important influences:

1. Its price.
2. Current prices of inputs needed to produce and market the good.
3. Current technology available to produce and market the good.
4. Prices of other goods that can be produced with inputs used or owned by the sellers.
5. Expectations about future prices.
6. The number of sellers serving the market.

In analyzing the quantity of a good made available for sale in a given period, we must isolate the effects of each of the separate influences. We'll pay special attention to the influence of price on the quantity sellers are willing to sell. The **quantity supplied** is the quantity of a good sellers are willing and able to make available in the market over a given period at a certain price, *other things being equal*. In this case the *other things* being held equal are all the previously listed supply influences other than the price of the good itself.

The concept of supply as used in economics is a relationship between the price of an item and the quantity supplied. Like demand, supply is not a fixed quantity. Instead, it signifies how the quantity sellers offer varies with price. The amount sellers bring to the market over any given period depends on the price of the product and the other supply influences.

The Market Supply Curve and the Law of Supply

3 The price is the payment a seller receives for each unit of a good sold. Just as changes in relative price influence incentives to buy a good, so do changes in relative price influence incentives to sell a good. The table in Box 4 provides hypothetical data for the price and quantity of eggs supplied in a local farmers' market each week. (Other supply influences are assumed not to change as price changes.) The data constitute the **supply schedule,** which shows how quantity supplied is related to the price. The first column of the table shows possible prices per dozen eggs. The second column shows the quantities supplied per week at each possible price. The data indicate a direct relationship between price and quantity supplied: the higher the price, the greater the quantity supplied. For example, as the price of eggs increases from $1 to $1.25 per dozen, the weekly quantity supplied increases from 5,000 dozen to 6,000 dozen.

Naturally, the higher the price per unit of a good, other things being equal, the greater the potential gain from supplying it. The law of supply states that, in general, other things being equal, the higher the price of a good, the greater the quantity of that good sellers are willing and able to make available over a given period.

The law of supply is an implication of a model based on the assumption that sellers seek to maximize net gains from their activities. The law represents a hypothesis that is widely supported by empirical evidence. Let's sketch out the idea underlying the law of supply by using an example. Over any given period, say a week, there are a given number of suppliers of stone-washed denims in the United States. Each supplier can make only a certain number of pairs of jeans available. Some inputs, such as factory space and machinery, can't easily be increased over such a short period. As sellers try to make more jeans available by hiring more labor and increasing other inputs that can be more easily obtained, their operations become

---

quantity supplied the quantity of a good sellers are willing and able to make available in the market over a given period at a certain price, other things being equal.

supply a relationship between the price of an item and the quantity supplied.

supply schedule a table that shows how the quantity supplied of a good is related to its price.

law of supply the principle stating that, in general, other things being equal, the higher the price of a good, the greater the quantity of that good sellers are willing and able to make available over a given period.

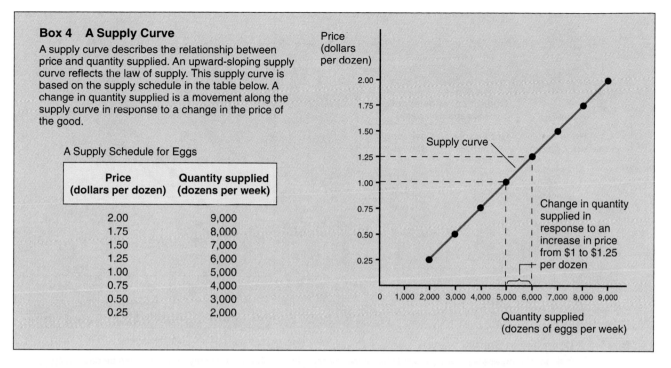

Box 4   A Supply Curve

A supply curve describes the relationship between price and quantity supplied. An upward-sloping supply curve reflects the law of supply. This supply curve is based on the supply schedule in the table below. A change in quantity supplied is a movement along the supply curve in response to a change in the price of the good.

A Supply Schedule for Eggs

Price (dollars per dozen)	Quantity supplied (dozens per week)
2.00	9,000
1.75	8,000
1.50	7,000
1.25	6,000
1.00	5,000
0.75	4,000
0.50	3,000
0.25	2,000

less efficient. Workers overutilize machines, which tends to make them break down more often. As the limit of productive capacity is approached, the costs per pair of jeans tend to rise, as does the marginal cost of making the jeans available to prospective buyers. These increasing marginal costs imply that sellers are unwilling to make more stone-washed denims available unless higher prices prevail to cover their increasing costs. Unless prices rise, sellers can't enjoy a net gain (profit) from producing more jeans. At higher prices each seller is likely to want to make more pairs of jeans available over a given period.

A **supply curve** is a graph of the data from a supply schedule that shows how quantity supplied varies with price. The graph in Box 4 plots the weekly supply curve for eggs based on the data in the table. Price is plotted on the vertical axis, while quantity supplied corresponds to points on the horizontal axis. For example, if the price were $2 per dozen, suppliers would be willing to make 9,000 dozen eggs available to the market. To see this, find the point on the price axis corresponding to $2 and draw a horizontal line across to the supply curve. Then draw a vertical line to the quantity axis that will intersect this axis at a quantity supplied of 9,000 dozen eggs per week. Assume that if the price fell below 25 cents per dozen, no one would be willing to sell eggs, so the quantity supplied would fall to zero. Understandably, sellers require a minimum price to cover their costs before they'll make goods available to buyers.

Note that you can also interpret points on a supply curve as indicating the price sellers will accept to make each possible quantity available to buyers. The greater the quantity buyers want to purchase, the higher the price necessary to induce sellers to make the desired quantity available.

supply curve a graph that shows how quantity supplied varies with the price of a good.

Changes in Quantity Supplied

The upward slope of the supply curve reflects the law of supply. As the price increases, the quantity supplied over a period goes up. A **change in quantity supplied** is a change in the amount sellers are willing to sell over a period in response to a

change in quantity supplied a change in the amount of a good sellers are willing to sell over a period in response to a change in the price of the good.

alternative goods change the opportunity cost of producing a given good, resulting in changes in its supply. For example, given the price of T-shirts, an increase in the price of sweatshirts could decrease the supply of T-shirts if manufacturers use their facilities to produce more sweatshirts and fewer T-shirts. This would shift the supply curve for T-shirts to the left. Similarly, a decrease in the price of sweatshirts could increase the supply of T-shirts, shifting the supply curve for this item to the right.

4. *Changes in the number of sellers serving the market.* Other things being equal, an increase in the number of sellers increases the supply of a good. For example, an increase in the number of firms producing compact discs increases the number of CDs available at any given price. Over long periods of time, changes in the number of sellers in a market are a very important determinant of supply. The number of sellers in a market changes with the profitability of producing a good.

Other important determinants can also affect the supply of particular goods. For example, weather can affect the supply of agricultural commodities. A frost in Florida that ruins the citrus crop can decrease the supply of oranges in the market over a year. Expectations about future prices of goods and services and inputs can also affect current supply, as can taxes and subsidies.

CONCEPT CHECK

☐

- Explain how a supply curve shows the law of supply. List the supply influences that must be held constant to draw a supply curve.

- What can cause a change in quantity supplied? What can cause a change in supply?

- An improvement in technology allows a given amount of inputs to produce more pocket TVs per week. Use a graph to show the impact of the improvement on the weekly supply of pocket TVs.

MARKET EQUILIBRIUM PRICE AND QUANTITY

4

equilibrium the situation that prevails when economic forces balance so that economic variables neither increase nor decrease.

market equilibrium the situation attained when the price of a good adjusts so that the quantity buyers are willing and able to buy at that price is just equal to the quantity sellers are willing and able to supply.

shortage the situation that exists in a market when the quantity demanded of a good exceeds the quantity supplied over a given period.

surplus the condition that exists in a market when the quantity supplied of a good exceeds the quantity demanded over a given period.

An **equilibrium** prevails when economic forces balance so that economic variables neither increase nor decrease. **Market equilibrium** is attained when the price of a good adjusts so that the quantity buyers will buy at that price is equal to the quantity sellers will sell. When a market equilibrium has been attained, forces of supply and demand balance, so that there's no tendency for the market price or quantity to change over a given period. The equilibrium price acts to ration the good so that everyone who wants to buy the good will find it available. Similarly, at the equilibrium price, everyone who wants to sell the good will be able to do so successfully. For example, equilibrium in the personal stereo market requires that the price of personal stereos be such that the quantity demanded equals the quantity supplied. When quantity demanded equals quantity supplied, the market is said to *clear*.

A **shortage** exists in a market when the quantity demanded of a good exceeds the quantity supplied over a given period. For example, there will be a monthly shortage of compact disc players if at the current market price the monthly number of players that sellers will make available falls short of the monthly number that buyers will purchase.

A **surplus** exists in a market when the quantity supplied of a good exceeds the quantity demanded over a given period. There would be a monthly surplus of gas if the monthly quantity supplied by sellers exceeded the monthly quantity demanded by buyers at a certain price. At the market equilibrium price of a good, there can be neither surpluses nor shortages in the market. When a market clears, the good is rationed, because there are neither surpluses nor shortages.

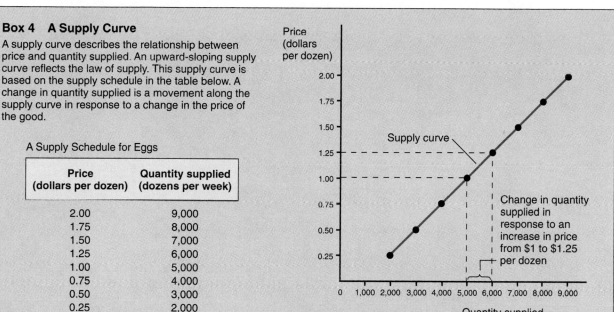

Box 4   A Supply Curve

A supply curve describes the relationship between price and quantity supplied. An upward-sloping supply curve reflects the law of supply. This supply curve is based on the supply schedule in the table below. A change in quantity supplied is a movement along the supply curve in response to a change in the price of the good.

A Supply Schedule for Eggs

Price (dollars per dozen)	Quantity supplied (dozens per week)
2.00	9,000
1.75	8,000
1.50	7,000
1.25	6,000
1.00	5,000
0.75	4,000
0.50	3,000
0.25	2,000

less efficient. Workers overutilize machines, which tends to make them break down more often. As the limit of productive capacity is approached, the costs per pair of jeans tend to rise, as does the marginal cost of making the jeans available to prospective buyers. These increasing marginal costs imply that sellers are unwilling to make more stone-washed denims available unless higher prices prevail to cover their increasing costs. Unless prices rise, sellers can't enjoy a net gain (profit) from producing more jeans. At higher prices each seller is likely to want to make more pairs of jeans available over a given period.

A **supply curve** is a graph of the data from a supply schedule that shows how quantity supplied varies with price. The graph in Box 4 plots the weekly supply curve for eggs based on the data in the table. Price is plotted on the vertical axis, while quantity supplied corresponds to points on the horizontal axis. For example, if the price were $2 per dozen, suppliers would be willing to make 9,000 dozen eggs available to the market. To see this, find the point on the price axis corresponding to $2 and draw a horizontal line across to the supply curve. Then draw a vertical line to the quantity axis that will intersect this axis at a quantity supplied of 9,000 dozen eggs per week. Assume that if the price fell below 25 cents per dozen, no one would be willing to sell eggs, so the quantity supplied would fall to zero. Understandably, sellers require a minimum price to cover their costs before they'll make goods available to buyers.

supply curve a graph that shows how quantity supplied varies with the price of a good.

Note that you can also interpret points on a supply curve as indicating the price sellers will accept to make each possible quantity available to buyers. The greater the quantity buyers want to purchase, the higher the price necessary to induce sellers to make the desired quantity available.

Changes in Quantity Supplied

The upward slope of the supply curve reflects the law of supply. As the price increases, the quantity supplied over a period goes up. A **change in quantity supplied** is a change in the amount sellers are willing to sell over a period in response to a

change in quantity supplied a change in the amount of a good sellers are willing to sell over a period in response to a change in the price of the good.

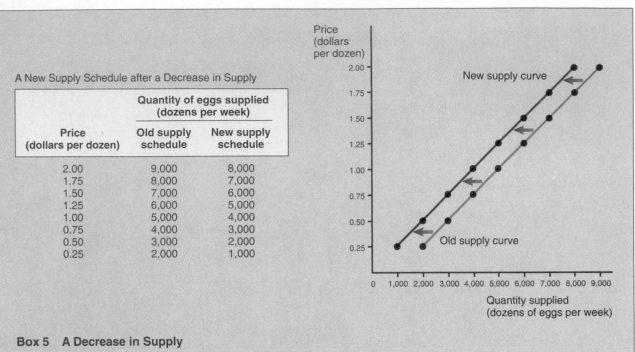

A New Supply Schedule after a Decrease in Supply

Price (dollars per dozen)	Quantity of eggs supplied (dozens per week)	
	Old supply schedule	New supply schedule
2.00	9,000	8,000
1.75	8,000	7,000
1.50	7,000	6,000
1.25	6,000	5,000
1.00	5,000	4,000
0.75	4,000	3,000
0.50	3,000	2,000
0.25	2,000	1,000

Box 5   A Decrease in Supply

A decrease in supply is represented by an inward shift of the supply curve. A change in supply of an item can be caused by:

- A change in the prices of inputs used to produce it: an increase in input prices decreases supply, while a decrease in input prices increases supply.
- A change in technology: an improvement in technology increases supply, while the unlikely event of a deterioration in technology (caused by some catastrophe) would decrease supply.
- A change in the prices of other items: an increase in the relative price of an alternative item that can be produced with the same resources decreases supply of the first item, while a decrease in the relative price of the alternative item would increase supply of the first item.
- A change in the number of sellers serving the market: a decrease in the number of sellers decreases supply, while an increase in the number of sellers increases supply.

change in the price of the good. Changes in quantity supplied represent movements along a given supply curve in response to price changes while all other factors affecting the willingness of sellers to sell are unchanged. For example, if the price of eggs declined from $2 to $1.75 per dozen, there would be a *decrease in quantity supplied* and the quantity sellers would make available to the market would decline from 9,000 dozen to 8,000 dozen per week. Similarly, if the price increased from $1 to $1.25 per dozen, there would be an *increase in quantity supplied* as sellers would be willing to increase the quantity available for sale from 5,000 dozen to 6,000 dozen per week.

Changes in Supply

change in supply a change in the relationship between the price of a good and the quantity supplied in response to a change in a supply determinant other than the price of the good.

A **change in supply** is a change in the relationship between the price of a good and the quantity supplied in response to a change in a supply determinant other than the price of the good. A change in supply implies a shift of the entire supply curve. A new supply schedule must be drawn up because the quantity supplied by sellers *at each price* will change. For example, in the table in Box 5, a change in supply means that the data in the second column will change.

Among the important changes in economic conditions that can cause changes in supply are the following:

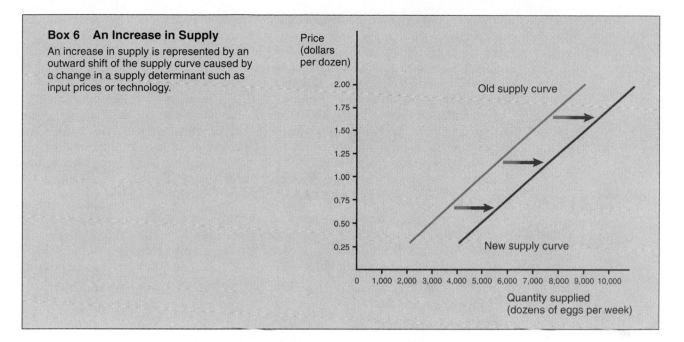

Box 6   An Increase in Supply

An increase in supply is represented by an outward shift of the supply curve caused by a change in a supply determinant such as input prices or technology.

Price (dollars per dozen)

Old supply curve

New supply curve

Quantity supplied (dozens of eggs per week)

1. *Changes in the prices of the inputs necessary to produce and sell a good.* The possible profit at any given price depends on the prices a seller must pay for the economic resources to produce a good. Increases in input prices and costs associated with selling the good result in less profit for selling any given quantity. This decreases the supply of the good. Conversely, a decrease in input prices increases the profitability of selling the good and results in an increase in supply. Suppose, for example, that there's an increase in the price of chicken feed. This is likely to decrease the willingness of egg producers to make eggs available at a given price because it is now more expensive to produce any given quantity of eggs. The table in Box 5 shows that the quantity supplied *at each price* is now less than was the case when the old supply schedule prevailed. The graph in Box 5 plots the new supply curve alongside the old one. The new supply curve, corresponding to the data in the table, is closer to the vertical axis at each possible price. A *decrease in supply* is therefore represented by an *inward* shift of the entire supply curve. Similarly, an *increase in supply* is represented by an *outward* shift of the entire supply curve, illustrated by the graph in Box 6. Note that the new supply curves do not have to be parallel to the old ones.

2. *Changes in the technology available to produce a good.* Improvements in technology tend to increase the output from economic resources used to produce a good. Assuming that input prices are unchanged, advances in technology lower the cost per unit of output and tend to increase the profit possible from selling the good at various prices. For example, an improvement in the technology of producing laser disc players lowers the unit and marginal costs of making laser disc players available. The lower costs increase the potential profit and thus encourage existing sellers to supply more laser disc players while attracting new sellers to the market. Improvements in technology shift the supply curve to the right, as you can see in Box 6.

3. *Changes in the prices of other goods that can be produced with the seller's resources.* The opportunity cost of producing and selling any one good is the sacrifice of the opportunity to sell some other good. Changes in the prices of

alternative goods change the opportunity cost of producing a given good, resulting in changes in its supply. For example, given the price of T-shirts, an increase in the price of sweatshirts could decrease the supply of T-shirts if manufacturers use their facilities to produce more sweatshirts and fewer T-shirts. This would shift the supply curve for T-shirts to the left. Similarly, a decrease in the price of sweatshirts could increase the supply of T-shirts, shifting the supply curve for this item to the right.

4. *Changes in the number of sellers serving the market.* Other things being equal, an increase in the number of sellers increases the supply of a good. For example, an increase in the number of firms producing compact discs increases the number of CDs available at any given price. Over long periods of time, changes in the number of sellers in a market are a very important determinant of supply. The number of sellers in a market changes with the profitability of producing a good.

Other important determinants can also affect the supply of particular goods. For example, weather can affect the supply of agricultural commodities. A frost in Florida that ruins the citrus crop can decrease the supply of oranges in the market over a year. Expectations about future prices of goods and services and inputs can also affect current supply, as can taxes and subsidies.

- Explain how a supply curve shows the law of supply. List the supply influences that must be held constant to draw a supply curve.

- What can cause a change in quantity supplied? What can cause a change in supply?

- An improvement in technology allows a given amount of inputs to produce more pocket TVs per week. Use a graph to show the impact of the improvement on the weekly supply of pocket TVs.

MARKET EQUILIBRIUM PRICE AND QUANTITY

4

equilibrium the situation that prevails when economic forces balance so that economic variables neither increase nor decrease.

market equilibrium the situation attained when the price of a good adjusts so that the quantity buyers are willing and able to buy at that price is just equal to the quantity sellers are willing and able to supply.

shortage the situation that exists in a market when the quantity demanded of a good exceeds the quantity supplied over a given period.

surplus the condition that exists in a market when the quantity supplied of a good exceeds the quantity demanded over a given period.

An **equilibrium** prevails when economic forces balance so that economic variables neither increase nor decrease. **Market equilibrium** is attained when the price of a good adjusts so that the quantity buyers will buy at that price is equal to the quantity sellers will sell. When a market equilibrium has been attained, forces of supply and demand balance, so that there's no tendency for the market price or quantity to change over a given period. The equilibrium price acts to ration the good so that everyone who wants to buy the good will find it available. Similarly, at the equilibrium price, everyone who wants to sell the good will be able to do so successfully. For example, equilibrium in the personal stereo market requires that the price of personal stereos be such that the quantity demanded equals the quantity supplied. When quantity demanded equals quantity supplied, the market is said to *clear*.

A **shortage** exists in a market when the quantity demanded of a good exceeds the quantity supplied over a given period. For example, there will be a monthly shortage of compact disc players if at the current market price the monthly number of players that sellers will make available falls short of the monthly number that buyers will purchase.

A **surplus** exists in a market when the quantity supplied of a good exceeds the quantity demanded over a given period. There would be a monthly surplus of gas if the monthly quantity supplied by sellers exceeded the monthly quantity demanded by buyers at a certain price. At the market equilibrium price of a good, there can be neither surpluses nor shortages in the market. When a market clears, the good is rationed, because there are neither surpluses nor shortages.

Box 7   Market Equilibrium

The market equilibrium price is $1 per dozen. The corresponding market equilibrium quantity is 5,000 dozen per week. Any price above $1 will result in a weekly surplus of eggs. Similarly, any price below $1 will result in a shortage.

Market Equilibrium

| Price (dollars per dozen) | Dozens of eggs per week | | | |
	Quantity demanded	Quantity supplied	Shortage or surplus	Pressure on price
2.00	1,000	9,000	Surplus	Down
1.75	2,000	8,000	Surplus	Down
1.50	3,000	7,000	Surplus	Down
1.25	4,000	6,000	Surplus	Down
1.00	5,000	5,000	Equilibrium	None
0.75	6,000	4,000	Shortage	Up
0.50	7,000	3,000	Shortage	Up
0.25	8,000	2,000	Shortage	Up

Graphic Depiction of Market Equilibrium

The graph in Box 7 plots the demand curve for eggs on the same set of axes as the supply curve. Suppose the price of eggs is $2 per dozen. At that price the weekly quantity supplied by sellers would be 9,000 dozen, the weekly quantity demanded by buyers would be 1,000 dozen, and there would be a surplus of 8,000 dozen. *It follows that the price of $2 per dozen cannot result in a market equilibrium because at that price quantity supplied exceeds quantity demanded.*

Now suppose instead that the price of eggs is 50 cents per dozen. Will this price result in a market equilibrium? To find out, just draw a horizontal line from that price to the demand and supply curves. The quantity demanded at a price of 50 cents per dozen is 7,000 dozen. However, the weekly quantity supplied at that price is 3,000 dozen. Because the quantity demanded exceeds the quantity supplied by 4,000 dozen, it's clear from the graph that at a price of 50 cents per dozen there will be a weekly shortage of eggs in the market. *It follows that the price of 50 cents per dozen cannot result in a market equilibrium because at that price the weekly quantity of eggs demanded exceeds the weekly quantity supplied.*

Finally, let's look at the price of $1 per dozen. Draw a horizontal line from that price to both curves. Note that this line just touches the demand curve and the supply curve where the two curves intersect (point *E*). At $1 per dozen, the weekly quantity supplied will be 5,000 dozen and the weekly quantity demanded will also be 5,000 dozen. *Because the weekly quantity demanded equals the weekly quantity supplied, it follows that the $1 price will result in a market equilibrium. At that price there is neither a weekly surplus nor a weekly shortage of eggs on the market.* Note that, given all other influences on demand and supply, the $1 per dozen price is the *only* price that will result in market equilibrium. To check your understanding, examine the relationship between quantity demanded and quantity supplied at any other price. You'll see that any price other than $1 per dozen will result in either a weekly shortage or a weekly surplus of eggs.

⑤ *Self-Equilibrating Markets*

If the equilibrium price is not initially established in a market, competition among buyers for goods, and among sellers for sales, will set up forces that cause the price to change. Whenever price exceeds its equilibrium level, there will be a surplus of goods on the market. Goods brought to market will go unsold. Sellers of eggs will accept lower prices rather than allow their weekly supply of eggs to spoil. In the case of goods whose quality doesn't deteriorate over time, sellers will accept lower prices to avoid the costs of maintaining inventory or transporting goods back to the point of production. *A surplus results in downward pressure on price.* As price falls, weekly quantity supplied declines and weekly quantity demanded increases, serving to eliminate the surplus. The weekly surplus in the egg market will be completely eliminated when the price reaches the equilibrium level, where quantity demanded equals quantity supplied each week.

A shortage implies that some buyers willing and able to pay the price of a good will find the good unavailable in the market. Although eggs seem to be a bargain when their price is below the market equilibrium level, there aren't enough of them to go around! Competition among consumers for the available weekly quantity of eggs supplied will inevitably increase the price. Some consumers will be willing to pay more than the prevailing price rather than go without eggs. *A shortage therefore results in upward pressure on market price.* As market price increases, weekly quantity supplied will also increase, while weekly quantity demanded will decline. This will continue until quantity demanded once again equals quantity supplied at the market equilibrium price and the shortage has been eliminated.

As you can see, a competitive market tends to be self-equilibrating as a result of the competition among many buyers and sellers. The competition among buyers for available goods and among sellers for sales ensures that prices will adjust to achieve an equilibrium.

The table in Box 7 summarizes the relationship between quantities demanded and supplied at various prices. The table shows that only at the equilibrium price of $1 per dozen is there neither upward nor downward pressure on price. The $1 price is the only price at which quantity demanded equals quantity supplied, given the current demand and supply curves.

The Impact of Changes in Demand on Market Equilibrium

⑥ Changes in either demand or supply can change market equilibrium prices and quantities. You can now begin to use supply and demand analysis to make forecasts about what will happen to prices and quantities sold in response to these changes in demand and supply.

Changes in demand affect market equilibrium. For example, suppose there's a decrease in demand for eggs because of growing concern about their high cholesterol content. Recall that a decrease in the demand for eggs means an inward shift of the entire demand curve.

The graph in Box 8 shows the impact of a decrease in demand for eggs on the egg market. As the demand curve shifts inward, the old price of $1 and quantity of 5,000 dozen eggs per week, corresponding to point E_1, no longer represent market equilib-

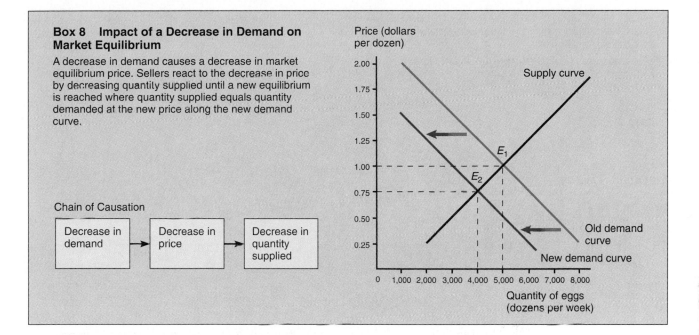

Box 8   Impact of a Decrease in Demand on Market Equilibrium

A decrease in demand causes a decrease in market equilibrium price. Sellers react to the decrease in price by decreasing quantity supplied until a new equilibrium is reached where quantity supplied equals quantity demanded at the new price along the new demand curve.

Chain of Causation

rium. To see why, move along the dotted horizontal line drawn from the point corresponding to $1 on the vertical axis. The quantity demanded at that price along the *new* demand curve is now 3,000 dozen eggs per week. The quantity supplied at that price is still 5,000 dozen eggs because there has been no change in supply. If the price remains at $1, there will be a weekly surplus of 2,000 dozen eggs. The market attains a *new* equilibrium in response to the decrease in demand as price declines to eliminate the surplus. The new market equilibrium corresponds to point E_2, at which the *new* demand curve intersects the supply curve. The price corresponding to that point is 75 cents per dozen. At the lower price the quantity supplied by sellers declines to 4,000 dozen per week, which exactly equals the quantity demanded by buyers along the new demand curve at that price.

The decrease in demand, other things remaining unchanged, sets up the following chain of events in the market: First, the price declines as a surplus develops at the original price. Second, sellers *respond* to the decrease in price by decreasing the quantity supplied. Finally, as the quantity supplied declines, a new equilibrium is attained at a price for which quantity demanded on the *new* demand curve equals quantity supplied on the existing supply curve. *Notice that sellers do not respond directly to the decrease in demand. Instead, they respond to the decline in price caused by the decrease in demand.* This illustrates the role of price as a *signal* through which buyers communicate a change in their desires to sellers.

There has been, in fact, a massive decline in the demand for eggs in the past few years because of health concerns. Egg consumption per person fell as many Americans now carefully watched their intake of cholesterol. As a consequence, the price of eggs also fell. In 1984 the average U.S. retail price for a dozen large eggs was $1.02. Four years later the equilibrium retail price was only 74 cents per dozen. Thousands of egg producers were driven out of business because they could no longer profitably sell eggs at that price.

Box 9   Impact of an Increase in Demand on Market Equilibrium

An increase in demand shifts market equilibrium from E_1 to E_2. The increase in demand raises price and induces an increase in quantity supplied as movement to the new equilibrium occurs.

Chain of Causation

Increase in demand → Increase in price → Increase in quantity supplied

The reasoning for an increase in demand is exactly the reverse. Suppose an increase in income causes an increase in the demand for stereo speakers. An increase in demand is a shift of the entire demand curve outward. The graph in Box 9 shows that an increase in demand for speakers will increase the market equilibrium price. As the price increases, there's a corresponding increase in quantity supplied until quantity demanded, on the new demand curve, once again equals quantity supplied. In the graph the initial equilibrium corresponds to point E_1, at which the price of a standard-quality speaker is $100 and 10,000 speakers are sold per month. After the increase in demand, the new equilibrium corresponds to point E_2, at which the price is $125 per speaker and the quantity supplied is 12,000 per month. The increase in price is a signal that induces sellers to increase the quantity supplied.

The Impact of Changes in Supply on Market Equilibrium
Remember that a change in the supply of a good is represented by a shift of the entire supply curve caused by a change in some influence other than price. For example, an increase in the price of chicken feed is likely to decrease the supply of eggs. The graph in Box 10 shows how a decrease in supply affects market equilibrium. Assume that the initial market equilibrium, corresponding to point E_1 on the graph, is once again a price of $1 per dozen and that 5,000 dozen eggs are sold per week at that price. As the supply curve shifts inward, the initial price can no longer result in an equilibrium. This is because the quantity supplied at that price along the *new* supply curve is now only 3,000 dozen per week. Because there's been no change in demand, the quantity demanded at that price is still 5,000 dozen per week. There will therefore be a weekly market shortage of eggs if the price remains at $1 per dozen. Competition among buyers eliminates the shortage and raises the price. As the price increases, quantity demanded declines until it equals quantity supplied. The new market equilibrium corresponds to point E_2, at which market price is $1.25 per dozen and quantity sold is 4,000 dozen per week. This is the point at which the *new* supply curve intersects the original demand curve. Note that *buyers do not respond directly to the decrease in supply. Instead, they respond to the increase in market price*

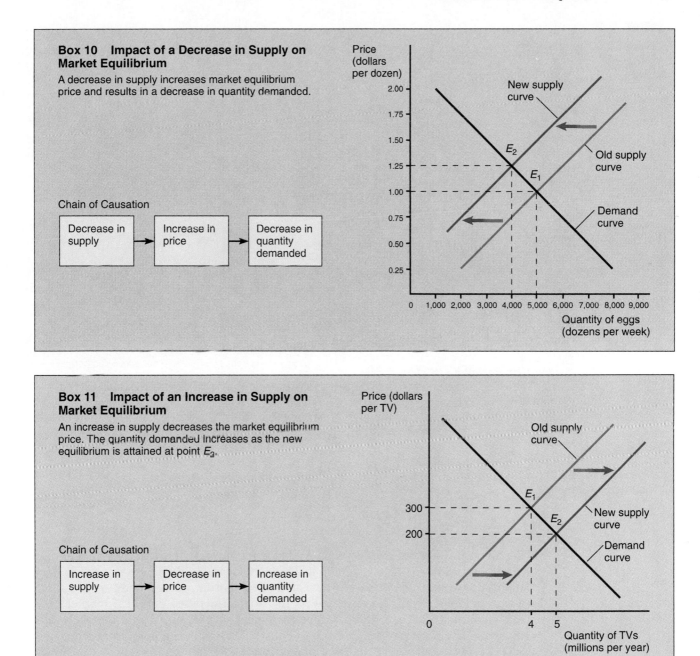

Box 10   Impact of a Decrease in Supply on Market Equilibrium

A decrease in supply increases market equilibrium price and results in a decrease in quantity demanded.

Chain of Causation

Decrease in supply → Increase in price → Decrease in quantity demanded

Box 11   Impact of an Increase in Supply on Market Equilibrium

An increase in supply decreases the market equilibrium price. The quantity demanded increases as the new equilibrium is attained at point E_2.

Chain of Causation

Increase in supply → Decrease in price → Increase in quantity demanded

caused by the decrease in supply. Once again, you can see how price serves as communication between buyers and sellers. Buyers are motivated to reduce the quantity demanded in response to the higher price caused by the decrease in supply.

The reasoning is similar for an increase in supply. For example, a number of years ago the equilibrium price for a standard 13-inch color TV was about $300. As advances in technology increased supply, there was downward pressure on the price of TVs. The graph in Box 11 shows the impact of an increase in supply on market equilibrium. Start out once again at point E_1, at which the original demand curve

principles in practice

The Market for Medical Services

How Health Insurance Increases Spending on Health Care
In 1992, Americans devoted a whopping 13.5 percent of the value of annual output to health care. U.S. households spent over $800 billion on medical services in that year. Most of that amount was paid to vendors of health care services through insurance programs. U.S. businesses now pay an average of more than $3,000 per employee in health insurance costs, and a major portion of government budgets in the United States is now allocated to pay for health care to the aged, the poor, and other groups, including veterans. More than 15 percent of the federal government's outlays are for medical payments and health care.

As of 1993 over 80 percent of the U.S. population was covered by health insurance or government programs that pay nearly three quarters of personal health care costs in the United States. The major government programs that pay for health care are Medicare (a government-subsidized system of health insurance for the elderly) and Medicaid (which pays medical bills for the poor). When an insured person requires medical services, all but a small portion (if any) of the bill is usually paid by the insurance company. Most insurance plans require the patient to incur a certain modest amount of expenditures (called the "deductible") for medical services before the plan starts paying. When the patient incurs the deductible expense, the plan usually pays

between 80 percent and all of the additional medical expenses each year.

Let's extend our use of supply and demand analysis to see how the system of health insurance in the United States has affected the expenditures for medical services. The bulk of payments for medical services in the United States is made by a *third party* other than the buyer or seller of the services. That third party is, of

intersects the original supply curve. At that point the market price of TVs is $300 and the quantity sold per year is 4 million. The increase in supply means that the original supply curve shifts outward. The new market equilibrium corresponds to point E_2, at which the *new* supply curve intersects the original demand curve. If market price remains at $300 per set, there will be an annual surplus of TVs on the shelves of retailers. The price must fall to clear the market. The new equilibrium price is now $200 per TV. Quantity demanded at that price is 5 million TVs per year, which exactly equals the quantity sellers are willing to supply at that price along the *new* supply curve. An improvement in technology therefore tends to lower the market price of a good and to increase the quantity demanded.

CONCEPT CHECK
☐

- Explain why shortages or surpluses of goods in a market imply that it is not in equilibrium.

- What opposing forces balance when market equilibrium is attained? How do markets self-equilibrate?

- An increase in the popularity of skiing increases the demand for skis. Use supply and demand analysis to forecast the impact of the increase in demand on the price and quantity of skis supplied by sellers.

course, the health insurer or the government. The graph shows the supply and demand curves for medical services. In the absence of any third-party payments, the equilibrium price, on average, for medical services is P_1 and the equilibrium quantity is Q_1. As a result of third-party payments, the price per unit of service (on average) to the patient falls from P_1 to P_B because the insurance company picks up most of the bill for doctors' visits, surgery, and hospital stays. As a result of the fall in the price per unit of service, the quantity demanded increases from Q_1 to Q_B as we move along the market demand curve to point A. As the quantity demanded of medical services increases, the quantity supplied must also increase to prevent shortages. This means that the price paid to medical suppliers must increase to P_S to induce suppliers to move from point E to point B on the supply curve. From the suppliers' point of view, the third-party payments increase the demand for medical services. The new market equilibrium is at point B, where medical services suppliers receive a price of P_S as the combined payment from both patients and insurers.

People do not choose to get sick more often because they have health insurance. However, in many cases insurance results in people not being as careful to avoid medical problems as they might be if they knew they had to pay the full price of medical services (this is called the "moral hazard" problem). Insurance also induces people to visit physicians for more minor ailments (such as the common cold) than they would if they had to pay the full price of each visit. Medical practitioners often have the incentive to prescribe more tests and medical procedures when they know a third party will pay.

Third-party payments for medical services therefore provide incentives for individuals to increase the quantity of medical services demanded. Also, because providers are compensated for their costs at a higher rate, such payments attract more resources into the provision of health care. Naturally, as expenditures on health care have increased, so have health insurance premiums used to finance private insurance and taxes used to finance Medicare and Medicaid. Because of third-party payments, both consumption and the price paid to medical services suppliers rise. Total expenditure on medical care also increases as both the price and the quantity provided increase. Even though the price of a unit of medical services is now P_S, buyers pay only P_B and the insurance companies pay the remainder.

Many insurers are now increasing the portion of medical services (called the copayment) that the patient must pay. Some insurers also limit their payments for certain kinds of services and require patients to get second, and even third, opinions before agreeing to pay for costly medical procedures. Other insurers seek to control costs by requiring their insured employees to obtain their medical care from an approved health maintenance organization.

Soon, government regulations may also be used to control health costs. As of 1993, the Clinton administration was working on a new government plan to help control the growth of medical expenditures.

 the global economy

The Dollar Has Its Price Too!

Demand for and Supply of the Dollar in Foreign Exchange Markets The dollar has its price in terms of foreign currencies—a price that fluctuates with changes in supply and demand. Demand for dollars is generated from foreigners' desires to purchase them so they can buy U.S. goods and services or acquire U.S. assets. The supply of dollars to the market is generated by the desires of U.S. households and businesses to acquire foreign currencies so that they can purchase foreign goods, services, and assets. There are markets for the dollar in exchange for many foreign currencies, but in this example we concentrate on the market for dollars in exchange for Japanese yen.

On February 26, 1985, it took 261.5 yen to buy one U.S. dollar. By early 1988, a dollar could be bought at a bargain rate of only about 125 yen. As of early 1990, the dollar was worth 145 yen, but by late 1992 it was worth only 120 yen. As you can see, the dollar's price fluctuates considerably over time. You might want to look up its current price. (You can find

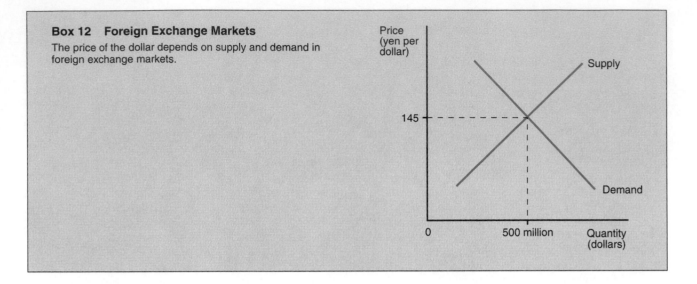

Box 12   Foreign Exchange Markets
The price of the dollar depends on supply and demand in foreign exchange markets.

Price (yen per dollar)

Supply

145

Demand

0   500 million   Quantity (dollars)

foreign exchange quotes in *The Wall Street Journal* or perhaps your local daily newspaper.)

The graph in Box 12 shows the supply and demand curves for the dollar in international markets. The vertical axis shows the price of a dollar in terms of Japanese yen. The horizontal axis shows the number of dollars exchanged for yen per day. Like the demand curve for almost any commodity, that for dollars is downward sloping. Similarly, the higher the price of dollars in terms of yen (the exchange rate), the greater the quantity of dollars supplied in exchange for yen, indicating an upward-sloping supply curve.

You can understand why the laws of supply and demand hold for dollars if you examine the consequences of changes in the exchange rate. Suppose the cost of production and the minimum acceptable profit for both Japanese and U.S. goods are given. The price U.S. farmers will accept for each bushel of wheat is $2. The price Japanese camera companies will accept for each camera is 50,000 yen. Suppose the current equilibrium price of the dollar is 250 yen. You can now use the equilibrium exchange rate to convert the price of wheat into yen and the price of cameras into dollars.

Case 1: $1 = 250 yen

Price of wheat in yen = $2(250 yen/$1) = 500 yen
Price of cameras in dollars = 50,000 yen ($1/250 yen) = $200

Now suppose the price of the dollar falls to 125 yen. *Assuming there is no change in the prices sellers of these goods will accept in terms of their own currencies:*

Case 2: $1 = 125 yen

Price of wheat in yen = $2(125 yen/$1) = 250 yen
Price of cameras in dollars = 50,000 yen ($1/125 yen) = $400

The *decrease* in the price of the dollar makes Japanese goods more expensive in dollars and makes U.S. goods less expensive in yen. This means that, other things being equal, the Japanese will be more eager to buy U.S. wheat and other goods when the price of the dollar falls. The increase in the demand for U.S. goods caused by the decrease in the price of the dollar induces holders of yen to increase the number of dollars demanded. Similarly, because a decrease in the price of the dollar makes Japanese goods more expensive in terms of dollars, the number of dollars supplied in exchange for yen will decrease as the price of the dollar falls.

The next obvious question is: What causes the demand for and supply of dollars offered for yen to change over time?

1. Interest rates in the United States and Japan affect the Japanese demand for dollars. The higher interest rates are in the United States relative to those in Japan, the greater the demand for dollars by the Japanese. This is because when interest rates are high on assets denominated in U.S. dollars, Japanese holders of yen can earn more by acquiring dollars to buy U.S. assets than by using yen to invest in Japanese assets. Relatively high interest rates in the United States therefore raise the price of the dollar by increasing Japanese demand for dollars. On the other hand, a decline in U.S. interest rates relative to those in Japan (as occurred in 1992) decreases the Japanese demand for dollars and puts downward pressure on the dollar's price in terms of the yen.

2. *The prices in domestic currencies that sellers in Japan and the United States will accept for products offered in international trade affect the supply of and demand for dollars.* An increase in the prices (in yen) Japanese automobile producers will accept for cars they want to export to the United States will, other things being equal, make those cars less attractive to U.S. citizens. An increase in Japanese prices in yen relative to those of competing U.S. products therefore decreases the supply of dollars offered in exchange for yen. The decrease in the supply of dollars tends to increase the price of the dollar in terms of the yen.

Sometimes a government steps in and buys and sells its own currency. The purpose is to adjust the price of the currency in terms of foreign exchange in order to improve the balance of exports and imports.

MASTERING THE ART OF SUPPLY AND DEMAND ANALYSIS

The forces of supply and demand determine prices in competitive markets. If you thoroughly understand how buyers and sellers respond to changes in opportunities for gains in markets and how market equilibrium prices serve to equate quantity demanded with quantity supplied, you're on your way to understanding the most basic of economic relationships.

Supply and demand analysis is relevant to all goods and services exchanged in markets. You must understand how to manipulate supply and demand curves so that, in later chapters, you'll be able to explain changes in product prices, interest rates, wages, and rents.

You'll also want to keep in mind that supply and demand influences are constantly changing. We usually base our analysis of a market on a "snapshot" of the market at a single point in time. We then make hypotheses about the way market equilibrium would change if a certain demand or supply influence were to change. In actuality, many changes occur simultaneously in a market. Supply and demand curves are constantly shifting. Perhaps the best example of this is the stock market, where prices can move quickly and often erratically over a short period of time as conditions in that market change (see the Principles in Practice box). However, you'll gain little understanding of the relationship between price and other variables by trying to analyze all variables at the same time. You'll find that the best way to understand the process of price determination in markets is to study one variable at a time. This will help you isolate the impact of important influences on price and quantities traded.

Part of the art of supply and demand analysis is knowing the relevant influences affecting the decisions of buyers and sellers in a market and their ability to purchase or sell goods. You need to understand the causes of changes in supply or demand so you can forecast market prices and trading. For example, weather is likely to be an important supply influence on an agricultural market, but it has little effect on the market for computers. Interest rates are likely to be an important influence on the net gains we can enjoy from buying homes and cars, and thus interest rates affect demand for those items. Improvements in technology are a major influence on the supply of electronic goods such as VCRs, microwave ovens, and personal computers.

principles in practice

Business Brief: The Stock Market

How It Works On Monday, October 19, 1987, a wave of selling triggered widespread price declines in stock markets from New York to Australia. On that day, now infamous as "Black Monday," over 600 million shares were traded on the New York Stock Exchange—more than twice the NYSE's average sales volume. The Dow Jones Industrial Average of the prices of 30 stocks of major U.S. companies lost 22.6 percent of its value on that memorable day, plunging 508 points in the panicky rush to sell.

What is the stock market, and how is it affected by the forces of supply and demand? The stock market is the means through which previously issued corporate stocks, shares of ownership in a corporation, are traded. Stock exchanges are organizations whose members act as intermediaries to buy and sell stocks for their clients. About 80 percent of all the stock trading in the United States takes place at the New York Stock Exchange. Stocks of smaller companies are traded on the over-the-counter market, a network of independent brokers who communicate by telephone and telex rather than meeting at a specific location. There are other stock exchanges in the United States as well as in such cities as Paris, London, Sydney, and Tokyo.

How are stock prices determined? The answer, as you might expect, is by supply and demand. However, the forces influencing the prices of corporate stocks are quite different from those influencing the prices of goods and services. People and organizations that buy and hold stocks do so for the incomes they hope to earn. The incomes depend on dividends paid to stockholders, changes in the price of stocks over time, and the expected return compared to the return on alternative investments.

On any given day in the stock market, there are orders to buy and orders to sell. The orders to buy constitute the quantity of stocks demanded at the current (or anticipated) prices per share, while the orders to sell constitute the quantity supplied at those prices. The chief influence on both the supply of and demand for stocks is the income potential of holding the stocks compared to the income potential of holding alternative assets such as bonds, other types of securities, or real property such as buildings and land.

The way in which the forces of supply and demand actually influence stock prices depends on the trading rules of the particular stock exchange. For example, the Paris stock exchange uses a "call market" method. Under this method, brokers have time to accumulate their orders to buy and sell specific stocks. When there's a call for a stock, a clerk acts like an auctioneer to establish an equilibrium price at the time of the call.

SUMMARY

1. Markets are arrangements through which buyers and sellers can communicate and conduct transactions to enjoy mutual gains.

2. The law of demand states that, in general, other things being equal, there is a negative relationship between the price of a good and the willingness and ability of buyers to purchase it.

3. A demand curve illustrates the relationship between price and quantity demanded.

4. A change in quantity demanded is represented by a movement along a demand curve in response to a change in a good's price. A change in demand is a response to a change in something other than price that shifts an entire demand curve. Changes in demand can be caused by changes in consumer income, prices of other goods, expectations, tastes, or population.

5. The law of supply states that, in general, other things being equal, there is a positive relationship between price and the amount of a good sellers will make available.

6. A supply curve shows how quantity supplied varies with the price of a good.

7. A change in quantity supplied is represented by a movement along a given supply curve caused by a change in a good's price. A change is supply implies a shift of an entire supply curve caused by a change in something other than the price of a good that affects the willingness and ability of sellers to make the good available. Changes in supply can be caused by changes in input prices, improvements in technology, changes in the prices of other goods that can be produced with the sellers' resources, and changes in sellers' expectations about the future.

8. A market equilibrium is attained when the price of a good adjusts so that the quantity of the good demanded equals the quantity supplied. If price of the

Average price
(dollars per share)

Demand
(October 16, 1987)

Supply
(October 16, 1987)

E_1

P_1

Supply
(October 19, 1987)

E_2

P_2

Demand
(October 19, 1987)

0   300   600

Shares traded
(millions per day)

The clerk may begin by calling out the most recent trading price of the stock, say 1,000 francs. If after the call all the selling orders are filled and brokers still have orders to buy, the clerk will call out a higher price. Similarly, if at the initial price of 1,000 francs all the orders to sell aren't matched by orders to buy, the clerk will call out a lower price. In this way the clerk acts to adjust price until quantity demanded equals quantity

supplied at the call session. Naturally, if there are more sell orders than buy orders at the current price, the price of the stock will tumble during the call.

On the New York Stock Exchange, trading in all stocks is continuous. A specialist is assigned to oversee trading in each stock. This specialist is a "broker's broker" who tries to adjust the price of the stock so that quantity demanded equals quantity supplied. However, the specialist is also allowed to purchase the stock to hold as a personal investment if no buyer can be found. In this way the specialist can exert some influence on the supply of and demand for stocks, and will do so if it's profitable.

When the orders to sell far outnumber the orders to buy, specialists and call clerks in the market must lower prices to equate quantity demanded with quantity supplied. On October 19, 1987, there were hardly any buy orders and the markets were flooded with sell orders. Because of the tremendous surplus of stocks at the prevailing prices, specialists and call clerks lowered prices until quantity demanded equaled quantity supplied. When Black Monday finally reeled to a close, many a portfolio had lost over a fifth of the value it had at the end of the previous trading day. The dollar value of outstanding stocks in the United States declined by a whopping $500 billion! In terms of supply and demand, the graph shows that the Crash of 1987 resulted from a sharp increase in the supply of stocks coupled with a decrease in demand.

good is above the market equilibrium level, a surplus will prevail. If price is below the market equilibrium level, a shortage will prevail. Surpluses put downward pressure on prices, while shortages put upward pressure on prices.

9. Market equilibrium prices ration goods by ensuring that everyone who wants to buy a good will find it available, while everyone who wants to sell a good will do so successfully. Prices accomplish this objective because they influence the personal gains possible from buying and selling goods.

10. Changes in demand or supply result in new market equilibrium prices. A change in demand affects the market equilibrium price of a good. A change in market price affects the gains possible from selling the good and causes sellers to respond by adjusting the quantity they supply. A change in supply also affects the market equilibrium price of a good. The resulting change in price affects the gains possible from purchasing the good and therefore causes buyers to respond by adjusting quantity demanded.

KEY TERMS

market *59*

supply and demand
 analysis *59*

quantity demanded *59*

demand *59*

demand schedule *60*

law of demand *60*

demand curve *61*

change in relative price *62*

change in quantity
 demanded *62*

change in demand *63*

substitutes *64*

complements *65*

quantity supplied *66*

supply *66*

supply schedule *66*

law of supply *66*

supply curve *67*

change in quantity supplied
 67

change in supply *68*

equilibrium *70*

market equilibrium *70*

shortage *70*

surplus *71*

CONCEPT REVIEW

1. Give an example of a market, and discuss how it functions.

2. What can cause a change in quantity demanded? What can cause a change in demand?

3. What can cause a change in quantity supplied? What can cause a change in supply?

4. How can you tell whether or not a market is in equilibrium?

5. Under what circumstances would there be a shortage in a market?

6. How will an increase in demand affect market equilibrium price and quantity supplied? How will a decrease in supply affect market equilibrium price and quantity demanded?

PROBLEMS AND APPLICATIONS

1. A new report by the surgeon general on the harmful effects of cholesterol decreases the demand for eggs. Suppose the resulting decrease in demand reduces by 50 percent the quantities buyers are willing to buy each week at each possible price for the demand schedule in Box 1. Graph the new demand schedule, and show the decrease in demand by drawing both the old and new demand curves. 6

2. An improvement in the technology of egg laying doubles the number of eggs each chicken can lay per week. Assuming that the improvement doubles the weekly quantity supplied at each price in the table in Box 4, graph the new supply schedule. Draw both the old and new supply curves to illustrate the change in supply. 6

3. Assuming that both the decrease in demand for eggs and the increase in supply of eggs described in Problems 1 and 2 occur simultaneously, use a graph to show the impact on the market equilibrium price of eggs and on the quantity sold per week. 6

4. Suppose the market for coffee is currently in equilibrium at a price of $3 per pound. An early frost in coffee-growing nations decreases the supply of coffee. Use supply and demand analysis to forecast the impact of the freeze on the market equilibrium price and quantity of coffee. 4, 6

5. Suppose the market rate of interest on car loans declines substantially. Use supply and demand analysis to predict the impact of the interest rate decline on the prices of cars and the quantity sold. 6

6. Suppose you want to buy a popular brand of compact disc player. Every store in town is out of stock. You are willing and able to pay the market price of $300 for a player, but you can't find any available. Is the market for this compact disc player in equilibrium? Use supply and demand analysis to explain your answer. 4

7. The federal government announces that it will pay $3 a loaf for all the bread that can't be sold in a competitive market at that price. At the end of each week, the government purchases 1 million loaves of bread. Use supply and demand analysis to show on a graph that the market equilibrium price is less than $3 per loaf. Why doesn't the market price fall in this case? 5

8. Using your graph in Problem 7, show how a decrease in the supply of bread can raise its market equilibrium price above $3 a loaf. How much bread would the government buy each week under these circumstances? 4, 5

9. Assume the market price of Mustang convertibles is $15,000. At that price the quantity demanded is 1 million per year, while the quantity supplied is only 500,000 per year. Is the market in equilibrium? Explain your answer. 4

10. A decrease in demand for personal computers results in a market surplus of PCs. Explain how market forces will act to eliminate the surplus. 4, 5, 6

chapter 4

Using Supply and Demand Analysis

W hat are the prospects for profitably marketing a new product? Will an increase in interest rates bring on an economic recession? Should the federal government continue to subsidize farmers by guaranteeing them minimum prices for their crops? Should landlords be bound by laws that place a ceiling on the rents they can charge?

Each of these actions or policies has predictable results that we can forecast using supply and demand analysis. In this chapter you'll have more opportunities to use supply and demand analysis, and to understand its relevance to a wide range of business, political, and social issues.

As you'll see after reading the chapter, the laws of supply and demand cannot be repealed. Because so many goods and services are bought and sold in markets, market outcomes influence our daily lives. Changes in supply and demand conditions change market prices. Changes in prices inevitably affect the gains possible from buying and selling goods, and thereby change the choices we make.

☐ CONCEPT PREVIEW

After reading this chapter, you should be able to:

1. Demonstrate how market equilibrium prices deal with the problem of scarcity by rationing goods and services, and explain why prices would be zero for nonscarce goods.

2. Explain how supply and demand conditions affect the price and sales potential of new products.

3. Show how wages and interest rates are determined in competitive markets.

4. Use supply and demand analysis to show how government control of prices in competitive markets can result in shortages or surpluses.

PRICES, SCARCITY, AND MARKETING PROSPECTS

1   Imagine that you could shop at all your favorite stores, pick out every item your heart desired, and sail right by the checkout counter without paying a dime. In this consumer's dream you could have the pleasure of acquiring at zero price as much as you wanted of any good or service: designer fashions, an expensive audio/video system, a home gym, a chauffeur-driven limousine. Surely, you'd obtain more and better goods and services in this fantasy world than you do when confronted with the reality of market prices and limited income.

Suppose *everyone* were given the privilege of bypassing the checkout counter at the local imported-car dealer. How would the available Porsches, BMWs, and Audis be allocated among the hordes of eager consumers clamoring for them? Would customers obediently wait in line, or would they be more likely to turn into an unruly and perhaps violent mob, fighting over 735i's and 944s? Who would make the cars available?

If business firms couldn't charge for their goods, they wouldn't make a profit. If they couldn't cover their production and distribution costs and make a profit, they wouldn't make products available to consumers. If you're looking for a sleek Corvette at zero price, you probably know you're out of luck! This fantasy of a giveaway world should make it clear to you how prices are necessary to cope with scarcity.

Nonscarce Goods

There's only one case in which zero prices for goods will not create hopeless shortages. This is the rather improbable case of a good that's not actually scarce. A **nonscarce (or free) good** is one for which the quantity demanded does not exceed the quantity supplied at zero price. In other words, a nonscarce good is available in amounts that result in no shortage even if the price of the good is zero.

Of course, few, if any, goods can be described as nonscarce. However, we can fantasize about situations in which nonscarcity might prevail. For example, coconuts might be so plentiful in an island nation that its few people could enjoy all they wished at zero price. (Assume that no resident of this island paradise thinks about exporting the coconuts to other areas of the world where the fruit is scarce in relation to desires to use it.) The graph in Box 1 shows you the demand and supply curves for coconuts in such a paradise. You'll notice that the demand curve intersects the horizontal axis without intersecting the supply curve first. At zero price 10 tons of coconuts per season are demanded. At zero price the quantity of coconuts available is 20 tons per season. Because at zero price the quantity supplied exceeds the quantity demanded, there's a surplus of coconuts even when they're available free. Anyone who tries to sell coconuts on the island will be unable to find any buyers, because at zero price the availability of the fruit exceeds the amount desired.

However, the laws of supply and demand are still relevant. The higher the price of coconuts on the island, the lower the quantity demanded, as you can see by the downward-sloping demand curve. For example, if the price were $5 per ton, a shown in the graph, the quantity demanded would fall below 10 tons per year. Similarly, the higher the price of coconuts on the island, the greater the quantity supplied as residents of other coconut-rich islands make their coconuts available. However, the quantity available at zero price exceeds the quantity demanded at that price, making it impossible for people with coconuts to sell them at a positive price.

Garbage is a negatively valued item that we pay someone to take away. However, with changes in either demand or supply items we currently toss away as garbage can become scarce goods. For example, the current quantity of plastic soft-drink bottles

nonscarce (or free) good a good for which the quantity demanded does not exceed the quantity supplied at zero price.

Box 1   Demand for and Supply of a Nonscarce Good

A nonscarce good is available in amounts that exceed the quantity demanded at zero price. As shown here, at zero price there is a surplus of coconuts on a desert island.

at zero price exceeds the quantity demanded. In the future, however, the supply curve for today's empty bottles will move to the left and the demand curve for such bottles by collectors will move to the right. If the supply and demand curves continue to shift in this way, they'll intersect at a positive price. Today's trash can end up being tomorrow's treasures—something you already know if your mother threw out your shoe box of baseball cards!

How Demand and Supply Conditions Affect the Success of New Products

We can use supply and demand analysis to evaluate the prospects for marketing new products profitably. The price of a new product influences the quantity demanded. Firms must be able to sell new products at prices that exceed costs sufficiently to allow a profit.

Suppose you're considering investing in a company that plans to market a product that utilizes a new and improved method of reproducing recorded sound. The company estimates that when it first puts the product on the market, the minimum price it can accept is $1,000 per unit. Will the product sell at that price? To find out, we need to guess how the supply and demand curves for the product look.

The demand curve for the product is like the one illustrated in the graph in Box 2. A number of supply curves are also drawn in the graph. Suppose the product is the compact disc player—first developed by Sony in 1982. The first supply curve shows the supply of CD players in 1980, when the technology for the product wasn't fully developed. However, let's assume that a prototype of the product could have been marketed at that time along with a reasonable number of selections on compact disc. The supply curve for 1980 hits the price axis at $2,000. The demand curve for that year hits the price axis at about $1,100. This implies that the minimum price sellers would accept to make available only one CD player per year exceeds the maximum price that any buyer would buy. *Using business jargon, this means that there is no market for the product.* The supply and demand curves don't intersect at a positive quantity.

This analysis illustrates an important business-related lesson: *The price of a new product is a crucial determinant of its success in a market.* You may develop an idea for a fantastic new electronic product, say a computerized household robot that cleans and cooks. However, unless you can price it at a level that allows you to make sufficient sales while at the same time at least covering your opportunity costs, your product will have no market.

It's worthwhile to continue this analysis because it illustrates how changing supply and demand conditions can expand the market for new products. Sony

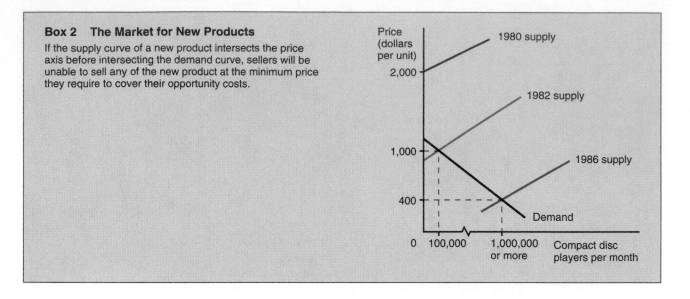

Box 2   The Market for New Products

If the supply curve of a new product intersects the price axis before intersecting the demand curve, sellers will be unable to sell any of the new product at the minimum price they require to cover their opportunity costs.

introduced its CD player in Japan in 1982 at a price of $1,000. At that price the company quickly sold 100,000 units in the first month! Apparently the demand and supply curves did intersect at a positive quantity. It's reasonable to assume that in 1982 the technology for mass-producing the new product had improved, resulting in an outward shift of the market supply curve, shown in the graph in Box 2. In that graph it's assumed that there was no change in demand for compact disc players between 1980 and 1982. However, the lower price made possible by the increase in supply caused an increase in the quantity demanded.

By the mid-1980s improvements in technology, coupled with growth in the number of firms producing compact disc players, caused the supply to increase, and a worldwide market opened up as the price fell. Assuming no change in demand and no change in the quality of the product, the graph in Box 2 shows the supply curve for 1986. At that time the average market price of CD players was about $400. At that price over a million units were sold, showing that the quantity demanded had increased. The graph in Box 2 doesn't consider possible increases in demand (outward shifts of the demand curve) caused by increased availability of CDs and aggressive advertising campaigns by Sony and other manufacturers. Increases in demand would have offset some of the price-depressing effects of the increases in supply by putting upward pressure on prices.

The expansion of markets as a result of improved technology has been common for electronic products in recent years. The hand-held calculator, the personal computer, and the home videocassette recorder were all unheard of 30 years ago. Thanks to improved technology, these products are now available at affordable prices.

MARKETS FOR LABOR AND CREDIT

3 We can also apply supply and demand analysis to markets for *economic resources*, such as the services of labor. Many macroeconomic issues deal with analysis of prices and employment of productive resources. To understand these issues, you need to understand how the laws of supply and demand operate in markets for economic resources.

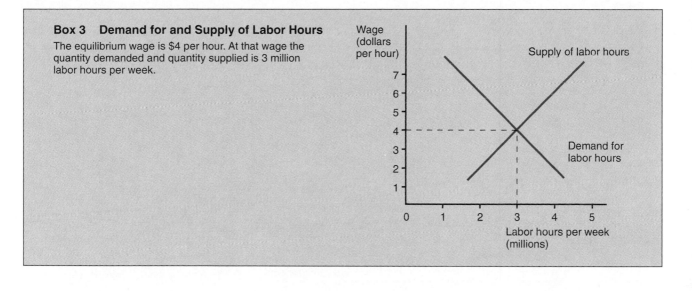

Box 3   Demand for and Supply of Labor Hours
The equilibrium wage is $4 per hour. At that wage the quantity demanded and quantity supplied is 3 million labor hours per week.

Labor Markets

In modern economies workers sell their services to employers in labor markets. In a competitive labor market many workers independently offer skills of a given quality to many employers who compete for the workers' services. As is the case in product markets, wages, the prices paid for labor services on an hourly or yearly basis, are important determinants of the amount of labor demanded and supplied over a given period.

wages the prices paid for labor services.

It's reasonable to expect the laws of demand and supply to prevail in labor markets as they do in product markets. The lower the wage, the greater the quantity of labor services demanded by employers. The demand curve for labor services is therefore downward sloping, because employers substitute other inputs, such as machines, for labor services as wages go up, while substituting labor services for other inputs as wages go down.

The higher the wage, the greater the quantity of labor services generally supplied. At higher wages individual workers are usually willing to work more hours per week. In addition, higher wages are likely to induce workers not currently looking for work, such as students, retirees, and homemakers, to enter the job market. Also, an increase in wages in one part of the country is likely to attract workers from other parts of the country who are looking for jobs at the higher wages.

The graph in Box 3 shows the demand and supply curves for labor services in a market for unskilled labor. Employers have no reason to prefer the services of one worker over another in such a market because labor services are standardized. In the graph the equilibrium wage is $4 per hour. At that wage 3 million labor hours per week are employed.

Our economy includes a multitude of labor markets for services that require many kinds of skills. There are, for example, markets for economics professors, heart surgeons, plumbers, musicians, grape pickers, and cruise directors. In each market workers have similar skills. Wages, of course, differ widely in these markets, depending on the value employers place on workers' skills and on the factors influencing the supply of each type of labor. Later in this book we'll investigate in greater depth the factors influencing the demand for and supply of labor.

principles in practice

Operation of Labor Markets in the United States

In practice, market wages don't always instantaneously adjust to eliminate surpluses and shortages of labor. For example, during a recession the demand for factory workers typically declines as the demand for factory output decreases. If wages were to adjust immediately after the decline in demand, the quantity of labor demanded would equal the quantity supplied at a lower wage, as shown in the graph.

However, the data on wage adjustment in the United States during recessions since the end of World War II indicate that wages adjusted for the effects of inflation actually *rise* slightly during recessions! This suggests that labor markets don't adjust quickly to temporary declines in labor demand. During a typical recession in the United States, the unemployment rate rises about 2 to 4 percentage points.[*]

As a result of downward rigidity in wages during recessions, employment declines by more than would otherwise be the case. In the graph employment would fall from Q_1 to Q_2 during a recession if wages fell in response to the decrease in labor demand. However, when wages don't fall quickly in response to the decline in demand, employment falls to Q_3. Rigid wages therefore result in a surplus of labor and excessive unemployment during a recession. However, workers who keep their jobs during recessions don't suffer a decline in income. The way U.S. labor markets operate, the work-

ers with the greatest seniority are laid off last during a recession. This implies that much of the loss of income caused by layoffs in a recession is borne by younger workers.

[*] See Thomas J. Kniesner and Arthur H. Goldsmith, "A Survey of Alternative Models of the Aggregate U.S. Labor Market," *Journal of Economic Literature* 25, no. 3 (September 1987), pp. 1241–80.

Notice how the market equilibrium wage rations the available number of labor hours per month. At the equilibrium wage of $4 per hour, the quantity of labor hours demanded just equals the quantity supplied. This means that all workers willing and able to work will find jobs, while all employers willing and able to hire workers at that wage will find them available. There's neither a shortage of labor services nor a surplus.

The demand for labor is derived from the demand for the products that labor produces. When a business enjoys an increase in orders, it will have to hire more labor to fill those orders. Consider the workers whose labor market is illustrated in Box 3. An increase in demand for labor caused by increased orders will increase wages. An increase in wages will make work more attractive to workers and cause an increase in the number of labor hours supplied per month.

You can see the effect of an increase in demand for labor services by looking at the graph in Box 4. The increase in demand for workers increases the wage from $4 to $5 per hour. If the wage were to remain at $4 after the increase in demand, the quantity demanded would be 4 million hours per month, while the quantity supplied would remain at 3 million hours per month. There would therefore be a shortage of workers. Competition among employers would put upward pressure on wages. As the wage increases from $4 to $5, the quantity of labor hours supplied increases. A

Box 4   Impact of an Increase in Demand for Labor Hours

An increase in the demand for weekly labor hours increases the market wage and increases the quantity of labor hours supplied. If the market wage did not increase to $5 per hour, there would be a weekly shortage of labor hours.

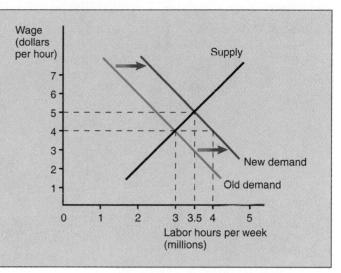

Box 5   Impact of an Increase in Supply of Labor Hours

An increase in the supply of labor hours decreases the equilibrium wage and increases the quantity of labor demanded. If the wage did not fall, there would be a weekly surplus of labor hours.

new labor market equilibrium is achieved, and 3.5 million labor hours per month are employed. As in product markets, the price of labor services (in this case, wages) acts as a signal to workers by increasing the gains possible from additional work. Workers respond to higher wages by increasing the quantity of labor supplied.

Conversely, a decrease in orders for products will cause a decrease in the demand for labor. Suppose the bicycle industry in the United States experiences a decline in orders because bikers are buying, as substitutes, inexpensive, foreign-produced bikes. The decrease in demand for American-made bikes will decrease the demand for bicycle workers. This will put downward pressure on workers' wages and thus decrease the quantity of labor supplied.

An increase in the supply of labor hours caused by, say, an increase in the working-age population will also affect labor market equilibrium. An increase in the supply of workers, other things unchanged, puts downward pressure on wages. As shown in the graph in Box 5, if market wages remain at $4 per hour after an increase in labor supply, there will be a surplus of labor hours at that wage. The surplus causes market wages to decline to $3 per hour, and the number of labor hours demanded by employers per month increases.

Box 6   Credit Market Equilibrium

In a market for credit, the equilibrium interest rate and loans extended depend on the demand for and supply of loanable funds.

Credit Markets: The Demand for and Supply of Loanable Funds

We can use supply and demand analysis to analyze markets for credit just as we used it to analyze labor markets. Credit is the use of loanable funds supplied by lenders to borrowers who agree to pay back the borrowed funds according to an agreed-upon schedule. The price for the use of loanable funds, called interest, is usually expressed as a percentage per dollar of funds borrowed. This percentage is referred to as the *interest rate*. For example, if you borrow money from a bank to buy a car, the bank is the creditor and you, as the debtor, will make monthly payments that include an interest charge. If you deposit money in an interest-bearing account, you are, in effect, lending money to the bank and the bank will pay interest to you. Most of us conduct transactions as both lenders and borrowers, and so we both earn and pay interest.

Interest is a price, and its level depends on the demand for and supply of loanable funds in financial markets where credit is available. The demand for loanable funds depends on the willingness and ability of consumers, business firms, and governments to borrow funds. Among the factors these potential borrowers consider are the general business outlook, the expected profitability of business investment, and the level of consumer income. As you'd expect, the total quantity of loanable funds demanded in any year depends on the interest rate. You can see the demand curve in the graph in Box 6. The lower the interest rate, other things being equal, the greater the quantity of loanable funds demanded.

The supply of loanable funds depends on the willingness and ability of lenders to make funds available to borrowers. In general, the gains possible from lending funds depend on the interest rate paid for the use of funds. The higher the interest rate, the greater the gains. The supply curve of loanable funds as shown in Box 6 is therefore assumed to be upward sloping. In general, the supply of loanable funds depends on the willingness and ability of individuals, businesses, and governments to save rather than spend all their current income in the current year. Such factors as consumer income, expectations of future price levels, population, and average age of people in the population affect the supply of loanable funds. As you'll see later in the book, the supply of loanable funds also depends on policies pursued by authorities that regulate banks and other financial institutions.

The graph in Box 6 shows the equilibrium in the market for loanable funds. The equilibrium market rate of interest is 8 percent, and at that rate $1,000 billion of funds

credit the use of loanable funds supplied by lenders to borrowers who agree to pay back the borrowed funds according to an agreed-upon schedule.

interest the price for the use of funds, usually expressed as a percentage per dollar of funds borrowed.

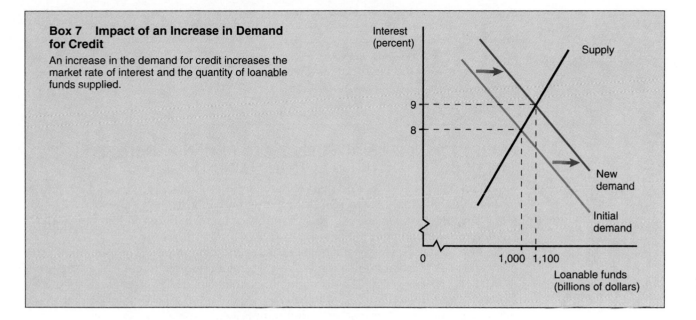

Box 7   Impact of an Increase in Demand for Credit

An increase in the demand for credit increases the market rate of interest and the quantity of loanable funds supplied.

are loaned out. The equilibrium interest rate rations available credit by adjusting to equate the quantity of loanable funds demanded with the quantity supplied.

Changes in conditions affecting the demand for or supply of loanable funds will result in shifts of either the demand curve or the supply curve. This will cause changes in the market rate of interest. For example, an increase in the demand for credit by consumers caused, say, by confidence that future income will increase will move the demand curve outward. As shown in the graph in Box 7, this will, other things unchanged, result in an increase in the market equilibrium interest rate. Lenders will respond by increasing the quantity of loanable funds supplied.

Upward pressure on interest rates can also result from increased business demand for credit and from government borrowing. Many economists argue that the enormous federal budget deficits of the 1980s were a significant factor in pushing interest rates up at that time. When federal tax revenues fell short of expenditures by more than $200 billion annually for some years in the mid-1980s, the U.S. Treasury borrowed heavily in financial markets, which increased the demand for credit. Other influences on the demand for and supply of loanable funds remaining unchanged, this borrowing tended to push equilibrium interest rates up. As you can see, borrowing to cover deficits has the potential to raise interest rates, which tends to choke off consumer spending and business borrowing for new equipment. Later, in the macroeconomic sections, we'll discuss the controversy surrounding government budget deficits. At this point, make sure you know how you can use the laws of supply and demand to understand the current controversy about the federal government's deficit spending.

Make sure you can also use supply and demand analysis to show that a decrease in the demand for credit will decrease the market interest rate and the quantity of loanable funds supplied. An increase in the supply of loanable funds will put downward pressure on interest rates by shifting the supply curve outward. Finally, a decrease in the supply of loanable funds will shift the supply curve inward and put upward pressure on interest rates. As you can see, forecasting movements in interest rates in competitive markets requires a solid understanding of the forces influencing both the supply of and demand for loanable funds.

PRICE CEILINGS: USING SUPPLY AND DEMAND ANALYSIS TO FORECAST THEIR EFFECTS IN MARKETS

4 Not all of us are satisfied with market outcomes. Undoubtedly, you'd like prices to be lower than actual equilibrium prices. You probably wouldn't complain if a law were enacted that would cut your monthly rent in half, provided you weren't adversely affected in any other way.

People dissatisfied with outcomes in unregulated markets often organize politically and seek legislation that allows government authorities to control or set prices in markets. A *price ceiling* is a maximum price that can legally be charged for a good or service. A price ceiling is said to be *effective* if it is set below the price that would otherwise emerge as the market equilibrium price.

price ceiling a maximum price that can legally be charged for a good or service.

Government control of prices inevitably prevents the market system from performing its function of rationing goods and services. In this section we'll look at the consequences of price control policies. As you'll see, the laws of supply and demand can't be repealed even by government action!

Rent Control

Rent control is a price ceiling that government authorities sometimes use for rental housing. Rent control can prevent housing markets from reaching equilibrium only when rents are set *below* market equilibrium rents. After the end of World War II, when there was a sharp increase in the demand for housing, many cities instituted rent controls to prevent the spectacular increases in rents that were anticipated. Rent controls were abandoned by most cities in the 1950s but have regained popularity, particularly in cities on the West Coast where rents have risen rapidly.

Typically, rent controls limit increases in monthly rental rates or establish rules used to determine "fair" monthly rental rates for housing of varying kinds and quality. They seek to keep rents lower than those that would prevail in equilibrium in a competitive market. Many supporters of rent controls believe that these controls benefit lower-income people who would otherwise have to pay higher percentages of their income for rent. There's no doubt that those fortunate enough to snare rent-controlled apartments do benefit; however, the beneficiaries aren't always in the low-income bracket!

Rent controls cause shortages. The graph in Box 8 uses supply and demand analysis to show how rent controls cause housing shortages when the rents set by law are below the market equilibrium rents. Suppose the market equilibrium rent per room in a certain city would normally be $100 and that at this rent 8,000 rooms per year would be rented.

Now suppose a local rent control ordinance establishes a ceiling of $50 per room. Because the controlled rent is below the market equilibrium rent, the result is a shortage of housing. At the $50 per room rent the number of rooms demanded per year is 10,000, while the number supplied is only 6,000, resulting in an annual shortage of 4,000 rooms. the shortage arises from an increase in the quantity of housing demanded over the quantity that would prevail at the equilibrium rent and

Box 8   The Effect of Rent Controls

If a ceiling on rents is below the market equilibrium rent, the inevitable result is a shortage of rental housing.

from a decrease in the quantity of housing space supplied below the quantity that would prevail at the equilibrium rent.

Rent controls do make rental housing less expensive to tenants. Landlords respond to the reduction in possible gain by decreasing the quantity and often the quality of rental housing supplied. The inevitable result is a shortage of rental housing. The gainers are those fortunate enough to have found rent-controlled apartments, many of whom are in the middle- and upper-middle-income brackets. The losers are often people just starting out who seek a rent-controlled apartment but fail to find one because the established tenants with rent-controlled apartments don't give up their leases!

Nonprice Rationing of Shortages Resulting from Price Ceilings

Price ceilings inevitably result in shortages when they are set below market equilibrium prices. Because prices can't increase to ration a shortage when a ceiling is enforced, other means must be developed to distribute available supplies to those willing and able to pay. These means often reflect a high degree of human ingenuity. Nonprice rationing devices distribute available goods and services on a basis other than willingness to pay. Many people argue that nonprice rationing gives lower-income people the opportunity to consume a good they otherwise wouldn't be able to afford. Although this is true in some cases, the poor aren't always the ones fortunate enough to obtain available supplies when there's a shortage.

nonprice rationing devices that distribute available goods and services on a basis other than willingness to pay.

The simplest form of nonprice rationing is the use of a "first come, first served" rule. Available supplies of a good are rationed by time spent waiting in line. There's no way of knowing whether low-income people will be first in line or last. The waiting rations the good by doling out supplies only as they become available. Of course, waiting in line is time consuming and annoying. People often choose to do without a good if the gain they expect from it is less than the price they must pay plus the value of their time and the annoyance of waiting.

Another method of rationing scarce goods is the use of eligibility criteria to select from a pool of people who are willing and able to pay the controlled price. This requires people to fill out forms to establish their eligibility. Government officials

principles in practice

Policy Perspective: How Landlords Respond to Rent Control

The Case of New York City   Rent control has been used in New York City since 1943. Nearly two thirds of the city's population lives in rental units, and 1.2 million of these units are subject to some form of rent control. Because rent control applies to units of housing and isn't based on the income or needs of individuals, its benefits extend to rich and poor alike. Ironically, many of the beneficiaries of rent control are middle-income and upper-middle-income families.

Rent controls in New York City prevented rents from rising from 1965 to 1975, a period of increasing housing maintenance costs. This contributed to the loss of nearly 200,000 housing units through abandonment during that period. Although tenants in rent-controlled apartments pay lower rents, the quality of their housing is often lower than that enjoyed by people whose units aren't under rent control. Vacancy rates in New York City for rental housing have consistently been below those of cities without rent controls, suggesting that the controls have in fact contributed to housing shortages.[*]

Rent control is a government-mandated subsidy from landlords to tenants. One study estimates the value of this subsidy in New York City at $20 billion between 1943 and 1976. Many of the landlords whose income is reduced as a result of rent control are small investors of modest means.[†]

One way landlords in New York City can avoid the unfavorable effects of rent control on their incomes is to convert rental housing to industrial and commercial property, for which rents are not controlled. During the 1980s landlords frequently responded to rent regulations by converting rental housing to condominiums, which they could then sell at the market price.

When a rent-controlled apartment becomes vacant, the landlord often chooses not to rerent it. (In 1987 it was estimated that as many as 90,000 of the city's 1.2 million rent-regulated apartments were being held off the market. Landlords were "warehousing" the units to avoid legal difficulties in converting them to condominiums.) Warehousing aggravates the shortage of rental units caused by controls in the first place. The landlords argue that it's their right to choose not to rent apartments they own. Critics of warehousing argue that it should be outlawed.

You can easily understand the motivation for warehousing if you look at some of the costs landlords incur in converting rental units to salable owner-occupied condominium units. When a building in New York City is converted to condominiums, the tenants in rent-regulated apartments are protected by law against eviction. Tenants have three options: retain the right to rent (and to renew the lease at a modest increase in rent), buy their apartments at discounted "insider" prices, or accept payments from the landlord in return for giving up their tenant rights. Before a condominium conversion can begin in New York City, a certain minimum number of apartments must be vacant or tenants must agree to vacate or purchase their units. Landlords gladly offer tenants discounts and payments to induce them to give up their legal rights to rent-controlled units.

One Manhattan tenant was given the option to purchase the apartment he currently leased at a price of $72,000, which represented a 28 percent discount from the outsider price. Alternatively, the landlord would have happily paid the tenant $36,000 to give up his tenant rights. This tenant chose to keep renting the apartment at the current regulated rent of about $400 a month. The tenant wasn't acting irrationally. The controlled rent was a good deal compared to the other alternatives. Had the tenant accepted the payment and bought the apartment, his monthly housing costs would probably have tripled![‡] About two thirds of the tenants in condominium conversions in New York City find keeping their rent-controlled apartments the best alternative compared to accepting payments to vacate or buying their apartments at the insider price.

The boom in condominium conversions in New York City came to a halt in 1990 as an economic slowdown in the city sharply reduced the demand for housing. As real estate values and rents began to fall, and maintenance costs rose, many landlords found it difficult to earn profits whether they rented apartments or tried to sell them as condos. In some cases in early 1990, market equilibrium rents fell enough so that rent-controlled apartments could not be rented for the legally authorized rents! There is little incentive to convert apartments to condominiums when rent controls are no longer effective.

[*] See Frank S. Kristof, "The Effects of Rent Control and Rent Stabilization in New York City," in *Rent Control: Myths and Realities*, ed. Walter Block and Edgar Olsen (Vancouver, B.C.: Fraser Institute, 1981).
[†] Ibid.
[‡] See Michael de Courcy Hinds, "For New Yorkers, Is There Life after Rent Regulation?" *The New York Times*, Real Estate, October 26, 1986, p. 2.

then decide who gets served first on the basis of predetermined criteria. For example, if price controls resulted in a shortage of milk, authorities might decide that families with children would get first priority to purchase available supplies. Similarly, if there were a shortage of housing, families might get priority over single people.

Prices are typically controlled in wartime, and the price ceilings result in shortages. A common method of rationing scarce goods is the use of special stamps, a certain number of which are issued to consumers each week. The stamps are usually valid for only a week to prevent people from hoarding them. Prices for goods are stated in both money and stamps. Under this system of nonprice rationing, it isn't enough to be willing and able to pay the money price. A person must also have the stamps. During World War II, for example, stamps issued to civilians limited gasoline consumption to 3 gallons per week. Other stamps limited food, and a system of "points" was used to limit purchases of scarce items such as meat and sugar.

With price ceilings and nonprice rationing there are always dissatisfied potential buyers willing to pay more than the legal price to get the goods or services they want. Selling goods at prices higher than those legally set is punishable by fines or even imprisonment. Nonetheless, there are always sellers willing to risk charging more than the ceiling prices. A market in which sellers sell goods to buyers for more than the legal prices is called a black market. In a black market, prices are invariably higher than those that would prevail if the controlled market were allowed to reach equilibrium. For example, it's not uncommon for eager people searching for housing in rent-controlled markets to make illegal payments in order to obtain choice apartments. In some cases these payments are outright bribes. In other cases they take the form of exorbitant security deposits or purchases of apartment improvements at greatly inflated prices.

black market a market in which sellers sell goods to buyers for more than the legal prices.

PRICE FLOORS: SUPPLY AND DEMAND ANALYSIS OF THEIR EFFECTS

The opposite of a price ceiling is a price floor, a minimum price established by law. Two commonly used price floors are minimum wages and agricultural price supports. Minimum wages prohibit employers from paying less than a certain stipulated wage. Agricultural price supports guarantee farmers a minimum price for their crops. As with price ceilings, providing benefits in this way impairs the rationing function of prices. When price floors are set *above* market equilibrium prices, the inevitable result is a surplus on the market. Again, we can use supply and demand analysis to see how such surpluses arise and to identify who gains and who loses as a result of the price floor.

price floor a minimum price established by law.

Minimum Wages

Minimum wages are an example of a price floor that governments establish for labor services. Governments enforce minimum-wage laws by penalizing employers who pay less than the stipulated hourly wage.

In modern industrial nations, skilled workers and people employed in factories typically earn equilibrium wages that exceed the minimum wage. However, equilibrium wages for unskilled workers are usually lower than the minimum wage. The graph in Box 9 shows you the effect of a minimum wage in a market for unskilled labor.

The market equilibrium wage for the services of unskilled workers is $4 per hour. At that wage the quantity of labor services demanded per week just equals the quantity supplied of 3 million hours. The minimum wage is set at $5 per hour. At that

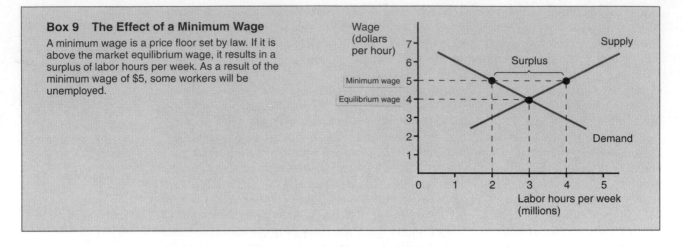

Box 9   The Effect of a Minimum Wage

A minimum wage is a price floor set by law. If it is above the market equilibrium wage, it results in a surplus of labor hours per week. As a result of the minimum wage of $5, some workers will be unemployed.

floor the quantity of labor supplied is 4 million hours per week, while the quantity demanded is only 2 million hours. There is therefore a weekly surplus of 2 million labor hours. This means that some workers seeking employment at the minimum wage will be unable to find jobs, an inevitable situation when minimum wages are set above market equilibrium wages. Of course, if the wage floor were set below or equal to the market wage, it would have no effect on the market equilibrium, because employers would pay more than the minimum wage to avoid labor shortages.

Minimum wages benefit workers who are fortunate enough to find work at wage levels that exceed the equilibrium wage. However, they harm workers who seek employment at the higher wage but can't find jobs. Evidence has linked minimum-wage laws with teenage unemployment. Each 10 percent increase in the minimum wage appears to be associated with about a 1 percent to 3 percent reduction in total teenage employment. Minimum wages also appear to reduce employment of young adults aged 20 to 24 and of the elderly. Some studies, however, have found that the minimum wage increases employment of some adults, particularly women, between the ages of 25 and 55.[1]

As you might expect, minimum wages have the most adverse effects on employment in low-wage industries such as retail sales. Employers often react to increases in minimum wages by decreasing the quality of working conditions and reducing fringe benefits. As minimum wages rise, the pace of work is increased and the number of vacation days tends to decline.[2]

Despite the adverse effects of minimum wages on employment opportunities for teenagers and on working conditions for workers in low-wage industries, many politicians and economists argue that minimum wages are an effective way of benefiting the working poor. Of course, employers whose marginal costs increase because of an increase in the minimum wage are likely to respond by decreasing the supply of their products in markets. Consequently, the prices of goods and services produced with unskilled labor will rise and consumers will pay part of the cost of the minimum wage.

---

[1] For a summary of these studies, see Charles Brown, Curtis Gilroy, and Andrew Kohen, "The Effect of the Minimum Wage on Employment and Unemployment," *Journal of Economic Literature* 20, no. 2 (June 1982), pp. 487–528.

[2] Walter J. Wessels, *Minimum Wages: Fringe Benefits, and Working Conditions* (Washington, D.C.: American Enterprise Institute for Public Policy Research, 1980).

As of April 1991, the minimum wage in the United States was set at $4.25 per hour based on legislation enacted by Congress. In an effort to reduce some of the adverse effects of minimum wages on employment opportunities for teenagers, the new legislation allows employers to pay a "subminimum training wage" of less than $4.25 per hour for a six-month period to workers below the age of 20. This provision is designed to encourage employers to hire and train teenagers.

Agricultural Price Supports

Agricultural price supports are another example of a price floor. These supports, which are common in the United States, are a direct benefit to farmers. However, when the supports are established above equilibrium prices, the inevitable result is a surplus of agricultural commodities. Usually the federal government acquires such surpluses (at taxpayer cost) and holds them in storage. Limited amounts are given away as foreign aid. You may wonder why the government doesn't simply give all the surplus commodities away, in light of the great need for food in famine-stricken Third World countries. The reason is that this would increase world food supplies tremendously and sharply reduce prices. This would create political problems, as the plummeting prices reduce incomes of farmers in other countries.

Later in the book we'll examine American agricultural price support programs. At this point we can easily use supply and demand analysis to outline the basic method of price supports to farmers and its effects.

Let's briefly sketch how the price floor works for one farm commodity: milk. For many years dairy farmers have benefited from price supports for milk set by the U.S. Department of Agriculture. Dairy farmers decide how much milk to supply on the basis of the price floor. The graph in Box 10 shows how a surplus of milk results when the actual market price turns out to be less than the price floor. Suppose that the price floor is $2 per gallon, while the market equilibrium price would be $1.50 per gallon. Dairy farmers produce 11 billion gallons of milk per year, which corresponds to point L on the supply curve. At a price of $2 per gallon, the quantity demanded is only 10 billion gallons per year (point M on the demand curve). As a result, there's a surplus of 1 billion gallons per year. To prevent this surplus from putting downward pressure on price, the government buys the 1-billion-gallon surplus at the official price floor each year and stores it. The shaded rectangle shows you the total cost of the program to taxpayers, which in this case is $2 billion. In addition, consumers pay $2 per gallon of milk rather than the $1.50 per gallon market equilibrium price. At the higher price the quantity demanded by consumers is 10 billion gallons per year instead of the 10.5 billion gallons per year that would be demanded if there were no government-established price floor.

You can note these important results of the price support policy:

1. The prices consumers pay for milk (and other agricultural commodities whose prices are supported by government programs) increase when the price floor is higher than the market equilibrium price.

2. Taxpayers foot the bill for purchase and storage of surplus commodities that result from the price floor. However, the government acquires the commodities as assets that it can sell later to generate revenue.

3. Farmers' incomes are higher when the government-established price floors exceed the equilibrium prices of the commodities they sell. As a result of the price supports, they can sell more output than they could otherwise and they receive higher prices than those that would prevail in free markets.

Box 10   Impact of Agricultural Price Supports

The agricultural support price of $2 per gallon is above the market equilibrium price of $1.50 per gallon. The support price reduces quantity demanded and increases quantity supplied, resulting in a 1-billion-gallon surplus per year. The surplus milk is purchased and stored by the government. The cost to taxpayers of purchasing the surplus is shown by the shaded rectangular area.

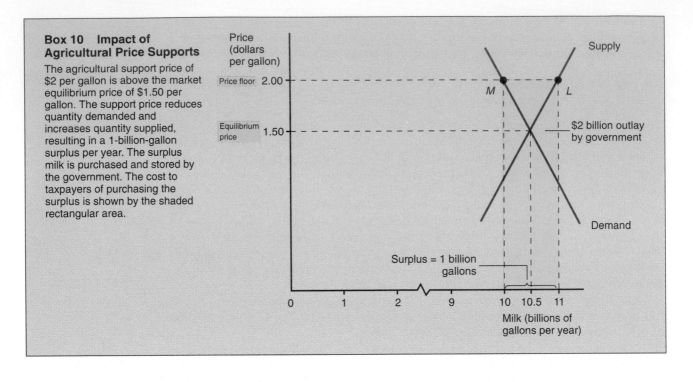

CONCEPT CHECK

- What are price ceilings? Under what circumstances do price ceilings cause shortages in competitive markets?

- What is nonprice rationing?

- A price floor is established for eggs. Under what circumstances would the price floor result in a surplus of eggs?

PRICE CONTROLS: THE COST OF GOVERNMENT INTERVENTION

Price ceilings and price floors prevent the price system from rationing goods and services. Seeking to provide benefits to certain groups through regulation of the market mechanism therefore always impairs the function of prices in allocating goods and services. Government intervention in otherwise competitive markets often has unfortunate consequences. In the case of price ceilings, otherwise honest people are often tempted to enter into illegal transactions to obtain scarce goods or services. When price controls cause severe shortages, the costs of preventing illegal transactions are often very high. Price ceilings can also cause the quality of goods to deteriorate as sellers who can't cover their opportunity costs at the controlled prices provide shoddier products.

In the case of price floors, inefficient, high-cost producers can still make profits as a result of government support of prices. The costs of dealing with stored surplus commodities purchased by the government can be quite high. Taxpayers end up subsidizing farmers as tax money is used to purchase and store surplus crops. Finally, consumers of products or services protected by price floors are made worse off because they must pay higher prices than would prevail without the floors.

As you can see, interference with the functioning of free and competitive markets is likely to result in resource allocation problems and reduced efficiency. However, you shouldn't conclude that government intervention in markets is never justified.

Making a judgment on the desirability of government intervention clearly depends on your point of view and your goals. In all the cases we've discussed, there were gainers as well as losers. Elimination of price controls always causes some business firms to fail as prices move to equilibrium levels. Obviously, you might rationally support rent control, minimum wages, interest rate ceilings, and agricultural price supports if you and people you care about gained as a result. *However, the important question is whether the gainers could have been made just as well off in other ways that didn't impair the rationing function of market prices.*

Finally, remember that the analysis in this chapter assumed that markets were in fact freely competitive. In many cases markets are not competitive, nor are buyers and sellers the only people who gain or lose when they transact their business. In such cases we must reassess the role of government in modifying market outcomes.

 the global economy

The Transition to Free Markets in the Former Communist Nations

A hallmark of communism was price controls for everything. Throughout much of the 20th century, the economies of Eastern Europe and the republics of the former Soviet Union lacked free markets. Under communism, a cumbersome system of central planning prevailed through which government determined what was produced and how it was produced and influenced living standards by controlling wages and salaries. The economies of Eastern Europe and the former Soviet Union were characterized by government ownership or control of productive resources. Under central planning, these economies were managed by governing authorities who set

prices and production targets to achieve political goals. All business was controlled by the government, and markets as means for the free exchange of goods and services were a rarity.

We can use our analysis of price controls to understand how the old system of central planning worked and some of the difficulties involved in the transition to free markets in the formerly communist nations. In most of these nations central planning allocated a disproportionate amount of resources to heavy industries, such as steel, to support a vast military establishment. Production of consumer goods was not given high priority by the planners. The prices of food and other basic items were kept low. The government, which owned many of the farms and all of the bakeries and food production facilities, often sold food below the costs of production as a way of subsidizing workers whose low wage levels were set by it.

Unfortunately, the low prices for such items as bread were well below equilibrium levels and vast shortages were common. Citizens of Eastern Europe and the former Soviet Union were accustomed to waiting in lines for many hours to obtain bread.

The graph in Box 11 shows the effect of setting prices below equilibrium levels under central planning. The supply of an item was usually determined at the beginning of the year by the planning authorities, and the amount made available each month was therefore fixed and independent of price. At the price set by the planners, quantity demanded far exceeded quantity supplied.

The prices set by the planners did not result only in shortages—they also resulted in waste. Bread was so cheap that farmers often used it instead of raw

Box 11   How Shortages Arise in a Centrally Planned Economy When Prices Are Set below Equilibrium Levels

When planners set the price of a product in fixed supply at a level below the equilibrium price, there will be a shortage. If prices are allowed to rise to equilibrium levels as part of a transition to a free-market economy, quantity demanded will fall. Shift to a free-market economy results in a more responsive supply as higher prices attract more suppliers and induce existing enterprises to expand production. The supply curve will become upward sloping as a free market is established.

grain to feed pigs! There was also waste because many items, such as unpopular, frumpy clothing, were priced above equilibrium levels and were therefore in surplus. Despite the surpluses, because of the rigid system of central planning, these items continued to be produced.

As communism ended, food prices were allowed to rise to equilibrium levels. In the early 1990s, for example, Poland was feeling the effects of the move to free markets. The food shops were well stocked with meat, bread, and cakes. There were no lines. Individual entrepreneurs set up makeshift markets selling goods they had acquired directly from factories in Poland. Others took advantage of newly opened borders and the freedom to acquire foreign currency. They traveled abroad, where they bought fresh produce to sell to eager Polish consumers with the ability to pay.

As prices rose, quantities demanded fell. The Polish people could now find what they wanted in the shops, but most people couldn't afford these items! The Poles were poor before the prices were allowed to rise—under the first come, first served principle, however, some of them were able to obtain basic goods in short supply *if they were lucky*. Now it took hard cash rather than time in line to obtain sausage.

To complete the move to free markets, the governments of the formerly communist nations must transfer their property rights in productive resources to private interests. "Privatizing" former government enterprises means selling them to domestic or foreign buyers who will operate them as business firms. The privatization process will result in the shutdown of unprofitable enterprises. As private ownership becomes the norm, the owners of firms will become independent suppliers of products to a system of markets in which prices are determined by supply and demand. Eventually, the rigid fixed-supply curves, such as that for bread illustrated in Box 11, will become upward sloping as profit-seeking entrepreneurs become responsive to price changes. When the economies of the formerly communist nations complete their transition to free markets, prices will serve as signals of scarcity and profitability to the new private enterprises that will supply goods and services.

However, the transition to free markets will not be painless. As old, inefficient state enterprises are privatized or shut down, many workers will lose their jobs and have to seek new ones while the prices of many of the products they need will be rising. Higher prices will eliminate shortages but will also reduce the purchasing power of already low incomes. Unemployment, reduced living standards, and soaring prices are the unfortunate consequences of the painful transition to free markets that will eventually improve resource use and raise incomes in the formerly communist nations.

insights on issues

How Will Changes Abroad, Especially the Movement away from Communism toward Free Markets in Eastern Europe and the Former Soviet Union, Affect the U.S. Economy? Talking with Abram Bergson

A professor of economics at Harvard University, Abram Bergson was born in Baltimore, Maryland, in 1914 and gained his A.B. at Johns Hopkins and his Ph.D. at Harvard. He is the author of numerous articles and books on economic theory and the economics of socialism. His most recent book is *Planning and Performance in Socialist Economies* (1989).

What effects will the movement toward free markets in Russia have on the average American? Will prices of products consumed by Americans be affected? The ongoing disintegration of Soviet and Eastern European communism and their resulting shifts toward a western-type market economy will affect the United States chiefly through the contraction that is induced by U.S. defense expenditures. The revolutionary developments in the former Soviet Union (FSU) are also causing a near-term contraction of its globally important oil exports, which should result in higher prices for oil in the United States. Russia and a number of other republics into which the FSU has dissolved apparently continue to suffer a grain deficit. As far as financing can be arranged, they must continue to import grain, which is by far the most important export from the United States to the FSU. The FSU is competing actively with the United States in world arms markets.

What opportunities for investment will open up for U.S. industries in economies in transition? What are the risks of such investments? Eastern Europe and the FSU are eager for U.S. investment. Because of the turmoil there, especially in the FSU, western commitments thus far have been on a modest scale, but some significant projects have been initiated and others are being negotiated. In the FSU, an outstanding case in point is the oil venture Chevron is arranging in Kazakhstan.

What are the pitfalls of the transition to free markets in former communist nations? There are many pitfalls. A primary one is the continual threat of high-level inflation resulting from the difficulty of observing budgetary and financial discipline. The transformation that is in process is often painful for the population, and there is intense pressure to ease the pain through budgetary subsidies and benefits and lax credit controls. Because of the difficulties encountered, especially in the FSU, public support for reform has tended to atrophy.

How will the economic development of former communist China and less developed nations affect U.S. exports and job opportunities? In contrast to the FSU and Eastern Europe, China has been enjoying notably rapid economic growth. By 1989 it had advanced to thirteenth place in the world in volume of foreign trade. China has been running a large trade surplus with us ($11.5 billion in 1990), which troubles some of our political authorities. As indicated, except for grain, the FSU is a very minor player in U.S. domestic markets. U.S. trade with Eastern Europe has been minute historically.

SUMMARY

1. Prices serve to ration scarce goods sold in competitive markets by preventing shortages and surpluses.

2. A nonscarce good is one for which quantity demanded will not exceed quantity supplied at zero price.

3. Successful marketing of a new item depends on conditions of supply and demand for the item. If the minimum price sellers will accept exceeds the maximum price buyers will pay for the first unit made available, the item is not marketable. Changes in technology lower the minimum prices sellers can accept for items and expand markets for these goods.

4. Wages and hours worked in competitive labor markets depend on the demand for and supply of labor. Similarly, interest rates and credit extended in competitive financial markets depend on the demand for and supply of loanable funds.

5. Price ceilings, maximum prices that can legally be charged in competitive markets, result in shortages

when they are below market equilibrium prices. Rent control laws are examples of price ceilings.

6. Nonprice rationing distributes available amounts of goods and services on a basis other than willingness to pay when shortages caused by price ceilings exist in competitive markets. The most common nonprice rationing device is "first come, first served."

7. Price ceilings usually result in illegal transactions in black markets at prices that exceed the legal limits.

8. Price floors establish minimum prices, which can result in surpluses when these prices exceed equilibrium prices in competitive markets. Minimum wages and agricultural price supports are common examples of price floor programs.

9. Price ceilings and price floors benefit certain groups but impair the rationing of goods and services by the price system in competitive markets.

KEY TERMS

nonscarce (or free) good *84*
wages *87*
credit *90*
interest *90*
price ceiling *92*
nonprice rationing *93*
black market *95*
price floor *95*

CONCEPT REVIEW

1 Why would a world in which scarce goods are free be chaotic?

2 Under what circumstances would the equilibrium quantity of a good be zero in a market?

3 Explain why downward rigidity of wages can result in surpluses of labor (excessive unemployment) during a recession when the demand for labor declines.

4 Why do rent controls result in shortages of housing?

PROBLEMS AND APPLICATIONS

1. A local record store advertises that it will give away Bruce Springsteen albums from 8 A.M. to 5 P.M., on Saturday. What is likely to happen? Why might you be better off waiting until Monday to buy your album at the market price? **1**

2. Residents on an island in which coconuts are a nonscarce good discover that people in the rest of the world don't consider coconuts nonscarce and will pay high prices to obtain them. Explain what is likely to happen to the demand for coconuts as island residents discover that they can export the fruit to foreign markets. **1**

3. The price of personal computers was well over $5,000 when they were introduced in the early 1980s. Since then the price has fallen drastically. Use supply and demand analysis to explain the likely cause of this fall. What was the effect of decreasing prices on the quantity demanded of this good? **2**

4. Rising enrollment in college accounting curricula causes a sharp increase in the supply of accountants four years later. Other things being equal, use supply and demand analysis to forecast the impact of the increase in the supply of accountants on annual salaries of accounting graduates. **3**

5. A drop in profits for oil companies results in a sharp decrease in the demand for chemical engineers. Use supply and demand analysis to predict the effect on salaries paid to chemical engineers and on the quantity of their labor supplied. **3**

6. Suppose the federal government finally balances the budget. The decrease in demand for loanable funds to cover the deficit is likely to have a significant effect on credit markets. Use supply and demand analysis to forecast, other things being equal, the impact of a decrease in government demand for loanable funds on interest rates and on borrowing by business firms and consumers. **3**

7. The market equilibrium rent per room in a small city is $50. A rent control law is passed that establishes a price ceiling of exactly $50 per room. What will be the impact of the law on the market for rental housing? How will your answer change if immediately after the rent controls have been passed, a major corporation announces that it will build a new factory employing 10,000 workers? The new plant is expected to sharply increase the demand for housing. **4**

8. A 50-cent-per-gallon price ceiling is established for gasoline. As a result of the ceiling, a weekly shortage of 10,000 gallons develops. How can the shortage be rationed? **4**

9. Although minimum wages prevent labor markets from rationing unskilled labor services, they are widely praised by labor leaders and are regarded as good by most people. How can you explain the political support for minimum wages? **4**

10. How could agricultural surpluses be eliminated in the United States? Use supply and demand analysis to show how agricultural price floors cause surpluses and how taxpayers pay the cost of the surpluses. Who would gain and who would lose if agricultural price support programs were phased out? **4**

chapter 5

The Price System
Free Markets and the Economy

The republics of the former Soviet Union and other economies that have relied on government plans to direct resource use and state ownership of the means of production are struggling to change. Leaders of these nations are moving toward a free-market system to help fill the empty shelves in their stores. Is this transition going to solve their problems?

In this chapter we will look at how prices guide economic decisions in a system of markets under which business firms seek to profit by supplying products that satisfy market demands. We will examine the basic components of a capitalist economy and how production of goods and services in such an economy generates the income necessary to buy these products.

The production or consumption of many products sold in markets often has undesirable side effects such as pollution. Governments often intervene in markets to reduce or eliminate such effects. International trade plays an important role in modern economies by allowing consumers to enjoy a greater variety of products and to obtain products at lower prices. To completely understand how modern economies function, it is therefore necessary to look at both government activity and the process of international trade.

□ CONCEPT PREVIEW

After reading this chapter, you should be able to:

1. Examine the framework of a pure market economy and show how the circular flow of income and expenditure in a capitalist economy keeps it functioning.

2. Explain the price system as a means of allocating resources in terms of what is produced, how it is produced, and how it is distributed.

3. Identify the defects of a pure market system.

4. Briefly outline the functioning of the modern mixed and open economy.

CAPITALISM AND THE MARKET ECONOMY

1

capitalism an economic
system characterized by
private ownership of
economic resources and
freedom of enterprise in
which owners of factories
and other capital hire
workers to produce goods
and services.

mixed economy an
economy in which
governments as well as
business firms provide
goods and services.

Capitalism is an economic system characterized by private ownership of economic resources and freedom of enterprise in which owners of factories and other capital hire workers to produce goods and services. Under capitalism, anyone is free to use economic resources to start a business and sell a product in a market. In a purely capitalist economy government's role is quite limited and the economy relies on the pursuit of profit through market sales to make goods and services available.

In most modern nations, however, governments control many resources and criteria other than personal gain and business profit are used to decide how resources will be employed. Most modern nations have a **mixed economy,** where governments as well as business firms provide goods and services. In such economies governments supply roads, defense, pensions, and schooling directly to citizens. In modern economies governments also commonly intervene in markets to control prices and correct for the shortcomings of a system in which prices and the pursuit of personal gain influence resource use and incomes.

price system a
mechanism by which
resource use in a market
economy is guided by
prices.

Let's look first at how resources would be allocated in an economy in which all useful goods and services are traded in competitive markets. In such an economy, prices would act as signals that influence the possibilities for gain. The **price system** is a mechanism by which resource use in a market economy is guided by prices. In such a system, changes in prices caused by changes in demand and supply affect opportunities for profit and personal gain and cause changes in resource use.

The driving force behind a capitalist economy is the pursuit of personal gain by both sellers and buyers who seek to get the most satisfaction from their income. In such an economy, people are free to organize business firms for the purpose of selling goods and services at a profit. There are few restrictions on what can be bought or sold. The people who manage and assume the risks of business enterprises are called *entrepreneurs*. They are innovators who develop new products and processes or reorganize production in ways that reduce costs or better satisfy consumers. Profit is both the reward and the incentive that motivates them.

The owners and managers of business firms acquire capital equipment and inventories of materials, and negotiate contracts to hire workers who produce goods and services for sale in markets. The private ownership of capital and other resources is a dominant feature of capitalism. In the capitalist system *freedom of enterprise* is the right of business firm owners to employ private economic resources for whatever purpose they want.

free markets the situation
that exists when there are
no restrictions that prevent
buyers or sellers from
entering or exiting a
market.

Capitalism is also characterized by *economic rivalry*, a situation in which large numbers of buyers are competing for available supplies of goods and services offered by large numbers of sellers. Economic rivalry implies a diffusion of economic power, so that no single buyer or seller can make a good significantly more abundant or scarce. **Free markets** exist when there are no restrictions that prevent either buyers or sellers from entering or exiting a market. No one is forced to enter into market transactions; therefore, only those transactions that provide mutual gains to buyers and sellers will be pursued.

Specialization and Exchange

Specialization and division of labor mean that workers and entrepreneurs devote most of their time to produce one or a few goods and services. These specialists sell the goods or services they specialize in and then use their incomes to buy goods and services they want that are offered for sale by other specialists. In this way specialization and voluntary exchange allow people to enjoy additional gains from existing production. Such exchange involves *mutual gains* to the traders. If no one else is

principles in practice

The Entrepreneurial Spirit in American Capitalism

In the United States entrepreneurs often attain the status of folk heroes. Entrepreneurs are opportunists, seeking to exploit the right moment for an innovation in products or processes. When successful, they are rewarded with spectacular profits that enable them to accumulate vast fortunes. Entrepreneurs are the dynamic and driving spirits who start businesses, satisfy demands for resources or products, and prosper from doing so.

Who are the great entrepreneurs of American history? Thomas Edison, the inventor of electric lighting and the phonograph, was foremost an entrepreneur interested in marketing his inventions. To make his inventions profitable, Edison had to acquire funds to purchase the necessary capital. He acted as an entrepreneur in doing so and capped his skill as an inventor with equal skills as an entrepreneur to translate his ideas into revenue and profit.* He engineered a profitable way to deliver electrical power to homes and businesses. The delivery system was the key, because electricity had to be *priceable* for it to be profitable. The Edison Electric Illuminating Company of New York was organized in 1880 to provide street lighting. By 1883 it was supplying electricity to more than 700 private customers.

Fred Smith is a modern-day entrepreneur who envisioned a profitable opportunity for a firm specializing in overnight delivery of small packages. Unlike Edison, Smith was not an inventor, but he too saw a demand and organized the resources needed to satisfy that demand. What Smith saw was an economy with dispersed production and service facilities that needed a quick and reliable means of shipping documents, drugs, discs and tapes, and small electronic components among those facilities.

In 1970 no one was providing such shipments. The U.S. Postal Service had a monopoly on the shipment of first-class mail. The performance of the Postal Service wasn't reliable enough for business firms that needed guaranteed 24-hour delivery. Private freight services likewise were incapable of providing guaranteed overnight delivery. Airmail and air freight were carried by a number of airlines, but the inevitable delays involved in loading and unloading made overnight delivery infeasible. In a term paper Smith wrote when he was a junior at Yale, he outlined his idea. The professor gave the paper a grade of "C."

In 1971, Smith began to put his idea into action. He succeeded in raising $90 million to start up his company, which he called Federal Express. He purchased 33 small Dassault Falcon jets and developed a hub at Memphis, Tennessee, for sorting packages, which were restricted in size and weight. All packages picked up during the day were sent to the Memphis hub for sorting. They were shipped out the same night to their ultimate destination for delivery the next morning. The company invested considerable resources in developing its distinctive logo and its reputation for reliability. When Federal Express began in 1973, it served 22 cities. It wasn't immediately profitable. In fact, it didn't turn a profit until 1976. After that time, changes in government regulations enabled it to expand more easily and to operate larger aircraft. In 1977 Federal Express earned $20 million. In 1980 it took in nearly $600 million revenues and earned $60 million.

As happens with most successful enterprises, competition stiffened. By the 1980s many other firms, such as Purolator, United Parcel Service, Airborne, and even the U.S. Postal Service, were offering overnight delivery service for small parcels. As you can see, the price system works in the long run both to create entrepreneurs and to encourage other firms to emulate the innovations of successful ones.

* For a more detailed account of Edison's achievements, see Robert Sobel and David B. Sicilia, *The Entrepreneurs: An American Adventure* (Boston: Houghton Mifflin, 1986), pp. 7–16.

harmed when people specialize and trade in goods and services and there is no deception, then more benefit can be obtained from an existing amount of production. For example, suppose a farmer produces more food than he can use. This farmer can gain if he is allowed to exchange the food that results from specialization for another item that he values more, such as clothing. Similarly, a tailor who produces more clothing that he needs can gain by exchanging some of the clothing for food. Even if both the tailor and the farmer produce their products without waste, they can both enjoy further gains by exchanging their food and clothing in a market trade.

barter the process of exchanging goods (or services) for goods (or services).

This process of exchanging goods (or services) for goods (or services) is known as **barter.** In a barter economy a farmer can truck his produce into a market and trade it for clothing offered by a tailor. Barter is an inconvenient means of exchange because it requires *double coincidence of wants*, which means that to exchange an item a trader must truck items around to find someone else who both wants what the trader offers and has what he or she desires. For example, suppose you have accounting skills. This week you want to buy a new stereo system. To exchange your accounting services for a stereo system, you'll need to find someone willing to exchange the stereo system you want for your accounting services. Making this exchange can require a time-consuming search. You may find someone who has the kind of stereo system you want but who has absolutely no desire for your accounting services. You may also find people who want your accounting services but don't have anything you want. With a barter system of exchange, each trader must seek out people who have the desired goods and want the goods offered in exchange for them.

Money exchange doesn't require this double coincidence of wants. All you have to do is sell your accounting services to anyone willing to pay for them. When you've earned enough money income, you go to the store and exchange it for a stereo system. *Money,* usually issued only by governments, is what sellers generally accept as payment for goods and services. The characteristics of money are so important that we'll devote an entire chapter to its function later in the book. At this point you should realize that a generally accepted medium of exchange serving as money greatly facilitates specialization and market exchange of goods and services.

How Production Generates Income in the Market Economy: Circular Flow of Income and Expenditure

Imagine an economy in which all goods and services are made available through markets. Business firms acquire resources from households, whose members provide labor services, entrepreneurial talent, and funds to acquire new capital. Household members also provide natural resources if they own land. The diagram in Box 1 gives you a simplified overview of a pure market economy.

In such an economy, business firms are buyers of resources offered for sale in input markets. Households supply economic resources as sellers in these input markets. The competition among the many buyers and sellers of inputs then results in market prices for labor, the use of funds, capital, and natural resources. The prices depend on conditions of supply and demand in each input market.

The sale of input services provides a flow of income in the form of wages, rent, interest, and profit to the members of each household supplying resources or owning businesses. For example, people in one household may earn wages as department store employees. They may also own land and buildings that they allow a business to use in exchange for rent. Income from both wages and rent flows into the household. Household members also earn interest income from bank deposits or bonds. If they own corporate stock, they may receive a flow of income as dividends on the stock. They may run a small business that generates profits. The flow of payments for labor and resource use plus distribution of profit to the members of households who own businesses equals the income earned in the economy.

Household members use the money income they earn to express their demand for goods and services. Firms respond to that demand by producing a variety of goods and services. The price of each good and service is determined by its supply and demand in product markets. Consumers' expenditures constitute revenue for firms that they use to finance outlays for inputs (wages to staff, purchases of inventories, rent) and profit payments to owners of the firms.

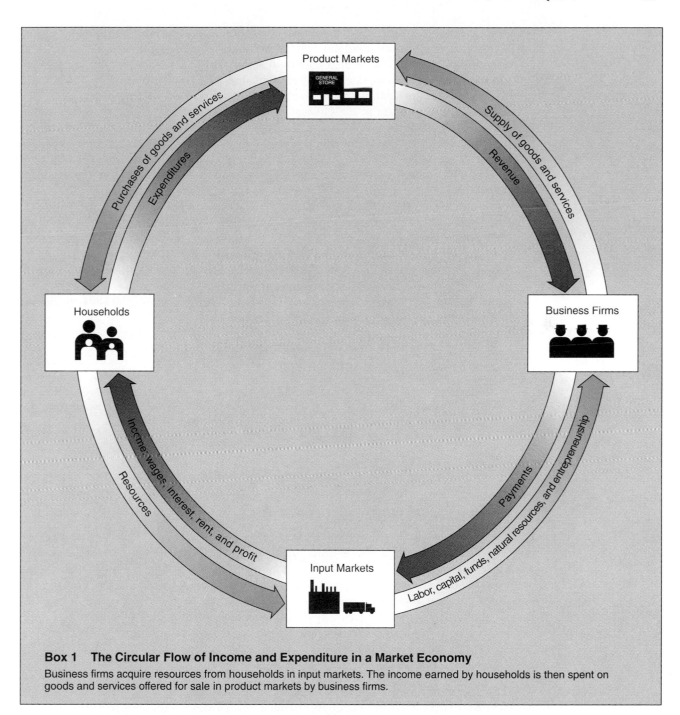

Box 1   The Circular Flow of Income and Expenditure in a Market Economy

Business firms acquire resources from households in input markets. The income earned by households is then spent on goods and services offered for sale in product markets by business firms.

The picture of the economy as a set of interrelated markets in which income and expenditure move in a circular flow between business firms and households is a simplified but enlightening view of a pure market economy. It points out that both households and business firms meet in two sets of markets—households are sellers in input markets but are buyers in product markets; business firms are buyers in input markets and sellers in output markets. Money lubricates the wheels of exchange. It is paid out as income to households that they in turn spend on products. It then becomes revenue to business firms that they use to pay for the items they need in order to make goods available. These payments provide income as the cycle goes on and on. Business firms also employ a steady flow of resources that are used to supply goods and services each day to households. The clockwise flow of expenditures, revenue, payments, and income fuels the counterclockwise flow of goods and services and resources in the circular flow diagram in Box 1.

The production of goods and services therefore generates income. The income then becomes the means by which households purchase the products produced by business firms. As production grows, so will income payments to households.

Box 1 does not show that business firms conduct market transactions among themselves. Some of the products firms purchase, such as machinery, structures, and vehicles, are intended for final use in production and will not be resold to consumers or governments. Others are used as materials and parts that will be incorporated into other products sold to final users. The diagram also ignores the role of government in the economy, since government has only a minor role in an economy where all useful goods and services are provided through markets. Finally, the circular flow analysis does not consider the effects of international trade. We will soon show how both government and international trade affect the flow of income and expenditure in the modern mixed economy.

CONCEPT CHECK

☐

- What are the basic features of a capitalist economy?
- Explain how the use of money facilitates exchange in a market economy, and describe the circular flow of money in a pure market economy.

- Briefly explain how production generates income in a market economy and how income and expenditure flow between business firms and households.

THE PRICE SYSTEM: HOW IT WORKS

2 We need to elaborate on the diagram in Box 1 to show you how the price system works and when it fails. Within the box labeled ''households,'' you and other individuals constantly weigh the costs and benefits of working or enjoying leisure, of using land for personal purposes or renting it out for use by others, and of providing funds for business firms to expand or spending those funds on consumer goods. Within the box labeled ''business firms,'' managers decide how to employ resources and what to produce. *The unifying feature of all these decisions is that they are influenced by prices determined by free play of the forces of supply and demand in competitive markets.*

How the Price System Influences What Is Produced
No one directs a market economy. Instead, the prices established in markets act as signals for personal gain and profit to which households and business managers respond. *What* gets produced in a market economy is determined chiefly by profitability. When demand for a particular good increases, so does its price. For example, other things being equal, an increase in the demand for exercise bikes increases their price. The higher price increases the profitability of producing them. Because entrepreneurs seek out profits and avoid losses, when more profits are possible from

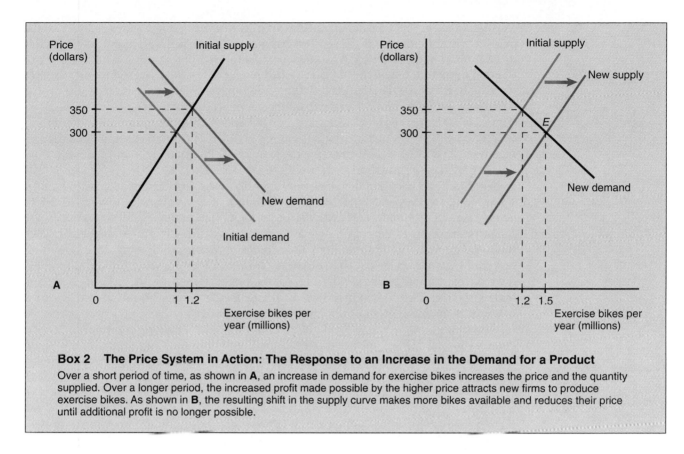

Box 2   The Price System in Action: The Response to an Increase in the Demand for a Product

Over a short period of time, as shown in **A**, an increase in demand for exercise bikes increases the price and the quantity supplied. Over a longer period, the increased profit made possible by the higher price attracts new firms to produce exercise bikes. As shown in **B**, the resulting shift in the supply curve makes more bikes available and reduces their price until additional profit is no longer possible.

making exercise bikes than from making cars, entrepreneurs will reallocate their resources from cars to exercise bikes. In this way, through the price system, suppliers respond to demand by producing the products that consumers want to purchase.

Box 2 shows how the price system responds to an increase in demand. Graph **A** shows that, given the initial demand and supply, at the market price of $300, 1 million exercise bikes per year are sold. An increase in demand increases the market price of exercise bikes to $350 and results in an increase in quantity supplied over the year to 1.2 million. This increase occurs as existing firms hire more workers and use material in existing factories to respond to the profit opportunities that arise when the price increases.

Over a longer period of time, the higher price makes it profitable for entrepreneurs to start new factories specializing in the production of exercise bikes. More resources are devoted to producing exercise bikes over time. As shown in graph **B,** this increases the supply of exercise bikes. The final equilibrium is at point *E* in graph **B,** at which the new supply curve intersects the new demand curve. The quantity of exercise bikes sold increases to 1.5 million per year, and the price falls from $350 to $300. No single person planned the increase in the supply of exercise bikes. Instead, competition among entrepreneurs for profit opportunities caused the increase in supply that ultimately lowered prices and made more exercise bikes available.

Adjustments like this occur all the time in markets. For example, in 1986 the market price of compact disc recordings remained fairly high and many popular titles were in short supply. Throughout the world factories were working around the clock to keep up with the demand. In that year, however, 15 *new* CD production facilities were being completed in the United States. Seeing the opportunity to increase profits by producing CDs, firms were expanding their productive capacity to do so. The supply of CDs increased substantially in 1987 and 1988, putting downward pressure on prices. Meanwhile, the markets for long-playing records and cassette tape recordings were also affected. Demand for these items declined, and fewer resources were devoted to their production.

We can conduct a similar analysis for a decrease in demand for a product. A decrease in the demand for a petroleum product such as gasoline lowers its price. This lessened demand decreases the profitability of producing oil and causes the quantity supplied to decrease over a short period of time. Over a longer period of time, the decrease in profitability causes oil production facilities to close down. As less labor, capital, and natural resources are devoted to drilling for oil, oil supply decreases, placing upward pressure on oil prices. Once again, no single person makes the decision to produce less oil. Instead, the change in oil prices sets up a chain of events that leads to the allocation of fewer resources to oil production. In fact, such a scenario was played out in 1986 and 1987. The long-term decline in the demand for oil caused oil prices to fall in 1986. Oil-drilling operations were abandoned. As fewer resources were devoted to oil production, the oil supply gradually decreased. In 1987 upward pressure on oil prices resulted from the withdrawal of resources from oil production. Higher oil prices in 1990 opened up the possibility of an increase in the oil supply over the long run if the prices were maintained. At the higher prices companies would be willing to devote more resources to oil exploration and to reexplore abandoned unprofitable oil wells.

In mid-1990, the price of oil briefly soared from $16 per barrel to over $40 per barrel as a result of Iraq's invasion of Kuwait and the trade sanctions against Iraq. By late 1990, however, increased supplies of oil from other nations caused the price of oil to fall to less than $25 per barrel. Because the price of oil was very unstable during this period, there was little incentive for major investments in new exploration.

Similarly, changes in resource prices can affect the profitability of producing certain items. For example, a decrease in the cost of fuel can make supplying air travel more profitable, causing a reallocation of resources toward air travel services. As shown in Box 3, a decrease in fuel prices increases the supply of air travel offered between two points: New York and San Francisco. The increase in supply lowers the price, and the decrease in input prices allows more profits to be made on this route. As firms compete for the extra profit, supply increases. In Box 3 you can see that the increase in supply lowers the airfare from $300 to $200. As a result of the lower price, the number of passenger-miles of travel demanded on this route increases from 3 million to 4 million per year.

Similarly, an improvement in technology can increase the supply of a good by lowering costs and increasing profit opportunities. For example, as the supply of personal computers, VCRs, and microwave ovens increased in response to the profit opportunities, their prices fell and the quantities demanded increased.

Changes in price signal changes in scarcity or demand, and both business firms and households respond by altering their choices. Later in the book, to gain more insight into the workings of the price system, we'll study the decisions made by business managers selling in competitive markets.

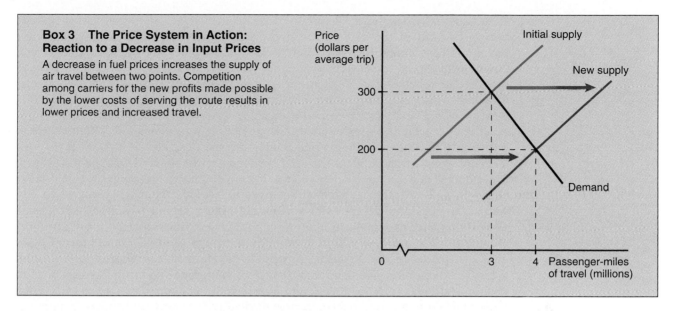

**Box 3   The Price System in Action:
Reaction to a Decrease in Input Prices**

A decrease in fuel prices increases the supply of air travel between two points. Competition among carriers for the new profits made possible by the lower costs of serving the route results in lower prices and increased travel.

How the Price System Influences Production Methods

The pursuit of profit also influences *how* goods and services are produced. Business firms can earn more profit by producing any given quantity of goods and services at lower cost. Managers therefore try to use the *least costly* techniques to supply a given quantity of goods. If they don't, their competitors will, resulting in lower costs that will enable rival firms to profitably increase supply. There will then be downward pressure on prices, which will make it more difficult for a firm using older techniques to enjoy a profit.

Entrepreneurs seek opportunities for profit by developing new techniques that lower costs in much the same way that they seize opportunities to earn additional profit by responding to changes in consumer demands. Once again, prices, in this case those of inputs, play an important role in entrepreneurial and managerial decisions. For example, an increase in the price of labor services is likely to induce firms to look for ways to reduce labor use. If wages paid to farm workers increase, farm operators will find it more attractive to switch to mechanized harvesting and cultivation. During the 1970s wages paid to agricultural workers increased substantially in states producing tobacco. As a result, tobacco growers shifted to a new mechanized method of harvesting.

Entrepreneurs can also make more profit by devising less costly methods of production. For example, Henry Ford developed mass production techniques that enabled him to sell automobiles at much lower prices than those of his competitors. These innovative methods expanded the market for automobiles, and soon competing sellers adopted similar techniques. In this way innovation in production methods resulted in the allocation of more resources to the production of automobiles. Similarly, in the 1980s some steelmakers in the United States began using scrap steel instead of blast furnaces to produce steel directly from iron ore and coal. This method, used in small mills, allowed cost reductions in steel production. As a result, there was more investment in the so-called mini-mills and less investment in the larger "integrated" steel mills as profit opportunities in the mini-mills expanded.

Who Gets the Goods and Services?

Who gets what in the capitalist system? Remember that in such a system your income is determined by your labor skills and the other economic resources you possess and choose to sell at market prices. Your ability to buy goods and services in product markets therefore depends on your ability to register a demand for products. Remember also that demand is much more than the desire for an item. Demand is desire that can be *backed up* with the willingness and ability to pay. It is on this basis that the price system allocates goods and services among consumers. Your ability to pay in turn depends chiefly on your money income.

People who are poorly skilled, lack funds, and own no land or capital will have low incomes in a pure market economy. They will receive low wages for their labor and will have no other economic resources to provide them with income to buy goods and services. People whose skills are highly valued will earn high wages. People who have accumulated funds through saving or inheritance, and are fortunate enough to own land and capital, will enjoy nonlabor income. Entrepreneurs often earn spectacular incomes if their profitable innovations allow them to accumulate a great deal of capital. The market system can't guarantee support and sustenance to people who don't (or can't) work and who have no economic resources aside from their own labor. As you can see, income inequality is a likely occurrence in a market economy.

A Recap: The Price System in Motion

Given the ownership of economic resources, the market system is driven by prices. Changes in prices or technology signal changes in opportunities for private gain. The market system is dynamic in the sense that the pursuit of gain results in changes in resource use as economic conditions change. Profits and personal gain fuel the system, while competition keeps it on course. Profitable innovations are inevitably copied. As long as profit is possible from making more of a good available in a market, supply will increase and prices will fall. The competition for profit eventually lowers prices and results in the elimination of profits. Competition eliminates profits after they have served the purpose of allocating resources to uses that are in the greatest demand.

CONCEPT CHECK
□

- Explain how resource use will be affected when the demand for gasoline decreases. Who makes the decisions to reallocate resources in a market system?

- An advance in technology lowers the cost of producing personal computers. How is this change communicated to consumers by the price system?

- How does the price system influence personal incomes?

SOME COMMON DEFECTS IN THE PRICE SYSTEM

The picture of the pure market economy painted earlier assumes that all useful goods and services can be sold in markets for a profit. However, such services as environmental protection, national defense, and police and fire protection are hard to sell by the unit in a market. You can't buy cleaner air and national security the way you can buy bread by the loaf! If we relied on competing sellers to produce these useful goods for profit in a competitive market, it's possible that none of them would be made available. For this reason people often find it convenient to have goods like national defense made available through government. The quantity and means of financing these goods are then determined politically by voters.

Public Goods and Externalities

Public goods are those consumed equally by all of us, whether we pay or not. Environmental protection and national security are good examples of public goods because they benefit all of us, regardless of whether we pay. Because we can't rely on competing sellers to provide public goods, revenue to make them available can be obtained only through a sharing arrangement such as taxation. In the modern mixed economy, we rely on government to provide roads, military defense, air traffic control, and many other public goods. In fact, purchases of economic resources by governments to provide various services amount to 20 percent of the value of all goods and services produced in the United States.

In a nutshell, one common problem in a pure market economy is that not all the goods we want and are willing to pay for can easily be sold in neat packages that can be priced. The market often fails to provide public goods even though net gains are possible from doing so.

A related problem with the price system is that production or consumption of goods and services often results in costs or benefits to people other than the buyers and sellers. For example, if a firm disposes of wastes in a stream, it imposes costs on people who want to use the stream for swimming, fishing, and drinking water. It's not easy to put a price on economic resources like streams, the ocean, and the atmosphere when these resources are used as convenient receptacles for industrial wastes. When natural resources that no single person owns are used to dispose of harmful waste products, the result is pollution. The inability to charge for the use of the environment as a waste dump often results in the degradation of air and water quality.

Externalities are costs or benefits of market transactions that are not reflected in the prices buyers and sellers use to make their decisions. For example, aircraft noise in a neighborhood near an airport is a *negative* externality (or external cost) of the transaction between airlines and their passengers. Insofar as you and other college students make all members of society better off by improving the quality of life, transactions between college students and the university result in *positive* externalities (external benefits) to third parties. Externalities prevail because the use of resources like streams and the air, or the external benefits resulting from education, can't easily be priced. To understand the failure of the price system to allocate resources efficiently when externalities exist, we first need to examine the prerequisites for market exchange.

Externalities and Resource Use

Buyers and sellers in competitive markets seek personal gains through market transactions. If no one other than the buyers and sellers is harmed or benefited by these transactions, then those personal gains will be the only gains in the society at large. However, when externalities prevail, there are *third parties* in addition to the buyers or sellers who are affected by market transactions. For example, suppose pollution from the purchase and use of gasoline makes people other than the buyers or sellers worse off by impairing their health. Part of the cost of making gasoline available is the impaired health of those harmed by pollution. The market prices of gasoline are *too low* because they are not based on *all* the costs of making gasoline available. In this case the price system fails to price a valuable environmental resource, and consequently a negative externality prevails.

public goods goods that are consumed equally by everyone, whether they pay or not.

externalities costs or benefits of market transactions that are not reflected in the prices buyers and sellers use to make their decisions.

Box 4   The Impact of Charges for Environmental Damage to Third Parties

A charge for pollution damage decreases the supply of gasoline and increases its market equilibrium price. After the charge is imposed, the quantity of gasoline demanded declines.

Similarly, you might not consider the fact that when you buy a particular item you benefit some third party other than you and the seller. For example, if you buy a smoke detector, you benefit your neighbors by reducing the risk of fire that can spread to their homes. The third parties in this case benefit from your purchase of the good but aren't charged for the benefit they receive. In this case the price system fails to price a benefit to third parties to a market transaction.

When a negative externality prevails, the unit and marginal costs that sellers consider in deciding quantity supplied are lower than the actual marginal costs because the sellers aren't charged for the damage they cause to third parties. As a result, the sellers produce more than they would if they were charged for the external costs they impose. If it were possible to price the use of the resources that are used free of charge, such as air or water, the marginal cost of any given output would increase. This increase in cost would cause sellers to decrease the supply of the product, and as a result price would increase. As a consequence of the higher price, the quantity of the good demanded would decline. For example, if the emissions of harmful pollutants resulting from the production of gasoline could be measured, sellers could be charged according to the damage the emissions cause. These charges would increase the sellers' marginal cost and would therefore decrease supply, resulting in an increase in price. The charges would also induce the sellers to change their productive methods to reduce the harmful emissions.

In the Box 4 graph you can see how charges for emitting damaging wastes affect the market for goods whose production or use causes such emissions. Suppose that when the externality prevails, the market equilibrium for gasoline corresponds to point E_1. At that equilibrium the price is $1 per gallon and 5 million gallons are sold. When sellers are charged for the damage they cause to third parties, they now have to include a previously unpriced input (the air) as part of the cost of producing and using gasoline. This results in a decrease in supply. The new market equilibrium is now at E_2, and the price of gasoline rises to $1.40 per gallon. As a consequence,

principles in practice

Property Rights, Transaction Costs, and Pricing

As a buyer, you have an incentive to buy something only if you're assured that you'll get certain benefits when you actually pay the price to purchase it. *Property rights* are privileges to use or own goods, services, and economic resources. As a consumer, you acquire property rights when you make market purchases. Similarly, sellers are induced to offer items for sale because they know they have the right to transfer the items in exchange for payments from buyers. *Markets can be established only for items for which property rights can be guaranteed and easily exchanged.* If you know you can enjoy the right to cleaner air and other public goods without purchasing that right from someone else, you have little incentive to pay a price for them. You'd scoff at an opportunity to buy the Brooklyn Bridge or an acre of the ocean because you know those items can't be bought. You'll engage in market transactions only when you can gain by obtaining something of value. Similarly, you'd be unwilling to invest in the production of a good if those who refused to pay for the good could obtain property rights of use or ownership. For example, the incentives to produce cable television programming for sale are affected by the ease with which those who don't pay can be prevented from benefiting from its availability. If all viewers can receive the programs even if they don't pay, sellers will have no incentive to make cable TV available.

If people are to be motivated to engage in market transactions, resources must be devoted to establishing and enforcing property rights. *Transaction costs* are those incurred in enforcing property rights, locating trading partners, and actually carrying out the transactions. Transaction costs are associated with exchanging, rather than producing, goods and services. One transaction cost to enforce property rights is the cost of scrambling satellite transmissions of television programs by firms like HBO. Examples of transaction costs to locate trading partners and carry out transactions are advertising and brokerage fees, the salaries of sales personnel, and the costs of transporting goods to and from the point of sale.

High transaction costs can prevent markets from being organized for the exchange of items. For example, the right to use the ocean for fishing is rarely sold in a market. Exclusive ownership rights to the use of the ocean can't be granted to a particular seller in ways that allow the ocean to be rented out to others for payment. Even if such rights were granted, the ocean is so vast that the seller would have to invest in a fleet of sophisticated vessels to monitor use. The high cost of actually enforcing these rights would make it infeasible to actually sell them in a market.

The concepts of property rights and transaction costs are intertwined. The establishment of property rights to own or use goods or services depends on the transaction costs of guaranteeing those rights. Government plays an important role in markets by using its power to guarantee and enforce agreements to exchange property rights. In effect, the government is the silent partner in all market transactions because its system of courts and police power is used to guarantee property rights acquired in market exchanges and to settle disputes concerning such exchanges. The effectiveness of government in establishing and facilitating the exchange of property rights is crucial to the smooth functioning of markets.

In addition, changes in technology often reduce transaction costs, thereby providing gains from market exchanges of new goods and services. For example, the right to park on city streets wasn't priced until the development of the parking meter.

But even that advance in technology can be further improved. New York City has over 60,000 parking meters that produce income of more than $30 million in coins annually. However, the city incurs nearly $2 million in transaction costs for collecting the coins and $8 million for maintaining the meters. It is currently considering replacing its meters with a new electronic meter that will be operated by a card similar to those used to operate gates at parking lots.* The card would be purchased at newsstands and convenience stores. Instead of putting coins in the meter, parkers would simply insert their electronically coded card. At the end of the month, each motorist would receive a bill in the mail for parking fees.

Another approach the city is considering is simply to abolish the meters. Instead, drivers would be required to buy disposable electric timers giving them the right to 10 hours of parking time. These timers would be displayed in their windshields.

* See James Brooke, "Time Is Running Out for the Coin-Operated Parking Meter," *The New York Times*, September 7, 1986.

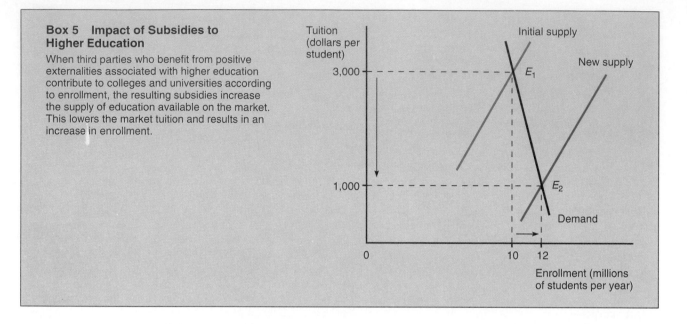

Box 5   Impact of Subsidies to Higher Education

When third parties who benefit from positive externalities associated with higher education contribute to colleges and universities according to enrollment, the resulting subsidies increase the supply of education available on the market. This lowers the market tuition and results in an increase in enrollment.

quantity demanded declines to 4 million gallons per year. Reducing the emissions provides benefits to third parties and results in more efficient resource use. Sellers must consider the marginal cost of emissions as well as other costs when choosing output. However, because they're now charged for the emissions, the price of gasoline goes up. Without such charges, the price of the product doesn't reflect the entire cost of producing it or using it, and more of the product is sold than would be sold if the price reflected all the costs.

Similarly, when a positive externality prevails, the sale of a good benefits someone other than the buyer or seller. If it were possible to charge these third parties for the benefit they receive, the seller could use the funds obtained to reduce the cost of making the good available. Such a subsidy to output would increase the gain from selling it and result in an increase in supply. The increase in supply would lower the price to buyers and increase the quantity demanded. For example, tuition is subsidized by citizens' taxes at state-supported schools. Taxpaying residents are third parties who eventually enjoy external benefits from students' education. Their tax dollars are used to lower tuition costs and increase the supply of higher-education services.

Box 5 shows you the impact of subsidies to encourage consumption of a good whose use results in a positive externality. When there are no means for third parties to contribute to the cost of higher education, the market equilibrium corresponds to point E_1. The corresponding tuition per year is $3,000, and the number of students enrolling in colleges and universities is 10 million. After third-party subsidies to higher education (such as the tax revenues a state government gives its colleges), the supply of higher-education services increases and the new market equilibrium corresponds to E_2. At that point the tuition per student declines to $1,000 per year and the number of students enrolled increases to 12 million per year. In the absence of any means for third parties to contribute toward the cost of higher education from which they benefit, the market devotes less than the efficient amount of resources to higher education.

In a later chapter we'll discuss the policies government employs to deal with externalities. We'll also analyze the consequences of current government regulations designed to cope with market failure resulting from externalities.

Other Common Problems in a Market System

There are other problems that are common in a market system. Three of the most important are lack of competition, income inequality and poverty, and instability.

Lack of Competition   Markets are not always free and competitive. In noncompetitive markets there are barriers that prevent gains from being achieved. For example, suppose there's only one seller of eggs in a market and that it's impossible for additional sellers to enter the market. Buyers now have only one source of supply. Additional sellers who might be able to gain by making more eggs available at the profitable price set by the single seller are prevented from doing so. Under these conditions, the seller who monopolizes the supply can control the price to buyers who have no other source of supply.

Lack of adequate competition impairs the ability of the price system to respond to changes in demand. Monopolization of supply prevents profits from serving as a signal for entry of new firms and more output in markets in which additional output would be profitable.

Income Inequality and Poverty   In a pure market economy income depends entirely on the quantity, quality, and types of resources people are willing and able to sell. Income influences willingness and ability to pay for goods. People with very low incomes may be unable to buy the minimal amounts of goods and services required for their survival. If a large number of people in the economy lack the skills that would enable them to earn labor income and the ownership of capital and land is concentrated in the hands of a few wealthy individuals, the masses will be poor, while an elite class will earn most of the income.

In the United States, for example, the top 20 percent of families ranked according to income account for nearly half of all the income earned each year. On the other hand, the poorest 20 percent earn less than 4 percent of the nation's annual income. As you can see, the gap between the rich and the poor is vast.

Many critics of the pure market economy argue that its outcomes can't be given high marks on the basis of normative criteria for evaluating income distribution, even when the results of market exchange rank high in terms of efficiency criteria. The paradox of poverty in the midst of wealth is a common criticism of the performance of the capitalist economy. In 1990, an astounding 13.5 percent of the U.S. population was estimated to have money income inadequate to attain minimum acceptable living standards. In a later chapter we'll discuss income distribution in the United States and government policies to influence it.

Instability   When markets react to changes in demand or supply, it often takes a considerable amount of time for them to achieve equilibrium again. For example, fluctuations in the demand for products result in fluctuations in the demand for labor. A decrease in demand for labor is likely during a recession. Market wages don't always decline quickly enough to eliminate the labor surplus that occurs at the initial wage after the decrease in demand. As a result, during recessions there is excessive unemployment.

Similarly, prices are sometimes quite unstable and subject to sharp and unpredictable increases. Unpredictable inflation of the price level can make planning for the future difficult and can result in price changes that distort the way we conduct our daily affairs. For example, fear of future price increases can cause us to stock up on certain items. By stocking up, we further increase the demand for those items, thereby putting more upward pressure on prices.

Fluctuations in demand and supply and consequent periods of market disequilibrium are an inherent problem that results from lack of coordination of decision making in the price system. Governments often regulate markets and seek to influence the demand for products and loanable funds in attempts to correct market instability.

CONCEPT CHECK
□

- Why is it difficult to establish a price for certain useful goods and services?
- What are externalities?

- Make a list of problems likely to prevail in an economy that relies exclusively on markets to allocate economic resources.

THE MODERN MIXED AND OPEN ECONOMY

The shortcomings of a pure market economy have led to the evolution of the modern mixed economy. When markets do a poor job of allocating resources, we look to government to improve matters. The impact of government on resource use and income distribution is a controversial question that we'll address in many parts of the book. However, the fact is that neither the United States nor any other nation can be regarded as having a purely capitalist economy.

In the United States the federal, state, and local governments levy taxes on both businesses and households to finance the provision of public goods and services. Governments also borrow funds to help meet their expenses. Finally, governments intervene in decisions made by households and business managers to protect environmental resources, prevent restraints on competition in markets, and correct for failures of the price system to account for the property rights of third parties to market transactions.

Governments in the United States acquire resources to provide hospital and health services, provide free and compulsory elementary and secondary education, assist the poor in maintaining minimum standards of living, provide for the national defense, and make pension and insurance services available to the elderly and other groups. About 20 percent of all workers in the United States are employed by governments.

The U.S. government supports the prices of some agricultural products. Government regulations influence the quality of such products as automobiles and new drugs, and through various taxes governments affect the prices of gasoline, cigarettes, and alcoholic beverages. Governments provide the legal structure that facilitates market transactions. Finally, governments seek to stabilize the general level of economic activity to correct for the difficulty that the price system often encounters in maintaining stable prices and full employment of labor and other economic resources.

Government and the Economy
Box 6 shows how government fits into the circular flow of expenditure and income. Governments participate in input markets by purchasing labor services and other productive resources. They also borrow funds from credit markets when their expenditures exceed their tax revenues. Governments also participate in product markets

Box 6   The Mixed Economy

In a mixed economy, governments compete in input markets and product markets to obtain the resources and products they need to supply goods and services. Governments obtain funds to finance their operations by taxing households and business firms and by borrowing in credit markets. Governments use some of their revenues to provide income support to the elderly, the poor, and other groups and also to subsidize some business firms.

to purchase the output of business firms. They purchase such goods as paper, aircraft, and machinery, and they contract with construction firms to build roads and structures. The vertical arrows in Box 6 show how governments participate in markets and provide income to workers, resource owners, and business firms.

The horizontal arrows show how governments tax households and businesses to obtain the funds necessary to purchase products and hire input services. The inputs and products are used to provide government goods and services that benefit both households and business firms. Governments provide national defense, education, police and fire protection, and a host of other services to the public at no direct charge. Most government goods and services are not sold by the unit in markets. Instead, governments make their goods and services available freely as public goods or establish criteria for the eligibility of individuals to obtain certain services. For example, government funds are used to provide income support to eligible persons. Social Security pensions, welfare payments to the poor, veterans' benefits, payments for medical care, and unemployment insurance payments are examples of government income-support programs financed by taxation. Finally, governments provide subsidies to business firms such as price support payments to farmers and loan guarantees.

open economy an economy linked to the rest of the world through international trade.

By bidding for resources, providing income support for the elderly, the poor, and veterans, subsidizing certain activities, and taxing businesses and households, governments influence market demand and affect prices. Thus, in the mixed economy governments, as well as households and business firms, influence resource allocation.

the global economy

International Trade

We have one more building block to set in place to get a full view of the modern economy. An **open economy** is one that is linked to the rest of the world through international input, product, foreign exchange, and credit markets. The United States and virtually all other nations today have open economies, although most nations place at least some government restrictions on international trade. Business firms export some of their products to buyers in the rest of the world. Similarly, American households, businesses, and even governments buy imported products. American businesses also own and operate production facilities abroad and regularly purchase foreign assets. At the same time, foreign businesses and individuals own and operate productive facilities in the United States and regularly supply funds to American credit markets. Box 7 provides a schematic view of the international links between the United States and the rest of the world. No nation today is self-sufficient. As we pointed out in the prologue to this book, international linkages are becoming more and more important to the functioning of the U.S. economy.

Exports are a source of revenue for American business firms. They provide income to workers and other resource owners whose services are used to produce exported goods and services. When we im-

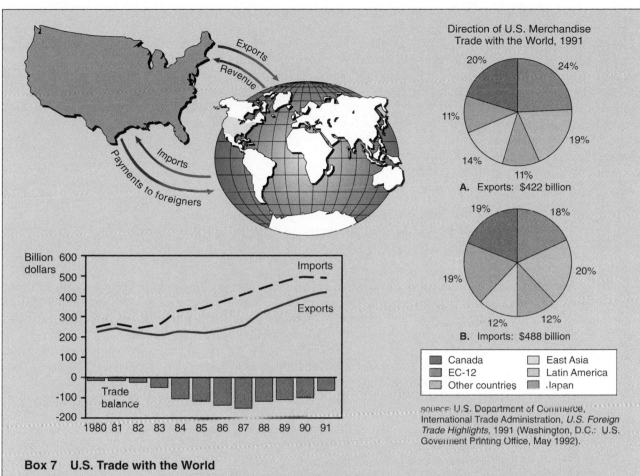

Direction of U.S. Merchandise
Trade with the World, 1991

20%   24%
11%
19%
14%
11%
A. Exports: $422 billion

19%   18%
19%   20%
12%   12%
B. Imports: $488 billion

■ Canada   □ East Asia
■ EC-12   □ Latin America
□ Other countries ▨ Japan

SOURCE: U.S. Department of Commerce,
International Trade Administration, *U.S. Foreign
Trade Highlights*, 1991 (Washington, D.C.: U.S.
Government Printing Office, May 1992).

Box 7   U.S. Trade with the World

In an open economy, some output of business firms is exported providing them with revenue from sales in foreign markets. Imports result in payments by U.S. citizens to foreign producers. Both imports and exports have been growing in importance for the U.S. economy. Our major trading partners are the 12 European Community nations (EC-12), Canada, Japan, and nations in Latin America and East Asia.

port goods and services, we place dollars in the hands of foreigners. When we import a greater dollar volume of products than we export, we place more dollars in the hands of foreigners than they return to us and there will be a deficit in the balance of trade. Under such circumstances, foreign holders of dollars choose to save or invest those funds in the United States by acquiring U.S. assets such as real estate, bonds, and bank deposits denominated in dollars. In effect, if we import more than we export, as has been the case in recent years, we must borrow from foreigners to make up the difference. Foreign saving

and investment in the United States grew rapidly in the 1980s because of a persistent balance-of-trade deficit.

Of course, it is also possible for a nation to incur a balance-of-trade surplus. In this instance the value of goods and services exported exceeds the value of imports. If the United States were to have a balance-of-trade surplus, it would earn more foreign currency than it uses to import goods and services during the year. The excess foreign currency would be saved and invested in foreign nations. In effect, the United States would be a net lender to the rest of the world.

Also shown in Box 7 is the upward trend in the dollar volume of both U.S. exports and imports from 1980 to 1991. Notice that the balance of trade has been negative throughout the period illustrated. Japan, Canada, and 12 nations of the European Community (EC) were the major customers for U.S. merchandise exports, accounting for 55 percent of the value of our exports, while 56 percent of the value of our imports came from the same group of nations. The pie charts in Box 7 show the direction of our trade with various trading partners.

The total share of both domestic production exported and of domestic income used to purchase imports has increased substantially in the United States since 1960. Also, because we have had a chronic balance-of-trade deficit for a number of years, foreigners have increased their holdings of U.S. assets. We will discuss international linkages between the U.S. economy and the rest of the world regularly in the following chapters.

CONCLUSION: ECONOMIC ACTIVITY AND ECONOMIC DECISIONS

The price system operates to influence resource allocation through a complex of input and product markets. Households and businesses operate rationally in these markets by weighing the marginal benefits and marginal costs of their actions. Citizens vote and engage in political activity to influence government policies. People like you are players in the economy, and each decision of these players is linked to others through the price system. The U.S. economy itself is linked to the rest of the world through international trade and international markets. Economic decisions by market participants affect both prices and the overall performance of the economy. As firms, households, and governments conduct their business in markets, their decisions are, in turn, affected by prices.

In the modern mixed and open economy, businesses must compete with foreign sellers in both domestic and global markets. Competition helps keep prices as low as possible over the long run.

The flow of production and income in the economy is affected by household saving and spending decisions, including decisions to purchase imported products. Government spending and taxing decisions also affect the level of economic activity. Finally, total production, income, and economic growth are closely intertwined with business investment decisions and the effectiveness with which domestic firms compete with foreign sellers.

As you can now see, the flows and interrelationships among American households, business firms, governments, and their counterparts in the rest of the world are quite complex. Ideally, we would like to see production and, therefore, income grow steadily each year. When production and income grow over time (after adjustment for inflation) more rapidly than population increases, then output and income per capita rise, contributing to higher living standards.

Later in the book we will study in greater detail the way the economy and its sectors operate. You'll see how the complex of markets comprised by the economy fit together. As we go through microeconomic analysis of production, consumption, and markets, you'll be in a better position to comprehend how the decisions of households, businesses, and resource owners work through the price system and how government acts to try to correct for the defects of the price system. As we discuss macroeconomics, you'll begin to understand the forces that influence economic growth, unemployment, and inflation in the mixed and open economy.

insights on issues

How Shall We Use Our Resources and Capabilities? Talking with Douglas Holtz-Eakin

A professor at Syracuse University, Douglas Holtz-Eakin received his undergraduate degree in mathematics and economics from Denison University and his Ph.D. from Princeton. He was born in 1958 in Bulter, Pennsylvania. Professor Holtz-Eakin recently focused on the study of state and local government spending on infrastructure. He served as a staff economist for the Council of Economic Advisers.

What aspects of resource use are likely to be public-policy issues as we approach the year 2000? Four key issues of public policy for the near future are (1) tax policy and international transactions, (2) health care, (3) worker training and education, and (4) urban issues, especially the decay of the large central cities. In vesting in the flexibility of our work-

ers will be this country's best social safety net.

How will the movement away from defense spending affect the economy? I believe the effects of the peace dividend will be minor. Real defense spending has been declining since 1986, so basically we've had the peace dividend already. The economy is a lot more flexible than we give it credit for. While restructuring away from military spending can be very hard on some individuals, it just won't have that large an effect on the big picture.

Are we overspending on health care? Underspending? The amount the government spends on health care seems about right in total. But we need to reallocate away from expensive end-stage procedures and toward covering the population comprehensively.

Are we underinvesting in public infrastructure? No. More spending on infrastructure might improve the quality of life, but it wouldn't boost productivity. Increased highway spending, for example, would not increase productivity much; our highways already are in good enough shape to carry products

where they need to go in a timely fashion. However, more spending on parks and other public facilities would make our lives better, which is a legitimate goal of public policy.

Does the government's spending and tax policy cause distortions in resource use? Absolutely. The most systematic biases involve the taxation of capital income. The tax code has been made far too intricate in an attempt to fine-tune the economy. We need to reorient the tax code to tax consumption, not income (a solution that would be politically unattractive, but administratively effective). We try to tax labor and income and returns on savings and investment, but the fact is we don't know how to measure such returns. For example, what is the value of a patent?

Should we be devoting more resources toward environmental protection? Because of the large-scale use of mandate and regulations, it is difficult to gauge the exact cost of our current policies. It would be useful to follow the lead of the permit-trading premises of the Clean Air Act, at a minimum.

SUMMARY

1. Capitalism is characterized by private ownership of economic resources and freedom of enterprise in competitive markets. the people who manage and assume the risks of business enterprises in a capitalist economy are its entrepreneurs.

2. Under capitalism, economic rivalry tempers market power. When economic rivalry prevails there are large numbers of buyers competing for available supplies of goods and services offered by large numbers of sellers. No single buyer or seller can make an item significantly more abundant or scarce so as to influence its price in a market. Free markets have no restrictions to prevent the entry or exit of buyers or sellers.

3. In modern economies people tend to specialize in specific productive endeavors. The resulting division of labor makes people dependent on each other to obtain items that they choose not to produce for themselves.

4. Mutual gains from exchange are possible when the minimum amount of goods or money a person will accept in trade for an item is less than the maximum amount a trading partner will surrender in exchange for that item.

5. In modern economies most exchange involves trades of money for goods (or services) rather than barter of goods for goods (or services). Barter is inconvenient because it requires double coincidence of wants.

6. In a market economy there is a circular flow of income and expenditure. Business firms employ economic resources offered for sale in input markets. The payments they make for the resources constitute income to members of the economy's households. Households use their income to buy goods and services offered for sale in markets by business firms.

7. The price system is the mechanism by which resource use is guided by prices in a market economy. Price changes occur in response to shifts in demand and supply. They affect the opportunities for personal gain in market transactions and result in resource reallocation until no further gain is possible. In this way prices guide what is produced and influence business managers' choice of production methods.

8. The amounts of goods and services you can enjoy depend on your money income, which you use to back up your desire for goods and services insofar as your income influences your ability to pay. Your money income is determined by the prices of the services or economic resources you have and are willing to sell.

9. Public goods are those consumed equally by all of us, whether we pay or not.

10. The price system fails when some goods people want and are willing to pay for can't be easily packaged into units that can be priced. Market exchange is feasible only for items for which property rights can be guaranteed and easily exchanged.

11. Externalities are costs or benefits of market transactions not reflected in market prices. Externalities are indicative of market failure to price the use of valuable resources.

12. Markets are not always competitive. For example, one or several buyers or sellers can control price in a market if entry into the market is limited. This can prevent the market from achieving allocative efficiency.

13. A market economy often results in significant poverty if the distribution of skills and ownership of capital is unequal. People with low incomes because of lack of marketable resources will live in poverty unless they receive assistance from charities or government authorities. In the early 1990s in the United States 13.5 percent of the population was classified as living in poverty.

14. In the modern mixed economy, governments supply goods and services and can use their power to attempt to correct for the shortcomings of the price system.

15. An open economy is linked to the rest of the world through international trade. International trade has become increasingly more important for the U.S. economy since 1980. Both exports and imports have grown. However, exports have fallen short of imports throughout the 1980s and early 1990s.

KEY TERMS

capitalism *104*
mixed economy *104*
price system *104*
free markets *104*
barter *106*
public goods *113*
externalities *113*
open economy *120*

CONCEPT REVIEW

1. How does specialization and exchange in markets contribute to providing additional gains from an existing amount of production?

2. How do prices and profit act in a capitalist economy as signals to allocate resources to the uses in which they are of highest value?

3. Why are public goods unlikely to be supplied in free markets?

4. What do we mean when we describe the United States as a mixed and open economy?

PROBLEMS AND APPLICATIONS

1. Suppose you start a new business distributing software for personal computers. The business proves to be extremely profitable. Explain how freedom of enterprise and economic rivalry are likely to come into play in a market economy in a way that will eventually reduce the profits of your business. **[1]**

2. The marginal benefit of a good represents the sum of money a consumer is willing and able to pay for one more unit of the good. The marginal cost of a good represents the minimum sum of money a seller is willing to accept to make more of the good available. Suppose the marginal benefit of color televisions is $200, while the marginal cost is only $100. Assuming that the marginal benefit of color TVs declines and the marginal cost increases as more are made available, show that more color TVs must be sold to achieve all possible mutual gains from exchange. **[1]**

3. An economy is producing a mix of food and clothing that corresponds to a point on, instead of within, its production possibilities curve. Explain how it's possible for this economy to achieve further net gains even though the economy is on its production possibilities curve. **[1]**

4. Use supply and demand analysis to show how an increase in the demand for four-wheel-drive recreational vehicles accompanied by a decrease in the demand for standard full-size passenger cars will affect resource allocation in the automobile industry. **[2]**

5. During the energy crisis of the early 1970s, the price of smaller cars actually increased above the price of gas-guzzling full-size models. How did the American automobile industry react to the change in prices? What do you expect will happen to the kinds of cars made available if the supply of gas increases substantially in the 1990s to push the price down permanently to an average of 75 cents per gallon? **[2]**

6. Use supply and demand analysis to trace out the impact of a sharp reduction in the price of electronic components on the price, use, and profitability of producing goods that use electronic components as inputs. What effect is the change in price likely to have on production techniques? **[2]**

7. Your parents own 1,000 acres of land. The land is in the flight path to an airport, and planes regularly fly over it as they make their approach to the airport. Why can't your parents charge the airlines for using their airspace? **[3]**

8. You plan to sell your bicycle at the end of the year when you graduate. You'd like to get $100 for it. List the transaction costs you must incur to find a buyer. Under what circumstances might you be better off giving the bike away instead of trying to sell it? **[2], [3]**

9. A firm that manufactures paper products dumps its wastes into a stream and doesn't pay for the right to do so. The stream is used by fishermen and boaters as a source of recreational enjoyment. The waste products dumped into the stream make it less useful for recreation. Explain why an externality exists, and identify the groups involved in the externality. In what sense is there a failure of the price system in this case? **[3]**

10. Make a list of the goods and services provided to you by governments. List the shortcomings of the pure market economy that each of these government goods and services is designed to correct. **[3]**

career profiles

Rhonda Williams "How economists understand human behavior has a major impact on our culture," says Rhonda Williams, an assistant professor jointly in the economics and Afro-American studies departments at the University of Maryland. "Economics must constantly be critiqued because it can be too confining, but it's a good lens through which to begin your critical thinking."

Williams became interested in economics at the early age of eight, when her family moved to Athens, Ohio, for her father's job as a professor at Ohio University. The move exposed her to rural white poverty in Appalachia. "I had already learned something about black poverty through my parents' work in the civil rights movement," she recalls. "But now I saw that even some of my white classmates lived in shacks and had no dental care. This led me to think about systematic inequality and the question of where wealth comes from."

This early interest was followed in due time by an undergraduate degree in economics from Harvard and a Ph.D. from the Massachusetts Institute of Technology in 1983. Williams's first teaching job was at the University of Texas at Austin. She then taught both at Yale and at the New School for Social Research in New York City. When she accepted her current job, she says, "I was glad to be back at a state institution. It was a conscious choice on my part due to the composition of the student body—more blacks and more students from working-class backgrounds."

Williams knew early in her college years that she wanted to be a teacher/scholar. "I'm at the more privileged end of the teaching spectrum," she observes. "I spend about 30 percent of my time teaching, 30 percent on professional activities, and the balance on research." She's enthusiastic about her current research project, a National Science Foundation–funded empirical analysis of race/gender job competition and interindustry wage differentials. So far she's spent four years on the theoretical research and nearly a year building the data set. "It's a slow process, but it's rewarding to be able to do work that is both interesting and important to me as a political economist," Williams says.

Her professional activities keep her quite busy too. Williams is a member of the economic policy task force of the Joint Center for Political and Economic Studies and of the pay equity advisory committee of the Institute for Women's Policy Research. She also served on the board of directors of the National Economic Association and is on the board of editors of the journal *Feminist Studies*. And she still finds time to write articles for a number of other journals, as well as organizing and speaking at conferences.

As for the third aspect of her career, Williams continues to enjoy teaching. "I consider education an active political process," she explains. Whether her students are conducting a voter registration drive or simply watching TV, she believes their knowledge of economics gives them an awareness of the contradictions and conflicts in what they observe and a sensitivity to change.

Williams opines that the most useful traits for master's or Ph.D. candidates in economics are self-confidence and good analytical skills. They should realize the university is as political as other major institutions where they will face the power plays, sexism, and racism endemic to hierarchies, so negotiating skills will also be useful. "Advanced study of political economics will help you put the world in context," she says.

inside information

Getting Information on Financial and Commodity Markets Do you own any shares of stock? Have you ever traveled to a foreign country? Are you interested in learning about ways to make money? If so, you'll be interested in the functioning of the financial and commodity markets that we will discuss in this part of the book.

If you want to follow the markets on a daily basis, you can look in your daily paper. You will be able to get most stock and mutual-fund prices in the financial section. If you're interested in the price of precious metals you can track the prices of gold, silver, and platinum.

Specialized newspapers have more detailed information than most regular daily papers. Two of the best are *Barron's* and *The Wall Street Journal*. The "Money & Investing" section of *The Wall Street Journal* is a major source of daily market information for thousands of businesses

and private investors. On the left side of this section's first page is a series of graphs and tables that show market trends based on the Dow Jones Industrial Average, the Standard & Poor's 500, and NASDAQ, as well as trends in prices on the London and Tokyo stock exchanges. You'll find data on bond prices and interest rates as well as the U.S. dollar's price against 15 major world currencies. Also in this section are recent prices of gold, West Texas intermediate crude oil, wheat, and steers.

Naturally, as you would expect for a newspaper like *The Wall Street Journal*, you will find a wealth of information on stocks, bonds, and mutual funds; but you will also find detailed information on commodities and foreign exchange rates. For example, the "Currency Trading" column will give you the U.S. equivalent for the currencies of nearly 50 countries and also will show you the price of foreign currency in terms of U.S. dollars. If you are traveling abroad, this is the first place to look to estimate the number of pounds, yen, or francs you'll need to purchase foreign goods and services.

Turn to the commodities section to find cash prices for grains, feeds, foods, fats and oils, fibers and textiles, regular and precious metals, and various grades of crude oil and refined petroleum products including gasoline, propane, No. 2 heating oil, and butane.

Finally, check the columns on credit markets. You can find key interest rates such as the federal funds rate (the interest rate banks pay for short-term loans from other banks) and the prime rate (the rate banks charge their most creditworthy customers). Also listed are interest rates for certificates of deposit, treasury securities, corporate bonds, municipal bonds, and mortgages. All this information, updated regularly, is in a single newspaper!

part III

Introduction to Macroeconomic Concepts

William Morris, *Compton Chintz,* 1896. Victoria and Albert Museum,
London/Art Resource, NY

CONCEPTS

Nominal and Real GDP

Aggregate Expenditure

Aggregate Real Income

Disposable Income

National Saving

Business Cycle

Contractions and Expansions

Recession

Unemployment Rate

Frictional, Structural, and
Cyclical Unemployment

Natural Rate of Unemployment
and Potential Real GDP

Price Level and Inflation

Consumer Price Index (CPI)

GDP Deflator

Nominal versus Real Income

Real Wages

Real Interest Rate

Hyperinflation

6 chapter

Gross Domestic Product and the Performance of the National Economy

If you follow the news about the economy, you know there are periods during which it appears to be bursting at the seams. At those times business firms can't keep up with orders. At other times the economy's performance is sluggish, so that inventories of unsold goods build up. When production declines in the economy, factories and offices are not fully utilized, workers are laid off, and incomes fall. The fact is your job prospects, your income, and the purchasing power of your hard-earned dollars all depend on the performance of the economy as a whole.

This part of the book shows how we measure the economy's growth and explains why a slowdown in growth, excessive unemployment, or inflation can be serious problems. In the next part of the book, we will analyze the forces that influence the performance of the economy.

In this chapter we will show how an economy's output is measured and how the elaborate National Income and Product Accounts of the United States keep track of how resources and income are used. By tracing the flows of expenditure and income through the economy, we will see how its various sectors and markets fit together and how decisions to save, invest, and allocate resources to government use influence production and income. We will also show how the U.S. economy is tied to the rest of the world through international trade.

☐ CONCEPT PREVIEW

After reading this chapter, you should be able to:

1. Explain what GDP is, how it can be viewed as the value added to intermediate products, and how real GDP differs from nominal GDP.

2. Understand why GDP must equal the sum of consumption, investment, government purchases, and net exports and how expenditure on the nation's output results in income to resource owners.

3. Explain how the concepts of gross national product, net national product, national in-come, personal income, and disposable income can be derived from GDP.

4. Understand how spending and income circulate among business firms, households, and governments and how international trade affects the economy.

5. Explain how national saving is computed and show how net foreign saving in the United States has helped finance domestic investment in recent years.

LOOKING AT THE ECONOMY FROM A MACROECONOMIC PERSPECTIVE

In Chapter 1 we defined *macroeconomics* as the study of the overall performance of the economy and the way various sectors of the economy relate to one another. Our goal in studying macroeconomics is to analyze the big issues relating to employment opportunities, inflation, and economic growth. But before we can accomplish that goal, we must have a means of measuring the performance of the economy, so we can tell how well it is doing and whether economic conditions are improving or deteriorating.

The performance of the economy depends on decisions made by millions of individuals. In macroeconomics we focus on the total value of a nation's production, ranging from safety pins to oil-drilling rigs and from haircuts to coronary bypass surgeries. Rather than looking at the purchases of one household or business firm alone, we examine influences on the total purchases of all households and all business firms. Rather than looking at production for sale in a specific market, we add up the total value of products produced during the year and offered for sale in all markets. We then show how changes in conditions of demand and supply can affect employment of workers, inflation, and growth of production and income.

During the 1930s, when the U.S. economy was performing dismally, economist Simon Kuznets helped create a system that became the basis for charting the course of the economy, for which he was later awarded a Nobel prize. The National Income and Product Accounts (NIPA) are the official system used for measuring economic activity in product and input markets in the United States. Our system of National Income and Product Accounts focuses on aggregates, which are broad totals of economic variables such as production, consumption, and investment.

The NIPA also provides information on what we're producing and which groups are reaping the rewards for producing those goods and services. It provides us with information about how much output is produced, how much income results from production, and what types of products are produced. You may be surprised to read that the bulk of the income resulting from production goes to workers and that only a very small share ends up as rents. It may not surprise you, however, to read that the United States devotes the bulk of its vast productive capability to satisfying the desires of consumers who save very little of their income.

The NIPA not only measure economic activity; they also show how households, business firms, and governments affect the flow of expenditure and income in product and input markets. We can use the accounts to discover how production influences income and how consumer spending, business investment, government policies, and international trade affect current and future output.

MEASURING AGGREGATE OUTPUT: GROSS DOMESTIC PRODUCT

In reading the newspapers and watching television news reports, you have probably been exposed to the term *gross domestic product,* the cornerstone of our system of National Income and Product Accounts. Gross domestic product (GDP) is the market value of the final goods and services produced by workers and other resources located within the borders of a nation over a period of one year. The goods and services whose values are included in GDP are the nation's final products that are sold to final users and not used as materials, parts, or services to be incorporated in the value of other items that are to be resold. Included in GDP is the value of domestic output produced by foreign workers with jobs in the United States and by foreign-owned property located within the borders of the nation. For example, the

National Income and Product Accounts (NIPA) the official system of accounting used to measure the flows of income and expenditure in the United States.

aggregates broad totals of economic variables such as production, consumption, and investment.

1

gross domestic product (GDP) the market value of the final goods and services produced by workers and other resources located within the borders of a nation over a period of one year.

final products goods and services sold to final users and not used as materials, parts, or services to be incorporated in the value of other items that are to be resold.

cars produced in a Japanese-owned Toyota factory located in Kentucky are part of America's GDP. By the same token, computers produced by a U.S.-owned Apple Computer factory in Singapore are included in the GDP of that nation.

Gross domestic product is a key economic variable that is closely watched in gauging the performance of the economy. Both job opportunities and earnings in a nation are linked to production. When the output of final products in the economy grows, so too will income and job opportunities. More production means greater use of inputs; and as more inputs are used, the earnings of those who supply them goes up—as do the opportunities for employment. Conversely, if GDP falls, fewer resources will be used and income in the nation will also fall.

How GDP Is Calculated

GDP is calculated by multiplying the quantity of each individual type of final product by its market price. The dollar values of all final products derived in this way are then added to obtain a sum that equals the market value of the economy's aggregate production of final products. We aggregate the value of loaves of bread, computers, tickets to football games, pizzas, televisions, new homes, new cars, bulldozers, drill presses, aircraft, insurance, medical services, and other items produced over a year to measure GDP.

Because GDP is a measure of the market value of aggregate production, transactions that don't involve production aren't included in it. For example, the value of sales of stocks and bonds is *not* part of GDP because these and other purely financial transactions don't involve actual production of goods and services. Changes in the value of existing assets are also excluded from GDP because they don't represent production of new goods and services. Likewise, the value of used goods sold during the year is not part of GDP because the value of these goods was counted in prior years. Finally, in most cases goods and services not sold through markets are not reflected in GDP. For example, if you clean your own apartment or cook your own meals, the value of these productive services you provide to yourself instead of purchasing them in a market will not be included in GDP.

By placing dollar values on output based on the market prices of final products, we measure the worth of those products to buyers. We also avoid the difficulties involved in adding up goods and services measured in different units. Does aggregate production go up or down, for example, if the economy produces 50,000 fewer cars and 100,000 more insurance policies in a given year? To answer this question, simply compare the market value of the 50,000 cars and the 100,000 insurance policies. If the market value of the insurance policies exceeds the market value of the cars, we would say that aggregate output has increased.

Intermediate Products and Value Added

intermediate products products produced by business firms for resale by other firms or for use as materials or services that will be included in the value of resold goods.

value added the extra worth that a business firm adds to intermediate products; measured by the difference between the market value of a firm's sales and the market value of intermediate products purchased.

In measuring GDP it's important to exclude the market value of production that is not for final use to avoid overestimating aggregate production. **Intermediate products** are those produced by business firms for resale by other firms or for use as materials or services that will be included in the value of resold goods. For example, steel purchased by General Motors from the USX Corporation is an intermediate product because the steel will be used by General Motors as an input in the production of automobiles. If the value of the steel and the value of the automobile it is used in are *both* counted in GDP, the value of the steel will be counted twice.

During the process of production, business firms add worth to the intermediate products they purchase from other firms. **Value added** is the extra worth that a business firm adds to intermediate products. It is measured by the difference between the market value of a firm's sales and the market value of the intermediate products that the firm purchases.

Value added comes from such inputs as labor, capital, land, and entrepreneurial expertise. Firms combine these inputs with intermediate products that they purchase from other firms. A carmaker buys steel, glass, tires, and other products from other firms and uses its workers, capital, and managerial expertise to produce a vehicle. Naturally, the vehicle is worth more than the intermediate products that the carmaker purchased from other firms.

Total value added in a nation is the difference between the market value of *all* products of business firms and the market value of all intermediate products.

$$\text{Total value added in a nation (GDP)} = \text{Market value of all products} - \text{Market value of intermediate products}$$

The market value of all products includes the value of both final and intermediate products. Therefore, when the value of intermediate products is subtracted from this sum, the result is the market value of the nation's final products. *Because the market value of final products is GDP, it follows that GDP can be viewed as total value added in a nation over a year.*

A simple example about the production of blue jeans will show you how value added is computed at each stage of production and how it is related to the receipts and payments of a business firm.

1. To make a pair of blue jeans available in product markets, cotton is first grown by farmers. If you assume that farmers produce cotton without purchasing any materials or services from other firms, the value added by farmers equals the market value of their sales of cotton. (The value of the intermediate products is zero.)

Suppose annual sales of the cotton to be used in producing blue jeans are $1 million. The value of these sales must be fully accounted for by the sum of the farmers' profit and costs incurred. Because the farmers are not purchasing anything from other firms, the value of wages paid to workers, rent paid to land and equipment owners, and interest paid to lenders are the only costs reflected in the $1 million sales receipts. Therefore, any part of the $1 million not accounted for by these costs is the profit. *The value added of the farmers is the income generated by the sale of cotton.*

2. Next weavers who convert the cotton to cloth purchase the cotton from the farmers. The weavers' only intermediate purchase is that of the $1 million worth of cotton they obtain from farmers. After processing the cotton into cloth, the weavers sell the cloth for $2 million to a manufacturer of jeans. The value added by the weavers is therefore the $2 million in sales less the $1 million purchase of cotton.

The logic of the concept of value added should be clear to you now. *Value added at each stage of production is the difference between the value of the product at that stage and the cost of products purchased from other firms for use as inputs.* The value added by the weavers is the worth they have added to the cotton by processing it into cloth. This worth must reflect the value of the inputs used to process the cotton into cloth that are *not* purchased from other firms.

3. The manufacturer of blue jeans sells the product it produces with the cloth to consumers who wear the jeans. Assume that the only intermediate purchase made by the blue jean manufacturer is the $2 million purchase of cloth. If the total market value of the jeans produced by the manufacturer is $4 million, then the value added at this final stage of production is $4 million less $2 million, which equals $2 million. Once again, the $2 million value added by the blue jean maker must equal the sum of

total value added in a nation the difference between the market value of *all* products of business firms and the market value of all intermediate products. Equivalent of GDP.

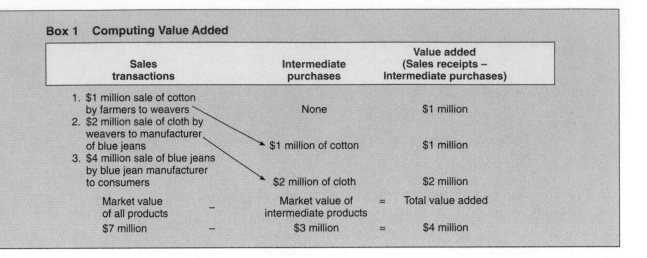

Box 1   Computing Value Added

Sales transactions	Intermediate purchases	Value added (Sales receipts – Intermediate purchases)
1. $1 million sale of cotton by farmers to weavers	None	$1 million
2. $2 million sale of cloth by weavers to manufacturer of blue jeans	$1 million of cotton	$1 million
3. $4 million sale of blue jeans by blue jean manufacturer to consumers	$2 million of cloth	$2 million
Market value of all products	– Market value of intermediate products	= Total value added
$7 million	– $3 million	= $4 million

incomes of workers and other input owners whose resources are used to produce the blue jeans, plus the manufacturer's profit.

The table in Box 1 shows how we arrived at total value added. Line 1 shows the sales transactions of farmers. The sum of product sales, including those of intermediate products, is $7 million, which is obtained by adding the numbers in Column 1. The sum of the market value of all intermediate purchases is $3 million, obtained by summing the dollar values of sales in Column 2. The sum of value added is $4 million (Column 3). *The sum of the value added associated with the production of blue jeans at its various stages exactly equals the market value of the final product sold by the blue jean makers to consumers.*

To summarize: GDP can be viewed as the sum of value added in all transactions involving new production in a nation over a year. Value added also equals the sum of payments to the owners of all resources used to produce the goods and services included in GDP and the profit of business firms, because value added at each stage represents the sum of payments to labor, capital, land, and all other inputs. When value added goes up in a nation, so will income.

Nominal GDP and Real GDP

nominal GDP the market value of a nation's final output based on current prices for the goods and services produced during the year.

Nominal GDP is the market value of a nation's final output based on *current prices* for the goods and services produced during the year. Nominal GDP is of only limited use in measuring changes in aggregate production over time. This is because nominal GDP can rise from one year to the next as a result of increases in the market prices of goods even when the nation's aggregate production of final products does not increase. In fact, nominal GDP can increase as a result of substantial increases in a broad array of market prices even when the nation's aggregate production of final output actually declines! Similarly, if market prices fall substantially during a year, nominal GDP might fall even if the nation's aggregate production goes up.

real GDP a measure of the value of a nation's final products obtained by using market prices prevailing for products during a certain base or reference year.

Real GDP is a measure of the value of a nation's final products obtained by *using market prices prevailing for products during a certain base or reference year.* Real GDP indicates the expenditure in dollars necessary to buy the economy's final products during a given year if they were sold at prices prevailing in the base year. The base year for U.S. real GDP as of 1993 was 1987. Calculation of real GDP allows more accurate measurement of changes in aggregate production in the economy over time by adjusting nominal GDP for the effects of inflation.

principles in practice

Policy Perspective: The Value-Added Tax

A New Way to Tax GDP or Its Components From the hallowed halls of Congress to the local diner, there's an ongoing debate about government spending and income taxes. Should we cut spending? Raise income taxes? Neither? Both?

Amid all the controversy, a new source of government revenue is being considered: the value-added tax. What is it? Where is it being used? And how does it work?

In European nations it's common to tax value added. Value-added taxes account for over 20 percent of tax revenue in most European Community nations. Such a tax has often been proposed as a means of providing additional revenue for the federal government without raising income tax rates.

A value-added tax (VAT) is sometimes called a national sales tax, because it's levied on every transaction as both intermediate and final products are sold. Under the value-added tax used in European nations, almost every transaction in the economy is subject to tax. Sellers must add the tax to the value of the goods they sell at each stage of production. Business firms that collect the tax then make tax payments quarterly on their value added over the period.

In European nations the "invoice method" is used to collect the tax. Under this method, no taxpayer has to compute value added (or understand what it is)! Each firm adds up the tax it has collected during the period as recorded on its sales invoices, where the tax is itemized. At the same time, the firm gathers all the invoices for the purchases it made from other firms during the period. The value-added taxes on these transactions are also itemized on the bills the firm has paid. The firm's accountants then sum the amounts of tax it *paid* on intermediate purchases from other firms. The firm's tax liability is the difference between the tax it collected from sales to other firms and the tax it paid on purchases from its suppliers.

$$\text{Tax liability} = \text{Tax payable on sales} - \text{Tax paid on purchases from other firms}$$

If the tax rate on each transaction is 20 percent, then the firm's tax liability is

20% (Sales receipts − Purchases from other firms)

Because the difference between a firm's sales receipts and its purchases of materials, parts, and services from other firms is its value added, the tax liability will be 20 percent of its value added.

Tax liability = 20% of value added

If *every* purchase is taxed at 20 percent, the government will collect 20 percent of GDP in tax revenue. Even the federal government's own purchases will be subject to the value-added tax. In other words, if a value-added tax is levied on all the components of expenditure in GDP, the federal government will collect the tax from itself as well as from state and local governments. The buyers of the final products will find that the price they pay for goods increases by 20 percent because the 20 percent tax is levied on all final sales as well as on intermediate sales. The tax will therefore collect 20 percent of the market value of the nation's final products, which is 20 percent of GDP.

In practice, the value-added tax as used in most European nations is not levied on most investment purchases and government purchases. In this case the value-added tax is really a tax on purchases of consumption goods! If the European version of the value-added tax were introduced in the United States, it would be equivalent to a national sales tax on consumption goods.

Viewing GDP as total value added in a nation thus helps us understand how a VAT would affect the economy. If a VAT that excludes investment and government purchases from taxation were introduced in the United States, those who allocate high percentages of their income to consumption would end up paying higher percentages of their income in taxes.

Calculating Nominal and Real GDP: A Simple Example

A simple numerical example will make clear the distinction between nominal and real GDP. Imagine an economy in which only two final products are produced each year: pizzas and jeans. Suppose that in 1987 the economy's final products were 2 million pizzas and 1 million pairs of jeans. The market price of a pizza in 1987 is $5,

Box 2   Nominal and Real GDP for a Two-Product Economy

Calculation of 1987 nominal GDP

Final products	1987 price	Market value
2 million pizzas	$ 5	$10 million = (2 million)($5)
1 million pairs of jeans	20	20 million = (1 million)($20)

Nominal GDP = $30 million = $10 million + $20 million

Calculation of 1994 nominal GDP

Final products	1994 price	Market value
4 million pizzas	$ 6	$24 million = (4 million)($6)
2 million pairs of jeans	25	50 million = (2 million)($25)

Nominal GDP = $74 million = $24 million + $50 million

Calculation of 1994 real GDP using 1987 prices

Final products	1987 price	Market value based on 1987 prices
4 million pizzas	$ 5	$20 million = (4 million)($5)
2 million pairs of jeans	20	40 million = (2 million)($20)

Real GDP = $60 million = $20 million + $40 million

and the market price of a pair of jeans is $20. The market value of pizzas that year is therefore $10 million, while the market value of jeans is $20 million. Nominal GDP is the sum of the market value of pizzas and jeans, which in this case is $30 million. The $30 million sum represents the market value of the economy's aggregate production using the prices prevailing during the year. Nominal GDP in the United States is calculated in a similar fashion by estimating the production of each industry and then multiplying units of production by current market prices and summing the market values of all the products.

The table in Box 2 shows how both nominal and real GDP can be computed for our imaginary economy for different years. Notice that in calculating nominal GDP in 1994, the output of both pizzas and jeans is significantly greater than it was in 1987. As you can see, production of both these goods has doubled over the seven-year period. Also note that the 1994 market prices of the two goods have increased from their 1987 levels. As the calculation in the table shows, based on the $6 market price prevailing in 1994, the market value of the 4 million pizzas produced that year is $24 million. Similarly, the market value of the 2 million pairs of jeans produced in 1994 is $50 million based on the price of $25 per pair prevailing that year. The market value of the economy's aggregate production of final products is therefore $74 million based on 1994 market prices.

If you now compare nominal GDP between 1987 and 1994, you can see why nominal GDP gives a misleading picture of the change in aggregate production between the two years. The output of each of the two products in the economy has doubled from 1987 to 1994; however, between 1987 and 1994 nominal GDP has more than doubled (from $30 million to $74 million). The discrepancy between growth in output

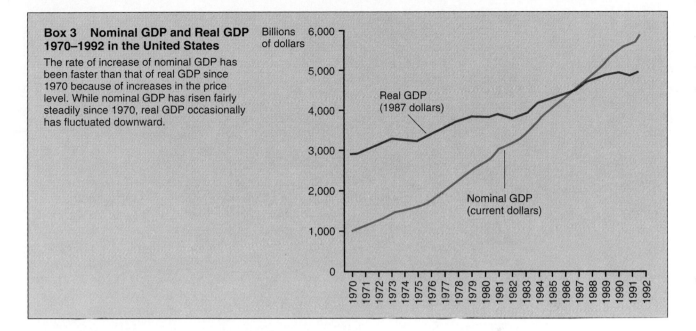

Box 3   Nominal GDP and Real GDP 1970–1992 in the United States

The rate of increase of nominal GDP has been faster than that of real GDP since 1970 because of increases in the price level. While nominal GDP has risen fairly steadily since 1970, real GDP occasionally has fluctuated downward.

and growth in nominal GDP stems from the fact that the growth in nominal GDP represents an amalgam of the changes in the prices of the products and the growth in output.

It's easy to obtain an accurate estimate of the change in aggregate production by valuing products produced in 1994 at the prices that prevailed in 1987. The market value of pizza in 1994 based on the $5 price that prevailed in 1987 is $20 million, while the market value of jeans produced in 1994 valued at the $20 price that prevailed in 1987 is $40 million. Summing these two market values gives a real GDP of $60 million, which is twice the real GDP that prevailed in 1987. The doubling of real GDP reflects the doubling of aggregate production. Note that 1987 nominal GDP is also 1987 real GDP when 1987 is used as the base year.

Let's look at the changes in actual real and nominal GDP in the United States between 1990 and 1991. Nominal GDP increased from $5,522 billion in 1990 to $5,677.5 billion in 1991. However, 1991 was really a bad year for the U.S. economy because aggregate production actually declined in that year. When U.S. aggregate production in both 1990 and 1991 is valued at the prices prevailing in 1987, we see that real GDP *declined* from $4,877.5 billion in 1990 to $4,821 billion in 1991. That decline in real GDP disrupted the operation of the economy as unemployment rose and income fell because of cutbacks in production.

The graph in Box 3 charts both real GDP and nominal GDP from 1970 to 1992. Note that nominal GDP increases at a more rapid rate over time than does real GDP. Nominal GDP has grown more quickly than real GDP since 1970 because prices have risen on average since that time. Also note that real GDP is more apt to decline than is nominal GDP. The graph shows sharp declines in real GDP during the periods 1973–75, 1981–82, and 1990–91. During these three periods production declined and job opportunities were therefore reduced. As a result, many workers lost their jobs and suffered declines in income.

How Good Is GDP as a Measure of National Well-Being?

How does GDP rate as a measure of the overall well-being of Americans? How does exclusion of nonmarket services affect the accuracy of GDP as an index of national well-being? Does GDP account for *decreases* in the quality of the environment that result from pollution? In this section we discuss important items affecting our well-being that are not included in GDP.

1. *Nonmarket production.* Many useful services are produced by members of households for the benefit of themselves or their families. Husbands and wives perform useful services for themselves and their families when they prepare meals, make household repairs, and handle their own financial affairs. The value of these services is *not* included in GDP because they do not represent services purchased through market transactions. The value of the work people do at home for themselves and their families has been estimated to be about one third of GDP.[1] If this estimate is correct, GDP significantly undervalues the total output of the nation by excluding nonmarket household production. Perhaps you can see this more graphically if you imagine each husband paying his wife for her services and each wife paying her husband for his services. These services would now become market services and would be included in GDP. Similarly, if more people remain single and hire housekeepers to do work that spouses would normally do without monetary compensation, GDP will increase!

Some nonmarket transactions, however, are included in GDP. For example, homeowners who live in their own homes enjoy the housing services their homes provide. In the National Income and Product Accounts, these owner-occupiers are viewed as being in the business of renting their homes to themselves. An estimate of the value of housing services enjoyed in this way *is included in GDP.*

In addition, GDP accountants impute values to farm products consumed on farms and food, clothing, and lodging furnished to employees. The imputed market values of these goods and services are also included in GDP. Of course, the goods and services made available by governments, such as national defense, are not sold in markets. However, their value is reflected in GDP because government purchases of labor and products are a component of GDP.

2. *The value of leisure.* All of you place some value on your time. You sell some of your time to employers for labor income; however, you retain much of it for your own use as leisure. Some of this leisure is used to produce household services that, as we discussed earlier, escape inclusion in GDP. The satisfaction you get from recreational activities and other uses of your leisure time also escapes inclusion in GDP.

3. *Cost of environmental damage.* We Americans may be able to enjoy more and better goods and services each year, but we must also put up with more congestion, dirty air, polluted waters, and other environmental costs that decrease the quality of our lives. Costs are associated with pollution and other aspects of industrial activity that damage the environment. The costs of environmental damage are not subtracted from the market value of final products when GDP is calculated. Some economists therefore believe that GDP overestimates the value of output by failing to account for environmental costs of production.

4. *The underground economy.* The United States has a vast *underground* economy. This economy consists of transactions that are never reported to tax and other

---

[1] See Oli Hawrylyshyn, "The Value of Household Services: A Survey of Empirical Estimates," *Review of Income and Wealth* 22, no. 2 (June 1976), pp. 101–31; and Reuben Bronau, "Home Production—A Forgotten Industry," *Review of Economics and Statistics* 63, no. 3 (August 1980), pp. 408–16.

government authorities. It includes transactions involving illegal goods and services, such as narcotics, gambling, and prostitution. These illegal goods and services are final products that are not included in GDP!

The transactions of the underground economy also include activities by people who don't comply with tax laws, immigration laws, or government regulations and who don't report their income to authorities. For example, a person might obtain a job and be paid in cash without paying any Social Security taxes or income taxes. Such transactions are not reported to the Internal Revenue Service, and because no record of the transactions is transmitted to governing authorities, the final product of the transactions often goes unvalued in GDP.

Estimates of the value of the transactions that take place in the underground economy and are not included in GDP range from as little as 1.5 percent of GDP to as high as one third of GDP.[2]

▪ What is measured in GDP?	▪ Why is real GDP a better measure of variation in aggregate production over time than nominal GDP?	**CONCEPT CHECK** ☐
▪ How is value added related to the market value of final products and intermediate products?		

THE EXPENDITURE AND INCOME COMPONENTS OF GDP

As we pointed out in Chapter 1, a major task of any economy is creating a mechanism for determining *what* is produced. The National Income and Product Accounts were designed not only to provide information on the total value of the final products produced over a year but also to keep track of the *kinds* of output produced. GDP can be broken down into components that show how much of our productive resources is being allocated to satisfy consumers' demands, to produce investment goods such as new machinery, to be used by governments, and to produce goods for export. It can also provide us with information about how much of our income we use to purchase imported products.

We can show how the receipts from the sale of final products are used to reward those who produce the output, thereby dividing GDP into income components. You will see that the bulk of the receipts that businesses receive for selling their products is allocated to paying their workers.

The Expenditure Components of GDP

GDP provides information on what we use our resources to produce by dividing expenditure on final products into components showing how much of our production we devote to consumption, investment, government activity, and exports.

Let's examine the kinds of output that are included in GDP and show how these aggregates are measured in the National Income and Product Accounts.

1. *Consumption.* If you were to browse through the National Income and Product Accounts, you could find out how much consumers spend on haircuts, beer, cosmetics, or anything else. **Personal consumption expenditures** are purchases of final products (except new homes) by households and individuals. The NIPA treats the purchase of a new home as an investment purchase (as opposed to a consumption purchase). Personal consumption consists of the purchase of both durable and

personal consumption expenditures household and individual purchases of both durable and nondurable goods and services.

---

[2] Carol S. Carson, ''The Underground Economy: An Introduction,'' U.S. Department of Commerce, *Survey of Current Business*, July 1984, pp. 106–17.

nondurable goods and services by people like you. Durable goods are items that last for a number of years, such as automobiles, kitchen appliances, and furniture. Nondurable goods are items that consumers use up soon after purchase, such as food and fuel. Services are nonmaterial items, such as the services of physicians and hospitals, lawyers, mechanics, banks, insurance companies, hotels, and educational institutions. Included in expenditures on services are housing rents, transportation costs, and household operating expenses for electricity, gas, and water. In recent years, services have become the dominant component of consumption in the United States, accounting for more than half the dollar value of consumption expenditures.

Personal consumption expenditures in the United States typically account for two thirds or more of GDP. A reduction in consumer spending can spell trouble for the economy because the reduced consumer demand for goods and services can reduce production and job opportunities.

2. *Investment.* Investment is the purchase of final products by business firms for use in production or as additions to inventories and the purchase of new homes by households. Investment involves the production of new capital goods by businesses, including changes in inventories of unsold goods, materials, and parts over the year.

gross private domestic investment expenditure by business firms on new machinery and equipment (producer durables), the value of new residential and nonresidential construction, and the change in business inventories during the year.

Gross private domestic investment includes purchases of new machinery, equipment, and structures by businesses, purchases of new homes by households, and the change in business inventories during the year. When inventories increase from one year to the next, they are added to investment. Reductions in business inventories during the year are treated as negative investment. Increases in business inventories represent goods that have been produced during the year but have not been sold to buyers in the market. These inventory accumulations must be included in GDP to accurately measure current production. In effect, the NIPA treats increases in business inventories as a final use of goods by businesses during the year. Similarly, when inventories decline during a year, the decline represents goods that were produced in previous years but sold during the current year. To accurately measure current GDP, the decline in inventories must be subtracted from investment.

Investment is *domestic* because it includes only that which takes place in the United States. For example, if IBM invests by building a new plant in Mexico, this investment is not part of U.S. GDP except to the extent that IBM purchases machinery in the United States for use in its Mexican plant.

depreciation an estimate of the value of capital goods that wear out or become obsolete during the year.

net private domestic investment gross private domestic investment less depreciation.

Investment is *gross* because it doesn't deduct the amount of purchases necessary to replace capital that wears out or becomes obsolete during the year. **Depreciation** (also called *consumption of fixed capital*) is an estimate of the value of capital goods that wear out or become obsolete during the year. **Net private domestic investment** is gross investment less depreciation. If gross investment were just equal to depreciation, net investment would be zero and there would be no net addition to the value of capital during the year.

Gross private domestic investment fluctuates quite a bit, but it typically accounts for between 12 and 15 percent of GDP in the United States.

3. *Government purchases.* A significant amount of resources are devoted to government use each year and government also purchases final products from business firms. **Government purchases of goods and services** include expenditure on final products of business firms and all input costs, including labor costs, incurred by all levels of government in the United States. Each paper clip, computer, fighter plane, filing cabinet, and aircraft purchased by government is included in the government purchases component of GDP. Also included is the entire payroll of all governments in the United States (local, state, and federal), representing purchases of labor services by governments.

government purchases of goods and services expenditure on final products of business firms and all input costs, including labor costs, incurred by all levels of government in the United States.

Governments themselves produce valuable goods and services, such as national defense, police and fire protection, roads, bridges, schooling, and environmental protection. However, government services are not sold in the marketplace. Such government services as national defense, public education, and garbage pickup are indirectly valued in computing GDP because the costs (including labor) of making these services available are included in the government purchases component of GDP.

Not all government expenditures represent purchases of final products. Governments often incur expenditures that disburse payments to individuals without requiring any services in return. **Transfer payments** are payments for which no good or service is currently received in return. Expenditures by governments for Social Security pensions, welfare payments to the poor, and subsidies to agriculture and industry are examples of transfer payments. These transfer payments constitute a source of income for the recipients and, when spent, show up as consumption or possibly as investment in the GDP accounts. In effect, transfer payments are negative taxes representing payments by governments to individuals instead of payments by individuals to governments. Government expenditures (which include transfer payments) far exceed government purchases.

transfer payments payments for which no good or service is currently received in return and that therefore do not represent expenditures for the purchase of final products.

The treatment of the government sector of the economy in the NIPA is often criticized for not providing sufficient information on the way governments affect both current and future economic performance. Governments also add worth to intermediate products by using labor and other inputs. In the NIPA all government purchases of intermediate products, investment goods, and labor are lumped together. This procedure makes it difficult to determine how much government activity is for investment (such as new roads) and how much is for direct consumption of goods and services.

There is no way to determine the worth added to intermediate products by government's use of labor and other inputs because government output is not typically sold in the marketplace. There is no measure of *depreciation* for government investment in the NIPA, so we cannot readily determine how much government investment is made to replace worn-out capital and how much represents a net addition to the nation's capital stock. The types of investments made by governments include roads, bridges, airports, structures, water resources development, sewers, mass transit, and other items referred to as the nation's *infrastructure*. Estimates indicate that government investment has not kept up with private investment in recent years.[3] Because infrastructure is an important input into the production process, the declining rate of government investment is likely to adversely affect private productivity. Government purchases account for about 20 percent of GDP in the United States.

4. *Net exports.* Exports represent expenditure on U.S. final products by foreigners and show us how much of our total production is sold abroad. Imports represent the value of goods and services produced abroad and purchased by Americans. **Net exports** represent the excess of expenditure on exports over imports. In measuring GDP, expenditure on imports by consumers, businesses, and governments must be subtracted from their total expenditures to avoid counting the value of other nations' production in the U.S. GDP. Exports must then be added to account for the portion of our domestic production that is sold to foreigners.

net exports any excess of expenditure on exports over imports.

---

[3] See David Alan Aschauer, "Public Spending for Private Profit," *The Wall Street Journal,* March 14, 1990.

When exports exceed imports, net exports are positive and foreign trade adds to GDP. When net exports are negative, imports exceed exports. In recent years U.S. imports have exceeded U.S. exports and net exports have been a negative component of GDP that is subtracted from the sum of consumption, investment, and government purchases to arrive at GDP.

Throughout the 1980s we spent more than the value of what we produced in the United States. As you will see, when a nation spends more than the value of its production, it must borrow from foreigners to make up the difference. In recent years the United States has, in fact, been a net borrower from the rest of the world.

aggregate expenditure
the sum of consumption expenditures, investment expenditures, government purchases, and net exports during the year. Equivalent to GDP.

Aggregate Expenditure   The sum of consumption expenditures (C), expenditures on investment goods (I), government purchases (G), and net exports (NE) during the year is **aggregate expenditure.** This represents the dollar value of the nation's final production and is therefore equivalent to GDP:

$$GDP = C + I + G + NE = \text{Aggregate expenditure}$$

Whenever some goods produced during the year are not sold and are added to inventory, the NIPA treats them as investment expenditures by businesses. In this way the accounts must always balance because the value of aggregate production (GDP) will always, by definition, equal aggregate expenditure.

When the expenditure components of GDP are valued at base year market prices, aggregate expenditure measures real GDP.

The Income Side of GDP

As we showed in Chapter 5, expenditure on output in product markets provides the funds for business firms to meet such expenses as wages, interest, and rents. You can therefore think of gross domestic product as also measuring *gross domestic income,* which is the costs incurred to pay for resources and profits earned in production of items included in GDP. Gross domestic income is the aggregate income earned annually from production. Aggregate expenditure on final products becomes the aggregate income of the nation. Every dollar spent on final products produced during the year ends up as income to either businesses or households.

The total income generated from production of final products is therefore equal to the value of those final products, which, as you saw in the previous section, is also equal to the value added to intermediate products by productive resources in the nation. Real GDP represents the value of final products produced during the year after adjustment for inflation. You can now see that real GDP also represents the **aggregate real income** of a nation, which is its nominal (money) income adjusted for inflation since the base year used to measure real GDP. If real GDP falls, so too will aggregate real income. If income, and living standards, in a nation are to grow, real GDP must also grow.

aggregate real income
the nominal (money) income of a nation, adjusted for inflation. Equivalent to real GDP.

One of the reasons economists are so concerned about gross domestic product and its rate of growth is that production generates income. The more production in a given year, the more jobs. More jobs mean more income for workers.

Dividing GDP into Income Components   Who earns the income that results from the production of goods and services in the economy? How much of that income is saved? How much goes to pay the taxes that finance government purchases and government transfer payments? The National Income and Product Accounts help us answer questions like these by keeping tabs on the way our aggregate expenditure on goods and services is channeled through the economy to businesses, resources owners, and governments.

principles in practice

How the Bureau of Economic Analysis Calculates GDP Every Three Months

There are two teams and a match. But there's no competition. The teams are composed of staff members of the Bureau of Economic Analysis of the U.S. Department of Commerce. One team measures GDP from the expenditure side, while the other measures it from the income side. When the two teams finish their independent work, a group of 15 economists meets to reconcile the two estimates. Aggregate expenditures on final products must equal aggregate income earned. On occasion the results don't match, and when the economists can't explain the source of the difference, it shows up as a statistical discrepancy on the GDP accounts.

The team that estimates GDP from the expenditure side uses data collected by the U.S. Bureau of the Census and other organizations. The team that estimates GDP from the income side uses the results of a number of income surveys.

In making estimates of real GDP, the Bureau of Economic Analysis staff members must value final products at prices prevailing in a base year. This often creates some serious problems when new products are developed or the quality of products changes over time. For example, in the early 1980s the base year used to estimate real GDP was 1972. By 1980, however, the economy was producing products that didn't exist in the early 1970s, such as personal computers. There was no 1972 price for personal computers because the product wasn't sold in markets at that time! To resolve such problems, the Bureau of Economic Analysis looks at how prices of similar products such as electric typewriters change over time and then deflates the current price of the new product to match the trend. For example, if electric typewriters in 1972 were priced at 70 percent of their 1980 market price, the bureau would value personal computers at 70 percent of their 1980 selling price when computing real GDP in 1980.

Quality changes in products also create headaches for the people who measure real GDP. Suppose a car sells for $20,000 in 1994 and the same model of that car sold for $16,000 in the 1987 base year used to estimate real GDP. However, the 1994 model has antilock brakes, a stereo cassette system, autolock doors, air bags, and other features that weren't available in 1987. To adjust for the quality change, the bureau must add on the market value of these features by estimating their value in 1987. Many judgments about the value of quality changes must be made in computing real GDP.

The Bureau of Economic Analysis takes its first stab at estimating GDP for each calendar quarter during the month following the end of that quarter. For example, the first, or "advance," estimate of the GDP at a seasonally adjusted annual rate for the third quarter is released toward the end of October. A revised estimate is issued the next month as more data become available. Finally, one month later, the bureau issues its "final" estimate of GDP for the third quarter. The final estimate of GDP for the third quarter would therefore not be available until December. The president and his economic advisers are privileged to obtain each GDP estimate one day before its official release.

Let's examine the income side of GDP by tracing out the uses of the receipts businesses take in during the year. Some receipts of business firms are used to pay sales taxes on output, such as gasoline taxes and state and local sales taxes, and some are plowed back into the businesses to finance investment. Most of the remainder is paid out as wages and salaries, interest on borrowings, and rents. Whatever is left over after making these payments is the profit of business firms.

The income components of GDP show how the receipts of business firms are allocated to pay for the resources used to produce final products during the year. The major income components of GDP are discussed below.

1. *Compensation of employees.* Employee compensation is the income from the sale of labor services during the year. It includes wages, salaries, and fringe benefits, such as employer-provided insurance and employer contributions to pension funds. Compensation of employees is the labor cost of producing final products and is by far the largest income component of GDP. It accounts for about 60 percent of the value of final products produced each year.

2. *Net interest.* The portion of business receipts used to pay for borrowed funds that finance investment purchases is called *net interest.* Interest payments provide earnings for savers and other suppliers of loanable funds for investment purchases. Interest paid by governments is not included in this category because it is financed by taxes rather than out of revenue from the sale of final products.

3. *Rental income.* Rental income is earned by those who supply the services of land, mineral rights, and buildings for use by others. Also included in rental income is an estimate of the imputed rent earned by homeowners who live in their own homes less the expenses of maintaining their homes. Rental income accounts for a near negligible share of GDP. In fact, rental income was actually negative in 1991 because in that year the depreciation on structures exceeded the rent payments for the use of those structures.

4. *Profits.* Before we can calculate the profit of corporations and unincorporated businesses, we have to make two additional deductions from business receipts in addition to payments for the use of productive resources:

   a. *Indirect business taxes.* Taxes levied on sales of final products that are reflected in the market value of goods and services sold by business firms are called indirect business taxes. These taxes include sales taxes, excise taxes, and other taxes that business firms treat as costs. Indirect business taxes account for about 8 percent of the value of receipts taken in from the sale of final products each year. They are really the portion of the receipts collected by business firms that are claimed by governments rather than used to pay for input costs or to be included as profit.

   b. *Consumption of fixed capital.* A surprisingly large portion of the receipts from the sale of final products is set aside by business firms as allowances for consumption of fixed capital. As we pointed out in our discussion of investments, this allowance accounts roughly for the value of capital goods that are "used up" in production during the year. Allowance for consumption of fixed capital accounts for about 11 percent of GDP and represents the second largest use of business receipts after compensation of employees. Capital consumption allowances are a major portion of *business saving,* which represents business receipts that are neither paid out to resource owners nor used to pay taxes or add to profits.

indirect business taxes taxes levied on sales of final products by business firms that increase the costs of these firms and are therefore reflected in the market value of goods and services sold.

After deductions from business receipts for indirect business taxes, capital consumption allowances, and costs for compensation of employees, net interest, and rents paid, the remainder is profit. Profit represents the income earned by owners of unincorporated corporate business (proprietors' income). Profit can be positive or negative. If costs exceed the receipts from the sale of final products, profit will be negative—implying that in the aggregate business firms incur losses during the year. As you know, the rate of profit is a very important determinant of the incentive firms have to supply goods and services.

The Economy's Income Statement

For the national economy we can use an income statement to show how receipts are allocated to pay expenses over a period. Such a statement shows how the receipts from expenditure on final products are accounted for by earnings of owners of resources and by other payments. Box 4 shows the *income statement* for the national economy in 1991.

The value of the final products represented by the sum C + I + G + NE must be accounted for as the flow of income and other payments generated by their sale. The

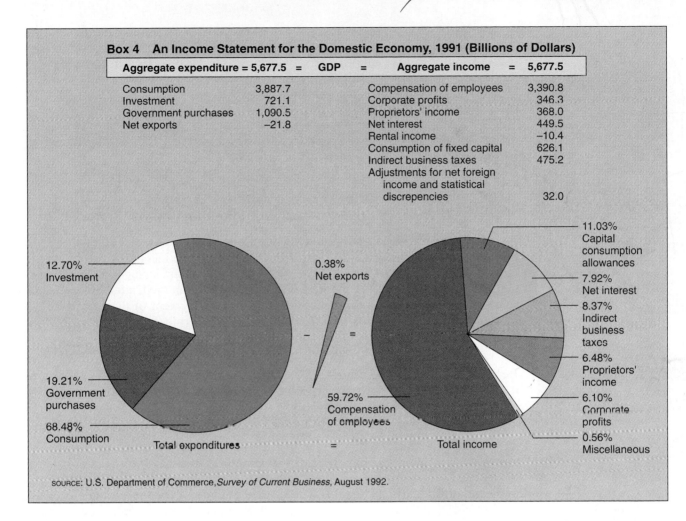

Box 4   An Income Statement for the Domestic Economy, 1991 (Billions of Dollars)

| Aggregate expenditure = 5,677.5 | = | GDP | = | Aggregate income | = | 5,677.5 |

Consumption	3,887.7	Compensation of employees		3,390.8
Investment	721.1	Corporate profits		346.3
Government purchases	1,090.5	Proprietors' income		368.0
Net exports	−21.8	Net interest		449.5
		Rental income		−10.4
		Consumption of fixed capital		626.1
		Indirect business taxes		475.2
		Adjustments for net foreign income and statistical discrepencies		32.0

12.70% Investment

19.21% Government purchases

68.48% Consumption

Total expenditures

0.38% Net exports

59.72% Compensation of employees

−   =

Total income

11.03% Capital consumption allowances

7.92% Net interest

8.37% Indirect business taxes

6.48% Proprietors' income

6.10% Corporate profits

0.56% Miscellaneous

SOURCE: U.S. Department of Commerce, *Survey of Current Business*, August 1992.

left side of the income statement in Box 4 shows how GDP is measured by aggregate expenditure. The right side of the income statement shows how receipts taken in from sales of final products are allocated to reward resource owners and to fund capital consumption allowances and pay indirect business taxes.

In effect, the economy is viewed as an enormous household in the NIPA. Aggregate expenditure must equal aggregate income.

Other Measures of Aggregate Expenditure and Income

The National Income and Product Accounts include other measures of expenditure and income that are used to keep tabs on the performance of the economy. This section discusses how gross national product, net national product, national income, personal income, and disposable income are related to GDP and how these accounting concepts are used.

Gross National Product   GDP is the primary measure used to gauge the growth of the domestic economy. However, a portion of the value of final output included in GDP reflects the worth of foreign resources employed within the boundaries of the United States. Moreover, GDP does not include the value of output produced by U.S. labor and property employed abroad. Let's now look at an NIPA concept that measures the value of output produced by U.S.-owned resources.

gross national product (GNP) the market value of final output produced annually by all labor and property supplied by a nation's households, no matter where those resources are employed. Measures the aggregate income of a nation's households.

Gross national product (GNP) is the market value of final output produced annually by all labor and property supplied by a nation's households, no matter where those resources are employed. GNP includes U.S. income from foreign sources (such as Ford's earnings on its foreign investments) but excludes the income of foreigners from work or investments in the United States (such as Toyota's profits from its U.S. production facilities).

GNP is calculated by adding to GDP income that U.S. households earn from work or investments in other nations and by subtracting from GDP income earned by foreigners from work or investments in the United States:

$$\text{GNP} = \text{GDP} + \begin{array}{c}\text{Foreign source}\\ \text{income of}\\ \text{U.S. households}\end{array} - \begin{array}{c}\text{Income earned}\\ \text{by foreigners in}\\ \text{the United States}\end{array}$$

Because GNP measures the total value of output produced by resources that U.S. households supply, it is the best measure of the aggregate income of Americans.

In 1991 the U.S. gross domestic product of $5,677.5 billion included $126 billion of income foreigners earned by working or owning property in the United States. In the same year Americans earned $143.5 billion from employment of their resources in foreign nations. Using the above formula, we can now calculate GNP for 1991:

$$\text{GNP} = \$5,667.5 \text{ billion} + \$143.5 \text{ billion} - \$126 \text{ billion} = \$5,695 \text{ billion}$$

Because in 1991 earnings from U.S. resources supplied abroad exceeded the earnings of foreign resources employed in the United States, GNP was greater than GDP in that year. If a nation's foreign earnings fall short of the earnings of foreigners in that nation, its GDP would exceed its GNP.

Net National Product   GNP includes investment purchases reflecting replacement of existing capital goods (including residential structures) that have worn out or become obsolete. To account for *net* new additions to capital stock, a measure of the depreciation of existing capital stock must be deducted from the estimate of gross investment. Net national product (NNP) is GNP less capital consumption allowances, which estimate depreciation:

net national product (NNP) GNP less capital consumption allowances.

$$\text{NNP} = \text{GNP} - \text{Capital consumption allowances}$$

Net national product is a measure of national production that includes only net additions to capital and excludes any purchases for replacement of worn-out or obsolete capital.

Similarly, by deducting an estimate of depreciation of existing capital stock from gross domestic product, we would obtain *net domestic product*.

Because capital consumption allowances are only very rough estimates of actual depreciation, most economists believe that NNP is not a very reliable indicator of net production. NNP is rarely used in economic analysis because of the dubious accuracy of the NIPA estimate of depreciation.

National Income   Some of the receipts shown on the income side of the statement in Box 5, such as indirect business taxes and capital consumption allowances, are not paid out to owners of productive resources. We can, however, make some adjustments to better gauge how much of the value of final products is actually paid out to those whose resources are used in production.

Box 5   From GDP to Disposable Income, 1991

	Billions of dollars
Step 1 Gross domestic product	5,677.5
Plus: Receipts of foreign income	143.5
Less: Payments of income to foreigners	126.0
Equals: Gross national product	5,695.0
Step 2 Gross national product	5,695.0
Less: Capital consumption allowances	626.1
Equals: Net national product	5,068.9
Step 3 Net national product	5,068.9
Less: Indirect business taxes and other adjustments	524.7
Equals: National income	4,544.2
Step 4 National income	4,544.2
Less: Social Security payroll taxes	528.8
Corporate profits	346.3
Net interest paid	449.5
Plus: Government transfer payments	748.3
Personal interest, dividends, and other transfers	860.4
Equals: Personal income	4,828.3
Step 5 Personal income	4,828.3
Less: Personal taxes	618.7
Equals: Disposable income	4,209.6

National income is a measure of household and business earnings from the use of productive resources over a period of one year. It can be calculated by subtracting indirect business taxes and capital consumption allowances from GNP:

$$\text{National income} = \text{GNP} - \text{Capital consumption allowances} - \text{Indirect business taxes}$$

national income the NIPA measure of annual household and business earnings from the use of productive resources.

It can also be calculated by summing the compensation of employees, rental income, net interest income earned by those who make loans to finance production, and profits.

Personal Income   How much income do households actually have available to spend before paying personal taxes? **Personal income** is the NIPA measure of the income available to households in a given year. To obtain personal income, the following subtractions from and additions to national income are required:

personal income the NIPA measure of annual income available to households.

1. Subtract all net interest and corporate profits from national income because these accrue to businesses rather than to households.

2. Subtract Social Security (payroll) taxes. These taxes are not paid out to individuals and therefore are not available for households to spend.

3. Add all personal interest income. This income exceeds the net interest that is initially subtracted because much of the interest earned by individuals is not used to finance production. Included in personal interest income is the interest paid by government to individuals who own government securities.

4. Add personal dividend payments, the portion of corporate profits that is paid to individuals.

5. Add all payments that individuals receive through government transfers (such as Social Security pensions) and business transfers (such as pensions).

After these adjustments have been made, the result is a measure of the income from production that actually gets paid out to households during the year along with income that does not necessarily reflect the sale of productive services. Note that personal income exceeds national income because the additions we make to national income to derive it exceed the subtractions.

Personal income is a useful measure of the ability of households to make purchases, save, and pay taxes. Retail sales forecasters eagerly await the monthly release of personal income estimates because they consider trends in personal income to be of great importance in influencing consumption.

disposable income the income individuals have to spend or save after payment of taxes.

Disposable Income   The income that individuals have to spend or save after payment of personal taxes is called **disposable income.** Officially designated *disposable personal income* in the NIPA, it is obtained by deducting personal tax and nontax payments to governments from personal income. Disposable income is closely watched by forecasters as a key determinant of consumers' ability to spend and save.

The table in Box 5 shows how GDP is related to NNP, national income, personal income, and disposable income. By moving from the first line to the bottom line, you can see how disposable income is derived from GDP in the 1991 National Income and Product Accounts.

CONCEPT CHECK
☐

- What are the expenditure components of GDP?
- What are the income components of GDP?
- What is measured by gross national product and net national product? Explain the differences

between national income, personal income, and disposable income as they are measured in the NIPA.

THE CIRCULAR FLOW OF EXPENDITURE AND INCOME: A MACROECONOMIC PERSPECTIVE

4 National income and product accounting demonstrates that expenditure on final products generates income; but this is not a onetime affair. Instead, the income in turn generates purchases of final products, which then result in more income as the process goes on and on. We can illustrate the continued flow of expenditure and income with a *circular flow diagram* similar to the one used in Chapter 5. However, with our enhanced knowledge of the NIPA accounts, we can now further investigate the relationship between the sources and uses of income by showing how the financial system, governments, and international trade affect the economy.

The enhanced circular flow diagram is drawn in Box 6. The upper loop of the big circle represents expenditures on final products, while the lower loop represents a flow of income generated by the purchases. Where does the expenditure that generates income originate? To find out, let's start at the box marked "Households."

Household consumption (C) in the United States accounts for about two thirds of GDP. Now move along the upper loop and notice that investment purchases (I) add to the flow of expenditures as funds from the nation's financial system are used to

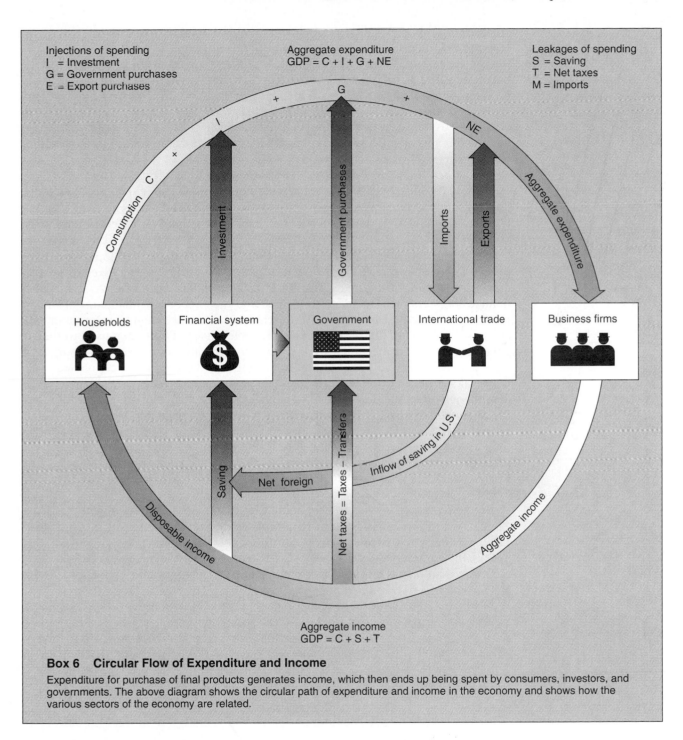

Box 6   Circular Flow of Expenditure and Income

Expenditure for purchase of final products generates income, which then ends up being spent by consumers, investors, and governments. The above diagram shows the circular path of expenditure and income in the economy and shows how the various sectors of the economy are related.

finance acquisition of machinery, new structures, and other investment goods. As you reach the top of the loop, government purchases (G) represent another addition to the flow of spending. Finally, moving down along the upper loop toward the box marked "business firms," notice that some spending is for import purchases (M) from international trade. Expenditures by U.S. buyers for such goods as Japanese computers and televisions, German automobiles, and Korean shoes end up as receipts to foreign sellers rather than to U.S. businesses. The spending for imports is therefore removed from the circular flow and does not end up as income to U.S. businesses and households. However, U.S. exports (E) are foreign purchases of U.S. products that help generate income in the United States from international trade. The difference E − M represents net exports (NE). By the time you get to the box marked "business firms," the total spending has grown to the sum C + I + G + NE, which you now know represents GDP expressed as the sum of its expenditure components.

The expenditure on final products generates the aggregate income earned by owners of business firms and members of households. This income is paid out as compensation to employees, net interest on funds borrowed, and rents, and a portion is set aside (saved) by business firms as capital consumption allowances. The remainder is profit.

We can now trace the uses of income by moving along the lower loop of the circle. Some of the income earned "leaks out" of the lower loop to pay taxes to governments. A portion of the taxes paid by U.S. households and businesses is used to finance transfers that are added to income and thus become available for spending. However, **net taxes,** which are the difference between taxes and transfer payments, are positive because taxes exceed transfers. Net taxes (T) are then used to finance government purchases, which were shown in the upper loop. Finally, a portion of income earned also flows out of the lower loop as saving, which is channeled to the financial system to provide funds for investment purchases. Some business saving (capital consumption allowances) is channeled to financial markets. **Personal saving** is the portion of household income that is not used to make purchases or pay taxes over the year. Governments also absorb some of the saving during the year when they run a budget deficit. When this is the case, the government must borrow through the financial system, as shown by the flow of funds from the financial system to government. In the early 1990s the federal government was absorbing over $200 billion of annual savings to finance its enormous deficits.

Some funds are supplied to the financial system by foreigners saving in the United States. When foreigners acquire more dollars during the year than they spend on U.S. products, the excess dollars end up as dollar deposits in U.S. banks. These dollars then enter the U.S. financial system as net foreign saving in the United States (see Box 6). When the net export component of GDP is negative, the United States runs a *balance of trade deficit*.[4]

Now you're back to the box marked "Households," and the process begins all over again. Expenditure on final products during the year has provided households with the income necessary to finance their consumption. Income is used for consumption purchases (C), household and business savings (S), or payment of the difference between taxes and government transfers (net taxes = T).

GDP expressed as the sum of income uses is

$$GDP = C + S + T$$

net taxes the difference between taxes and transfer payments.

personal saving the portion of household income that is not used to make purchases or pay taxes.

---

[4] Net foreign saving in the United States typically exceeds the balance of trade deficit for goods and services. This is because foreign holders of dollars also earn interest income on their U.S. investments and because some foreigners also receive transfer payments from governments in the United States. For example, in 1986 the balance of trade deficit was $105.5 billion, but that year the excess of dollars earned by foreigners over their expenditure on U.S. products was $148.7 billion.

Leakages and Injections of Purchasing Power and the Demand for U.S. Final Products

A **leakage** of spending represents a portion of income that is not used to purchase domestically produced products during the year. There are three types of leakage of spending power from the circular flow:

1. Net taxes—the difference between total taxes paid to governments and transfer payments made by governments.

2. Saving.

3. Import purchases.

Leakages of spending from the circular flow cause decreases in the current demand for U.S. final products. Other things being equal, the more saving, the greater the difference between taxes and transfers, and the greater the import purchases, the less national income is used to buy U.S. goods and services during the year.

An **injection** of spending is a purchase made by business firms, governments, or foreign buyers that increases the flow of income in a nation. Injections of purchasing power for purposes other than consumption by U.S. households increase demand in the economy. The injections illustrated in the circular flow diagram are:

1. Investment.

2. Government purchases.

3. Exports.

A reduction in business investment purchases during the year or a decline in export purchases could spell trouble for the economy by causing a reduction in current income. On the other hand, an increase in government purchases increases the demand for goods and services.

You can think of real GDP as a volume of liquid flowing through the tubes of the circular flow diagram in Box 6. When the injections of spending exceed the leakages of spending, the volume of liquid in the tubes will increase, meaning that current real GDP will increase. On the other hand, when the injections of spending fall short of the leakages of spending, the volume of liquid in the tubes will decline, meaning that current real GDP or the price level will decrease. The task of macroeconomic theory is to understand the economic forces that influence these leakages and injections in order to forecast changes in real GDP and to develop policies that minimize fluctuations in real GDP.

Flows of Saving and Investment in the United States: Do We Save Enough?

In Chapter 2 we showed how a nation's *future* production possibilities depend on investment. Individuals in the economy must refrain from devoting all of their resources to purchases of consumption goods so that some resources can be devoted to investment. When we save rather than consume, we can allocate some of our resources to the production of new machinery, equipment, education, research and development, and other uses that help us provide more output in the future. The more we save, the more of our resources we can devote to investment and the greater will be our output in the future. How does the United States shape up against other nations in terms of its recent saving and investment performance?

National saving is the sum of household saving, business saving, and government saving. Box 7 shows how national saving has varied as a percentage of GNP (used

leakage (of spending) a portion of income that is not used to purchase domestically produced goods during the year.

injection (of spending) a purchase made by business firms, governments, or foreign buyers that increases the flow of income in a nation.

national saving the sum of household saving, business saving, and saving by the government sector.

Box 7   National Saving, Investment, and Net Foreign Saving Inflow

	Average annual rate of national saving (percent of GNP)	
	1950–1979	1980–1991
Gross private domestic investment	16.0	15.5
Equals:		
National saving	16.3	14.0
Household	5.0	3.7
Business	11.8	12.8
Government	−0.4	−2.5
Plus:		
Net foreign saving inflow	−0.3	1.5

NOTE: Detail may not add to totals because of rounding.
SOURCE: Department of Commerce, Bureau of Economic Analysis.

here as a measure of aggregate income) since 1950. From 1980 to 1991, national saving in the United States averaged only 14 percent of GNP—down from the 16.3 percent average that prevailed from 1950 to 1979. The U.S. saving rate has dropped substantially (by 13.5 percent) from the average that prevailed from 1950 to 1979.

Now let's examine the saving rate of three sectors of the domestic economy: households, businesses, and government. Notice that the bulk of national saving is accounted for by business firms, mainly in the form of capital consumption allowances and undistributed corporate profits. The business saving rate has actually increased since the 30-year period from 1950 to 1979, averaging 12.8 percent of GNP from 1980 to 1991. Next look at how household (or personal) saving has declined substantially from its 1950–79 average. From 1980 to 1991, household (personal) saving was only 3.7 percent of GNP.

But households don't bear the sole responsibility for the decline in national saving. To illustrate, look at saving by the government sector of the economy. Notice that government saving is *negative*. This simply means that the government sector in the United States spends more than it takes in. On net the government sector absorbs savings in the United States because it must borrow to cover expenses not financed by taxes, fees, and charges. The saving rate of the government sector averaged −2.5 percent from 1980 to 1991. This negative saving rate largely reflected the federal budget deficits during this period. In fact, state and local governments actually ran surpluses during the same period and contributed 1.2 percent of GNP to national saving. *The federal budget deficit on average from 1980 to 1991 subtracted 3.7 percent of GNP from the national saving rate!*

After looking at Box 7, we can conclude that the national saving rate has declined substantially in recent years and that lower saving by households and increased borrowing by the federal government are largely responsible for the poor saving performance of the United States from 1980 to 1991.

The U.S. national saving rate is now considerably lower than that of some other advanced nations. For example, since 1975, national saving in the United States has averaged less than half the saving rate in Japan, which exceeds 30 percent of aggregate income. The U.S. saving rate is also less than the saving rates of Canada and nations of the European Community. Because savings fuel the process of investment, which in turn fuels the process of economic growth, many economists are concerned that the declining rate of national saving in the United States means that U.S. living standards will not rise as quickly as they have risen since the end of World War II. There is also concern that other nations will surge ahead of the United States in productivity and the improvement of living standards. The decline in the national saving rate in the United States could affect your future living standards. If we do not improve our savings performance soon, you may not enjoy the improvements in the standard of living that your parents have enjoyed over their lives!

How Foreigners Helped Finance U.S. Investment between 1980 and 1991

Between 1980 and 1991, national saving averaged only 14 percent of GNP, while investment averaged 15.5 percent of GNP. Americans have not saved enough to finance investment purchases by U.S. businesses. This shortfall in national saving has been overcome by the net inflow of foreign saving. Foreigners save in the United States when they use the dollars they acquire during the year in foreign exchange markets to purchase U.S. assets instead of spending those dollars on U.S. exports. *Net foreign saving in the United States* is the difference between total foreign saving in the United States and U.S. saving abroad and is positive whenever we have a balance of trade deficit.

The table in Box 7 shows that the net inflow from foreign saving in the United States averaged 1.5 percent of U.S. GNP from 1980 to 1991. When these funds are added to national saving, total saving in the United States exactly equals gross private investment. Total saving in the United States is the sum of national saving and net foreign saving in the United States. The circular flow diagram in Box 6 shows how foreign saving in the United States is added to national saving to help finance investment purchases.

total saving in the United States the sum of national saving and net foreign saving in the United States.

You have probably read quite a bit about foreign saving in the United States. Some of it takes the form of direct investment in the United States, as is the case when Japanese savers use dollars they have acquired in foreign exchange markets to buy U.S. real estate and U.S. businesses. Most foreign saving in the United States, however, involves the acquisition of paper assets, such as stocks, bonds, and certificates of deposit. In recent years foreign saving, including the portion of such saving that is direct investment in the United States, has served a valuable function in the U.S. economy by allowing the rate of investment to exceed the national saving rate.

Because of foreign saving, we have been able to create more jobs and we are likely to have more rapid economic growth in the future than would otherwise have been possible. In effect, foreign saving in the United States since 1980 has allowed U.S. spending to exceed U.S. income! The low supply of savings from U.S. households makes funds for investment scarce and puts upward pressure on interest rates. Foreign saving offsets the low rate of U.S. saving and puts downward pressure on interest rates by increasing the supply of loanable funds. By purchasing U.S. government securities such as Treasury bonds, notes, and bills, foreign savers keep the huge federal budget deficit from exerting still more upward pressure on interest rates.

By making direct investments in U.S. industries, which is what foreigners do when they acquire U.S. firms and plants, foreigners will in the long run enable U.S. firms to compete in international markets. This is because the new equipment and technology that U.S. firms acquire with funds supplied by foreign investors will enable these firms to produce at lower cost in the future. And foreign producers are finding it in their interest to use the U.S. dollars they acquire in trade to build their own plants in the United States. The Toyota Camry you buy may very well have been produced in Georgetown, Kentucky, where Toyota has a plant. Honda also has plants in the United States. Since 1982 manufacturing costs per unit have fallen in the United States, while they have risen in other nations. This makes direct investment in the United States a good deal for foreign producers, who in the late 1980s actually found that in many cases they could *reduce* their labor costs by producing in the United States instead of at home! On the flip side, the more U.S. assets owned by foreigners, the more income earned in the United States will accrue to foreign citizens instead of U.S. citizens in the future. In perspective, the United States owns lots of foreign assets. For example, a substantial portion of the Canadian economy consists of assets owned by U.S. businesses and households. In recent years U.S. businesses and individuals have invested heavily in such nations as Switzerland, the United Kingdom, and the Netherlands. It's all part of increased globalization of business—a trend that shows no signs of subsiding.

Foreign business interests actually play a relatively small role in the United States as measured by the extent of their controlling interest in U.S. companies. Only 4 percent of the U.S. labor force in the late 1980s was employed by companies with foreign ownership of 10 percent or more.

the global economy

The Growing Importance of Exports and Imports for the U.S. Economy

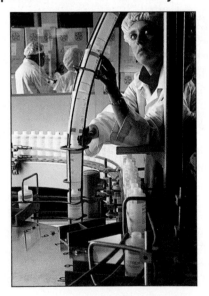

How many Japanese or other foreign cars were on the American roads 25 years ago? Practically none. Likewise, there were few foreign TV sets, shoes, or cameras in comparison to what's available today.

In recent years the U.S. economy has become increasingly linked with the rest of the world through international trade. Americans have enjoyed gains from foreign trade because foreign trade has enabled them to buy quality goods at lower prices than would have otherwise been possible. In the 1980s the growth in the value of imported products exceeded the growth in the value of exported products, which contributed to huge balance of trade deficits in the United States.

The graph in Box 8 documents the spectacular rise in the importance of exports and imports for the U.S. economy since 1960. In 1960 real exports amounted to 4.5 percent of real GDP. By 1991, 11.2 percent of U.S. output was exported. A similar trend is observed for real imports which grew from 4.9 percent of real GDP in 1960 to a whopping 11.6 percent of real GDP in 1991. Both imports and exports fluctuate from year to year as a result of changes in economic conditions. For example, both imports and exports are responsive to changes in the international value of the dollar. A rise in the value of the dollar in terms of foreign currency from 1980 to 1986 was responsible, in part, for the sharp decline in real exports as a share of real GDP in the United States over that period. During the same period the higher-valued dollar caused the price of imports to fall to U.S. buyers, and we observe a sharp increase in real imports as a share of real GDP from 1980 to 1986.

The U.S. economy is now enmeshed in the global economy through the strong appetite of U.S. buyers

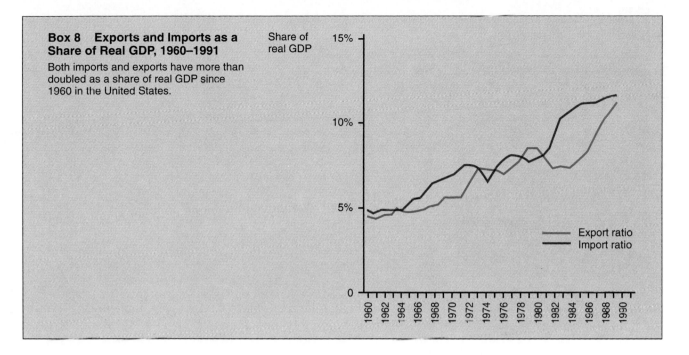

Box 8   Exports and Imports as a Share of Real GDP, 1960–1991

Both imports and exports have more than doubled as a share of real GDP since 1960 in the United States.

Share of real GDP

— Export ratio
— Import ratio

for imports and through the reliance of U.S. industry on export demand as a source of revenue. More income is now generated from the sale of exports, and more income is spent on imported goods and services.

As we have just demonstrated, the negative net export position of the United States throughout the 1980s and early 1990s has enabled foreigners to increase their holding of U.S. assets. Our balance of trade deficit is mirrored by a net inflow of foreign saving in the United States. Of course, if the United States were to begin exporting more than it imported, it would convert the balance of trade deficit into a *balance of trade surplus,* as a result of which the net inflow of foreign saving into the United States would become negative and foreign ownership of U.S. assets would decline.

Exports have been a driving force of the U.S. economy in recent years. Merchandise exports accounted for 20 percent of U.S. industrial output as of 1992 and were estimated to have added 1.5 million jobs to the U.S. economy from 1989 to 1991.[5] The U.S. share of world exports rose from 15.3 percent in

1986 to 22 percent in 1992. Investment goods (such as machinery) and industrial supplies (such as chemicals, paper, and metals) have accounted for much of the growth in U.S. exports in recent years. However, exports of consumer goods, food, and even automobiles have also increased. Among the products that foreigners have been buying in increased volume from American sellers are pharmaceuticals, tobacco products, toys, sporting goods, kitchen appliances, and electronic items. Markets for U.S. exports have been growing in Europe, Latin America, and Asia. Even the beleaguered General Motors Corporation has been increasing its exports by selling more full-size cars in Europe and the Middle East.

In recent years the improved export performance of the U.S. economy has contributed to GDP growth and reduced balance of trade deficits. However, increased reliance on exports for growth of jobs and income also means that the U.S. economy is increasingly subject to fluctuations in foreign demand. Recessions in Germany and other European nations in 1992 along with a slowdown in Japanese economic growth could dampen growth in the United States.

[5] See A. Ehrbar, ''Trading Up: Many U.S. Companies Expect Strong Exports despite Talk of Slump,'' *The Wall Street Journal,* January 18, 1993.

insights on issues

Will Standards of Living in the United States Continue to Improve? Talking with
Kenneth J. Arrow and Robert E. Litan

Kenneth J. Arrow is a professor of economics emeritus at Stanford University. He received the Nobel Memorial Prize in economics in 1972 for his theories on the rationale of government policy decisions and on the interconnectedness of the economy, including business risks. Robert E. Litan is an economist with The Brookings Institution who recently coauthored a book on American standards of living.

How are living standards measured? Are these measures accurate?
Kenneth Arrow: In principle, the quantities of goods and services used by consumers are combined into a single measure by being weighted by the prices paid for them. As the quantities change from year to year, the prices used as weights remain constant. There can, in principle, be no perfect representation of a disparate group of goods and services by a single number, and there are many practical problems. Nevertheless, I consider the measures reasonably accurate for the purposes for which they are used.
Robert Litan: Two of the most common measures of living standards are income per capita and consumption per capita, both measured at market prices. Income per capita is the average earning power of citi-

zens in a country; consumption per capita indicates how well the average citizen is living at any particular time. The latter measure can be deceptive when savings rates are declining (as in the United States during the past decade), since many citizens may be temporarily living beyond their means.

All measures of living standards using conventional national income and product account data also may be deceiving in that they exclude the values of things and attributes not traded in the market—for example, clean air, safe residences and workplaces, lack of congestion, and household labor.

Some economists say the rate of growth of living standards has stagnated, and children today will be poorer as adults than their parents were. Do you agree?

CONCEPT CHECK

☐

- What are the leakages and injections of spending in the economy's circular flow of income and expenditure?

- What are the components of national saving?

- How did foreigners help finance investment in the United States from 1980 to 1991? How is the net inflow of foreign saving in the United States related to the U.S. balance of trade deficit?

SUMMARY

1. Macroeconomics is the study of the overall performance of the economy and the way its various sectors are related.

2. The National Income and Product Accounts represent the official system of national accounting in the United States. Statistics on these accounts are published quarterly by the U.S. Department of Commerce and are used to measure the performance of the national economy.

3. Gross domestic product is the market value of the final goods and services produced in a nation over a period of one year.

4. Nominal GDP is the market value of a nation's aggregate production of final goods and services based on current prices, while real GDP measures the value of aggregate production using base year prices. Changes in real GDP reflect changes in aggregate production over time more accurately than do changes in nominal GDP.

5. Total value added in a nation over the year is the difference between the market value of all products of business firms and the market value of all intermediate products and is equivalent to GDP. Value added at each stage of production is the worth added to items purchased from other firms.

Kenneth Arrow: The rate of growth of living standards certainly has been slower in the last 15 years than before, but I see no reason to believe it will turn negative. Of course, there are always some children who are worse off than their parents, just as there are some who are better off. If the rate of growth slows, the first group will grow and the second will fall. Nevertheless, I expect most children will still be better off than their parents.

Robert Litan: When measured by conventional economic data, living standards in the United States have improved at a less rapid rate in the past two decades than during the previous 25 years. But this slowdown in improvement also is found in other industrialized countries. Whether today's children will be poorer as adults than their parents are now will depend on both their level of education and the future rate of economywide productivity growth. The faster overall productivity grows, the more likely it is that even less well-educated children will be better off than their parents.

Do you expect that the rate of income growth in the United States will fall behind those of other nations? Why or why not?

Kenneth Arrow: Rates of income growth have dropped all over the world. In some dimensions, particularly creation of new jobs, the United States has done better than European countries. The present period of cost-cutting augurs well for increased output in the next five to seven years. Beyond that, the chief problem will be educating competent, ambitious workers; here I am more pessimistic.

Robert Litan: If productivity growth in the United States continues at the pace of the last 20 years (around 1.2 percent annually) while productivity growth in Japan and Europe continues at its recent rate (ranging from 2 to 3 percent), it is a mathematical certainty that sometime in the early part of the 21st century, average living standards abroad will be higher than here.

What can be done today to improve living standards for the future?

Kenneth Arrow: Improvement in education, including vocational training, is the most important step. To achieve this requires, among other elements, reversing the decline of the family. The family is the first place of socialization and achievement orientation, and its effect on educational attainment is very clear. We also need an increase in our rate of national saving, for which reducing the budget deficit is a major prerequisite.

Robert Litan: The United States must significantly increase its anemic savings rate, devoting greater resources toward investment rather than consumption. "Investment" must broadly include physical equipment, R&D, and training (especially of workers who do not go to college).

6. From the expenditure standpoint, GDP is the sum of consumption, investment, government purchases, and net exports. Net exports are the difference between exports and imports of goods and services over the year.

7. From the income standpoint, GDP is the sum of annual compensation of employees, profits, net interest, rental income, capital consumption allowances, and indirect business taxes. Capital consumption allowances are a form of business saving. Capital consumption allowances, indirect business taxes, and corporate profits taxes are not paid out as income to members of households.

8. The circular flow of expenditure and income in an economy stems from the fact that expenditures on final products end up as income, which is then used to make purchases. Disposable income is the income available to households for spending or saving after payment of taxes.

9. In the circular flow of income and expenditure, the financial system acts to channel savings so that they can be used to finance investment purchases. The government collects taxes and makes transfers of income among citizens. Net taxes are the difference between taxes and transfers. Net taxes finance government purchases. Some income earned during the year is used to purchase imports, and U.S. businesses export some of their products through international trade. When net exports are negative, a net inflow of foreign saving into the United States helps finance investment purchases.

10. National saving is the sum of household saving, business saving, and government saving.

11. In recent years national saving in the United States has fallen short of gross private domestic investment. The national saving rate is lower in the United States than in other advanced nations.

KEY TERMS

National Income and
   Product Accounts
   (NIPA) *131*
aggregates *131*
gross domestic product
   (GDP) *131*
final products *131*
intermediate products *132*
value added *132*
total value added in a
   nation *132*

nominal GDP *134*
real GDP *134*
personal consumption
   expenditures *139*
gross private domestic
   investment *140*
depreciation *140*
net private domestic
   investment *140*
government purchases of
   goods and services *142*

transfer payments *141*
net exports *141*
aggregate expenditure *142*
aggregate real income *142*
indirect business taxes *144*
gross national product
   (GNP) *146*
net national product
   (NNP) *146*
national income *147*

personal income *147*
disposable income *148*
net taxes *150*
personal saving *150*
leakage (of spending) *151*
injection (of spending) *151*
national saving *151*
total saving in the United
   States *153*

CONCEPT REVIEW

1 Explain how GDP is measured and how nominal GDP differs from real GDP.

2 Suppose that personal consumption expenditures are $3 trillion, gross private domestic investment is $1 trillion, and government purchases are $2 trillion. If GDP is $5 trillion, what is the value of net exports?

3 What is the best NIPA measure of income earned by owners of productive resources? What is the best NIPA

measure of after-tax income available for household spending?

4 How does expenditure on final products end up as income to households and businesses?

5 What is national saving, and how does it differ from total saving in the United States?

PROBLEMS AND APPLICATIONS

1. During the year a small nation produces the following final products: 1 million automobiles, 5 million clothing outfits, 10 million pounds of food, rental of 2 million dwelling units, 1 million hours of attorneys' services to households, and 2 million hours of medical services to households. The current market price for these products are:

   $10,000 per automobile

   $100 per clothing outfit

   $2 per pound of food

   $4,000 per year per dwelling unit

   $20 per hour of attorneys' services

   $30 per hour of medical services

   Calculate the nation's nominal gross domestic product. **1**

2. Suppose nominal GDP in the U.S. economy increases from $5,000 billion to $5,500 billion. Can you conclude that aggregate production, income, and job opportunities have increased as well? Explain your answer. **1**

3. Explain why GDP would be overestimated if the market values of both final products and intermediate products were included in it. **1**

4. The market value of all sales in an economy, including those of intermediate products, is $10,000 billion. If the market value of intermediate products is $6,000

billion, what is the total value added in the nation? Why is the value added equal to gross domestic product? **1**

5. GDP is currently equal to $4,500 billion. Consumption is $3,000 billion, and government purchases are $1,000 billion. If net exports are zero, how much is gross private domestic investment? What are the major components of gross private domestic investment? Under what circumstances would net private domestic investment be negative? **2**

6. During 1985, total government expenditures in the United States amounted to $1,400 billion. In the same year the government purchases component of GDP was only $815 billion. Explain why the government purchases component of GDP falls short of actual government expenditures. List some of the important government expenditures that are not included in the government purchases component of GDP. What is the logic of excluding these expenditures? **2**

7. GDP is $5,000 billion in the current year. During the year employee compensation is $3,000 billion, net interest earned is $300 billion, and rental income is $50 billion. Calculate the sum of corporate profits and proprietors' income, assuming that capital consumption allowances are $400 billion and indirect business taxes are $300 billion. **3**

8. Suppose investment, government purchases, and exports are expected to decline this year. Can you conclude that real GDP will also decline? Why would you look at growth in disposable income to predict changes in consumer spending? **4**

9. Suppose that gross private domestic investment in 1995 is $900 billion. That year personal saving is $250 billion, business saving is $650 billion, and the government sector runs a $200 billion budget deficit. Calculate national saving. What is the net inflow of foreign saving into the United States in 1995? **4** , **5**

10. Suppose that gross domestic purchases, which are the sum of consumption, investment, and government purchases, are equal to $6,000 billion. Gross domestic product is equal to $5,500 billion in the same year. Calculate net exports. How can an increase in the government budget deficit contribute to a balance of trade deficit? **5**

inside information

Where to Find Current Information on the Performance of the U.S. Economy

Economic forecasters measure the performance of the U.S. economy by examining data on gross domestic product, disposable income, unemployment rates, and inflation. You will become familiar with these concepts in Part VI. Where can you get current information on these important measures of economic performance?

If you are really eager to get the latest releases of information on the economy, you can tap into the *Electronic Bulletin Board* of the U.S. Department of Commerce, a computer information service available for those who have modems. If you can wait a bit longer, three major periodicals published monthly by the federal government have just about all the data you might want to write term papers or satisfy your own curiosity about statistics on the U.S. economy:

1. The *Survey of Current Business,* published monthly by the U.S. Department of Commerce, provides information about production, spending, and income, together with articles on national income accounting. The July issue usually contains more comprehensive information about the performance of the economy than do other issues. This is an excellent source if you want information about gross domestic product, spending, or disposable income.

2. The *Monthly Labor Review,* a publication of the Bureau of Labor Statistics of the U.S. Department of Labor, provides information about employment, unemployment, the price level, and inflation. It also carries interesting articles on labor market issues and publishes information on unemployment rates and the consumer price index, the most widely used cost-of-living indicator in the United States. If you want to find out what the rate of inflation in the United States is for a current month, your first stop in the library should be the government documents section, where you can get a copy of the latest *Monthly Labor Review.*

3. *Employment and Earnings,* another publication of the Bureau of Labor Statistics, provides detailed information about labor market indicators. This publication has complete information about employment and earnings by region and by occupation. For example, you can find information on unemployment rates in your own metropolitan area and compare those rates with national averages.

7 chapter

Business Cycles, Unemployment, and Economic Growth

You've undoubtedly heard the terms *recession* and *unemployment* talked about on the nightly news. In 1990 the United States fell into a recession, and the consequences for the economy were increased unemployment and declining incomes. By early 1991 unemployment rates were moving upward throughout the country and businesses were complaining about sluggish sales.

A major goal of this chapter is to discuss the history of fluctuations and growth of real GDP and show the links among real GDP growth, employment of workers, and living standards. The chapter will show how unemployment is measured and will explain why some unemployment is normal in a dynamic economy that doesn't instantaneously adjust to change.

When excessive numbers of workers are unemployed, it's difficult for new entrants into the labor force to find jobs and more people have difficulty meeting their expenses. Excessive unemployment is wasteful because the labor services of idle workers are not being used to produce goods and services. Lack of employment can disrupt the lives of families and threaten the social fabric of a nation. For this reason the United States pursues policies designed to minimize unemployment and reduce its cost.

☐ CONCEPT PREVIEW

After reading this chapter, you should be able to:

1. Discuss the business cycle and give examples of recent periods of recession and expansion of the U.S. economy.

2. Explain how unemployment is measured and how the unemployment rate can be viewed as the sum of frictional, structural, and cyclical unemployment.

3. Define the concept of *full employment* and show how it is related to the natural rate of unemployment.

4. Explain *potential real GDP* and the difficulties involved in estimating it.

5. Discuss the social costs of unemployment and the programs designed to cushion these costs.

6. Discuss the record and sources of economic growth in the United States.

FLUCTUATIONS IN REAL GDP: THE HISTORICAL RECORD

Increases in real GDP from one year to the next indicate that the economy's aggregate production of final products has also increased. More production means more goods and services available for people to consume. Given a growing population, increases in real GDP are necessary to maintain the standard of living as measured by the average of goods and services per person. When real GDP falls from one year to the next, final output per person will also fall, implying a reduced average standard of living. When output falls from one year to the next, employers won't use as much input as they did the year before. This means some workers will lose their jobs and new entrants into the labor force will have difficulty finding jobs. *Declines in real GDP therefore also imply declines in income, employment opportunities, and the standard of living on average in a nation as output per person falls in the economy.*

The Business Cycle

Real GDP is estimated quarterly by the U.S. Department of Commerce. The quarterly estimate is then multiplied by 4 (after adjusting for normal seasonal variation) to obtain the annual rate of GDP over the three-month period.[1] Unfortunately, real GDP doesn't always steadily increase. There are irregular fluctuations in real GDP over time that have consequences for you and for everyone else.

Business cycle is the term used to describe the fluctuations in aggregate production as measured by the ups and downs of real GDP. The fluctuations, although not subject to easy predictability or regularity, can be readily identified. Box 1 contains a stylized graph depicting the recurrent business cycle that shows the periodic ups and downs of real GDP.

business cycle the term used to describe the fluctuations in aggregate production as measured by the ups and downs of real GDP.

The business cycle is characterized by peaks and troughs and periods of contraction or expansion:

1. *Peak.* The *peak* is the highest level of real GDP in the cycle. Each peak (two are illustrated in the graph) indicates an economy operating at close to full capacity, so that national product and national income correspond to a very high degree of utilization of labor, factories, and offices. During a peak of the cycle, there are likely to be shortages of labor, parts, and materials in certain markets. On occasion the economy booms to such a degree that factories and offices are utilized around the clock, with two or more shifts of labor.

2. *Contraction or recession.* A contraction is a downturn from peak economic activity during which real GDP declines from its previous value. During a contraction, real GDP and therefore earnings also decline. Business profits also typically decline. As profitability falls, so does business demand for investment goods.

contraction a downturn from peak economic activity in the business cycle during which real GDP declines from its previous value.

Sometimes the decline in real GDP that occurs during a contraction is particularly severe or prolonged. The U.S. Department of Commerce usually considers a contraction to be a recession when the decline in real GDP measured at an annual rate occurs for two consecutive three-month reporting periods. In 1982, which was a recession year, real GDP fell by 3.3 percent of its 1981 value. Real GDP fell by 2.2 percent during the 1990–91 recession. As a consequence of a decline in real GDP, the percentage of the work force classified as unemployed usually rises by anywhere from 2 to 4 percentage points. In a typical nonrecession year only 4 percent to 6

recession exists when the decline in real GDP measured at an annual rate occurs for two consecutive three-month reporting periods.

---

[1] In some quarters real GDP is normally expected to be higher because of seasonal production patterns. To avoid overestimating the *annual* rate of GDP during quarters when GDP is higher because of seasonal increases, actual data are adjusted downward before multiplying by 4 to obtain annual real GDP. A similar upward adjustment is made for quarters during which real GDP is normally expected to be lower.

percent of the labor force may be unemployed, while during a recession 1 out of every 10 workers may be unemployed.

During recessions (which, since the end of World War II, have typically lasted for 10 to 12 months), increased unemployment can turn families topsy-turvy. As earnings fall, so do living standards. Work routines are broken up, and the idleness that goes with joblessness often leads to mental illness. Divorces and suicides increase along with the increase in unemployment. From an economic standpoint, the waste of labor and other resources capable of both producing goods and services and earning incomes for their suppliers is lamentable.

3. *Trough.* A *trough* is the lowest level of real GDP observed over the business cycle. A trough is reached when the economy begins to pull out of a contraction or recession. During this time there is an excessive amount of unemployment and idle productive capacity. Businesses are more likely to fail because of low demand for their products.

Although a trough is the pits, it's also the point at which things start looking up. Once a trough has been reached, things can't get much worse and the economic health of the nation begins to take a turn for the better.

4. *Expansion or recovery.* An **expansion** is an upturn of economic activity between a trough and a peak during which real GDP increases. During an expansion, demand for goods and services increases and real GDP rises as firms expand production, hire more workers, and purchase more investment goods. Employment opportunities increase during an expansion. The expansion in economic activity after a trough is called a **recovery** if it follows a period of contraction severe enough to be classified as a recession. During an expansion the economy moves toward a new peak, at which the cycle begins again.

expansion an upturn of economic activity between a trough and a peak during which real GDP increases.

recovery the term used to describe an expansion in economic activity after a trough if the expansion follows a period of contraction severe enough to be classified as a recession.

The cycle of peak-contraction-trough-expansion-peak is never as regular and predictable as in the graph shown in Box 1. However, the fluctuations in real GDP actually occur even if they don't do so in a clear pattern. Notice that an upward-sloping trend line has been fitted through the peaks and troughs of the cyclical pattern of real GDP. This line shows that, although real annual GDP fluctuates, the trend is upward over the long run.

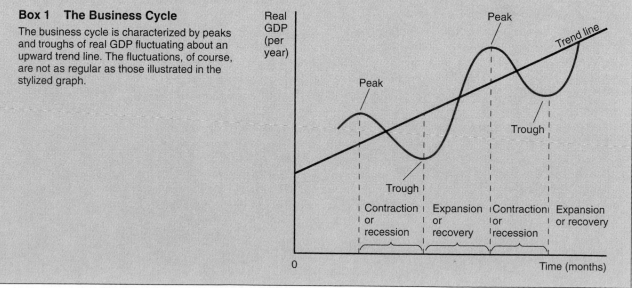

Box 1   The Business Cycle

The business cycle is characterized by peaks and troughs of real GDP fluctuating about an upward trend line. The fluctuations, of course, are not as regular as those illustrated in the stylized graph.

Actual Fluctuations and Trend of Real GDP in the United States

The graph in Box 2 shows the variation in real GDP over time. A trend line has been fitted through the data to reflect the average rate of increase in real GDP since 1900.

The general upward trend in real GDP is clear in Box 2. On average, real GDP grew by 3.1 percent per year from 1900 to 1990. *Real GDP has increased more than tenfold since 1900.* However, the growth has not been steady. There are clearly ups and downs in real GDP that can be identified as peaks, contractions, troughs, and expansions, although they're not as regular as those shown in the stylized graph in Box 1. A number of historical periods have been identified on the Box 2 graph.

1. *The Great Depression.* The Great Depression of the 1930s is clearly identifiable as a prolonged recession with a deep trough. It was unquestionably the trough of troughs.

The Great Depression hit in 1929 as a stock market crash late that year wiped out a substantial portion of the nation's accumulated savings. From the end of 1929 through 1933, real GDP fell by nearly one third of its 1929 value. During many severe recessions it isn't uncommon for prices to fall on average. From the end of 1929 through 1933, prices fell to only 75 percent of their 1929 level. Those who could spare a dime in 1933 knew it was worth more then than it had been in 1929.

During the Great Depression there were virtually no business investment purchases. The decline in aggregate real income made the prospects for selling goods bleak. Given the gloomy outlook, few investors were willing to build new plants or purchase new equipment.

But the worst part of the Great Depression was the unemployment. One out of every four workers in the labor force was jobless in 1933. Imagine the terrible waste of having one quarter of the able-bodied workers in the nation without jobs. You can also imagine the plight of the unemployed at a time when our nation didn't have the unemployment insurance and welfare programs we take for granted today. If you think there are a lot of street people today, you should have been around in the 1930s. The increased unemployment of the early 1930s is all the more dramatic when you realize that in 1929 only 3 percent of the labor force had been unemployed.

To anyone who lived through it, the Great Depression was a period of social unrest as well as economic contraction. The depression was worldwide, and the social instability it caused in Europe helped spawn the Nazi party and bring Hitler to power. As you'll see in the next part of this book, the Great Depression also affected

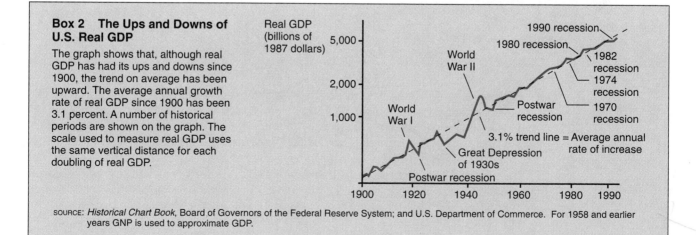

Box 2   The Ups and Downs of U.S. Real GDP

The graph shows that, although real GDP has had its ups and downs since 1900, the trend on average has been upward. The average annual growth rate of real GDP since 1900 has been 3.1 percent. A number of historical periods are shown on the graph. The scale used to measure real GDP uses the same vertical distance for each doubling of real GDP.

SOURCE: *Historical Chart Book*, Board of Governors of the Federal Reserve System; and U.S. Department of Commerce. For 1958 and earlier years GNP is used to approximate GDP.

principles in practice

Business Brief: What Is a Recession, and Who Can Predict When One Will Arrive?

Who decides whether the United States is in a recession? The Business Cycle Dating Committee, which meets under the auspices of the National Bureau of Economic Research (NBER), dates the beginnings and ends of recessions after they have actually occurred. The committee consists of a panel of seven experts that meets periodically to assess business conditions.

A recession is usually defined as a period in which output, income, and employment decline nationally over a period of at least six months. During a recession there is a widespread contraction of economic activity affecting many sectors of the economy. Orders for new plants and equipment and for materials and inventories typically plummet. Real GDP, industrial production, and personal income usually decline, while unemployment increases. Almost all recessions are preceded by a decline in stock market prices, but not all declines in stock market prices are followed by a recession.

Predicting when a recession will start isn't easy. Most forecasters failed to predict the two worst recessions of the 1970s and 1980s—the recessions of 1974–75 and 1981–82. However, the recession that began during 1990 was widely anticipated. In fact, the Dating Committee of the NBER in a rare early ruling declared that a recession "probably" began in August 1990. However, the official designation of the beginning of the recession was not made until 1991. The committee waited until late 1992 before designating March 1991 as the end of the 1990–91 recession.

What do you look for when trying to determine whether a recession is brewing? Most economists regard overexpansion of business investment—overstocks of parts and materials—as a prelude to contraction. Sudden increases in the prices of key inputs, such as oil, can also precipitate a recession.

Experts who try to forecast changes in real GDP keep a close watch on various sectors of the economy.

Leading economic indicators are economic variables whose values are normally expected to decline prior to a decline in real GDP and to rise prior to a rise in real GDP. In other words, leading economic indicators can sometimes (but not always) be useful in forecasting economic contractions or expansions. Among the important leading economic indicators watched in the United States are:

1. Average workweek of production workers in manufacturing.
2. Average weekly initial claims for unemployment insurance.
3. New orders for manufacturing, consumer goods, and materials.
4. A measure of vendors reporting slower deliveries.
5. Plant and equipment contracts and orders.
6. Building permits for new residential housing.
7. Changes in manufacturers' unfilled orders for durable goods.
8. Changes in the prices of certain materials used in production.
9. Common stock prices (an index of 500 stock prices).
10. Checking deposits, currency in circulation, and certain liquid assets.
11. An index of consumer expectations about the future.

The U.S. Department of Commerce regularly compiles a composite index of these 11 leading indicators. The year 1982 is used as a benchmark year, so its indicators are set equal to 100. Other years are then compared with 1982. Some of the indicators enter negatively in the index. For example, an increase in initial claims for unemployment insurance forebodes a decline in real GDP, so the index will go down whenever such claims go up. Similarly, a decline in materials prices will

the thinking of economists, most of whom prior to the 1930s thought that recessions would quickly cure themselves without assistance from the government. Their revised views led to the birth of macroeconomics—a policy-oriented branch of economics that would help formulate government programs to prevent severe recessions.

2. *Wartime prosperity and the post–World War II expansions.* The peaks, just before the 1920s and the early 1940s, when the economy was working at full steam producing goods for the war efforts, have also been clearly marked in Box 2. Notice that after World War I and World War II ended, there was a recession as the economy readjusted.

Ratio scale (1982 = 100)

NOTES: Peak (P) indicates the end of business cycle expansion and the beginning of recession (shaded area). Trough (T) indicates the end of business cycle recession and the beginning of expansion. Business cycle peaks and troughs are designated by the National Bureau of Economic Research, Inc. The numbers and arrows indicate length of leads (−) in months from business cycle turning dates.

SOURCE: U.S. Department of Commerce.

decrease unit costs of production and thus will cause the index to go up. Other components of the index can signify increases in economic activity and real GDP for fairly obvious reasons. For example, an upturn in the average workweek, building permits, bank deposits and other liquid assets, or the number of new contracts and orders implies more demand for final products and upward pressure on real GDP. Similarly, if vendor companies have difficulty getting deliveries of parts and equipment, a peak level of economic activity may be approaching.

Other components of the composite index are more difficult to interpret. For example, declines in stock prices decrease wealth and can adversely affect demand. Declines in stock prices can also mean reductions in future business profits. However, stock prices change in response to investors' perception of the profitability of holding stocks compared to other assets.

The index of leading indicators does occasionally decline without a subsequent decline in real GDP, so it must be used with caution. Forecasting the ups and downs of real GDP is riddled with pitfalls.

The graph shows movements in the index of leading indicators from 1970 to 1992. The shaded areas in the graph correspond to periods classified as recessions. Notice how the index tends to turn downward just prior to each recession. It begins to rise again after the recession has run its course and an expansion begins. However, you should also note that in some cases the index declines for an extended period, as long as one year, before a recession occurs. In other cases, such as in 1984, declines in the index are not followed by a recession. Typically, once a recession does hit, the index plummets. For example, see how sharply the index dropped during the 1974 and 1982 recessions.

Like any measure employed in forecasting, the index of leading economic indicators is useful but not infallible.

The 1950s were a period of prolonged and markedly steady growth in real GDP. However, the postwar expansion wasn't entirely uninterrupted by contractions and recessions. There was a recession immediately after World War II, and there were also recessions in 1949, 1954, 1958, and 1961. However, these five recessions were remarkably mild and much shorter than earlier recessions.

3. *The booming 60s.* After the recession of 1961 ended, the economy moved into a period of expansion. The 1960s were a period of military expansion and the Vietnam conflict. The increase in government purchases fueled the economy and also resulted in rising inflation.

4. *The curious 70s.* The 1970s came in with a recession. Although the recovery began in 1971, something strange happened in the economy in 1973. At that time the Organization of Petroleum Exporting Countries (OPEC) instituted an embargo on oil shipments to the United States and other nations. Inflation increased, and the price of petroleum products skyrocketed. Not only did inflation go up in the 1970s, but, curiously, so did unemployment! By 1974 the economy was buffeted by double-digit inflation and a severe recession. This was viewed as highly unusual. In the past inflation had usually eased up during a recession and sometimes prices had actually fallen, as was the case during the Great Depression. Real GDP fell substantially between 1973 and 1975, and unemployment soared to 9 percent of the labor force. It was all over by the end of 1975, when the economy recovered, and an expansion led to a 5 percent growth in real GDP in 1976. Inflation continued at a rampant rate during the remainder of the 1970s, but the nation avoided another recession.

5. *The expanding 80s.* Like the 1970s, the 1980s came in with a recession. The recession of 1980 was brief, lasting only six months, but extraordinary because it took place when inflation was still in double digits. As was the case for the 1974 recession, inflation and high unemployment sat side by side. The recession of 1980 was quite mild, with real GDP declining by only 0.5 percent that year. However, inflation remained a serious problem for the economy, running at 10 percent annual rates. At the end of 1981, the economy was plunged into the deepest recession it had experienced since the Great Depression of the 1930s. In that year real GDP fell by 2.2 percent and the unemployment rate soared to 11 percent.

The recession ended in late 1982, and the economy was well on its way to recovery. Starting in November 1982 and continuing to the end of the decade, the U.S. economy enjoyed a period of unprecedented peacetime expansion. In March 1989 the unemployment rate bottomed out at 5 percent—the lowest level that had been achieved since the early 1970s. Despite a major crash of the stock market in 1987, the economy remained resilient and continued to expand. Nearly 20 million new jobs were created during this period, and aggregate real income grew in a generally prosperous economy.

6. *The ominous 90s.* The 1990s began with a distinct slowdown in the growth rate of real GDP. By the second quarter of 1990, real GDP growth had slowed to a 0.4 percent seasonally adjusted annual rate. The economy was buffeted by declines in real estate values, bank failures, and a growing federal budget deficit. Declining profits in a heavily debt-burdened corporate sector contributed to a market slow-down in hiring. Unemployment rates began to creep up from their low of 5 percent in March 1990.

In August 1990 Iraq invaded Kuwait. The crisis sent oil prices soaring from less than $20 a barrel to as much as $40 a barrel. The increased oil prices caused gasoline prices and other prices to increase. The resulting increase in the price level adversely affected real incomes and caused a general decrease in the demand for a variety of goods and services. The oil price increase came at a time when the economy was already suffering from slowing growth. By September 1990 it was becoming very clear that the economy was slipping into a recession. During the last three months of 1990, real GDP in the United States fell at an annual rate of 2 percent. As the expansion of the 1980s ended, the unemployment rate increased to over 7 percent of the labor force. In the aftermath of the Gulf War, however, oil prices fell to less than $20 a barrel, which helped stimulate the sluggish U.S. economy. The recession of 1990–91 officially ended in March 1991. The recession was mild by historical standards, but it was followed by an uncharacteristically weak recovery. Throughout 1991 and 1992 real GDP grew at a relatively slow rate and there was no surge in job creation to help the unemployment rate decline. By early 1993, as the Clinton administration took power, unemployment rates were still in the range of 7 percent and economic growth was improving, but the expansion was still sluggish compared to other postrecession periods.

The ups and downs of real GDP depend on changes in market conditions of supply and demand. In the next part of this book, we will begin to develop the economic theory that shows how the forces of aggregate supply and demand influence real GDP. You will see that changes in economic and political conditions as well as changes in labor and other inputs, financial markets, and foreign exchange markets affect the level of both real GDP and prices.

CONCEPT CHECK
□

- How are a nation's living standards affected by a decline in real GDP from one year to the next when population is growing?
- How would you identify the peaks and troughs of the business cycle from quarterly data on real GDP?
- What has the trend of growth in real GDP been in the United States since 1900?

UNEMPLOYMENT

Increased unemployment is a major consequence of cyclical declines in real GDP during periods of contraction or recession. Workers in some industries are more apt to be unemployed during recessions than others. Those who produce producer-durable goods, consumer-durable goods, and construction are typically hard hit by economic contractions and recessions because investment purchases by businesses and purchases of durable goods by consumers decline. However, unemployment is not limited to a few industries. As unemployed workers cut back on their spending, other workers soon find their jobs in jeopardy.

Some unemployment naturally exists even during periods of peak economic activity. The portion of unemployment attributable to a cyclical downturn or to production below the economy's potential can, however, be identified once agreement has been reached on what constitutes "normal" unemployment. In this way the concept of "full" or high employment for the economy can be defined.

Macroeconomic stabilization policies seek to minimize excessive unemployment. However, to intelligently formulate such policies, it is first necessary to understand what unemployment is and how it is measured. This makes it possible to distinguish excessive or cyclical unemployment from normal unemployment.

The Unemployment Rate

The **labor force** is the number of people over the age of 16 who are either employed or actively seeking a job. The **unemployment rate** measures the ratio of the number of people classified as unemployed to the total labor force. An **unemployed person** is defined as one over the age of 16 who is available for work and has actively sought employment during the previous four weeks. Note that this definition excludes people who *choose not* to have or seek jobs and therefore are not part of the labor force. By definition, full-time students over the age of 16, people who choose to devote their time to household chores or to raising their children, retired people, people unable to work because of disability, and people in mental or correctional institutions, although not working for pay, are not part of the labor force.

The U.S. Department of Labor estimates the unemployment rate each month with a sample of about 60,000 households. The households in the sample are changed periodically. A person is classified as unemployed if he or she did not do any work

2

labor force the number of people over the age of 16 who are either employed or actively seeking a job.

unemployment rate the ratio of the number of people classified as unemployed to the total labor force.

unemployed person a person over the age of 16 who is available for work and has actively sought employment during the previous four weeks.

during the previous week. Note that people who have suffered reductions in paid work *hours* because of employer work cutbacks are *not* counted as unemployed. For example, a person whose work hours were cut from 40 to 20 a week because of slack demand for the product his employer manufactures is not counted as unemployed. However, a 50 percent reduction in the paid hours of work of two such workers amounts to the loss of a 40-hour workweek for the economy! This type of work loss isn't picked up by the unemployment statistics. Because the statistics don't measure the "underemployment" of workers who are not working full time but would like to be, they tend to underestimate actual unemployment.

The U.S. Department of Labor's monthly survey asks those in the sample whether they are actively looking for work. Some of the people who answer no to this question would be looking for work if wages were higher. Similarly, some of those classified as unemployed because they answer yes to this question may have unrealistic ideas about the value of their services and the wages they can reasonably expect. They may therefore be holding out for a job that they are unlikely to ever be offered.

discouraged worker
a worker who leaves the labor force (stops actively seeking a job) after unsuccessfully searching for a job for a certain period.

A **discouraged worker** is one who leaves the labor force (stops actively seeking a job) after unsuccessfully searching for a job. It's not unusual for more than 1 percent of those surveyed by the Department of Labor to respond that they aren't looking for a job because they don't believe one can be found. It's difficult to objectively determine why workers respond in this way. However, by not counting discouraged workers among the ranks of the unemployed, the official unemployment statistics tend *to underestimate* actual unemployment. Because of the way it treats part-time and discouraged workers, the official unemployment rate is an imperfect indicator of actual unemployment as a percentage of the labor force.

Frictional, Structural, and Cyclical Unemployment

When a worker quits a job, is fired, or is laid off, a *job separation* occurs. Unemployment would always be zero if the time between a job separation and the discovery of a new job were zero for each worker and if new entrants and reentrants into the labor force immediately found a job. The time, effort, and transaction costs required to find a new job guarantee that there will always be some unemployed workers looking for jobs. *Job search* is the process of looking for a suitable job either by those who have just entered the labor force or have just experienced a job separation. *Job finding* occurs when an unemployed worker accepts an offer of a new job.

frictional unemployment
the usual amount of unemployment resulting from people who have left jobs that did not work out and are searching for new employment, or people who are either entering or reentering the labor force to search for a job.

Members of the labor force search for jobs that best suit their skills and preferences. It's normal for workers to leave jobs they find unsuitable and for employers to fire workers who aren't performing their tasks up to required standards. **Frictional unemployment** represents the usual amount of unemployment resulting from people who have left jobs that didn't work out and are searching for new employment, or people who are either entering or reentering the labor force to search for a job. For example, if you spent six months looking for the right job after graduation, you would have been counted among the frictionally unemployed during that period. If a worker who is dissatisfied with a job managing a fast-food restaurant quits and takes two months to find a new job, that worker would be among the frictionally unemployed during that period.

structural unemployment unemployment resulting from permanent shifts in the pattern of demand for goods and services or from changes in technology.

Structural unemployment is unemployment resulting from permanent shifts in the pattern of demand for goods and services or from changes in technology such as automation or computerization. Structurally unemployed workers have skills that are not in demand by employers because of permanent changes in the economy. Structural unemployment often requires that workers who lose their jobs as a result of such changes learn new skills or move to other locations to find satisfactory new jobs. For example, the automobile workers who lost their jobs in the 1980s as result of a permanent decline in the demand for U.S.-made cars and increased automation of production facilities would be counted among the structurally unemployed. A permanent decline in the demand for petroleum products that resulted from improved conservation methods and higher oil prices in the 1980s caused structural unemployment for oil field and refinery workers in the United States. In the 1990s structural unemployment increased as a result of a permanent reduction in defense-related spending by the federal government and of corporate "downsizing" of work forces to reduce costs and increase productivity in a more competitive environment. To regain employment, some workers in the pool of the structurally unemployed have to find jobs in other industries or learn new skills.

The economy is always in flux because the pattern of demand and technology changes almost monthly. Both the industrial and regional patterns of demand for workers also change, implying that some workers will lose their jobs and have to search for new ones as a result of normal changes in the economy.

It's inevitable that a certain percentage of the labor force will experience job separation over the year. Forcing workers to stay in their jobs forever and preventing employers from ever cutting back employment, going out of business, or firing or laying off workers would involve losses in efficiency just as surely as excessive unemployment would result in waste.

Some unemployment, however, is directly attributable to cyclical declines in real GDP. **Cyclical unemployment** is the amount of unemployment resulting from declines in real GDP during periods of contraction or recession or in any period when the economy fails to operate at its potential. In macroeconomic policy analysis, cyclical unemployment receives the greatest amount of attention because cyclical unemployment is viewed as controllable. Policies that help prevent cyclical declines in real GDP can prevent cyclical unemployment.

Cyclical unemployment is characterized by layoffs. A **layoff** is the temporary suspension of employment without pay for a period of seven consecutive days or more. Workers who are on layoff are not fired. Instead, they are let go because of temporarily reduced demand for the product they are employed to produce. A worker who is laid off has some expectation of being recalled by his or her employer should business pick up again. Of course, a layoff may end up being permanent, in which case the worker must search for a new job to regain employment.

The total amount of unemployment in any month is the sum of frictional, structural, and cyclical unemployment. Frictional and structural unemployment result from natural and, perhaps, unavoidable occurrences in a dynamic economy. Cyclical unemployment, however, is the result of imbalances between aggregate purchases and the aggregate production corresponding to full employment.

The Natural Rate of Unemployment and Potential Real GDP

The **natural rate of unemployment** is the percentage of the labor force that can normally be expected to be unemployed for reasons other than cyclical fluctuations in real GDP. In other words, the natural rate of unemployment is the sum of the frictional and structural unemployment expected over the year. When the economy operates so that there is only structural and frictional unemployment, it is viewed as achieving the potential productive capacity normally expected at the peak of the business cycle. When the actual rate of unemployment is no more than the natural

cyclical unemployment the amount of unemployment resulting from declines in real GDP during periods of contraction or recession, or in any period when the economy fails to operate at its potential.

layoff the temporary suspension of employment without pay for a period of seven consecutive days or more.

3

natural rate of unemployment the percentage of the labor force that can normally be expected to be unemployed for reasons other than cyclical fluctuations in real GDP.

---

[2] The *natural rate of unemployment* can also be defined as the unemployment rate that would prevail if all wages and prices were instantaneously adjustable to changes in market conditions.

full employment the situation that occurs when the actual rate of unemployment is no more than the natural rate of unemployment.

rate of unemployment, the economy operates at **full employment**. *Because the natural rate of unemployment is not zero, full employment does not mean zero unemployment!*[3]

In 1985 the natural rate of unemployment was generally believed to be about 6 percent. If this was the case, cyclical unemployment would have been 1.1 percent because the actual unemployment rate that year, based on monthly averages, was 7.1 percent. In 1992 the natural rate of unemployment was estimated to be 5.5 percent. Because actual unemployment was 7.3 percent on average in 1992, there was cyclical unemployment of 1.8 percent in that year. Of course, when the economy attains full employment, as it did in 1989, the actual unemployment rate is close to the natural rate of unemployment and cyclical unemployment is close to zero.

[4]

potential real GDP the level of real GDP that would prevail if the economy achieves the natural rate of unemployment over a period of one year.

overheated economy an economy in which the actual unemployment rate is less than the natural rate of unemployment.

Potential real GDP is the level of real GDP that would prevail if the economy achieves the natural rate of employment over a period of one year. When the economy's performance is below its potential, such as during recessions, the unemployment rate exceeds the natural rate of unemployment.

An **overheated economy,** on the other hand, is one for which the actual unemployment rate is *less* than the natural rate of unemployment. In an overheated economy factories are run around the clock and many workers put in overtime. Typically, unit costs of production rise rapidly and labor shortages occur, putting upward pressure on wages and labor costs. When actual GDP rises above potential real GDP, the typical result is rapidly rising prices. The higher prices, as you will soon see, tend to decrease the aggregate quantity of goods and services demanded and cause real GDP to decline.

You should understand the following basic facts about potential real GDP:

1. *Potential real GDP is not the economy's "capacity" output.* The economy can produce *more* than potential real GDP when the actual unemployment rate falls below the natural unemployment rate. Even though capacity output exceeds potential real GDP, most economists believe that the economy cannot exceed potential real GDP for long periods without consequences that impair its future performance and ultimately cause actual real GDP to decline to its potential level.

2. *It's not easy to measure potential real GDP.* The natural rate of unemployment can vary from year to year. The number of hours worked per year when the natural rate of unemployment has been attained can also vary, depending on the mix of employment. In addition, it's hard to determine the level of output associated with the natural rate of unemployment, because the output depends on the productivity of workers. It's often only possible to guess at the level of real GDP that corresponds to the natural rate of unemployment. When we discuss economic policy to stabilize the economy, you will see that if policies are based on erroneous estimates of potential real GDP, they can destabilize the economy instead. For example, if policymakers mistake an increase in the natural rate of unemployment for an increase in cyclical unemployment and seek to expand the economy to get back to full employment, they could cause the economy to overheat and start a process of inflation that would impair the functioning of the economy for several years!

3. *Potential real GDP grows over time.* Remember that the long-term growth rate of real GDP in the United States has been slightly greater than 3 percent per year

---

[3] Actually, it's a matter of simple arithmetic to calculate the natural rate of unemployment when there are no movements of workers in or out of the labor force. The natural rate of unemployment, U, under these circumstances is the rate of job separation, s, divided by the sum of the rate of job finding, f, and the rate of job separation: $U = s/(f + s)$. For example, if 1 percent of the labor force experiences job separation during the year and 15 percent of the unemployed find jobs, the natural rate of unemployment is $0.01/0.16 = 6.2\%$. See Robert J. Barro, *Macroeconomics*, 3rd ed. (New York: John Wiley & Sons, 1990), pp. 256–59.

What Influences the Natural Rate of Unemployment?

Changes in the natural rate of unemployment can easily be mistaken for cyclical unemployment. For this reason it's important to understand the forces influencing the natural rate of unemployment in an economy. The natural rate of unemployment is related to the willingness of workers to voluntarily separate from their jobs, job loss, the duration of unemployment periods, the rate of change in the pattern of demand, and changes in technology.

Younger workers are more likely to quit their jobs than older workers. It takes some time for them to match their skills with their employment. It's therefore reasonable to assume that the younger the average age of workers in the labor force, the higher the natural rate of unemployment, because frictional unemployment increases when job separations increase. Teenagers in particular are likely to quit their jobs after only a short period. The higher the percentage of teenagers in the labor force, therefore, the higher the natural rate of unemployment.

The high unemployment rates observed in the United States in the late 1970s were partly the result of the entry of a disproportionately high number of younger workers into the labor force. At that time the baby boomers were in their 20s. These younger workers had higher quit rates than did older workers. The natural rate of unemployment will probably fall in the 1990s as the bulk of the baby boomers hit 40 and are snugly matched to the right jobs. Workers over 40 are much less likely than younger workers to quit their jobs.

Increased fluctuation in the pattern of demand for domestic goods increases structural unemployment and, in turn, contributes to a higher natural rate of unemployment. For example, the increase in energy prices that occurred in the mid-1970s disrupted hiring in many U.S. industries. Increased foreign competition also hurt the U.S. automobile and steel industries at that time. One researcher estimated that the changes in the structure of demand in the late 1970s increased the natural rate of unemployment by 1 to 2 percentage points.*

Rapid changes in technology designed to cut costs can also result in greater job separation. In an effort to compete more effectively with foreign firms, many U.S. firms have shifted to new technology that requires fewer workers per plant and results in slower hiring of new workers.

In recent years the number of married women in the labor force has increased sharply, thereby increasing the number of two-earner families. The existence of a second income prevents income from falling to zero when one of the spouses quits a job to search for a better one. Also, the second income allows a longer period to find a new job than would otherwise be possible. Thus, an increase in the number of two-earner families increases the natural rate of unemployment because it increases job separation through quitting and the duration of unemployment.

Tendencies toward moving in and out of the labor force can also affect the natural rate of unemployment, because such movement can affect the rate of job separation and job finding in the future. Workers who frequently move in and out of the work force have a high rate of job separation because they're less experienced than other workers. As a result, they're more likely to quit or be fired from a job.

In the early 1990s structural unemployment increased due to reductions in defense spending and corporate downsizing. These changes increased the natural rate of unemployment. However, aging of the work force in the 1990s will contribute to a decline in frictional unemployment, which will decrease the natural rate of unemployment. As of 1992, most economists estimated the natural rate of unemployment for the U.S. economy to be within the range of 5.5 percent to 5.8 percent of the labor force.

* David M. Lilien, ''Sectoral Shifts and Cyclical Unemployment,'' *Journal of Political Economy* 90, no. 4 (August 1982), pp. 777–93.

since 1900. Potential real GDP also grows on average from year to year. In some years the economy may grow slower than the growth in potential real GDP, and in some years it may grow faster. Potential real GDP growth depends on growth in the labor force and other resources, improvements in technology, and general improvements in the quality of productive resources (such as those that result from improvements in the educational level of workers). Potential real GDP will also grow if labor market conditions lower the natural rate of unemployment. For example, there is currently some concern that the growth rate of potential real GDP will decline in the future because of declines in the growth rate of the labor force. However, a decline in the growth rate of the labor force can be offset by improvements in technology that will either increase labor productivity or reduce the natural rate of unemployment.

Potential real GDP is the benchmark we will use throughout our study of macroeconomics to gauge the performance of the economy. Ideally, we would like to see the economy operate most of the time at potential real GDP.

CONCEPT CHECK

□

- Under what circumstances is a person officially classified as unemployed in the United States?

- Why is the economy considered to be operating at full employment when as much as 5.5 percent of the labor force is unemployed?

- What is potential real GDP, and why is it difficult to measure?

CYCLICAL UNEMPLOYMENT

Excessive unemployment is a sign that the economy is operating below its potential. When this is the case, there is cyclical unemployment. Not only is there idle labor, but machines and factories are also idle when real GDP is below its potential. The main cost is a reduction in output; when output falls, so does aggregate real income. The decline in income stems mainly from the workers who are unfortunate enough to lose their jobs. However, owners of other inputs, particularly capital, also experience declines in income, because the profit rate of many businesses declines when the economy contracts. Some industries are more sensitive to cyclical declines in output than others. For example, income tends to fall sharply in the construction and automobile industries when there is a recession.

How Unemployment Varies with the Business Cycle

One source of unemployment is a predictable pattern of quits and layoffs. Layoffs tend to increase, as you would expect, during contractions and recessions. Typically, during a recession about 3 percent of the labor force will be unemployed because of layoffs. In February 1986 less than 1 percent of the labor force was unemployed because of layoffs. However, in 1982, a recession year, about 3 percent of the labor force was unemployed because of layoffs. The unemployment rate in 1982 averaged more than 9 percent. The 1982 unemployment rate can be thought of as the sum of a natural rate of about 6 percent and the cyclical rate of 3 percent. Layoffs represent the cyclical component of the unemployment rate.

Unemployment resulting from quitting tends to drop during recessions but increases during expansions. Obviously, you wouldn't want to quit a job when the probability of finding another one is low, as it is during a recession. However, when times are good, you and many workers like you (typically as high as 3 percent) take the chance and quit to find a new job. In February 1986 less than 1 percent of the labor force was unemployed because of quitting.

The pie charts in Box 3 show that during a peak in the business cycle, the percentage of unemployed workers who lost their jobs because of layoff is typically not more than 12 percent of the unemployed. The chart at the left shows that, during 1978, a year generally classified as one of peak economic activity, only 11.5 percent of the job losers were on layoff. During a peak year the percentage of the unem-

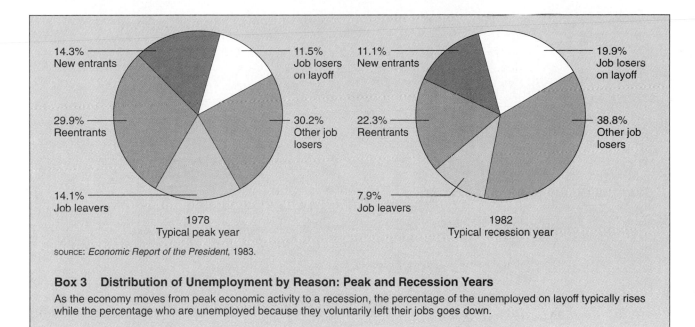

14.3% New entrants		11.5% Job losers on layoff
29.9% Reentrants		30.2% Other job losers
14.1% Job leavers		

1978
Typical peak year

11.1% New entrants		19.9% Job losers on layoff
22.3% Reentrants		38.8% Other job losers
7.9% Job leavers		

1982
Typical recession year

SOURCE: *Economic Report of the President*, 1983.

Box 3   Distribution of Unemployment by Reason: Peak and Recession Years

As the economy moves from peak economic activity to a recession, the percentage of the unemployed on layoff typically rises while the percentage who are unemployed because they voluntarily left their jobs goes down.

ployed who quit their jobs (job leavers) also tends to increase. In 1978, 14.1 percent of the unemployed voluntarily left their jobs.

During a recession year such as 1982 (a particularly severe period of recession), the proportion of unemployed who are on layoff approaches 20 percent. At such times people who have voluntarily left their jobs account for a much smaller percentage of the unemployed. In 1982 only 7.9 percent of the unemployed were people who left their jobs voluntarily. Box 4 shows how U.S. unemployment rates have varied since 1950.

The Costs of Unemployment

Unemployment means a drop in national production. This implies a reduction in income for the nation. When business receipts decline and firms have unused capacity, profits decline. When workers lose their jobs, they also lose the labor income they would have otherwise earned. The loss in wages and profits is part of the costs of unemployment. As income and business revenues decline during a recession, governments also suffer, because they experience a decline in their tax revenues.

But still more costs are associated with unemployment. Unemployment can be a depressing experience. Research provides evidence that increases in the cyclical unemployment rate are associated with increased suicide, crime, mental illness, and physical illness.[4] During recessions the average period of unemployment tends to double from the normal two-month duration. During recessions it's also more probable that in many families both spouses will lose their jobs. This tends to compound the stress and other social problems stemming from unemployment.

---

[4] See Barry Bluestone and Bennett Harrison, *The Deindustrialization of America* (New York: Basic Books, 1982). Chap. 3.

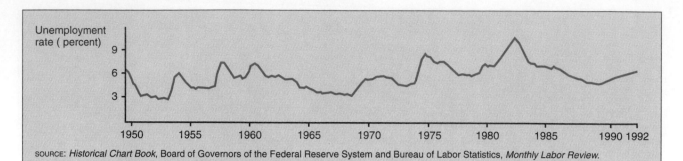

SOURCE: *Historical Chart Book*, Board of Governors of the Federal Reserve System and Bureau of Labor Statistics, *Monthly Labor Review*.

Box 4   Unemployment Rates 1950–1992

The official unemployment rate in the United States follows a cyclical pattern with ups and downs over time.

Cushioning Unemployment Costs

Unemployment insurance benefits available to eligible workers cushion the loss of income associated with temporary unemployment. These benefits vary from state to state, but they average about 35 percent of previous earnings. Usually the benefits last for a maximum of 26 weeks. Because the average duration of unemployment is only about eight weeks, workers seldom collect for the full period. In a recession, however, the duration of unemployment increases dramatically, to more than four months. In periods of unusually high unemployment, Congress extends the benefits for an additional 13 weeks.

Unemployment insurance was established in the United States as part of the Social Security Act of 1935. The program is managed by individual states, each of which has a separate trust fund used to support unemployment insurance benefits. The unemployment insurance tax is collected from employers by the federal government, which returns most of the funds to the states for deposit in their trust funds.

Unemployment insurance puts a floor on income and eases the costs of unemployment, but unemployment insurance is not available to all the unemployed. Eligibility varies from state to state. However, in all states only *covered* workers are eligible. How does a worker obtain coverage under unemployment insurance? He or she must have worked for a specified period at a job for which an employer paid the payroll tax for unemployment insurance.

New entrants and reentrants into the labor force are *not* eligible. For example, if it takes you six months to find a job after graduating from college, don't count on getting unemployment insurance to tide you over until you gain employment! Job quitters almost without exception are not eligible, nor in most cases are people who are fired because of poor performance. Who, then, gets the benefits? The answer is mainly people who lose their jobs temporarily because of layoffs or permanently because of shutdowns of business firms or contractions in business operations. In other words, the insurance alleviates the costs of cyclical and structural unemployment.

Finally, to remain eligible for benefits, an unemployed worker must be actively looking for a new job and cannot reject an offer of a suitable job. This last provision, however, is hard to enforce.

Recently there has been a significant decline in the proportion of the unemployed receiving unemployment insurance benefits. As of 1990, only about one third of the unemployed were receiving unemployment checks, compared to 75 percent of the unemployed in 1975. To reduce the tax bill for unemployment insurance, most state governments now require workers to work longer and earn more wages before they can qualify for unemployment insurance benefits. In addition, today's work force comprises more service workers, many of whom are part-timers and some of whom change jobs frequently. These workers are less likely to be eligible for unemployment insurance benefits.

Unemployment insurance benefits have not kept pace with inflation. The average benefits paid have declined from half of previous earnings in the 1970s to only a bit more than one third of previous earnings today. There are concerns among many that unemployment insurance has become a less effective cushion against the costs of unemployment than it once was.

▪ How does the pattern of laid-off workers, reentrants into the labor force, and new entrants into the labor force as a percentage of the unemployed vary with the phases of business cycle?	▪ What are the costs of unemployment, and how are they cushioned in the United States? ▪ Who is eligible for unemployment insurance?	**CONCEPT CHECK** ☐

ECONOMIC GROWTH AND ITS SOURCES

Over the long run, the ability of the economy to create job opportunities for a growing population depends on its rate of growth. There are always periods of recession, but their effects tend to be offset occasionally by boom periods during which the economy exceeds its potential. Over a long period, real GDP *on average* grows along with growth in potential real GDP. However, because of the tendency of prices to rise more in expansion periods than they fall during contraction periods, the price level rises along with the growth in real GDP.

Economic growth in a nation is measured by the annual percentage increase in its level of real GDP. Economic growth is the key to improvements in a nation's standard of living. Since 1900 real GDP growth in the United States has averaged 3.1 percent per year. Thus, the nation's ability to produce goods and services has increased at slightly more than 3 percent per year since 1900. The table in Box 5 shows the growth rates of real output in the United States for selected years from 1933 to 1991.

economic growth expansion in production measured by the annual percentage increase in a nation's level of real GDP.

The Sources of Growth

Ultimately, actual economic growth depends on the growth of the potential of the economy to produce goods and services. Actual real GDP may fluctuate around potential real GDP, but over a long period the economy on average comes reasonably close to producing a potential real GDP. As potential real GDP grows, so too do employment opportunities and potential aggregate real income. To understand the process of economic growth, therefore, we must understand the important influences on a nation's potential real GDP.

The major influences on a nation's potential to produce goods and services are:

1. *The productive resources available to the nation.* The labor, capital equipment, natural resources, and other inputs available in any year influence productive potential. The more workers and equipment available, given a nation's population and natural resources, the greater the nation's productive potential.

The U.S. labor force has grown considerably over the past 40 years. In recent years immigration, maturation of the baby-boom generation, and increased employ-

Box 5   Annual Growth Rate of Real Output in the United States, 1933–1991 (Percent Change from Previous Year)

Year	Growth rate	Year	Growth rate
1933	−2.1	1965	5.5
1939	7.9	1966	5.9
		1967	2.6
1940	7.8	1968	4.2
1941	17.7	1969	2.7
1942	18.8		
1943	18.1	1970	0
1944	8.2	1971	2.9
1945	−1.9	1972	5.1
1946	−19.0	1973	5.2
1947	−2.8	1974	−0.6
1948	3.9	1975	−0.8
1949	0	1976	4.9
		1977	4.5
1950	8.5	1978	4.8
1951	10.3	1979	2.5
1952	3.9		
1953	4.0	1980	−0.5
1954	−1.3	1981	1.8
1955	5.6	1982	−2.2
1956	2.1	1983	3.9
1957	1.7	1984	6.2
1958	−0.8	1985	3.2
1959	5.5	1986	2.9
		1987	3.1
1960	2.2	1988	3.9
1961	2.7	1989	2.5
1962	5.2		
1963	4.1	1990	0.8
1964	5.6	1991	−1.2

SOURCE: U.S. Department of Commerce.

ment of women have contributed to economic growth. In 1992 nearly 60 percent of working-age women participated in the labor force, compared to only 34 percent in 1950.

2. *The quality of productive resources available to the nation.* The quality of a productive resource is measured by its **productivity,** which is a measure of output per unit of input. The more productive workers, natural resources (such as agricultural land), and capital equipment, the greater the real GDP possible from a given amount of productive resources. Because labor is the dominant productive input, growth in labor productivity is a key to economic growth. When output per worker increases in a nation, output per person also tends to go up! Therefore, steady growth in a nation's labor productivity ensures steady growth in final products per person and in the material well-being of individuals in the nation.

The skills of a nation's labor force represent "human capital." The quality of a nation's human capital depends on the education and experience of its workers. Years and quality of schooling and on-the-job experience increase both output per worker and wages. Recent concerns about the quality of education in the United States reflect the fact that education is a key influence on worker productivity and living standards.

productivity a measure of output per unit of input.

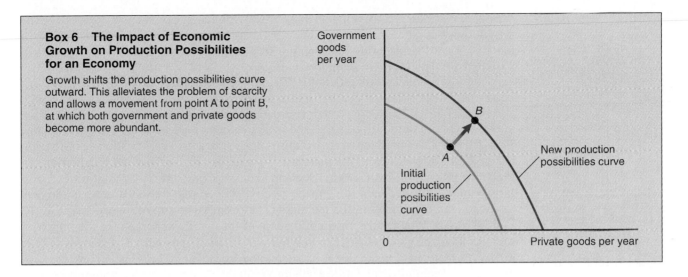

Box 6   The Impact of Economic Growth on Production Possibilities for an Economy

Growth shifts the production possibilities curve outward. This alleviates the problem of scarcity and allows a movement from point A to point B, at which both government and private goods become more abundant.

3. *Improvements in technology.* As technology advances, the output available from a given quantity of productive resources increases. Technological progress requires investment in research and development.

4. *Improvements in the efficiency with which available inputs are used.* Policies that promote efficiency in resource use allow the economy to obtain the greatest possible output of final products from available resources. Changes in management or policies that reduce waste in production and conserve resources can therefore contribute to increases in the economy's productive potential.

A favorable change in any of the preceding factors can be viewed as shifting the nation's production possibilities curve outward (see Chapter 2). As the nation enjoys improvements in the quality of resources, the quantity available, or technology, its potential to produce any combination of goods also increases. The production possibilities curve drawn in Box 6 illustrates the economy's potential to produce two broad classes of goods: private goods available to individuals and business firms for their exclusive use and government goods whose benefits are shared by all. You can see that growth helps deal with the problem of scarcity by allowing an increase in both government goods and private goods as the economy moves from point *A* to point *B*.

Improvements in Productivity

As suggested earlier, a key to the growth process is annual improvements in labor productivity. Output per worker goes up when worker skills or education improves, or when workers have improved tools to work with. Because workers gain more experience as they spend more time on their jobs, productivity growth is also influenced by the age composition of the labor force. When the percentage of younger workers in the labor force increases, the influx of inexperienced workers can adversely affect productivity.

Improvements in technology allow a given amount of capital or natural resources to be more productive when used by a labor force of given size. The sources of growth just listed are therefore not independent. Steady improvements in the quality of resources depend on steady improvements in technology and steady growth in capital per worker. Improvements in the quality of management can also improve the productivity of workers. Better productive management can improve the division of labor in ways that generate more output from a given work force. Improvements in personnel management procedures can give workers incentives to acquire more skills and to produce more efficiently. Economic growth has an important *allocative* component that is influenced by both business management techniques and public policies. In any given year growth is greater when resources are used in ways that allow maximum output to be squeezed from available inputs. Improvements in labor productivity accounted for over two thirds of the growth in real GDP over the period 1929 to 1982.[5] Increases in the quantity of available labor accounted for the remaining third. Research by Edward Denison indicates that the most important factor influencing improvements in labor productivity over that period was technological advance. Improvements in the technology of production and of management in the United States have been estimated to account for nearly 40 percent of the improvement in labor productivity. Keep in mind that it takes considerable business investment to create new technology, so technological advance and investment are not unrelated. Technological improvements result in new and better equipment, machines, and techniques that enhance worker productivity. New computers, machines, and modes of transportation have made workers much more productive in recent years.

Increases in the amount of capital available to workers, according to Denison, account for nearly 30 percent of the increase in labor productivity. Another 21 percent is accounted for by improved education and training. The bulk of the gains in labor productivity are therefore accounted for by improvements in technology, growth of capital equipment, and better education and training.

Saving, Investment, and Economic Growth

A nation's growth rate is influenced by the portion of national income that is invested. The process of investment involves the sacrifice of current consumption so that resources can be devoted to creating new capital, technology, or skills that will increase productivity and income in the future.

Business investment requires the outlay of funds that are obtained through financial markets or through capital consumption allowances or retained earnings. Capital consumption allowances (depreciation) are a form of saving through which businesses finance investment by setting aside earnings to replace worn-out or obsolete capital. Retained earnings are corporate savings used to finance the acquisition of capital goods.

Personal savings are also used to finance investment. They are channeled through financial markets to investors who borrow funds to make investments.

Investment in *human* capital often requires that people forgo opportunities for current income by attending colleges, universities, or training institutes. When people study to obtain new skills, they give up opportunities for current consumption in the hope that the extra education and skills they acquire in school will allow them to enjoy more annual future consumption.

The Trade-Off between Current and Future Consumption

The process of economic growth depends on the willingness of people in a nation to give up current consumption in exchange for the possibility of greater future consumption. The funds and labor hours allocated to investment can be used to develop

---

[5] Edward F. Denison, *Trends in American Economic Growth, 1929–1982* (Washington, D.C.: Brookings Institution, 1985).

principles in practice

The Costs versus the Benefits of Economic Growth

Can economic growth in a nation be anything other than a positive development? Can it actually have a down side? Let's see why the answers to these questions are yes by examining some of the negative consequences of economic growth.

Increases in output per capita benefit people in a nation by allowing higher average levels of material well-being over the long run. Such growth means more job opportunities for workers. It causes an outward shift of a nation's production possibilities curve that allows the economy to have more of both government goods and private goods. This allows a nation the luxury of using government services to deal with social problems without increasing tax rates.

But what about the costs of economic growth? More output each year can mean more pollution, more stress, and the development of a materialistic philosophy. Preoccupation with economic growth can prevent social progress that improves job safety and human health. Growth-oriented politicians are likely to oppose social programs that increase business costs if these programs slow growth in output.

Many of the amenities of life are not included in real GDP. In fact, some of the costs of economic growth require expenditures of funds to solve such problems as congestion and pollution. These expenditures to offset the side effects of economic growth are actually included in real GDP.

It's clear that social programs designed to cope with pollution, congestion, income inequality, and abuse of workers' rights do slow down the rate of economic growth. Estimates by Edward F. Denison conclude that improvements in the legal and human environment stemming from government regulations and other measures to control the social costs of economic growth contributed to a decline in such growth in 1973 and 1976.* A trade-off clearly exists between economic growth and policies to correct its undesirable effects. People must decide whether they are willing to give up some of the material benefits of economic growth in exchange for increased allocation of resources to correct the social problems of a growing economy.

* Edward F. Denison, *Trends in American Economic Growth, 1929–1982* (Washington, D.C.: Brookings Institution, 1985).

new technology, new factories and equipment, and more productive labor that will increase future real GDP. Of course, all investment entails risks and the actual payoff to investment is uncertain.

A nation with a higher saving rate is more likely to have a higher growth rate of output per capita over the long run than a nation with a lower saving rate. But a high saving rate can exert downward pressure on aggregate demand in a given year when the business outlook is poor and saving exceeds intended investment. High saving can thus exert downward pressure on equilibrium real GDP in some years because it detracts from demand. Over the long run, however, when the ups and downs of the business cycle average out, high saving rates will be matched by high investment rates. High saving over the long run will contribute to growth in productive capacity for the nation and increased future output per capita.

Recent Trends in Investment and Productivity Growth in the United States
Since 1975 the United States has been investing a percentage of GDP lower than the percentage invested by other advanced nations. The lagging investment rate in the United States could spell trouble for the international competitiveness of U.S. industries. In general, higher investment contributes to the productivity of workers and plants. When the U.S. investment rate lags behind that of other nations, unit costs of production in some industries could rise above those of industries in competing nations. U.S. firms could lose their competitive edge and sales in world markets, which would translate into slower growth of job opportunities at home.

During the 1980s, net investment in the United States, a measure of the investment purchases over and above the amount necessary to replace worn-out or

Box 7   Growth Rates of Capital per Worker and Labor Productivity in the United States, 1959–1991 (Average Annual Percentage Change)

Period	Capital per worker	Labor productivity
1959–1973	2.0	2.8
1974–1991	0.6	1.0

SOURCE: *Economic Report of the President*, 1993.

obsolete equipment, was also below average. The result of this lower net investment could be a lower rate of economic growth, spelling trouble for improvement in living standards. If the rate of growth of real GDP falls below the rate of population growth in the United States, average living standards could actually decline in the long run—a dismal prospect. The lagging investment rate in the united States is beginning to take a toll on labor productivity. There are fears that it could diminish the growth of future job opportunities and living standards.

A nation's physical stock of capital depends on past investment decisions. The physical stock of capital includes equipment, buildings, inventories, and transportation and communication networks. The growth of capital per worker is correlated with growth in labor productivity. As shown in Box 7, since 1973 the rate of growth of capital per worker has fallen substantially in the United States as U.S. investment rates have fallen. The decline in the growth of capital per worker has been accompanied by a sharp decline in annual productivity growth.

CONCEPT CHECK
☐

- What are the major sources of economic growth over the long run?

- What is productivity, and why is productivity growth important to growth in real GDP and real GDP per person?

- Why is national saving important for economic growth?

SUMMARY

1. The material well-being of a nation's citizens depends on real GDP. Declines in real GDP reduce both national production and national income. In a nation with a growing population, declines in real GDP result in decreases in final production per person.

2. The business cycle describes the periodic fluctuations in national production as measured by the ups and downs of real GDP.

3. The business cycle consists of movements from peaks to contractions and occasional recessions, then to troughs, and then expansions and recoveries from recessions. A recession is a decline in real GDP that occurs over at least a six-month (two consecutive quarters) reporting period.

4. Despite the ups and downs of the business cycle, there has been a general upward trend in real GDP since 1900. On average, real GDP has grown at the rate of 3.1 percent per year in the United States since 1900.

5. A consequence of declines in real GDP is excessive unemployment. The unemployment rate measures the ratio of the number of people classified as unemployed to the total labor force, which consists of the sum of employed and unemployed people over the age of 16. An *unemployed person* is a person over the age of 16 who is available for work and has actively sought employment during the past four weeks. The unemployment rate is estimated each month from a sample of 60,000 households. Not included in the ranks of the

unemployed are people who suffer reductions in hours worked but are employed part time during a period because of production cutbacks.

6. A layoff is a temporary suspension of employment without pay for a period of seven days or more.

7. A job separation occurs whenever a worker quits, is fired, or is laid off. Job separations are normal occurrences resulting from poor matches of workers to jobs and from changes in the pattern of demand for goods and services. *Frictional unemployment* is the usual amount of unemployment that occurs when people have left jobs and are searching for new employment or are entering the labor force. *Structural unemployment* is the unemployment that results from permanent shifts in the pattern of demand for goods and services or from changes in technology that affect the profitability of hiring workers in specific industries. *Cyclical unemployment* is the unemployment that results from declines in real GDP when the economy fails to operate at its potential. The excessive unemployment observed during a recession is cyclical unemployment. Layoffs are the major source of cyclical unemployment.

8. The natural rate of unemployment is the percentage of the labor force that can normally be expected to be unemployed for reasons other than cyclical fluctuations in real GDP. Natural unemployment is the sum of frictional and structural unemployment. The economy is viewed as operating at full employment when cyclical unemployment is zero. At full employment the actual unemployment rate is not zero, because some frictional and structural unemployment is normal even when the economy is operating at its potential. The natural rate of unemployment varies, but in recent years it has been estimated to be between 5 and 6 percent.

9. Potential real GDP is an estimate of the level of production that would prevail in an economy if the natural rate of unemployment were achieved.

10. The costs of unemployment include a reduction in national output and tax revenues. Increases in unemployment appear to be associated with increased mental and physical illness and other social problems. Unemployment insurance cushions the declines in well-being that result from excessive unemployment.

11. Economic growth is measured by the annual percentage change in a nation's real GDP. The most important sources of economic growth are increases in the quantity and quality of economic resources, improvements in technology, and more efficient resource use.

12. Improvement in labor productivity is a driving force behind economic growth. Improvements in workers' skills or education or the capital that workers use can improve their productivity.

13. The process of investment involves the sacrifice of current consumption so that resources can be devoted to creating new capital, technology, or skills that will in the future increase productivity and therefore real GDP and real income.

KEY TERMS

business cycle *161*
contraction *161*
recession *161*
expansion *162*
recovery *162*
labor force *167*
unemployment rate *167*

unemployed person *167*
discouraged worker *168*
frictional
 unemployment *168*
structural
 unemployment *168*

cyclical
 unemployment *169*
layoff *169*
natural rate of
 unemployment *169*

full employment *170*
potential real GDP *170*
overheated economy *170*
economic growth *175*
productivity *176*

CONCEPT REVIEW

1 What is the business cycle?

2 How is the unemployment rate measured in the United States?

3 Explain why the unemployment rate is not zero when the economy achieves "full employment."

4 How is the concept of potential real GDP related to the natural rate of unemployment and the economy's "capacity" output?

5 How does the system of unemployment insurance operate in the United States?

6 What could cause a slowdown in the rate of economic growth in the United States?

PROBLEMS AND APPLICATIONS

1. Following are seasonally adjusted data for real GDP for each of 10 quarters:

Period	Quarterly real GDP (billions of seasonally adjusted dollars)
1st quarter, year 1	1,000
2nd quarter, year 1	900
3rd quarter, year 1	800
4th quarter, year 1	700
1st quarter, year 2	700
2nd quarter, year 2	750
3rd quarter, year 2	850
4th quarter, year 2	1,100
1st quarter, year 3	1,150
2nd quarter, year 3	1,100

Calculate the real GDP at an annual rate for each quarter, and plot the points associated with each quarter. Trace a curve through the points to illustrate the phases of the business cycle. Was there a recession over the period covered by the data? How would you calculate the long-term trend in growth in real GDP over that period? **2**

2. Can real GDP decline even though there is no recession? What are the consequences for the economy of declines in real GDP? **1** , **2**

3. In January there are 60 million employed workers and 2 million unemployed workers in the economy. Calculate the January unemployment rate. **2**

4. Why can the official unemployment rate be criticized for underestimating actual unemployment in the economy? **2**

5. Explain why it is unreasonable to expect an economy's unemployment rate ever to fall to zero. Why can unemployment be decreased by an improvement in the job search process that decreases the time required for job finding? **3**

6. Suppose the natural rate of unemployment in 1995 is 6 percent and corresponds to 320 billion hours of labor for the year. When that unemployment rate has been achieved, output per labor hour is $20 measured in 1987 prices. Calculate potential real GDP for 1995. **4**

7. The current unemployment rate is 7 percent. If the sum of structural and frictional unemployment is 6 percent, how much cyclical unemployment prevails? **3**

8. Explain how the pattern of quits and layoffs varies predictably with the business cycle. **3** , **5**

9. Why does a slowdown in the rate of economic growth imply that future living standards may deteriorate? **6**

10. Why is the rate of productivity growth in a nation likely to be tied to the rate of saving and investment in the nation? **6**

chapter 8

The Price Level and Inflation

In 1975 you could buy a hot dog for 65 cents. Nowadays try to find a decent hot dog for less than $1.25. Just think about how much more you could buy with your allowance or earnings if prices were what they were when you were a kid. A pair of jeans priced at $35 today would cost only $24 if it were still available at the price that prevailed 10 years ago. In fact, prices on average have more than tripled in the United States since 1970!

Inflation can make it difficult to plan for the future and can adversely affect the purchasing power of our income and savings. When the prices of goods and services we buy are subject to erratic increases, the result is distortions in resource use as we seek ways to protect the purchasing power of our dollars.

In this chapter we will show how the economy's price level and inflation are measured and how inflation can damage the functioning of the economy by affecting incentives to save, invest, and allocate resources. We will also examine who loses and who gains as a result of inflation. Our goal will be to understand the impact of fluctuations in the average level of prices on the economy and on people. In the next part of this book, we will consider the causes of inflation, and later we will evaluate policies designed to keep it under control.

☐ CONCEPT PREVIEW

After reading this chapter, you should be able to:

1. Understand how price indexes are used to measure the price level and inflation.

2. Deflate nominal income using a price index to derive real income and know the distinction between real and nominal wages.

3. Explain how inflation affects workers, employers, creditors, and debtors.

4. Explain how inflation affects interest rates and know the distinction between real and nominal interest rates.

5. Explain how inflation affects economic decisions and the functioning of the economy.

THE PRICE LEVEL AND INFLATION

[11]

price level an indicator of how high or low prices are in a given year compared to prices in a certain *base period.*

Before discussing inflation, we need to define what we mean by the level of prices in the economy in a given year. The **price level** is an indicator of how high or low prices are in a certain year compared to average prices in a certain *base period*. Given the bewildering variety of goods and services available in markets, the government chooses a representative group (or aggregate) of goods and services, called a *market basket,* and calculates the cost of purchasing the items in the basket. The cost of the market basket of goods and services in the current year is then compared with the cost of the same market basket in a certain base year.

price index a number used to measure the price level. The value of the index is set at 100 in the base year or period.

A **price index** is a number used to measure the price level. The value of the index is set at 100 in the base year or period. If the price index in a given year exceeds 100, the price level in that year is higher than it was in the base year. Similarly, a price index of less than 100 for a given year means the price level in that year is lower than it was in the base year.

inflation the rate of upward movement in the price level for an aggregate of goods and services.

Inflation is the rate of upward movement in the price level for an aggregate of goods and services. Inflation occurs when prices on average are increasing over the year. Of course, not all prices increase at the same rate during periods of inflation, and it's quite common for some items to fall in price even during periods when prices are generally rising. For example, during the late 1970s and early 1980s (a period of rapid inflation), prices of televisions and other electronic goods actually declined. Rising prices make it difficult to plan for the future and cause distortions in decisions as people seek to protect themselves against the effect of inflation on the purchasing power of their money income and savings.

deflation the rate of downward movement in the price level for an aggregate of goods and services.

Although you're accustomed to a rising price level, there have been periods when the price level actually declined. During the Great Depression of the 1930s, for example, there was a sharp decline in prices. **Deflation** is the rate of downward movement in the price level for an aggregate of goods and services.

The Consumer Price Index

A price index measures how the cost of purchasing a standard market basket of goods and services varies from the cost of purchasing the same market basket in the base period. It is calculated as the ratio of the current cost of a given market basket to the cost of the same market basket in the base period multiplied by 100:

$$\text{Price index} = \left(\frac{\text{Cost of a market basket of products at current prices}}{\begin{array}{c}\text{Cost of the same basket of products} \\ \text{at prices prevailing over the base period}\end{array}} \right) 100$$

The value of the index is always 100 in the base period because the numerator and denominator of the equation are the same in the base period.

consumer price index (CPI) the price index most commonly used to measure the impact of changes in prices on households. This index is based on a standard market basket of goods and services purchased by a typical urban family.

The **consumer price index (CPI)** is the price index most commonly used to measure the impact of inflation on households. This index is based on a standard market basket of goods and services purchased by a typical urban family. The CPI market basket does not include exported goods, investment goods, or items purchased by governments. However, changes in the prices of imported goods purchased by the typical urban family are considered when calculating the CPI.

The goods in the CPI market basket are based on a survey conducted once a decade by the Bureau of Labor Statistics. The most recent survey resulted in a revision of the goods in the market basket in 1987 (see Principles in Practice box). Since 1988 an average of prices for the years 1982 to 1984 has been used in calculating the base period cost of the market basket.

The CPI is actually a *weighted average* of a number of component price indexes. Price indexes for such items as housing, transportation, food and beverages, and other broad categories for expenditure are computed separately. Then the price index for each item receives a weight that indicates the relative importance of the item in consumer spending. For example, housing is presumed to account for 42.6 cents of each dollar spent by the urban family. The index measuring the aggregate price level of housing services is therefore multiplied by 0.426 when calculating the "all items" CPI. Entertainment is currently assumed to absorb 4.4 cents of each dollar spent. The price index for entertainment is therefore multiplied by 0.044 when calculating the "all items" index.

Because the weight attached to housing exceeds the weight attached to entertainment, a given percentage increase in the price of housing will have a much greater impact on the CPI than the same percentage increase in the price of entertainment. For the current CPI, a 4 percent increase in the aggregate price level of housing services will receive nearly 10 times as much weight in calculating the "all items" CPI as a 4 percent increase in the aggregate price level of entertainment items.

Measuring Inflation

Annual rates of inflation are measured by the percentage change in a price index, such as the CPI, from one year to the next. For example, the monthly average of the CPI in 1989, using the average of prices between 1982 and 1984 as the base, was actually 124.0. In 1988 the monthly average of the CPI was 118.3. To calculate the percentage change in the CPI, first take the change in the price index over the year, which in this case is $(124.0 - 118.3)$. Next divide the change in the price index by its value in the initial year, 1988, and multiply the result by 100 percent to convert to a percentage increase. The rate of inflation between 1988 and 1989 was therefore

$$\left(\frac{\text{CPI in 1989} - \text{CPI in 1988}}{\text{CPI in 1988}}\right) \times 100\%$$

$$\left(\frac{124.0 - 118.3}{118.3}\right) \times 100\% = 4.8\%$$

Changes in the Price Level versus Changes in Relative Prices

You should always keep in mind that the official inflation rate is a measure of the average rate of change in the prices of a broad aggregate of products. For example, in 1986, when the official inflation rate was 1.9 percent measured by the percentage change in the CPI, energy prices *fell* by 19.7 percent, which helped pull the average of all prices down. However, that year food prices rose by 3.7 percent and the price of medical care rose by 7.7 percent. The economy rarely experiences **pure inflation,** during which the prices of *all* goods rise by the same percentage over the year.

The *change in the relative price of a good* is a change in its price relative to the prices of an average of all goods. If the economy experienced pure inflation, there would be no changes in the relative prices of goods because the price of every good would rise by the same percentage. Under pure inflation, the price of any one good does not change more or less than the average rate. This means that over the year no particular good becomes any cheaper or more expensive relative to other goods than it was at the beginning of the year. Pure inflation therefore does not provide consumers with any incentive to substitute one good for another in their budget, nor does it change the profitability for sellers of one good rather than another. On the other hand, changes in the relative prices of goods in the economy are signals that provide incentives to adapt to changing conditions.

pure inflation a condition that occurs when the prices of all goods rise by the same percentage over the year.

principles in practice

The CPI Market Basket

The shopping cart you steer down the supermarket aisles today probably contains items that differ from those used by a family 50 years ago. For example, most people are buying less red meat and fewer eggs because of health concerns, and disposable shavers have replaced old-fashioned straight razors.

The consumer price index (CPI) is designed to measure changes in a weighted average of prices for goods and services purchased by a typical urban family. Because consumers' needs and purchases change, every 10 years the consumer price index gets an overhaul by the Bureau of Labor Statistics. The way a typical urban family spends each dollar of earnings also changes over time. The weights used in the consumer price index reflect the percentage of each dollar an urban family allocates to particular groups of items. When the CPI is updated, so are the weights given to various prices for groups of products included in the CPI.

The most recent version of the CPI market basket was introduced in January 1987. It was based on interviews with nearly 10,000 American families from 1982 to 1984. The new CPI is calculated for the cost of a market basket that consists of 184 different goods and services consumed by the typical urban family.

The new basket of goods reflects changes in the working, living, and spending patterns of Americans since 1978. Families are now smaller, and over half the women in families are employed outside the home. As a result, food eaten away from home is now a larger component of consumer budgets than was the case in 1978. People tend to drive less than they did in 1978, so transportation is now a smaller component.

In computing the CPI, the item given the most weight is housing. Of each dollar spent on consumer goods and services, the typical urban family spent 43 cents for housing over the period 1982 to 1984. In 1978 housing represented only 38 cents of each consumption dollar.

New goods and services creep into the CPI each time it's revised. For example, the latest model of the CPI includes day care for children. Personal computers, VCRs, and compact disc players didn't exist in 1978. However, these goods are now purchased regularly by Americans, and they're included in the new CPI. Other new services in the CPI are videocassette rentals, pet services, and home care for the elderly and the disabled.

The table shows the percentage of consumer spending for each category in the latest model of the CPI and in the old CPI. These percentages represent the broad categories of weights that are used in computing all the items in the CPI from the individual price indexes of its components.

The CPI is called a base period weight index because the importance of each price in determining the value of the index each month depends on how much income consumers spent on that item *during the base period survey.* The higher the percentage of income spent on an item, the greater the weight given to a change in the price of that item. The survey for 1982 to 1984 is therefore very important because it will influence the way inflation is measured until 1997.

The CPI is published monthly. The data used to calculate the index each month are gathered by about 250 "price collectors" employed by the Bureau of Labor Statistics who check prices at about 18,000 stores in 56 cities. The average prices of each product included in the index are then computed and combined into the overall CPI using the weights based on the most recent survey. A complicated exercise—but useful!

Expenditure	1972–1973	1982–1984
Housing	38.2%	42.6%
Transportation	19.1	18.7
Food and beverages	20.8	17.8
Apparel and upkeep	7.5	6.5
Other goods and services	4.8	5.1
Medical care	5.0	4.8
Entertainment	4.6	4.4

The GDP Deflator

The CPI is the best measure of the price level for determining changes in the cost of living for typical urban households in the United States. Sometimes, however, we want to use a broader measure of the price level to determine the effects of inflation on producers' incentives to supply all goods and services. Remember, GDP does not include only consumption goods—it also includes goods and services produced for use as final products by businesses, governments, and foreign buyers that demand our exports. A broader index of inflation would include the effects of changes in the prices of all investment goods, government purchases, and net exports.

The **GDP deflator** is the ratio of nominal GDP to real GDP (multiplied by 100); it is an index of the average of the prices used to deflate nominal GDP. Remember that nominal GDP measures aggregate production of final products valued at their current market prices. Real GDP measures aggregate production of final products valued at base year prices. The Department of Commerce currently uses 1987 as the base year in calculating real GDP. The GDP deflator is therefore:

GDP deflator the ratio of nominal GDP to real GDP (multiplied by 100); an index of the average of the prices used to deflate nominal GDP.

$$\text{Implicit GDP deflator} = (\text{Nominal GDP/Real GDP})100$$

For example, in 1991 the GDP deflator stood at 110.9, which implies that, *on average,* final products priced at $100 in 1987 would have been priced at $110.90 in 1991.

The aggregate of products used to compute the GDP deflator differs from that used to compute the CPI. Imported products are not part of GDP, because they are produced in foreign nations. Therefore, a change in the price of a VCR imported from Japan will have no impact on the GDP deflator. However, the price change will affect the CPI if the VCR is purchased by a typical urban family.

The GDP deflator will also change with the mix of products in the current GDP. Unlike the CPI, the GDP deflator does not measure the change in the cost of a standard market basket of a given combination of products.

A History of the Consumer Price Level and Inflation

The graph in Box 1 shows fluctuations in the consumer price index from 1913 to 1990. The base period is 1982–84. As you can see in the graph, consumer prices rose sharply during World War I. Immediately after the war there was a period of deflation followed by price stability during the 1920s. Consumer prices plummeted, however, during the Great Depression of the 1930s. Prices began to increase again in 1933, but at a very slow rate. After World War II began, the price level shot up again. There was a mild deflation of the price level in 1948.

Since 1948 consumer prices have risen. The rate of increase was greatest in the 1970s. During the 1980s prices continued to rise, but at a much slower rate than during the 1970s.

The graph in Box 2 shows the quarterly percentage changes in the consumer price index from 1950 to 1992. As you can see, the pattern of inflation measured by the annual percentage changes in the CPI has been quite erratic since 1950. After a sharp increase in the inflation rate in the early 1950s, during the Korean War, the price level was relatively stable, with inflation seldom exceeding 5 percent per year. There was even a brief period of deflation. However, the 1970s were a period of high and erratic inflation. The average annual rate of inflation ranged between 3.3 percent and 11.3 percent. In 1980 inflation was roaring at an average annual rate of 13.5 percent.

From 1983 to 1989, inflation averaged 3.64 percent per year based on year-to-year percentage changes in the CPI. In fact, mainly because of sharp drops in the prices of gasoline and other energy-related products, there was even deflation of the price level in some months during 1986. In 1992 the rate of inflation was only 2.9 percent.

Box 3 shows the average annual rate of inflation for consumer prices during periods from 1960 to 1992. As you can see, inflation was quite low in the early 1960s, when it averaged 1.26 percent per year. It peaked in 1975 to 1980, when it averaged 8 percent per year. Between 1980 and 1985 inflation averaged a bit less than 6 percent per year, and between 1985 and 1989 inflation averaged 3.6 percent per year.

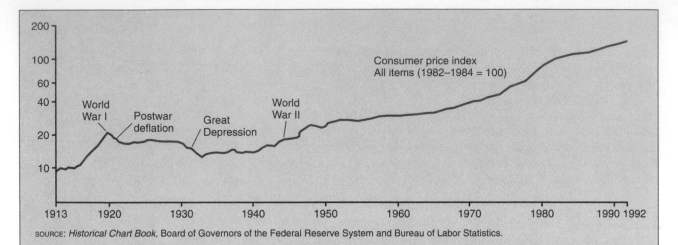

SOURCE: *Historical Chart Book*, Board of Governors of the Federal Reserve System and Bureau of Labor Statistics.

Box 1   Consumer Prices, 1913–1992; Quarterly Averages, 1982–1984 = 100

Consumer prices have risen steadily since 1950. However, prior to 1950 there were periods in which prices fell. There was a sharp drop in consumer prices during the Great Depression of the 1930s. The scale used to measure prices uses the same vertical distance for each doubling of the price level.

Box 2   Quarterly Percentage Changes in the Consumer Price Index: Seasonally Adjusted Annual Rates 1950–1992

Since 1950 the pattern of inflation has been erratic. Inflation was very high during the period 1974–1975 and between 1978 and 1981.

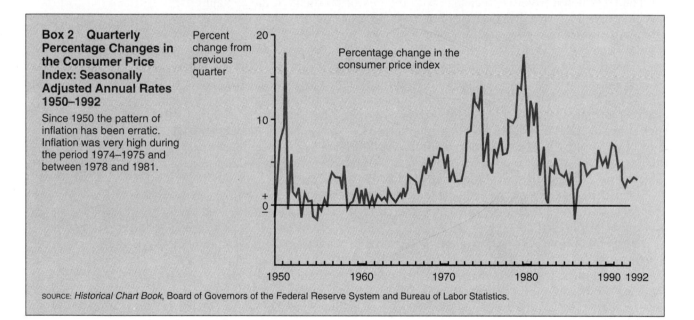

SOURCE: *Historical Chart Book*, Board of Governors of the Federal Reserve System and Bureau of Labor Statistics.

Box 3   Average Annual Rate of Inflation, Five-Year Averages

Period	Average annual percentage change in consumer price index
1960–1964	1.26
1965–1969	3.46
1970–1974	6.10
1975–1979	8.06
1980–1984	7.50
1985–1989	3.60
1990–1992	4.17

SOURCE: *Economic Report of the President*, 1993.

How is inflation measured?

How do the GDP deflator and the CPI differ as measures of the price level?

Inflation during the year has been 4 percent. However, the relative price of clothing has fallen during the year. Does this necessarily mean that clothing costs less in dollars than it did last year?

CONCEPT CHECK

□

THE DISTORTIONS AND COSTS OF PRICE INSTABILITY

Why all the concern about price instability? Who gains and who loses as a result of inflation or deflation? What distortions in decision making are associated with price instability?

Inflation can significantly affect the national standard of living. It can also cause changes in behavior that can have serious effects on resource use and the functioning of the economy. To analyze the costs of inflation, we must examine its effects on both incomes and decisions. There are always gainers and losers from inflation, but it is not always easy to predict who will lose and who will gain.

Real Income: Using the CPI to Deflate Nominal Income

Fluctuations in the price level affect the quantity of goods and services that can be purchased with a given sum of money. The **purchasing power of a dollar** (or any other unit of currency) is a measure of how much it can buy. An increase in the price level means a decrease in the purchasing power of a dollar. For example, if the price level were to double over a year, the purchasing power of a dollar would be cut in half because it would take $2 to buy what a year earlier could have been bought for $1. In any given year, the greater the rate of inflation, the greater the decline in the purchasing power of a dollar for the year.

To measure changes in the purchasing power of income over time, it is necessary to adjust nominal income for changes in the price level. **Nominal income** is the actual number of dollars of income received over a year. **Real income** is the purchasing power of nominal income. Real income is usually expressed in terms of the market value of the final products it can purchase when those products are valued in *base period* prices rather than current period prices.

Real income is obtained by deflating nominal income by the current CPI to adjust for rises in the price level since the base period. To deflate nominal income, divide it by the current CPI/100:

$$\text{Real income} = \frac{\text{Nominal income}}{\text{Current CPI}/100}$$

For example, suppose your nominal income in 1989 was $10,000. To find out what your *real* income was in 1989, first divide the 1989 CPI of 124 by 100, which gives 1.24. This tells you that the price of a market basket of goods purchased by a typical urban family was 1.24 times higher in 1989 than it was on average between 1982 and 1984. Your real income is

$$1989 \text{ real income} = \frac{\$10,000}{1.24} = \$8,064.52$$

Real income measures income in base period (in this case 1982–84) dollars rather than current dollars. Your $10,000 nominal income for 1989 has the same purchasing power that $8,064.52 had on average between 1982 and 1984! A person who earned $10,000 in 1989 had the same purchasing power as a person who earned about $8,000 in 1983, when the CPI was 99.6.

purchasing power of a dollar a measure of how much a dollar can buy.

nominal income the actual number of dollars of income received over a year.

real income the purchasing power of nominal income.

Knowing how to deflate nominal values is extremely important in making comparisons of salaries from one period to another. For example, suppose your sister graduated from college in 1983 and got a job paying $12,000 per year. In 1983 the CPI was approximately equal to 100, so her real salary was also $12,000. Now suppose you graduate from college in 1995 and you get a job that pays $20,000 per year. Suppose the value of the CPI in 1995 is 200. It is clear that your nominal starting salary is greater than your sister's. However, your real salary deflated to 1983 dollars is only $20,000/2 = $10,000. Your sister's starting salary, therefore, had greater purchasing power than your starting salary does.

You can also use the preceding formula to deflate $1 to find out the purchasing power of a current dollar after adjusting for inflation since the base year:

$$\text{Purchasing power of a current dollar} = \frac{\$1}{\text{CPI}/100}$$

In 1989 the purchasing power of a dollar was

$$\frac{\$1}{1.24} = 80.64 \text{ cents}$$

On average, each dollar in 1989 bought what could have been purchased for only about 80 cents at the prices that prevailed, on average, over the period 1982–84.

The graph in Box 4 shows how the purchasing power of a dollar has varied from 1960 to 1992. Because the price level has increased substantially since 1960, the purchasing power of a dollar has fallen. The more rapid the rate of inflation in a given year, the greater the decline in the purchasing power of a dollar.

Of course, conclusions about the impact of inflation on the purchasing power of a dollar for particular consumers must be qualified. Not all consumers buy exactly the same mix of goods. If you spend more of your income than the average urban consumer on goods whose prices have not increased as fast as the average, such as televisions, calculators, and stereo equipment, inflation is less of a problem for you than for the typical urban consumer. Also, because not all prices rise by the same percentage during inflationary periods, consumers adjust their buying habits in response to changes in prices. They buy more goods whose prices have increased less than the average and fewer goods whose prices have increased more than the average. To say that the purchasing power of a dollar in 1989 was one third what it was in 1967 means that a dollar bought only one third as many goods in 1989 as it did in 1967 *for the consumer who bought exactly the same goods in the CPI market basket year after year.*

When the rate of inflation of consumer prices exceeds the rate of increase of a person's nominal income, a person buying the standard market basket of goods used to calculate the CPI will find that his money income buys less this year than it bought the year before. *When a person's annual rate of increase in nominal income lags behind the annual rate of increase in the price level, the person's real income declines.* A decline in a person's real income implies a decline in his standard of living as measured by the quantity of goods and services his income can buy. To find out the effect of inflation on a person's standard of living, we must therefore analyze its impact on that person's real income. As you'll soon see, inflation can have some rather capricious and unpredictable effects on the distribution of real income. Inflation affects everyone, but not equally!

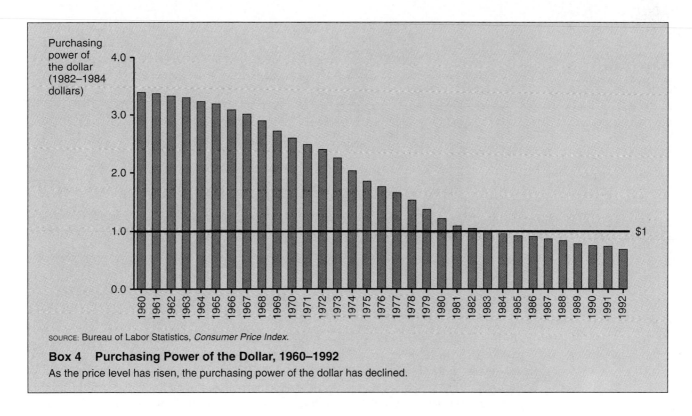

SOURCE: Bureau of Labor Statistics, *Consumer Price Index.*

Box 4   Purchasing Power of the Dollar, 1960–1992

As the price level has risen, the purchasing power of the dollar has declined.

Nominal Wages versus Real Wages

Wages are a measure of both hourly payments for labor services by business firms and hourly compensation to workers. Nominal wages are hourly payments to workers in current dollars. Real wages are nominal wages deflated to adjust for changes in the purchasing power of a dollar since a certain base period. Real wages give hourly compensation in terms of base period dollars. For example, suppose nominal hourly wages in 1995, including the hourly dollar value of fringe benefits, are $20. If the consumer price index is 200 in 1995 (and 1982–84 is the base), then the purchasing power of a 1995 dollar is only one half the purchasing power of a 1982–84 dollar. It follows that the real wage expressed in terms of base period dollars is only $10.

The graph in Box 5 shows the percentage changes in consumer prices and the percentage changes in hourly employee compensation (the hourly nominal wage and the nominal value of hourly fringe benefits) from 1960 to 1991. In most years, the percentage change in hourly employee compensation exceeds the percentage change in prices. In most years, therefore, the growth rate of nominal wages (including the value of fringe benefits) exceeds inflation, because employers compensate workers not only for changes in the price level but also for changes in productivity. The graph shows that, on average, competition for labor services has resulted in a nominal wage growth exceeding the inflation rate. On average, real wages in the United States have increased each year. The increase in the real wage reflects increases in labor productivity.

You should also observe that the annual percentage change in labor compensation and the inflation rate move together. However, there's often a lag between the increase in consumer prices and the increase in nominal hourly labor compensation.

3

nominal wages hourly payments to workers in current dollars.

real wages nominal wages deflated to adjust for changes in the purchasing power of a dollar since a certain base period.

Box 5   Annual Percentage Changes in Hourly Labor Compensation and in Consumer Prices 1960–1991

Changes in annual consumer prices and annual hourly labor compensation move together. In some years, however, increases in the prices of consumer products do exceed increases in labor compensation.

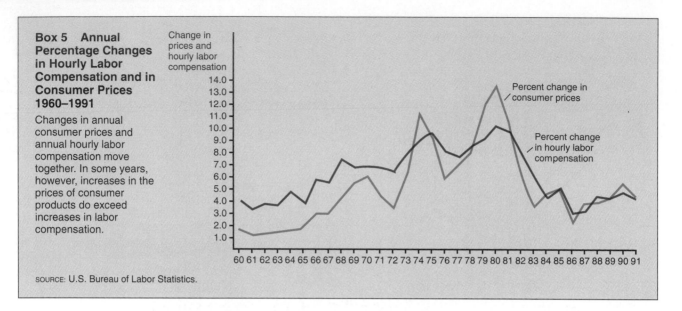

SOURCE: U.S. Bureau of Labor Statistics.

During periods of rapid inflation, the rate of increase in consumer prices often exceeds the rate of increase in nominal hourly labor compensation. For example, during the periods of rapid inflation from 1973 to 1975 and from 1979 to 1981, inflation outstripped increases in hourly labor compensation. Real wages therefore fell over that period. Similarly, in 1984 inflation outstripped the growth of nominal wages, resulting in a decline in real wages.

During periods of rapid inflation, when real wages decline, workers' hourly compensation falls. Who gains? The answer is employers, who end up paying less in hourly labor costs. *As a result, during periods in which inflation exceeds the percentage increase in nominal wages (hourly labor compensation), there is a redistribution of income from workers to their employers.* This is one of the capricious effects of inflation on the distribution of income.

Workers consider inflation when engaging in contract negotiations that set wages. By and large, the growth in nominal wages and inflation move together because workers demand increases to offset the effects of inflation. Nominal increases in hourly compensation lag behind inflation only in periods when inflation heats up rapidly.

How Inflation Can Redistribute Income and Wealth from Creditors to Debtors

Inflation is great for people who are in debt, because the purchasing power of dollars will decline over the life of their loans. Debtors will therefore pay back principal and interest in dollars that are worth less each year in terms of purchasing power. *Inflation tends to decrease the burden of paying off loans because debtors make payments in dollars that have less purchasing power than the dollars they borrowed!*

Inflation decreases the wealth of creditors, who experience a reduction in the purchasing power of the outstanding balances on the loans they carry on their books as assets. For example, suppose you borrowed mortgage money in 1967. Assume the outstanding balance on your loan in 1987 was $10,000. Because the purchasing power of a dollar in 1987 was only about one third of its purchasing power in 1967, the outstanding balance valued in 1967 dollars (when you borrowed money to buy the house) was only $3,333. In this way inflation redistributes wealth (asset values) from creditors to debtors.

In effect, savers can be regarded as creditors. Those who have savings accounts in banks, such as 10-year certificates of deposit, are harmed by inflation because the purchasing power of their savings will be eroded unless the interest they earn is high enough to compensate them for the effects of inflation. For example, suppose you purchase a five-year certificate of deposit that yields 10 percent interest per year. If inflation is 20 percent per year, you'll lose purchasing power on your savings each year. Although the balance will go up by 10 percent per year because of interest payments, the 20 percent inflation will outstrip the interest payments. The net effect will be a fall in the purchasing power of your savings.

Nominal Interest Rates versus Real Interest Rates

The preceding analysis of the impact of inflation on debtors and creditors assumes that the interest rate doesn't adjust for the effects of inflation. You should recall the analysis of the impact of inflation on wages. Inflation is considered in the bargains struck between workers and employers. By the same token, inflation is considered in the bargains struck between borrowers and lenders. Lenders are less willing to make loans when they see inflation coming, because they know that inflation will reduce the purchasing power of the dollars that will be repaid. As lenders anticipate the adverse effects of inflation on the profitability of lending, they decrease the supply of loanable funds and thus put upward pressure on interest rates.

The **nominal interest rate** is the annual percentage amount of money that is earned on a sum loaned by or deposited in a bank. The nominal interest rate is the contract interest on the face of the loan or deposit and is always positive. For example, if you buy a $5,000 certificate of deposit that yields 10 percent annual interest, you are a creditor who loans the bank that sum for a period of time at a 10 percent nominal annual rate of interest. The **real interest rate**[1] is the actual annual percentage change in the *purchasing power of interest income* earned on a sum of money that is loaned out. When inflation is present, the real rate of interest will be less than the nominal rate. The real rate of interest is the nominal rate adjusted for the decrease in purchasing power that results from inflation.

The earned real rate of interest can be thought of as the nominal interest rate minus the rate of inflation.[2] For example, suppose the nominal interest rate you earned over a one-year period on a $5,000 certificate of deposit was 9 percent. If inflation averaged 6 percent over the same period, then the real interest rate you earned was 3 percent.

$$\begin{array}{ccccc} \text{Real interest earned} \\ \text{on a loan} & = & \text{Nominal interest rate} & - & \text{Inflation rate} \\ \text{over its life} & & \text{per year} & & \text{per year} \\ 3\% & = & 9\% & - & 6\% \end{array}$$

The $5,000 principal plus the interest it earned over the period that the bank held it, after adjustment for inflation, was worth only 3 percent more than it was worth when you deposited it.

Although nominal interest rates are always positive, real interest rates are negative when the actual rate of inflation exceeds the nominal interest rate. Lenders will

> **nominal interest rate** the annual percentage amount of money that is earned on a sum loaned by or deposited in a bank.

> **real interest rate** the actual annual percentage change in the purchasing power of interest income earned on a sum of money that is loaned out.

---

[1] The definition refers to the "earned" or *ex post* real interest rate. In contrast, the *ex ante* real interest rate is the nominal interest rate minus the anticipated rate of inflation. The "earned" real interest rate is important for calculating the actual real return on an outstanding loan. The *ex ante* real interest rate is important when parties are considering a new loan or investment.

[2] The real interest rate can be shown to equal the nominal interest rate minus the rate of inflation plus the product of the rate of inflation and the nominal interest rate. However, when both inflation and the nominal interest rate are less than 20 percent, the product of inflation and the nominal interest rate is so low that it can be ignored.

incur losses on loans during periods when the nominal interest rate on the loans is less than the rate of inflation. Of course, given the nominal interest rate, lenders need not incur losses in future years on loans made when real interest rates are negative. Changes in the inflation rate over the life of the loans will affect the real interest rate earned in future years.

Despite the fact that nominal interest rates soared to double digits in the late 1970s, borrowing was a good deal at that time because roaring inflation actually resulted in negative real interest rates! In 1978, for example, the real interest rate on three-month Treasury bills, which represent short-term borrowing by the federal government, was estimated to be −1.5 percent. In such periods, when nominal interest rates increase less rapidly than prices, borrowers benefit greatly, while lenders are harmed.

Naturally, creditors seek to anticipate the rate of inflation when lending funds over a long period. If creditors expect inflation to heat up in the future, they are going to be very cautious about making long-term loans. This decreases the supply of long-term credit in the markets for loanable funds and pushes up nominal interest rates in those markets to compensate for expected inflation. Because market forces tend to adjust nominal interest rates in response to inflationary expectations, it is very difficult to conclude whether creditors or debtors gain as a result of inflation. For example, if actual inflation turns out to be less than is anticipated by the creditors when they make long-term loans, the debtors could be harmed by inflation because they will end up paying relatively high real interest rates over the life of their loans.

If all long-term contracts involving loanable funds had clauses allowing automatic adjustment for inflation, no redistribution of income from creditors to debtors would arise from changes in the inflation rate. In fact, after the rapid unanticipated inflation of the 1970s, many banks became reluctant to make long-term loans (such as mortgages) at fixed interest rates. Instead, they made long-term loans with variable interest rates tied to current interest rates. Both individual consumers and business managers learn from their mistakes!

CONCEPT CHECK
☐

- Under what circumstances is inflation likely to result in a decline in real wages?
- Under what circumstances will inflation redistribute wealth and income from creditors to debtors?
- What is the real interest rate? Under what circumstances will real interest rates be negative?

HOW PRICE INSTABILITY AFFECTS THE PERFORMANCE OF THE ECONOMY

5 Price instability, or, more accurately, the actions taken in anticipation of it, can adversely affect the performance of the economy. When buyers and sellers try to guess what price instability will do to the purchasing power of the dollar in the future, they also base their decisions in part on the gains or losses they might incur as a result of inflation (or deflation). The resulting shifts in supply and demand in individual markets cause distortions in market prices. For example, suppose everyone thought that inflation would erode the real value of savings. This would cause the supply of savings to decrease, which would make interest rates higher than they would be in the absence of these inflationary expectations.

Anticipated Inflation and Economic Decisions

You've undoubtedly become used to the fact of inflation over your lifetime. If you're like most people, you've probably made purchases that you might otherwise have put off, because you *anticipated* that inflation would increase the prices of the product. For example, if you anticipate a 10 percent price increase in the stereo system you want to have next year, when you move out of your dorm into an apartment, you might choose to buy it now rather than next year. Similarly, when signing a lease for an apartment or borrowing money, you've probably considered what inflation would do to rent or interest charges.

Inflation makes it hard to collect information about what constitutes a reasonable price for an item. You never know whether the price of an item has gone up because of shifts in the supply of and demand for that item or because of general inflation. This makes it difficult to decide what to buy and when to buy it.

Anticipated inflation affects the choices we make as individuals. Those who correctly anticipate the impact of inflation on their incomes can avoid the reduction in real income and wealth that inflation will cause. For example, if lenders correctly anticipate inflation, they can avoid its undesirable effect on their real income by attaching an inflation "premium" to the nominal interest rate they charge for new loans. Businesses consider inflation when placing orders. For example, businesses that expect future price increases may stock up on parts and raw materials.

When inflation is steady and predictable, many people correctly anticipate its effects on the purchasing power of the dollar. However, when inflation is erratic, fewer people succeed in anticipating its effects. The actual impact of inflation on the distribution of income between workers and their employers and between borrowers and lenders will depend on how accurately inflation is anticipated by each of these groups.

Inflationary Distortions in Saving and Investment

Erratic inflation is particularly troublesome for long-term contracts. It increases the risk involved in estimating the returns on investment projects by making it difficult to anticipate future input and output prices. This may lead to distortions in decisions to save and invest and cause investment to be reduced below the efficient level.

Let's first look at how inflation can reduce investment by increasing the cost of acquiring new plant and equipment. Capital consumption allowances (depreciation) represent a cost of production that can be deducted from business income before taxes are computed. The sum of capital consumption allowances deducted over the life of an asset equals its purchase price. The *real value* of capital consumption allowances falls as a result of inflation. This means the tax deduction that business firms get for purchasing capital is worth less and businesses will pay more in taxes. The higher the rate of inflation, the less will be the gain in after-tax profits for businesses from purchasing investment goods. Inflation therefore reduces the incentives of businesses to make investments and could adversely affect the economy's growth rate.

Now let's look at how inflation can reduce the supply of saving to fund investment. Remember that inflation erodes the value of bank deposits and other assets that are fixed in monetary value, such as funds. If inflation soars, savers may liquidate their financial assets and purchase land or antiques and other collectibles because when inflation soars, the prices of land and collectibles are also likely to soar. This makes less funds available for productive investments such as new factories that ensure future increases in labor productivity and employment opportunities for workers. This puts further upward pressure on interest rates.

Inflation not only distorts current choices but also can decrease confidence in the nation's financial markets, thereby adversely affecting future opportunities as the amount of saving channeled into productive investment is reduced. A nation's real GDP growth rate can be adversely affected if inflation reduces business investment.

When inflation reaches excessive levels, the central banking authorities of a nation, such as the Board of Governors of the Federal Reserve System in the United States, are usually obliged to take action to raise interest rates and reduce the supply of credit. If monetary authorities tighten credit severely to achieve their objective of reducing the rate of inflation, the result could be a recession. This has happened in the past. For example, the recession of 1982 in the United States was a direct result of economic policies designed to reduce the rate of inflation.

The Disastrous Effects of Hyperinflation

Extraordinarily high rates of inflation are likely to be more costly than modest rates of inflation. If people expect very high inflation, they'll try to spend their earnings as quickly as possible so as to avoid holding money whose purchasing power will be quickly eroded. For example, if you anticipate that prices will rise 10 percent per week, you'll be eager to be paid once or twice a day so you can spend your earnings before the purchasing power of the dollar deteriorates!

hyperinflation inflation at very high rates of usually 200 percent or more prevailing for at least one year.

During the 1920s, inflation in the German Weimar Republic reached such astronomical rates that it was dubbed hyperinflation, defined by the International Monetary Fund now as inflation at an annual rate of 200 percent or more prevailing in a nation for at least one year. In 1922 the annual inflation rate in Germany exceeded 5,000 percent because the Weimar government sought to pay its bills by printing money. In 1922 the money stock in Germany grew by about 30 percent per month. Prices rose almost hourly! German currency became worthless and was used as kindling for stoves. Once people began to anticipate the inflation, they tried to unload cash balances, which caused further inflationary pressures by increasing the demand for goods and services.

The cost to Germany was tremendous. Credit markets virtually collapsed, as no one was willing to take the risk of lending money. A massive redistribution of income wiped out the savings of millions and benefited people who were heavily in debt. Employees demanded to be paid at least once a day and spent an inordinate amount of time each day trying to unload their earnings before the price level rose again! The ultimate solution for Germany was a monetary reform in 1923 that changed the currency and limited printing of the new currency.

Hyperinflation is not a historic relic. In 1985 the rate of inflation in Bolivia was 11,749 percent! An item that sold for the equivalent of 50 cents at the beginning of 1985 cost more than $5,000 at the end of the year! In 1992 hyperinflation was on the verge of rearing its ugly head in Russia!

Bolivia managed to get its inflation under control by 1990. However, another South American nation, Argentina, was still struggling with the horrors of hyperinflation in that year. Prices in Argentina increased by over 5,000 percent in 1989, and in some months of 1989 the annual rate of inflation was over 12,000 percent. The result was social chaos and a collapse of monetary and financial markets. As of 1990, many prices in Argentina were quoted in U.S. dollars and Argentines who wished to pay in their own national currency had to pay at the current rate of exchange for dollars, which fluctuated hourly!

According to the International Monetary Fund's definition, the nations of Peru, Brazil, Nicaragua, Poland, and Yugoslavia also suffered from hyperinflation in 1989.

the global economy

Hyperinflation in the Computer Age

In May and June 1989 there were riots and looting in the streets in Argentina. The printing machines in Argentina's National Mint were running around the clock to keep up with the incredible demands for currency in a nation whose inflation was estimated to be running at an annual rate of 12,000 percent per year. A new 50,000 austral note (the *austral* is the Argentine monetary unit) was designed to help ease the demand for currency whose purchasing power declined hourly. A 100,000 austral note was being planned. The machines at the mint were breaking down regularly from the strain of overuse.[3] Even the paper the money was printed on was being debased—cheap paper from Brazil and Yugoslavia instead of the fine 100 percent rag paper the mint used to use! The Argentines themselves preferred U.S. dollars to their own currency, but dollars quickly became expensive—the price of a dollar rose from 17 australes in January 1989 to 175 australes in early June 1989, and some black market sellers were getting nearly twice as many australes to the dollar. By early 1990 it took nearly 6,000 australes to buy a U.S. dollar.

Hyperinflation encountered the computer age in Argentina—an event on a par with Godzilla meeting King Kong. Supermarket managers could increase prices daily and even hourly if they wanted to because of the computerized checkout counters. Prices in Argentine supermarkets were going up in May 1989 at the rate of 1 percent every four hours.[4] However, the salaries of Argentine workers did not enjoy the same computerized adjustment for inflation. Argentine workers saw the purchasing power of their wages and salaries fall daily. In May 1989 riots and looting of supermarkets resulted in 15 deaths and 170 arrests.

The situation in Argentina is testimony to the way rampant inflation can rip the social fabric of a nation. In May 1989 prices in Argentina rose 80 percent and expectations of further inflation led shoppers to run to supermarkets as soon as they were paid. Banks were paying interest on deposits at the rate of 2 percent *per day*. Businesses tried to delay paying their bills as long as possible to earn interest on their outstanding balances and to pay back in australes whose purchasing power was less than that of the day before. The Argentines were accustomed to triple-digit inflation, but the hyperinflation of 1989 was the straw that broke the camel's back.

Attempts to control hyperinflation by the government led to a severe economic slowdown. In 1990 Argentina's prospects still appeared bleak. Inflation was still raging, unemployment was soaring, and poverty was increasing. The economic planning secretary of the Argentine government described his country as "on the way to underdevelopment."[5]

Unemployment in some regions of Argentina was as high as 25 percent as of early 1990. In a nation noted for its beef, few workers could afford meat; its consumption dropped sharply.

Cutbacks in government spending designed to control inflation caused cutbacks in public services. In the first quarter of 1990, inflation was still running at an annual rate of nearly 1,200 percent! The inflation triggered a recession. Argentina may have been the first nation in the world to have experienced *staghyperinflation*—hyperinflation coupled with an economic slowdown.

---

[3] See James Brooke, "Fodder for a Ravenous Inflation," *The New York Times,* June 12, 1989.

[4] See James Brooke, "Argentina in Chaos as Prices Rise Hourly," *The New York Times,* June 2, 1989.

[5] See Thomas Kamm, "Argentina's Economy Is Caught in Downward Spiral," *The Wall Street Journal,* April 26, 1990.

CONCEPT CHECK

☐

- How can inflation decrease the supply of credit and contribute to higher nominal and real interest rates?
- How can inflation influence household allocation

- of income between current and future consumption?
- Can the impact of inflation on the distribution of income be easily predicted?

SUMMARY

1. Inflation is the rate at which the general price level increases for goods and services produced in a nation. When inflation exists, the purchasing power of a nation's currency declines over time. A dollar buys fewer goods and services over time as a result of increases in the price level. Deflation is the opposite of inflation. When deflation exists, the price level declines and the purchasing power of a dollar increases.

2. The percentage change in the consumer price index (CPI) over a year is the most common measure of inflation. The CPI is a weighted average of the prices of a market basket of goods purchased by a typical urban family relative to a weighted average of the prices of the same basket of goods in a base period. Measured in this way, inflation is an average of the increases in the prices of all goods in the CPI market basket. The greater the weight attached to an item in the CPI, the greater the impact of a change in its price on the CPI.

3. Some goods can actually decrease in price even when inflation is positive. Pure inflation prevails in an economy if the prices of all goods rise by the same percentage over the year. The relative price of a good increases when its price rises at a more rapid rate than the prices of all goods.

4. Nominal income is the number of dollars received as income during a year. Real income is the purchasing power of nominal income measured by the quantity of goods and services that can be bought with that income. Real income is measured in base period prices and is obtained by dividing nominal income by the CPI/100. When there is inflation is an economy, increases in nominal income do not necessarily imply increases in real income.

5. When the rate of inflation exceeds the growth rate of nominal income, real income declines. The real wage for an hour of work declines if the nominal wage increases at a rate less than the rate of inflation. In the U.S. economy nominal wages tend to increase with inflation. However, there is a lag between increases in the price level and increases in nominal wages, particularly during periods of rapid inflation. Under those circumstances, workers suffer temporary reductions in real wages.

6. Inflation can result in a redistribution of income and wealth from creditors to debtors. As a result of inflation, borrowers can pay back loans in dollars that have less purchasing power than the dollars they borrowed. This makes debtors better off at the expense of creditors, who are repaid in dollars that are worth less than those they lent. Inflation can also harm savers, who, in effect, are creditors, because the purchasing power of dollars in savings decreases as a result of inflation.

7. The effect of inflation on debtors and creditors also depends on how much the nominal interest rate adjusts for inflation. The real interest rate on a loan is the annual percentage change in the purchasing power of interest income earned on a sum of money loaned out. As a result of inflation, the real interest rate is less than the nominal interest rate. The real interest rate earned on a loan can be thought of as the annual nominal interest rate less the annual inflation rate over the life of the loan. Real interest rates can be negative.

8. Actions taken in anticipation of inflation can adversely affect the performance of the economy. When buyers and sellers try to anticipate inflation, they base their economic decisions, in part, on the gains or losses they expect to incur. This can affect the supply of and demand for particular goods and services, thereby distorting market prices.

9. Anticipated inflation can distort consumer choices by causing buyers to purchase goods now that they might otherwise prefer to purchase in the future. Hyperinflation seriously impairs the functioning of the economy by causing credit markets to collapse and by wiping out the purchasing power of accumulated savings.

10. Inflation is a distorter of choices and a capricious redistributor of income. Erratic inflation has both gainers and losers, but it is difficult to predict who will gain and who will lose.

KEY TERMS

price level *184*

price index *184*

inflation *184*

deflation *184*

consumer price
index (CPI) *184*

pure inflation *185*

GDP deflator *187*

purchasing power of a
dollar *189*

nominal income *189*

real income *189*

nominal wages *191*

real wages *191*

nominal interest rate *193*

real interest rate *193*

hyperinflation *196*

CONCEPT REVIEW

1 What is the consumer price index (CPI)?

2 How can the CPI be used to deflate nominal income to real income measured in base year dollars?

3 How can inflation harm workers and creditors (including savers)?

4 How do real interest rates differ from nominal interest rates?

5 How can very high and erratic inflation reduce an economy's rate of growth?

PROBLEMS AND APPLICATIONS

1. Suppose the consumer price index is 200 in 1995. Assuming an average of prices for 1982–84 is the base, explain the implication of the CPI for prices and the cost of living in 1995 as compared to the 1982–84 average. **1**

2. Suppose nominal income for young urban professionals averaged $30,000 per year in 1982–84 and $50,000 per year in 1995. Using 1982–84 as the base period, calculate the real 1995 income of an average yuppie measured in base period dollars, assuming the CPI is 200 in 1995. **2**

3. Suppose the rate of inflation is 5 percent. Does this mean that all the goods you purchase will cost 5 percent more than they did the year before? How would you determine the rate of inflation for goods and services that are included in your personal budget? What can cause a decline in the relative price of a good? **1**

4. Suppose the consumer price index goes up from 300 to 310 during the year. At the beginning of the year, your nominal wage is $10 per hour. At the beginning of the following year, you get a raise that increases your nominal wage to $11 per hour. Calculate your real wage in each year, and indicate whether your real wage has gone up or down. **2**

5. How are real wages in the United States affected by inflation on average over a period of several years? What is the implication of a decline in real wages for both workers and their employers? Under what circumstances does inflation redistribute income from workers to employers? **2**, **3**

6. A borrower negotiates a $20,000 loan at 3 percent interest in 1983, when the value of the consumer price index is 100. In 1990 the outstanding balance on the loan is $10,000. If the CPI is 130 in 1990, how much is the outstanding balance of the loan in 1983 dollars? How has inflation since 1983 affected the borrower? **2**, **3**

7. In what sense does inflation redistribute income from the holders of the federal debt to current taxpayers? **3**

8. The nominal interest rate on bank deposits is 6 percent. During the year the inflation rate is 3 percent. What is the real interest rate earned on bank deposits that year? Suppose depositors and banks anticipated 4 percent inflation during the year. How did real interest rates differ from those anticipated, and how did the difference between actual and expected inflation affect the distribution of well-being between borrowers and lenders? **4**

9. The nominal interest rate in a certain nation is not permitted to exceed 10 percent. During the year most lenders anticipate 14 percent inflation. Predict the impact of these expectations on decisions to lend funds. **4**, **5**

10. Suppose you live in a nation where hyperinflation prevails. If you are given a choice between two jobs, both paying the same wage and having the same fringe benefits, explain why you would be more likely to choose the job that pays you every week instead of the one that pays you every month. **5**

part IV

Aggregate Demand/ Aggregate Supply

CONCEPTS

Aggregate Demand

Aggregate Supply

Macroeconomic Equilibrium

Recessionary GDP Gap

Inflationary GDP Gap

Classical Model of Macroeconomic Equilibrium

Keynesian Model of Macroeconomic Equilibrium

Wage-Price Spiral

Supply-Side Shock

Stagflation

Consumption Function and Marginal Propensity to Consume

Aggregate Purchases

Marginal Respending Rate and the Multiplier

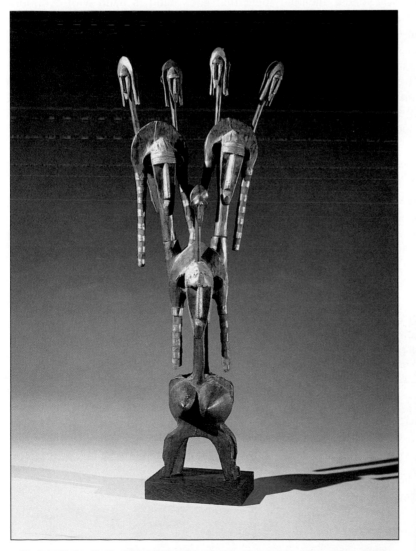

Bambara Marionette Headdress from N'tieko Society. Found at the village of Sela mar San, northeastern Bambaraland, Private collection/Art Resource, NY

9 chapter

Aggregate Demand and Aggregate Supply

You now know how real GDP, the price level, and their fluctuations are measured. You also know that the economy is subject to the ups and downs of the business cycle. But what causes excessive unemployment and inflation? Is it possible to avoid recessions and the cyclical unemployment that goes hand in hand with economic contractions? Can the ravages of inflation be kept under control? How can we explain why an economy suffers simultaneously from both high unemployment and high inflation, as was the case during the recessions of the 1970s and 1980s. In this chapter we begin an investigation of these questions.

You have already seen how supply and demand analysis can be used to explain prices and quantities exchanged in individual markets. In macroeconomics the basic tools of supply and demand are adapted to explain fluctuations in and growth of aggregate production (real GDP) and fluctuations in the price level.

☐ CONCEPT PREVIEW

After reading this chapter, you should be able to:

1. Distinguish an aggregate demand curve from a market demand curve and discuss changes in aggregate demand.

2. Distinguish an aggregate supply curve from a market supply curve and discuss changes in aggregate supply.

3. Use aggregate supply and demand analysis to show how the equilibrium level of real GDP and the price level over a given year are determined.

4. Use aggregate supply and demand analysis to show how changes in aggregate demand and aggregate supply affect the equilibrium levels of real GDP and the price level for a given year and to explain the causes of recessions, excessive unemployment, and inflation.

AGGREGATE DEMAND AND AGGREGATE SUPPLY

In macroeconomics, supply and demand analysis is used to help us understand how changes in the economy can result in expansions or contractions and price instability. Instead of trying to explain the quantity of an individual item produced over a certain period, macroeconomics tries to explain the forces that influence *aggregate* production, measured by real GDP. Similarly, instead of trying to explain how the price of one good is established in a market, macroeconomics tries to explain how the price *level*, measured by a price index such as the GDP deflator or the CPI, is established.

When you understand the forces influencing demand and supply in the aggregate, you'll be in a better position to make your own forecasts about where the economy is headed. You will better understand the mysteries of inflation, recession, and why the economy sometimes suffers simultaneously from both excessive inflation and increasing unemployment. You'll then be able to comprehend newspaper articles and evening news reports more clearly to formulate your own ideas about what the government and banking authorities should do to help stabilize the economy.

AGGREGATE DEMAND

The demand for goods and services is an important influence on the performance of the economy. Aggregate demand depends on the willingness and ability of consumers, business firms, and governments to purchase the goods and services produced nationally and available for sale in domestic and foreign markets.

The amount of the final products that will be demanded in any given year depends on a variety of factors, including the price level, consumer confidence, wealth, and the availability of credit. In analyzing the overall demand for final products in the economy, we first isolate the relationship between the amount that will be demanded and the general level of prices for products, holding all other influences on demand fixed. The amount of final products (measured as real GDP) that buyers will purchase at a given price level is called the **aggregate quantity demanded.**

Aggregate demand is a relationship between aggregate quantity demanded and the economy's price level. In macroeconomics we depict this relationship using an **aggregate demand curve,** a graph that shows how aggregate quantity demanded varies with the price level for the economy. A downward-sloping aggregate demand curve implies that the lower the price level, the greater the aggregate quantity demanded, other things being equal.

The graph in Box 1 shows the aggregate demand curve prevailing for a given year. The vertical axis measures the price level for the aggregate of final goods and services included in real GDP. The horizontal axis measures the quantity of final products demanded measured in base year dollars, representing the quantity of aggregate production that will be demanded for the year at each possible price level.

Although the aggregate demand curve may look like a market demand curve, it's really quite different. It describes a relationship between an *index* of prices and an *aggregate* of the final products demanded in a nation instead of a relationship between the price and quantity of a single good. For example, when you move down an aggregate demand curve, there is an increase in an *aggregate* of the goods and services demanded in the nation. When the price level falls, it means that the cost of purchasing an *aggregate* (or "market basket") of many products falls. Some individual prices may actually rise when the price level falls, and vice versa.

1

aggregate quantity demanded the amount of final products that buyers are willing and able to purchase at a given price level.

aggregate demand a relationship between aggregate quantity demanded and the economy's price level

aggregate demand curve a graph that shows how the amount of aggregate domestic production demanded, measured by real GDP will vary with the price level.

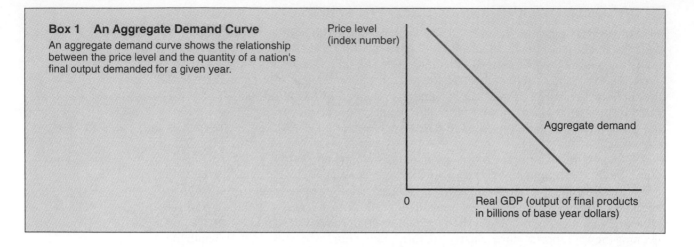

Box 1   An Aggregate Demand Curve

An aggregate demand curve shows the relationship between the price level and the quantity of a nation's final output demanded for a given year.

Price level (index number)

Aggregate demand

0   Real GDP (output of final products in billions of base year dollars)

Because changes in real GDP mean changes in input use in the nation, income earned in the nation also changes when you move along an aggregate demand curve. Therefore, income is not held constant as you move along an aggregate demand curve as it is held constant when you move along the market demand curve for a single product.

The downward-sloping aggregate demand curve means that an increase in the price level will decrease the willingness and ability of at least some buyers to purchase the products included in real GDP. The reasons for the downward slope of an aggregate demand curve are much more complex than those that explain downward-sloping market demand curves for a single product. Three basic reasons for the inverse relationship between the aggregate quantity demanded and the price level are:

1. *The real wealth effect: A higher price level can decrease real wealth in a nation and reduce consumer spending on final products.* The purchasing power of accumulated savings denominated in fixed dollar amounts declines when the price level goes up. For example, suppose you have $100 in cash in a cookie jar in your apartment. If the price level rises, the real value of this currency falls. The reduction in purchasing power associated with the rise in the price level will make you less wealthy and can decrease your willingness and ability to purchase final goods and services. The aggregate reduction in wealth caused by an increase in the price level is likely to decrease the willingness and ability of all consumers to purchase currently produced final products during the year.

A higher price level can also increase saving. If savers have specific goals, such as accumulating enough funds to make a down payment on a house or to finance their children's college education, an increase in the price level can induce them to save more of their current income for those purposes. When the price level rises, they must accumulate more dollars to achieve the same goal. For example, if the goal is to save enough to pay a child's college tuition costs, an increase in the price level that includes an increase in tuition costs means that more dollars must be saved to achieve that goal. As saving increases because of the higher price level, consumer purchases in the *current year* decrease, resulting in a decrease in the aggregate quantity demanded.

2. *The real interest rate effect: A higher price level can increase interest rates, making credit more expensive and reducing the quantity of investment goods demanded.* The ability of business firms and households to purchase goods and ser-

vices produced depends on the cost of credit, which is measured by the real interest rate. Naturally, at a higher price level the dollar amount of credit necessary to purchase any given quantity of goods and services also increases. The increased demand for credit resulting from the higher price level puts upward pressure on real interest rates. As real interest rates rise, business firms cut back their purchase of investment goods and households cut back their spending. These actions decrease the aggregate quantity of goods and services demanded.

3. *The foreign trade effect: A higher price level reduces foreign demand for U.S. exports and increases domestic demand for imports.* Because the higher domestic price level implies that U.S. goods become more expensive relative to foreign goods, consumers in the United States tend to substitute imported goods for domestic goods. For example, rapid increases in the price level over the year mean an increase in the price of domestically produced cars. Assuming the increase in the price level in the United States has little effect on the dollar prices Korean sellers are willing to accept for cars they export to the United States, there will be a decrease in the quantity of U.S. cars demanded and an increase in the demand for Korean cars.

The increase in the price of U.S. items also decreases the quantity of U.S. exports demanded, other things being equal. The net effect of the increase in the price level is therefore a decline in the demand for the final products of U.S. firms in foreign markets and a further decline in the quantity of final products of U.S. firms demanded in domestic markets as buyers substitute foreign goods for domestic goods. Both the increase in U.S. demand for foreign products and the decrease in demand for U.S. products abroad contribute to a decline in the aggregate quantity of U.S. final products demanded during the year.[1]

Changes in Aggregate Demand

The amount of final products demanded does not depend on the price level alone. Aggregate demand is also influenced by such economic variables as wealth, interest rates, foreign exchange rates, and expectations about the future. A **change in aggregate demand** is a change in the amount of a nation's final products that will be purchased caused by something other than a change in the price level.

A change in aggregate demand is represented by an inward or outward shift of the economy's aggregate demand curve. The distinction between a *change in aggregate demand* and a *change in aggregate quantity demanded* is similar to the distinction between change in demand and change in quantity demanded for market demand curves. A change in aggregate quantity demanded is a movement along a given aggregate demand curve that occurs in response to a change in the price level. A *change in aggregate demand, however, implies a movement of the entire aggregate demand curve.* When aggregate demand increases or decreases, the relationship between the price level and aggregate quantity demanded is altered. The graphs in Boxes 2 and 3 illustrate changes in aggregate demand. An increase in aggregate demand implies an outward shift of the aggregate demand curve, while a decrease in aggregate demand implies an inward shift of the curve.

Influences on Aggregate Demand

Changes in the economy cause changes in aggregate demand by affecting the willingness of consumers to spend their income on the final products of domestic producers. Business demand for investment goods fluctuates, as do government

change in aggregate demand a change in the amount of a nation's final products that will be purchased caused by something other than a change in the price level.

---

[1] This analysis assumes that the exchange rate of the dollar for foreign currency does not immediately adjust to cancel out the effect of the increase in the domestic price level. In practice many foreign nations manipulate the demand for and supply of their currencies in ways that prevent the exchange rate of those currencies from changing immediately in response to changes in the U.S. price level.

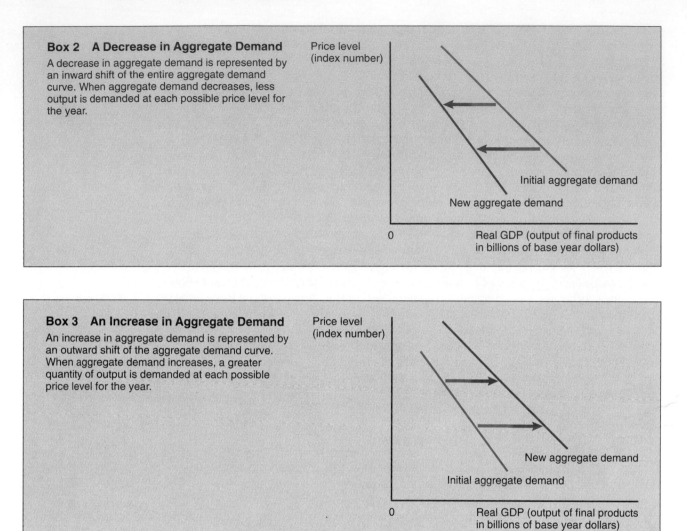

Box 2   A Decrease in Aggregate Demand

A decrease in aggregate demand is represented by an inward shift of the entire aggregate demand curve. When aggregate demand decreases, less output is demanded at each possible price level for the year.

Price level (index number)

Initial aggregate demand

New aggregate demand

0   Real GDP (output of final products in billions of base year dollars)

Box 3   An Increase in Aggregate Demand

An increase in aggregate demand is represented by an outward shift of the aggregate demand curve. When aggregate demand increases, a greater quantity of output is demanded at each possible price level for the year.

Price level (index number)

New aggregate demand

Initial aggregate demand

0   Real GDP (output of final products in billions of base year dollars)

purchases. Similarly, changes in the demand for our exports can influence aggregate demand for the products of domestic producers.

Much of the macroeconomic analysis in the next few chapters will examine in depth the various influences on aggregate demand. At this point we will briefly list them.

1. *Real interest rates*. When real interest rates go up, businesses cut back on their plans to buy new equipment and structures, and households find they cannot afford the monthly payments necessary to buy such items as furniture, cars, and new homes. An increase in real interest rates therefore causes a decrease in aggregate demand, while a decrease in real interest rates causes an increase in aggregate demand.

2. *The quantity of money in circulation*. Suppose the government were to suddenly declare that each dollar people held in their pockets as currency or on deposit in banks was now worth two dollars. As a result, aggregate demand would increase because people would have more money to spend. On the other hand, a decrease in

the quantity of money would decrease aggregate demand. As you will soon see, unrestrained increases in the quantity of money in circulation are a major cause of inflation and hyperinflation.

3. *Changes in the international value of the dollar.* As the price of the dollar goes up in terms of foreign currencies, our exports become more expensive in foreign markets, while imports become cheaper (other things being equal) to U.S. buyers. A higher dollar decreases aggregate demand by decreasing the demand for our exports and stimulating domestic demand for imports. As the price of the dollar goes down, the prices of our exports fall in terms of foreign currencies, stimulating demand for them, while the prices of imports go up in dollars, thereby encouraging U.S. consumers to substitute domestic products for imports. A decrease in the price of the dollar therefore results in an increase in aggregate demand. Changes in foreign exchange rates can have a major impact on an economy like the United States, where increasing proportions of spending are accounted for by imports and exports.

4. *Wealth.* Wealth consists of assets that can be sold, if necessary, to provide money for spending, such as stocks, bonds, and real estate. When stock prices are high, consumers who hold stocks are likely to be more willing to spend their current income rather than save it. Conversely, when the prices of stocks and other assets (such as land and homes) fall, aggregate demand can decrease. For example, when stock prices fell in 1929, aggregate demand plummeted as the savings of millions of stockholders were wiped out. However, the link between short-term changes in wealth and aggregate demand is not always clear cut. In 1987, when there was another major stock market crash, many economists predicted a sharp cutback in aggregate demand. The effects, however, proved negligible, and aggregate demand continued to increase in 1987 and 1988. By 1990, however, declining real estate values and increased debt burdens did contribute to a decline in aggregate demand

5. *Government purchases, taxes, and transfers.* An increase in government purchases of goods and services increases aggregate demand, while a decrease in such purchases decreases aggregate demand. Taxes take a portion of income earned by households and businesses out of the spending stream. An increase in tax rates, other things being equal, decreases disposable income to households and is likely to decrease aggregate demand. Conversely, a decrease in tax rates is likely to increase aggregate demand because it increases disposable income. Transfer payments are a source of income to millions of Americans on Social Security pensions and to those who depend on welfare or unemployment benefits. Transfers influence consumption expenditures, and when they increase, aggregate demand also increases. For example, when the unemployment rate goes up, aggregate demand tends to decrease because labor earnings decline. However, unemployment insurance compensation (which is a transfer) goes up when the unemployment rate increases. The increase in transfer payments from unemployment insurance acts to increase aggregate demand, thereby cushioning the impact of increased cyclical unemployment on the economy.

6. *Expectations about the future.* If the outlook for future increases in disposable income is bleak, consumers are likely to cut back on spending. The decrease in aggregate demand resulting from a decline in the demand for consumption goods can reduce the demand of business firms for investment goods. If business firms do not think they can sell all their current production, they are unlikely to purchase more inventory, machines, or equipment or to plan new plants. When expectations turn up, aggregate demand is also likely to increase.

7. *Income and other economic conditions affecting demand in foreign countries.* When income goes up in foreign nations, their demand for such U.S. products as aircraft, beef, and lumber also goes up. This will increase aggregate demand in the

---

Box 4   Factors Influencing Changes in Aggregate Demand

Changes in aggregate demand are caused by changes in the demand for domestically produced consumption goods, investment goods, changes in the demand for exports or imports, and changes in government purchases.

Changes that can cause an increase in aggregate demand	Changes that can cause a decrease in aggregate demand
■ A decrease in real interest rates.	■ An increase in real interest rates.
■ An increase in the quantity of money in circulation.	■ A decrease in the quantity of money in circulation.
■ A decrease in the international value of the dollar.	■ An increase in the international value of the dollar.
■ An increase in the general level of wealth.	■ A decrease in the general level of wealth.
■ An increase in goverment purchases.	■ A decrease in goverment purchases.
■ A decrease in tax rates.	■ An increase in tax rates.
■ An increase in government transfers.	■ A decrease in government transfers.
■ Improved expectations about the future.	■ Deteriorating expectations about the future.
■ Higher income and improvements in economic conditions in foreign nations.	■ Lower income and worsening economic conditions in foreign nations.

United States. Conversely, if income in the rest of the world declines, there will be a decrease in the demand for U.S. exports and the aggregate demand curve will shift inward.

Box 4 summarizes the major factors that can result in a change in aggregate demand.

CONCEPT CHECK

□

- How does an aggregate demand curve differ from a market demand curve?

- Why does an aggregate demand curve slope downward?

- What can cause aggregate demand to increase? What can cause aggregate demand to decrease?

AGGREGATE SUPPLY

2   Sellers, like buyers, respond to incentives. How much they are willing to produce in a given year depends on their assessments of the profitability of selling their products. The amount sellers are willing and able to supply to product markets is influenced by the price of their products and by such considerations as wages, other input prices, and technology. In macroeconomic analysis we begin by isolating the influence of product prices on production decisions. The **aggregate quantity supplied** is the quantity of final products (measured by real GDP) that will be supplied by producers at a given price level. **Aggregate supply** is a relationship between the price level and aggregate quantity supplied.

An **aggregate supply curve** shows the aggregate quantity supplied for each possible price level over a given period. When drawing an aggregate supply curve, we assume that all input prices and the general availability and quality of productive resources in the economy are fixed. We also assume that technology does not advance over the given period.

An upward-sloping aggregate supply curve, illustrated in Box 5, implies that an increase in the price level will increase the aggregate of the final products, measured by real GDP, that domestic business firms will produce. As was the case for

aggregate quantity supplied the quantity of final products that will be supplied by producers at a given price level.

aggregate supply a relationship between the price level and aggregate quantity supplied.

aggregate supply curve a graph showing how aggregate quantity supplied varies with the price level, other things being equal.

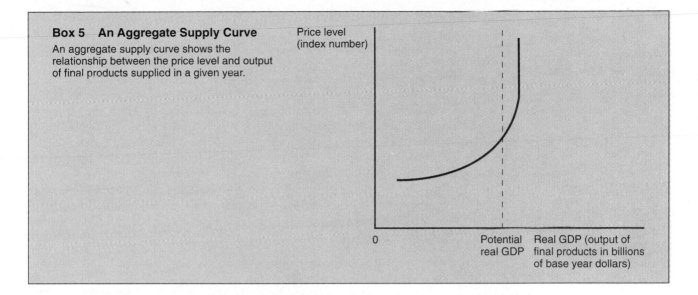

Box 5   An Aggregate Supply Curve

An aggregate supply curve shows the relationship between the price level and output of final products supplied in a given year.

Price level (index number)

0   Potential real GDP   Real GDP (output of final products in billions of base year dollars)

aggregate demand, the shape of the aggregate supply curve cannot be as easily explained as that of a market supply curve for a particular item. A market supply curve slopes upward because higher prices imply greater opportunities for profit, thereby attracting new sellers to enter the market over the long run. When we discuss aggregate supply, the number of sellers and the resources available during the year are more or less fixed, so it's not possible to explain the increase in output in terms of the attraction of additional sellers or resources into production.

However, there is reason to believe that profit opportunities from supplying more output do increase in the aggregate, at least over a period of a year, when the price level rises. Over a short period a higher price level increases the amount businesses receive from selling additional output, *while input prices stay the same*. Naturally, if product prices rise but *input* prices remain constant, opportunities arise for additional profit from producing more. This leads producers to produce more until the costs of additional output rise to match the higher prices (this is the marginal cost of output). The costs of additional output eventually rise because firms must work their existing facilities more intensely and must hire less experienced workers to produce more. As this occurs, unit costs of production tend to rise because of overuse of facilities and because of the lower skill and productivity of less experienced workers. If you've already studied microeconomics, you know that the marginal cost of output for a firm tends to increase as more output is supplied.

In the graph in Box 5, the level of real GDP corresponding to potential real GDP is indicated on the horizontal axis. Recall that potential real GDP is the level of real GDP that would be produced if the economy were at full employment. As potential real GDP for the economy is approached, factories, offices, and other productive facilities are pushed beyond the levels at which the unit cost of production is at a minimum. This impairs the overall efficiency of operation. These factors contribute to the higher unit production costs that occur, even though input prices are constant.

In addition, as an economy's potential real GDP is approached, businesses often have difficulty in obtaining all of the input they require. To operate facilities around the clock, firms must use overtime labor, which is often difficult to obtain without paying bonuses. The aggregate supply curve becomes steeper as output increases, because the costs of producing the additional units increase as potential real GDP is approached.[2]

Notice that the aggregate supply curve goes through the line corresponding to potential real GDP. The economy can produce more than the amount of final products corresponding to potential real GDP when the actual unemployment rate falls below the natural rate of unemployment. However, there is a physical limit to the amount of output that can be produced in a given year. When the economy surpasses potential real GDP, firms hire less experienced workers and work their plants around the clock. As this occurs, unit costs of production tend to soar. These higher costs are reflected in the steeply rising aggregate supply curve beyond the level of real GDP corresponding to the natural rate of unemployment.

The aggregate supply curve eventually becomes vertical (see Box 5). The level of real GDP corresponding to that point is the physical limit of production for the economy for the year. At that point it is virtually impossible to obtain the labor and other inputs necessary to increase output anymore.

Segments of the Aggregate Supply Curve

The slope of the aggregate supply curve differs depending on how much slack there is in the economy at the beginning of a year (or any other production period). The aggregate supply curve drawn in Box 6 has been divided into three distinct segments for corresponding levels of real GDP:

Segment 1: *The economy is operating well below its potential, with considerable cyclical unemployment.* When actual real GDP is considerably below the level that corresponds to potential real GDP, there will be cyclical unemployment and idle capacity. Under these circumstances, aggregate production can increase without much upward pressure on unit costs. If the economy is operating in this segment, business firms can easily produce more by bringing idle plant capacity and equipment back into service. It's also easy for business firms to obtain materials and labor under these circumstances, so they can increase output without increasing the costs of additional units of output. In this segment there is considerable slack in the economy and, other things being equal, little or no increase in the price level will suffice to increase aggregate quantity supplied.

Segment 2: *The economy is close to full employment.* As idle capacity is eliminated and the economy is approaching the level of aggregate production corresponding to potential real GDP, costs of additional units of output begin to rise more quickly. Under these circumstances, more substantial increases in the price level are necessary to induce firms to increase aggregate quantity supplied. It follows that as the economy approaches full employment, inflation will heat up if aggregate quantity supplied increases further.

Segment 3: *The economy is overheated.* The aggregate quantity supplied will exceed potential real GDP. Unit costs of production will rise very rapidly and much higher prices will be necessary to cover those higher unit costs if the economy is to produce more. An economy operating at the beginning of the year in the nearly vertical portion of its aggregate supply curve will be bursting at the seams through overproduction.

---

[2] Just as the marginal cost of output for an individual producer increases when output goes up, so too does the marginal cost of real GDP for the economy increase as the economy approaches full employment.

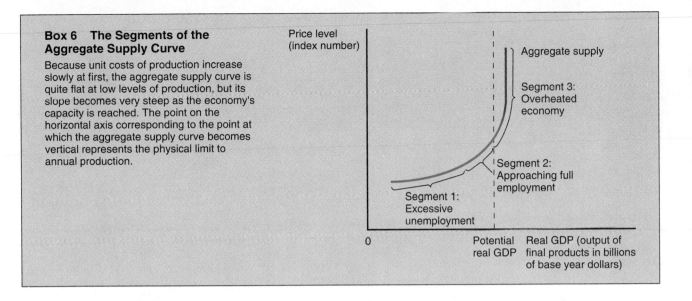

Box 6   The Segments of the Aggregate Supply Curve

Because unit costs of production increase slowly at first, the aggregate supply curve is quite flat at low levels of production, but its slope becomes very steep as the economy's capacity is reached. The point on the horizontal axis corresponding to the point at which the aggregate supply curve becomes vertical represents the physical limit to annual production.

Price level (index number)

Aggregate supply

Segment 3: Overheated economy

Segment 2: Approaching full employment

Segment 1: Excessive unemployment

0   Potential real GDP   Real GDP (output of final products in billions of base year dollars)

Changes in Aggregate Supply

The amount that sellers will produce does not depend on the price level alone. Changes in wages and other input prices, changes in the quality and quantity of resources available, and advances in technology will change the aggregate quantity supplied at each possible price level. A **change in aggregate supply** is a change in the amount of national production resulting from something other than a change in the price level. A change in aggregate supply implies a shift of the economy's aggregate supply curve. Remember that the aggregate supply curve is drawn under the assumption that the level of all input prices, including the price of labor (nominal wages), the availability and quality of inputs, and technology are fixed. A decrease in aggregate supply is represented by an *inward* shift of the aggregate supply curve, and an increase in aggregate supply is represented by an *outward* shift of the aggregate supply curve.

How Changes in Input Prices Affect Aggregate Supply   Some changes in the economy that change aggregate supply have little impact on the level of real GDP that corresponds to potential real GDP and the nation's physical limit to output for the year. Consider the impact of a change in nominal wages on aggregate supply. As nominal wages go up, the unit and marginal costs of production also go up, decreasing the profitability of selling output at any given price level. Because firms now require higher prices to make any given level of output available, the aggregate supply curve shifts inward, just as a market supply curve shifts inward in response to an increase in wages. However, the wage increase itself affects neither the economy's potential real GDP nor the level of output corresponding to the economy's physical limit to production.

The graph in Box 7 illustrates a decrease in aggregate supply that results from an increase in nominal wages or an increase in other input prices (such as fuel prices). Notice that the curve shifts inward but that the level of output for which the curve becomes vertical does not change. The level of output corresponding to potential real GDP and the economy's physical limit to output does not change.

change in aggregate supply a change in the amount of national production resulting from something other than a change in the price level.

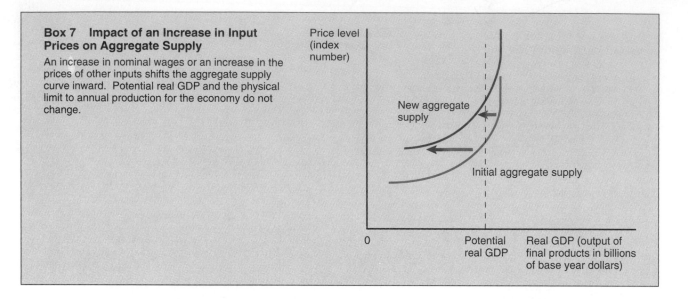

Box 7   Impact of an Increase in Input Prices on Aggregate Supply

An increase in nominal wages or an increase in the prices of other inputs shifts the aggregate supply curve inward. Potential real GDP and the physical limit to annual production for the economy do not change.

Price level (index number)

New aggregate supply

Initial aggregate supply

0   Potential real GDP   Real GDP (output of final products in billions of base year dollars)

A decrease in nominal wages or a decrease in fuel prices would increase aggregate supply without affecting potential real GDP or the level of real GDP corresponding to the economy's capacity output. Lower input prices increase profit opportunities and induce businesses to increase the aggregate quantity supplied at each possible price level. The graph in Box 8 shows how a decrease in input prices affects the aggregate supply curve. For example, suppose the price of oil, a key input used in production, falls by 20 percent during the year. This means the unit and marginal costs of production will also fall. This induces businesses to increase the aggregate quantity supplied at any given price level. The decrease in oil prices itself, however, does not change the level of real GDP corresponding to potential real GDP or to the physical limit to output during the year.

How Changes in the Quantity or Productivity of Inputs Affect Aggregate Supply
Changes in the availability or productivity of resources and advances in technology increase or decrease aggregate supply and also change the levels of output corresponding to potential real GDP and the nation's capacity output. The graph in Box 9 shows an increase in aggregate supply that results when changes in the economy affect the nation's potential real GDP and the level of real GDP corresponding to capacity output. For example, an increase in the size of the labor force means that more labor hours are available for production. Because of the increased labor, potential real GDP is greater, and so too is the capacity of the economy to produce goods and services. Similarly, an increase in the nation's capital stock will increase aggregate supply because more capital means that a given labor force has more tools with which to work. Naturally, with more tools labor will be more productive. The graph in Box 9 shows that as a result of the increase in the availability of inputs, both potential real GDP and the level of real GDP corresponding to the physical limit to production (for which the aggregate supply curve becomes vertical) increase as aggregate supply increases.

An increase in the availability of raw materials can also increase aggregate supply, as illustrated in Box 9. Improvement in the *quality* of inputs is another important cause of increases in aggregate supply that also increase potential real GDP. For example, improvement of the educational level of the labor force is a major cause of

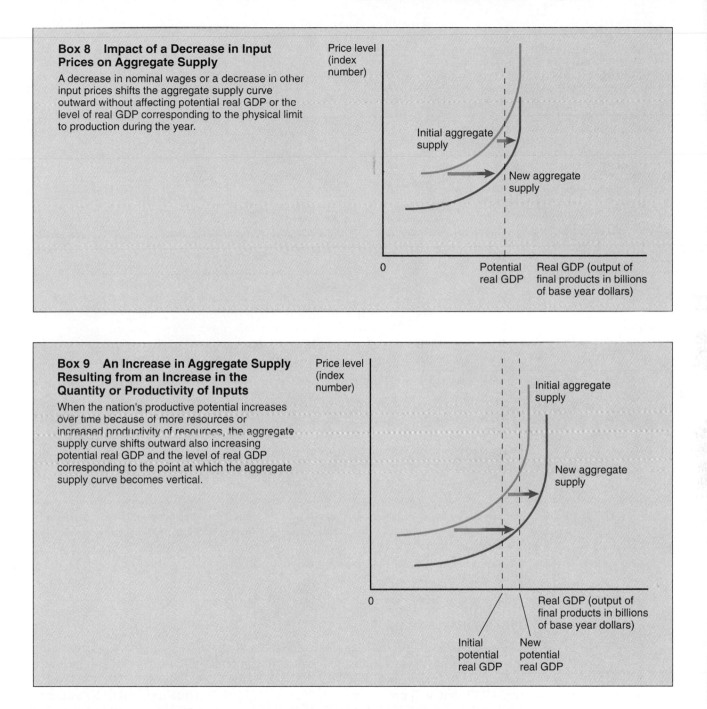

Box 8   Impact of a Decrease in Input Prices on Aggregate Supply

A decrease in nominal wages or a decrease in other input prices shifts the aggregate supply curve outward without affecting potential real GDP or the level of real GDP corresponding to the physical limit to production during the year.

Price level (index number)

Initial aggregate supply

New aggregate supply

0   Potential real GDP   Real GDP (output of final products in billions of base year dollars)

Box 9   An Increase in Aggregate Supply Resulting from an Increase in the Quantity or Productivity of Inputs

When the nation's productive potential increases over time because of more resources or increased productivity of resources, the aggregate supply curve shifts outward also increasing potential real GDP and the level of real GDP corresponding to the point at which the aggregate supply curve becomes vertical.

Price level (index number)

Initial aggregate supply

New aggregate supply

0   Real GDP (output of final products in billions of base year dollars)

Initial potential real GDP

New potential real GDP

such increases in aggregate supply. Advances in technology, such as new and faster computers and automated production techniques, also contribute to such outward shifts in aggregate supply.

Although it is normal for aggregate supply to increase over time as the availability and productivity of resources increase, natural or social catastrophes occasionally result in decreases in aggregate supply. For example, in 1988 a severe drought in the United States resulted in a decrease in aggregate supply. Wars and natural disasters, such as earthquakes and hurricanes, can destroy productive resources and decrease

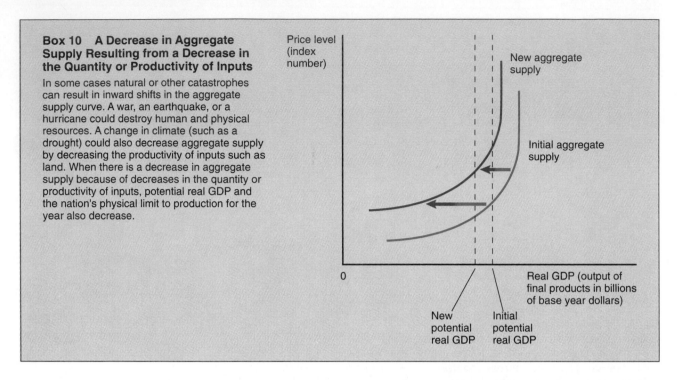

Box 10   A Decrease in Aggregate Supply Resulting from a Decrease in the Quantity or Productivity of Inputs

In some cases natural or other catastrophes can result in inward shifts in the aggregate supply curve. A war, an earthquake, or a hurricane could destroy human and physical resources. A change in climate (such as a drought) could also decrease aggregate supply by decreasing the productivity of inputs such as land. When there is a decrease in aggregate supply because of decreases in the quantity or productivity of inputs, potential real GDP and the nation's physical limit to production for the year also decrease.

aggregate supply. The sharp cutoff in imported supplies of oil that occurred in the 1970s in the United States as a result of the OPEC oil embargo caused a decrease in aggregate supply. Box 10 shows a decrease in aggregate supply resulting from a decrease in resource availability; it also shows how both potential real GDP and the nation's capacity output decline as a consequence.

CONCEPT CHECK
☐

- Explain why an aggregate supply curve is upward sloping, and discuss the economic significance of its three segments.

- Other things being equal, how will an increase in nominal wages affect aggregate supply?

- How will an improvement in the productivity of workers affect aggregate supply?

MACROECONOMIC EQUILIBRIUM

[3]   The preceding analysis of aggregate demand and aggregate supply shows that both the amounts buyers are willing to buy and the amounts sellers are willing to produce depend on the price level. But what determines the actual price level and the level of real GDP that will prevail over a given period? Will actual real GDP be equal to potential real GDP over that period? Will increases in aggregate demand result in inflation that sends the price level skyrocketing, or will they merely result in an increase in aggregate production? How will an oil embargo affect real GDP and the price level over the period?

To answer these questions, we have to examine whether the spending plans of buyers match the production plans of sellers over the given period. We must also examine how changes in aggregate demand and aggregate supply will affect the balance between aggregate quantity demanded and aggregate quantity supplied. In

Box 11   Macroeconomic Equilibrium

Point *E* is a macroeconomic equilibrium because at the price level of 120, aggregate quantity demanded and aggregate quantity supplied are equal to $5,000 billion.

this way we can forecast how changes in the economy will affect unemployment and inflation. We can also examine the way government stabilization policies can affect the economy through their impact on the balance between aggregate quantities demanded and supplied.

A **macroeconomic equilibrium** is attained when the aggregate quantity demanded equals the aggregate quantity supplied. When aggregate supply and demand balance at the equilibrium price level, there is neither widespread unplanned buildup of product inventories nor an unexpected rapid reduction in inventories because businesses cannot fill orders quickly enough. When a macroeconomic equilibrium is achieved, the aggregate production made available for sale over a given period is, on average, willingly purchased in markets at the prevailing price level.

The phrase *on average* is important when discussing macroeconomic equilibrium, because both the price level and real GDP are aggregates. Some *individual* markets can be out of equilibrium even when a macroeconomic equilibrium is attained. For example, the demand for personal computers may fall, resulting in a surplus of computers and an unanticipated buildup of inventories. At the same time, an increase in the demand for compact discs may result in an unanticipated depletion of producer inventories. There would therefore be downward pressure on the price of personal computers and upward pressure on the price of compact discs as these markets move to a new equilibrium.

When a macroeconomic equilibrium exists, there may be shortages in some product markets and surpluses in other product markets. *In the aggregate,* however, there is neither upward nor downward pressure on the price level or the level of real GDP once macroeconomic equilibrium is attained.

The graph in Box 11 illustrates the concept of macroeconomic equilibrium, using the aggregate demand and aggregate supply curves prevailing for a given year. The macroeconomic equilibrium corresponds to the point at which the aggregate demand and aggregate supply curves intersect. The equilibrium level of real GDP corresponding to the point of intersection, *E,* is $5,000 billion. Aggregate production of

macroeconomic equilibrium a situation that occurs when the aggregate quantity demanded equals the aggregate quantity supplied.

$5,000 billion (measured in base year dollars) also corresponds to the quantity of final products demanded at the equilibrium price level of 120 as measured by a price index such as the GDP deflator. Because the entire aggregate quantity supplied of $5,000 billion is willingly purchased at the current price level of 120, there is, on average, no upward or downward pressure on prices or production.

The Results of Unintended Inventory Changes

Suppose the quantity of final products demanded fell short of aggregate quantity supplied at the existing price level during the year. Under these circumstances, there would be an abundance of unsold goods. Many industries would experience slack demand for the final products they produced during the year. Manufacturing firms would find that their orders were less than anticipated. As inventories built up, these firms would lay off workers and cut back on orders for materials. Service firms, such as banks, insurance companies, and brokerage houses, would find that their staffs were excessive for the volume of their business, and they too would lay off workers. Production and employment would begin to fall, and there would be downward pressure on the price level.

Now imagine a scenario in which the quantity of final products demanded exceeded aggregate quantity supplied. Inventories would be rapidly drawn down. Manufacturing firms would experience difficulty in keeping up with orders. These firms would hire more workers or work their plants around the clock with existing workers as goods were reordered. Service firms would expand their staffs or offer overtime bonuses to existing workers. There would be upward pressure on the price level and upward pressure on the output of final products as the economy moved to a macroeconomic equilibrium.[3]

In a market economy no one coordinates the production decisions of business firms with the purchase decisions of buyers. For example, business firms may anticipate a strong holiday selling season. Then an unanticipated event, such as a sharp increase in real interest rates or a stock market collapse, may cause buyers to buy less than anticipated. As a result of the unexpected decline in sales, business firms that are stuck with lots of inventory cancel their orders for more goods. Business firms may also reduce their investment purchases. As orders are canceled, aggregate production and aggregate real income will decline. There might also be downward pressure on the price level as sellers stuck with inventories of unsold goods lower prices. Real GDP, and possibly the price level, will adjust until an equilibrium is attained. On the other hand, if sellers *underestimate* the aggregate quantity demanded during a period, there will be upward pressure on real GDP and the price level as reorders of goods and additional hiring of workers increase aggregate quantity supplied and aggregate real income.

How a Decrease in Aggregate Demand Can Affect the Economy

4 A decrease in aggregate demand can result in a decrease in equilibrium real GDP and a consequent decrease in earnings and employment in the economy. If the decrease in aggregate demand is severe enough, it can cause the economy to operate well below its potential and thereby result in excessive unemployment. If the decline in aggregate demand is prolonged, it pushes the economy into a recession.

---

[3] In the National Income and Production Accounts, final sales are a measure of the quantity of final products actually purchased in markets. Remember that changes in business inventory at the end of the year are treated as an investment purchase by the firms holding the inventory even though they do not actually buy the goods from themselves. For example, real GDP in 1991 was $4,821 billion. Real final sales in the same year were $4,830.3 billion. Because final sales exceeded real GDP, that year there was a decline of $9.3 billion in real business inventories.

Box 12   Impact of a Decrease in Aggregate Demand

Other things being equal, a decrease in aggregate demand reduces the equilibrium price level and real GDP. The decrease in aggregate demand shown causes the economy to contract. Equilibrium real GDP falls below potential real GDP opening up a recessionary GDP gap.

The graph in Box 12 shows the impact of a decrease in aggregate demand in an economy. Suppose the economy is initially in equilibrium at point E_1, at which the price level is 120 and real GDP is at the full-employment level of $5,000 billion. When aggregate demand decreases, the economy moves to an equilibrium at point E_2, at which real GDP declines to $4,500 billion and the price level falls to 115. The decline in aggregate demand during the year means that a level of output corresponding to $5,000 billion real GDP cannot be sustained, because at the new level of aggregate demand it is not possible to sell that much output. As inventories build up unexpectedly during the year, firms cut back orders, and both real GDP and employment decline as the economy moves to the new equilibrium at point E_2. The decline in real GDP means the economy moves into a contraction as a result of the decrease in aggregate demand. *A decline in aggregate demand is a possible cause of contractions or recessions and can explain increases in cyclical unemployment.* We can now begin to unravel the mysteries of the causes of excessive unemployment and recessions.

Recessionary GDP Gap

A macroeconomic equilibrium need not occur at a level of real GDP that corresponds to potential real GDP. If potential real GDP were attained, the economy would be at full employment. However, in Box 12 the level of aggregate demand is not high enough to generate full employment. The equilibrium level of real GDP is $500 billion below potential real GDP, implying that there is some cyclical unemployment in the economy. In other words, if the level of real GDP corresponding to full employment were attained, the result would be a widespread buildup of inventory, which would set up forces that cause production to decline and move the economy to equilibrium at point E_2. The difference between the equilibrium level of real GDP and potential real GDP when the economy is operating at less than full employment is called a **recessionary GDP gap.** The recessionary GDP gap in Box 12 amounts to $500 billion.

recessionary GDP gap
the difference between the equilibrium level of real GDP and potential real GDP when the economy is operating at less than full employment.

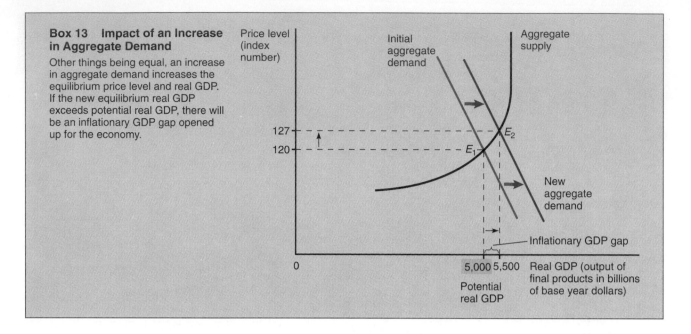

Box 13   Impact of an Increase in Aggregate Demand

Other things being equal, an increase in aggregate demand increases the equilibrium price level and real GDP. If the new equilibrium real GDP exceeds potential real GDP, there will be an inflationary GDP gap opened up for the economy.

It's quite possible for the aggregate demand curve to intersect the aggregate supply curve along the latter's flat portion. In this case the macroeconomic equilibrium would correspond to considerable unemployment of workers and idle capacity in the economy.

How an Increase in Aggregate Demand Can Affect the Economy

An increase in aggregate demand puts upward pressure on equilibrium real GDP and the price level. The graph in Box 13 shows how an increase in aggregate demand moves the economy to a new macroeconomic equilibrium corresponding to point E_2, at which both real GDP and the price level are higher than at the initial equilibrium, corresponding to point E_1. The increase in aggregate demand is sufficient to overheat the economy. As a result, equilibrium real GDP rises above potential real GDP, creating an **inflationary GDP gap,** which is the difference between equilibrium real GDP and potential real GDP when the economy is overheated.

inflationary GDP gap
the difference between equilibrium real GDP and potential real GDP when the economy is overheated.

demand-pull inflation
inflation caused by increases in aggregate demand.

Demand-pull inflation is inflation caused by increases in aggregate demand. When, given aggregate supply, the aggregate demand curve continually shifts outward, the result is upward pressure on prices, which means inflation. A general increase in the availability of money and credit in the economy is a common cause of demand-pull inflation that we'll investigate later on. Increases in the stock of money measured by currency in circulation and bank deposits can cause inflation through their impact on aggregate demand.

The extent to which changes in aggregate demand cause changes in aggregate production and the price level depends on how close the economy is to the level of real GDP that corresponds to full employment. Suppose the economy starts the year operating in segment 3 of its aggregate supply curve. Factories and offices are already operating around the clock, and there is little unemployment. Under these circumstances, the main impact of the increase in aggregate demand will be upward pressure on the price level. There will be little, if any, effect on equilibrium real GDP. The economy will move along the portion of its aggregate supply curve that is

A. An economy operating close to capacity

B. An economy operating with unused capacity

Box 14   How the Response to Changes in Aggregate Demand Can Vary with the Extent of Capacity Utilization in an Economy

A change in aggregate demand in an economy operating close to capacity will mainly change the price level with little effect on real GDP. In an economy with lots of unused capacity, changes in aggregate demand will mainly affect real GDP with little effect on the price level.

nearly vertical, as shown in graph **A** in Box 14. Demand-pull inflation will be a very serious problem. When the economy is operating in equilibrium above potential real GDP, steady increases in aggregate demand will surely put sharp, steady upward pressure on the price level. On the other hand, if there is considerable unused capacity in the economy and excessive unemployment during the year, then the main effect of the increase in aggregate demand will be an increase in real GDP, with little upward pressure on the price level. For example, government stabilization policies that seek to increase real GDP by increasing aggregate demand can do so with little fear of generating inflation in an economy operating in segment 1 of its aggregate supply curve. In such a case, the increase in aggregate demand moves the economy along the relatively flat portion of its aggregate supply curve, as shown in graph **B** of Box 14.

If the economy is in equilibrium at a level of real GDP at which factories and offices are utilized well below capacity levels and there is excessive unemployment, a decrease in aggregate demand will decrease real GDP with little downward pressure on the price level.

How a Decrease in Aggregate Supply Can Affect the Economy

Suppose there is a decrease in aggregate supply resulting from an increase in the general level of nominal wages not matched by productivity increases or from a sharp increase in the price of a key input such as oil. The decrease in aggregate supply shown in graph **A** in Box 15 moves the economy from its initial equilibrium at point E_1 to a new equilibrium at point E_2.

Note that at the new equilibrium real GDP is lower than it was initially and the price level is higher. Decreases in aggregate supply are particularly harmful because they result in *both* decreased production and upward pressure on the price level. Thus, a decrease in aggregate supply can simultaneously contribute to increased

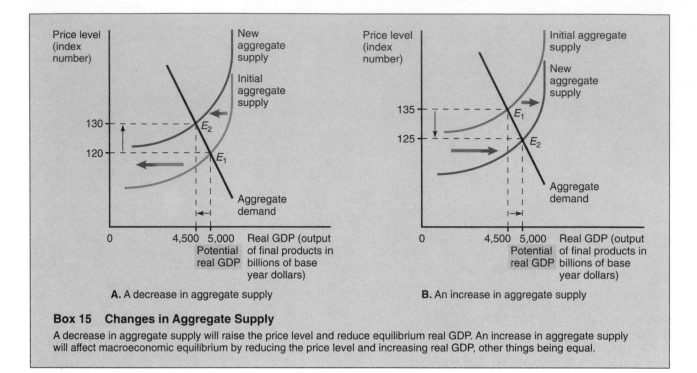

A. A decrease in aggregate supply

B. An increase in aggregate supply

Box 15   Changes in Aggregate Supply

A decrease in aggregate supply will raise the price level and reduce equilibrium real GDP. An increase in aggregate supply will affect macroeconomic equilibrium by reducing the price level and increasing real GDP, other things being equal.

cost-push inflation
inflation caused by
continual decreases in
aggregate supply.

unemployment *and* to increases in the price level that erode the purchasing power of income! Thus, recessions can be caused not only by decreases in aggregate demand but also by decreases in aggregate supply. For example, the soaring price of oil in 1990, triggered by Iraq's invasion of Kuwait, caused a decrease in aggregate supply that increased the price level and cut job growth in the United States.

Inflation caused by *continual* decreases in aggregate supply is called cost-push inflation. Cost-push inflation is usually found in an overheated economy whose actual unemployment rate has fallen below the natural rate of unemployment. Except for cases in which the economy overheats, cost-push inflation is relatively rare. In most cases a decrease in aggregate supply results in a *onetime* increase in the price level that increases the rate of inflation only during the year the decrease in aggregate supply occurs. In later years, unless aggregate supply decreases again, there is no acceleration in the rate of inflation.

How an Increase in Aggregate Supply Can Affect the Economy
An increase in aggregate supply can improve the performance of the economy by simultaneously increasing production and putting downward pressure on the price level. In graph **B** of Box 15, the economy is in equilibrium at point E_1, at which real GDP is \$4,500 billion and the price level is 135. As aggregate supply increases, the economy moves to a new equilibrium at point E_2. Real GDP is equal to \$5,000 billion, its potential level, while during the year the price level falls to 125.

Increases in aggregate supply are particularly desirable for the economy because they can reduce cyclical unemployment and keep inflationary pressures down. In early 1988, for example, news of decreasing oil prices was greeted very favorably by the people who evaluate the economy. Because a decrease in aggregate demand was feared at that time, the forecast of a likely increase in aggregate supply was viewed as reducing the likelihood that there would be a recession in 1988. An increase in

principles in practice

What Caused the Recession of 1990–1991?

In July 1990 the longest peacetime expansion in the history of the United States came to an abrupt halt. It was followed by eight months of declining real GDP and a relatively weak recovery that began in March 1991. During the first 12 months of the recovery, economic growth averaged less than 2 percent per year.

Although the beginning of the recession coincided with the beginning of the Gulf War and a consequent temporary run-up in the price of oil, it is now clear that the fundamental cause of the recession was a decline in aggregate demand. The following factors contributed to decreasing aggregate demand in 1990 and 1991:

1. *Growing corporate and household debt and new tax laws that increased borrowing costs.* The 1980s left a legacy of large debt burdens for consumers and corporations that decreased their willingness to spend or to take on new debt. The ratio of household interest payments to income had climbed to 18 percent by 1989. Many corporations had borrowed heavily in the late 1980s to restructure their operations. Moreover, tax law changes that were enacted in 1986 increased the cost of borrowing to consumers by limiting the deductibility of interest payments and to investors by changing the depreciation rules.

2. *A credit crunch.* Because of an increase in bank failures and more stringent regulatory standards for banks, financing for new business ventures became more difficult by 1990. The growing reluctance of banks to make loans constrained the growth of aggregate demand.

3. *Declining spending for defense and constraints on the growth of government spending.* The end of the cold war in the early 1990s resulted in significant reductions in defense spending that had particularly adverse effects in the states of Connecticut, Virginia, Massachusetts, and California, whose economies had many defense-related industries. In addition, demands that the federal budget deficit be kept under control led to federal tax increases in 1991 and prevented new government spending from adding significantly to aggregate demand. In many states slowdowns led to tax increases and reductions in state and local government spending that also adversely affected aggregate demand.

4. *Industry restructuring.* Because of increased global competition, many industries were compelled to restructure in the early 1990s so as to remain profitable and survive. The restructuring involved attempts to increase productivity by reorganizing, adapting to changing technology, and reducing the size of their work forces. The restructuring contributed to job losses and to a decline in the rate of formation of new jobs. There was also a slowdown in the construction industry as a combination of demographic changes and tax law changes decreased the demand for new homes. Overbuilding of office space in the 1980s resulted in a decrease in commercial construction as markets worked off the surplus of space. As the demand for new homes and new office space declined, so too did the demand for furniture and other durable goods.

The effects of all these events were to decrease aggregate demand in 1990 and early 1991 while contributing to a slow recovery through most of 1992. When the recovery finally gained steam in early 1993, much of the growth in real GDP came as a result of an increase in productivity rather than an increase in jobs. Corporate downsizing resulted in the retention of the most productive workers and thus increased worker productivity. However, unemployment rates remained stubbornly high in late 1992 and 1993 because many large corporations were still downsizing. The recovery from the recession of 1990–91 was going down as one of the weakest recoveries in history.

aggregate supply also occurred as a result of decrease in oil prices in 1991, after it became clear that the conflict in the Persian Gulf could not disrupt oil supplies.

A Recap: Economic Fluctuations and Their Causes

Recessions can be caused by *both* decreases in aggregate supply and decreases in aggregate demand. A recession induced by a decrease in aggregate supply is likely to be accompanied by *both* inflation and excessive unemployment. A recession caused by a decrease in aggregate demand will result in both excessive unemployment and some downward pressure on the price level. As you'll soon learn, except for very severe economic contractions (such as the Great Depression of the 1930s), there's usually little, if any, decline in the price level during a typical recession.

the global economy

Exports and Macroeconomic Equilibrium

The death sentence for U.S. manufacturing that was passed by many observers in the early 1980s was off the mark. The falling value of the dollar in 1987 and 1988 spurred an enormous export boom. The output of U.S. factories, much of which was for export, rose by nearly 5 percent in 1987. Exports accounted for more than 11 percent of real GDP in 1987. The growing demand for U.S. exports, particularly manufactured products, fueled the economy and helped the unemployment rate fall below 6 percent for the first time in the 1980s.

U.S. export sales grew by a remarkable 11.4 percent in 1987, and manufacturing plants were operating at peak capacity. Industries producing paper, metals, plastics, lumber and wood products, electronic items, office equipment, and machine tools enjoyed booming sales in foreign markets in 1987. Over 50 percent of the total revenue taken in by IBM

in the United States was from foreign sales and operations. Even U.S. automakers, which never cultivated foreign sales in the past, were getting into the act. Chrysler Corporation hoped to export close to $1 billion worth of its cars to foreign markets in 1988.

The low value of the dollar also affected production decisions of U.S. firms. In 1987 the Tandy Corporation shifted assembly operations of its Color Computer 3 from South Korea to the United States. The Otis Elevator division of United Technologies moved its escalator production operations from West Germany to the United States.[4]

In addition, the changing international trade picture in 1987 and 1988 affected U.S. markets. Caterpillar Tractor, which had lost much of its share of the U.S. earthmover market to Japan's Komatsu, regained what it had lost. The U.S. specialty steel industry found that as a result of the dollar's decline, its products were more competitively priced in both U.S. and foreign markets.

The U.S. economy has become more sensitive to changes in economic conditions abroad. Just as the U.S. economy was beginning to recover from its recession of 1990–91, high interest rates and other factors pushed the economies of Canada and the United Kingdom, two of its major trading partners, into a recession. Both Germany and Japan, two other major buyers of U.S. exports, began drifting toward recession in 1992. As the major trading partners of the United States suffered declines in income growth, the growth rate of U.S. exports also suffered.

The U.S. economy will continue to be tied to world markets. To remain competitive, U.S. industries must invest in new technologies allowing productivity gains that keep production costs low. Changes in international currency markets can cause real GDP to fluctuate to a greater extent than has been the case in the past.

Inflation can be explained by either increases in aggregate demand or decreases in aggregate supply. Both demand-pull and cost-push inflation occur, and sometimes both occur simultaneously.

In the following chapters we'll be carefully examining the underlying forces that cause aggregate demand and aggregate supply to fluctuate. A good understanding of these forces is essential in formulating macroeconomic stabilization policies.

---

[4] See "Big Wheels Turning," *Time*, March 14, 1988, pp. 46–50.

- Under what circumstances will an economy achieve a macroeconomic equilibrium?

- Explain why unintended inventory buildup during the year implies that the economy has not achieved macroeconomic equilibrium. What will happen to aggregate production and earnings in the economy in such a case?

- How can recessions be caused by either changes in aggregate demand or changes in aggregate supply? How can increases in aggregate demand cause inflation when aggregate supply is relatively stable?

CONCEPT CHECK
☐

SUMMARY

1. Aggregate demand is a relationship between the price level and the aggregate quantity of final products demanded that is depicted by an aggregate demand curve. Aggregate supply is a relationship between the price level and the aggregate quantity of final products supplied that is depicted by an aggregate supply curve.

2. An aggregate demand curve slopes downward because increases in the price level can result in decreases in real wealth, increases in real interest rates, and changes in prices of exports and imports that decrease people's willingness and ability to purchase a nation's aggregate output of final products.

3. An aggregate supply curve slopes upward because the unit costs of additional production tend to increase as more is produced over a given year. The aggregate supply curve is quite flat when the economy has considerable slack, but it is very steep when the economy is operating above the level of aggregate production corresponding to potential real GDP.

4. A change in aggregate demand is a change in the relationship between the price level and aggregate quantity demanded caused by something other than a change in the price level. An increase in aggregate demand is represented by an outward shift of the aggregate demand curve, while a decrease in aggregate demand is represented by an inward shift of the aggregate demand curve. Aggregate demand can change in response to changes in real interest rates, the quantity of money in circulation, the foreign exchange rate of the dollar, government purchases, taxes or transfers, and factors influencing the demand for exports.

5. A change in aggregate supply is a change in the relationship between the price level and aggregate quantity supplied caused by something other than a change

in the price level. An increase in aggregate supply is represented by an outward shift of the aggregate supply curve, while a decrease in aggregate supply is represented by an inward shift of the aggregate supply curve. Changes in aggregate supply result from changes in input prices, changes in the quantity and quality of inputs, and advances in technology.

6. A macroeconomic equilibrium is attained for the economy when the aggregate quantity demanded equals the aggregate quantity supplied at the prevailing price level. Under macroeconomic equilibrium, there are no unintended inventory changes that can cause changes in business orders for new goods or services.

7. Equilibrium real GDP can differ from potential real GDP. When equilibrium GDP is less than potential real GDP, a recessionary GDP gap equal to the difference exists. When equilibrium real GDP exceeds potential real GDP, an inflationary GDP gap equal to the difference exists.

8. Decreases in aggregate demand put downward pressure on real GDP and the price level, while increases in aggregate demand put upward pressure on real GDP and the price level. A recession can be caused by a decrease in aggregate demand or a decrease in aggregate supply.

9. Inflation can be caused by continual increases in aggregate demand (demand-pull inflation) or by continual decreases in aggregate supply (cost-push inflation).

10. Decreases in aggregate supply exert upward pressure on the price level and downward pressure on real GDP, while increases in aggregate supply exert downward pressure on the price level and upward pressure on real GDP.

KEY TERMS

aggregate quantity demanded *203*

aggregate demand *203*

aggregate demand curve *203*

change in aggregate demand *205*

aggregate quantity supplied *208*

aggregate supply *208*

aggregate supply curve *208*

change in aggregate supply *211*

macroeconomic equilibrium *215*

recessionary GDP gap *217*

inflationary GDP gap *218*

demand-pull inflation *218*

cost-push inflation *220*

CONCEPT REVIEW

1. What is aggregate demand, and how it is depicted by an aggregate demand curve? List some major influences on aggregate demand that can cause it to increase or decrease.

2. Explain the shape of an aggregate supply curve, and list the major influences that can cause aggregate supply to change.

3. Under what circumstances will an economy be in macroeconomic equilibrium?

4. Other things being equal, how will an increase in aggregate demand affect the economy? How is the economy affected by an increase in aggregate supply?

PROBLEMS AND APPLICATIONS

1. An increase in aggregate demand occurs during 1995. Under what circumstances would you expect the increase in aggregate demand to increase real GDP while having little or no effect on the price level of the economy? **1**, **4**

2. Potential real GDP in the current quarter is $5,000 billion. Equilibrium real GDP in the current quarter is also $5,000 billion. There is a sharp increase in the demand for U.S. exports during the year. Other things being equal, forecast the effect of that increase on unemployment and inflation in the economy. **1**, **4**

3. Assume that an economy exists in which all assets held by the public are automatically adjusted for inflation or deflation whenever the price level changes, there is no international trade, and real interest rates do not change when the price level changes. What would the aggregate demand curve for such an economy look like? **1**

4. The economy is currently operating at full employment. At the beginning of the year, all nuclear power plants are shut down because of protests about the risk of environmental contamination. As power companies shift to more expensive sources of electricity, the price of electricity triples. Predict the effect of the power plant closings on macroeconomic equilibrium. **2**, **4**

5. Suppose that after a period of labor unrest the workers in a nation succeed in getting governing authorities to order a 25 percent increase in nominal hourly wages. Other things being equal, predict the impact of this settlement on macroeconomic equilibrium for the economy. Under what circumstances will the increase in the wage level reduce labor earnings? **2**, **4**

6. The economy is in a deep recession. After extensive negotiations, labor unions and all other workers agree to a 25 percent cut in nominal wages at the beginning of the next year. Use a graph to show the impact of the wage cut on macroeconomic equilibrium. **3**, **4**

7. Suppose the aggregate supply curve for an economy is a flat line. What would this imply about the relationship between real GDP and the price level? Show how a decrease in aggregate demand will affect the economy if the aggregate supply curve is a flat line. **2**, **4**

8. The economy is currently in a deep recession. The Federal Reserve System, which influences the supply of credit, takes actions to lower real interest rates. As real interest rates fall, business firms increase their demand for investment goods. Use a graph to show how the increase in demand can pull the economy out of the recession with little or no resulting inflation. **4**

9. Suppose there is a severe drought in a nation whose agricultural output accounts for a large percentage of real GDP. Show the impact of the drought on the nation's aggregate supply curve and its macroeconomic equilibrium. Why is the drought likely to result in both inflation and a recession? **3**, **4**

10. Typically, there are increases in both aggregate demand and aggregate supply for a growing economy. Use aggregate demand–aggregate supply analysis to show how aggregate demand can increase in an economy without causing inflation if the quantity and productivity of resources are also growing. **3**, **4**

chapter 10

Aggregate Demand–Aggregate Supply Analysis of Economic Fluctuations and Growth

How resilient is the U.S. economy—can it automatically stay on a steady path of growth close to full employment? What would happen to the economy if the stock market were to crash again as it did in 1929? Can there be another depression as serious and as long-lived as the Great Depression of the 1930s? Why are we likely to be in for an unfortunate combination of both inflation and increased unemployment if the economy overheats? What effect will a rise or fall in the international value of the dollar have on the economy? Why is economic growth important in increasing living standards and keeping inflation under control? We are now ready to use macroeconomic analysis to answer questions like these.

In this chapter we will use aggregate demand–aggregate supply analysis to understand why the economy is sometimes in macroeconomic equilibrium at levels of real GDP that fall short of or exceed potential real GDP. We will also show how the economy is affected by increases or decreases in nominal wages or fluctuations in the price of fuel and how these changes can affect the inflation rate and employment. We will also examine how changes in the foreign exchange rate of the dollar can affect macroeconomic equilibrium. Finally, we will use the analysis to further understand economic growth and its impact on living standards.

□ CONCEPT PREVIEW

After reading this chapter, you should be able to:

1. Understand the classical model of macroeconomic equilibrium and explain why the self-correction mechanism implied by the model does not always work quickly and reliably.

2. Discuss the Keynesian model of macroeconomic equilibrium and explain why Keynes thought that the economy could stagnate in equilibrium at a level of real GDP well below potential real GDP.

3. Discuss the process of self-correction in an overheated economy and explain how that process results in a wage-price spiral and a period of stagflation.

4. Explain how supply-side shocks affect the economy and understand the consequences of a supply-side recession.

5. Use aggregate demand–aggregate supply analysis to explain how changes in the international value of the dollar affect macroeconomic equilibrium.

6. Discuss the process of economic growth using aggregate demand–aggregate supply analysis.

MACROECONOMIC EQUILIBRIUM: THE CLASSICAL MODEL VERSUS THE KEYNESIAN MODEL

The classical economists of 19th-century England were inspired by Adam Smith's concept of the "invisible hand," which implied that individuals pursuing their own self-interest would unintentionally contribute to the general interest. David Ricardo, Thomas R. Malthus, John Stuart Mill, and other classical economists believed that prices for both products and resources would adjust quickly in markets to avoid general shortages or surpluses of goods. They also believed that the production of goods and services generated enough income to buy all the output produced—that supply created its own demand (based on the ideas of J. B. Say—see Economic Thinkers box). According to the classical economists, if the economy was not in equilibrium at full employment, changes in prices would eventually adjust market outcomes to get the economy back to full employment without any need for government intervention to stimulate aggregate demand. The economy would self-correct to assure equilibrium at potential real GDP.

The views of the classical economists were naturally subject to criticism during the Great Depression of the 1930s, when much of the world appeared hopelessly stuck in macroeconomic equilibrium at a level of real GDP much lower than potential real GDP. At the trough of the Great Depression in the United States, one out of every four workers was unemployed. It was during this period that the great English economist John Maynard Keynes (1883–1946) developed a new theory of macroeconomic equilibrium. Keynes (pronounced "Kains") presented reasons for believing that the economy could stagnate in equilibrium at a level of output well below the level that could provide full employment. He argued that during a recession government should use its powers to increase aggregate demand so as to restore full employment.

The controversy between the Keynesian (pronounced "Kainsian") and classical views of the economy still rages. Many modern economists believe that the powers of the economy to regulate itself have become stronger in recent years. These economists argue that attempts to stabilize the economy through changes in government spending or tax policy or changes in the supply of money and credit often do more to destabilize the economy than to stabilize it.

The Classical Model of Macroeconomic Equilibrium

When an economy is in macroeconomic equilibrium with excessive unemployment, why don't the markets where there are excess supplies reequilibrate to eliminate the surpluses? In other words, how is it that an economy can stay locked in a deep depression, as it did during the Great Depression of the 1930s? This problem perplexed economists for much of the 19th and early 20th centuries.

Economists of the 19th century believed that when the level of aggregate demand was insufficient to purchase the output of final products that would provide full employment, the resulting surpluses in input markets would cause input prices to decline. The declines in nominal wages, interest rates, rents, and other input prices would then increase aggregate supply to increase equilibrium real GDP. The model of macroeconomic equilibrium of the 19th-century classical economists maintained that price flexibility in the economy would prevent it from stagnating in a macroeconomic equilibrium with excessive unemployment.

The **classical model of macroeconomic equilibrium** implied that excessive unemployment and unused productive capacity would set up market forces that would eventually increase real GDP and eliminate cyclical unemployment. In other words, the economy has a self-correcting mechanism that keeps it working at full employ-

classical model of macroeconomic equilibrium a theory implying that excessive unemployment and unused productive capacity would set up forces that would eventually increase real GDP and eliminate the cyclical unemployment of workers.

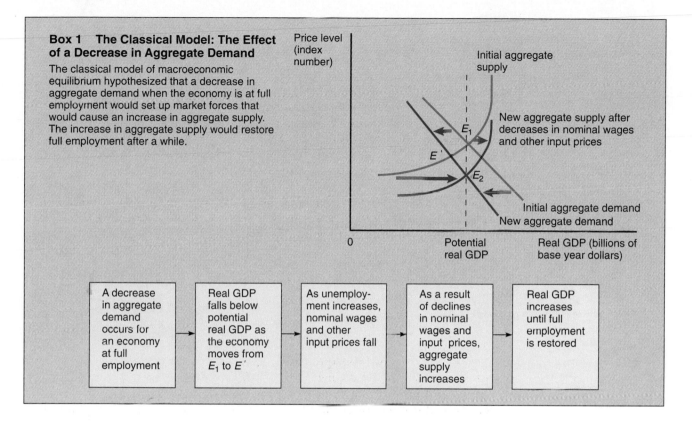

Box 1   The Classical Model: The Effect of a Decrease in Aggregate Demand

The classical model of macroeconomic equilibrium hypothesized that a decrease in aggregate demand when the economy is at full employment would set up market forces that would cause an increase in aggregate supply. The increase in aggregate supply would restore full employment after a while.

| A decrease in aggregate demand occurs for an economy at full employment | Real GDP falls below potential real GDP as the economy moves from E_1 to E' | As unemployment increases, nominal wages and other input prices fall | As a result of declines in nominal wages and input prices, aggregate supply increases | Real GDP increases until full employment is restored |

ment most of the time. A key assumption of the classical model is that in response to decreases in aggregate demand causing cyclical unemployment, nominal wages and other input prices fall sufficiently to shift aggregate supply outward enough to restore full employment quickly.

Think about why a decrease in aggregate demand reduces equilibrium real GDP and causes unemployment to increase. Given the level of input prices, a decline in aggregate demand reduces the profitability of supplying final products in markets. The decline in profitability causes firms to reduce output. As we showed in the preceding chapter, a decrease in aggregate demand moves the economy to a new macroeconomic equilibrium at which real GDP is lower. Of course, the decrease in real GDP that occurs in response to the decrease in aggregate demand also implies a decrease in the demand for labor and other inputs used to make products available. What would happen if nominal wages and other input prices (measured by some index of *input* prices) *also* fell when the price level fell? Such declines would reduce the unit costs of any given level of aggregate production and would therefore make it more profitable for firms to supply output.

Declines in nominal wages and other input prices cause the aggregate supply curve to shift outward. For example, suppose a decrease in aggregate demand moves an economy initially in equilibrium at potential real GDP (implying full employment) to a new equilibrium along the initial aggregate supply curve. As shown in Box 1, the economy moves from point E_1 to point E'. According to the classical economists, the equilibrium at point E' is only temporary. The decrease in aggregate demand that caused real GDP to decline below potential real GDP results in cyclical unemployment. The resulting surplus of labor then causes nominal wages to decline. As this

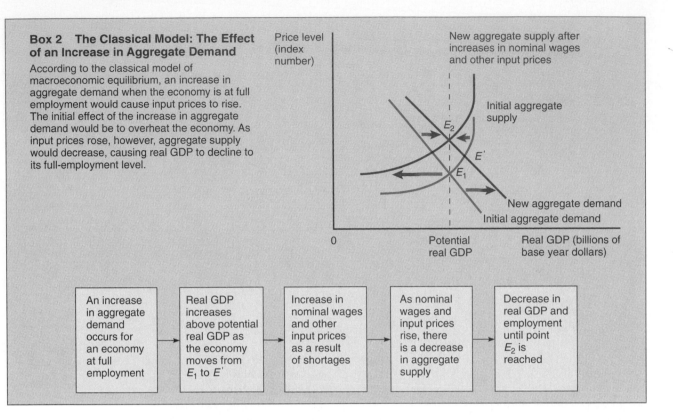

Box 2   The Classical Model: The Effect of an Increase in Aggregate Demand

According to the classical model of macroeconomic equilibrium, an increase in aggregate demand when the economy is at full employment would cause input prices to rise. The initial effect of the increase in aggregate demand would be to overheat the economy. As input prices rose, however, aggregate supply would decrease, causing real GDP to decline to its full-employment level.

| An increase in aggregate demand occurs for an economy at full employment | Real GDP increases above potential real GDP as the economy moves from E_1 to E' | Increase in nominal wages and other input prices as a result of shortages | As nominal wages and input prices rise, there is a decrease in aggregate supply | Decrease in real GDP and employment until point E_2 is reached |

happens, the aggregate supply curve shifts out. The increase in aggregate supply continues until nominal wages decline enough to restore full employment. Downward flexibility of nominal wages and other input prices, including interest rates, ensures that the economy will soon return to a new equilibrium at point E_2.

The increase in aggregate supply in response to the decrease in nominal wages and other input prices (including interest rates) puts upward pressure on real GDP and further downward pressure on the price level. This counteracts the unfavorable effects on real GDP of the initial decrease in aggregate demand.

The logical conclusion of the classical model is that equilibrium real GDP can never deviate for long below the level that corresponds to the full employment of labor and all other economic resources, as long as product prices, input prices, and interest rates are flexible. As long as nominal wages are flexible, they must fall enough to eliminate cyclical unemployment.

The key to the classical model is the assumption that *prices and quantities in all markets are flexible*. The classical economists presumed that price flexibility would eliminate all surpluses or shortages in markets and that markets were competitive enough to adjust to changes in economic conditions. If markets quickly adjusted to changes in economic conditions, widespread surpluses of labor would be rare and excessive unemployment would be unlikely.

The classical model also implies that an *increase* in aggregate demand will put upward pressure on real GDP only temporarily if the increase causes the economy to overheat. An increase in aggregate demand can cause the economy to exceed its potential real GDP as overtime labor is used and physical facilities are operated around the clock. This will, of course, put upward pressure on the price level. An increase in aggregate demand moves the economy to a temporary equilibrium at a

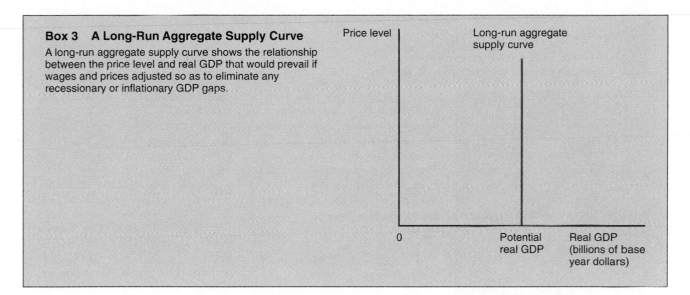

Box 3   A Long-Run Aggregate Supply Curve

A long-run aggregate supply curve shows the relationship between the price level and real GDP that would prevail if wages and prices adjusted so as to eliminate any recessionary or inflationary GDP gaps.

level of real GDP that exceeds the level for which full employment is attained. Because of the increase in aggregate demand, the economy becomes temporarily overheated. As shown in Box 2, the economy moves along its initial aggregate supply curve from point E_1 to point E'. The resulting increase in demand for labor puts upward pressure on nominal wages (and other input prices). Temporary shortages occur in labor markets until nominal wages rise sufficiently. The wage increase continues shifting the aggregate supply curve inward until labor shortages have been eliminated. The aggregate supply curve shifts inward until equilibrium is attained at point E_2, at which equilibrium real GDP has declined to potential real GDP corresponding to full employment. At the final equilibrium at point E_2, both nominal wages and the price level have increased.

The Classical Long-Run Aggregate Supply Curve

According to the classical economists, equilibrium real GDP can deviate from potential real GDP only temporarily. Any recessionary or inflationary real GDP gaps are quickly eliminated through changes in aggregate supply that eliminate the discrepancy between equilibrium and potential real GDP. The classical economists therefore argued that except for short-lived episodes the economy could be expected to achieve equilibrium at full employment. The **long-run aggregate supply curve (LRAS)** shows the relationship between the aggregate quantity supplied and the price level that would be observed if nominal wages and other money prices were flexible enough to allow the classical self-correction mechanism to work. Because equilibrium real GDP over the long run would equal potential real GDP if all prices were flexible, the long-run aggregate supply curve would be a vertical line corresponding to potential (full-employment) real GDP.

The graph in Box 3 shows the long-run aggregate supply curve for the economy. This curve can be thought of as simply indicating the economy's potential real GDP at any point in time. Points on the long-run aggregate supply curve correspond to full employment. Points of temporary equilibrium (such as E' in Boxes 1 and 2) are not points on the LRAS.

In the long run, an increase in real GDP is possible only if potential real GDP increases. When potential GDP increases, the long-run aggregate supply curve shifts

long-run aggregate supply curve (LRAS) a curve showing the relationship between the aggregate quantity supplied and the price level that would be observed if nominal wages and other money prices were flexible enough to allow the classical self-correcting mechanism to work.

economic thinkers

Jean Baptiste Say and "Say's Law"

He was French but his influence was greatly felt by the classical economists of 19th-century England. Jean Baptiste Say was born in Lyon, France, in 1767. Because of religious persecution, his family moved to England when Jean was a child. There he learned about Adam Smith's view about a market system in which an "invisible hand" led individuals (who intended to benefit only themselves) to benefit others and about how the economy was regulated by this process.

Say returned to France to work in an insurance firm. As a supporter of the French Revolution, he became active in politics but continued to study economics. However, the spark kindled in his mind by the clever and well-turned prose of Smith would not die easily. Say was destined to stimulate the thinking of Adam Smith's successors—the classical economists, a group that included David Ricardo. Thomas R. Malthus, and John Stuart Mill—and to create a controversy that to this day rages in macroeconomics.

In 1803 he published his *Treatise on Political Economy: Or, The Production, Distribution and Consumption of Wealth*. In this book Say developed the basic idea behind the circular flow of production and income. Say developed the "law of markets," which implies that supply creates its own demand. Commonly referred to as "Say's Law," this idea that production creates income was a major contribution to economic thought.

Say's Law is actually more complex than the simple interpretation given to it here. Naturally the income from the production of goods and services is adequate to purchase all that has been produced. Say, however, realized there can be a discrepancy between what has actually been produced and the *willingness* of the public to buy it. He concluded, however, that these discrepancies were merely mismatches between the mix of output and the mix of demand that would soon correct themselves.

The classical economists agreed with Say's Law. They believed markets would always adjust so prices would assure that the total quantity produced would eventually be sold. They argued that a "general glut" of goods and services or of labor (excessive unemployment) was unlikely but, if it did occur, market prices would quickly adjust to eliminate any surpluses. Therefore, extended recessions were thought to be impossible. The best policy would be to let supply create its own demand in the long run. The economy would achieve potential GDP most of the time, although there would be temporary periods of cyclical unemployment that would not last long.*

Although Say's Law was widely discredited in the 1930s when the economy stagnated in a deep depression, today there are many economists who think the basic idea behind Say's Law is correct and that the best policy to stabilize the economy is to leave it alone. These economists argue that the economy is likely to achieve full employment and that economic policy should encourage improvements in productivity and create incentives for work and investment. According to these modern "supply-side" economists, policies that encourage growth in the labor force, improvement in technology, and gains in labor productivity, and provide incentives to work and invest will eventually result in the income to buy the extra output that will be produced.

Jean Baptiste Say was active in business and taught economics later in his life. He coined the word "entrepreneur" and analyzed the entrepreneur's role as a risk taker and an organizer. Say was the author of *Cours Complete d'Economie Politique Pratique,* a major textbook designed to teach citizens about economics. He died in 1832 at the age of 65 after a productive life as an entrepreneur, politician, and teacher-scholar.

* For an excellent discussion of the classical economists' views regarding Say's Law, see George J. Stigler, *Essays in the History of Economics* (Chicago: University of Chicago Press, 1965), pp. 311–25.

outward. In the long run, increases in productive potential arise from improvements in productivity, resource availability, technology, and other supply-side forces. Although the economy occasionally produces more than potential GDP over the short run when aggregate demand increases, an increase in aggregate demand cannot permanently increase output beyond potential GDP over the long run. Temporary inflationary GDP gaps are eventually eliminated by increases in wages and prices.

Reductions in aggregate demand may never reduce the price level enough to get to points on the long-run aggregate supply curve! Even over relatively long periods, downward rigidity in prices and wages can prevent the economy's self-correcting mechanism from working. This situation is what Keynes had in mind when he said: "In the long run we are all dead." Recessions often require short-run action to increase aggregate demand because the long-run self-correcting mechanism of the economy doesn't work well in the downward direction!

Outward shifts of the long-run aggregate supply curve imply growth in potential and equilibrium real GDP on average over time. Increases in aggregate demand contribute to short-term economic growth because such increases give businesses the confidence necessary to make investments that expand the economy's productive capacity. Annual shifts in aggregate demand therefore exert an influence on the year-to-year performance of the economy. Ultimately, however, the growth of an economy depends on the expansion of its productive capacity and is therefore a supply-side phenomenon. Growth in aggregate demand can prevent an economy from falling into a recession and can occasionally cause the economy to exceed its potential temporarily, but the real engine of economic growth is an outward-shifting long-run aggregate supply curve.

The Keynesian Model of Macroeconomic Equilibrium

Although the logic of the classical model is correct, the evidence indicates that ⎘ nominal wage levels, which measure unit labor costs (an important determinant of aggregate supply since they constitute more than 70 percent of production costs), are quite inflexible over a period of one year. This is not to say that nominal wages never fall in response to sharp declines in aggregate demand. Based on past evidence, however, nominal wages don't appear to fall *enough* to increase the profitability of production and aggregate supply sufficiently to restore full employment when the U.S. economy operates below potential real GDP. As a consequence, declines in aggregate demand tend to reduce real GDP in the United States without setting up a process of rapid self-correction. For example, although there was a 21 percent decrease in nominal wages between the end of 1929 and 1933, that decrease wasn't sufficient to shift the aggregate supply curve outward enough to restore full employment.

The reason for downwardly inflexible nominal wages is not completely understood. However, it's believed that labor market characteristics, such as long-term wage contracts and seniority rules dictating which workers are laid off first, prevent wages from falling quickly in response to declines in labor demand. Whatever the reasons for downward rigidity of the nominal wage level in the United States and other economies, the phenomenon is well documented.

Downward nominal wage rigidity plays an important role in the theory of macroeconomic equilibrium developed by John Maynard Keynes. Keynes believed that an economy could become locked in a macroeconomic equilibrium with high cyclical unemployment, and that the classical self-correcting mechanism would not work. The Keynesian model of macroeconomic equilibrium assumes that because of rigid nominal wages the economy's self-correction mechanism cannot be expected to automatically restore full employment when aggregate demand declines. The Keynes-

Keynesian model of macroeconomic equilibrium a model assuming that because of rigid nominal wages the economy can be in equilibrium at less than full employment.

principles in practice

Business Brief: How Long-Term Labor Contracts Prevent Wage Flexibility in the U.S.

Union workers in the United States today account for less than 15 percent of the labor force. Although the influence of organized labor on the U.S. economy has waned over the last several years, unions still exert considerable power over wage levels in the nation by negotiating long-term labor contracts with employers. Union wage levels tend to influence wages in nonunion jobs as well. The existence of labor contracts prevents nominal (money) wages from fluctuating daily as prices do in stock markets and commodity markets.

Because of long-term contracts, nominal wages are likely to be quite unresponsive to changes in the price level over a period of at least one year. Most union contracts are for a three-year period, and sometimes contain inflation-linked cost-of-living adjustments in wages, but such adjustments are usually made at the *end* of the contract year.

Why do workers agree to contracts that fix nominal wages over a period of a year? The reason lies in the costs of negotiating wages. A three-year contract that specifies yearly increases in wages economizes on the costs incurred in reaching wage agreements. Such a contract also reduces the losses incurred in strikes and lockouts by limiting their incidence to once every three

years. For these reasons both workers and employers gain when long-term contracts are negotiated even though they run the risk that real wages will fluctuate over the contract period.

Rapid cost-of-living adjustments are rare in U.S. labor agreements. Firms fear that as the price level increases, rapid automatic increases in nominal wages will force them to raise the prices of their products. This, they fear, will cause a large reduction in sales volume that will adversely affect their profits. Similarly, unions fear that a reduction in sales resulting from nominal wage increases will cut the demand for labor and increase unemployment. Both workers and employers prefer not to take the risks associated with automatic cost-of-living adjustments.

These labor market practices keep the aggregate supply curve from shifting inward rapidly when the U.S. economy overheats. Over a period of one year, nominal wages are not only inflexible in the downward direction, but also appear to be inflexible in the upward direction. The rigidity of wages in the U.S. economy implies that over a relatively short period (say one year) the economy's self-correcting mechanism is unlikely to operate to stabilize real GDP at its full-employment level.

ian model implies that corrective measures are necessary to restore aggregate demand to the level that ensures full employment and to avoid declines in aggregate real income and employment opportunities. Therefore, government policies influencing aggregate demand are necessary. When there is considerable slack in the economy, increases in aggregate demand result primarily in increases in real GDP, with little upward pressure on the price level.

Modern Keynesians also believe that because of the way labor contracts are negotiated, over a period of one year nominal wages tend to be upwardly inflexible as well (see Principles in Practice box). This tends to reduce the effectiveness of the economy's self-correcting mechanism during periods in which the economy is overheated.

THE GREAT DEPRESSION: USING AGGREGATE DEMAND–AGGREGATE SUPPLY ANALYSIS TO UNDERSTAND WHAT HAPPENED

The Great Depression hit the U.S. economy suddenly and unexpectedly. In early 1929 the economy was operating at full employment, with an unemployment rate of only 3.2 percent. Then, in October 1929, the stock market crashed; the value of corporate stocks plunged to two thirds of the value that prevailed early in the year. Panicky traders sold stocks to meet the demands of creditors who wanted their loans paid off. Many loans were uncollectible and some banks failed. In an era without

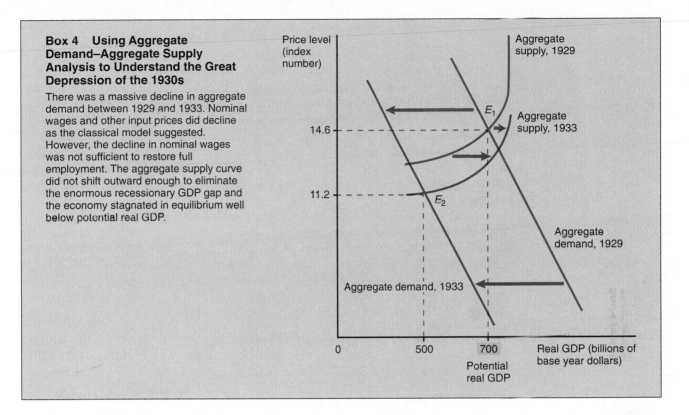

Box 4   Using Aggregate Demand–Aggregate Supply Analysis to Understand the Great Depression of the 1930s

There was a massive decline in aggregate demand between 1929 and 1933. Nominal wages and other input prices did decline as the classical model suggested. However, the decline in nominal wages was not sufficient to restore full employment. The aggregate supply curve did not shift outward enough to eliminate the enormous recessionary GDP gap and the economy stagnated in equilibrium well below potential real GDP.

federal deposit insurance, households lost their savings when banks could not meet demands for withdrawals. The end result of the decline in wealth was a massive decline in aggregate demand, which was particularly acute for housing and construction. Thousands of firms in the building industry were forced out of business.

A number of mistakes made by policymakers aggravated the decline in aggregate demand and prevented the economy from recovering. The supply of money in circulation was sharply reduced as a result of bank failures, and the nation's monetary authorities made no effort to reverse the trend. As the money supply declined, spending declined. Interest rates remained high as the supply of loanable funds dried up.

Box 4 shows the aggregate demand and aggregate supply curves prevailing in early 1929, prior to the stock market crash, and then in 1933 at the trough of the Great Depression. The initial equilibrium at point E_1 corresponds to potential real GDP in 1929. After the decline in aggregate demand, the unemployment rate soared and a substantial recessionary GDP gap opened up. The price level fell in 1930. In response to the general decline in the demand for inputs, there was some decline in input prices—just as the classical economists would have predicted. As nominal wages, land prices, and other input prices declined, there was an increase in the aggregate supply, as suggested in the classical model of macroeconomic equilibrium. However, the increase in aggregate supply was *not* sufficient to restore full employment. In 1933 the economy was in equilibrium at point E_2, at a level of real GDP well below potential real GDP.

By 1933 one out of every four workers was unemployed and real GDP was only 70 percent of its 1929 value. The price level had fallen to about 75 percent of its 1929 value. The classical self-correcting mechanism failed to restore full employment, and for most of the 1930s the economy stagnated in equilibrium at well below potential real GDP.

By 1933 the amount of money in circulation declined by 20 percent of the amount available in 1929, and prices of real estate and other assets fell. More policy blunders were made that made the contraction worse. Congress passed the Smoot-Hawley tariff, which was designed to stimulate U.S. industry by protecting it from foreign competition. Instead, the tariff had the opposite effect. By depriving the rest of the world of an enormous export market in the United States, it spread the recession around the world. As income and aggregate demand declined in European nations, so too did their demand for American products. The decline contributed to a further decline in aggregate demand in the United States, thus further reducing real GDP and the price level.

It was in the environment of the 1930s that Keynes developed his model of macroeconomic equilibrium, offering a unique solution to the problem of an economy stagnating in equilibrium at a level of real GDP below full employment. Keynes recommended that the government increase its purchases even if it had to borrow to do so. Keynes reasoned that if the government purchases component of real GDP were increased without increasing taxes, aggregate demand would increase, so that the economy could move toward full employment.

Why Another Great Depression Is Unlikely

We have learned a great deal from the Great Depression, and it is unlikely that such a massive contraction can occur again. It is no longer possible to borrow extensively to purchase corporate stocks. This restraint has eased speculation in the stock market and reduced the risk of overinflated stock prices. The monetary authorities are now more careful about assuring an adequate supply of money and credit in times of financial stress. When stock prices collapsed in 1987, Alan Greenspan, the chairman of the Board of Governors of the Federal Reserve System, was careful to assure banks and the financial community that the system would provide the money and credit banks needed to meet their withdrawal demands. Despite the increase in bank failures in recent years, particularly failures of savings and loan associations, bank deposits are insured so that household savings are not wiped out if banks fail. However, bailing out failed banks has increased the federal budget deficit as the government has had to increase borrowings to pay deposit insurance claims. In addition, the government purchases component of real GDP is much larger than it was in 1929. Government purchases are a much more stable component of aggregate expenditures than investment, exports, or even consumption. When we study stabilization policies, you will learn that the federal government budget contains built-in stabilizers such as unemployment insurance, that maintain private spending even when earnings decline. Because of both institutional changes in the economy and improved methods of stabilization in times of crisis, aggregate demand is much less likely to decline as sharply as it did in the period 1930–33.

CONCEPT CHECK

☐

- Briefly describe how the self-correcting mechanism envisioned by the classical economists would restore the economy to full employment when equilibrium real GDP fluctuates from potential real GDP.

- How does the Keynesian model of macroeconomic equilibrium differ from the classical model of macroeconomic equilibrium? How did the Great Depression of the 1930s show the flaws in the classical self-correcting mechanism?

- How does a long-run aggregate supply curve differ from the aggregate supply curve that prevails for a given year?

AN OVERHEATED ECONOMY AND STAGFLATION

Sometimes aggregate demand increases enough so that at the equilibrium level of real GDP, aggregate quantity supplied exceeds potential real GDP. When that happens, the economy booms and inflationary pressures build up. Recall from the preceding chapter that an economy can produce more than its potential real GDP in a year. An *inflationary GDP gap* prevails for the economy when equilibrium real GDP exceeds potential real GDP. The inflationary gap puts upward pressure on the price level, which then reduces aggregate quantity demanded as a new equilibrium is attained. Eventually, the inflationary gap is eliminated. Now, by analyzing shifts in aggregate supply, we can obtain greater insight into what is likely to occur in the economy when an inflationary gap prevails.

The process of reequilibration that results when an inflationary gap prevails involves shifts in aggregate supply that can cause the economy to experience stagnation or declines in the growth of real GDP at the same time that the price level rises. If the price level increases enough during the year, business firms find it profitable to increase production to levels that actually *exceed* the economy's potential. An economy *overheats* when it operates beyond its potential in much the same way that an engine overheats when it's run faster than its potential. When an economy is overheated, factories and offices are worked around the clock. Under these circumstances, total labor hours used during the year exceed the level that corresponds to the natural rate of unemployment. This occurs as workers put in overtime and some workers normally out of the labor force are induced to enter it.

The graph in Box 5 shows the process by which an overheated economy reequilibrates to eventually eliminate an inflationary gap. At the beginning of the year, the economy is in equilibrium at a price level of 120 and a real GDP level of $5,500 billion. Assume that potential real GDP is $5,000 billion. There is now an *inflationary*

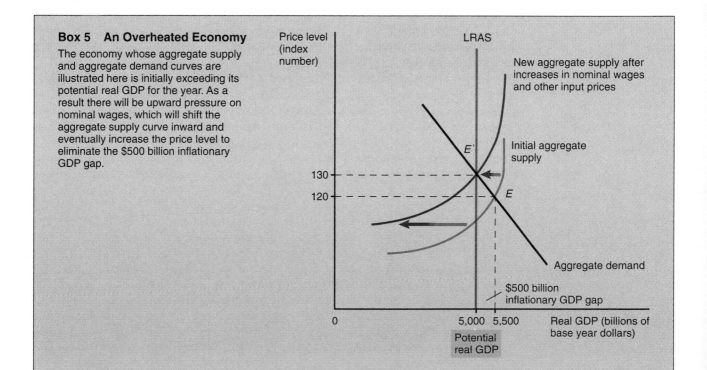

Box 5   An Overheated Economy

The economy whose aggregate supply and aggregate demand curves are illustrated here is initially exceeding its potential real GDP for the year. As a result there will be upward pressure on nominal wages, which will shift the aggregate supply curve inward and eventually increase the price level to eliminate the $500 billion inflationary GDP gap.

Price level (index number)

LRAS

New aggregate supply after increases in nominal wages and other input prices

E'

Initial aggregate supply

130

120

E

Aggregate demand

$500 billion inflationary GDP gap

0   5,000 5,500   Real GDP (billions of base year dollars)

Potential real GDP

GDP gap, measured by the difference between the equilibrium real GDP of $5,500 billion and the potential real GDP level of $5,000 billion. This $500 billion inflationary GDP gap is illustrated along the horizontal axis. The current equilibrium corresponds to point E. Assume that during the past year the price level has increased from 112 to 120, implying inflation of just over 7 percent.

As a result of the higher prices caused by the increase in aggregate demand, workers whose wages have lagged behind the rate of inflation during the past year are likely to demand wage increases when contract talks are opened up again. The labor market is likely to be tight when the economy is overheated, and workers will be in short supply. Under these conditions, employers are likely to grant worker demands for wage increases that at least keep pace with inflation. Similarly, materials will be in short supply in an overheated economy, and the prices of these inputs will rise over the year. *Because of increases in wages and other input prices that take place over the year in an overheated economy, the aggregate supply curve will shift inward.* As this process occurs, the economy will move toward an equilibrium, given the aggregate demand curve, at point E', at which real GDP falls to its potential level. But the decrease in aggregate supply *also* further increases the price level during the year! Eventually, real GDP will decline by $500 billion and the price level will increase from 120 to 130, implying 8 percent inflation. The preceding year's inflation caused the economy to stretch beyond its potential. The wage increases negotiated by workers to keep up with inflation then resulted in cost-push inflation in the following year as the aggregate supply curve steadily shifted inward.

Wage-Price Spirals in an Overheated Economy

Whenever aggregate demand is so excessive that is causes an economy to overheat, the result is an inflationary process. In some cases an economy can remain overheated for a number of years. For example, the U.S. economy was overheated between 1966 and 1968, when the government was engaged in a military buildup for the Vietnam conflict. During those years, when equilibrium real GDP exceeded potential real GDP, a process of demand-pull inflation followed by cost-push inflation had the economy in its grip. Between 1965 and 1970 inflation surged. Relatively high inflation continued in 1969 and 1970 despite a brief recession that hit the economy in 1969.

wage-price spiral a situation that exists when higher product prices result in higher wages, which in turn increase prices still further through a decrease in aggregate supply.

A **wage-price spiral** exists in the economy when higher product prices result in higher wages, which in turn increase prices still further through a decrease in aggregate supply! When a wage-price spiral exists, increases in aggregate demand cause an inflationary GDP gap, which in turn causes wages to increase. The resulting decrease in aggregate supply causes further increases in the price level. Further increases in aggregate demand then cause the price level to increase again, and the process starts all over. The process continues until the inflationary gap has been eliminated.

The U.S. economy was caught in a wage-price spiral exactly like this during the period from 1966 to 1970. From the beginning of 1966 to the end of 1969, the economy was clearly overheated, with the official unemployment rates over that four-year period averaging only 3.6 percent. Workers were in short supply, and it's likely that the economy was exceeding its potential. Inflation increased from a mere 2 percent per year in 1965 to nearly 6 percent per year in 1970. Each year workers negotiated labor contracts that pushed wages higher. In fact, workers began to anticipate inflation and usually demanded a little more in wages so their nominal wages wouldn't lose purchasing power over the next year. The result was a wage-price spiral. Cost-push inflation followed from the demand-pull inflation that overheated the economy.

Stagflation

Stagflation is the term that has been coined to describe an economy in which real GDP stagnates at a given level or actually declines from one period to the next while inflation ensues at relatively high rates. Stagflation is a combination of stagnation of economic growth in real GDP and rising prices. The process described in Box 5, as the economy moved from an equilibrium at point *E* to the one at *E'*, was one of stagflation. After the economy overheated, the consequence was a decrease in aggregate supply, which in turn caused a decrease in real GDP and an increase in the price level.

When workers start to anticipate the effect of inflation on their real wages and succeed in getting large nominal wage increases, the aggregate supply curve can shift inward enough to cause equilibrium real GDP to be below potential real GDP. This effect can be compounded, as you'll soon see, when other changes in economic conditions result in further inward shifts of the aggregate supply curve.

Stagflation implies that an economy, after overheating, can suffer from both a recession and inflation. For example, during the period 1974–75 the U.S. economy experienced a recession after achieving huge increases of 5 percent in real GDP in both 1972 and 1973. In 1974 real GDP declined by 0.5 percent of its 1973 value, and in 1975 real GDP fell by nearly 1 percent of its 1974 value. The unemployment rate soared to 8.3 percent of the labor force in 1975. At the same time, however, inflation roared at record levels. The rate of inflation measured by the annual percentage change in the consumer price index was 11 percent in 1974 and 9.1 percent in 1975.

Stagflation occurred again in 1980, when real GDP suffered a slight decline and inflation was in high gear at an annual rate of 13.5 percent. Then, during the severe 1982 recession, real GDP fell by 2.5 percent, and in 1983 unemployment rose to 9.5 percent, while inflation still continued at an annual rate of 6.1 percent.

Stagflation is particularly harmful to consumers because at the same time real GDP declines, so does the purchasing power of the dollar. As people seek to protect themselves against inflation, decision making is distorted.

Supply-Side Shocks

In some cases a **supply-side shock,** a sudden and unexpected shift of the aggregate supply curve, occurs. In 1973, as the economy was reequilibrating from an inflationary gap, it also got socked with a supply-side shock in the form of the OPEC oil embargo that sent the price of a key input skyrocketing. The result was an inward shift of the economy's aggregate supply curve. In 1979 higher oil prices caused another unexpected and unfavorable supply-side shock that raised prices and decreased real GDP. In August 1990 the price of crude oil skyrocketed after Iraq's invasion of Kuwait. This shock caused the price level to rise and put downward pressure on real GDP just when aggregate demand was beginning to slow its rate of outward growth.

Supply-side shocks result from either increases in input prices or decreases in the availability of resources. In the preceding chapter we traced the effect of a price shock in which aggregate supply curve decreased as a result of an unexpected increase in the price of a key input. Now let's examine the effect of a supply-side shock that results from a decrease in the availability of a key input—perhaps because of a cutoff (as opposed to a simple price increase) in the supply of oil or a disaster (an earthquake or a war) that destroys human life and capital.

The graph in Box 6 shows how the economy reacts to an unfavorable supply-side shock. Suppose the economy is initially in equilibrium at point *E* at a real GDP of $5,000 billion and a price level of 120. As aggregate supply decreases because of the

stagflation term coined to describe an economy in which real GDP stagnates at a given level or actually declines from one period to the next while inflation ensues at relatively high rates.

4

supply-side shock a sudden and unexpected shift of the aggregate supply curve.

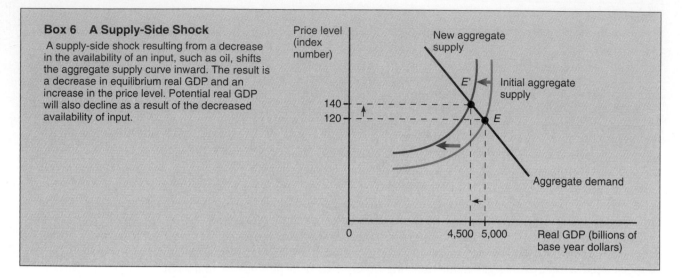

Box 6   A Supply-Side Shock

A supply-side shock resulting from a decrease in the availability of an input, such as oil, shifts the aggregate supply curve inward. The result is a decrease in equilibrium real GDP and an increase in the price level. Potential real GDP will also decline as a result of the decreased availability of input.

reduced availability of resources, both potential real GDP and the level of real GDP corresponding to the economy's capacity output also decrease. The economy adjusts during the year by moving to a new equilibrium at point E'. At the new equilibrium the price level increases to 140. Notice that the effect of the shock is a *onetime* increase in the price level. Because the shock is a onetime event, it does not add to the inflation rate in the following year. In other words, a supply-side shock does not start an inflationary process in the same way as it would in an overheated economy. Note also that a supply-side shock that results from a decrease in the availability of input also reduces potential real GDP and the capacity output of the economy.

CONCEPT CHECK

☐

- Under what circumstances will an economy "overheat"?

- How can stagflation result when an economy becomes overheated? Show how a supply-side shock can cause an economy to suffer from both a recession and inflation.

- How can supply-side shock cause a recession while causing the price level to rise?

EXCHANGE RATES AND MACROECONOMIC EQUILIBRIUM

5 As imports and exports have increased in importance for the U.S. economy since 1960, macroeconomic equilibrium has become more sensitive to changes in the international value of the dollar. Recall from our discussion of exchange rates in Chapter 3 that the price of the dollar affects the selling price of our exports to foreigners, who must buy dollars to buy our goods. Other things being equal, the higher the price (the foreign exchange rate) of the dollar, the higher the price of our exports in terms of foreign currency. When the exchange rate of the dollar changes, so does the price of imported goods. For example, as the price of the dollar in terms of Japanese yen increased in 1990, Japanese imports became cheaper for American buyers. The impact of changes in the international value of the dollar on macroeconomic equilibrium can be traced using aggregate demand–aggregate supply analysis.

Box 7   Impact of an Increase in the Exchange Rate of the Dollar on Aggregate Demand

An increase in the exchange rate of the dollar decreases aggregate demand. This puts downward pressure on real GDP and on the price level.

Impact of a Higher Dollar on Aggregate Demand

When the exchange rate of the dollar increases, our exports, other things being equal, will become more expensive to foreigners, while imported goods will become less expensive for us (although there's sometimes a lag in the change in the prices of imports). Other things being equal, we expect increases in the exchange rate of the dollar against a broad group of currencies to contribute to lower net exports. As net exports decline, there is a reduction in employment in export industries and in industries facing strong competition from foreign suppliers.

An increase in exchange rates therefore decreases aggregate demand, with the extent of the decrease depending on the size of the economy's export sector and the extent to which domestic industries must compete with foreign sellers at home. A decrease in aggregate demand caused by an increase in the exchange rate of the dollar is illustrated in the graph in Box 7. As you can see, the decrease in aggregate demand results in downward pressure on both real GDP and the price level. The unemployment resulting from the decline in real GDP is concentrated in export industries and industries facing strong foreign competition from imports. From 1981 to 1985, for example, the U.S. automobile and textile industries were particularly hard hit by the high price of the dollar. U.S. agriculture, which relies heavily on export sales, was also adversely affected.

Similarly, a decrease in the exchange rate of the dollar can increase aggregate demand by increasing the demand for U.S. exports while decreasing the U.S. demand for imports. This increases employment in U.S. export industries and, after a lag, in U.S. industries that compete with imports. The decline in the exchange rate of the dollar after 1985 resulted in a boom in U.S. export industries in 1987 and 1988. However, because of the delayed effect of the decline on import prices, import demand was slow to respond, which dampened the expansionary effect.

Impact of Changes in Exchange Rates on Aggregate Supply

Changes in exchange rates can also affect macroeconomic equilibrium through effects on aggregate supply. The United States and many other nations import substantial amounts of raw materials and machinery. An increase in the exchange rate of the dollar means that the prices of imported inputs, after adjustment for inflation, will decline. A higher priced dollar can therefore contribute to lower input prices and cause the aggregate supply curve to shift outward, as shown in the graph in Box 8.

The increase in aggregate supply that results from a higher exchange rate of the dollar puts upward pressure on real GDP and downward pressure on the price level. A higher-valued dollar therefore contributes to both increased employment and lower inflation through its impact on aggregate supply. On the other hand, a decline in the exchange rate of the dollar contributes to a decrease in aggregate supply by raising the prices of imported inputs. The decrease in aggregate supply is a contractionary influence on the economy and puts upward pressure on the price level. Of course, the magnitude of the supply-side effects will depend on the importance of imported inputs in production.

Conclusion: The Impact of Changes in Foreign Exchange Rates on Macroeconomic Equilibrium

As you can see from the preceding analysis, changes in exchange rates have a complex impact on macroeconomic equilibrium in the economy. A higher-priced dollar, through its effect on aggregate demand, is a contractionary influence on the economy. But through its effects on aggregate supply, the higher-priced dollar is an expansionary influence on the economy because it lowers the prices of imported inputs. Depending on whether the demand-side or supply-side effects are stronger, a higher-priced dollar can either increase or decrease real GDP.

However, there's no doubt that a higher-priced dollar will moderate inflationary pressures in the U.S. economy. The reason for this is that both the demand-side and supply-side effects of the increase in the exchange rate put downward pressure on the price level.

There's one other complication in the analysis that we must consider and that we'll investigate later in greater detail. You'll recall from our analysis of the circular flow of income and expenditure that whenever net exports are negative, foreign saving in the United States must increase. An increase in the exchange rate of the

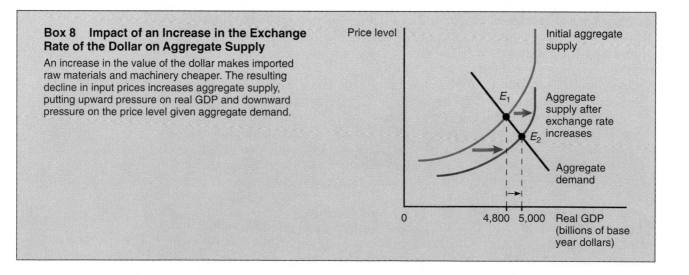

Box 8   Impact of an Increase in the Exchange Rate of the Dollar on Aggregate Supply

An increase in the value of the dollar makes imported raw materials and machinery cheaper. The resulting decline in input prices increases aggregate supply, putting upward pressure on real GDP and downward pressure on the price level given aggregate demand.

dollar that contributes to a further deterioration of the U.S. balance of trade therefore increases the supply of foreign saving in the United States. This puts downward pressure on real interest rates by increasing the supply of loanable funds in U.S. credit markets. The lower real interest rates can increase the quantity of investment goods demanded by U.S. businesses, which increases aggregate demand in the United States. This interest rate effect moderates the contractionary influence of the negative net exports on U.S. real GDP.

The graph in Box 9 shows a case where a higher exchange rate acts to decrease equilibrium real GDP. The aggregate demand curve shifts inward in response to lower net export demand by a greater amount than the aggregate supply curve shifts outward in response to lower input prices. As real GDP declines, there is an increase in the unemployment rate in the economy.

We can analyze the impact of a decrease in the exchange rate of the dollar in a similar fashion. You know that, other things being equal, a lower-priced dollar increases demand for U.S. exports and decreases U.S. demand for imports. This tends to increase aggregate demand, putting upward pressure on U.S. real GDP and the price level. Similarly, a lower-priced dollar contributes to higher input prices as a result of increases in the prices of imported raw materials and machinery. As this occurs, aggregate supply will decrease, which in turn puts downward pressure on real GDP and upward pressure on the price level. We can conclude that a decrease in the exchange rate of the dollar contributes to inflationary pressures in the United States and either increases or decreases real GDP, depending on whether the demand-side or supply-side effects are stronger. As the exchange rate of the dollar declined in 1987 and 1988, the demand for U.S. exports boomed. The demand-side effects were quite strong at that time, and real GDP increased, as did inflationary pressures in the economy. The graph in Box 10 shows how a decline in the exchange rate of the dollar can result in an increase in equilibrium real GDP.

Finally, a lower-priced dollar means that foreign saving in the United States will decline as the U.S. balance of trade improves. There will be upward pressure on real interest rates in the United States in response to a decrease in the foreign supply of loanable funds in credit markets.

Box 9   How a Higher Dollar Can Decrease Equilibrium Real GDP

When the effect on aggregate demand is stronger than the effect on aggregate supply when the dollar appreciates on international foreign exchange markets, equilibrium real GDP will fall.

Box 10   How a Lower Dollar Can Increase Equilibrium Real GDP

When the impact of the lower dollar on aggregate demand is stronger than its effect on aggregate supply, real GDP will increase. In 1987 and 1988 the strong increase in aggregate demand resulting from increased exports dominated the U.S. economy and acted to increase equilibrium real GDP, as shown in the graph, while at the same time putting upward pressure on the price level.

MACROECONOMIC EQUILIBRIUM IN A GROWING ECONOMY

In a growing economy both the aggregate demand and aggregate supply curves shift outward yearly. Normally, assuming that there are no supply-side shocks, the process of economic growth results in fairly steady increases in aggregate supply. There are, of course, occasional cyclical downturns in aggregate demand. However, as population and income grow, aggregate demand on average also increases as the increased aggregate income in the economy results in more purchases by households, businesses, and government.

In any given year, the changes in equilibrium real GDP and the price level depend on how far out aggregate demand shifts relative to the outward shift in aggregate supply (from increases in the labor force or increases in labor productivity). This situation is illustrated in the graph in Box 11. If aggregate supply were fixed, the increase in aggregate demand that occurred during the year would increase the price level from 120 to 126 and equilibrium real GDP would increase from $5,000 billion to $5,200 billion. However, because aggregate supply also shifts outward, the price level ends up increasing to only 124 during the year and real GDP increases to $5,300 billion. As you can see, outward shifts in aggregate supply resulting from normal economic growth have favorable effects on macroeconomic equilibrium.

1. Supply-side shifts from economic growth moderate inflationary pressures as outward shifts in aggregate supply offset the upward pressure on the price level resulting from outward shifts in aggregate demand.

2. Supply-side shifts from economic growth increase real GDP beyond the equilibrium level that results from normal increases in aggregate demand.

Of course, in a given year what actually happens to aggregate demand depends on the spending plans of households, businesses, and governments. In some years aggregate demand shifts outward more quickly than does aggregate supply. When that is the case, the inflationary pressures from increased aggregate demand are strong. In years when there is little economic growth, increases in aggregate demand can result in substantial inflationary pressure that can overheat the economy. Given the rate of growth in aggregate supply, the more rapid the outward shift of the

Box 11   Shifts in Aggregate Demand and Aggregate Supply in a Growing Economy

In a growing economy both aggregate demand and aggregate supply increase yearly. Despite cyclical decreases in aggregate demand, on average, aggregate demand increases. Economic growth in productivity means that outward shifts in aggregate supply help dampen inflationary pressures caused by increasing aggregate demand and also result in higher equilibrium real GDP than would otherwise be possible.

aggregate demand curve for the economy, the greater is the rate of inflation and the more likely it is that the economy will overheat.

Increases in productivity and the labor force also tend to increase potential real GDP. When increases in productivity and other positive supply-side influences are shifting the aggregate supply curve outward, it's less likely that an increase in aggregate demand will overheat the economy.

Noninflationary Growth

The situation depicted in Box 11 is a good representation of economic growth in the U.S. economy since the end of World War II. Real GDP has increased at a rate of about 3 percent per year on average, but growth in real GDP has also been accompanied by inflation of the price level. Real GDP increased by 71 percent from 1970 to 1989, while over the same period the price level increased by over 200 percent.

It is, however, possible to have noninflationary growth. Box 12 shows the case of an economy enjoying noninflationary growth. In this economy the growth that results from supply-side influences is strong enough to counter the inflationary effects of increases in aggregate demand that occur over time. As a result, this economy achieves equilibrium year after year at the price level of 120. At the same time, real GDP increases. For the economy illustrated in Box 12, equilibrium occurs at potential real GDP.

Noninflationary growth is possible when economic policies restrain aggregate demand and keep it from becoming excessive. For example, controlling the growth rate of money and credit to keep it in line with the growth rate of potential real GDP is one way of achieving noninflationary growth. This policy was quite effective in West Germany from 1983 to 1989, when that nation enjoyed annual real GDP growth rates of nearly 3 percent, while inflation rates were less than 1.5 percent.

In the United States, a slowdown in the rate of growth of the labor force and in productivity leads many economists to predict that the U.S. economy's rate of growth of potential real GDP could be as low as 2 percent pear year throughout the 1990s. If this is the case, the growth in aggregate demand will have to be restrained at 2 percent per year as well to avoid inflation.

principles in practice

U.S. Macroeconomic Equilibrium, 1970–1991

Let's look at the actual equilibrium points for the U.S. economy from 1970 to 1991. Each point in the graph is assumed to correspond to the intersection of the aggregate demand curve and the aggregate supply curve for the given year. (We have drawn in the curves corresponding to 1970 and 1991 for reference.) The points shown give the level of real GDP and the value of the GDP deflator for the year (assuming the economy is in equilibrium). As you can see, there have been increases in both aggregate demand and aggregate supply since 1970, but the race has clearly been won by aggregate demand, indicated by the more rapid rise in price level than in real GDP. Based on data up to 1991, real GDP has increased by 68 percent, while the GDP deflator has increased by 237 percent!

Follow the dots in the graph, and you will take a ride on the economy! Each dot represents a snapshot of the economy for the given year. Notice how the economy expanded steadily with only moderate inflation from 1970 to 1973. Then, in 1973, it was hit by a massive decrease in aggregate supply caused by sharply increased oil prices. The oil price increases decreased aggregate supply and resulted in sharp increases in the price level in 1974 and 1975. In 1975 inflation hit double-digit levels mainly as a result of the decrease in aggregate supply, which also caused a recession in 1974. This

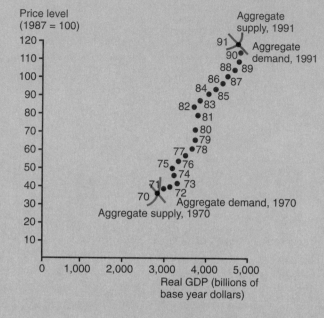

was a supply-side-induced recession. The decrease in aggregate supply outpaced the normal increase in aggregate demand in 1974, and real GDP fell sharply.

From 1975 to 1982, real GDP grew only moderately

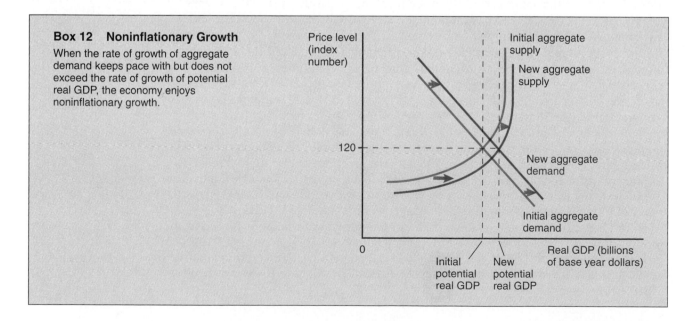

Box 12   Noninflationary Growth

When the rate of growth of aggregate demand keeps pace with but does not exceed the rate of growth of potential real GDP, the economy enjoys noninflationary growth.

because productivity did not increase greatly. Over the same period there was strong inflation. That inflation was the result of both decreases in aggregate supply and increases in aggregate demand. The increases in oil prices over the period 1974–79 contributed to shifts in the aggregate supply curve that put upward pressure on the price level. The Federal Reserve System, the nation's central bank in charge of controlling the supply of money and credit, allowed the quantity of money in circulation to increase over the same period. This provided the public with the credit to buy higher-priced goods and services resulting from the higher oil prices. The increased supply of money and credit contributed to increased aggregate demand that allowed the economy to expand moderately (to avoid a recession) but also contributed to a high rate of inflation.

In 1979 the nation's central banking authorities decided to apply the brakes. From 1980 to 1981, the growth rate of aggregate demand slowed, but the price of oil and other raw materials continued to increase. The consequent continual decreases in aggregate supply resulted in strong inflation, while slow productivity growth prevented strong outward movement in aggregate supply. The slow growth rate of potential real GDP coupled with slower growth in aggregate demand meant that the growth rate of equilibrium real GDP slackened quite a bit between 1979 and 1981. However, inflation remained strong during these years because of the decreases in aggregate supply.

In 1982 the growth rate of aggregate demand was sharply curtailed by a slowdown in the growth rate of money and credit. This situation was engineered by Paul Volcker, Chairman of the Board of Governors of the Federal Reserve System. Because aggregate supply was still decreasing that year due to increases in oil prices, inflation continued at a strong pace, and the economy was plunged into another supply-side recession. *Stagflation*, the unfortunate pairing of high inflation with high unemployment, was the outcome.

The recession of 1981–82, the most severe economic downturn the U.S. economy had experienced since the Great Depression of the 1930s, was bitter medicine for the U.S. economy. However, the recession managed to reduce the growth rate of aggregate demand enough to keep inflation under control. Since 1983 oil prices have increased more slowly. In fact, during the 1980s they often declined! With increases in aggregate supply occurring more often than decreases, the economy prospered and inflation moderated. From 1983 to 1990, the economy enjoyed an uninterrupted period of economic expansion, with moderate growth in real GDP and moderate, but steady, inflation (in the range of 4–5 percent per year). From 1983 to 1990, steady increases in aggregate supply coupled with steady but moderate increases in aggregate demand contributed to expansion of real GDP and moderate inflation. In 1991 a decrease in aggregate demand reduced real GDP. Since 1990 inflation has been at moderate levels.

- Explain how a change in the international value of the dollar, other things being equal, can shift both the aggregate supply curve and aggregate demand curve.

- Will a decrease in the international value of the dollar always increase real GDP?

- Explain how increases in aggregate supply that result when resources and their productivity grow from year to year can moderate inflationary pressures caused by increases in aggregate demand.

SUMMARY

1. The classical model of macroeconomic equilibrium is based on an assumption of flexible nominal wages and prices. The classical model suggests that a self-correcting mechanism guarantees the return of the economy to full employment when equilibrium GDP moves temporarily above or below potential real GDP.

2. Downwardly rigid wages can prevent the economy's self-correcting mechanism from working when aggregate demand decreases and equilibrium real GDP falls below potential real GDP.

3. The Keynesian model of macroeconomic equilibrium explains how real GDP and aggregate real income are determined in an economy in which there is downward rigidity in nominal wages.

4. The long-run aggregate supply curve shows the relationship between the price level and real GDP that prevails if wages and prices adjust in order to eliminate any recessionary or inflationary GDP gaps. The long-run aggregate supply curve is a vertical line that intersects the horizontal axis or potential real GDP.

5. When the economy produces beyond its potential, an inflationary GDP gap prevails. When the economy overheats in this way and workers are in short supply, wage levels are likely to be renegotiated. As wage levels and other input prices increase, the aggregate supply curve prevailing for the year shifts inward. Continual inward shifts of the aggregate supply curve cause a process of cost-push inflation. A wage-price spiral exists when higher prices result in higher wage levels, which then shift the aggregate supply curve inward and result in still higher prices.

6. A supply-side shock is a sudden and unexpected shift of the prevailing aggregate supply curve. A decrease in aggregate supply caused by an increase in the price or a decrease in the availability of a key input can throw the economy into a recession.

7. Changes in the international value of the dollar can cause both the aggregate demand curve and the aggregate supply curve to shift. When the price of the dollar falls, the demand for exports increases and the demand for imports decreases, causing an outward shift of the aggregate demand curve. A fall in the price of the dollar causes aggregate supply to decrease because it increases the price of imported inputs. The overall effect is an increase in the price level, but equilibrium real GDP can either increase or decrease.

8. In a growing economy annual increases in aggregate supply help moderate inflationary pressures by counteracting the effect of increases in demand on the price level.

KEY TERMS

classical model of macroeconomic equilibrium *226*

long-run aggregate supply curve (LRAS) *229*

Keynesian model of macroeconomic equilibrium *231*

wage-price spiral *236*

stagflation *237*

supply-side shock *237*

CONCEPT REVIEW

1 Briefly summarize the implications of the classical model of macroeconomic equilibrium.

2 Briefly summarize the implications of the Keynesian model of macroeconomic equilibrium.

3 Why is the rate of inflation in an overheated economy likely to accelerate while real GDP declines?

4 Give an example of a supply-side shock, and trace out its effects on the economy.

5 Forecast what is likely to happen to the equilibrium price level and real GDP if the foreign exchange rate of the dollar falls against all other currencies.

6 How does economic growth affect aggregate supply and macroeconomic equilibrium?

PROBLEMS AND APPLICATIONS

1. What is the underlying logic of the classical model of macroeconomic equilibrium? Explain why this model does not fit the facts for the U.S. economy very well when aggregate demand decreases. **1** , **2**

2. Assume an economy in which all input and output prices instantaneously adjust whenever there are shortages or surpluses in markets. Draw the aggregate supply curve for such an economy. **1**

3. Real GDP is currently $4,500 billion, and potential GDP is $4,600 billion. At the beginning of the year, new labor contracts are negotiated that increase the general level of wages in the economy by 10 percent. Other things being equal, show the impact of the new labor contracts on the aggregate supply curve. What effect will the shift in the aggregate supply curve have on macroeconomic equilibrium? **1**

4. An improvement in technology increases labor productivity in the economy. Show the impact of the improvement on the economy's long-run aggregate supply curve. Why is the economy less likely to overheat in response to an increase in aggregate demand after the improvement in technology is adopted? **3** , **6**

5. In the next 10 years the average age of the labor force will increase. Workers are expected to be more experienced and better educated. What effects are the improvements in the quality of the labor force likely to have on aggregate supply and macroeconomic equilibrium? **6**

6. The economy is currently operating with a recessionary GDP gap of about $500 billion. Under what circumstances can economic policies designed to eliminate the recessionary gap cause a wage-price spiral? **3**

7. Potential real GDP is $5,000 billion per year. A surge in aggregate demand causes the equilibrium level of

real GDP to equal $5,500 billion for the year. Show how the resulting inflationary gap is eliminated over time by a shift of the aggregate supply curve. **1**, **3**

8. Suppose an international disturbance disrupts the shipment of petroleum products into the United States. As a consequence, the prices of energy resources increase sharply. Forecast the impact of the increase in energy prices on aggregate supply and macroeconomic equilibrium. Show how, if the price increases are severe enough, they can cause a recession coupled with very high inflation. Why does a nation like Japan have to be very concerned about supply-side shocks resulting from increases in the price of petroleum? **4**

9. Suppose the price of the dollar soars next year. Trace out the possible effects of the higher dollar on the equilibrium level of real GDP and the rate of inflation for the year. **5**

10. Explain why both aggregate demand and aggregate supply tend to increase yearly. Use aggregate demand and supply analysis to show how an increase in the rate of outward shift of the economy's aggregate supply curve prevailing each year helps keep inflation down while putting upward pressure on equilibrium real GDP and potential real GDP. **6**

inside information

The State of the "Stats": How Accurate Are Government Economic Statistics?

Because so many economic decisions, including those relating to the federal budget, credit availability, and international trade, are based on federal statistics, their accuracy is a prerequisite to informed decision making. Yet there are some disturbing indications that both the quality and the accuracy of government economic statistics have fallen in recent years. For example, between the preliminary and revised reports on quarterly real GDP for the second quarter of 1989, the Commerce Department changed its estimate for that period's growth rate from 1.7 to 2.7 percent. A 1.7 percent growth rate showed a slowing economy. However, a 2.7 percent growth rate showed an economy that was still steaming ahead, perhaps overheating, thereby causing inflation to accelerate. Two very different pictures! Concern about the quality of economic statistics led President Bush to establish a working group in 1989, headed by the chairman of the President's Council of Economic Advisers, to improve the data collection and data processing procedures.

Here are a number of reasons why data on GDP are less reliable today than they were 30 years ago:

1. *A larger share of the nation's output is accounted for by services (instead of manufactured goods), where output is difficult to measure and output growth is easier to underestimate.* It's fairly easy to add up the number of cars or tons of aluminum or bushels of wheat to get an output measure, but how do we measure the output of banking, insurance firms, or the software industry?

For some service industries the U.S. Department of Commerce measures output by labor input because it can't get a reliable unit of service. Where output per unit of labor goes up, the increase in output is not reflected in the NIPA accounts. In addition, because service industries are dominated by small firms, it is more difficult to collect data on sales. In 1987, by surveying only three U.S. automakers, the U.S. Department of Commerce was able to obtain data on $150 billion in sales. The Department of Commerce would have had to survey 189,000 firms in the eating and drinking industry to obtain the same data on $150 billion in sales—a much more difficult task.

2. *Rapid technological change in some industries results in quality improvements that are not easily measured in the NIPA accounts.* Increases in prices often reflect quality improvements rather than inflation. For example, the 1994 American auto has better brakes, better safety features, and less emissions than its 1970 counterpart. However, much of that quality increase is measured as an increase in price that affects only nominal GDP and does not translate into an increase in real GDP. When the U.S. Department of Commerce recently changed the way it adjusted for quality changes in estimating price changes for computers, that change resulted in an increase in the level of real GDP in 1988 of $70 billion (measured in 1982 dollars).

3. *Deregulation of the economy and cost-cutting programs by many businesses have made it more difficult to get business firms to voluntarily report data to the federal government.* In the past the Commerce Department could get data on telephones produced in the United States by simply calling AT&T, which had a monopoly on the sale of telephones. Now, due to deregulation, so many firms in the United States produce telephones that it is much more difficult to collect such data.

11 chapter

Keynesian Analysis of Aggregate Purchases

The truth is that most Americans are big spenders and their purchases keep the wheels of commerce grinding away. Decisions made by people like you, as well as by investors, governments, and those who buy U.S. exports, influence the demand for the products of U.S. business.

Analysis of aggregate purchases is a major contribution of John Maynard Keynes to macroeconomics. You have already been introduced to some of Keynes's ideas in our discussion of the controversy between the Keynesian and classical models of macroeconomic equilibrium. In his macroeconomic analysis Keynes concentrated on the relationship between *income* and the willingness and ability of households and businesses to purchase goods and services. He then showed how the relationship between income and aggregate purchases changes in response to other changes in the economy.

In this chapter we further examine influences on decisions to consume and show how purchases of investment goods, government purchases, exports, and imports influence macroeconomic equilibrium. Keynesian analysis shows how fluctuations in spending affect the performance of the economy.

□ **CONCEPT PREVIEW**

After reading this chapter, you should be able to:

1. Discuss the Keynesian consumption function and the distinction between induced consumption and autonomous consumption.

2. Know how to measure the marginal propensity to consume and the marginal propensity to save.

3. Explain why investment purchases are extremely unstable from year to year.

4. Understand why government purchases in a given year are independent of disposable income, discuss how imports are likely to vary with disposable income, and draw a nation's net export function graph.

5. Draw an aggregate purchases line and explain how purchases of final products will vary with disposable income in a given year.

THE CONSUMPTION FUNCTION

In many ways the consumer is king in the modern economy because the bulk of production is to satisfy consumer desire. Consumer purchases account for about two thirds of real GDP in the United States. These purchases are largely influenced by the income households have available to spend during the year.

John Maynard Keynes, a 20th-century English economist, recognized the importance of the consumer in influencing macroeconomic equilibrium. Aggregate spending, in Keynes's view, is the most important influence on the performance of the economy. In his macroeconomic analysis Keynes gave special attention to the way consumption is influenced by changes in income. He developed the idea of the **consumption function,** which is the relationship between aggregate consumer purchases and disposable income for the year, given all other influences on consumption. We now begin a more in-depth analysis of aggregate purchases by first examining how disposable income influences consumer spending.

consumption function the relationship between aggregate consumer purchases and disposable income for the year, given all other influences on consumption.

Income and Consumption

Just as your income largely determines how much you can buy during the year, so too does aggregate income largely determine aggregate consumer purchases in the economy each year. As income available for spending has increased over time in the United States, so has personal consumption.

Disposable income is the best National Income and Product Accounts measure of the income available for spending by households. Recall that disposable income is income available for spending by households after payment of personal taxes. There is a clear historical relationship between real disposable income and real consumption in the United States. The graph in Box 1 shows how real disposable income and real consumption (both measured in 1987 dollars) have moved together. Over the period from 1960 to 1991, Americans, on average, have used slightly over 90 percent of their real disposable income annually for consumer purchases. As disposable income increases, so do consumption expenditures.

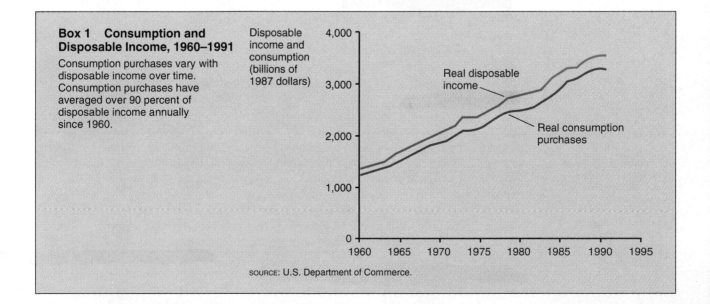

Box 1   Consumption and Disposable Income, 1960–1991

Consumption purchases vary with disposable income over time. Consumption purchases have averaged over 90 percent of disposable income annually since 1960.

Disposable income and consumption (billions of 1987 dollars)

Real disposable income

Real consumption purchases

SOURCE: U.S. Department of Commerce.

Other Determinants of Consumption

Income is not the only determinant of consumer purchases in a given year. You can readily understand this if you examine your own behavior. If you have a savings account at a bank, you can use your accumulated savings from past years to finance the purchase of a car or a stereo system this year. If you have accumulated a "fat" savings account from past earnings, you can actually spend more than your current income on consumer purchases during a year by drawing on your savings. Perhaps your parents financed your college education by drawing down savings accumulated in past years for that purpose.

A person's wealth is the sum of the current values of all assets owned. Examples of such assets are bank deposits, corporate stock, bonds, and real estate. Do not confuse wealth with income. Wealth is a *stock* of accumulated purchasing power stored up from past income. It's possible to have a great deal of wealth but very little income. For example, many elderly people have very low incomes and draw on accumulated savings to make consumer purchases.

aggregate household wealth the purchasing power of all assets owned by households.

Aggregate household wealth is the purchasing power of all assets owned by households. Aggregate wealth is a very important determinant of consumption in the economy. Just as you're more likely to spend more of your current income when you have a sizable bank account and a large portfolio of valuable stocks, so is aggregate consumption likely to be greater, at any given annual income, as aggregate household wealth increases. For example, when the stock market goes up, the value of stocks owned by households increases. The resulting increase in wealth is likely to increase annual consumption. A general decrease in stock prices decreases the wealth of households and is likely to cause them to decrease annual consumption, given their current annual income.

The sharp rise in stock prices in the United States in the 1980s helped fuel consumer purchases. Similarly, increases in home prices in the late 1970s increased the wealth of many households and made them more willing to spend their current income on consumer purchases. The serious stock market crash of 1929 forced many people to sharply reduce their spending. Declines in stock prices and real estate values in 1990 reduced consumer spending and helped bring on a recession.

Changes in the price level affect household wealth and thereby indirectly affect annual consumption. An increase in the price level erodes the purchasing power of accumulated savings that are fixed in dollar value. Each dollar of savings held in certificates of deposit has its purchasing power reduced when the price level goes up. A reduction in the purchasing power of aggregate household wealth caused by an increase in the price level can adversely affect consumer purchases in a given year.

Debt accumulated by households can also influence consumption. The more debt, the more current income must be allocated to repaying debt. For example, if your monthly income after taxes is $1,000, you'll have less to spend when you have to make a car payment of $200 each month than you'd have if you had no debt. **Aggregate household debt** is the purchasing power of the money households have borrowed and are currently obligated to repay. Given the aggregate wealth and disposable income in the economy, an increase in debt can reduce the willingness and ability of households to make consumer purchases out of current income. Increased household debt in the late 1980s gave rise to fears that consumer spending would fall, thereby putting downward pressure on aggregate demand.

aggregate household debt the purchasing power of the sums of money outstanding that households have borrowed and are currently obligated to repay.

Consumer purchases in a given year also depend on household *expectations* about the future course of their income and wealth. The reason for this is very simple: If you think bad times are ahead, you're likely to want to save more of your current income to help you get by in the future. If many workers feel the same way, saving will increase, which means less consumer purchases out of current disposable income. On the other hand, if you think your income will rise in the future and that the value of your assets will also rise, you may save very little and indulge in greater purchases of goods and services. The greater the expectations of future increases in income and wealth, the greater are consumer purchases in the current year.

Graphing the Consumption Function

We can draw a graph to show how consumption in the economy is related to disposable income, given all other influences on income. The first step in drawing such a graph is to estimate autonomous consumption, the portion of annual consumer purchases that is independent of, and not affected by, current disposable income. Your consumption would not fall to zero even if you had zero income during the year, because you could draw on savings or find other means to continue buying the necessities of life even though you had no income. You could rely on your savings to support yourself. For example, retired people draw on accumulated savings to finance some or all of their purchases. Similarly, in a given year, a number of families dip into their savings to finance college tuition costs or purchase a new car. Because these purchases are made with dollars saved from earnings in previous years, they are not affected by changes in current disposable income.

autonomous consumption the portion of annual consumer purchases that is independent of, and not affected by, current disposable income.

Induced consumption is the portion of annual consumer purchases in a given year that responds to changes in current disposable income. For example, suppose you do well during the first year on a new job and as a reward receive a whopping $3,000 raise from your employer. You use part of the raise to buy a new surround-sound unit for your home audio-video system. Your purchase of the new sound unit is *induced* consumption because it is a direct result of increased disposable income. Similarly, for the economy as a whole, as annual disposable income increases, the added income *induces* people to make more purchases.

induced consumption the portion of annual consumer purchases in a given year that responds to changes in current disposable income.

The data in Box 2's table show the relationship between possible levels of annual disposable income and aggregate consumer purchases for a hypothetical economy. The first column shows possible levels of disposable income (*DI*) for a certain year. The second column shows the consumer purchases (*C*) associated with each of these income levels. It's assumed that $400 billion of consumption expenditure is independent of income and occurs during the year even if disposable income is zero. The $400 billion is the amount of annual autonomous consumption that depends on wealth (or other factors) rather than income. The rest of the column 2 data are obtained by assuming that each $1,000 billion increase in income available for households to spend will increase annual consumer purchases by $800 billion.

The table in Box 2 also shows how saving varies with possible levels of disposable income over a given year. Saving is simply the difference between disposable income and consumption expenditures associated with each level of income. Whatever is saved is not spent by consumers on current production. Other things being equal, therefore, an increase in saving decreases aggregate demand.

Saving and consumption are mutually exclusive uses of disposable income. Whatever portion of disposable income is not used for consumption purposes is saved. Note that saving can be negative when households draw more from previously accumulated savings than they save in the current year. Saving is negative whenever consumer purchases exceed disposable income.

Showing the Relationship between Income and Saving

The consumption function based on the data in Box 2 is plotted in the upper graph. Notice how consumer purchases increase in a given year when the actual level of

Box 2 The Relationship between Disposable Income, Consumption, and Saving for a Given Year (Hypothetical Data)

The higher disposable income is for a year, the higher consumption and saving will be for that year. However, saving will be negative at low levels of income. Points *A* and *A'* show that at a level of disposable income of $2,000 billion for the year, saving would be zero. As disposable income increases above this level, households save some of their income.

Disposable income ($ billions) (*DI*)	Consumption ($ billions) (*C*)	Saving ($ billions) (*S*)
0	400	−400
1,000	1,200	−200
2,000	2,000	0
3,000	2,800	200
4,000	3,600	400
5,000	4,400	600
6,000	5,200	800
7,000	6,000	1,000
8,000	6,800	1,200

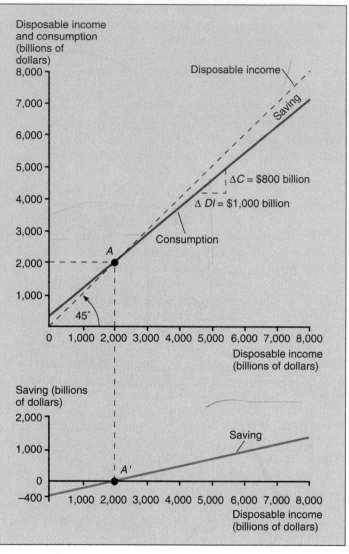

disposable income increases in that year. The unbroken line drawn in the upper graph shows the relationship between possible levels of income and the consumption associated with each of them for *a given year*. At the end of the year, disposable income will be at a certain level. The consumption observed will be the amount associated with that level of disposable income.

The lower graph plots the relationship between saving and disposable income. If disposable income is very low in a given year, households reduce their savings and sell some of their assets to maintain their consumption over that year. The table and graphs show that saving in the economy is negative if disposable income is less than $2,000 billion for the year. As observed earlier, negative saving means people consume more than their current income by converting some of their saving from past years into cash and using it to make purchases. In this example, saving is zero if disposable income is $2,000 billion for the year. For each $1,000 billion increase in disposable income, saving increases by $200 billion. Remember that disposable income already has taxes deducted from it. The sum of saving and consumption must therefore equal disposable income at each possible level of disposable income.

Using a 45-Degree Guideline to Measure Savings

A 45-degree dashed line from the origin has been drawn in the upper graph in Box 2 to help you see the relationship between the consumption and saving graphs. Disposable income (*DI*) minus consumption (*C*) always equals saving (*S*):

$$DI = C + S$$

Therefore,

$$S = DI - C$$

Take any point on the 45-degree line and draw a straight line from that point to each of the axes. The result will be a square whose sides are the two lines you drew and a portion of each of the axes. Because all sides of a square are equal in length, it follows that the length on the horizontal axis corresponding to disposable income equals the distance from the origin to the point at which your horizontal line cuts the vertical axis. The 45-degree line therefore enables you to compare disposable income with consumption. The vertical distance between the consumption line and the 45-degree line represents saving for any given level of disposable income on the horizontal axis. For example, at point *A* the consumption line intersects the 45-degree line. At that point annual consumption of $2,000 billion equals annual disposable income of $2,000 billion. (If the actual level of disposable income were $2,000 billion, there would be no saving in the given year.) When disposable income exceeds $2,000 billion per year, annual consumption is less than annual disposable income. This conclusion is reflected in the fact that points on the 45-degree line correspond to greater dollar amounts on the vertical axis than points on the consumption line when disposable income exceeds $2,000 billion per year. The vertical difference between the 45-degree line and the consumption line therefore measures annual saving at each possible level of disposable income. You can verify this by looking at the lower graph, in which saving is positive whenever national income exceeds $2,000 billion but is negative when national income is less than $2,000 billion.

Just as consumption increases with income, so too does saving. If annual disposable income is $2,000 billion, the percentage of income saved is zero. If disposable income is $4,000 billion, the fraction of income saved is $400 billion/$4,000 billion, which is 0.1, or 10 percent of disposable income. However, if disposable income is $8,000 billion, the fraction saved is $1,200 billion/$8,000 billion, or 15 percent. The greater the disposable income for a year, the greater the ability of consumers to save and the higher the percentage of their disposable income they are likely to save.

The Marginal Propensities to Consume and to Save

The **marginal propensity to consume** is the fraction of each additional dollar of annual disposable income that is allocated to consumer purchases. The marginal propensity to consume can be calculated from the following formula:

$$MPC = \frac{\text{Change in consumption}}{\text{Change in disposable income}} = \frac{\Delta C}{\Delta DI}$$

where the symbol Δ signifies "change in" the variable it precedes. In Box 2 every $1,000 billion of additional income earned each year results in $800 billion of additional consumption that year. In this case $MPC = $800 billion/$1,000 billion$ $= 0.8$.

2

marginal propensity to consume the fraction of each additional dollar of annual disposable income that is allocated to consumer purchases.

The **marginal propensity to save** is the fraction of each additional dollar of annual disposable income that is saved. The formula for calculating the marginal propensity to save is

$$MPS = \frac{\text{Change in saving}}{\text{Change in disposable income}} = \frac{\Delta S}{\Delta DI}$$

In Box 2 each $1,000 billion of additional disposable income earned in a year results in $200 billion in additional saving. In this case MPS = $200 billion/$1,000 billion = 0.2. If only 80 cents of each extra dollar is used for consumer purchases, it follows that 20 cents is saved.

Because additional disposable income available during the year is either consumed or saved, the sum of the marginal propensity to consume and to save is always 1:

$$MPC + MPS = 1$$

Note that the marginal propensity to consume is the *slope* of the consumption line drawn in the upper graph. Each additional dollar of disposable income, ΔDI, will increase consumption by ΔC along the consumption line. The slope of the line is therefore

$$\text{Slope} = \frac{\Delta C}{\Delta DI} = \frac{\text{Change in consumption}}{\text{Change in disposable income}} = MPC$$

The consumption line has a constant slope because the marginal propensity to consume is assumed to be constant at 0.8. Similarly, the marginal propensity to save is the slope of the savings line. The slope of this line is 0.2, because 20 cents of each additional dollar of disposable income is assumed to be saved.

How Changes in Wealth Can Shift the Consumption Line

A consumption function describes the relationship between possible levels of disposable income and consumption for a certain year, given *all other influences on consumption*. What happens if, over time, property values in a nation soar or stock prices rise, thus increasing household wealth from one year to the next? If wealth increases, autonomous consumption at each possible level of disposable income will also increase. An increase in aggregate household wealth therefore shifts the consumption line in Box 3 upward. Increases in wealth, other things being equal, increase aggregate demand by increasing consumer purchases.

If the consumption line shifts upward, it follows that the savings line, also shown in Box 3, must shift downward, because when more disposable income is used for consumer purchases, less is allocated to saving. *An increase in aggregate household wealth therefore tends to increase the consumption but decrease the saving associated with each possible level of annual disposable income.*

A decrease in wealth has opposite effects. Declines in real estate values and stock prices in 1990 had an adverse affect on consumption in that year.

How a Change in Household Debt Outstanding Can Affect Current Consumption

Given the value of assets owned by households, an increase in aggregate household debt can reduce the willingness and ability of households to consume out of current income. The greater the debt of households, the greater the proportion of current

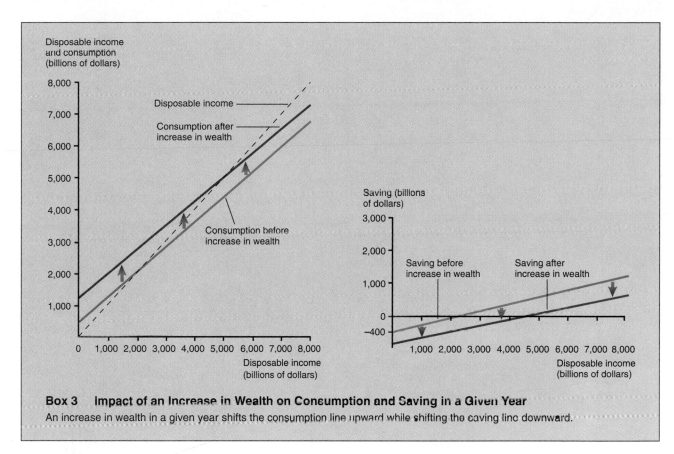

Box 3   Impact of an Increase in Wealth on Consumption and Saving in a Given Year
An increase in wealth in a given year shifts the consumption line upward while shifting the saving line downward.

income that households must allocate to make payments to creditors. An increase in aggregate household debt is therefore likely to shift the consumption line downward and the savings line upward. This result is illustrated in Box 4. When consumers devote higher proportions of their current income to paying off previous debts, they are, in effect, increasing current saving at each level of disposable income, because repayment of debt represents a use of disposable income for a purpose other than consumption. Consumers have to decrease current consumption to pay off the borrowing that helped them increase consumption in previous years. Increased consumer indebtedness in the late 1980s shifted the economy's consumption line downward in 1990, thereby putting downward pressure on aggregate demand and contributing to a recession in that year.

The Influence of Expectations on Current Consumption
Consumers consume more in a year if they think the purchasing power of their future income will increase. They're less likely to spend current income if they think bad times are ahead. Anticipation of bad times is likely to shift the consumption line downward as consumers try to save more of any given current level of disposable income to supplement future income. Decreased consumer confidence will therefore result in the shifts of the savings and consumption lines illustrated in Box 4. On the other hand, increased consumer confidence about future well-being will result in the shifts illustrated in Box 3.

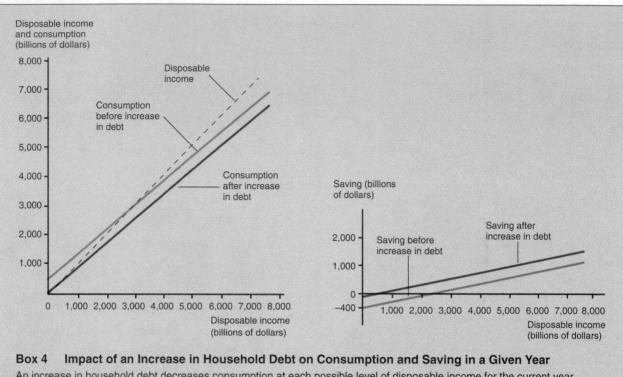

Box 4   Impact of an Increase in Household Debt on Consumption and Saving in a Given Year

An increase in household debt decreases consumption at each possible level of disposable income for the current year while having the opposite effect on saving as consumers must devote higher proportions of current income to repaying debt instead of making purchases.

CONCEPT CHECK
☐

- What are the major influences on annual consumption expenditures in a nation?

- How are saving, consumption, and disposable income related in a given year? If the marginal propensity to consume is 0.9, how will a $1,000 billion increase in annual disposable income be used?

- List three possible causes of an upward shift in a nation's consumption line, and explain why the nation's savings line will shift downward when the consumption line shifts upward.

INVESTMENT PURCHASES

3 Investment purchases of final products by business firms are a very unstable component of aggregate demand compared to consumption. Investment purchases include expenditures for new machinery, equipment, structures, and inventories. Although consumer purchases are closely related to disposable income, investment purchases are not. The variability of real gross private domestic investment is obvious when it is expressed as a percentage of real GDP. For example, in 1933, when the economy was in the doldrums, real gross private domestic investment accounted for only 5 percent of real GDP. In the recession year of 1982, real gross private domestic investment accounted for 14 percent of real GDP. In a typical boom year, however, real gross private domestic investment approaches 20 percent of real GDP.

Movements in investment purchases are quite erratic and not easily predictable. In fact, investment is even more variable than is suggested by the data from the National Income and Product Accounts. The reason for this is that the official accounting system of the United States includes all net additions to or reductions in business inventories as part of gross private domestic investment. Additions to business inventories that result from the fact that firms sell *less* than they had anticipated during the year are included in the official statistics on investment. The official statistics view business firms as purchasing their own net additions to inventories at the end of the year. This is clearly misleading since some of the increments (or declines) in business inventories occur because businesses end up selling more or less of their stocks of final products than they intended to sell during the year.

Planned investment purchases are purchases of new or replacement residential and nonresidential structures, producer durable equipment, and additions to inventories that business firms intentionally make during the year. Gross private domestic investment differs from planned investment by the extent to which firms end up with unintended net changes in their business inventories. In discussing the determinants of investment, the relevant economic variable that must be explained is *planned* investment purchases. When planned investment deviates from actual investment, the economy is in a state of macroeconomic disequilibrium that results in pressure for change in real GDP and/or the price level (see the preceding and following chapters).

planned investment purchases purchases of new or replacement residential and nonresidential structures, producer durable equipment, and additions to inventories that business firms intentionally make during the year.

Investment Demand and the Real Interest Rate

When a firm makes an investment, it incurs expenditures for current purchases of investment goods that will be employed to provide future revenue. Business firms typically borrow funds to make investments and repay their borrowings out of future revenues. Even if they don't borrow, managers know that if they use current revenues to finance investment purchases, they forgo the opportunity to earn interest. The annual opportunity cost of using a dollar to make an investment can therefore be represented by the real interest rate. The real interest rate is the "price" of using a dollar to make an investment purchase.

The real marginal return to investment is an estimate of the percentage of each dollar invested that will be returned to a firm as additional revenue per year (adjusted for the effects of changes in the price level). Naturally, a firm that seeks to maximize profit compares the marginal return on each dollar invested, which is that dollar's percentage marginal return, with the opportunity cost of using another dollar for an investment purchase, which is the real rate of interest. As long as the real marginal return to an invested dollar (adjusted for inflation) is higher than the real rate of interest, businesses can add to their profits by increasing annual investment purchases. For example, if purchasing a new computer system would earn you revenue that returned the price of the system plus an additional 7 percent after adjustment for inflation over the three-year life of the system, then you would gain by borrowing to finance the system if the real rate of interest were only 4 percent.

real marginal return to investment an estimate of the percentage of each dollar invested that will be returned to a firm as additional revenue per year (adjusted for the effects of changes in the price level).

The graph in Box 5 shows the demand for investment goods in the economy as a function of the real interest rate. The lower the real interest rate, the lower the opportunity cost of making investment purchases and the greater the quantity of investment goods demanded. The demand curve for investment goods is therefore downward sloping. In Box 5 the real interest rate is currently 3 percent and the equilibrium level of annual investment purchases in the economy is $600 billion. If the real interest rate fell to 2 percent, investment purchases not profitable at the 3 percent rate would be undertaken during the year.

Now that you see how important the real interest rate is in determining investment purchases, you can also begin to understand one source of investment purchase

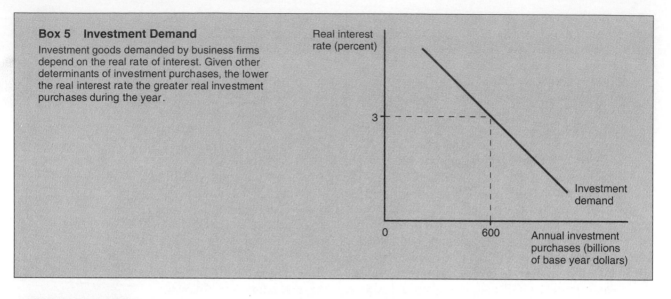

Box 5   Investment Demand

Investment goods demanded by business firms depend on the real rate of interest. Given other determinants of investment purchases, the lower the real interest rate the greater real investment purchases during the year.

instability by looking at the variability of real interest rates. The real interest rate that business firms anticipate paying over the life of an investment depends not only on the nominal interest rate but also on the fluctuation in the price level over the life of the investment. Real interest rates tend to fluctuate widely, often going from positive to negative values. This fluctuation contributes to instability in equilibrium investment purchases, which, in turn, contributes to instability in aggregate demand. Investment purchases are therefore unstable, in part, because real interest rates have been quite unstable over time.

Shifts in Investment Demand

Investment demand is notoriously unstable. The investment demand curve shifts inward and outward regularly in response to changes in business perceptions about the future profitability of expansion in productive capacity. When the investment demand curve shifts outward, businesses will invest more dollars each year at each possible real interest rate. At a 3 percent real interest rate, for example, annual investment rises from $600 billion to $700 billion per year in response to the outward shift in the investment demand curve shown in the graph in Box 6. It would also rise at any other possible interest rate. In view of the importance of investment demand, it's useful to outline influences on business confidence in the future that can contribute to steady outward shifts in the investment demand curve.

Among the important influences on investment demand, given the level of real interest rates in the economy, are:

1. Expectations about shifts in aggregate demand.
2. Expectations about input and product prices and other considerations affecting the profitability of adding to productive capacity and inventory.
3. Current capacity utilization.
4. Technological advance in the economy.
5. Tax treatment of investment purchases and income.

The future revenue from an investment purchase depends on the future prospects of sales. If firms expect future declines in aggregate demand, the revenues they anticipate from investment purchases will sag and the demand for investment goods

principles in practice

Personal Consumption and Saving in the United States

American Households Are Saving Less of Their Disposable Income For a variety of reasons, Americans are known around the world as big spenders—and our reputation, if not always flattering, is certainly well deserved. On average over the past 60 years, we Americans have spent approximately 90 percent of our disposable income each year on consumer purchases. In the last several years we've become even more self-indulgent.

American consumers piled up debt at record levels during the 1980s. Armed with credit cards and mortgage loans, they amassed household debt equal to 86 percent of disposable income in 1986, when they owed $2.2 trillion to creditors.

In 1975 personal saving in the United States was nearly 9 percent of disposable income. In the 1980s personal saving in the United States fell to less than 5 percent of disposable income, as shown in the accompanying graph. The U.S. personal saving rate is much lower than those of Western Europe and Japan. In Western Europe personal saving averages 7 percent to 10 percent of disposable income, while in Japan personal saving amounts to 15 percent of disposable income.

The saving habits of American households have important implications for the functioning of the economy. first of all, consumption constitutes the bulk of aggregate demand, amounting to over 65 percent of purchases of real GDP. High consumption rates therefore fuel expansion of the economy by bolstering aggregate demand. On the other hand, saving constitutes a source of loanable funds for investment purchases that stimulate growth in the economy's productive capacity. As personal saving declines, other things being equal, the supply of loanable funds for investment diminishes, thereby putting upward pressure on real interest rates. Higher real interest rates in turn tend to decrease investment purchases that fuel future economic growth.

In recent years the decline in personal saving has been offset by increased foreign saving in the United States, which results when there is a balance of trade deficit. If net exports in the United States eventually become positive, foreign saving will dry up and the low saving rate in the United States can then begin to have unfavorable effects on investment purchases.

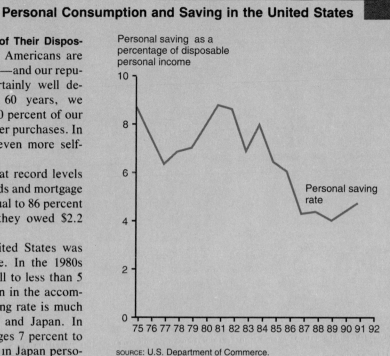

Personal saving as a percentage of disposable personal income

SOURCE: U.S. Department of Commerce.

The low saving rate in the United States can be explained in part by demographic trends. In the mid-1980s, 30 percent of the country's population was under age 35. People in this age group tend to be big spenders as they establish their households. Typically, the biggest savers are people between the ages of 35 and 65. People over 65 are dissavers who draw down savings accumulated in past years as they retire. It's likely that as the percentage of the population between the ages of 35 and 65 increases by the year 2000, the saving rate will increase. In the 21st century, however, the portion of the population accounted for by people over 65 is expected to double from the current level of about 12 percent to nearly 25 percent! As the elderly become a larger portion of the population, the saving rate could decline. In light of these realities, you might want to think about spending less and saving more!

Box 6   Shifts in Investment Demand

A shift in investment demand will change the amount of real investment purchases associated with any given real interest rate.

will decline. A decline in investment demand means an inward shift in the investment demand curve. When investment demand decreases in this way, the quantity of investment purchases at any given real interest rate will be less. Conversely, expectations of a future increase in aggregate demand shift the investment demand curve outward.

Business expectations about future prices also affect the demand for investment goods. If businesses believe that input prices will fall relative to output prices, the profitability of supplying output in the future will increase. As a result, they will seek to add to productive capacity when they anticipate declines in input prices that decrease marginal cost. Thus, decreases in input prices relative to product prices tend to increase investment demand, while increases in input prices relative to product prices tend to decrease investment demand.

Business investment demand is also likely to be related to current capacity utilization. When there's considerable slack in the economy and existing plant and equipment are not being used, firms are less likely to make new investment purchases. During the contraction in economic activity between 1979 and 1982, for example, investment purchases in the United States declined by nearly 20 percent. On the other hand, when the economy is in an expansion phase, firms will want to add to inventories and increase plant capacity, thus shifting the investment demand curve outward.

The rate of technological advance is also likely to affect investment demand, because as technology advances, so do opportunities for making profit from new investments. During periods of rapid advances in technology, firms are more likely to replace obsolete equipment and processes with newer ones that reduce unit and marginal costs of production. Rapid advances in technology therefore shift the demand curve for investment outward at a rapid rate.

Finally, tax treatment of investment purchases and income also affects investment demand. The tax law often subsidizes investment purchases through generous depreciation rules that allow firms to deduct large portions of their investment outlays from their taxable income. However, tax treatment of investment changes from time to time, and this results in changes in investment demand. For example, the Economic Recovery Tax Act of 1981 introduced very generous deprecation allowances

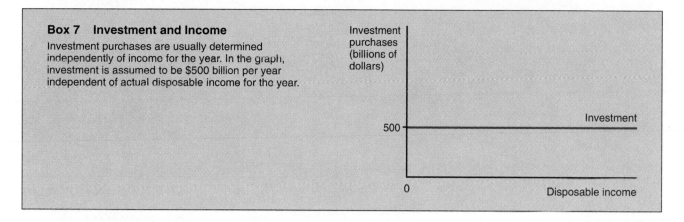

Box 7   Investment and Income

Investment purchases are usually determined independently of income for the year. In the graph, investment is assumed to be $500 billion per year independent of actual disposable income for the year.

and investment subsidies that encouraged investment at that time. However, the Tax Reform Act of 1986 substantially reduced depreciation allowances and investment subsidies.

You saw in the preceding section that investment purchases fluctuate first of all because real interest rates are highly variable, often shifting from positive to negative values. Now you see that investment purchases also fluctuate because the investment demand curve itself tends to shift inward and outward rather unpredictably in response to changes in business expectations about future revenues, costs, and changes in tax rules.

Planned investment purchases are usually formulated at the beginning of the year based on the current economic outlook for real interest rates and other conditions affecting business demand. In analyzing aggregate purchases, the level of planned investment purchases is assumed to be the same no matter what the actual level of disposable income for the year. This assumption is reflected in the graph in Box 7, which shows planned investment purchases as a fixed amount for the year independent of annual disposable income. Investment purchases are assumed to be $500 billion for the year no matter what the disposable income for the year.

- List the major influences on investment purchases.
- Why will an increase in real interest rates decrease investment purchases?

- Why are purchases of investment goods more volatile than purchases of consumer goods?

CONCEPT CHECK
☐

GOVERNMENT PURCHASES AND NET EXPORTS

Consumption and investment both fluctuate, but on average they account for about 80 percent of aggregate demand in a given year. The remaining 20 percent comes from government purchases and net exports. In recent years U.S. net exports have been negative, thereby putting downward pressure on aggregate demand. In this section we look at the influence of government and international trade on aggregate demand.

Government Purchases and the Influence of Taxes and Transfers on Spending

To provide national security, health, education, transportation, and other essential services, state and local governments and the federal government purchase aircraft,

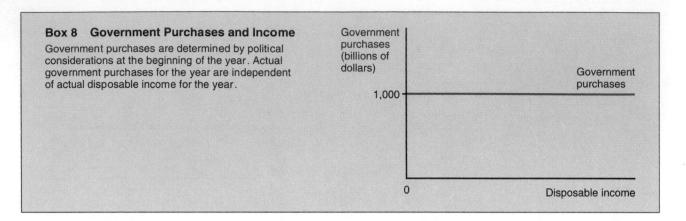

Box 8   Government Purchases and Income

Government purchases are determined by political considerations at the beginning of the year. Actual government purchases for the year are independent of actual disposable income for the year.

foods, clothing, medical supplies, and the services of workers and capital. Governments also purchase new structures and durable goods produced by business firms during the year. The government purchases component of aggregate demand accounted for about 20 percent of real GDP in 1990.

Government purchases for a given year are determined by political considerations. The actual amounts of purchases for a given year are usually set in budgets approved by the U.S. Congress and by various state legislatures and city or town councils. It's reasonable to assume that government purchases, like investment purchases, are not affected in any clear-cut way by changes in disposable income in a given year. The graph in Box 8 reflects this assumption and shows that actual government purchases in a given year are the same no matter what the actual level of disposable income in that year. In the graph it's assumed that annual government purchases are $1,000 billion no matter what disposable income is for the year.

You should note, however, that government also affects aggregate demand indirectly through the influence of its tax and transfer policies on disposable income. For example, given government purchases and transfers, an increase in taxes levied on households decreases the disposable income associated with any given level of real GDP and aggregate real income. Government can therefore affect consumption purchases by changing its tax policy to change the relationship between real GDP and disposable income. Similarly, if government increases transfer payments to households while not increasing taxes, it increases the disposable income associated with any level of real GDP and therefore influences consumption. As you saw in the analysis of investment purchases, taxes affecting business income can affect aggregate demand indirectly by changing investment demand. Both investment and consumer demand are therefore influenced by government policies relating to taxes and transfers.

The ability of government to affect aggregate purchases gives it the opportunity to stabilize aggregate demand. The use of government spending and taxing policy to affect aggregate purchases and equilibrium real GDP is called *fiscal policy* and will be examined in the part of this book entitled "Stabilizing the Economy."

Net Exports

If you've been following the newspapers and the evening news broadcasts, you probably know that in recent years the United States has been importing more goods than it has exported. But why all the concern about the fact that U.S. buyers spend more on Japanese VCRs, German automobiles, Polish ham, and other foreign goods

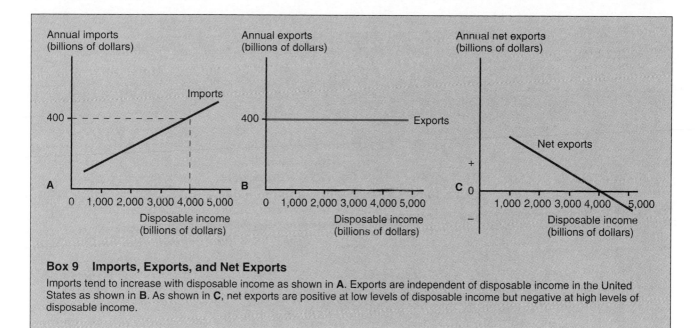

Box 9 Imports, Exports, and Net Exports

Imports tend to increase with disposable income as shown in **A**. Exports are independent of disposable income in the United States as shown in **B**. As shown in **C**, net exports are positive at low levels of disposable income but negative at high levels of disposable income.

than U.S. firms earn from selling their goods abroad? The answer is that negative net exports represent a subtraction from aggregate demand.

The graphs in Box 9 show how exports, imports, and the difference between the two are likely to vary with disposable income in a given year. Like consumer purchases, purchases of imported goods are greater when disposable income is high than when it is low. Graph **A** shows that imports increase with disposable income. Just as your spending on goods in general is likely to increase when you have a lot of income to spend, so too is aggregate spending on imports likely to increase as disposable income increases. In a boom year, other things being equal, BMW, Mercedes, Denon, and other foreign manufacturers are likely to enjoy good sales in the United States. On the other hand, in a recession year, when disposable income is low, consumers are likely to cut back on their purchases of imports as they do on most purchases.

Exports of U.S. goods, however, are unlikely to be related to disposable income in the United States. Instead, they are determined, in part, by disposable income in foreign nations. An increase in disposable income in the United States during the year does nothing to increase the ability of Mexicans and Italians to purchase IBM computers and Boeing 767s. Graph **B** shows that exports for a given year are constant no matter what U.S. disposable income is in that year.

In graph **C,** the imports associated with any given level of disposable income are *subtracted from exports to obtain a graph showing how net exports,* which are exports minus imports, vary with disposable income. Exports are assumed to be $400 billion no matter what disposable income is for the year. However, when disposable income is relatively low, imports will also be low and exports will exceed imports. As disposable income increases in the United States, U.S. imports grow. For example, if disposable income for the year turned out to be $4,000 billion, then imports would be $400 billion (see graph **A**). Graph **C** shows that at that level of imports net exports are zero because exports also equal $400 billion, as shown in graph **B**. When disposable income is less than $4,000 billion for the year, imports will be less than $400 billion. This means that exports exceed imports and net exports are positive. If disposable income is greater than $4,000 billion for the year, imports exceed exports and net exports are negative, as shown in graph **C.**

The level of disposable income is not the only determinant of net exports. The quantity of imported products that U.S. buyers will buy at any given level of disposable income also depends on the prices of imported goods relative to the prices of domestically produced substitutes. As you learned in Chapter 3, the prices of imported goods depend in part on the international value of the dollar. When the dollar increases in value relative to foreign currencies, the prices of our imports decrease, while the prices of our exports go up. This makes the price of Japanese-produced Toyotas fall relative to the price of U.S.-produced Fords. The net exports line, shown in Box 10, shifts downward because imports increase and exports decrease as a result of a rise in the price of the dollar. During the period 1980 to 1986, when the price of the dollar went up in most international markets, U.S. imports soared, while U.S. exports dipped. A similar shift could occur as a result of any other change that makes our imports cheaper and our exports more expensive. When the net exports line shifts downward, the level of disposable income associated with zero net exports declines to $3,000 billion. This means that if disposable income for the year were $4,000 billion, net exports would be negative.

Similarly, anything that makes our imports more expensive and our exports cheaper will shift the net exports line upward. By early 1988, for example, the decrease in the price of the dollar that occurred in 1987 was beginning to have an effect on net exports. In the first half of 1988, exports increased substantially and the net exports line shifted upward. Note in Box 10 that after the net exports line has shifted upward, net exports are positive if disposable income is $4,000 billion for the year.

Whether net exports are positive or negative in a given year doesn't depend only on disposable income in the United States. It also depends on disposable income in foreign nations and on factors that influence the prices of imports and exports.

Aggregate Purchases: $C + I_P + G + NE$

5 **Aggregate purchases** are the market value of final goods and services that will be purchased at any given level of income. Therefore,

aggregate purchases
the market value of final goods and services that will be purchased at any given level of income.

$$\text{Aggregate purchases} = C + I_P + G + NE$$

where I_P are investment purchases planned for the year. Both consumer purchases, C, and net exports, NE, will vary with income. Planned investment and government purchases, G, are assumed to be independent of income, as is likely.

The graph in Box 11 shows how aggregate purchases will vary with income. First, the levels of investment and government purchases for the year are added to consumption for each possible level of income. Net exports are then added to the line labeled $C + I_P + G$ for each possible level of income. The sum of $C + I_P + G$ is equal to aggregate income when net exports are zero, as is the case in Box 11 when income for the year is $5,000 billion. When income is less than $5,000 billion, net exports will be positive and aggregate purchases will exceed $C + I_P + G$. However, when income is greater than $5,000 billion, net exports will be negative and aggregate purchases will be less than the sum of $C + I_P + G$.

You can now see that the level of aggregate purchases in a given year in the economy depends on consumer, investment, government, export, and import purchases for the year. In addition, the actual amount of consumption and net exports for the year depends on the equilibrium level of disposable income.

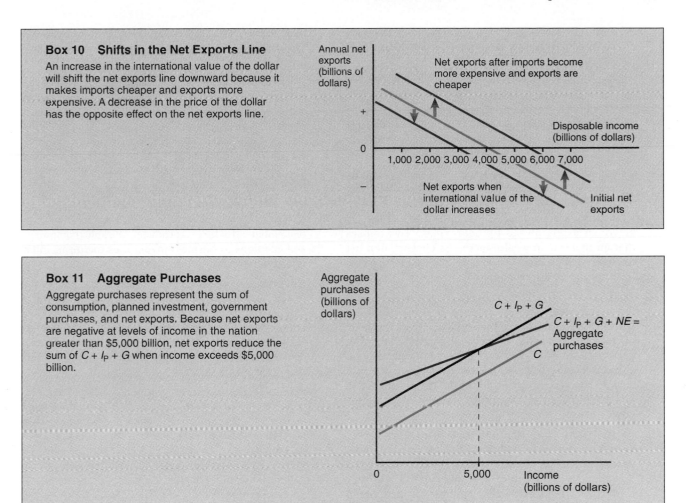

Box 10   Shifts in the Net Exports Line

An increase in the international value of the dollar will shift the net exports line downward because it makes imports cheaper and exports more expensive. A decrease in the price of the dollar has the opposite effect on the net exports line.

Annual net exports (billions of dollars)

Net exports after imports become more expensive and exports are cheaper

Disposable income (billions of dollars)

1,000 2,000 3,000 4,000 5,000 6,000 7,000

Net exports when international value of the dollar increases

Initial net exports

Box 11   Aggregate Purchases

Aggregate purchases represent the sum of consumption, planned investment, government purchases, and net exports. Because net exports are negative at levels of income in the nation greater than $5,000 billion, net exports reduce the sum of $C + I_p + G$ when income exceeds $5,000 billion.

Aggregate purchases (billions of dollars)

$C + I_p + G$

$C + I_p + G + NE =$ Aggregate purchases

C

0   5,000   Income (billions of dollars)

Now that you know the components of aggregate purchases and aggregate demand, the next step is to investigate the important role that aggregate purchases play in determining equilibrium real GDP and income. In the following chapter we examine the Keynesian model of macroeconomic equilibrium by focusing on the role of aggregate purchases in the economy.

- How does the government sector of the economy influence aggregate demand?

- Explain why net exports vary with disposable income.

- What are the components of aggregate purchases?

CONCEPT CHECK

☐

SUMMARY

1. Consumption is the most important component of GDP, typically accounting for two thirds of annual purchases. Annual disposable income is the major determinant of the annual quantity of goods and services that consumers are willing and able to purchase at the current price level.

2. Total annual consumption is the sum of the amount attributable to disposable income and the amount attributable to other influences during the year.

3. The consumption function describes the relationship between annual disposable income and consumption

expenditures for the economy in a given year. Annual consumption increases as annual disposable income increases.

4. The marginal propensity to consume is the fraction of each additional dollar of annual disposable income that is consumed. The marginal propensity to save is the fraction of each additional dollar of annual disposable income that is saved. The marginal propensity to consume is the slope of the consumption line.

5. The consumption line showing the relationship between annual consumption and annual disposable income shifts upward in response to an increase in annual household wealth, which is the purchasing power of assets owned by households. This implies that an increase in wealth increases consumption but decreases the saving associated with each possible level of annual disposable income.

6. Aggregate household debt is the purchasing power of the money that households have borrowed and are currently obligated to repay over time. Given the value of household wealth, an increase in household debt decreases the willingness and ability to consume out of current income because they must allocate more of current income to repayment of debt. An increase in household debt therefore shifts the consumption line downward.

7. Expectations about the future are likely to influence current annual consumption. Consumers are more willing and able to spend on goods and services when they believe their future real income will increase. Consumer confidence about increases in their future real income shifts the consumption line upward, while the line shifts downward if consumers think hard times are ahead.

8. Planned investment in a given year is a highly unstable component of real GDP. Fluctuations in real interest rates and investment demand explain fluctuations in planned investment purchases. Investment demand shifts in response to changes in expectations about aggregate demand and prices and to changes in capacity utilization, technology, and tax treatment of investment purchases and income.

9. Planned investment during a year represents purchases for new and replacement residential and nonresidential structures, producer durable equipment, and additions to business inventories that firms intentionally make during the year.

10. Government purchases for a given year are determined by political considerations and are likely to be independent of disposable income for the year. Governments also influence aggregate demand indirectly because their tax and expenditure policies influence disposable income and the profitability of investment.

11. Net exports are the difference between exports and imports. Net exports vary with disposable income because imports tend to increase as disposable income increases. The greater the disposable income for the year, the smaller the net exports components of aggregate demand, all else being equal. Net exports are also influenced by changes in the international value of the dollar and in other factors affecting the prices of exports and imports.

KEY TERMS

consumption function *249*

aggregate household wealth *250*

aggregate household debt *250*

autonomous consumption *251*

induced consumption *251*

marginal propensity to consume *253*

marginal propensity to save *254*

planned investment purchases *257*

real marginal return to investment *257*

aggregate purchases *264*

CONCEPT REVIEW

1. What relationship is illustrated by the consumption function? What is the distinction between autonomous consumption and induced consumption?

2. Each year households in the United States consume 95 percent of each additional dollar of disposable income they earn. What are the marginal propensity to consume and the marginal propensity to save?

3. What can cause investment purchases to fluctuate?

4. How are imports, exports, and government purchases likely to vary with disposable income in a nation?

5. Under what circumstances will aggregate purchases exceed the sum of consumption, investment, and government purchases?

PROBLEMS AND APPLICATIONS

1. The consumption function for households in a certain nation can be expressed by the following equation:

$$C = (800 \text{ billion} + 0.7DI)$$

where C is annual consumption and DI is annual disposable income. How much annual consumption is dependent on factors other than annual disposable income such as aggregate wealth? What are the nation's marginal propensity to consume and its marginal propensity to save? **1**

2. Suppose disposable income is $3,000 billion for the year. Use the consumption function from Problem 1 to calculate annual consumption. Calculate annual consumer purchases for annual disposable income of $4,000 billion, $5,000 billion, and $6,000 billion, and show how the percentages of income consumed and saved vary as disposable income varies. **1**

3. Graph the consumption function whose equation is given in Problem 1. Use your graph to show the level of annual disposable income at which household saving would be zero. How could consumers afford to purchase goods and services even if their annual disposable income were zero? **1**

4. Suppose an increase in household wealth increases the amount of autonomous consumption each year from $800 billion to $1,000 billion. Assuming the marginal propensity to consume remains 0.7, write the equation of the new consumption function and show how the increase in wealth affects the consumption line you drew in answer to Problem 3. **1**, **2**

5. Suppose the marginal propensity to consume increases from 0.7 to 0.8. Assuming the amount of annual consumption independent of annual income remains $800 billion, show the impact of the increase in the marginal propensity to consume on the consumption line you drew in answer to Problem 3. **2**

6. The current real rate of interest is 5 percent. Draw an investment demand curve, and show the equilibrium quantity of investment purchases. What is the real marginal return to investment in equilibrium? **3**

7. Assuming no change in the real rate of interest during the year, what can cause investment purchases to increase? Use the graph you drew in answer to Problem 6 to show how an increase in investment purchases can come about. What can cause a decrease in investment purchases? **3**

8. Suppose the real rate of interest income increases from 5 percent to 7 percent. Use the graph you drew in answer to problem 6 to show the impact on investment purchases. **3**

9. Suppose net exports are negative for the U.S. economy. Explain how a recession in the United States could result in positive net exports in the following year. **4**

10. Draw an aggregate purchases line, and show how aggregate purchases fall short of the sum of consumer, investment, and government purchases when net exports are negative. **5**

12 chapter

Keynesian Analysis of Macroeconomic Equilibrium

Your prospects for finding a job when you graduate are tied to the level of spending in the economy. In late 1990 and early 1991, consumers in the U.S. economy cut back on their purchases and suddenly thousands of workers were being laid off and opportunities for new jobs were drying up. Cross your fingers that when you are ready to look for your first full-time job, total spending is going to be strong enough to keep the economy grinding away at a level of real GDP high enough to guarantee full employment.

Keynesian analysis of the economy's performance concentrates on the role of fluctuations in aggregate purchases of domestic products in causing cyclical unemployment, recessions, and inflation. When the economy is in a recession, policies that encourage spending can help achieve full employment. As long as the economy is operating well below its potential, there is little risk of inflation from new purchases that bolster aggregate demand. Keynes advocated government policies to increase aggregate demand during recessions as a way of eliminating the unemployment that the economy's own self-correcting mechanism could not.

The Keynesian analysis does not consider the role of aggregate supply in causing inflation, recessions, or stagflation. However, it does examine how inflation can result when aggregate purchases in a given year exceed potential real GDP. In this chapter we will examine Keynes's macroeconomic analysis of the causes of unemployment and inflation and his prescriptions for dealing with these problems.

☐ CONCEPT PREVIEW

After reading this chapter, you should be able to:

1. Show how macroeconomic equilibrium is influenced by the level of aggregate purchases of domestic products by consumers, investors, governments, and foreigners.

2. Show how a decrease in the aggregate purchases associated with any given level of real income can cause equilibrium real GDP to decline.

3. Understand the concept of the multiplier and how it is related to the rate at which income is respent on the final products of domestic sellers.

4. Show how an increase in the price level can affect aggregate purchases and discuss Keynes's analysis of the causes of inflation.

AGGREGATE PURCHASES AND MACROECONOMIC EQUILIBRIUM

Fluctuations in any component of aggregate purchases (consumption, investment, government purchases, or net exports) can cause changes in macroeconomic equilibrium. The most likely sources of such fluctuations are changes in investment purchases and net exports, the most fickle and unpredictable components of spending. However, even small fluctuations in consumer purchases at any given level of income (changes in autonomous consumption) can also have major effects on aggregate purchases, because consumption accounts for over two thirds of real GDP.

Keynesian analysis of macroeconomic equilibrium shows how declines in aggregate purchases can cause recessions and cyclical unemployment. Such analysis also shows how increases in aggregate purchases can cause inflation when the economy is operating at or close to its potential. Keynes assumed that in an economy operating below its potential, increases in aggregate purchases would increase equilibrium real GDP with little or no inflation. Spending is the key determinant of real GDP and therefore of income in the Keynesian analysis.

To simplify that analysis at the outset, we'll assume that aggregate purchases consist only of consumption and investment. We'll also assume that government purchases, net taxes (taxes minus transfers), capital consumption allowances (depreciation), undistributed corporate profits, and indirect business taxes, exports, and imports are all equal to zero in the economy. These simplifying assumptions eliminate the distinction between real GDP, national income, and disposable income based on their definitions in the National Income and Product Accounts. We can now view real GDP, which equals the aggregate real income earned in a nation, as the major influence on consumer purchases.

Keynesian Analysis of Macroeconomic Equilibrium

The table in Box 1 provides hypothetical data on the components of aggregate purchases that prevail at alternative levels of income earned in a given year at a given price level. The first column of the table shows possible levels of real GDP during the year. The second column gives consumption purchases based on the consumption function discussed in the preceding chapter. The third column gives planned investment, which is assumed to be $600 billion per year no matter what the level of real GDP. The fourth column shows the aggregate purchases of final products, given the price level prevailing during the year.

Aggregate purchases in this simple economy are the sum of consumer purchases (C) and planned investment purchases (I_P) by business firms during the year:

$$\text{Aggregate purchases} = \text{Consumption} + \text{Planned investment}$$

$$= C + I_P$$

The equilibrium level of real GDP is the one for which the forces of aggregate demand and aggregate supply balance, so that there is no upward or downward pressure on real GDP and income. Note that as income increases, aggregate purchases increase at a slower rate than aggregate production because a portion of the income earned from additional production is always saved.

The data in Box 1 show that when real GDP is less than $5,000 billion, aggregate purchases (shown in column 4) exceed aggregate production (shown in column 1). Aggregate quantity demanded will therefore exceed aggregate quantity supplied if real GDP is less than $5,000 billion during the year. Under these circumstances, firms will sell more than they produced during the year and will unexpectedly deplete their inventories. Such unintended inventory reductions are shown as negative unintended inventory investment in the fifth column of the table.

Box 1   Aggregate Production, Aggregate Purchases, and Determination of Macroeconomic Equilibrium Real GDP in a Simple Economy (Hypothetical Data, Billions of Dollars)

(1)	(2)	(3)	(4)	(5)	(6)	(7)
Aggregate production (Real GDP = Income)	Consumption purchases (C)	Planned investment purchases (I_P)	Aggregate purchases ($C + I_P$)	Unintended inventory investment	Employment (billions of hours per year)	Pressure on real GDP and employment
1,000	1,200	600	1,800	−800	50	Up
2,000	2,000	600	2,600	−600	100	Up
3,000	2,800	600	3,400	−400	150	Up
4,000	3,600	600	4,200	−200	200	Up
5,000	4,400	600	5,000	0	250	Equilibrium
6,000	5,200	600	5,800	200	300	Down

Remember from the analysis of macroeconomic equilibrium in the chapter entitled "Aggregate Demand and Aggregate Supply" that any imbalance between aggregate quantities demanded and supplied will affect both hiring plans and business orders for goods and services. For example, suppose real GDP and income are only $1,000 billion for the year. At that level of aggregate production and income, the table shows that aggregate purchases for the year are $1,800 billion. Because aggregate purchases exceed aggregate production by $800 billion, an unanticipated reduction in business inventories equal to this amount is shown in column 5. As inventories fall during the year, producers increase output and real GDP and income increase. When inventories are unexpectedly being depleted, firms will seek to produce more by hiring additional labor. Column 6 shows billions of labor hours utilized at various levels of real GDP.

Similarly, notice that when real GDP exceeds $5,000 billion, aggregate purchases fall short of aggregate production. Sellers are unable to sell everything they produce at current prices. The unsold goods pile up as unintended inventory investment (column 5). Firms will soon cut back production, and real GDP and income earned in the nation will tend to fall. Then firms will tend to lay off workers. For example, if aggregate production is $6,000 billion, aggregate purchases amount to only $5,800 billion. As a result, $200 billion worth of final products go unsold and firms cut back production in response to the unintended inventory buildup.

Column 7 shows how real GDP and income will move according to the relationship between aggregate production and aggregate purchases at each possible level of real GDP. *Real GDP is in equilibrium, meaning there is no tendency for it to increase or decrease, when aggregate purchases just equal aggregate production.* Equilibrium occurs when the quantity of goods supplied at current prices just equals the quantity that consumers and businesses are willing to purchase. When equilibrium has been reached, there will be no unintended inventory increase or decrease and no tendency for income and employment in the economy to increase or decrease. In the table in Box 1, equilibrium real GDP is reached at $5,000 billion.

A Graphic Analysis

The graph in Box 2, based on the data in Box 1, plots aggregate purchases and shows how they vary during the year at each possible level of income. The upward-sloping curve representing aggregate purchases is obtained by summing the consumption and planned investment at each level of income. Because planned investment is

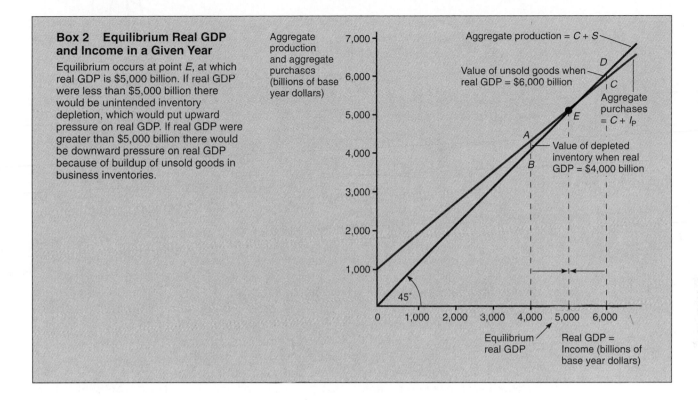

Box 2   Equilibrium Real GDP and Income in a Given Year

Equilibrium occurs at point *E*, at which real GDP is $5,000 billion. If real GDP were less than $5,000 billion there would be unintended inventory depletion, which would put upward pressure on real GDP. If real GDP were greater than $5,000 billion there would be downward pressure on real GDP because of buildup of unsold goods in business inventories.

[Graph labels:]
Aggregate production and aggregate purchases (billions of base year dollars)

Aggregate production = $C + S$

Value of unsold goods when real GDP = $6,000 billion

Aggregate purchases = $C + I_P$

Value of depleted inventory when real GDP = $4,000 billion

45°

Equilibrium real GDP

Real GDP = Income (billions of base year dollars)

---

assumed to be $600 billion no matter what the level of income for the year, the upward slope of the aggregate purchases line reflects the upward slope of the consumption line.

The 45-degree line represents aggregate production because when measured on the vertical axis, points on this line (corresponding to the numbers in column 1 of the table in Box 1) correspond to the level of real GDP and income on the horizontal axis. Points on the 45-degree line correspond to the sum of consumption and saving at any level of income, as was the case for the 45-degree line drawn in the preceding chapter.

The vertical difference between the aggregate purchases line and the 45-degree line represents unintended inventory investment (positive or negative). For example, if real GDP were $4,000 billion per year, aggregate purchases would be $4,200 billion per year and there would be $200 billion of unintended inventory depletion, shown as the distance *AB* on the graph. Because aggregate purchases would exceed aggregate production if real GDP were $4,000 billion, the consequent reordering of goods and services to replenish inventories would result in upward pressure on real GDP. Similarly, if real GDP were $6,000 billion per year, there would be unintended inventory buildup of $200 billion per year, represented by the distance *DC* on the graph, because aggregate production would exceed aggregate purchases for the year. This would result in downward pressure on real GDP because firms would cut back orders. Only at point *E* are aggregate purchases equal to aggregate production. At that point the forces of aggregate demand and aggregate supply balance and the corresponding equilibrium level of real GDP and income is $5,000 billion per year.

Conditions for Macroeconomic Equilibrium

When macroeconomic equilibrium is achieved, saving (which is the portion of income not used to purchase final products in this simple model with no government sector and no international trade) equals planned investment purchases. To see this, remember that real GDP must also equal real income, which is either used for consumer purchases or saved:

$$\text{Real GDP} = \text{Income} = C + S$$

In *equilibrium*, real GDP must also equal the sum of consumer purchases plus planned investment purchases (I_P):

$$\text{Real GDP} = \text{Aggregate purchases} = C + I_P$$

It follows that in equilibrium

$$\text{Real GDP} = C + S = C + I_P = \text{Aggregate purchases}$$

Subtracting C from both real GDP and aggregate purchases shows that in equilibrium

$$S = I_P$$

You can understand this by reasoning that whatever households don't spend is saved, assuming that taxes are zero, as is the case in this simple model. Saving provides funds for investment purchases. However, when the amount saved exceeds the amount that businesses plan to invest, some output will not be purchased. Saving constitutes a portion of income that is not used for purchases. Unless the amount saved is exactly matched by planned investment purchases, aggregate supply will not balance aggregate demand and the economy cannot be in equilibrium.

The relationship between saving and planned investment based on the data in Box 1 is shown in the graph in Box 3. Because planned investment is $600 billion, the equilibrium level of saving must also be $600 billion. If saving exceeds $600 billion, aggregate purchases fall short of aggregate production and there is downward pressure on real GDP because of unintended inventory accumulation. Similarly, if saving falls short of investment, aggregate purchases exceed aggregate production because the sum of consumption and planned investment exceeds real GDP. In that case there is unexpected inventory depletion and real GDP increases.

Saving will equal $600 billion only when real GDP, and therefore income, is equal to $5,000 billion. It follows that equilibrium real GDP will be $5,000 billion, which is exactly the same as the conclusion reached by using the aggregate purchases equals aggregate production approach.

CONCEPT CHECK
□

- What are the components of aggregate purchases in an economy with no government sector and no international trade?

- At the end of the year, business firms have $200 billion worth of unintended inventory accumulation. Is the economy in macroeconomic equilibrium?

- Aggregate purchases are currently $5,000 billion for the economy. Aggregate production for the year is $4,500 billion. Is the economy in equilibrium?

KEYNESIAN ANALYSIS OF CONTRACTIONS OR RECESSIONS

The core of the Keynesian theory of recessions is that both product prices and wages tend to be downwardly inflexible as a result of market imperfections. Long-term labor contracts, particularly those negotiated by powerful unions, don't allow for quick downward adjustment in wages when aggregate demand slacks off. Similarly, many firms are reluctant to reduce prices even when inventories pile up.

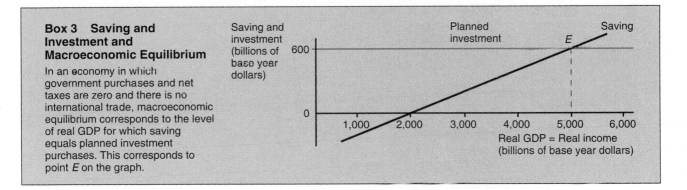

Box 3   Saving and Investment and Macroeconomic Equilibrium

In an economy in which government purchases and net taxes are zero and there is no international trade, macroeconomic equilibrium corresponds to the level of real GDP for which saving equals planned investment purchases. This corresponds to point *E* on the graph.

Keynes didn't dispute the view of the classical economists that the economy would eventually pull itself out of recessions through downward pressure on nominal wages and prices, but he pointed out that "eventually" could be a very lengthy period. Keynes argued that an immediate solution was required to alleviate the misery caused by excessive unemployment during deep recessions. In this regard Keynes's often-quoted remark about the classical prescription of doing nothing for recessions was, "In the long run we are all dead!" By this he meant that the economy's tendency to self-equilibrate through price adjustment took too long and was too unreliable.

How a Decline in Planned Investment Can Cause Equilibrium Real GDP to Fall

Suppose the equilibrium level of real GDP ($5,000 billion in Box 2) is also potential real GDP. At that level of real GDP, 250 billion labor hours will be employed in the economy during the year. Under these conditions, the actual unemployment rate equals the natural unemployment rate and there is no cyclical unemployment.

Now suppose business firms revise their plans and decide to spend only $400 billion on new investment purchases instead of $600 billion. The table in Box 4 shows how aggregate purchases vary with real GDP at the current price level, given the new level of planned investment and assuming no change in the consumption function.

It's easy to see that $5,000 billion will no longer be the equilibrium real GDP after the decline in planned investment purchases. If real GDP is $5,000 billion, aggregate purchases are only $4,800 billion after the decline in investment demand. *There is unintended inventory investment at potential real GDP.* It follows that aggregate purchases at a potential real GDP of $5,000 billion are insufficient to purchase all of the aggregate production. The $200 billion worth of unintended inventory investment results in downward pressure on real GDP. The equilibrium level of real GDP is now only $4,000 billion at the current price level. The economy will therefore be in equilibrium at a level of real GDP that is $1,000 billion below potential real GDP. The decline in real GDP over the year means that the reduction in planned business investment has caused a contraction. The result will be job layoffs. Cyclical unemployment will increase the actual unemployment rate above the natural rate. As real GDP falls to its new equilibrium level, employment in the economy falls from 250 billion to 200 billion labor hours during the year.

A decline in planned investment in the United States in 1981 caused exactly such a scenario. As aggregate demand fell, firms were stuck with inventory they couldn't sell. The automobile industry was particularly hard hit that year, and unplanned accumulations of inventories were in evidence at dealerships and manufacturers'

Box 4   Macroeconomic Equilibrium: The Response to a Decline in Planned Investment (Hypothetical Data, Billions of Dollars)

(1) Aggregate production (Real GDP = Income)	(2) Consumption purchases (C)	(3) Planned investment (I_P)	(4) Aggregate purchases ($C + I_P$)	(5) Unintended inventory investment	(6) Employment (billions of hours per year)
1,000	1,200	400	1,600	−600	50
2,000	2,000	400	2,400	−400	100
3,000	2,800	400	3,200	−200	150
4,000 = Equilibrium real GDP	3,600	400	4,000	0	200
5,000 = Potential real GDP	4,400	400	4,800	+200	250
6,000	5,200	400	5,600	+400	300

Box 5   How a Decline in Aggregate Purchases in a Given Year Causes a Recessionary GDP Gap

A decline in planned investment shifts the aggregate purchases curve downward. The new equilibrium level of real GDP is $1,000 billion less than potential real GDP. The same effect could result from a decline in wealth or other unfavorable effects that reduce consumer spending.

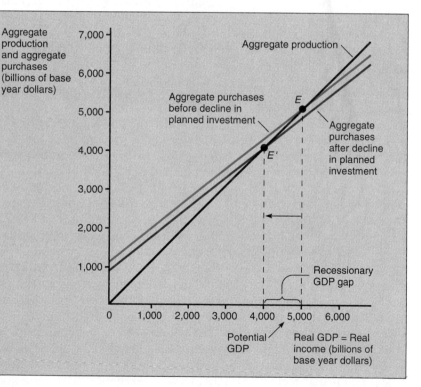

lots. As inventories of cars and other goods built up, the recession of 1982 hit with a vengeance. Firms laid off workers, and the economy moved to a lower equilibrium level of real GDP.

The graph in Box 5 shows that the decline in planned investment shifts the aggregate purchases line downward. This results in a new equilibrium at point E'. At E' the economy is in equilibrium at the new lower level of real GDP of $4,000 billion for the year. Only at E' is unintended inventory accumulation zero. The *recessionary*

Box 6   Macroeconomic Equilibrium: The Response to a Decline in Consumer Spending (Hypothetical Data, Billions of Dollars)

Aggregate production (Real GDP = Real income)	Consumption (C)	Planned investment (I_p)	Aggregate purchases ($C + I_p$)	Unintended inventory investment	Employment (billions of hours per year)
1,000	1,000	600	1,600	−600	50
2,000	1,800	600	2,400	−400	100
3,000	2,600	600	3,200	−200	150
4,000 = Equilibrium real GDP	3,400	600	4,000	0	200
5,000 = Potential real GDP	4,200	600	4,800	+200	250
6,000	5,000	600	5,600	+400	300

GDP gap of $1,000 billion shown on the graph measures the difference between potential real GDP and equilibrium real GDP. Whenever a recessionary gap exists for the economy, there will be cyclical unemployment.

How a Decline in Consumer Spending Intentions Can Cause a Contraction or a Recession

A contraction or recession can also be induced by a decline in the willingness and ability of consumers to spend their income. Suppose that because of a decrease in household wealth, an increase in household debt, or a decline in consumer confidence about future income, the autonomous consumption associated with each possible level of real GDP declines by $200 billion. The table in Box 6 shows the impact of a shift in the consumption function and assumes that planned investment is $600 billion, as it was initially.

The table in Box 6 shows that the level of aggregate purchases at a real GDP level of $5,000 billion is once again only $4,800 billion. Equilibrium real GDP will therefore decline over the year to $4,000 billion to eliminate the unintended inventory accumulation. The aggregate purchases curve will shift downward as a result of the decline in consumer spending. As before, a $1,000 billion recessionary GDP gap occurs as the economy moves into a contraction. If the contraction is severe enough, the economy can be plunged into a recession as a result of the decline in autonomous consumption. A recession can be caused by a decline in consumer spending in just the same way that it can be caused by a decline in planned investment spending!

Keynes's insight into the way the economy works not only explained why an economy could stagnate in a recession, but also suggested a way out of recessions. *A recession could be cured by stimulating aggregate demand.* This stimulation could be accomplished either by encouraging more private investment or consumer purchases or by using government purchases to bolster aggregate demand. Keynes argued that business confidence during a deep recession would probably be so low that even decreases in real interest rates might be ineffective in increasing planned investment. After all, when there was a great deal of excess capacity in the economy, business firms would probably be reluctant to add still more! Similarly, the decline in income and wealth that occurred during a deep recession made it unlikely that government policies could effectively stimulate consumption. Therefore, Keynes strongly advocated that government purchase final products and labor services

economic thinkers

John Maynard Keynes

In the darkness of worldwide depression, economists might well have expected help to come from someone who had struggled in its bowels. Certainly not from a buoyant, successful British phenomenon who once claimed his only regret was not drinking enough champagne. John Maynard Keynes was a dynamo of sorts who revolutionized economics as did no other in the 20th century.

This darling of Britain's most avant-garde intellectuals wrote a highly acclaimed book on mathematical probability while working for the British government, made a fortune speculating in international currencies and commodities by phoning orders from his bed the first half hour of the morning, climbed mountains, married a beautiful Russian ballerina, and set the economic world on its head with his masterwork, *The General Theory of Employment, Interest and Money.*

Written during the Great Depression, it explained what classical economics could not: perpetual unemployment and a stagnating economy. The most depressing part of the Great Depression was that it seemed without end. Keynes's theory explained how this phenomenon could occur and offered a solution in the form of increased government spending.

Keynes was famous long before this masterpiece was published. He worked for the British Treasury during World War I and attended the conference at Versailles. He wrote a book, *Economic Consequences of the Peace,* that claimed the treaty would lead to further instability and war in Europe. His perception of the historical consequences of the harsh financial treatment of Germany in reparation for the war was prophetic.

Keynes studied economics at Cambridge University under Alfred Marshall, whom he later lovingly described as an absurd old man. His father was also a noted economist, and Keynes followed in his footsteps, teaching at Cambridge.

Ironically, this man who sold champagne at discounted prices to support its consumption was born the year Karl Marx died. Both were revolutionary economists, but while Marx viewed capitalism with despair, Keynes—even in its blackest hour—looked for explanations, hope, and a cure. And being the man he was, he found them.

during a recession by engaging in deficit spending if necessary. In this way government could shift aggregate demand outward and move the economy back to full employment with little fear of causing inflation to heat up.

CONCEPT CHECK ☐

- At the economy's potential GDP level of $5,000 billion, consumption expenditure is $4,000 billion and planned investment is $500 billion. Assuming that consumption and investment are the only components of aggregate purchases, will the economy produce at its potential for the year?

- Suppose $500 billion of goods and services that business firms had planned to sell during the current year remain unsold. Explain how downward rigidity in product prices contributes to slow elimination of the unintended increase in business inventories.

- Suppose a sharp decline in the stock market cuts household wealth in half. How could this contribute to a recession?

THE MULTIPLIER: WHAT IT IS AND HOW IT WORKS

The variability of investment purchases is both a curse and a blessing. On the one hand, as was shown earlier, the economy can be thrown into recession when such purchases suddenly swing down in response to a decrease in business confidence or an increase in real interest rates. On the other hand, if an economy is stagnating in a recession, increases in investment purchases can help move the economy up to its potential.

Suppose the economy is in equilibrium at a level of real GDP below potential real GDP. As a consequence, there is excessive unemployment and unused productive capacity. One way to increase aggregate demand is to pursue policies that *increase* investment purchases.

Although it may seem strange, it's quite reasonable to expect that each $1 increase in investment purchases will increase real GDP and income in the nation by more than $1 for the year! Why? Well, it's because $1 of additional purchases during a year results in increases in income that are *respent* many times. For example, suppose that after a decline in real interest rates, many business firms put in orders for new investment goods. Automakers decide to purchase new machines for their factories, airlines decide to order new aircraft to replace their aging fleets and to expand service, trucking firms order new tractors and trailers, and railroads order new locomotives. As the new orders come in, production increases. Laid-off employees are recalled, and existing employees enjoy overtime work. As earnings increase because of the new production, households increase their purchases, which, in turn, increases aggregate demand for retail goods and services. As goods disappear from shelves, retailers put in more orders and hire more staff, thereby generating still more income and production.

Autonomous purchases are purchases such as investment or autonomous consumption that cause the economy's aggregate purchases line to shift. A change in planned investment represents a change in autonomous purchases because it shifts the aggregate purchases line. Similarly, a change in wealth can cause a change in autonomous consumption that shifts the aggregate purchases line. A change in government purchases or net exports can also shift the aggregate purchases line, and net exports and government purchases are therefore also considered autonomous purchases.

The **multiplier** is a number that indicates how many dollars of increase in real GDP result from each dollar of new autonomous purchases. For example, a multiplier of 5 indicates that each $1 increase in investment purchases will increase equilibrium real GDP by $5. Any increase in purchases that results in an upward shift of the economy's aggregate purchases line, implying an outward shift in its aggregate demand curve, can result in a multiplier effect on real GDP. The multiplier can be expressed as the ratio of the change in equilibrium real GDP to the change in autonomous purchases:

$$\text{Multiplier} = \frac{\text{Change in equilibrium real GDP}}{\text{Change in autonomous purchases}}$$

autonomous purchases purchases such as investment or autonomous consumption that cause the economy's aggregate purchases line to shift.

multiplier a number that indicates how many dollars of increase in real GDP result from each dollar of new autonomous purchases.

The Respending Process

The multiplier effect stems from a process through which an initial round of autonomous purchases generates income, which in turn generates more purchases, which then generate more income, and so on. To see how the multiplier works, suppose the initial level of equilibrium real GDP is $4,000 billion and potential real GDP is $5,000

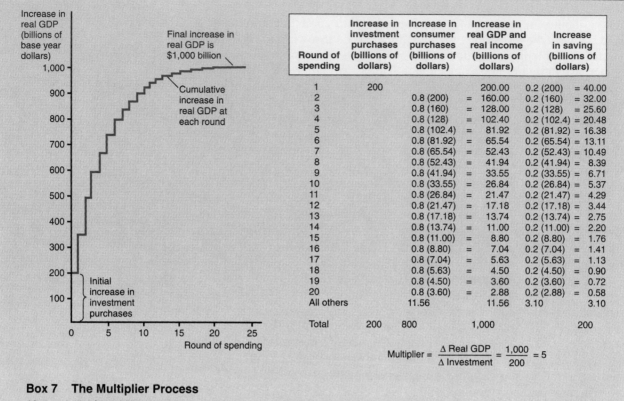

Round of spending	Increase in investment purchases (billions of dollars)	Increase in consumer purchases (billions of dollars)	Increase in real GDP and real income (billions of dollars)		Increase in saving (billions of dollars)	
1	200			200.00	0.2 (200)	= 40.00
2		0.8 (200)	=	160.00	0.2 (160)	= 32.00
3		0.8 (160)	=	128.00	0.2 (128)	= 25.60
4		0.8 (128)	=	102.40	0.2 (102.4)	= 20.48
5		0.8 (102.4)	=	81.92	0.2 (81.92)	= 16.38
6		0.8 (81.92)	=	65.54	0.2 (65.54)	= 13.11
7		0.8 (65.54)	=	52.43	0.2 (52.43)	= 10.49
8		0.8 (52.43)	=	41.94	0.2 (41.94)	= 8.39
9		0.8 (41.94)	=	33.55	0.2 (33.55)	= 6.71
10		0.8 (33.55)	=	26.84	0.2 (26.84)	= 5.37
11		0.8 (26.84)	=	21.47	0.2 (21.47)	= 4.29
12		0.8 (21.47)	=	17.18	0.2 (17.18)	= 3.44
13		0.8 (17.18)	=	13.74	0.2 (13.74)	= 2.75
14		0.8 (13.74)	=	11.00	0.2 (11.00)	= 2.20
15		0.8 (11.00)	=	8.80	0.2 (8.80)	= 1.76
16		0.8 (8.80)	=	7.04	0.2 (7.04)	= 1.41
17		0.8 (7.04)	=	5.63	0.2 (5.63)	= 1.13
18		0.8 (5.63)	=	4.50	0.2 (4.50)	= 0.90
19		0.8 (4.50)	=	3.60	0.2 (3.60)	= 0.72
20		0.8 (3.60)	=	2.88	0.2 (2.88)	= 0.58
All others		11.56		11.56	3.10	3.10
Total	200	800		1,000		200

$$\text{Multiplier} = \frac{\Delta \text{ Real GDP}}{\Delta \text{ Investment}} = \frac{1,000}{200} = 5$$

Box 7   The Multiplier Process

After an initial $200 billion investment purchase, the responding process results in successive increases in real GDP until equilibrium real GDP increases by $1,000 billion. The graph plots the cumulative increase in real GDP for each round of spending based on the data in the table.

billion. The economy therefore suffers from a $1,000 billion recessionary GDP gap. The marginal propensity to consume measures the extra consumption purchases that result from each extra dollar of disposable income.

Assume that the marginal propensity to consume for the economy is 0.8 at all levels of real GDP. Also assume that the only components of aggregate demand are consumer and investment purchases and that there are no government purchases, no international trade, and no net taxation. Under these circumstances, the only way income will not be respent is if it is saved. Therefore, the marginal propensity to consume is also the rate at which each dollar of income is respent. When the marginal propensity to consume is 0.8, an annual increase in investment of only $200 billion will be sufficient to increase real GDP by $1,000 billion to eliminate the recessionary gap and restore full employment.

To see why this is so, think about what happens in the economy as annual investment purchases increase during the year. The orders for $200 billion worth of new machines, new vehicles, and new structures result in $200 billion worth of real GDP and income as firms hire inputs and earn profits filling the orders. An equal increase in income therefore results from the $200 billion in investment purchases, but the increase in *equilibrium* income is much larger than the initial income generated. Those who earn the $200 billion income will spend it on food, clothing, new cars, insurance policies for new cars, and hairstyling services. Some of the income will be saved. If the marginal propensity to consume is 0.8, then 0.8($200 billion), or $160 billion, will be respent in a second round of spending. As was the case for the investment purchases, the $160 billion of new consumer purchases will result in reorders by retailers and still more employment opportunities to satisfy the increased demand for consumer goods and services. In the second round of spending, $160 billion worth of consumer purchases will generate an additional $160 billion in income to resource owners. But the process doesn't end here. The $160 billion will result in 0.8($160 billion) = $128 billion in consumer purchases and $32 billion in additional saving. The $128 billion in consumer purchases will then generate $128 billion of income, and the spending process will commence again.

The table in Box 7 shows how each additional round of respending results in more consumption, more production, and therefore still further increases in income. However, notice that as the process continues, the change in income for subsequent rounds becomes smaller and smaller. The total cumulative increase in real GDP approaches $1,000 billion as the increase in income from subsequent rounds of spending approaches zero. The graph in Box 7 shows the cumulative growth in real GDP at each round of spending. It shows that as the process goes on and on, equilibrium real GDP eventually grows by $1,000 billion.

In equilibrium, the initial increase in investment purchases will have generated enough additional income to increase saving by $200 billion and to increase consumption by $800 billion. The $200 billion increase in saving restores the economy to equilibrium because it raises saving by an amount equaling the increase in planned investment that started the respending process. The last column of the Box 7 table shows the increase in saving resulting from the induced increases in income as the respending process works itself out. The bottom line of the last column shows that the cumulative increase in saving for the economy is $200 billion.

The Multiplier Effect and Macroeconomic Equilibrium

The graphs in Box 8 show how the multiplier effect results in a new macroeconomic equilibrium for the economy. In graph **A,** the economy is in equilibrium at point E_1, at which real GDP is $4,000 billion and the price level is 100. At that equilibrium level of real GDP, there is a $1,000 billion recessionary GDP gap. The increase in planned investment purchases shifts the aggregate purchases line upward by $200 billion at each possible level of real GDP for the year. Note that an increase in any type of autonomous purchases would have the same effect. For example, a $200 billion increase in autonomous consumption resulting from an increase in wealth would also shift the line upward. So too would the introduction of $200 billion worth of government purchases.

As the aggregate purchases line shifts upward, $4,000 billion is no longer the equilibrium level of real GDP, because after the new investment orders have been made, aggregate purchases exceed aggregate production at that level of real GDP. As inventories are drawn down, firms reorder and there is upward pressure on real GDP. The economy moves to a new equilibrium at point E_2, at which real GDP has increased by $1,000 billion to move to its potential level of $5,000 billion. As the new equilibrium is reached, consumption purchases rise by $800 billion, as shown in graph **A,** and saving increases by $200 billion. The $200 billion increase in investment purchases therefore eliminates the recessionary gap.

Graph **B** uses aggregate demand and supply analysis to show how the increase in investment purchases eliminates the recessionary gap. As investment purchases and then consumer purchases increase, the aggregate demand curve shifts outward. If the economy is in a deep recession (as Keynes assumed in his analysis of the

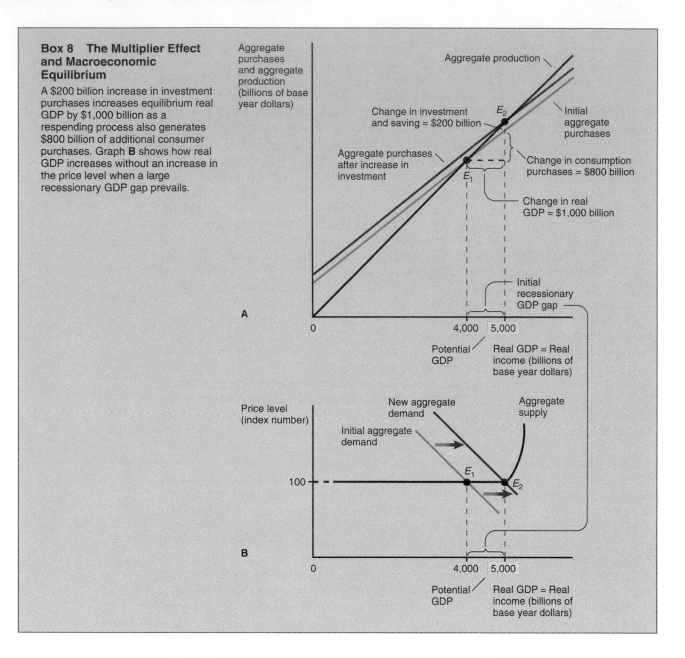

Box 8   The Multiplier Effect and Macroeconomic Equilibrium

A $200 billion increase in investment purchases increases equilibrium real GDP by $1,000 billion as a respending process also generates $800 billion of additional consumer purchases. Graph **B** shows how real GDP increases without an increase in the price level when a large recessionary GDP gap prevails.

multiplier effect), the slack in productive capacity and the excessive unemployment permit real GDP to grow without putting upward pressure on the price level. As a result, the economy moves from its initial equilibrium at E_1 to its new equilibrium at E_2 as real GDP increases from $4,000 billion to $5,000 billion and the price level remains at 100.

In Keynes's view an economy stagnating in a recession attains a macroeconomic equilibrium in the flat portion of its aggregate supply curve, as shown in graph **B** in Box 8. Keynes drew two important implications from this idea. First, it implies that wages and the price level don't decline in a relatively short time in response to declines in aggregate demand. This prevents the self-correcting mechanism envisioned by the classical economists from operating to quickly cure a recession by restoring full employment. Because wages don't decline, there is no incentive for firms to increase production and labor surpluses in the economy are not easily eliminated in labor markets. Second, when an economy is operating in the flat portion of its aggregate supply curve, increases in aggregate demand increase real GDP and therefore increase income and employment *without* putting upward pressure on the price level. The excessive unemployment and slack in productive capacity that exist in the economy during a recession mean that unused capacity can easily be put back into use without a rise in prices.

The multiplier works backward for decreases in spending as well as forward for increases. Suppose investment orders fall by $200 billion for the year. There will be an initial reduction of $200 billion in real GDP. A reduction in orders means that production, and therefore income, will decline. As workers are laid off, they will have to cut back consumption. As they cancel plans to buy new clothes, new cars, and new TVs, there will be a second-round effect of a $160 billion reduction in consumer purchases, assuming a marginal propensity to consume of 0.8. If the economy is initially in equilibrium at its potential real GDP of $5,000 billion, a decrease in investment of $200 billion will result in a $1,000 billion decline in real GDP. You can check this reasoning by looking at the example in Box 4 that showed how a $200 billion decline in planned investment resulted in a $1,000 billion decrease in equilibrium real GDP.

A Formula for the Multiplier

The size of the multiplier depends on the extent to which each extra dollar of earned income results in additional purchases of final products to generate additional production and income. When the only two uses of earned income are consumption and saving, the marginal propensity to consume equals the rate at which each extra dollar of income is respent. Using the data in Box 7, we can show how the value of the multiplier depends on the marginal propensity to consume when the only alternative is saving. The sum representing the cumulative increase in real GDP, and therefore income, can be written as

$$\Delta\text{Real GDP} = \$200 \text{ billion} + 0.8(\$200 \text{ billion}) + 0.8[0.8(\$200 \text{ billion})]$$
$$+ 0.8[(0.8)0.8(\$200 \text{ billion})] + \ldots$$

At each stage, 0.8 of the previous change in income is respent. At the second round the $160 billion increase in income that results from induced consumption purchases can be written as 0.8($200 billion). Similarly, the $128 billion increase in real GDP and income that results at the third round of spending can be written as $(0.8)^2(\$200$ billion). The fourth-round increase in real GDP can be written as $(0.8)^3(\$200$ billion). Note that each successive term in the sum will be smaller than the previous term because the marginal propensity to consume is less than 1.

A mathematical formula can be used to solve for the end product of such an infinite progression of numbers when the number raised to successively higher powers in the sum is greater than zero but less than 1. In this case the number raised to successively higher powers is the marginal propensity to consume. The formula for solving for this total increase in real GDP resulting from the $200 billion injection of investment purchases is

$$\Delta\text{Real GDP} = \left(\begin{array}{c}\text{Increase in investment} \\ \text{purchases}\end{array}\right) \left[\frac{1}{(1 - \text{Marginal propensity to consume})}\right]$$

marginal respending rate (MRR) the extra purchases that result from each extra dollar of income.

where the marginal propensity to consume represents the **marginal respending rate (MRR),** the extra purchases that result from each extra dollar of income. In this case the increase in investment purchases is \$200 billion and the marginal propensity to consume is 0.8, so the increase in real GDP is

$$\$200 \text{ billion} \left[\frac{1}{(1 - 0.8)} \right] = \frac{\$200 \text{ billion}}{0.2} = \$1,000 \text{ billion}$$

which is the result that was obtained in Box 7.

The formula for the multiplier in an economy with no government sector and no international trade is

$$\text{Multiplier} = \frac{1}{(1 - \text{Marginal propensity to consume})}$$

$$= \frac{1}{(1 - MPC)}$$

Because the marginal propensity to save (*MPS*) is equal to 1 minus the marginal propensity to consume, the multiplier can also be written as

$$\text{Multiplier} = \frac{1}{MPS}$$

When the marginal propensity to consume is 0.8, the multiplier for a simple economy is $1/0.2 = 5$. Notice that the higher the marginal propensity to consume, the smaller the denominator of the formula and the larger the multiplier.

CONCEPT CHECK
☐

- A \$300 billion increase in planned investment results in a \$900 billion increase in equilibrium real GDP over the year. Assuming that income earned is either consumed or saved, what is the multiplier?

- Calculate the impact of a \$300 billion reduction in annual planned investment on equilibrium real GDP, assuming the marginal propensity to consume is 0.7.

- A sharp increase in stock prices increases household wealth by 25 percent. The result is a \$100 billion increase in annual autonomous consumption. Assuming the marginal propensity to consume is 0.9, calculate the increase in equilibrium real GDP and use graphic analysis to show how the aggregate purchases line and the aggregate demand curve shift.

INTERNATIONAL TRADE, THE GOVERNMENT SECTOR, AND MACROECONOMIC EQUILIBRIUM

In reality, aggregate purchases depend not only on consumption and planned investment but also on government purchases and net exports. It's easy to incorporate government purchases, the impact of taxes and transfers, and international trade into the Keynesian analysis.

The graph in Box 9 adds government purchases and net exports associated with each possible level of income to consumption and planned investment to show how aggregate purchases vary with income. The line labeled "aggregate purchases" represents the sum. Government purchases are assumed to be a constant amount independent of real GDP and income. Net exports, however, add to aggregate purchases only at relatively low levels of income and must be subtracted from the sum of $C + I_P + G$ at relatively high levels of income (see the preceding chapter).

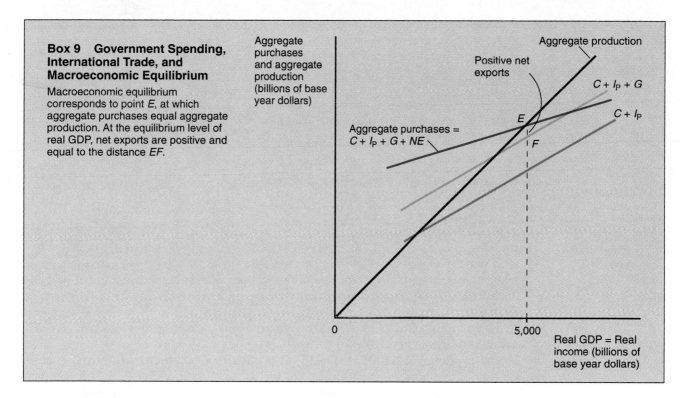

Box 9   Government Spending, International Trade, and Macroeconomic Equilibrium

Macroeconomic equilibrium corresponds to point *E*, at which aggregate purchases equal aggregate production. At the equilibrium level of real GDP, net exports are positive and equal to the distance *EF*.

The amount of consumption associated with each level of income depends on taxes and transfers because these items affect disposable income.

Government Purchases, Taxes, International Trade, and Macroeconomic Equilibrium

The criterion for macroeconomic equilibrium remains the same even when international trade, government spending, and taxation are considered: in equilibrium, aggregate purchases must equal aggregate production. In Box 9 the macroeconomic equilibrium corresponds to point *E*, at which real GDP and income equal $5,000 billion. Positive net exports at the equilibrium level of real GDP are shown as the distance *EF*.

When international trade and the government sector are considered,

$$\text{Aggregate purchases} = C + I_P + G + (E - M)$$

where *E* represents purchases of exports and *M* represents purchases of imports. The difference $(E - M)$ represents net exports.

Aggregate production equals real earnings from goods and services produced. These earnings are used for consumption, saving, or taxes. When earnings are saved or used to pay taxes, they are not directly used to purchase final products produced during the year and thus detract from aggregate demand. Aggregate production therefore measures income and can be expressed as

$$\text{Aggregate production} = C + S + T$$

where *C* includes purchases of imported products as well as those produced domestically and *T* represents the difference between taxes paid and transfers received from government during the year.

In equilibrium, aggregate purchases must equal aggregate production; otherwise, there will be unintended changes in inventories that will cause real GDP and income to adjust. Therefore, real GDP and income adjust until

$$\text{Aggregate purchases} = C + I_\text{P} + G + (E - M) = C + S + T = \text{Aggregate production}$$

Because C is a component of both aggregate production and aggregate purchases, it can be subtracted from both sides of the preceding equation, so that

$$I_\text{P} + G + (E - M) = S + T$$

By adding M to both sides of the preceding equation, we get

$$I_\text{P} + G + E = S + T + M$$

The left side of the equation represents injections into the economy, other than spending (consumption). The right side represents uses of income for purposes other than purchasing current domestic production. These must exactly equal the sum of planned investment, government, and export purchases in equilibrium. If the preceding equality is not met, unanticipated changes in inventories will cause changes in aggregate production, which, in turn, will change income until saving, tax collections, or import purchases adjust to equal the sum of planned investment, government, and export purchases.

The preceding equation is similar to the one derived earlier that showed macroeconomic equilibrium requiring saving to be equal to investment. In the simpler model, saving is the only possible use of income other than consumption of final products produced domestically. In this more complex and realistic model, income earned during the year is used to pay taxes and purchase imported products as well as being saved. The sum $S + T + M$ therefore represents the portion of income not spent on domestic final products.

Also in the simpler model, producing investment goods is the only alternative to producing consumer goods. In reality, however, business firms also produce goods for governments and for export. Unless the amount of income that is not spent on consumer goods is offset by investors (business firms), governments, and buyers in foreign markets who purchase a portion of our real GDP, aggregate production will exceed planned aggregate purchases and real GDP will fall.

We also have to modify our estimate of the multiplier when we consider international trade and taxation. In the simple formula, the marginal propensity to consume is the marginal respending rate because the only alternative to consuming income is to save it. In this more realistic depiction of the U.S. economy, however, we know that some of the extra income earned during the year must go to pay taxes and that some will be used to buy imported products. The **marginal propensity to import (MPI)** is the fraction of each extra dollar of income that is used to purchase imported products. The marginal propensity to import has been more than 0.1 for the U.S. economy, where more than 10 percent of income has been spent on imports in recent years. If taxes absorb 25 cents of each extra dollar earned and imports absorb another 10 cents, the marginal respending rate is less than the marginal propensity to consume. If 15 cents of every extra dollar earned in the United States is saved,[1]

marginal propensity to import (MPI) the fraction of each extra dollar of income used to purchase imported products.

---

[1] This includes business as well as personal saving. Remember that capital consumption allowances represent business saving.

25 cents is used to pay taxes, and 10 cents is used to buy imported products, only 50 cents is respent. Thus, the marginal respending rate on national production of each additional dollar earned is only 0.5. Based on MRR of 0.5, the multiplier would therefore be

$$\text{Multiplier} = \frac{1}{(1 - \text{Marginal respending rate})} = \frac{1}{(1 - 0.5)} = 2$$

the global economy

How a Decline in Exports or an Increase in the Marginal Propensity to Import Can Cause a Recessionary GDP Gap

Many nations rely on the sale of exports for significant portions of their income. (Even in the United States exports have become a more important source of income in the past 20 years.) Fluctuations in export demand can have a considerable effect on equilibrium real GDP and income of such nations. This is particularly true for many less developed nations that export basic materials such as petroleum and tin. It's also true for some prosperous nations, such as Japan and Germany, that import much of their raw materials and export a large portion of their real GDP for sale in foreign markets. International transactions account for more than 50 percent of the value of real GDP in Germany and South Korea.

You saw earlier how a contraction or recession can be caused by a decline in planned investment or

by a decline in the dollar amount of consumption attributable to influences other than income. It's easy to demonstrate how a contraction (or possibly a recession if net exports are a major component of aggregate demand) can be induced by a decline in net exports. Suppose the initial equilibrium level of income is $5,000 billion, which corresponds to potential GDP, so there is no cyclical unemployment. At the beginning of the next year, there is a decline in the net exports associated with any given level of real GDP.

It's now easy to show that the equilibrium level of real GDP, other things remaining unchanged for the year, will be below potential real GDP. The decline in net exports associated with each possible level of real GDP causes the aggregate purchases line to shift downward, as shown in the graph in Box 10. Over the year unintended inventory accumulation will put downward pressure on real GDP and income at the full-employment level of $5,000 billion.

The equilibrium level of real GDP declines below its potential level, and the equilibrium moves from point E to point E'. The result is a recessionary GDP gap, as shown in the graph. As real GDP falls below its potential level, some cyclical unemployment will result.

You can now begin to understand the concern about the balance of trade deficit in the United States and other countries. Negative net exports put downward pressure on real GDP. In recent years U.S. net exports have been negative, amounting to as much as 4 percent of real GDP. Other nations, such as Japan, Germany, South Korea, and many Latin American countries, rely on exports to generate a very large portion of their real GDP and income. Declines in world demand for basic products (such as oil and tin) have plunged such nations as Mexico and Bolivia into deep recessions in recent years.

Box 10   A Decline in Aggregate Purchases Caused by a Decrease in Net Exports

A downward shift in the aggregate purchases line can be caused by a decrease in net export demand or a decrease in government purchases for the year. Higher taxes, as well as declines in consumption or investment, also cause the aggregate expenditure line to shift downward. A decline in aggregate purchases decreases equilibrium real GDP and can open up a recessionary GDP gap.

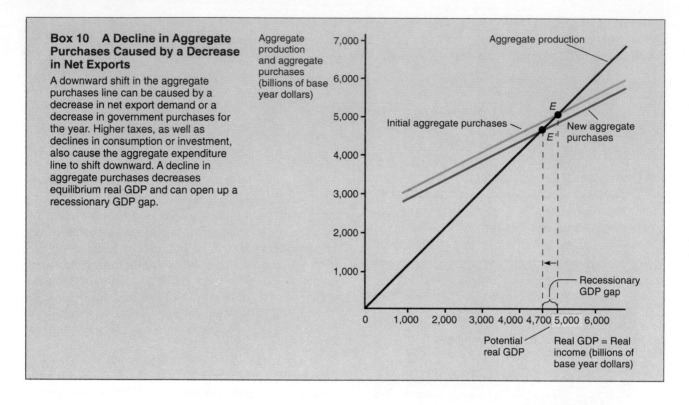

CONCEPT CHECK

☐

- What are possible uses other than consumption for income earned during the year?

- Explain why an increase in the demand for U.S. exports, other things being equal, will increase equilibrium real GDP.

- Why is the marginal respending rate for the U.S. economy actually lower than the marginal propensity to consume, and how does that fact affect the value of the multiplier?

THE PRICE LEVEL, AGGREGATE DEMAND, AND INFLATIONARY GAPS

4   Thus far the price level has been assumed to be fixed in the Keynesian analysis of aggregate demand. Keynesian analysis of macroeconomic equilibrium argues that shifts in aggregate purchases are not only responsible for recessions but are also responsible for inflation! In this section we will analyze the effect of changes in the price level on the aggregate quantity of real GDP demanded. In addition, we will analyze movements in the price level that result when the economy is operating at a level above potential real GDP.

Shifts of the Aggregate Purchases Line Caused by Price Changes

Suppose the prices of *all* goods and services produced in the economy were suddenly *doubled*. These price increases are applicable only to *domestically* produced goods and services that are part of real GDP and don't apply to imported goods, whose prices depend on the price levels in foreign nations.

The increase in the domestic price level is likely to decrease aggregate purchases for the reasons we first discussed in the chapter on aggregate supply and demand:

principles in practice

The Multiplier for the Globally Integrated U.S. Economy of the 1990s

If investment suddenly declines, by how much will real GDP fall in the United States? If government purchases increase, what increase in real GDP will result from the ensuing respending process? To answer questions like these, we need a realistic estimate of the multiplier for the U.S. economy. To obtain this estimate, we must have a reasonably accurate estimate of the marginal respending rate. How much of each dollar of real GDP earned is spent on domestically produced final products that generate income for U.S. households?

The best way to estimate the marginal respending rate is to examine recent data about U.S. saving, imports, and taxes. Of each dollar of GDP earned as income in the 1980s, approximately 14 percent was saved. The bulk of this saving (about 12 percent of GDP) was contributed by business firms in the form of capital consumption allowances and retained earnings. Household saving was notoriously low (the marginal propensity to consume has been running close to 95 percent in recent years). Government saving was negative throughout the 1980s and the early 1990s because of large federal budget deficits that required borrowing (negative saving). Of each dollar spent in 1990 in the United States, about 16 cents was spent on imported products instead of domestically produced final goods and services. Another 24 cents was used to pay business and personal taxes, including sales and excise taxes, corporate profits taxes, payroll taxes, and personal income taxes.

If we add up the numbers, we find that of each extra dollar of GDP generated,

> 14 cents is saved
> 16 cents is spent on imports
> 24 cents is paid in taxes
> _____
> 54 cents = Total leakage

Total spending on U.S. final products = $1 − 54 cents = 46 cents.

Forty-six cents of each extra dollar earned in recent years was used to purchase final products produced by domestic businesses. The marginal respending rate for the U.S. economy in the early 1990s was therefore about 0.46 after considering total national saving, spending on imports, and taxes, which represented *leakages* from the spending stream.

Using the formula we developed in this chapter, a realistic estimate for the multiplier of the U.S. economy in the early 1990s is

$$\text{Multiplier} = \frac{1}{(1 - 0.46)} = \frac{1}{0.54} = 1.85$$

Each dollar of increase in autonomous spending, such as government purchases, will increase real GDP by $1.85. This estimate assumes that there are no other effects that could choke off spending when aggregate demand increases, such as increases in the price level or increases in real interest rates.

Don't be fooled into thinking that the multiplier is 10 or more because the marginal propensity to consume is greater than 0.9. There is more to the respending process than just consumption. Because of leakages, the multiplier for the modern globally integrated U.S. economy is much less than it would be for an economy with no international trade and no government sector.

Is the multiplier likely to increase or decrease as we approach the 20th century? Although it is hard to forecast future trends, it is very likely that the multiplier will decrease. If current policies are successful, the budget deficit is likely to fall. If the federal government succeeds in balancing its budget, national saving will go up because the government sector will no longer be a net dissaver. It is also likely that state and local tax rates will rise because of increased demand for government services and reduced aid from the federal government. Finally, the U.S. economy is becoming more intertwined with the global economy, so the marginal propensity to import could increase still more in the 1990s, inching closer to 0.2. Increased taxes, a higher national saving rate, and a higher marginal propensity to import would all act to reduce the multiplier.

Suppose the United States succeeds in getting its national saving rate up to 20 percent of GDP—the level of other advanced nations. Also assume that the marginal propensity to import goes up to 18 percent of GDP and the marginal tax rate goes up to 26 percent of GDP. Under these circumstances, the total leakage of spending from the circular flow of income would be 64 cents and the marginal respending rate would be only 36 cents. Thus, the multiplier would be a mere 1/0.64 = 1.56!

1. A higher price level can decrease the real wealth in a nation, thereby decreasing consumer purchases. As a result of the increase in the price level, the purchasing power of money is reduced (in this example it is actually cut in half). There is a decrease in real wealth, which puts downward pressure on consumer purchases, shifting the aggregate purchases line downward.

2. A higher price level can increase real interest rates, making credit more expensive. At a higher price level, households and businesses demand larger cash balances to finance their everyday transactions. This decreases the supply of loanable funds, which puts upward pressure on real interest rates. The higher real interest rates in turn cause businesses to reduce the quantity of their planned investment purchases for the year.

3. A higher price level can reduce foreign demand for U.S. exports and can increase domestic demand for imports. Assuming the international value of the dollar doesn't immediately adjust to a change in the price level, U.S. goods rise in price relative to foreign substitutes, thus causing an increase in imports and a decrease in exports.

Graph **A** in Box 11 shows how an increase in the price level shifts the aggregate purchases line downward. Initially, the economy is in equilibrium at a real GDP level of \$5,000 billion, corresponding to point E_1. As the price level increases from 100 to 200, the aggregate purchases line shifts *downward*. As this happens, real GDP declines from its initial equilibrium of \$5,000 billion to a new equilibrium of \$4,000 billion as the economy moves to a new equilibrium at point E_2.

If the economy is initially in equilibrium at the potential level of real GDP, the increase in the price level will result in a recessionary GDP gap and some cyclical unemployment. An increase in the price level can cause a cyclical downturn in the economy, at least in the short run, by decreasing household real wealth, increasing real interest rates, and causing net exports to decline. A sudden sharp increase in the price of a basic input such as oil spells trouble for the economy. A contraction of economic activity can result in a recession.

Deriving the Aggregate Demand Curve

A higher price level decreases aggregate purchases by causing a reduction in real wealth, by making imports relatively cheaper for domestic consumers, and by making exports more expensive in foreign markets. Note that when the price level goes up, input prices rise along with output prices. The initial increase in prices doesn't affect income. Although people are paying higher prices for the items they consume, they're also receiving higher prices for the input services they sell. It's the reduction in aggregate purchases caused by the higher price level and the consequent reduction in wealth that causes a decline in real GDP, and thus income, in the nation.

The preceding analysis of the impact of a change in the price level on aggregate purchases showed how an increase in the price level shifts the aggregate purchases line downward and reduces equilibrium real GDP. Graph **B** in Box 11 simply plots the level of equilibrium real GDP associated with the initial price level of 100 and the new price level of 200. Other things being equal, an increase in the price level, as shown earlier, decreases equilibrium real GDP. Conversely, a decrease in the price level will increase equilibrium real GDP. Connecting the two points in graph **B** traces out the downward-sloping aggregate demand curve.

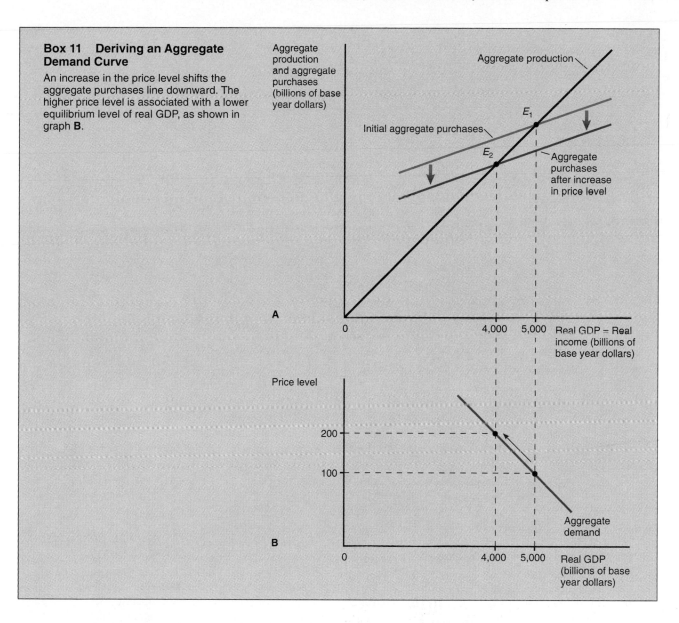

Box 11   Deriving an Aggregate Demand Curve

An increase in the price level shifts the aggregate purchases line downward. The higher price level is associated with a lower equilibrium level of real GDP, as shown in graph **B**.

Inflationary GDP Gaps

Keynes recognized that although prices and wages are quite inflexible in the downward direction, they are flexible in the upward direction. Increases in aggregate demand can therefore cause inflation when the economy is close to full employment. As a consequence, the economy's self-correcting mechanism seems to work much better when the economy overheats than when it stagnates in a recession.

As you learned in the chapters on aggregate supply and demand, an *inflationary GDP gap* is the difference between equilibrium real GDP and the level of real GDP corresponding to full employment for an economy that is operating beyond its potential. In Box 12 the inflationary gap is $1,000 billion.

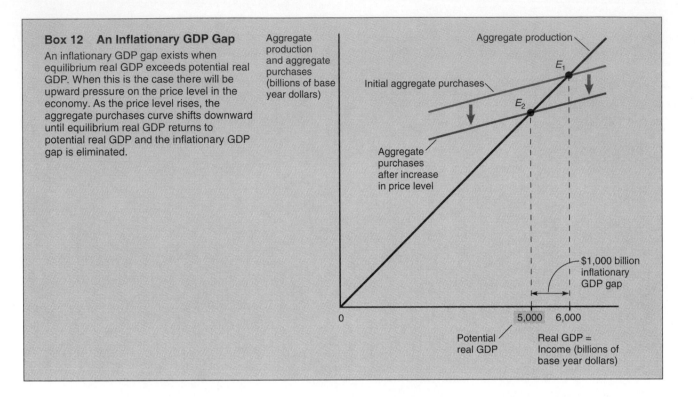

Box 12   An Inflationary GDP Gap

An inflationary GDP gap exists when equilibrium real GDP exceeds potential real GDP. When this is the case there will be upward pressure on the price level in the economy. As the price level rises, the aggregate purchases curve shifts downward until equilibrium real GDP returns to potential real GDP and the inflationary GDP gap is eliminated.

The inevitable result of an inflationary gap is upward pressure on the price level—a bout of inflation. As the price level increases, the aggregate purchases line shifts downward. As this happens, there is downward pressure on real GDP until the economy returns to equilibrium at the level of real GDP corresponding to full employment.

SUMMARY

1. Real GDP is in equilibrium when aggregate purchases equal aggregate production for the year. When real GDP is in equilibrium, there is no unintended inventory investment and no tendency for real GDP and income to increase or decrease.

2. A decline in planned investment or autonomous consumption can cause a contraction or a recession. When real GDP falls below its potential, the economy suffers from a recessionary GDP gap.

3. When the price level does not fall in response to a decline in aggregate demand, unintended inventory accumulations cannot be sold off quickly. The buildup of inventory caused by downward price rigidity causes firms to cut back production. Lengthy recessions can result when wages and prices do not respond to decreases in aggregate demand.

4. The Keynesian model of macroeconomic equilibrium assumes that the economy operates in the horizontal portion of its aggregate supply curve when stagnating in recession. Because both the price level and wages are downwardly inflexible, excessive unemployment is not quickly eliminated and the economy's self-correcting mechanism cannot operate. Keynes argued that policies that increase aggregate demand can restore full employment without upward pressure on the price level when the economy is in a recession.

5. The multiplier is a number used to multiply a change in autonomous purchases to obtain the change in equilibrium real GDP that results from those purchases. It indicates that an increase of $1 in planned investment or in other types of autonomous purchases will increase real GDP by more than $1.

6. The multiplier effect stems from a respending process as income earned from increased production is spent and respent over a period.

7. Planned investment purchases, government purchases, and exports of final products increase aggre-

gate demand for real GDP. Saving, taxes, and imports decrease aggregate demand for real GDP.

8. A decrease in net exports decreases aggregate purchases and aggregate demand. This decreases equilibrium real GDP and contributes to a recessionary GDP gap.

9. Changes in the price level cause shifts in the aggregate purchases line for the economy. An increase in the price level reduces the purchasing power of some assets denominated in dollars, such as cash. This reduces household real wealth and contributes to a decline in consumption. In addition, an increase in the

price level decreases foreign demand for exports, increases domestic demand for imports, and increases real interest rates. An increase in the price level therefore causes a decrease in aggregate quantity demanded.

10. When an inflationary GDP gap prevails, the economy operates at a level of real GDP that exceeds potential real GDP. An inflationary gap puts upward pressure on the price level, which shifts the aggregate purchases line downward, thus restoring the economy to the level of real GDP corresponding to full employment.

KEY TERMS

autonomous purchases *277*	multiplier *277*	marginal respending rate (MRR) *281*	marginal propensity to import (MPI) *284*

CONCEPT REVIEW

1 Planned investment this year is $40 billion. If there is no government sector and no international trade, what is the amount of saving this year?

2 List the possible causes of a recession, using the Keynesian analysis of macroeconomic equilibrium.

3 If the marginal respending rate for an economy is 0.6, what is the value of the multiplier for the economy?

What can cause the value of a nation's multiplier to decline?

4 Under what circumstance can an increase in aggregate purchases increase the rate of inflation?

PROBLEMS AND APPLICATIONS

1. An increase in real interest rates is forecast to reduce investment purchases by $300 billion next year. Assuming the forecast is correct, what do you predict will happen to real GDP, other things being equal? **1**, **2**

2. Use the data in the table in Box 1 to show what will happen to real GDP, income, consumption, and aggregate purchases and employment if planned investment purchases double for the year. **1**, **2**

3. Suppose autonomous consumption falls by $400 billion. Use the data in Box 1 to show how this fall in autonomous consumption can cause a recession. What will be the new equilibrium real GDP, income, and employment, assuming that nothing else changes? **1**, **2**

4. Explain why an increase in the amount of saving consumers want to set aside at each possible level of real GDP can cause an economic contraction. **2**

5. Suppose the marginal propensity to consume represents the marginal respending rate of additional income. If the marginal propensity to consume is 0.9, what will happen to real GDP if planned investment increases by $300 billion? **2**, **3**

6. Why is the marginal propensity to consume likely to overstate the marginal respending rate in the economy when the impact of government and international trade on the economy is considered? **3**

7. All indications are that consumers plan to devote higher proportions of their income to repayment of debt next year. Business firms have little optimism about the current outlook, and planned investments for next year are down. What is your prognosis for the economy? **2**

8. Why do you think the decline in the international value of the dollar against the yen could cause a recession in Japan? What effect will a recession in Japan have on U.S. exports to Japan, given the current international value of the dollar? **1**

9. Explain how a decrease in the price level in the economy will affect the aggregate purchases line and equilibrium real GDP. **4**

10. Under what circumstances will an inflationary gap prevail for an economy? How will the economy's self-correcting mechanism eliminate the inflationary gap? **4**

chapter appendix

A Complete Keynesian Model

In this appendix we extend our analysis by explicitly considering how tax collections and net exports vary with real GDP for a given year. The extension allows a more precise derivation of the conditions for macroeconomic equilibrium and an equation for the multiplier that shows how import demand and taxation affect the rate at which earned income is respent.

AGGREGATE PURCHASES: EXPLICIT CONSIDERATION OF TAXES, GOVERNMENT PURCHASES, AND INTERNATIONAL TRADE

The table in Box 1 can be used to derive an aggregate purchases line that explicitly considers how net tax receipts and net exports vary with income. Because taxes are now explicitly considered in the analysis, disposable income is no longer equal to income earned during the year.

The first column shows possible levels of aggregate production measured by real GDP, which also equals earned income (Y) for a given year. The second column calculates net taxes at alternative levels of income earned for the year. In making the calculation, it's assumed that net taxes are always 20 percent of income earned. Remember that net taxes are taxes minus government transfer payments. Tax collections are higher at higher levels of real GDP when taxes are proportional to income, as is the case in many modern economies. This means that government net tax collections can vary with real GDP, an important point in balancing government budgets because actual tax collections depend on how close the economy is to its potential real GDP. In 1982, for example, the federal budget deficit turned out to be much larger than government economists anticipated, because given the level of government purchases that year, tax collections plummeted when a recession hit. Equilibrium real GDP and income fell.

The third column of the table calculates disposable income by subtracting net taxes from each possible level of income. Notice that because net taxes are 20 percent of income, disposable income is always 80 percent of real GDP.

The relationship between aggregate income and disposable income depends on how net taxes vary with aggregate income. In general, disposable income (DI) is equal to income (Y) less the portion of income paid in taxes. The *marginal tax rate (t)* is the fraction of each extra dollar of income earned in a nation that is collected as taxes. In the table it's assumed that the marginal tax rate is always equal to 0.2. Although this is a simplifying assumption, it isn't too far off the mark. When all federal, state, and local taxes are considered, U.S. taxes do tend to stay within the range of 20 percent to 30 percent of earnings for the economy as a whole. It's reasonable to assume that of each extra \$1 of aggregate income, 20 cents in the aggregate must be used to pay taxes. Therefore, \$1,000 billion of extra aggregate income generates extra taxes of \$200 billion for households. If the tax rate is a fixed proportion of income earned, as it is in this example, taxes paid at any level of income will be

$$t(Y) = \text{(Marginal tax rate)(Income)} = \text{Net taxes collected}$$

Disposable income is simply earned income less net taxes collected:

$$DI = Y - (t)Y = (1 - t)Y$$

For example, when $t = 0.2$,

$$DI = (1 - 0.2)Y = 0.8Y$$

Box 1   Aggregate Production, Aggregate Purchases, and Macroeconomic Equilibrium (Hypothetical Data, Billions of Dollars)

(1)	(2)	(3)	(4)	(5)	(6)	(7)	(8)	(9)	(10)
Aggregate production (Real GDP = Real income) Y	Net taxes $tY = 0.2Y$	Disposable income $DI = (1 - t)Y = 0.8Y$	Consumption purchases $C = 400 + 0.8DI$	Saving $S = DI - C$	Planned investment I_p	Government purchases G	Net exports $NE = 400 - 0.1Y$	Aggregate purchases $C + I_p + G + NE$	Pressure on real GDP
1,000	200	800	1,040	−240	500	1,000	300	2,840	Up
2,000	400	1,600	1,680	−80	500	1,000	200	3,380	Up
3,000	600	2,400	2,320	80	500	1,000	100	3,920	Up
4,000	800	3,200	2,960	240	500	1,000	0	4,460	Up
5,000	1,000	4,000	3,600	400	500	1,000	−100	5,000	Equilibrium
6,000	1,200	4,800	4,240	560	500	1,000	−200	5,540	Down

Disposable income (Column 3) is therefore always 80 percent of earned income in this example.

At each possible level of income, consumption (C) consists of $400 billion in autonomous purchases that are independent of income plus 80 percent of disposable income, as shown in Column 4. The consumption function is therefore

$$C = (\$400 \text{ billion} + 0.8 \ DI)$$

This equation tells how consumption varies with *disposable* income. Because of taxes, however, only 80 cents of each $1 of aggregate income, Y, is available to households for spending as disposable income. Because the marginal propensity to consume disposable income is 0.8, each $1 of additional earnings will result in (0.8)80 cents, or 64 cents, of additional consumer purchases.

The extra consumer purchases resulting from an extra dollar of income are therefore $MPC(1 - t)$ dollars, where $(1 - t)$ is the proportion of each extra dollar of earnings that ends up as disposable income. In this example $(1 - t)$ dollars is $0.80. You can easily see this by substituting the expression for disposable income into the equation for the consumption function. Because $DI = (1 - t)Y$.

$$C = \$400 \text{ billion} + MPC[(1 - t)Y]$$

Because $MPC = 0.8$ and $t = 0.2$,

$$C = \$400 \text{ billion} + 0.64Y$$

Each $1,000 billion of aggregate income results in $640 billion more consumption and $200 billion in extra taxes. The total of additional consumption and taxes therefore accounts for $840 billion of each $1,000 billion increase in aggregate income. What happens to the remaining $160 billion of each $1,000 billion increase in aggregate income? Because it's used neither to pay taxes nor to pay for consumption of products, the remainder must be saving. Sixteen cents of each extra $1 earned ends up as saving. Column 5 shows how saving varies as income increases. Note that saving is negative at low levels of income but increases by $160 billion for each $1,000 billion increase in income for a given year. Column 6 shows planned investment (I_P), which is assumed to be $500 billion at all possible levels of aggregate income. Government purchases (G), shown in the seventh column, are assumed to be $1,000 billion at all possible levels of aggregate income over the year.[1] Typically, government purchases for a year are determined at the beginning of the year without regard to economic conditions for the coming year.

---

[1] It should be emphasized that constancy of planned investment and government purchases during the year is a simplification. Both planned investment and government purchases could vary with income as much as consumption does.

How Exports and Imports Affect Aggregate Purchases

To obtain aggregate purchases of domestic final products, export sales must be added to the sum of consumer, investment, and government purchases. However, because these purchases also include expenditure on goods produced in foreign nations, imports must be netted out of aggregate purchases, because expenditure on imports doesn't generate domestic production and therefore doesn't result in income for U.S. firms and households. The difference between expenditure on U.S. exports (E) and U.S. expenditure on imported goods (M) is net exports (NE):

$$NE = E - M$$

Aggregate purchases of real GDP during the year are therefore the sum of consumption, planned investment, government purchases, and net exports:

$$\text{Aggregate purchases} = C + I_P + G + NE$$

Net exports can be positive or negative. In the table in Box 1, net exports have been calculated by assuming that foreign purchases of U.S. products (exports) are $400 billion, independent of the level of real GDP and income in the United States. This is quite realistic because current year demand for U.S. exports is dependent on income and other demand influences in foreign nations that are export customers. Import purchases, however, are assumed to be 10 percent of income in the United States. *The dollar purchases of imports by Americans will increase as the level of real GDP and income increases for the year.* This assumption is also quite realistic for the United States, where purchases of imports have been over 10 percent of real GDP in recent years. As income rises, other things being equal, U.S. consumers typically demand more Toyotas, Volvos, Sony Camcorders, and other foreign goods. Just as consumers purchase proportionately more domestic goods as their income increases, so too do they purchase proportionately more imported goods. *In the U.S. economy, imports vary with income, while exports are independent of income.*

The fraction of each extra dollar of income that is spent on imported goods is the *marginal propensity to import* (MPI). In this example the marginal propensity to import is 0.1 because 10 cents of each extra dollar of national income is assumed to be spent on goods produced in foreign nations.

Because exports are assumed to be $400 billion no matter what the actual aggregate income is during the year, while imports are always assumed to be 10 percent of income, Y, the following equation can be used to calculate net exports at each possible level of aggregate income:

$$NE = (\$400 \text{ billion} - 0.1Y)$$

As you can see in column 8, net exports are positive at low levels of aggregate income but become negative at high levels of income as import expenditures outstrip export sales receipts. *Net exports therefore tend to decline as income, Y, increases.*

Column 9 gives the aggregate purchases for the year for each possible level of aggregate production. Aggregate purchases are obtained by summing the individual categories of expenditure ($C + I_P + G + NE$) at each possible level of income for the year.

Determination of Equilibrium Real GDP and Income

Aggregate purchases at the current price level must equal aggregate production in equilibrium. Aggregate production is represented by real GDP (which also equals aggregate real income) in column 1, while aggregate purchases (the sum of consumption, planned investment, government purchases, and net exports) are represented by the numbers in column 9. The equilibrium condition is met when income and real GDP are equal to $5,000 billion for the year, which is assumed to be the level of potential real GDP that will provide full employment. If real GDP were less than $5,000 billion, aggregate purchases would exceed aggregate production at the current price level and the resulting depletion of inventories would put upward pressure on real GDP. You can see this by comparing the numbers in column 9 with those in column 1. If real GDP were $3,000 billion, aggregate purchases of real GDP would be $3,920 billion and firms would be forced to draw down inventories to meet aggregate demand. The consequent reordering of products to replenish inventories would put upward pressure on real GDP. Similarly, if real GDP exceeded $5,000 billion, aggregate purchases would fall short of real GDP at the current price level and the unintended inventory accumulation would put downward pressure on real GDP. If real GDP were $6,000 billion, aggregate purchases would be only $5,540 billion and there would be unintended accumulation of inventories. The resulting cutback in production would put downward pressure on real GDP.

At the equilibrium level of real GDP, annual net taxes will be $1,000 billion. Notice from the data in the table that this is exactly equal to government purchases during the year, so the government budget will be balanced. However, if real GDP is lower, tax collections will fall and the budget will be thrown into deficit. For example, if real GDP were $4,000 billion, tax collections would fall to $800 billion. Because the data in the table assume constant government purchases of $1,000 billion, this would imply a budget deficit of $200 billion. This points out an important characteristic of budget balance for the government sector of the economy. The state of budget balance (surplus or deficit) is influenced by the level of aggregate production in a given year. In the chapter on fiscal policy, you'll study in detail how government tax collections and government purchases vary with real GDP.

Also notice that at the equilibrium level of real GDP in this case, net exports are negative, implying a *balance of trade deficit*. Income earned in nations in which U.S. firms sell exported products affects the business receipts for exports. In this analysis income in other nations is assumed to be given, so export receipts are assumed to be fixed and independent of the possible levels of U.S. income.[2] If demand for U.S. exports were stronger and/or if the marginal propensity to import were lower, net exports could very well be positive at the equilibrium level of real GDP. Net exports depend on a variety of factors, including economic conditions in foreign nations, the unit costs of U.S. goods compared to the unit costs of competing foreign goods, and the international rates of exchange of the dollar into foreign currencies.

The Balance of Trade, the Government Budget Balance, and the Savings-Investment Balance

Recall from the analysis of the simple economy with no international trade and no government sector that equilibrium required a balance between saving and planned investment. A similar but somewhat more complex condition can be derived for the economy by considering both the balance of international trade and the government budget balance. Aggregate purchases of real GDP are

$$\text{Aggregate purchases} = C + I_\text{P} + G + (E - M)$$

where $(E - M)$ represents net exports, the difference between exports and imports.

Aggregate production, which represents income (Y), is the sum of consumption, saving, and taxes over the year:

$$\text{Aggregate production} = Y = C + S + T$$

In equilibrium, aggregate production must equal aggregate purchases, which implies that

$$C + I_\text{P} + G + (E - M) = C + S + T$$

Because C is a component of both aggregate production and aggregate purchases, it can be subtracted from both sides of the preceding equation to obtain the following equilibrium condition:

$$I_\text{p} + G + (E - M) = S + T$$

---

[2] Once again, this is a simplification. An economic downturn in the United States could reduce real income in nations that purchase our exports. If there is such a linkage, the demand for U.S. exports could decline when U.S. income declines.

This equation can be written in the following form by rearranging terms:

$$(E - M) + (G - T) = S - I_\mathrm{P}$$

The term $(E - M)$ represents net exports, which can be positive or negative. When imports exceed exports, net exports are negative. Similarly, the term $(G - T)$ represents the government budget deficit that prevails when net taxes (T) are less than government purchases (G). The equilibrium condition states that the sum of net exports (the balance of trade) and the government budget deficit must equal the difference between saving and planned investment in the economy.

To understand the relevance of this condition, assume that in equilibrium there is a balance of trade deficit and a budget deficit, as has in fact been the case for the U.S. economy in recent years. This implies that

$$\text{Balance of trade deficit} = S - (I_\mathrm{P} + \text{Budget deficit})$$

When there is a balance of trade deficit, both sides of the preceding equation are negative in equilibrium. *A balance of trade deficit implies that domestic saving falls short of the sum of planned investment purchases and the budget deficit.* The balance of trade deficit equals the foreign saving in the United States that fills in the gap between domestic saving and the sum of investment and the government budget deficit in equilibrium.

The equilibrium condition just derived suggests that the trade deficit and the budget deficit can be connected. Given planned investment and export demand, an increase in the budget deficit associated with each possible level of real GDP is an expansionary influence on the economy because it increases aggregate purchases. As equilibrium real GDP increases, more import demand is generated in the economy. The increased import demand increases the balance of trade deficit. However, the expansionary influence of the budget deficit need not increase the trade deficit if it results in a sufficient increase in private saving or a decline in planned investment.

Given planned investment, to the extent that the increase in the budget deficit doesn't result in a substantial increase in saving, the difference must be made up by an increase in the balance of trade deficit. In effect, this means that increases in income in the economy contribute to a trade deficit because consumers choose to spend a higher percentage of their earnings on imported products instead of saving. However, as you'll see in the chapter on the federal budget deficit, it's also possible that an increase in the government budget deficit can result in a decline in private investment that also restores macroeconomic equilibrium. The greater the decline in private investment that results from the budget deficit, the less the increase in earnings and the lower the trade deficit, because imports will be correspondingly less.

ANALYSIS OF CHANGES IN AGGREGATE DEMAND AND THE MULTIPLIER IN THE MIXED AND OPEN ECONOMY

How the Multiplier Is Related to the Marginal Propensity to Consume, the Marginal Tax Rate, and the Marginal Propensity to Import

An algebraic calculation of the marginal respending rate allows us to derive a general formula for the multiplier. If the marginal tax rate is t, then disposable income resulting from each $1 of extra earnings is

$$(1 - t)Y$$

For example, if the marginal tax rate is 0.2, then each $1 increase in income will result in $(1 - 0.2) = 0.8$ of a dollar, or 80 cents, of additional disposable income. The extra consumer purchases that result from an extra dollar of earned income are obtained by multiplying the marginal propensity to consume by $(1 - t)$:

$$MPC(1 - t) = \text{Extra consumption purchases resulting from each \$1 increase in income}$$

For example, if the marginal propensity to consume is 0.8 and the marginal tax rate is 0.2, then each $1 of extra income will result in $0.8(1 - 0.2) = \$0.64$ of additional consumer purchases.

The preceding expression includes consumer purchases of *both* domestically produced and imported final products. Income used to purchase imported goods is not respent on domestic production and thus does not generate domestic income that fuels the respending process. Purchases of imports must therefore be netted out of extra consumption to accurately measure the marginal respending rate in the economy.

The marginal propensity to import (MPI) represents the portion of each extra dollar of earnings that is used to purchase imports. Subtracting MPI from the portion of each dollar respent on consumer purchases gives the extra consumption purchases of *domestic* products resulting from each $1 increase in income, which represents the marginal respending rate (MRR):

$$MRR = MPC(1 - t) - MPI$$

To convince yourself that this is correct, note that when the marginal propensity to consume is 0.8, the marginal tax rate is 0.2, and the marginal propensity to import is 0.1, the marginal respending rate is

$$MRR = 0.8(1 - 0.2) - 0.1 = 0.64 - 0.1 = 0.54$$

A marginal respending rate of 0.54 means that 54 cents of each extra dollar earned is spent on domestic final products and therefore increases income by that amount.

The general formula for the multiplier is

$$\text{Multiplier} = \frac{1}{(1 - MRR)} = \frac{1}{[1 - (MPC(1 - t) - MPI)]}$$

The marginal respending rate is influenced by the marginal propensity to consume, the marginal tax rate, and the marginal propensity to import. The greater the marginal respending rate for the economy, the greater the value of the multiplier. In general, the marginal respending rate increases with increases in the marginal propensity to consume, decreases in the marginal tax rate, and decreases in the marginal propensity to import.

The assumptions made in this appendix about the marginal tax rate and the marginal propensities to consume and import are quite close to the conditions that exist in the U.S. economy. The multiplier for injections of spending into the U.S. economy is somewhat larger than 2 but less than 3.

Determination of Equilibrium Real GDP: An Algebraic Approach

The computations that follow show how to derive a general formula for solving for equilibrium real GDP and income, assuming a fixed price level that is unresponsive to changes in aggregate demand.

The condition for macroeconomic equilibrium is

$$\text{Aggregate production} = \text{Aggregate purchases}$$

If this condition does not hold, there will be unintended inventory accumulation or depletion and forces will be set up to increase or decrease real GDP.

Use the symbol Y for real GDP. Because real GDP is also equal to aggregate income, Y also stands for income earned during a year. Aggregate purchases are the sum of consumption purchases (C), planned investment purchases (I_P), government purchases (G), and net exports (NE):

$$\text{Aggregate purchases} = C + I_P + G + NE$$

In equilibrium,

$$Y = C + I_P + G + NE$$

Consumption depends on the consumption function, which may be written in general as

$$C = A + MPC(DI)$$

where A is autonomous consumption, MPC is the marginal propensity to consume, and DI is disposable income. Assuming the marginal tax rate (t) is constant, disposable income is

$$DI = (1 - t)Y$$

The consumption function can therefore be written as

$$C = A + MPC[(1 - t)Y]$$

Both planned investment and government purchases are assumed to be autonomous purchases independent of income. However, net exports, which represent the difference between exports and imports, do depend on Y because imports vary with income. The expression for net exports is

$$NE = E - MPI(Y)$$

where E is exports and MPI is the marginal propensity to import.

Substituting the preceding equations in the expression for aggregate purchases gives the following equilibrium condition:

$$Y = A + MPC[(1 - t)]Y + I_P + G + [E - MPI(Y)]$$

Solving this equation for Y gives

$$Y = \frac{A + I_P + G + E}{1 - [MPC(1 - t)] + MPI}$$

$$= \frac{A + I_P + G + E}{1 - [MPC(1 - t) - MPI]}$$

$$= \frac{A + I_P + G + E}{1 - MRR}$$

where MRR is the marginal respending rate for the economy.

To check this formula, substitute the values from the table in Box 1 for the variables in the preceding equation for Y to solve for equilibrium real GDP:

$$Y = \frac{\$(400 + 500 + 1,000 + 400)\text{billion}}{1 - 0.8(1 - 0.2) + 0.1} = \frac{\$2,300 \text{ billion}}{0.46} = \$5,000 \text{ billion}$$

which is the same as the result obtained earlier.

The equilibrium condition derived algebraically shows how real GDP depends on autonomous consumption, planned investment, government purchases, and exports, given the marginal propensities to consume and import and the marginal tax rate in the economy. The equation implies that each extra $1 of autonomous purchases (A, I_P, G, or E) will result in $1/(1 - MRR)$ dollars of increase in real GDP, which is the multiplier for the economy.

part V

Money, Financial Markets, and Macroeconomic Equilibrium

CONCEPTS

Money and Near Money

Checkable Deposits

M1, M2, and M3

Demand for Money

Depository Institutions

Fractional Reserve Banking

Required and Excess Reserves

The Monetary Base

Federal Reserve Open Market Operations

Money Supply

Hans Hofmann, *The Gate*, 1959–1960. Solomon R. Guggenheim Museum, New York. Photo: David Heald © Solomon R. Guggenheim Museum, New York

13 chapter

The Functions of Money

Money may not make the world go round, but it sure does lubricate the wheels of exchange. In this chapter we'll explore the functions of money and how the amount in circulation can be measured. We'll examine why people and businesses hold money as an asset rather than using it to make purchases of goods or financial assets such as stocks and bonds. The amount of money in circulation is important because it can affect credit availability, aggregate demand, and the price level in the economy. Finally, we'll see how changes in the supply of money can affect the performance of the economy by influencing interest rates over the short run, aggregate demand, and the price level over the long run. The Federal Reserve System, the nation's central banking authority, uses its control of the nation's money supply to stabilize the economy by influencing aggregate demand.

Historically, many commodities, ranging from precious metals to cigarettes, have been used as money. In most modern societies, however, commodities are rarely used as money. Instead, money consists mainly of paper currency issued by governments and deposits in checking accounts that are accepted as a means of making payments for goods and services.

☐ CONCEPT PREVIEW

After reading this chapter, you should be able to:

1. List the four major functions of money in the economy.

2. Discuss the major components of the money stock in an economy, the concept of *near money,* and the official measures of the U.S. money stock.

3. Discuss the determinants of the demand to hold money.

4. Explain how, given the demand for money, changes in the available money stock can affect credit and interest rates and influence spending decisions and how, given the stock of money, changes in money demand can affect interest rates.

WHAT IS MONEY, AND WHAT ARE ITS FUNCTIONS?

Money is something you've been familiar with throughout your life. In fact, you may already consider yourself an expert on the subject. You regularly use money to measure the value of things you own. You also have some of it (in the form of currency) in your pocket and in bank accounts. It may surprise you to learn that there's a great deal of disagreement among economists about what money is and how to measure it. Money serves a number of functions, and any definition of money must consider all of its functions.

The four major functions of money are to serve as a medium of exchange, a standard of value, a standard of deferred payment, and a store of value. It's useful to begin our analysis of the fascinating concept of money by looking into its functions.

1. *A medium of exchange.* As a generally accepted medium of exchange, money eliminates the need for *barter,* the direct exchange of one item for another. Barter is a very inconvenient means of trading because it requires the *double coincidence of wants.* A trader with a good or service to offer must search for a buyer who has exactly what the trader desires. Under a barter system, for example, if a baker wants meat, he must search for a butcher who wants bread. Because money is generally accepted as payment for any purchase, a baker who sells bread for money can use the money to buy meat or anything else the baker wants. Money facilitates specialization and the division of labor in an economy by avoiding the inconvenience of barter. As a generally accepted medium of exchange, money cuts down on the transaction costs of trading.

2. *A standard of value.* Money provides a unit of account (in the United States it's the dollar) that serves as a standard for the measure of value. The value of an item is a measure of what a person will sacrifice to obtain it. How much is a two-week vacation in Hawaii worth to you? If you're like most people, you'll probably answer this question by valuing the vacation in dollars—say $2,000—rather than in terms of other things (such as your car). Whether or not you're conscious of it, you're constantly valuing items in dollars. You measure your income and the value of things you own in terms of dollars. You measure the opportunity cost of most of your purchases in terms of the dollar values of expenditure on other things. As a *standard of value,* money allows the addition of the values of such diverse items as automobiles and haircuts and of all other goods and services. The concept of GDP would be useless without a standard of value such as the dollar.

3. *A standard of deferred payment.* Many contracts involve promises to make payments in the future. The unit of account for *deferred payment* of debts is money. If you borrow money to buy a car, the loan contract specifies how much money you must pay back per month and the number of such payments that are required to satisfy your obligation. However, money serves its function as a standard of deferred payment only if its purchasing power remains fairly constant over time. If the price level rises, the purchasing power of money will decline over time. Similarly, a decrease in the price level will increase the future purchasing power of money.

4. *A store of value.* Money serves as a store of value that can be quickly converted into goods and services. As the actual medium of exchange, money is completely *liquid,* which means that it can be converted into goods and services without any inconvenience or cost. Other assets that serve as stores of value, such as stocks, bonds, or real estate, must first be liquidated (sold) to be converted into a generally accepted medium of exchange. Costs (such as brokerage fees) and inconvenience (a time delay) are often associated with the liquidation of other assets. Thus, holding money as a store of value can reduce the transaction costs involved in

everyday business. When inflation is present, however, the purchasing power of money declines. In holding money as a store of value, we weigh the gains of doing so against the possibility of loss in its purchasing power from inflation.

In Chapter 5 we offered a simple definition of money that emphasized its role as a medium of exchange. Now we can offer a more comprehensive definition of money that emphasizes its four functions. Money is anything that is generally accepted as payment in exchange for goods or services. It also serves as a standard of value, a standard of deferred payment, and a store of value.

Commodity Money

When you think of money, you probably think of the green dollar bills and coins that are used as currency in the United States. Yet a variety of *commodities* have been used as money in the course of history. Commodity money is an item that serves the functions of money but also has *intrinsic* value as a marketable item in addition to its value as the medium of exchange. In the early days of America, tobacco, corn, and other agricultural commodities were accepted as payment for goods and services. Gold and silver were most commonly used by European and other nations as money throughout much of their history.

Many strange items have cropped up as commodity money. For example, in ancient Russia furs were used as money and stamped pieces of leather were sometimes used as tokens of the furs and circulated as money. The Zulus of South Africa used cattle as money. The American Indians used *wampum,* a form of money consisting of trinkets made out of shells. In Rumania Kent cigarettes were recently used as money for black market transactions! It had to be Kent; no other brand would do! The packs were exchanged unopened, no one would dream of smoking the cigarettes. A Rumanian lighting up a Kent in the mid-1980s would have been considered as crazy as a person who burned dollar bills in the United States.

Fiat Money

Fiat money is money that is accepted as a medium of exchange because of government decree rather than because of its intrinsic value as a commodity. The dirty dollar bill in your pocket is really just a piece of high-quality 100 percent rag paper whose market value is virtually nil. You value it because you know that it will be accepted for a dollar's worth of goods and services at current prices.

In the past U.S. coins were made of silver. However, as the market price of silver increased, the market value of the silver in those coins increased to more than their face value. This meant that the silver in a 50-cent piece was worth more than 50 cents (see Principles in Practice box). Under these circumstances, it was profitable to melt down the coins into silver bullion because they were more valuable as raw silver than as money! Now the market value of the metal in a quarter is only a fraction of a cent.

Paper money was apparently invented by the Chinese in the 13th century. If you're fortunate enough to have paper money in your wallet, pull out a bill and look at it closely. You'll observe, on the dark-colored side, above a picture of a famous American, that the bill is a "Federal Reserve Note." This means it's issued by one of the 12 regional banks of the Federal Reserve System, the central banking system of the United States. Toward the upper left corner you'll see these words: "THIS NOTE IS LEGAL TENDER FOR ALL DEBTS, PUBLIC AND PRIVATE," a proclamation (or decree) by the government that this piece of paper is the legal medium of exchange in the United States. In effect, whenever you purchase an item, you incur a debt to the seller. You can pay off that debt immediately with Federal Reserve notes, which serve as fiat money in the United States.

principles in practice

Silver Coins in the United States

Good Money, Bad Money, and Gresham's Law Less than 30 years ago in this country, it was common for people to hand a teller or cashier a $1 bill, ask "a dollar's worth of silver"—and get it. That's because up until the 1960s dimes, quarters, and half-dollars were actually made of silver.

Those days are gone. There's no silver in the dimes, quarters, and half-dollars used in everyday transactions. When the price of a precious metal rises above its face value as money, the metal becomes more valuable in alternative uses. Silver dimes, quarters, and half-dollars are no longer in circulation because the silver in these coins is worth much more than the denominations of the coins. If such coins were still issued, an enterprising silver firm would find it cheaper to obtain silver by melting down coins than by buying it on the commodity market! Coins today are made of an alloy of nonprecious metal sandwiched around a layer of copper.

Gresham's Law, named after Sir Thomas Gresham, argues that "good money" is driven out of circulation by "bad money." Good money has higher value as a commodity than bad money.

Gresham, an Englishman, lived in the 16th century, when it was common for gold and silver coins to be *debased*. Governments did this by mixing nonprecious metals with the gold and silver. Governments could thus make a profit by issuing coins that had less precious metals than their face value indicated. Because different mintings of coins had varying amounts of gold and silver, even though they bore the same monetary denomination, some coins were *worth more* than others as *commodities*. People who dealt in gold and silver could easily see the difference between the "good money" and the "bad money." Even the common folk could get a rough idea about the value of coins by testing their malleability. Because gold and silver are softer than other metals, this was a good test of the precious metal content of coins. Gresham observed that coins with a higher content of gold and silver were melted down for their precious metal or were hoarded rather than being used in exchange.

In the mid-1960s, when the United States issued new coins to replace silver coins, Gresham's Law went right into action. Whenever a silver coin was found, it was hoarded or sold as silver rather than spent. Of course, old coins were also hoarded because they became valuable as collector's items. In any event it didn't take long for the new nonsilver coins to quickly replace the old coins. The "bad" alloy coins drove the "good" silver coins out of circulation, just as Gresham would have predicted!

Inflation always speeds up the action of Gresham's Law when both commodity money and paper money are used. When the price level rises, the money value of silver or gold rises as well. A bout of inflation therefore increases the rate at which gold and silver coins are hoarded. Today few nations use gold and silver coins for money.

Fiat money, like Federal Reserve notes, can serve the function of money simply because it's generally accepted in exchange for goods and services. Again, look at a Federal Reserve note. Nowhere on the note will you find any promise that the Federal Reserve banks will redeem it for gold, silver, or anything else. Of course, if you take a $20 bill to a Federal Reserve bank, you may be able to exchange it for two $10 bills. You can also use your money to *buy* gold or silver as you would use it to buy any other commodity.

Technically, Federal Reserve notes are a liability (or debt) of the Federal Reserve banks. You'll see in the chapter on the Federal Reserve System that the liabilities of the Federal Reserve banks are balanced by their assets, which include government bonds and some gold. However, by law the Federal Reserve banks are not required to exchange Federal Reserve notes held by the public for anything other than more currency (either paper money or coins).

Monetary authorities in central banks must be careful to keep confidence in money. When the public loses confidence in the official money of a nation, it seeks alternative forms of money. This impairs the functions of money as a medium of exchange, a standard and store of value, and a standard of deferred payment. If you expected rampant inflation, you wouldn't want to hold any money, and whenever you got some, you'd quickly exchange it for commodities whose value would keep up with the inflation rate.

Checkable Deposits as a Form of Money

Federal Reserve notes, along with the coins minted by the federal government, which constitute the nation's *currency,* are not the only means of paying off debts. A check serves the same function as currency because it can be used to pay for purchases and pay off debts. **Checkable deposits** are money deposited in bank accounts that can be used to write checks accepted to pay debts or that can easily be converted to currency. Paying by check has the advantage of safety. A check is made payable to a specific party and must be endorsed by that party before it can be converted to currency or before funds can be transferred from the payer's account to the recipient's account. Paying by check also avoids the risks associated with transporting sums of currency. Thieves find currency a more desirable target than checks, which require endorsement before they can be cashed or deposited.

Checkable deposits are money because they are accepted as a means of payment for goods and services and also perform the other major functions of money. The convenience of paying by check (or electronic transfer of checkable deposits), particularly when large sums of money are involved, explains why, as you'll soon see, the bulk of the money stock is held in the form of checkable deposits rather than currency.

Checkable deposit accounts are offered by various types of specialized firms called *depository institutions*. These institutions are commonly called "banks" and include commercial banks, savings and loan associations, savings banks, and credit unions. **Commercial banks** are firms that acquire funds by accepting checkable deposits and savings deposits from households and business firms and use these funds to make loans. Commercial banks, such as the Chase Manhattan Bank and the Bank of America, make both short-term and long-term loans to businesses and individuals seeking credit. Such banks also extend credit to governments by purchasing government bonds. **Savings and loan associations** are depository institutions that acquire funds chiefly by attracting savings deposits and that in the past specialized in making mortgage loans. **Mutual savings banks** are depository institutions operating in some states that are similar to savings and loan associations because they primarily attract savings deposits and in the past specialized in making mortgage loans. Mutual savings banks are owned by their depositors and are concentrated in New York State and the New England states. **Credit unions** are depository institutions whose depositors, called *members,* belong to a particular organization such as a business firm or government. Credit unions make loans only to their members for the purpose of financing homes or personal goods and services (such as cars). Savings and loan associations, mutual savings banks, and credit unions are called "thrift institutions" because they encourage saving by households and small businesses.

Prior to the late 1970s, checkable deposits in the United States were mainly available at commercial banks. Up to that time, funds in checkable deposits didn't earn interest. Since that time, changes and reforms in the U.S. financial industry have allowed thrift institutions to issue checkable deposits and have modified the restrictions on the types of loans that all depository institutions can make. Checkable deposits are now available at thrift institutions as well as commercial banks, and some checkable deposit accounts pay interest. For example, checkable deposits are available at savings and loan associations and mutual saving banks as *NOW* (nego-

checkable deposits money deposited in bank accounts that can be used to write checks accepted to pay debts or that can easily be converted to currency.

commercial banks firms that acquire funds by accepting checkable deposits and savings deposits from households and business firms and use these funds to make loans to businesses and individuals.

savings and loan associations depository institutions that acquire funds chiefly by attracting savings deposits and that in the past specialized in making mortgage loans.

mutual savings banks depository institutions operating in some states that are similar to savings and loan associations in that they primarily attract savings deposits and in the past specialized in making mortgage loans.

credit unions depository institutions whose depositors belong to a particular organization. Credit unions make loans only to their members.

tiable order of withdrawal) *accounts,* which permit writing checks on the sums deposited in interest-bearing savings accounts.[1] Commercial banks offer *ATS* (automatic transfer of savings) *accounts,* which transfer funds from an interest-bearing savings account to a non-interest-bearing checking account when a check is written. The funds in an ATS account therefore earn interest until checks written on the checking account result in the transfer of funds from the savings account to the checking account. *Demand deposits* are non-interest-bearing checkable deposits held at commercial banks. Over two thirds of demand deposits at commercial banks are held by business firms. These demand deposits largely represent the deposit accounts of corporations.

The nation's total checkable deposits are the sums in demand deposits, NOW accounts, ATS accounts, and other checkable deposits.

What Money Is Not

You should review the preceding discussions of money and its function and make sure you understand how the functions of money can be used to define *money* itself. Be careful not to confuse money with other important economic concepts. Although money is a store of value, it is not a productive input. Do not confuse money with capital. Money can be used to purchase investment goods that add to the nation's capital stock. However, this is simply because money *is* the medium of exchange. Also, do not confuse money with bonds and other debts of corporations. Bonds can be sold for money, but in themselves they are not a medium of exchange. **Bonds** are securities issued by corporations and governments representing the promise to make periodic payments of interest and to repay borrowed funds at a certain time.

Do not confuse money with income. Income is measured as a *flow* of dollars over a given period. It's convenient to measure income as a money sum because, after all, money is the standard of value. However, money itself is merely an asset that is held mainly in bank accounts and as currency in people's pockets and purses or in vaults.

Do not confuse credit cards with money. If you've ever used a credit card, you know it's accepted almost as readily as currency as a means of purchasing goods and services. However, when you make a purchase with a credit card, you are really incurring a debt that must be paid with money at a later time. Most credit card companies give you a specified period in which to repay your loan. After that period has elapsed, you must pay interest on your debt. You cannot use credit cards as a store of value. But credit cards have allowed many Americans to economize on the amount of money they hold. Rather than having to use money in checkable deposits *each day* for purchases, they can hold more bonds and other interest-bearing assets that they liquidate on a monthly rather than daily basis to pay their credit card bills.

bonds securities issued by corporations and governments representing the promise to make periodic payments of interest and to repay borrowed funds at a certain time.

MEASURING THE STOCK OF MONEY

Money is a stock rather than a flow. A *stock* is a variable that can be measured only at a given point in time. For example, the stock of money can be measured as the amount held by the public on a certain day. The stock of money can vary from day to day with conditions of supply and demand. To delve further into the mysteries of money, let's examine the method used to measure the stock of money available at a given point in time.

[2]

---

[1] Credit unions issue checkable deposits similar to NOW accounts. Checkable deposits issued by credit unions are called *share draft accounts.*

Measuring the Money Stock: M1

M1 a measure of the money stock that includes only currency and account balances commonly used to pay for goods and services; the sum of the currency, traveler's checks, and checkable deposits.

The Federal Reserve System has developed several measures of the money stock. The narrowest measure includes only items that serve as a medium of exchange. **M1** is a measure of the money stock that includes only currency and account balances commonly used in payment for purchases of goods and services. M1 is the sum of the currency, traveler's checks, and checkable deposits held by the public.

Box 1 shows the components of the money stock measured as M1 based on daily averages of the amounts actually held by the public during November 1992. You may be surprised to learn that currency constitutes only a bit more than one fourth of the available dollars used as a means of payment. Checkable deposits are by far the most important component of the available stock of money. Demand deposits at commercial banks and other checkable deposits, mainly NOW and ATS accounts held at commercial banks and thrift institutions, accounted for 80 percent of the money stock. Traveler's checks outstanding (such as those issued by the American Express Company) are a very small part of M1, accounting for less than 1 percent of the money stock.

Adding Near Money to M1: M2

near monies assets that are easily converted to money because they can be liquidated at low cost and little risk of loss.

Deposits in noncheckable savings accounts, certificates of deposit, bonds, and other types of financial assets are usually not considered to be money because they cannot readily be used to make payments. These assets must be *liquidated* into currency or demand deposits before the sum they represent can be used to make payments. **Near monies** are assets that are easily converted into money because they can be liquidated at low cost and little risk of loss.

M2 a measure of money including M1 and liquid assets that cannot be used directly as a medium of exchange but can be easily converted into checkable deposits or other components of M1. The sum of M1 and certain near monies.

Because near monies can be easily converted into money, some economists prefer to include them in a measure of the nation's stock of liquid assets available to make purchases. The Federal Reserve System measures the sum of M1 and certain near monies to obtain a measure of liquid assets held by the public that constitute a store of readily available purchasing power. **M2** is a broader measure of money than M1. It includes M1 and liquid assets that cannot be used directly as a medium of exchange but can be easily converted into checkable deposits or other components of M1. M2 is the sum of M1 and certain near monies:

$$M2 = M1 + \text{Money market deposit accounts at banks} + \text{Money market mutual fund accounts} + \text{Savings accounts and small-denomination certificates of deposit} + \text{Certain other near monies}$$

time deposits interest-bearing accounts at commercial banks and thrift institutions for which the bank can legally request a 30-day notice before paying out the funds.

Money market mutual fund accounts, offered by investment companies, give owners a share in financial assets and allow them limited check-writing privileges on their accounts. Savings accounts are noncheckable savings deposits. Certificates of deposit (CDs) are deposits made in banks for a specified time, with a penalty charged for early withdrawal. Savings deposits and certificates of deposit are examples of **time deposits,** which are interest-bearing accounts at a commercial bank or a thrift institution for which the bank can legally request a 30-day notice before paying out the funds. In practice, banks rarely ask for the 30-day notice, but they do have the legal right to do so. Only insured certificates of deposit in amounts less than $100,000 are included in M2. Certificates of deposit in excess of $100,000 are not insured by an agency of the federal government. The other near monies mainly include certain types of debts issued by commercial banks.

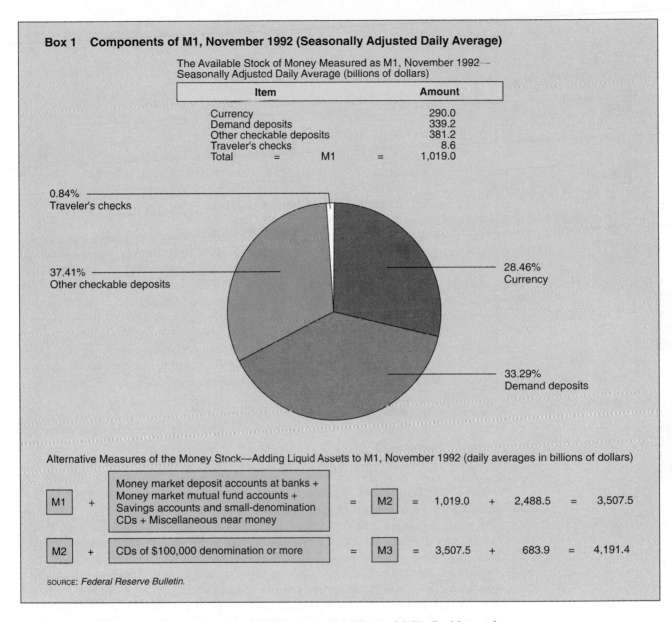

Box 1   Components of M1, November 1992 (Seasonally Adjusted Daily Average)

The Available Stock of Money Measured as M1, November 1992—
Seasonally Adjusted Daily Average (billions of dollars)

Item	Amount
Currency	290.0
Demand deposits	339.2
Other checkable deposits	381.2
Traveler's checks	8.6
Total = M1 =	1,019.0

0.84%
Traveler's checks

37.41%
Other checkable deposits

28.46%
Currency

33.29%
Demand deposits

Alternative Measures of the Money Stock—Adding Liquid Assets to M1, November 1992 (daily averages in billions of dollars)

M1 + Money market deposit accounts at banks + Money market mutual fund accounts + Savings accounts and small-denomination CDs + Miscellaneous near money = M2 = 1,019.0 + 2,488.5 = 3,507.5

M2 + CDs of $100,000 denomination or more = M3 = 3,507.5 + 683.9 = 4,191.4

SOURCE: *Federal Reserve Bulletin.*

The table in Box 1 shows the relationship between M1 and M2. In November 1992, average daily balances of funds included in M2 amounted to 3.5 times M1! Going one step further, you can add the large-denomination certificates of deposit and other large-denomination liquid assets to M2 to obtain still another measure of the stock of liquid assets held by the public called **M3.**

M3 = M2 + Large-denomination ($100,000 or more) certificates of deposit and other large-denomination liquid assets

M3 the sum of M2 and large-denomination ($100,000 or more) certificates of deposit and other large-denomination liquid assets.

Throughout this book we will be referring to M1 when we discuss the money stock. Although M2 and M3 are good measures of liquid assets available to the public, they include assets that cannot be readily used to make payments, such as savings deposits, and therefore cannot fulfill all the functions of money.

- List the four functions of money, and explain how funds in your checking account fulfill these functions.

- Which functions of money are not fulfilled by funds in your savings accounts?

- What is included in M1 as a measure of the nation's money stock? How does M2 differ from M1?

THE DEMAND FOR MONEY

3 Why do people desire to hold demand deposits and currency? After all, holding these two forms of money deprives them of the opportunity to earn interest on the sum held. Similarly, money held in the form of interest-bearing checkable deposits usually earns less interest than can be earned on near monies, bonds, and other less liquid assets that can be purchased with money.

The *opportunity cost* of holding a dollar in money over the year is the interest income that is forgone. For example, if you can earn 8 percent per year in a savings account, the opportunity cost of holding a dollar in cash is 8 cents over the year, assuming interest is computed once annually. The higher the interest rate you can earn in the next best alternative you have, such as investing in bonds or certificates of deposit, the greater the opportunity cost of holding money.

People hold money because they receive benefits from doing so. In deciding how much to hold, people consider both the benefits and the costs of holding money. In the following sections we analyze the benefits of holding money and we look at various motives for choosing to hold money as an asset.

Transaction Demand for Money

At any given level of interest rates, people demand a certain amount of money to carry out the basic transactions associated with everyday business. The level of interest rates is an average of a broad array of interest rates that can be earned on a variety of assets. The greater the dollar volume of transactions during the year, the greater the sum of money that is willingly held each day over the year at each possible level of interest rates.

By holding money, you avoid the inconvenience and the possible embarrassment of settling your debts late. You also avoid the need to incur other costs involved in liquidating assets to make payments. For example, suppose you have both a savings account and a checking account. To pay for your periodic purchases, you must be sure to have at least a minimum amount of currency and checkable deposits on hand. Your savings deposits do you little good as a means of payment unless you go to the bank and transfer some of these funds to your checking account or withdraw them as currency. The **transaction demand for money** is the sum of money people want to hold per day as a convenience in paying their everyday bills. The benefit of holding money in this form is the avoidance of the transaction costs of converting other assets into currency and checkable deposits.

Suppose you're paid once a month, your expenses require daily expenditure of money, and you don't borrow to meet any of your expenses. You can deposit *all* of your monthly money income in a savings account on the day you're paid to avoid the loss in interest income associated with holding it. However, every time you need to pay for an item, you'll have to go to the bank and wait in line to convert some of your savings deposits into checkable deposits or currency. In some cases you may incur penalties for early withdrawal that reduce your interest income. The time (the trip to the bank, for example) and the money costs involved in liquidating the savings deposits are your transaction costs. In managing the money you keep for transac-

transaction demand for money the sum of money people want to hold per day as a convenience in paying their bills.

tions, you must weigh these transaction costs against the income you forgo by holding money instead of interest-bearing assets. You may decide to always keep a certain sum each month as checkable deposits and currency rather than as less liquid assets. The interest you forgo by doing so is worth less to you than the inconvenience of having to liquidate those assets to make payments every day.

The yearly transaction demand for money at any given level of interest rates depends on the dollar volume of transactions over the year. In general, the greater the level of nominal GDP over the year, the greater the transaction demand for money. After all, if your monthly bills increase from $1,000 to $1,500 this year, you'll need to hold more money to make payments. Similarly, when nominal GDP increases from $6,000 billion to $7,000 billion per year, the transaction demand for money in the economy also increases even if interest rates don't change.

Money as an Asset

Money is one of many alternative assets people can choose to hold as a store of purchasing power. In deciding how much money to hold, people weigh the opportunity cost of holding it against the purchasing power of the interest income they forgo by doing so. However, benefits are associated with holding money rather than holding alternative assets. In deciding how much of a money stock to hold, people weigh the marginal benefits of holding additional money against the marginal cost of doing so.

The main advantage of money over alternative assets is its liquidity. Many people usually find that the benefits of holding money are worth the opportunity cost of doing so. By holding money, they have an asset they can quickly and conveniently draw upon to make payments when emergencies arise. People also hold money because of uncertainty about future flows of income and required payments. They hold it as a *precaution* against lack of synchronization between inflow of income and outflow of payments. You never know when your income over a certain period will fall short of the bills you must meet over that period. Holding money allows you to make payments quickly even when your income falls short of your expenditures. Would you run the risk of letting your checking account balance run down to zero and encountering embarrassing delays in meeting your bills?

Business firms have a similar precautionary motive for holding money. They do so to ensure a way of quickly paying their bills even when their cash receipts from sales are abnormally low. Because receipts of income and the due dates of bills are rarely synchronized, no household or business firm can expect to have income readily available to pay bills exactly at the time the bills come due.

Another reason why people hold money has to do with uncertainty about the future level of prices and interest rates in the economy. Although financial assets such as stocks and bonds yield income, the prices of these assets fluctuate with economic conditions. Therefore, people evaluate the riskiness of stocks, bonds, and other assets by trying to forecast movements in their prices. Considering economic conditions, people often find money an attractive alternative to stocks and bonds. In periods during which bond prices are expected to fall, other things being equal, the stock of money that people want to hold is likely to increase. Uncertainty concerning the future prices of stocks and bonds leads to a *speculative* motive for holding money.

For example, suppose that people expect stock and bond prices to fall in the future. In that case they may hold money instead of stocks and bonds. A modest positive return on money may be better than a negative return on stocks and bonds! Typically, the speculative demand for money increases when the prices of such assets as stock, bonds, or real estate are expected to fall. When the speculative demand for money increases, people try to hold more money and less alternative assets. Conversely, when it is generally believed that the prices of assets such as stock, bonds, and real estate will rise in the future, the speculative demand for money decreases. When the speculative demand for money decreases, people seek to hold less money and increase their demand for alternative assets.

The Money Demand Curve

demand for money the relationship between the sums of money people willingly hold and the level of interest rates in the economy, given all the other influences on the desirability of holding money instead of other assets.

The **demand for money** is the relationship between the sums of money that people willingly hold and the level of interest rates in the economy, given *all other influences* on the desirability of holding money instead of other assets. Among the other influences on the demand for money, aside from the level of nominal interest rates in the economy, are all the factors that affect the transaction, precautionary, and speculative demand for money. Among these factors are the degree to which payments and receipts can be synchronized in the economy, expectations about future levels of interest rates, stock and bond prices, inflation, and the level of nominal GDP.

money demand curve a curve that shows a relationship between the level of interest rates in the economy and the stock of money demanded at a given point in time.

A **money demand curve** shows a relationship between the level of interest rates in the economy and the stock of money demanded at a given point in time. In effect, the cost of holding a dollar is measured by the interest rate because the interest forgone on money balances is the opportunity cost of holding money. The higher the level of interest rates in the economy, the greater the opportunity cost of holding money and the lower the quantity of money demanded.

The graph in Box 2 shows a money demand curve that illustrates how the stock of money demanded on a given day varies inversely with the level of interest rates. The lower the interest rate, the lower the opportunity cost of holding money and the greater the quantity of money demanded on any given day as balances in checkable deposits or as currency. The actual responsiveness of the desired stock of money to changes in the level of interest rates is hotly debated among economists. Some economists believe the money demand curve looks like the one in Box 2. Other economists believe the money demand curve is nearly vertical, which implies that changes in the level of interest rates have little effect on the quantity of money demanded.

Changes in Money Demand

change in money demand a change, caused by a change in economic conditions, in the relationship between the level of interest rates and the stock of money demanded in the economy.

A **change in money demand** is a change, caused by a change in economic conditions, in the relationship between the level of interest rates and the stock of money demanded in the economy. When there's a change in money demand, the entire demand curve for money shifts inward or outward. A change in the transaction demand for money at any given interest rate level results in a change in money demand. As pointed out earlier, a change in nominal GDP results in a change in the transaction demand for money. Nominal GDP increases when either real GDP or the price level goes up. It follows that either an increase in real GDP or an increase in the price level shifts the money demand curve outward, as shown in graph **A** in Box 3. Similarly, a decrease in real GDP or a decrease in the price level shifts the money demand curve inward, as shown in graph **B**.

Given the price level, it's therefore reasonable to expect an increase in real GDP to increase money demand. During periods of economic expansion, the money demand curve shifts outward. Similarly, given the price level, decreases in real GDP imply decreases in the demand for money. During periods of contraction or recession, it's therefore reasonable to expect the demand for money to decrease.

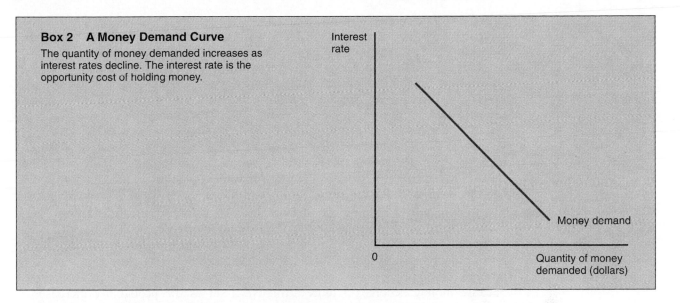

Box 2   A Money Demand Curve

The quantity of money demanded increases as interest rates decline. The interest rate is the opportunity cost of holding money.

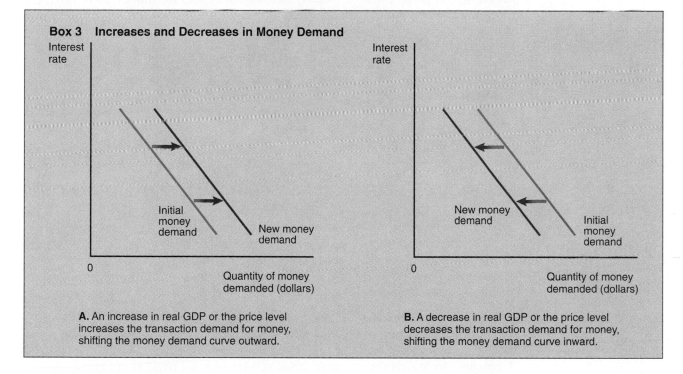

Box 3   Increases and Decreases in Money Demand

A. An increase in real GDP or the price level increases the transaction demand for money, shifting the money demand curve outward.

B. A decrease in real GDP or the price level decreases the transaction demand for money, shifting the money demand curve inward.

The money demand curve can also shift in response to other changes in economic conditions. For example, the invention of automatic teller machines has reduced the transaction cost of obtaining currency. You can now easily obtain currency from your savings account even when banks are closed. This innovation has probably affected your demand to hold currency and checkable deposits.

The proliferation of credit cards is another financial innovation that has affected the demand for money. With a credit card you can consolidate many bills into one bill that you can pay each month, and if you pay it in full, you'll incur no interest expense. By using a credit card, you can hold less money in checkable deposits and more in savings accounts or money market accounts that yield interest. You can then withdraw funds from these accounts as needed to meet credit card bills.

A decrease in the transaction cost of converting near money into money decreases the demand for money. The cost of converting bonds, savings deposits, and other assets into currency and checkable deposits falls when the time required to do so or the penalties involved in doing so are reduced. People hold less money when the transaction costs of converting near money into money fall, because it's then less advantageous to hold money. They therefore shift some of their wealth to bonds and near money. A decrease in the transaction cost of converting near money into money thus shifts the money demand curve inward. Similarly, an increase in the transaction cost of converting near money into money shifts the money demand curve outward.

The demand for money also changes with changes in the risk associated with holding assets other than money. For example, in periods when bond prices are expected to rise, the demand for money is likely to decline as people seek to hold lower money balances at any given interest rate so they can acquire more bonds. If, however, bond prices are expected to fall, the demand for money is likely to increase because money becomes a more attractive asset as the probability increases of incurring a loss from holding bonds. The demand curve for money therefore shifts inward when bond prices are expected to rise and shifts outward when bond prices are expected to fall.

THE STOCK OF MONEY, MONEY DEMAND, AND INTEREST RATES

4 Given the demand for money, changes in the money stock available can affect the interest rate level for the economy over short periods of time. To understand the link between the available stock of money and interest rates each day, assume the price level, real GDP, and all the other determinants of money demand are fixed in the short run. These assumptions simplify the analysis by ensuring that the money demand curve doesn't shift at the same time the available stock of money shifts.

The Effect of an Increase in the Available Money Stock

Suppose the stock of money available on average each day in January is $600 billion and this is exactly equal to the quantity demanded at the current interest rate level of 8 percent. In March the available stock of money is up to $700 billion on average each day. If the interest rate remains at 8 percent, there will be no change in the quantity of money demanded. This means that the $700 billion stock of money available will exceed the $600 billion demanded at the 8 percent interest rate level.

The graph in Box 4 shows the excess stock of money at the 8 percent interest rate. What will holders of the excess $100 billion worth of money seek to do with it? They could put the extra funds in savings accounts or use them to buy bonds. Everyone tries to get rid of the excess money, but like a hot potato it ends up in someone's hands or checking account whenever it's used to buy bonds. As banks find they have more funds on deposit than they had before the money stock increased, the supply of

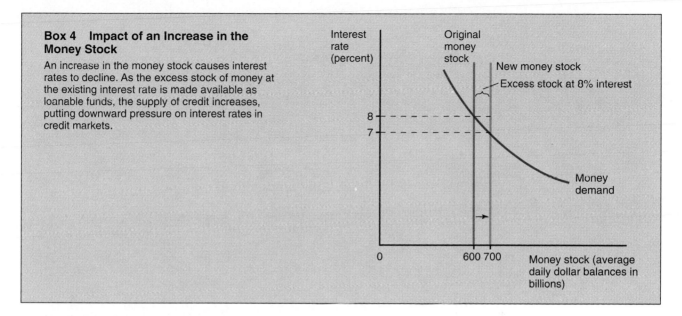

Box 4   Impact of an Increase in the Money Stock

An increase in the money stock causes interest rates to decline. As the excess stock of money at the existing interest rate is made available as loanable funds, the supply of credit increases, putting downward pressure on interest rates in credit markets.

funds available for loans increases. The increased supply of loanable funds puts downward pressure on interest rates. At lower interest rates, the opportunity cost of holding money is also lower and the existing larger stock is willingly held. In the graph in Box 4, the increase in the available stock of money will be willingly held only if the market rate of interest falls to 7 percent. Other things being equal, an increase in the available stock of money must increase the supply of credit and put downward pressure on the level of interest rates. Over a short period, therefore, given the level of nominal GDP, the price level, and the other determinants of money demand, the immediate effect of an increase in the available supply of money is a decrease in interest rates in the economy. The lower interest rates will encourage more purchases of investment goods and thus will increase aggregate demand and put upward pressure on real GDP.[2]

The Effect of a Decrease in the Available Money Stock

Other things being equal, a decrease in the available stock of money puts upward pressure on the interest rate in the short run. Given the money demand curve, a decrease in the available stock of money results in a shortage (excess demand) of money available at the current interest rate. The graph in Box 5 shows the impact of a decrease in the supply of money from $600 billion per day to $500 billion per day. The initial equilibrium interest rate is 8 percent. As the available stock of money decreases, the quantity available at the 8 percent interest rate will fall short of the quantity demanded. There will be a $100 billion excess demand for money. How will the difference between the quantity the public wants to hold and the quantity available be made up? Individuals and corporations will seek to liquidate near money such as bonds so as to add funds to their money balances. As the public tries to increase its holdings of money, the funds available for credit and new bonds will decrease. The decrease in the supply of loanable funds will then put upward pressure

---

[2] As you'll see in the chapter entitled "Stabilization of the Economy through Monetary Policy," the long-run effects of an increase in the available supply of money are more complex because over longer periods of time the added money stock could also increase the price level.

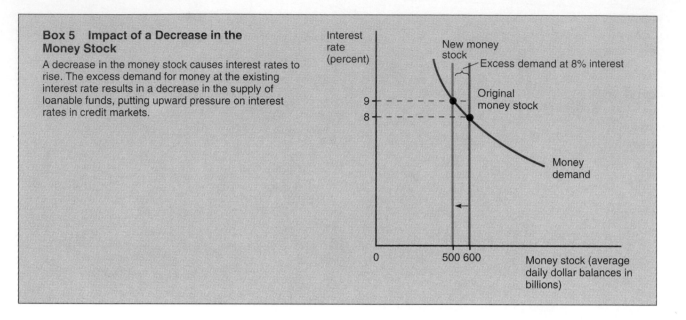

Box 5   Impact of a Decrease in the Money Stock

A decrease in the money stock causes interest rates to rise. The excess demand for money at the existing interest rate results in a decrease in the supply of loanable funds, putting upward pressure on interest rates in credit markets.

on interest rates, which will continue to rise until the reduced money stock is willingly held without further liquidation of near monies. In the graph, interest rates must rise to 9 percent before the quantity demanded declines to equal the $500 billion of available money per day. Decreases in the stock of money therefore put upward pressure on interest rates in the short run. The higher interest rates reduce the availability of credit in the economy. This is likely to put downward pressure on aggregate demand over a longer period and therefore tends to reduce real GDP.

How Shifts in Money Demand Can Affect Interest Rates

Given the available stock of money, an increase in money demand puts upward pressure on interest rates. An increase in money demand can be caused by an increase in real GDP, the price level, or the transaction costs of converting other assets into money or by expectations that the prices of bonds and other assets will fall.

The graph in Box 6 illustrates the effect of an increase in money demand on interest rates, assuming a fixed stock of money. As the money demand curve shifts outward, interest rates tend to rise, other things being equal. For example, an expanding economy in which real GDP is increasing is likely to be characterized by upward pressure on interest rates because the transaction demand for money increases during the expansion. An increasing price level will also increase money demand and puts upward pressure on interest rates.

You can expect downward pressure on interest rates as an economy moves into a recession, because a decline in real GDP reduces the transaction demand for money and shifts the money demand curve inward. If there is no change in the money stock, the interest rate will fall, as shown in the graph in Box 7. Similarly, a decrease in the transaction costs of converting near money into money puts downward pressure on interest rates over a short period, because the decrease in these transaction costs means the demand curve for money shifts inward.

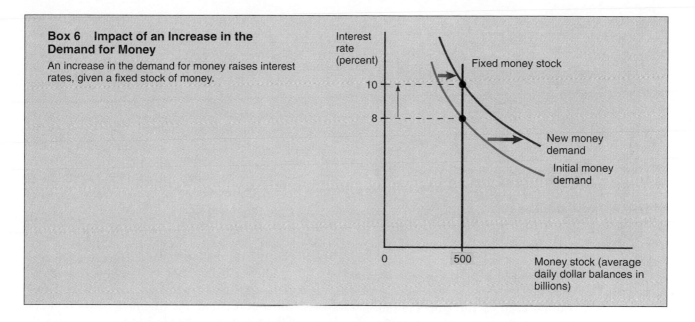

Box 6   Impact of an Increase in the Demand for Money

An increase in the demand for money raises interest rates, given a fixed stock of money.

Interest rate (percent)

Fixed money stock

10

8

New money demand

Initial money demand

0   500

Money stock (average daily dollar balances in billions)

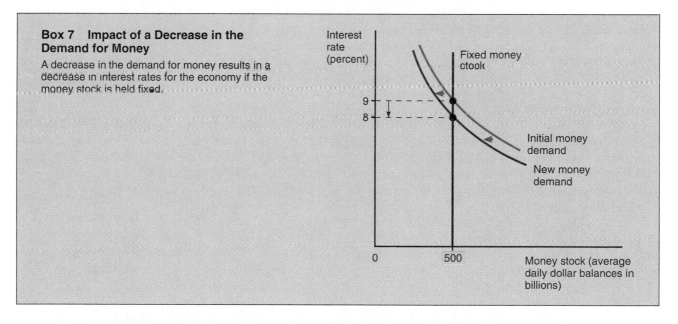

Box 7   Impact of a Decrease in the Demand for Money

A decrease in the demand for money results in a decrease in interest rates for the economy if the money stock is held fixed.

Interest rate (percent)

Fixed money stock

9

8

Initial money demand

New money demand

0   500

Money stock (average daily dollar balances in billions)

- Why does an increase in the stock of money put downward pressure on interest rates, given all the influences on money demand?

- Why does a decrease in the stock of money exert upward pressure on interest rates when money demand is fixed?

- Given the available stock of money (M1), how will money demand and interest rates be affected by an increase in the transaction costs of converting near money into money?

CONCEPT CHECK
◻

the global economy

Eurodollars

How the U.S. Dollar Circulates Overseas as a Medium of Exchange The U.S. dollar is an *international reserve currency* that is often used by foreigners in international transactions not involving U.S. traders. Its status has created a huge "offshore" demand for U.S. currency and checkable deposits. For example, oil and coal are always priced in U.S. dollars when they are sold on international markets. An Italian firm buying crude oil from Saudi Arabia pays in dollars. The Saudis then hold the dollars as deposits in foreign or U.S. banks until they are ready to spend them. Similarly, in nations in which the official foreign exchange rate of the national currency is set at artificially high levels or is not freely convertible into other currencies, many international and domestic transactions involve trades of goods or services for U.S. dollars. Foreigners visiting Russia and Eastern European nations are often amazed by the amount of U.S. dollars that circulate as money within those nations. The dollar is also heavily used in nations with high inflation.

Because a substantial demand for dollars exists overseas, an organized market has developed. *Eurodollars* are deposits denominated in U.S. dollars at banks and other financial institutions outside the United States. The name "Eurodollar" was coined because most of these foreign deposits of dollars were located at banks in Western Europe. Today, however, similar deposits held in other parts of the world are also referred to as "Eurodollars." For example, a large French corporation creates a Eurodollar account when it deposits in its Paris bank a $2 million check denominated in U.S. dollars.

The *Eurodollar market* is a market in foreign nations for exchange of bank deposits denominated in U.S. dollars. The total amount of Eurodollars outstanding is over $1 trillion dollars! The principal center for trading Eurodollars is London; however, Eurodollars are also traded extensively in Hong Kong, Singapore, and the Bahamas. Many U.S. banks with foreign branches in Europe actively compete for Eurodollars, which are easily transferred to the United States, where they can be used by U.S. banks to make loans. In recent years Eurodollars have been used by U.S. banks to extend credit in the United States amounting to more than $100 billion per year.

The prime buyers in the Eurodollar market are large corporations that usually purchase a minimum of $1 million in each transaction. Foreigners can also purchase "Eurodollar bonds," which are bonds denominated in dollars and traded in Europe.

Eurodollars are not included in the M1 definition of the money stock. However, some Eurodollars held by U.S. residents are included in both M2 and M3. The demand for Eurodollars adds to the overall demand for U.S. money. Changes in that demand can have some impact on U.S. interest rates.

THE NEED TO UNDERSTAND CHANGES IN THE MONEY STOCK

As you can see, the demand for money and the available stock of money exert an important influence on interest rates in the economy. The impact of changes in the money stock on the economy is complex, because changes in interest rates are likely to affect aggregate demand. Consumers find it more attractive to borrow as interest rates decline, so they spend more on homes, cars, and other durable goods. Similarly, business firms find it more attractive to make investments as interest rates decline. As a result, over longer periods, changes in the national money stock are likely to affect nominal GDP. As nominal GDP changes, so does the demand for money.

The next step in our quest to understand how the economy works is to examine the process by which the money stock changes in the economy. To do this, we need to begin an in-depth look at the nation's financial system and to learn how banks conduct their business. We also need to examine how the Federal Reserve System, the central bank of the United States, regulates the financial system and affects the ability of financial institutions to make loans and provide credit in financial markets. Once you understand how the financial system operates, you can begin to see how the policies pursued by the Federal Reserve System can influence macroeconomic equilibrium in the nation. Our goal in the next two chapters therefore is to develop the necessary background for an economic analysis of the impact on real GDP and the price level of policies that affect the money supply.

SUMMARY

1. Money serves four basic functions—medium of exchange, standard of deferred payment, and store of value. Currency is the paper money and coins that serve as a medium of exchange. Paper money in the United States is issued by Federal Reserve banks. Checkable deposits represent money held in checking accounts that can be used to pay debts or can be converted to currency.

2. M1 is a measure of the money stock that consists of the sum of checkable deposits and currency held by the public on average each day over a certain period.

3. Near monies are assets that can be liquidated at low cost and little risk of loss. An asset is liquidated when it is redeemed for currency or a checkable deposit. M2 is a broader measure of the money stock than M1, representing the sum of M1 and certain near monies.

4. The opportunity cost of holding a dollar of money over a year is the interest income that is forgone by doing so.

5. The demand for money is the relationship between the sums of money that people willingly hold and the level of interest rates, given all the other influences on the desirability of holding money instead of other assets. Money is held for precautionary and speculative motives and also to facilitate transactions. Money is part of the stock of wealth existing in the economy at a certain point in time.

6. A money demand curve shows a relationship between the level of interest rates in the economy and the stock of money demanded on a given day. The interest rate measures the cost of holding each dollar in terms of the annual interest income forgone.

7. The transaction demand for money is the sum that people wish to hold per day as a convenience in paying their everyday bills. Holding money economizes on the transaction costs of liquidating alternative assets to make payments. In general, the greater the nominal GDP over the year, the greater the transaction demand for money.

8. A decrease in the transaction costs of converting near money into money decreases the demand for money.

9. Changes in the available stock of money are likely to result in changes in the level of interest rates in the economy, given the demand for money. An increase in the stock of money is likely to increase the supply of loanable funds as holders of money use the excess supply of money at the current interest rate level to buy bonds and extend credit. This puts downward pressure on interest rates. Similarly, a decrease in the stock of money puts upward pressure on interest rates.

10. The level of interest rates in the economy can be affected by shifts in the demand for money. An increase in money demand puts upward pressure on interest rates, while a decrease in money demand puts downward pressure on interest rates.

KEY TERMS

money *302*
commodity money *302*
fiat money *302*
checkable deposits *304*
commercial banks *304*

savings and loan
  associations *304*
mutual savings banks *304*
credit unions *304*
bonds *305*

M1 *306*
near monies *306*
M2 *306*
time deposits *306*
M3 *307*

transaction demand for
  money *308*
demand for money *310*
money demand curve *310*
change in money
  demand *310*

CONCEPT REVIEW

1 What is money?

2 How does the M1 measure of the money stock differ from the M2 measure?

3 What can cause a change in money demand?

4 Explain why interest rates change when the demand for money changes while the stock of money is fixed.

PROBLEMS AND APPLICATIONS

1. What is the difference between commodity money and fiat money? Explain why U.S. currency is fiat money. **1**

2. Explain how currency and checkable deposits fulfill the functions of money for the U.S. economy. What are some advantages of currency and checkable deposits over gold and silver as a form of money? What are some disadvantages of currency and checkable deposits compared to commodity money? **1**

3. Suppose you open an account with a mutual fund composed of corporate bonds. The company managing the mutual fund gives you a checkbook that allows you to write checks against the market value of the bonds in the account. Is the value of the assets held in the mutual fund part of M1? **2**

4. Suppose inflation is expected to heat up in the future. How does inflation affect the function of money as a medium of exchange, standard of value, and store of purchasing power? **1**

5. What can U.S. currency be redeemed for if it is presented to the U.S. Treasury or a Federal Reserve bank? **1**

6. The level of interest rates in the economy increases on average over the year from 6 percent to 8 percent.

What effect will this change have on the quantity of money demanded? **3**

7. Explain how a decrease in the level of interest rates affects the quantity of money demanded in the economy. **3**

8. Nominal GDP is $5,000 billion, and the average daily stock of money measured by M1 during the year is $1,000 billion. What is likely to happen to the demand for money and interest rates if, as a result of an increase in government purchases, nominal GDP increases to $5,500 billion and M1 is held fixed at $1,000 billion? **2** , **4**

9. Use a graph to show how a decrease in the demand for money will affect interest rates if the money stock is held fixed. **3**

10. This year there is a 10 percent reduction in the stock of money measured as M1. Use a graph to show how the reduction in the stock of money will affect the quantity of money demanded and the equilibrium level of interest rates in credit markets. How could such a sharp reduction in the money supply precipitate a recession? **4**

inside information

Federal Reserve Bulletin The Federal Reserve System is the U.S. central banking authority. It influences the availability of money, credit, and the level of interest rates in the economy. It also collects and publish the data on which the decisions are based.

Information collected by the Federal Reserve System is published monthly in the *Federal Reserve Bulletin*. Each issue contains financial and business statistics along with reports on monetary policy, economic studies by the staff of the Federal Reserve System, and other information relating to production, income, banking, and monetary policy in the United States.

The *Federal Reserve Bulletin* is available at your college or university library. You will find it an important resource as you study money and banking, the topics in this part of your text. For example, check the *Bulletin* to obtain current information on the money stock in the United States. Look for information on liquid assets held by the public and on the assets and liabilities of U.S. banks and other depository institutions. The *Bulletin* publishes information

on the types of loans made by banks—how banks extend and allocate credit to governments, businesses, real estate, and individuals. You can find the reserve requirements for deposits of various maturities and amounts.

A considerable amount of data on financial markets is published in each issue of the *Bulletin*. You can discover how business firms are financing their purchases through banks and through direct lending in financial markets. You can also get facts about current interest rates, the stock market, real estate loans, and consumer credit.

The *Bulletin* contains data on federal budget receipts and outlays, federal debt, and the federal government's creditors. It also has data on industrial production, capacity utilization of plants, construction activity, and prices. Among the important international statistics you can find are data on foreign exchange rates, interest rates in foreign nations, the liabilities of U.S. banks and citizens to foreigners, and the claims U.S. banks and citizens have on foreign assets.

chapter 14

The Banking System

How old were you when you opened your first savings account? If you were grade-school age, you probably had a child's-eye view of the bank as a vast place where the coins and crumpled bills you handed the teller were stored in a box neatly labeled with your name. When you wanted to make a withdrawal, the teller would take down your box from a high shelf, remove the amount of money you requested, and replace the box.

You've long since discovered that banks are far more than a cool, dry place to store money. But how exactly do banks function—and where does money come from?

In this chapter we concentrate on the activities of banks. In the following chapter we'll explicitly consider the role in the economy played by the central bank of the United States, the Federal Reserve System.

□ CONCEPT PREVIEW

After reading this chapter, you should be able to:

1. Discuss the origins of banking and explain the concept of fractional reserve banking.

2. Examine the balance sheets of a bank and show how the balance sheets are affected when the bank makes loans.

3. Show how multiple expansion of the money stock can result from an inflow of excess reserves into banks and calculate the reserve multiplier.

4. Discuss bank portfolio management practices.

BANKING

11

depository institutions
institutions that make
loans and offer checkable
deposit and time deposit
accounts for use by
households and business
firms.

In the preceding chapter we saw that the bulk of the money stock, measured as M1, at any given point in time is held as checkable deposits in depository institutions. **Depository institutions** are those that make loans and offer checkable deposit and time deposit accounts for use by households and business firms. They are members of a broad class of firms that seek to make profits by linking savers who supply loanable funds to investors and other borrowers.

financial intermediaries
firms that specialize in
borrowing funds from
savers and lending those
funds to investors and
others.

Financial intermediaries are firms that specialize in borrowing funds from savers and lending those funds to investors and others. Depository institutions such as commercial banks, savings and loan associations, mutual savings banks, and credit unions are financial intermediaries. Brokerage houses, mutual fund companies, insurance companies, pension funds, and a host of other institutions and firms also provide financial intermediation services. However, only the banking system can actually create money.

The Evolution of Banking

In the Middle Ages, gold and silver were used as money in most European nations and for international trade. To avoid the inconvenience (and risk) of carrying around a wheelbarrow full of gold and coins, most merchants preferred to keep their money in a safe place. They usually left it with goldsmiths or money changers who first placed it on benches (or counters) so it could be examined and weighed. This practice evolved into what is now known as *banking*. The word *bank* is derived from the Italian word for bench, which is *banco*.

The goldsmiths of medieval England and the money changers of medieval Italy assessed the purity of the gold or coins before issuing depositors official receipts certifying the deposits. The depositors paid a fee for the storage service, just as you pay a fee for your checking account and other services at your bank. The deposit receipts soon began to circulate as a medium of exchange, which reduced the transaction costs by avoiding the inconvenience and risk of physically transporting gold in payment for goods and services. The holders of the receipts could at any time go to the goldsmiths and redeem the receipts for the stored gold. In effect, the receipts for the gold became paper currency.[1]

At first, the early bankers issued receipts for no more than the gold they had in the vault. If they stored 10,000 ounces, the total receipts in circulation were for no more than 10,000 ounces. However, some of the more astute goldsmiths observed that while receipts were presented each day for redemption of gold, new deposits of gold offset the decline from the outflow and resulted in the issuance of new receipts. *This meant, the goldsmiths could either loan out a portion of the gold on deposit for the use of others or issue more gold receipts than the actual gold available in the vault.* On any given day the inflows and outflows of gold were quite predictable, and it was rare for more than 25 percent of the gold receipts outstanding to end up as net withdrawals on a given day. By making loans, the goldsmiths could add to profits but would run little risk of being unable to meet the demand for withdrawals.

The goldsmiths made loans by issuing receipts for more gold than the actual amount of gold in the vault. *Because the gold receipts circulated as money, the goldsmiths actually created money by issuing receipts to borrowers for more gold than was in the vault!*

---

[1] For a discussion of the activities of goldsmiths in medieval England, see A. Andreades, *History of the Bank of England, 1640–1903*, 4th ed., with a new introduction by Paul Einzig (New York: Augustus M. Kelley, 1966), pp. 20–26 (first published in 1909).

Fractional Reserve Banking

The medieval goldsmiths and money changers were the first people to practice fractional reserve banking, in which a banking system creates checkable deposits by making loans in some multiple of the reserves it actually has on hand to pay withdrawals.

fractional reserve banking a process in which a banking system creates checkable deposits by making loans in some multiple of the reserves it actually has on hand to pay withdrawals.

If goldsmiths had fully backed all their receipts (used 100 percent reserve banking), they would have been unable to issue gold receipts for more than the amount of gold in their vaults. They would have had to keep enough reserves on hand to pay out *all* their deposits in cash on a given day. But suppose the goldsmiths made loans equal to *all* the gold they had in their vaults. They would have created receipts for deposits even though the people receiving the loans would not have actually deposited gold in their vaults. If a goldsmith with 10,000 ounces of gold in the vault makes loans of 10,000 ounces to people who don't actually deposit gold, the goldsmith, who can now be called a *banker,* credits the accounts of the people receiving the loans with "deposits" of 10,000 ounces of gold even though those people don't actually deposit any gold. The borrowers are now free to use receipts for these "created" deposits as money in making purchases.

The fractional reserve ratio the banker is operating under is the ratio of actual cash reserves (which in this case is gold) in the vault to total receipts for deposits. In this case the fractional reserve ratio would be

fractional reserve ratio the ratio of actual cash reserves to total receipts for deposits.

$$\begin{aligned} \text{Fractional reserve ratio} &= \text{Cash reserves/receipts for deposits} \\ &= 10{,}000/20{,}000 \\ &= 0.5 \end{aligned}$$

The gold held in the vault is sufficient to pay out only half the actual receipts the banker has issued. The fractional reserve is only 50 percent of the actual deposit receipts. This sounds very risky, but it really isn't. The banker knows from experience that because of daily inflows of new deposits, the new outflow of the reserves is almost never more than 25 percent of the gold receipts that have been issued.

A banker who wants to earn even more interest income on loans may use a lower fractional reserve ratio. If it's highly unlikely that more than 20 percent of the receipts issued for deposits will be redeemed in gold on any given day, the banker may find it prudent and profitable to loan out *four times* as much gold as is actually in the vault! The fractional reserve ratio for this banker would be 0.20. The banker would issue receipts for the 10,000 ounces of gold on deposit plus receipts for an additional 40,000 ounces of loans for which no gold has been deposited. The fractional reserve ratio is therefore 10,000/50,000 = 0.20.

A banking system that held 100 percent cash reserves for currency deposited by its customers would be unable to create checkable deposits to make loans. The 100 percent reserve system would be very safe for a banking system because the system could meet its customers' demand for currency in the unlikely event that all customers simultaneously closed their accounts. But like most businesses, banks must weigh safety considerations against profitability. Banks therefore use a fractional reserve system and earn interest income on the checkable deposits they create when they make loans.

In the United States, banking operations and practices are closely supervised by the Federal Reserve System, the U.S. Comptroller of the Currency, the Federal Deposit Insurance Corporation, and a multitude of state regulatory agencies. The purpose is to maintain confidence in the banking system to prevent "panics" that might cause depositors to try to withdraw abnormally high percentages of the total deposits on a given day.

HOW BANKS MAKE LOANS AND CREATE CHECKABLE DEPOSITS

🔲 The term **bank** generally refers to commercial banks and thrift institutions that offer checkable deposits. In fact, the banking industry in the United States consists of about 12,000 commercial banks, 3,000 savings and loan associations (some of which are now simply called *savings banks*), 400 mutual savings banks, and 20,000 credit unions. Each of these institutions offers checkable deposits, time deposits, loans to businesses and households, credit to governments, and other financial services.

bank a commercial bank or thrift institution that offers checkable deposits.

How a Bank Accepts Deposits and Makes Loans

To understand how the banking system of a modern nation operates, it's useful to begin by analyzing the operations of a single bank in a fractional reserve banking system. By examining the way a single bank accepts deposits and makes loans, you'll begin to understand how a modern banking system can actually create money in the same way the ancient goldsmiths created receipts.

reserves the balances that a modern U.S. bank keeps on deposit with the Federal Reserve bank in its district or as currency in its vault.

The **reserves** of a modern bank in the United States consist of the balances the bank keeps on deposit with the Federal Reserve bank in its district or as currency in its vault. Each of the 12 regional Federal Reserve banks serves the function of a "banker's bank" in which banks have accounts just as you have accounts at your bank. The Federal Reserve System seeks to control the money stock and, as you'll see shortly, *requires* banks to maintain a certain minimum fractional reserve ratio.

A bank's operations can be greatly clarified by examining its *balance sheet,* a statement of its assets and the claims against those assets. A balance sheet summarizes the financial position by showing the relationship between the bank's loans, property, and reserves and the claims that can be made on the bank by its creditors and owners. A bank's most important creditors are its depositors, who place their funds in the bank for safekeeping and have the right to withdraw those funds. The funds that depositors place in the bank are part of the bank's *liabilities;* they are debts of the bank to the depositors.

The bank's *assets* are property, cash, and debts owed to the bank, which include loans and any marketable securities the bank holds, such as Treasury bills and other notes of indebtedness. The *net worth* of the bank is the difference between its assets and its liabilities. Liabilities and net worth are two types of claims made against a bank's assets. The liabilities of a bank are the claims of its depositors and other creditors who are not owners of the bank. The net worth of a bank is the claim the bank's owners have to its assets after the claims of its creditors have been met. To understand how a bank can create money, we need to examine the relationship between its assets, liabilities, and net worth.

The function of a balance sheet is to divide the claims against assets into two mutually exclusive categories—liabilities and net worth. In other words, the bottom line of a balance sheet always shows that

$$\text{Assets} = \text{Liabilities} + \text{Net worth}$$

The balance sheet equation is actually an *identity,* because it must always hold by definition.

Box 1 shows the balance sheet of a bank that has just opened for business. After one week the bank has attracted $10 million in deposits. Assume these are all deposits of currency. The deposits don't actually increase the money stock. They simply convert currency into checkable deposits, which are the bank's liabilities. The bank has yet to extend any loans. The $10 million in currency that the bank accepts is deposited as reserves in the bank's own account at its district Federal Reserve bank. These reserves constitute part of the bank's assets because they are a

Box 1 Bank Balance Sheet—End of Week 1: No Loans			
Assets		**Liabilities and Net Worth**	
Reserves		Deposits	$10,000,000
Required	$ 2,000,000	Net worth	500,000
Excess	8,000,000		
Loans	0		
Property	500,000		
Total assets	$10,500,000	Total liabilities and net worth	$10,500,000

sum of money owed to the bank. When the bank needs currency to meet the demands of its depositors, it can draw on its account at the Federal Reserve bank and request a delivery of currency. (Remember that currency is issued by the Federal Reserve banks.) The bank also has assets in the form of the structures and equipment that constitute its physical plant. Assume the value of the bank's property is $500,000.

As shown in Box 1, the bank's assets consist of $10 million of reserves and $500,000 of property. Its liabilities are $10 million of checkable deposits. Its net worth, which is the portion of its assets not owed to creditors or other nonowners, is $500,000. The total assets of $10.5 million exactly equal the sum of liabilities and net worth.

With reserves equal to its deposits, the bank is like the goldsmith who doesn't issue receipts for any more gold than the gold on deposit. The bank cannot make any loans as long as it keeps reserves equal to 100 percent of its deposits. Its only source of income will be the fees it charges its depositors for the services it provides.

Making Loans: Deposit Creation by a Single Bank

During the second week of business, the executives of the newly organized bank in this example will advertise their services and drum up some loan business. But how much can they loan out? Suppose the bank's managers believe it's safe to keep 20 percent reserves against its deposits. Also assume that the regulatory authorities overseeing bank operations will not permit bank reserves to fall below 20 percent of deposits. The regulators set a **required reserve ratio,** which is the minimum percentage of deposits that a bank must hold in reserves. *A bank can hold more than this minimum percentage of deposits in reserves, but it cannot hold less.* The required reserve ratio is one of the tools the Federal Reserve System uses to control the amount of money in circulation.[2]

Required reserves are the dollar value of the currency and deposits in Federal Reserve banks that a bank must hold to meet current regulations. For our example the bank's required reserves are $2 million, which equals 20 percent of current deposits. **Excess reserves** represent the difference between total reserves and required reserves against deposits. Our bank currently holds $8 million in excess reserves. This is the excess of its $10 million total reserves over its $2 million required reserves. *An individual bank can make loans in an amount up to the value of its excess reserves.* Our bank can therefore make up to $8 million in loans out of its initial deposits of $10 million when it operates under the 20 percent required reserve rule.

required reserve ratio
the minimum percentage of deposits that a bank must hold in reserves to comply with regulatory requirements.

required reserves
dollar value of currency and deposits in Federal Reserve banks that a bank must hold to meet current regulations.

excess reserves
difference between total reserves and required reserves of a bank held against deposits.

---

[2] As you'll see in the following chapter, the required reserve ratio is actually much less than 0.2 for most types of deposits at banks.

default nonrepayment of the principal and interest on a loan.

Many local business firms that want funds to finance expansion, inventories, new equipment, and other investments come to the bank and fill out applications for credit. The managers of the bank carefully examine the applications and choose the most creditworthy businesses as their loan clients. Bank managers must be concerned about the risk of default, which is nonrepayment of the principal and interest, on each of its loans. They must carefully balance the risk of default against the interest income the bank obtains from making any given loan.

After the bank sorts through the applications and makes its decisions, it creates deposits for the clients to whom it makes loans. Usually a bank requires that its loan clients have an account at the bank. When a loan is approved, the bank simply adds the amount of the loan as a checkable deposit to the client's account.

Assume that our bank actually lends out *all* of its excess reserves by creating deposits for its clients on the first day of business of its second week of operation. The resulting balance sheet is shown in Box 2. The bank now has $18 million in deposits, of which $8 million represents the proceeds of the loans it has just made. Because the newly created deposits didn't result from inflows of currency or from an increase in deposits in the bank's Federal Reserve account, reserves do not increase. Total reserves remain $10 million on the day the loans are made. The bottom line of *both sides* of the bank's balance sheet increases by $8 million on the first day of business of week 2 as the bank acquires assets in the form of $8 million of loans balanced by $8 million of newly created liabilities in the form of deposits. *By making loans in this way, the bank has created $8 million of checkable deposits. It has therefore created money equal to its initial amount of excess reserves.*

How Checks Drawn on Newly Created Deposits Affect an Individual Bank's Balance Sheet

If the $8 million of newly created deposits were to remain in the bank, the required reserves would be $1.6 million and the bank would still have $6.4 million of excess reserves. However, the newly created deposits resulting from the $8 million in loans will be quickly withdrawn as the business firms use their loaned funds to finance their investments. *Because the banking system comprises many banks, spent loan proceeds are unlikely to be redeposited in the bank that initially created the checkable deposits.*

For example, suppose our bank is located in Denver and a firm receiving a loan of $1 million from it uses the funds to purchase a conveyor system from a firm in Detroit. The $1 million check that the firm writes to pay for the conveyor system is therefore deposited in a Detroit bank. The Detroit bank sends the check to its district Federal Reserve bank and requests that the check be deposited in its account there. The Federal Reserve bank then sends the check to the Denver bank's district Federal Reserve bank, where it will reduce the balance in the Denver bank's account by $1 million. When the Denver bank finally gets the check back, it will reduce by $1 million the sum in the account of the firm that wrote the check.

check clearing the process of transferring Federal Reserve deposits among banks as checks are paid.

The process of transferring Federal Reserve deposits among banks as checks are paid is called check clearing. Because the Federal Reserve deposits held by banks constitute their reserves, the clearing of the $1 million check will reduce the Denver bank's reserves by $1 million and increase the Detroit bank's reserves by $1 million. Check clearing, which is handled by specialized firms and the Federal Reserve banks, usually takes a few days. The Denver bank can expect *all* of its $8 million of newly created deposits to clear through the banking system in this way and end up as deposits in *other* banks. Box 3 shows the Denver bank's balance sheet at the end of

Box 2   Bank Balance Sheet—Beginning of Week 2: $8 Million in Loans Not Yet Withdrawn

Assets		Liabilities and Net Worth	
Reserves	$10,000,000	Deposits	$18,000,000
Loans	8,000,000	Net worth	500,000
Property	500,000		
Total assets	$18,500,000	Total liabilities and net worth	$18,500,000

Box 3   Bank Balance Sheet—End of Week 2: All Newly Created Deposits Drawn and Paid to Other Banks

Assets		Liabilities and Net Worth	
Reserves		Deposits	$10,000,000
Required	$ 2,000,000	Net worth	500,000
Excess	0		
Loans	8,000,000		
Property	500,000		
Total assets	$10,500,000	Total liabilities and net worth	$10,500,000

week 2, *after all its newly created deposits have been drawn on by the loan clients and the checks have cleared.*

Look at the liability side of the balance sheet. The bank now has only $10 million of deposits because its $8 million of newly created deposits has been drawn down and paid to other banks. Its net worth remains $500,000. Its assets now consist of $8 million in loans, $500,000 in property, *and only $2 million in reserves.* What happened to the $8 million in excess reserves that the bank had during its first week? These were paid out to *other* banks as the checks drawn on the loans cleared. The Denver bank's account at its district Federal Reserve bank was debited by $8 million after all of the checks written on the newly created checkable deposits were cleared. The bank no longer has any excess reserves. it therefore cannot make any more loans. When the excess reserves of a bank are zero, the bank is said to be *loaned up.* This bank will remain loaned up until it obtains more reserves from cash deposits or from deposits of checks drawn on other banks that increase the sums in its Federal Reserve account.

There's an important difference between the deposits that a single bank creates by making loans and those it obtains from customers who actually deposit cash or from checks drawn on other banks. Deposits of the latter type increase the bank's reserves, while created deposits do not. This bank cannot create any more checkable deposits by making loans until it receives more deposits that increase its reserves. In general, its reserves will go up if it receives deposits of cash or of checks drawn on other banks. Any type of deposit that increases the cash in the bank's vault or its deposits at its Federal Reserve bank will increase the bank's excess reserves and allow it to make more loans.

CONCEPT CHECK

□

- What is fractional reserve banking?
- What does a bank's balance sheet show?
- A bank currently holds reserves equal to 25 percent of its total deposits of $5 million. Assuming the required reserve ratio is 15 percent, how much of its deposits can the bank loan out? Why are deposits created by one bank likely to end up as new reserves for other banks?

MULTIPLE EXPANSION OF THE MONEY STOCK FOR THE ENTIRE BANKING SYSTEM

A truly amazing fact is that the *entire* banking system can create checkable deposits by an amount equal to a multiple of existing reserves available to all banks. To see how this process works, we need to trace the progress of newly created checkable deposits resulting from loans as they filter their way down through many banks. Suppose the deposits that the Denver bank received during its first week of operation increase *total reserves* for the banking system by $10 million. This would be the case if the $10 million in new deposits consisted of currency from the mattresses of local misers! The $10 million in deposits would then increase excess reserves in the banking system by $8 million. In the previous section we saw how this $10 million in deposits supported $8 million of newly created checkable deposits as the Denver bank loaned out its excess reserves. To see how these initial deposits can support still *more* loans and more money creation, assume that *all* of the $8 million of new checkable deposits created by the Denver bank is deposited in the Detroit bank.

The table in Box 4 shows the changes in assets and liabilities of the Detroit bank. The $8 million increases the Detroit bank's liabilities by $8 million. As the deposited checks clear, the Detroit bank's reserves also increase by $8 million as $8 million in deposits at the Federal Reserve bank is transferred from the Denver bank's account to the Detroit bank's account. Remember that the deposits held by banks at their district Federal Reserve banks constitute the bulk of their reserves.

The Detroit bank must hold 20 percent of its new reserves as required reserves against its $8 million in new deposits. This amounts to $1.6 million. The remaining $6.4 million is excess reserves that can be loaned out. *The initial $10 million in deposits at the Denver bank that has already supported $8 million in loans can now be used to support an additional $6.4 million in loans.* As the Detroit bank makes these loans, it will create checkable deposits equal to $6.4 million for its clients, assuming it loans out of its excess reserves. The total expansion in the money stock as a result of the initial $10 million increase in bank reserves is now $8 million plus $6.4 million, which equals $14.4 million.

The process of expansion doesn't stop here! As the checkable deposits created by the Detroit bank are spent by the people who obtain the loans, they will be deposited in other banks, increasing the reserves of still more banks and allowing additional money creation. For example, suppose all of the $6.4 million is deposited in a New York bank. After the checks clear, the New York bank will find that both its deposits and its total reserves have increased by $6.4 million. This bank must keep 20 percent of these funds, or $1.28 million, in required reserves, and can loan out amounts up to the excess reserves of $5.12 million as newly created checkable deposits. The initial change in the New York bank's balance sheet is shown in Box 5. Assuming the New York bank loans out all its excess reserves, the money stock will increase by an additional $5.12 million.

Box 4 Changes in Assets and Liabilities—Detroit Bank			
Changes in Assets		**Changes in Liabilities**	
Reserves	+$8,000,000	Deposits	+$8,000,000
Required	+$1,600,000		
Excess	+$6,400,000		

Box 5 Changes in Assets and Liabilities—New York Bank			
Changes in Assets		**Changes in Liabilities**	
Total reserves	+$6,400,000	Deposits	+$6,400,000
Required	+$1,280,000		
Excess	+$5,120,000		

The Money Creation Process

By now you can probably see how the process works. At each stage, as a result of new loans made by banks, the initial $10 million injection of reserve allows more money creation. At each stage, however, the loans that can be made become smaller and smaller, because only 80 percent of the deposits created from new loans end up as excess reserves that can be used to make more loans. The increase in checkable deposits becomes smaller and smaller as the funds work their way through the banking system. Eventually, the new loans that can be made approach zero.

The table in Box 6 shows how newly created checkable deposits decline at each stage, assuming that all excess reserves created at each stage of redeposit of loan proceeds are used to make new loans. It's also assumed, in the process of deposit and redeposit of checks among banks, that no reserves leak out of the banking system. For example, at each stage some of the people presenting checks to the banks may not deposit the full amount in their checking accounts. Instead, they may ask the bank to give them a portion of the funds in currency. If the currency is held by customers instead of being deposited in banks, the growth of excess reserves at each stage will be less and the amount of new checkable deposits that can be created will also be less.

The sum of additional deposits eventually reaches a limit as the additional excess reserves for the banking system that result from redeposit of funds eventually approach zero. The table in Box 6 shows how additional checkable deposits fall to $4.10 million when the checks drawn on the New York bank's $5.12 million of deposits are deposited in a Chicago bank. The table also shows how the maximum amount of checkable deposits that can be created becomes smaller as the Chicago bank makes loans that are then deposited in a St. Louis bank. The last column traces out the process for a number of other stages and shows how the maximum sum of new checkable deposits that can be created approaches $40 million when banks find it profitable to loan out all the excess reserves they acquire at each stage of the process.

Box 6   Growth in Checkable Deposits from an Initial $10,000,000 of New Bank Reserves with a 0.2 Required Reserve Ratio (millions of dollars)

Stage	Bank	New reserves acquired	Required reserves	Excess reserves	Checkable deposits that can be created from new excess reserves
1	Denver	10.00	2.00	8.00	8.00
2	Detroit	8.00	1.60	6.40	6.40
3	New York	6.40	1.28	5.12	5.12
4	Chicago	5.12	1.02	4.10	4.10
5	St. Louis	4.10	0.82	3.28	3.28
6	San Francisco	3.28	0.66	2.62	2.62
7	Los Angeles	2.62	0.52	2.10	2.10
8	Seattle	2.10	0.42	1.68	1.68
9	Cleveland	1.68	0.34	1.34	1.34
10	All other				5.36
Total increase in money stock					40.00

The Reserve Multiplier

For the entire banking system, an injection of $8 million in new excess reserves can be used to support a maximum of $40 million in new deposits when the required reserve ratio is 0.2! An individual bank can create no more checkable deposits than the amount of the excess reserves it acquires. However, the *entire banking system* can create new checkable deposits that amount to a *multiple* of the initial injection of excess reserves into the banking system. Any individual bank is likely to lose the excess reserves it acquires when it creates a checkable deposit for a loan customer. However, except for currency withdrawal, the excess reserves are not withdrawn from the banking system. When the new checkable deposits are deposited in another bank, that bank also acquires reserves of which another 80 percent can be loaned out.

Notice that the money creation process is just like the one described for the multiplier effect in the chapter on Keynesian analysis. The maximum amount of new checkable deposits that can result from a new injection of excess reserve dollars into the banking system can be expressed as an infinite geometric progression. After the $8 million in initial deposits created by the initial injection of new excess reserves, $6.4 million is the second-stage maximum of new deposits that the Detroit bank can create. The $6.4 million can be expressed as (0.8)($8 million). Similarly, the $5.12 million maximum of new deposits that can be created at the third stage by the New York bank can be expressed as 0.8[0.8($8 million)], which equals $(0.8)^2$($8 million). In the same way the $4.10 million in maximum checkable deposits that the Chicago bank can create at the fourth stage, assuming it loans out all of its newly acquired excess reserves, can be expressed as $(0.8)^3$($8 million). The infinite geometric progression is

Newly created checkable deposits = $8 million + 0.8($8 million)
$$+ 0.8^2(\$8 \text{ million}) + 0.8^3(\$8 \text{ million})$$
$$+ 0.8^4(\$8 \text{ million}) + \cdots$$

As the sum continues, each successive term becomes smaller, because any number less than 1 becomes smaller when it is raised to a higher power. The maximum possible increase in checkable deposits, and hence the money stock (ΔM), resulting from the initial increase in excess reserves for the banking system can be calculated by using the following formula to solve for the sum of an infinite geometric progression:

$$\Delta M = \frac{\Delta ER}{(1 - 0.8)} = \frac{\Delta ER}{0.2}$$

where ΔER is the change in excess reserves for the banking system. In this example, ΔER is $8 million, which represents the increase in excess reserves resulting from an initial $10 million deposit of currency into the banking system. The maximum increase in the money stock resulting from new checkable deposits that can be created from this amount of excess reserves is therefore

$$\Delta M = \frac{\$8 \text{ million}}{0.2} = \$40 \text{ million}$$

When the required reserve ratio is 0.2, each dollar of excess reserves that enters the banking system can support *five times* as much in new checkable deposits when banks find it profitable to loan out all their excess reserves at each stage of the process. Under these circumstances, an injection of $8 million in *new excess reserves* into the banking system can therefore ultimately support $40 million of new money stock in the form of checkable deposits.

The **reserve multiplier** is the maximum amount of new money stock that can be created from each dollar increase in the excess reserves available to the banking system. In the example just given, the reserve multiplier was 5. In general, the reserve multiplier can be calculated simply by dividing the number 1 by the required reserve ratio:

$$\text{Reserve multiplier} = \frac{1}{\text{Required reserve ratio}}$$

In this case the reserve multiplier is

$$\frac{1}{0.2} = 5$$

If the required reserve ratio were 0.1 instead of 0.2, the reserve multiplier would be increased to

$$\frac{1}{0.1} = 10$$

The maximum amount of new checkable deposits, ΔM, that can result from any increase in excess reserves can also be expressed as

$$\Delta M = \Delta ER(\text{Reserve multiplier})$$

This gives the amount of checkable deposits that the banking system can create from any increase in excess reserves when all excess reserves are loaned out and there is no withdrawal of currency from the banking system. In the previous example the maximum increase in checkable deposits is 5 times $8 million, which is $40 million.

Notice that the maximum possible increase in the money stock depends *both* on the excess reserves injected into the banking system and on the required reserve ratio. Other things being equal, the larger the increase in excess reserves or the lower the required reserve ratio, the greater the increase in the money stock. The *actual* increase in the money stock depends on the willingness of banks to lend out the

reserve multiplier the maximum amount of new money stock that can be credited from each dollar increase in the excess reserves available to the banking system.

excess reserves they acquire as a result of the money creation process and the amount of loan proceeds that end up in other banks (that is, the public's taste for currency). Thus, the preceding equation represents the maximum possible creation of deposits; in reality, the amount of money created will be less than is implied by the formula.

As a further illustration of the way to use the formula, suppose the Denver bank borrows $5 million from its district Federal Reserve bank. When it does, the Denver bank's account at the district Federal Reserve bank will be credited by $5 million. This $5 million represents new bank assets in the form of reserves that are balanced by a liability in the form of a $5 million debt to the Federal Reserve bank. Since no new deposits were acquired, the entire $5 million becomes excess reserves for the Denver bank. Assuming a required reserve ratio of 0.1, the maximum increase in the money stock that can result from the Denver bank's loan from the Federal Reserve bank is

$$\Delta M = \frac{\$5 \text{ million}}{0.1} = \$50 \text{ million}$$

Assuming that banks find it profitable to loan out all their excess reserves at each stage of the money creation process, a $5 million loan to a bank by the Federal Reserve bank will increase the money stock by $50 million.

Deposit Contraction: The Process in Reverse

The banking system's capacity to create money by making loans is impaired if its reserves are reduced. Suppose misers decide to withdraw $10 million in bank deposits and stuff the $10 million into their mattresses. There will be no change in the money stock at first. The amount of checkable deposits will decline by $10 million, but the amount of currency will increase by the same amount even if the currency stays in mattresses. However, bank reserves will also decline by $10 million as a result of the withdrawal of currency that is not redeposited into the banking system. The $10 million withdrawal from the banking system reduces excess reserves by $8 million.

If the banking system is fully loaned up, to make up for its loss it will have to obtain more reserves or to reduce the amount of loans it has outstanding or the securities it holds. Certain types of loans can be called in. This means the bank tells the borrowers they must repay their loans. As loans are repaid, the banks in the system find that their deposits decline and the required reserves they must hold also decline. Of course, if there are excess reserves in the system, the decline in deposits will be less drastic than it would be otherwise.

In practice, banks rarely have to call in loans when reserves fall. There's a constant turnover of loans as old loans are paid off and new loans are negotiated. The decline in reserves caused by the $10 million withdrawal will force the banks in the system to refuse to renew existing loans as their terms expire. As existing loans are paid off, the banks will also make fewer new loans than they would have otherwise. Finally, banks typically supply credit in an impersonal way by buying government securities and other notes of indebtedness. Banks can easily and quickly obtain additional reserves to meet their reserve requirements by selling securities they hold. If government securities are sold to the Federal Reserve banks, the banks will be credited with an increase in deposits that serve as reserves at the district Federal Reserve banks.

Assuming a required reserve ratio of 0.2, the maximum reduction in the money stock, ΔM, resulting from an $8 million withdrawal of excess reserves from the banking system will be

$$\text{Maximum reduction in checkable deposits} = \frac{\text{Loss in excess reserves}}{\text{Required reserve ratio}}$$

$$\Delta M = \frac{-\$8 \text{ million}}{0.2}$$

$$= -\$40 \text{ million}$$

The maximum decline in the money stock that results from the $10 million withdrawal from the banking system will therefore be $40 million. Of course, the decline in checkable deposits will be less if the banking system has excess reserves than would be the case if it were fully loaned up.

Bank Demand for Excess Reserves

Why do banks give up the opportunity to earn interest income by holding excess reserves instead of using the reserves to create checkable deposits for loan customers? One reason is to meet expected deposit outflows. If banks anticipate a heavy net outflow of deposits, they may retain more excess reserves so they will be able to meet that demand without calling in loans, selling securities, or borrowing. When excess reserves are on hand, banks avoid the transaction costs of obtaining the funds they need in other ways. The savings realized by avoiding these transaction costs often more than offset the forgone interest income on the excess reserves.

A bank's opportunity cost of holding each dollar of excess reserves is the interest income it forgoes by not lending that dollar out. Naturally, the higher the interest rate, the lower the quantity of excess reserves demanded. The lower the interest rate, the greater the willingness of banks to hold excess reserves.

Remember that banks are motivated to make profits. During a recession, interest rates typically decline and business failures tend to rise. It's both less profitable and riskier for banks to make loans during periods of economic downturn than during periods of recovery, when aggregate demand and real GDP are increasing. Banks are therefore more likely to hold excess reserves during a recession, when lower interest rates and the increased risk of loan defaults make lending money less profitable. Similarly, they're less likely to hold excess reserves during a recovery, when interest rates increase and the risk of loan default declines. The graph in Box 7 illustrates the downward-sloping bank demand curve for excess reserves and shows how changes in the market rate of interest affect bank holdings of excess reserves.

The cyclical fluctuation in bank demand for excess reserves has important implications for the money stock. The more excess reserve banks hold, the less the amount of checkable deposits that banks create by making loans and therefore the smaller the money stock. For example, if the required reserve ratio is 0.1, each dollar increase in the excess reserves *held by banks* rather than used by them to make loans or buy securities will prevent the money stock from increasing by $10! During recessions, when banks seek to increase the excess reserves they hold, there is downward pressure on the money stock. Because, as you'll soon see, the available stock of money influences aggregate demand, the decline in the money stock could further decrease aggregate demand during the recession, thereby causing a further decline in real GDP. By the same token, the eagerness of banks to make loans with

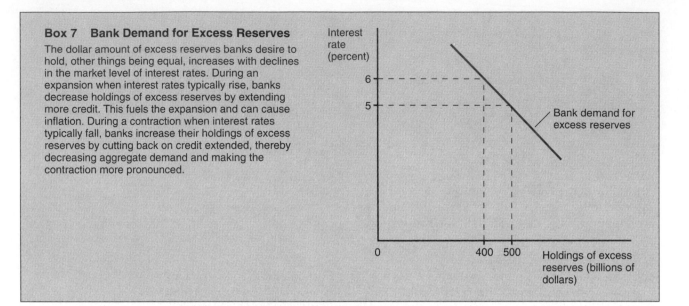

Box 7   Bank Demand for Excess Reserves

The dollar amount of excess reserves banks desire to hold, other things being equal, increases with declines in the market level of interest rates. During an expansion when interest rates typically rise, banks decrease holdings of excess reserves by extending more credit. This fuels the expansion and can cause inflation. During a contraction when interest rates typically fall, banks increase their holdings of excess reserves by cutting back on credit extended, thereby decreasing aggregate demand and making the contraction more pronounced.

their excess reserves during periods of peak economic activity tends to increase the money stock. This puts upward pressure on aggregate demand and can contribute to inflation.

The profit-motivated banking system can therefore cause destabilizing swings in aggregate demand that exaggerate the ups and downs of the business cycle. In an attempt to minimize the swings, the Federal Reserve System seeks to manage the total reserves available to the banking system. The role of the Federal Reserve System in influencing the money stock in this way is the subject of the following chapter.

The Federal Funds Market

In addition to holding excess reserves, banks lend these reserves to other banks that require reserves to support loans and security purchases. Banks with excess reserves often find it convenient to loan out these reserves to other banks on an overnight basis. Because these loans are repaid the following day, they allow the lending banks to maintain high liquidity. At the same time, they allow the lending banks to earn interest on their reserves, thereby reducing the opportunity cost of holding them. When excess reserves are lent out, the total reserves available to the banking system do not increase. However, the loan of excess reserves by one bank to another bank that uses the borrowed reserves to support loans to its customers acts to reduce the excess reserves in the banking system by converting the excess reserves of the lending bank into required reserves of the borrowing bank.

federal funds reserves loaned out on a short-term basis by one bank to another.

Federal funds are reserves loaned out by one bank to another bank on a short-term basis (usually overnight and rarely more than one week). Note that federal funds are funds belonging neither to the federal government nor to the Federal Reserve System. They are deposits that banks make at the Federal Reserve banks. Any bank that maintains a deposit account at a Federal Reserve bank can either lend or borrow federal funds. Special brokers arrange loans of federal funds among banks. When a loan is made, the Federal Reserve bank simply transfers deposits from the account of the lender to the account of the borrower. When the loan is repaid, the borrowing

principles in practice

Business Brief: Nonbank Financial Intermediaries

All banks are financial intermediaries, but not all financial intermediaries are banks. What are nonbank financial intermediaries? How do they differ from banks, and what role do they play in the financial system?

Nonbank financial intermediaries are those that make loans and provide other financial services but do not offer checkable deposits included in the M1 definition of money. These intermediaries channel funds from savers to borrowers. Some of them also help individuals and firms manage their cash balances in ways that are likely to affect the demand for money balances. Nonbank financial intermediaries include insurance companies, pension funds, mutual funds, and brokerage houses.

Insurance companies invest the premiums paid on policies in government securities, corporate stocks and bonds, mortgages, and real-estate. Life insurance companies also allow their policyholders to borrow funds against the cash value of life insurance.

Pension funds invest the contribution of employers and employees in various assets. In effect, these funds channel savings for the retirement of workers to finance investment by corporations and other businesses.

Finance companies that loan money to consumers and small businesses raise funds by borrowing on the open market and by issuing their own stocks and bonds. They use the funds they raise in this way to finance small loans. General Motors Acceptance Corporation is a finance company set up for the sole purpose of financing cars. Consumer finance companies such as Household Finance finance the purchase of such consumer durables as furniture and appliances. Business finance companies specialize in providing credit to business firms.

Mutual funds are financial intermediaries that channel the funds of savers into a variety of assets. These firms enable small investors to purchase part of a diversified portfolio of stocks, bonds, or other types of assets. One of the most significant developments in financial markets has been the organization of *money market mutual funds*. These funds invest in various kinds of short-term debt of business firms and governments and also purchase bank certificates of deposit. They were first organized in the late 1970s. By 1992 they held about $550 billion in assets. A unique feature of money market mutual funds is that they often allow their investors to write checks on the balances in their mutual fund accounts! In other words, these funds are often as liquid as checkable deposits for the savers who invest in them. They are redeemable at a fixed price per share. However, most of the funds don't permit checks to be written for less than $500 or $1,000.

Money market accounts with check-writing privileges are not considered legal checkable deposits. They are not subject to reserve requirements. Money market funds enable small investors to earn interest on funds they would normally hold in checkable deposit accounts. By reducing average daily cash balances that households hold, the funds contribute to quicker turnover of the available money stock. In other words, they tend to decrease the demand for money represented by M1.

bank's Federal Reserve account is debited by the amount of the loan and an amount equal to the interest on the loan. That sum is then transferred to the account of the bank that lent the funds. Most transactions in the federal funds market are very large, involving transfers of millions of dollars of reserves among banks.

The federal funds rate is the interest rate charged for the loan of reserves from one bank to another. This rate is a closely watched indicator of the availability of credit in the economy. It is published daily in such financial newspapers as *The Wall Street Journal*. Because the federal funds rate represents the market price of reserves to banks, its level varies with the scarcity of those reserves relative to the demand for their use to support loans. When reserves are scarce relative to demands for their use, the federal funds rate increases. On the other hand, when there is an increased availability of bank reserves relative to demands for their use and a consequent easing of credit conditions, the federal funds rate decreases. Because the federal funds market is very competitive, the federal funds rate fluctuates readily in response to changes in the demand or supply of bank reserves.

federal funds rate the interest rate charged for the loan of reserves from one bank to another.

principles in practice

Deposit Insurance and Bank Failures

The Staggering Cost of the Savings and Loan Industry Disaster When he was asked why he robbed banks, outlaw Willie Sutton said, "Because that's where the money is!"

Perhaps because banks are where the money is, they're among the most regulated firms in the economy. The reason for stringent regulation by various state and federal agencies is to prevent the horrifying specter of a collapse of the banking system. A *bank failure* occurs when a depository institution cannot meet its obligations to depositors who want to withdraw funds. Because one bank often has deposits and loans at other banks, a major bank failure can set up a chain reaction that causes chaos in the financial payments system.

A loss of confidence in the banking system can cause a *bank panic* in which depositors flock to banks to convert their deposits to cash. The increase in withdrawals on a given day can deplete the banking system's reserves. During the Great Depression of the early 1930s, thousands of bank failures wiped out the savings of millions of people. In 1934, to prevent future bank failures and to maintain confidence in the banking system, the Federal Deposit Insurance Corporation (FDIC) was established to guarantee bank deposits. The FDIC currently insures all deposits up to $100,000 per account against loss as a result of bank failure. Because many corporations maintain deposit accounts well in excess of $100,000, this insurance provides protection mainly to households. If a bank should fail, the FDIC has the right to dismiss its management and take over the bank to oversee the sale of its assets to pay off depositors.

Like any insurance system, the FDIC works if there is a small, predictable number of bank failures in any year. The insurance fund held by the FDIC amounts to about 2 percent of insured deposits and only a fraction of a percent of total deposits. If a panic spread through-

out the banking system, it would be difficult for the FDIC to meet all of its insurance obligations without help from the federal government, which would have to use tax revenues to bail out the banks.

In the 1980s bank failures in the United States rose dramatically, placing a tremendous burden on the deposit insurance system. By 1989 the Federal Savings and Loan Insurance Corporation (FSLIC), which insured deposits at savings and loan associations, was insolvent and the FDIC was running a loss. Major legislation was enacted by Congress to deal with a savings and loan (S&L) industry in which bank failure had become almost epidemic. The 1990 legislation (1) established a new Office of Thrift Supervision to regulate thrift institutions, (2) transferred the insurance functions of the FSLIC to the FDIC (organizing the Savings Association Insurance Fund for S&Ls and the Bank Insurance Fund for commercial and savings banks), and (3) created two funds to deal with failed thrift institutions. The FSLIC Resolution Fund manages the remaining assets of S&Ls taken over prior to 1989, while the Resolution Trust Corporation manages the assets and liabilities of thrifts that have become insolvent since 1989.

In 1989 and 1990 hundreds of insolvent thrift institutions were taken over by the new government agencies. By mid-1990 they estimated that it would take between $350 billion and $500 billion, depending on interest rates and real estate prices, to pay off insured deposits at insolvent savings and loan associations even after the assets of these institutions were sold. The bulk of the funds for the bailout, from the U.S. Treasury, were raised directly from taxpayers; other funds were obtained from loans on which taxpayers would ultimately pay the interest. In 1990 Treasury borrowings to finance the S&L bailout were putting distinct upward pressure on interest rates. It was estimated that 40 years would

---

CONCEPT CHECK
☐

■ The required reserve ratio is 0.1. If the reserves available to the banking system increase by $10 million, what is the maximum possible increase in checkable deposits that can result?

■ How does a decrease in bank reserves lead to a decrease in the money stock?

■ Why do banks choose to hold some of their assets in the form of excess reserves?

BANK PORTFOLIO MANAGEMENT

4 The picture of bank deposit creation just presented is highly simplified. In actuality, banking is a very complex business. Banks must be concerned with both the *liquidity* and the *profitability* of their operations.

be needed to finance the losses incurred by the old FSLIC!

What caused this incredible and expensive fiasco? Why are billions and billions of government dollars necessary to bail out these failed depository institutions? Are we in for a period of bank failures that could threaten the stability of the U.S. economy?

To understand the causes of the savings and loan disaster, we have to go back to 1980. In that year Congress enacted the Depository Institutions Deregulation and Monetary Control Act, which allowed savings and loan associations and other thrift institutions to issue checkable deposits and compete more aggressively for loanable funds. The increased competition caused a rise in the interest rates that thrift institutions paid to attract loanable funds. Although most thrift institutions had previously specialized in low-yielding mortgage loans, they were now pressured to seek more lucrative loans to compensate for the low-interest loans in their portfolios. Many thrifts made riskier loans on which they charged higher interest rates. The Garn–St Germain Act of 1982 increased the trouble by allowing S&Ls to expand their lending into commercial ventures and speculative land development.

In many ways the deposit insurance provided by the FDIC and FSLIC contributed to the risk-taking of depository institutions and precipitated many of the bank failures in the late 1980s. Many depositors believed that amounts in excess of $100,000 would be protected in the event of a bank failure. Most of the people who supplied their loanable funds to the thrifts were fully protected by deposit insurance and therefore cared little about their bank's financial health or the way it was managed! The net worth of a poorly managed bank that becomes insolvent is negative. The bank's owners therefore have none of their own capital at risk and become more willing to take risks with the funds they obtain from insured depositors. In some notorious cases, officers of thrift institutions contributed to the insolvency of their institutions by using the funds of depositors for extravagant and sometimes fraudulent personal purposes.

In the mid-1980s a number of unfortunate events triggered the failure of many savings and loan associations, particularly those located in oil-producing states such as Texas, Louisiana, and Oklahoma. As oil prices and land prices tumbled, risky loans based on the prospects of a prosperous oil industry turned sour. Many S&Ls discovered that their assets were insufficient to meet their deposit liabilities. Weak institutions offered higher interest rates to attract depositors, and depositors continued to supply funds to insolvent institutions because of deposit insurance. *The system of deposit insurance that prevented bank panics also encouraged risk-taking that ultimately led to bank failures!* The losers were not the depositors or the owners—the losers were the taxpayers and the economy itself, whose operation was severely impaired.

There is no easy solution for the S&L disaster. Some experts recommend more regulation of the thrift industry to control risk-taking and bank failure, while others argue that the whole U.S. banking system should be overhauled. Others recommend that deposit insurance coverage be reduced or that banks pay premiums for deposit insurance that more accurately reflect the riskiness of their portfolios. Currently, all banks pay the same rate of insurance per $100 of deposits, no matter how risky their assets. Finally, some experts propose that owners of thrift insurance institutions have more of their own money at stake (more net worth).

The price you pay for having the peace of mind that your money in the bank is safe may be higher taxes and higher interest rates in the future! However, if you've got lots of money in the bank, you need to be careful in the future. Since 1992 Congress has mandated that the FDIC limit insurance to accounts below $100,000. If you have an account of more than $100,000 at a bank that fails, you could lose your savings! This new provision is designed to encourage large depositors to monitor the loss policies of their banks and to withdraw funds from poorly managed banks. This prevents such banks from easily obtaining deposits to squander on bad loans.

Banks earn profits because they can make loans at interest rates higher than the rates they pay to depositors. In fact, for most checkable deposit accounts, banks pay no interest to depositors. Instead, they charge fees for checking services and other financial services. For time deposit accounts, such as savings accounts and certificates of deposit, banks pay interest to compete with other financial intermediaries and attract deposits.

A bank whose management makes loans only to the least creditworthy applicants is able to charge higher interest rates than it could charge if it made safer loans. In this way the bank will make higher profits, provided the borrowers actually repay their loans. However, the bank risks the possibility that a high percentage of its loans will default. Loan default means the bank earns no interest and also loses the funds it lent out. Banks must balance their desire for increased profitability against the risk of default and the risk of having assets that cannot be easily converted into reserves to meet unexpected withdrawals. To do this, most banks are careful to have a diversified *portfolio,* or mix, of assets.

Typically, a bank will make some risky loans at high interest rates. The riskiest types of loans are those made in exchange for unsecured promises to repay. Consumer loans on credit card accounts are an example of such loans. Banks also make short-term loans to creditworthy businesses at lower interest rates than they charge consumers. The prime rate is the interest rate a bank charges its most creditworthy customers, usually large corporations, for short-term loans of less than one year.

prime rate the interest rate a bank charges its most creditworthy customers for short-term loans of less than one year.

A bank often demands collateral, which is an asset a borrower pledges to a lender in case of default. For example, if you borrow money to buy a car, the bank typically asks you to pledge the car as collateral. The bank usually has a formal *lien* on the car, which means you can't sell the car without the bank's permission or repayment of the loan. If you default on the loan, the bank can seize the car and sell it to obtain the outstanding balance on your loan. Similarly, a *mortgage* is a loan a bank makes to finance the purchase of a house or other real estate, with the loan secured by that asset as collateral. The interest rate a bank charges on a loan depends on the collateral offered by the customer, the customer's credit history (as rated by independent credit bureaus), and various other factors. In general, loans are not very liquid. Most loans cannot be easily called in to be converted into reserves when the need arises. However, very short-term loans, those made for a period of, say, one to three months, turn over quickly and give the bank some flexibility in adjusting the amount of loans outstanding when the need for reserves arises.

collateral an asset a borrower pledges to a lender in case of default.

The business of banking involves careful portfolio management to balance risks, profits, and liquidity. Most banks carry 10 percent to 20 percent of their assets in the form of government securities that can be sold quickly at very low transaction costs to obtain reserves when the bank needs them. Government securities are interest-bearing debts of the federal government in the form of Treasury bills, Treasury notes, and Treasury bonds. The interest earned on these securities is typically lower than the interest the bank can earn on loans. However, their liquidity is worth the loss in profitability to the bank.

government securities interest-bearing debts of the federal government in the form of Treasury bills, Treasury notes, and Treasury bonds.

Commercial banks typically hold about 20 percent of their assets in the form of highly liquid government securities, often called secondary reserves. The sum of cash and government securities is the banking system's *liquidity base,* which is used to meet deposit withdrawal demands. About two thirds of bank assets are in loans, the bulk of which is commercial and industrial credit.

secondary reserves government securities held by banks.

Thrift institutions differ from commercial banks in that they specialize more in the provision of credit to real estate markets. As of the early 1990s, approximately 70 percent of the assets of thrifts was in mortgages or mortgage-backed securities. The bulk of the assets of thrifts was in the form of loans for the purchase of homes. Thrift institutions developed primarily to supply credit to homeowners and consumers rather than to commerce and industry. This legacy still dominates the balance sheets of these institutions even though they have moved into other types of loans.

The bulk of the liabilities of commercial banks and thrift institutions is deposits, which account for over 70 percent of the sum of their liabilities and their net worth.

Although the U.S. banking system remains sound for the most part, it is clear that changes in financial markets have adversely affected the profitability of commercial banks. Bank failures, which were rare in the United States in 1980, had climbed to over 200 per year by 1989.

The banking industry is facing more competition than ever before in credit markets. In 1990, large corporations, once the major clients of commercial banks, were borrowing directly from individual lenders by issuing commercial paper and raising more funds through direct issue of stock. When corporations did borrow from banks, many of the outstanding loans seemed in trouble as some debt-ridden corporations faced bankruptcy. Real estate loans were also souring as land values in many metropolitan markets began to fall. The lucrative consumer credit business was getting more difficult because companies such as Sears and AT&T entered credit card markets, and auto companies used their own subsidiaries to finance car loans. In 1990 the Chase Manhattan Bank began writing off some bad loans and laying off thousands of workers.

Commercial banks still have a relatively large net worth to cushion losses. It is generally agreed that U.S. commercial banks are better managed than the undercapitalized savings and loan industry and lack the problems of fraud that plagued it. But because of increased competition in the credit market, banks have had to cut the rates they charge on loans, which has cut into profits. Losses on loans increased from a bit more than one quarter of 1 percent per year in 1980 to slightly more than 1 percent in 1989. Much of the $40 billion in loans to Third World nations has decreased substantially in value because of the inability of those nations to make full payment.

In 1991 there were 12,000 commercial banks in operation. Many experts argued that the industry was larger than it had to be and that costs could be trimmed through mergers. Mergers would allow banks to share overhead facilities and cut costs but would require major changes in federal and state banking laws. One estimate indicated that if two large New York banks were to merge, the cost saving would be as much as $700 million per year.[3]

There are likely to be significant changes in U.S. banking as pressure mounts to allow banks to expand into new markets in order to increase profits. The number of banks is likely to decrease as mergers and some bank failures occur. Ultimately, in a free market economy, a sound banking system must be a profitable banking system. Unless measures are taken to allow the U.S. banking system to cover costs and earn a reasonable rate of return, bank failures will increase and the viability of the U.S. financial system will suffer.

the global economy

International Banking and the Global Economy

As the U.S. economy has become more integrated into the modern global economy, banking's international operations have increased. In 1960 only 8 U.S. banks operated branches in foreign nations; by 1990 more than 200 U.S. banks had branches in Europe, Latin America, the Far East, and the Caribbean. More than 600 banking offices in the United States are operated by foreign banks, whose assets in this country represent 15 percent of total U.S. banking assets.

U.S. banks with international operations and branches in foreign nations assist U.S. business firms in exporting products. These banks also offer their customers international payment services that facilitate both importing and exporting. They serve as dealers in foreign exchange, earning a profit from exchanging the currency of one nation for that of another. By operating branches abroad, they can also compete for Eurodollars. Eurodollars, which are not subject to any reserve requirements, can easily be transferred to the United States, where they can be

---

[3] See Douglas R. Sease and Robert Guenther, "Big Banks Are Plagued by a Gradual Erosion of Key Profit Centers," *The Wall Street Journal,* August 1, 1990.

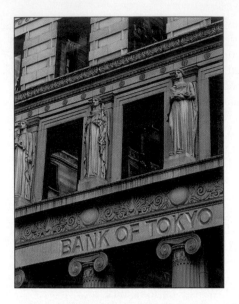

used to support domestic credit demands and add to the profit of U.S. banks.

Banking laws in the United States provide certain special concessions to U.S. international banks. Since 1919, with the passage of the Edge Act, U.S. international banks that specialize in international financial services (Edge Act banks) have been granted the privilege of interstate banking, which is not generally available to other banks in the United States. International banking facilities (IBFs), other types of international banking operations within the United States, can accept deposits from and make loans to foreigners and are not subject to reserve requirements. IBFs are treated like foreign branches of U.S. banks, which are not subject to U.S. regulations or taxes.

Foreign banks maintain offices in the United States to assist their customers in export and import operations. An agency office of a foreign bank cannot accept deposits from domestic residents, but it is allowed to lend funds. In addition, some foreign banks operate subsidiaries within the United States. These banks offer all banking services and compete with American-owned banks. The International Banking Act of 1978 subjects these full-service foreign banks to the same rules and regulations as U.S.-owned banks, including taxation. Foreign banks can also operate full-service branches in the United States, subject to U.S. rules and regulations. Foreigners can also operate Edge Act and IBFs that compete with U.S.-owned and -operated counterparts.

In financing international trade, U.S. banks make loans to foreigners. In the 1980s, many of the loans made to less developed countries by banks with international operations went sour as the economies of many of these debtor nations, especially those in Latin America, faltered. These bad loans contributed to lower profits for many U.S. banks and could contribute to bank failures in the future.

CONCEPT CHECK
□

- How do banks earn profit?
- What are secondary reserves?

- Why do banks seek to have a diversified portfolio of assets?

TOWARD UNDERSTANDING HOW THE MONEY SUPPLY CHANGES

The decisions made by the firms that constitute the nation's banking system exert an important influence on the money stock. In this chapter we've concentrated on the process by which the banking system actually creates money in the form of checkable deposits. As you have seen, the excess reserves available to the system and the willingness of banks to loan out these excess reserves are the major factors influencing daily money supplies.

To understand how the quantity of money available to the public changes, our next step is to examine how changes occur in the reserves available to the banking

principles in practice

Managerial Methods: Using Balance Sheets

Understanding How a Depository Institution becomes Insolvent The *net worth* of a depository institution is the claim its owners have on its assets. Net worth measures how much the owners of the institution have, over and above the value of assets, to pay the claims of depositors. In the 1980s regulations required that thrift institutions have a net worth of a mere 3 percent of total assets—a very small ownership stake. Therefore, defaults on loans or general economic difficulties that hamper the abilities of clients to repay loans can quickly wipe out the meager net worth of a savings and loan institution and even make it negative!

To see how this happens, let's take a look at the change in the balance sheet of a typical depository institution when a loan defaults.

Assets	**Liabilities and Net Worth**
Reserves: No change	Deposits: No change
Loans: −$2 million	Other liabilities: No change
Government securities: No change	Net worth: −$1 million
Other assets at market value: +$1 million	

When a default takes place, the loan no longer produces a stream of income and becomes worthless. Under these circumstances, if the borrower has pledged collateral for the loan, such as real estate, the bank can claim the right to sell the collateral. However, when the value of the collateral is less than the loan balance, as might be the case in a declining real estate market, the total asset value will decline.

For example, suppose a developer borrowed $2 million from a bank, using a shopping center as collateral. When building is finished, suppose the shopping center can't find any tenants willing to lease stores and the developer defaults on the loan. When the bank forecloses on the mortgage, it finds that the most it can get for the shopping center on the free market is $1 million. Therefore, the value of the loans declines by $2 million, while the value of other assets (property) increases by $1 million. The net decline of $1 million in assets must be matched by a $1 million decline in the sum of liabilities and net worth. Because deposits do not decline as a direct result of the foreclosure, the accountants debit the decline in assets against net worth. The balance sheet shows how the default causes the bank's net worth to decline by $1 million. If the depository institution's assets fall short of its liabilities, its net worth then becomes negative. When this situation occurs, it is declared insolvent.

When the economies of oil-producing states such as Texas, Louisiana, and Oklahoma went into a tailspin after 1985, hundreds of depository institutions in those states became insolvent. The difference between the value of their assets and their liabilities for insured deposits then became the responsibility of the deposit insurance agencies. The burden of making up the difference between the value of assets and liabilities is effectively transferred to taxpayers.

Notice that a bank whose net worth turns negative has nothing to lose by taking risks. It has none of its own funds at stake because they have already been wiped out! Depositors care little about the fact that an institution has become insolvent, because they know that their deposits (up to the limit of $100,000 per account) are insured by the federal government. As is always the case when someone else's money is at stake (in this case that money belongs to taxpayers), managers and their creditors can afford to be more careless because they will not bear the costs of their mistakes!

system. The Federal Reserve System manages the nation's money stock by determining the reserves available to the banking system and thus influencing the level of interest rates in the economy. To understand the role of money in the economy, we must analyze how the Federal Reserve System can control bank reserves and influence the willingness of banks to lend excess reserves.

In the following chapter we examine the operations of the Federal Reserve System. This examination will give you the necessary background to understand how the monetary policies pursued by the Federal Reserve System can influence macroeconomic equilibrium in the economy.

insights on issues

How Solid Is the U.S. Financial System? Talking with Edward J. Kane

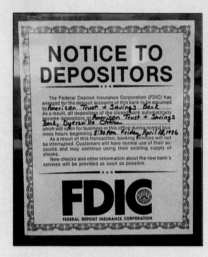

Edward J. Kane is James F. Cleary Professor in Finance at Boston College and an expert in banking and associated regulatory issues. He is author of *The Gathering Crisis in Federal Deposit Insurance* (1985) and *The S&L Insurance Mess: How Did It Happen?* (1989). He is a past president of the American Finance Association and a former Guggenheim fellow.

Are many American banks likely to fail in the near future? Authorities and the press wrongly fixate on bank failure rather than on the market value of the losses to which bank risk-taking exposes the FDIC's Bank Insurance Fund (BIF). Failures reveal and settle losses the FDIC actually has accrued in the past. Despite record profits in 1992, at year-end the FDIC deemed 863 banks, with over $550 billion in assets, to be troubled enough to label them as "problem" institutions. At least one third of these problem institutions eventually will fail. Many problem banks already are economi-

cally insolvent in the sense that the market value of stockholder-contributed assets is not large enough to pay off the firm's deposit and nondeposit obligations. Accounting values tend to show an overly rosy picture of net worth at a troubled bank. This is because managers can underreserve for anticipatable loan losses and other contingencies.

Today many problem banks are taking substantial amounts of interest-rate risk in an effort to gamble themselves back to health in a hurry. By not forcing weak banks to curtail this type of risk-taking, banking regulators are forcing other banks and the general taxpayer to underwrite endgame gambles. Such gambles pay off in a few cases at most times and in most cases a few times. However, considered as an investment, each imposes an expected loss on stronger banks and taxpayers. Assigning the deep downside of bank risk-taking to the FDIC leads one to calculate that in mid-1992 the FDIC was in the red to the tune of between $40 billion and $55 billion in net reserves.

What is the root problem in deposit insurance today? The root problem is a scandal in bank and government accounting. In tough times, the valuation and itemization principles that accountants and regulators use contain reporting options that encourage hiding large opportunity losses from public view. They also let discretionary nonrecurring profits be recorded in ways that can overstate current profits and net worths for years on end. The rosy bias in these readings has much in common with the rigged scales dis-

honest butchers use to overcharge their customers. With a show of apparent precision, they systematically and repeatedly mismeasure the cost of deposit insurance to taxpayers.

Are there any reforms in the works to make sure the banking industry does not face another crisis? Congress passed the FDIC Improvement Act of 1991, which insists that if the accounting value of an insured institution's capital position declines, its managers must recapitalize the bank promptly, or else. This exit-policy mandate subjects a weakening bank to the same sort of discipline its creditors would impose if they weren't insured against loss by the FDIC. Recapitalization does not imply the disappearance of a bank's asset or even of its franchise. What it does imply is a timely repricing of bank assets and a market testing of the value of keeping a troubled institution in play. The central purpose of FDICIA is to inhibit the doubling and redoubling of deposit-institution losses that (though hidden by accounting gimmicks) have occurred already.

Although FDICIA makes a good start, the FDIC needs to do more. It should strive to pattern its risk-management, capital valuation, and pricing decisions on those that a well-managed private deposit-insurance corporation would follow in a competitive market. The organizing principle for premium assessments and risk-control policies should be the need to price and reserve for the insurer's exposure to loss from each client.

SUMMARY

1. Financial intermediaries are firms that specialize in borrowing funds from savers and lending those funds to investors and others. The nation's banking system includes financial intermediaries that offer checkable deposits, such as commercial banks and thrift institutions.

2. Modern banking originated in the Middle Ages with the practice of issuing receipts for gold on deposit with goldsmiths and money changers. The receipts began to circulate as money. By observing inflows and outflows of gold deposits, the goldsmiths realized that only a small fraction of the gold on deposit was likely to be withdrawn on average each day. The issuers of gold receipts, who acted as bankers, ran little risk of running out of gold to meet depositors' demands for withdrawals. As a result, they could issue receipts for more than the actual amounts of gold they held in their vaults.

3. Fractional reserve banking allows a banking system to create checkable deposits by making loans in some multiple of the reserves that banks actually have on hand to meet withdrawals. The fractional reserve ratio is actual reserves divided by total deposits.

4. The banking industry in the United States consists of about 12,000 commercial banks and 3,000 savings and loan associations, 400 mutual savings banks, and other thrift institutions that offer checkable deposits. The reserves of modern banks consist of cash on hand and balances kept on deposit with the regional banks of the Federal Reserve System, the nation's central bank, which serves as a bank for bankers.

5. A bank balance sheet is a statement of its assets and the claims against those assets in the form of liabilities and net worth. A bank's liabilities consist mainly of deposit accounts, which represent the debt of the bank to depositors. A bank's major assets are its loans, government securities, and reserves in the form of cash on hand and deposits at a Federal Reserve bank. Its net worth is the difference between the value of its assets and the value of its liabilities.

6. The required reserve ratio for a bank is the legal minimum percentage of its deposits it must hold in reserves. Required reserves are the dollar value of the currency and deposits in a Federal Reserve bank that a bank must hold to meet current regulations. Excess reserves represent the difference between total reserves held against deposits and required reserves. A bank can use its excess reserves to make loans.

7. When a bank uses excess reserves to make a loan, it creates a deposit for the borrower. When the borrower spends the newly created deposit, excess reserves are likely to flow out of the borrower's bank and into another bank. The process of check clearing involves the transfer of deposits at the Federal Reserve banks. Excess reserves that one bank loses after making a loan are likely to end up as excess reserves for another bank in the banking system. A bank that uses up all of its excess reserves to make loans is said to be "loaned up." Banks typically hold at least some of their assets as excess reserves.

8. The banking system can create checkable deposits by an amount equal to a multiple of existing reserves available to all banks. As deposits created through loans are drawn down to make purchases, they increase deposits and reserves in other banks, which can use the excess reserves to make more loans. The reserve multiplier is the maximum number of new dollars in checkable deposits that can be created from each dollar increase in the excess reserve available to the banking system. The reserve multiplier is the inverse of the required reserve ratio.

9. Just as an increase in excess reserves can cause an increase in checkable deposits, a decrease in excess reserves can cause a decrease in checkable deposits. Because checkable deposits are the major component of the money stock, the excess reserves available to the banking system are an important influence on the money stock.

10. Banks choose to hold some of their assets as excess reserves instead of using those reserves to make loans. The opportunity cost of holding excess reserves depends on the interest that banks forgo by not using the funds to make loans. The demand for excess reserves typically increases during economic downturns and decreases during economic upturns. The greater the bank demand for excess reserves, the smaller the money stock.

11. Banks are motivated to make profits, but they must also maintain enough liquidity in their assets to permit adjustments in the composition of their asset portfolio as business conditions change. Banks are concerned about the riskiness of their assets and seek to minimize the risk of default on loans. Most banks hold 10 percent to 20 percent of their assets in government securities—assets that can be easily liquidated at low transaction cost. In their day-to-day operations, banks balance considerations of profitability, risk, and liquidity.

KEY TERMS

depository institutions *320*
financial
  intermediaries *320*
fractional reserve
  banking *321*

fractional reserve
  ratio *321*
bank *322*
reserves *322*
required reserve ratio *323*
required reserves *323*

excess reserves *323*
default *324*
check clearing *324*
reserve multiplier *329*
federal funds *332*

federal funds rate *333*
prime rate *336*
collateral *336*
government securities *336*
secondary reserves *336*

CONCEPT REVIEW

1 Why does fractional reserve banking give depository institutions the power to create money?

2 A bank has assets of $5 million and liabilities of $4 million. What is the net worth of the bank?

3 What is the reserve multiplier?

4 Under what circumstances does a bank become insolvent?

PROBLEMS AND APPLICATIONS

1. A banker operates under a 20 percent fractional reserve ratio. What amount of deposits can be supported by $5 million of reserves? In what form does a bank hold its reserves? Explain why a bank is unlikely to ever have to pay out all of its deposits in a single day. **1**

2. Suppose you deposit $3,000 in cash from your mattress in your local bank. Show the impact of your deposit on the bank's balance sheet. Explain why the bank cannot increase the loans it makes after it receives your deposit by more than a certain percentage of $3,000. If the required reserve ratio is 0.1, what is the maximum increase in checkable deposits that will result *in the entire banking system* as a result of your deposit? **1**, **2**, **3**

3. Suppose you have accounts at two banks. During a particular week you write a check on one of your accounts for $1,000 and deposit it in your account at the other bank. Will the money stock increase as a result of your transaction? **2**

4. Suppose the Federal Reserve bank lends funds to the First National Bank of Toledo. It does so by crediting the Toledo bank's account at the Federal Reserve by $2 million. Show the impact of the loan on the Toledo bank's balance sheet. What will happen to the Toledo bank's excess reserves as a result of the loan? If the required reserve ratio is 0.1, what is the maximum increase in the money stock that can result from the loan? **2**, **3**

5. Suppose that during the holiday season households withdraw $10 billion from their accounts in banks to hold as cash in their pockets to facilitate shopping. What will happen to bank excess reserves and the capacity of the banking system to make loans as a result? **2**, **3**

6. The required reserve ratio is 0.1, and current available bank reserves are $40 billion. Explain why checkable deposits in the banking system are likely to be less than the maximum possible $400 billion. **3**

7. Following is the balance sheet of the First National Bank of Jonesville:

Assets	**Liabilities and Net Worth**
Reserves, $100 million	Deposits, $180 million
Securities, $50 million	Net worth, $20 million
Loans, $50 million	

If the required reserve ratio is 0.1, what is the amount of the bank's excess reserves? How many dollars' worth of additional loans or securities can the bank acquire as assets? How much of an increase in the money stock could the bank's excess reserves support if all banks in the banking system were to hold zero excess reserves? **2**, **3**

8. Suppose the bank demand curve for excess reserves is a horizontal line. What will be the effect on the money stock of an increase in the amount of excess reserves available to the banking system? **3**

9. Explain why bank demand for excess reserves tends to increase during recessions. Why does the fact that bank demand for excess reserves varies with general business conditions tend to destabilize the economy? **3**

10. How do banks choose their portfolio of assets to balance considerations of profitability, liquidity, and risk? **4**

chapter 15

The Federal Reserve System and Its Influence on Money and Credit

It's nicknamed "the Fed," and its chairman is a highly visible and powerful person whose pronouncements can change the course of the world's securities markets. It's the Federal Reserve System, and its policies and activities play a central role in the economies of the United States and the world.

As the nation's central banking system, the Fed engages in activities that influence the money stock available in the nation. The 12 regional Federal Reserve banks provide deposit accounts for commercial banks and thrift institutions and supply them with currency and check-clearing services. The Federal Reserve System charges banks fees for its services and earns interest on government securities it holds. However, unlike an ordinary bank, the Fed isn't motivated to maximize profits. It's an independent agency charged with promoting the public interest. In its efforts to promote economic stability, the Fed pursues policies that influence the stock of money in circulation, interest rates, and other macroeconomic variables.

In this chapter we'll outline the organization and operations of the Federal Reserve System. Our main goal is to see how the Fed can influence the money stock and the level of interest rates in the economy. In the following chapter we'll examine how the Fed's activities can affect aggregate demand in the economy and influence real GDP and the price level.

☐ CONCEPT PREVIEW

After reading this chapter, you should be able to:

1. Discuss the organization and structure of the Federal Reserve System.

2. Describe the techniques used by the Fed to influence the money supply.

3. Show how the Fed's open market operations affect bank reserves, securities prices, interest rates, and the money supply.

4. Analyze the nation's money supply curve and show how the desire of banks to hold excess reserves affect the quantity of money supplied.

THE FEDERAL RESERVE SYSTEM

1 The Federal Reserve Act of 1913 established the Federal Reserve System and the 12 regional Federal Reserve banks. The system was organized in response to a series of bank panics in the late 19th and early 20th centuries. One of the most serious of these panics occurred in 1907. The loss in savings resulting from bank failures at that time led to strong political support for a central banking authority. Since it was established in 1913, the Federal Reserve System has acted in the public interest to promote the stability of the nation's banking and monetary system. Its role in the economy has evolved gradually since its organization. Currently, the Fed's day-to-day operations constitute an essential mechanism in the functioning of the economy. To gain a complete understanding of how the economy operates, it's necessary to examine the organization and functions of the Federal Reserve System.

The Federal Reserve System: How It Is Organized

Board of Governors of the Federal Reserve System the governing body that supervises the operation of the nation's banking system and acts as an authority to regulate the money supply. The Board consists of seven governors, each appointed by the president to serve a 14-year term.

The **Board of Governors of the Federal Reserve System,** located in Washington, D.C., supervises the operation of the nation's banking system and acts as an authority to regulate the money supply. It consists of seven governors, each of whom is appointed by the president of the United States, after approval by the Senate, for a 14-year term. One of the governors serves as chairman of the Board. The chairman is appointed by the president for a four-year term.

The Board of Governors operates as an independent, self-supporting authority. It does not receive funding from Congress, and it does not take orders from the president or any other political official! The Board has broad policymaking functions. For example, within certain limits the Board makes decisions about reserve requirements for banks.

regional Federal Reserve banks banks that perform central banking functions for banks within each of 12 Federal Reserve districts.

The **regional Federal Reserve banks** perform central banking functions for banks within each of 12 Federal Reserve districts. The regional Federal Reserve banks are located in San Francisco, Minneapolis, Kansas City, Dallas, Chicago, St. Louis, Atlanta, Cleveland, Richmond, Philadelphia, New York, and Boston. The maps in Box 1 show the boundaries of the 12 Federal Reserve districts.

Each of the regional Federal Reserve banks is a corporation. The stockholders in each of these corporations are the banks of the region that are members of the Federal Reserve System. All national banks—those with charters from the U.S. Office of the Comptroller of the Currency—must be members of the Federal Reserve System. Commercial banks whose charters are approved by state governments can choose to become members of the system. Currently, all depository institutions— both commercial banks and thrift institutions—are *required* to keep deposits at their regional Federal Reserve banks as reserves. All depository institutions have the privilege of borrowing funds from the Fed. From the standpoint of the control the Fed exercises over banks, there is little distinction between member and nonmember banks.

The Federal Reserve banks are very unusual corporations. Member banks can neither sell their shares on the stock market nor expect to receive a large share of the Fed's profits, most of which are given to the U.S. Treasury. Member banks earn a 6 percent annual dividend on their stock, no matter how much the Fed actually earns in a given year.

The regional Federal Reserve banks also issue currency. Although commercial banks and thrift institutions cannot issue currency, they can draw down their deposit accounts at the Fed in exchange for crisp, clean dollar (or any other denomination) bills when they want to hold cash. Both currency and the deposits banks hold at their

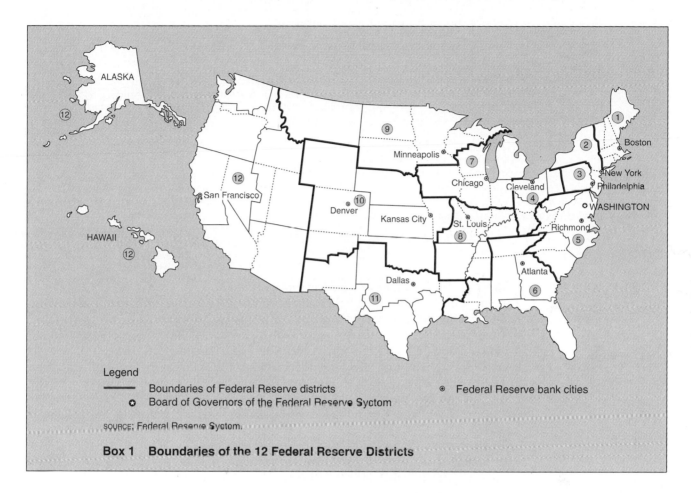

Legend

—— Boundaries of Federal Reserve districts
⊙ Board of Governors of the Federal Reserve System
◎ Federal Reserve bank cities

SOURCE: Federal Reserve System.

Box 1   Boundaries of the 12 Federal Reserve Districts

regional Federal Reserve banks are merely the liabilities issued by the Federal Reserve System.

The most important policymaking component of the Fed is the Federal Open Market Committee (FOMC), which makes decisions that influence the amount of excess reserves available to banks. The FOMC is composed of the seven governors of the Federal Reserve System, the president of the Federal Reserve Bank of New York, and the presidents of four other Federal Reserve banks. The committee's decisions and their implementation are a major determinant of interest rates and the availability of credit each day. The committee issues directives to the Federal Reserve Bank of New York to buy or sell government securities on the open market. As you'll soon see, adjustments in the amount of government securities held by the Federal Reserve banks are the major means used by the Fed to influence the stock of money in circulation.

There is also the *Federal Advisory Council,* which represents the owners of the Fed—its member banks. This council, which consists of 12 bankers, has virtually no policymaking power. Its function is purely advisory, and its members have no direct influence on the Fed's day-to-day operations.

Box 2 contains a convenient chart that shows how the Federal Reserve System is organized.

Federal Open Market Committee (FOMC)
an arm of the Federal Reserve System affects the amount of excess reserves available to banks by instructing the Federal Reserve Bank of New York to buy or sell government securities on the open market.

Box 2   Major Components of the Federal Reserve System

Board of Governors of the Federal Reserve System
1. Supervises the nation's banking system.
2. Regulates the money supply by setting reserve requirements and approving discount rate changes.

Regional Federal Reserve Banks
1. Perform central banking services for banks.
2. Issue currency and hold bank deposits to serve as reserves.

Federal Open Market Committee
1. Makes decisions that influence bank excess reserves by determining open market operations.
2. Is the policy arm of the Fed.

Is the Fed Independent of Political Interference?

The intent of the original Federal Reserve Act of 1913 was to diffuse central banking power among the 12 regional Federal Reserve banks. However, the Federal Reserve System has evolved into an organization that is responsible for promoting economic stability. The Fed's Board of Governors now has a considerable degree of power in establishing policies that affect the performance of the economy. The Board can also influence the activities of the regional banks, and it has substantial input in the choice of the presidents of these banks. Thus, the Federal Reserve System has become a much more centralized decision-making organization than was originally intended.

The chairman of the Board of Governors wields considerable power. That power rests in his control over professional staff members and advisers to the system. This control enables the chairman to influence the information and analysis upon which policy decisions are based.

In an attempt to eliminate political pressures on the governors, each of the seven governors is appointed for a *nonrenewable* 14-year term. Therefore, the governors have little incentive to pursue policies that always please the president or senators. To avoid possible regional bias, each of the governors must be from a different Federal Reserve district. Finally, the Fed is not dependent on Congress for funds. It earns interest income from its holdings of securities and from loans it makes to depository institutions. It earns, on average, more than $10 billion per year, but it returns the bulk of these earnings to the Treasury.

Despite the precautions that have been taken to ensure its political independence, the Fed is under constant and considerable political pressure. Congress can reduce the Fed's independence by changing the law. The threat of such legislative change can influence the Fed's behavior, thereby subjecting it to indirect and subtle political interference. In 1975, for example, Congress passed a resolution that requires the Fed to periodically announce its money supply growth targets. The Humphrey-Hawkins Bill, passed in 1978, requires the Fed to explain how its objectives coincide with the president's economic policies. The president can influence the Board of Governors by appointing governors and by his choice of the chairman. The president can also exert political pressure on the Fed in much the same way Congress can.

The issue of the Fed's political independence is highly controversial. Critics of an independent central bank argue that decisions affecting the functioning of the economy should be made by elected representatives rather than long-term appointees.

However, those who favor an independent central banking authority argue that political control of the Fed can result in expansion of the money stock and credit in periods before elections to help the dominant political party win. Expansion of the money stock before an election may contribute to short-term increases in aggregate demand that result in expansion of the economy. If this causes the economy to overheat, there may be a period of inflation after the election.

- How is the Federal Reserve System organized?
- What are the functions of the Fed?

- How is the Federal Reserve System insulated from political interference?

CONCEPT CHECK
☐

THE FED'S INFLUENCE ON THE MONETARY BASE

In the preceding chapter we saw that the banking system's potential to create money depends on the excess reserves available for loans. The Fed uses a variety of techniques to control the excess reserves available to depository institutions. The monetary base is the sum of currency in circulation and total bank reserves outstanding at any given time. Note that both currency and bank reserves, which consist mainly of vault cash and bank deposits at the Federal Reserve banks, are *liabilities* of the Federal Reserve System. The Fed can vary the monetary base by adjusting its liabilities and assets and by regulating banks through control of reserve requirements.

monetary base the sum of currency in circulation and total bank reserves outstanding at any given time.

By controlling the monetary base, the Fed can exert a strong influence on the equilibrium money stock. However, the equilibrium quantity of money held by the public at any point in time depends on a variety of factors, not just the actions taken by the Fed. An increase in the monetary base that increases bank excess reserves will increase the money stock only if banks choose to use those reserves to extend credit, thereby creating new deposits. The decisions made by profit-maximizing banks are therefore an important influence on the equilibrium money stock. The equilibrium money stock also depends on the public's demand for money balances. Shifts in the demand for money can affect interest rates and the desire of banks to create checkable deposits by extending credit.

In this section we concentrate only on the techniques available to the Fed to control the monetary base and, through that control, to influence excess reserves and the banking system's potential to create money. Once you understand how the Fed can achieve this, the next step is to show how Federal Reserve policies that control the monetary base also influence the equilibrium money stock and the equilibrium level of interest rates.

The Fed's major tools to control the monetary base are:

1. Control of *required reserve ratios,* the legally mandated ratios of reserves to deposits for banks.
2. Control of the **discount rate,** the interest rate Federal Reserve banks charge member banks for loans.
3. **Open market operations,** the Fed's purchases and sales of government securities on financial markets that affect the amount of excess reserves available to banks.

discount rate the interest rate Federal Reserve banks charge member banks for loans.

open market operations the Federal Reserve System's purchases and sales of government securities conducted by the Federal Open Market Committee.

Control of Required Reserve Ratios

The Board of Governors of the Federal Reserve System sets reserve requirements for depository institutions. Within certain limits established by Congress, the Fed

Box 3   Reserve Requirements of Depository Institutions, December 1992

Type of deposit	Statutory limits	Requirement as of December 1992
Checkable deposits		
0–$42.2 million	3%	3%
Over $42.2 million	8–14	10
Business time and Eurocurrency deposits	0–9	0

SOURCE: *Federal Reserve Bulletin.*

can raise or lower the required reserve ratio for checkable deposits, savings deposits, and time deposits. The table in Box 3 summarizes the reserve requirements for depository institutions in effect as of December 1992.

Recall that the maximum amount of checkable deposits supported by any given amount of bank reserves is inversely related to the required reserve ratio. If the average reserve requirement is, say, 10 percent, the maximum amount of checkable deposits can be computed by dividing the excess reserves by the required reserve ratio. If excess reserves are $20 billion and the required reserve ratio on average is 0.1, a maximum of $200 billion ($20 billion/0.1) in checkable deposits can be supported by those reserves. If the required reserve ratio were to fall to 0.05, the maximum amount of checkable deposits that could be supported by the available excess reserves would *double* to $400 billion ($20 billion/0.05).

Suppose checkable deposits at depository institutions are currently $400 billion. An increase in the required reserve ratio of a mere 0.005 for these deposits would increase required reserves by a whopping $2 billion ($400 billion × 0.005). Excess reserves would fall by $2 billion. If the required reserve ratio were 0.1005 after this increase, the potential decrease in the money supply resulting from the increase in the required reserve ratio would be

$$- \Delta M = \frac{- \Delta ER}{\text{Required reserve ratio}} = \frac{\$2 \text{ billion}}{0.1005} = \$19.9 \text{ billion}$$

The increase in required reserves would therefore have the potential to reduce the ability of the banking system to create checkable deposits by nearly $20 billion, which is almost 5 percent of the amount outstanding prior to the increase in the required reserve ratio.

The effects of manipulating reserve requirements on excess reserves and the money supply are so powerful and pronounced that they prevent small adjustments in the money supply. A very small increase in reserve requirements can cause serious disruptions in the loan business of banks with low excess reserves as it may force them to call in loans or clamp down on new credit. However, the Fed occasionally reduces reserve requirements as a dramatic way of signaling its intention of following an expansionary monetary policy. In late 1990, for the first time since 1983, the Fed reduced the reserve requirement on business time deposits, from 3 percent to 0 percent, as it became clear that the economy was in a recession. This increased bank excess reserves by $11.7 billion. Then, in April 1992, in response to a very sluggish recovery from the recession of 1990–91, the Fed reduced the reserve requirement for checkable deposits at large banks from 12 to 10 percent.

Discount Policy: The Fed as Lender of Last Resort

Bank borrowings from the Federal Reserve System are called discount loans or *advances*. These constitute a fraction of a percent of the assets of Federal Reserve banks usually amounting to less than 2 percent of the reserves of the banking system.

discount loans bank borrowings from the Federal Reserve System; also called *advances*.

When Federal Reserve banks make loans to creditworthy institutions, they create deposits for those institutions. Because deposits at the Fed are part of the reserves of banks, these loans increase the reserves available to the banking system. Therefore, discount loans to banks have the potential to increase the money stock by a multiple of the amounts loaned. Increased willingness of the Federal Reserve System to loan funds to banks, as evidenced by a decrease in the discount rate, will increase excess reserves and the supply of loanable funds. By the same token, an increase in the discount rate will tend to decrease the potential supply of loanable funds.

The Fed is very careful to regulate banks' use of the *discount window,* the Federal Reserve facility at which discount loans to banks are actually made. For example, if the discount rate is 8 percent and the market rate of interest that can be earned on three-month Treasury bills is 10 percent, banks will be tempted to borrow from the Fed to buy Treasury bills. They'll earn an easy and safe 2 percent on these transactions without risking any of their own funds. The Fed is well aware of this temptation, and it limits the frequency with which banks can avail themselves of the discount window loan facilities. By borrowing too much for short-term profit opportunities like investing in Treasury bills, a bank runs the risk of being turned down for credit in the future. Regulating the use of the discount window by refusing or discouraging borrowing is sometimes called *moral suasion* by the Fed. The Fed simply uses its discretionary power to say no to banks so that it can keep the supply of reserves down.

The discount window is also used by the Fed to maintain confidence in the banking system. The Fed lets it be known that it is the "lender of last resort." By creating new reserves for a bank when it is in danger of failing, the Fed can maintain confidence in the bank and prevent a bank run. For example, in 1970 the bankruptcy of the Penn Central Railroad rendered worthless much of that firm's short-term marketable loans, or *commercial paper*. Other companies that relied on short-term marketable loans as a means of raising funds had trouble selling their marketable loans in financial markets. The Fed solved this problem by announcing that it would gladly make discount loans to banks willing to make direct loans to firms that had difficulty in marketing their commercial paper. This avoided a chain reaction of bankruptcies that might have developed otherwise. Similarly, immediately after the stock market crash of 1987, the chairman of the Fed, Alan Greenspan, announced that the Fed would take measures to assure banks of access to the discount window. His motive was to bolster public confidence in the banking system's ability to obtain funds. Greenspan thereby hoped to prevent fears that banks that couldn't get quick repayment of loans to securities dealers would be unable to meet deposit withdrawal demands.

Changes in the discount rate don't always imply a change in Fed policy to influence the monetary base. Sometimes the Fed raises the discount rate simply because short-term market interest rates have risen. The Fed's objective may be merely to discourage overuse of the discount window for profit making rather than to slow down economic activity and decrease bank reserves.

How Open Market Sales of Government Securities by the Fed Affect Bank Reserves

The most flexible and most commonly used method of controlling the monetary base in the United States is Federal Reserve open market operations. These operations consist of daily sales and purchases of government securities by the Federal Reserve System. All open market operations are conducted through the Federal Reserve Bank of New York. The Fed's trading partners, about 40 securities dealers (many of which are banks), trade for their own accounts or act as agents for banks, for business firms, or for individuals who want to buy and sell government securities.

Any purchases of government securities by the Fed are purchases of securities *already outstanding* and held by the public. The Fed *does not* have the authority to purchase new Treasury issues of government securities.

Suppose, for example, that on a given day the Fed decides to reduce its holdings of government securities. It will sell securities on that day to dealers that are also depository institutions or through dealers that act as agents for such depository institutions (banks). To see how this affects the reserves available to the banking system, we need to examine both the balance sheet of the Federal Reserve banks and the consolidated balance sheet of all depository institutions.

Government securities held by the Federal Reserve banks are part of their assets. When they sell these securities to depository institutions, the Fed's asset holdings decline. As any accountant will tell you, when an entity's assets decline, its liabilities must also fall unless it acquires other assets to replace the ones that were sold. But how do the Fed's liabilities decline in this case? Well, the depository institutions pay for the purchases of government securities by drawing down their account balances (which serve as banking system reserves) at their district Federal Reserve banks. The Fed uses an electronic wire service (Fedwire) to simultaneously transfer securities to the banks and debit their accounts at their regional Federal Reserve banks. The Fed's liabilities therefore decline by the net sales of government securities. As a result, sales of government securities by the Fed to depository institutions will *decrease bank reserves. It follows that sales of government securities will decrease the monetary base and the potential of the banking system to create money.*

For example, a $1 billion sale of government securities by the Fed to banks will reduce bank reserves by that $1 billion. If the required reserve ratio is 0.1, the $1 billion sale will reduce the potential amount of checkable deposits in the banking system by $10 billion ($1 billion/0.1). Box 4 shows the effect of the $1 billion sale of securities on the balance sheets of the Federal Reserve banks and the banking system. For the Fed, the sale of securities reduces both its assets and liabilities by $1 billion. For the banking system, $1 billion of assets in the form of reserves are exchanged for $1 billion of assets in the form of government securities. This decreases the reserves in the banking system and thus reduces the banking system's potential to extend credit. There is no direct change in the liabilities of the banking system as a result of the transaction.

How Open Market Purchases of Government Securities Affect Bank Reserves

It's easy to show that the Fed's *purchase* of government securities from banks or the public will increase the monetary base. For example, suppose the Fed acts through its dealers to buy $1 billion of government securities from the portfolios of depository institutions. The Fed pays for the purchase by crediting the deposit accounts of these banks at regional Federal Reserve banks. These deposits, of course, are part of the banking system reserves. *The purchase of government securities from banks therefore increases the excess reserves of the banking system.* The creation of these excess reserves has the potential to allow multiple expansion of checkable deposits if the banks are willing to use the excess reserves to make loans. For example, if the required reserve ratio is 0.1, the $1 billion increase in excess reserves can support an increase of up to $10 billion in checkable deposits.

Box 4   Changes in Balance Sheets of Federal Reserve Banks and the Banking System as a Result of Net Open Market Sales to Banks

FEDERAL RESERVE BANKS
(billions of dollars)

Assets		Liabilities and net worth	
Government securities	−1	Reserves of depository institutions	−1

BANKING SYSTEM
Commercial Banks and Thrift Institutions
(billions of dollars)

Assets		Liabilities and net worth
Government securities	+1	No change
Reserves	−1	

Box 5   Changes in Balance Sheets of Federal Reserve Banks and the Banking System as a Result of Net Open Market Purchases

FEDERAL RESERVE BANKS
(billions of dollars)

Assets		Liabilities and net worth	
Government securities	+1	Reserves of depository institutions	+1

BANKING SYSTEM
Commercial Banks and Thrift Institutions
(billions of dollars)

Assets		Liabilities and net worth
Government securities	−1	No change
Reserves	+1	

The table in Box 5 shows the impact of the Fed's purchase of government securities on its balance sheet and the consolidated balance sheet of the banking system. The purchase of $1 billion of government securities increases the Fed's assets by $1 billion. Of course, whenever assets increase, liabilities must increase by an equivalent amount unless other assets decline. The new liabilities for the Fed in this case are the $1 billion in bank reserves that the Fed creates when it credits the accounts of banks that have sold securities. The Fed can also pay for its purchase of government securities by issuing more Federal Reserve notes. This is another neat trick of the central bank—it can actually create currency. All the Fed needs to do is put in a call to the Bureau of Engraving and Printing and order a crisp, clean batch of new $10, $20, $50, and $100 bills to ship out to the banks in payment for the securities. The currency, of course, is just as much a liability of the Fed as the deposits it creates for banks.

Box 5 also shows the change in the balance sheet of the banking system. When the banks sell government securities to the Fed, their assets in the form of securities

principles in practice

The Fed's Open Market Operations

A Visit to the Trading Desk If you read *The Wall Street Journal*, you know that securities trading is a fast-paced, high-stakes business that demands keen minds and nerves of steel. You certainly need those qualities in abundance if you're in charge of trading for the Federal Open Market Committee (FOMC). Let's see what this job entails.

Policies of the FOMC are executed by the Federal Reserve Bank of New York. The responsibility for actually making the daily purchases and sales of government securities is that of the manager for domestic operations at the trading desk of the New York Fed. The manager supervises a staff of traders who telephone securities dealers to conduct transactions on the open market.

The Treasury securities that the trading desk of the New York Fed deals in are held in electronic book entry form. When transactions take place, ownership of securities is transferred through the electronic Fedwire system and payment is also made through Fedwire. The volume of securities transfers that take place through Fedwire is very large, averaging over $350 billion per day. The trading desk moves around lots of cash and securities each day.

The manager keeps track of available reserves in the banking system and also watches the federal funds rate to get an idea of changes in bank demand for excess reserves. The federal funds rate is the interest rate banks charge for overnight loans of funds on deposit at Federal Reserve banks. The federal funds rate tends to fall when banks have increasing excess reserves, and it tends to rise when excess reserves are decreasing.

A day at the trading desk begins at 8:30 A.M., when staff members review changes in market conditions and analyze the effects of current economic reports on the demand for bank reserves.* Some staff members of the trading desk then meet with government securities dealers who arrive at the Fed from their nearby Wall Street offices to discuss forces at work in the financial markets that day. At around 10:30, the manager and the staff of the trading desk call the U.S. Treasury to get some idea of the effect of government payments on the banking system that day. By 10:45 A.M. the open market manager and other members of the trading desk start developing their preliminary trading plan.

At around 11:15 A.M., a conference call is put in to the office of the director of the Division of Monetary Affairs at the Board of Governors of the Fed. This puts the staff of the trading desk in touch with members of the FOMC. The conference call, which usually lasts 15 to 20 minutes, gives the members a chance to comment on the trading plan for the day.

At around 11:30, the Fed begins executing its trading program by contacting dealers and making an announcement of its plan to the press. At that time the traders on the eighth floor of the Federal Reserve bank begin making their telephone calls to dealers in government securities for price quotations. The Fed usually collects quotes on prices and makes all its trades by 12:15 P.M.

* This description is based on Ann-Marie Meulendyke, *U.S. Monetary Policy and Financial Markets* (New York: Federal Reserve Bank of New York, 1990).

fall by $1 billion. In exchange, the banks receive new reserves in the form of the $1 billion that the Fed creates for them as deposits at regional Federal Reserve banks. These are now new excess reserves that the banks can use to make loans and create checkable deposits.

A Recap: The Operations of the Federal Open Market Committee

The Federal Open Market Committee (FOMC) meets regularly (about once every six weeks) in Washington to decide on targets for M1 (currency and checkable deposits) and bank reserves in an attempt to help stabilize economic fluctuations. The FOMC directs the Federal Reserve Bank of New York, which is located in the center of the financial district in Manhattan, to buy or sell securities to achieve the Fed's objectives. The trading desk of the Federal Reserve Bank of New York (located on the eighth floor of the New York Fed, in case you want to visit) is the hub of the Fed's trading of government securities. The manager of the trading desk communicates

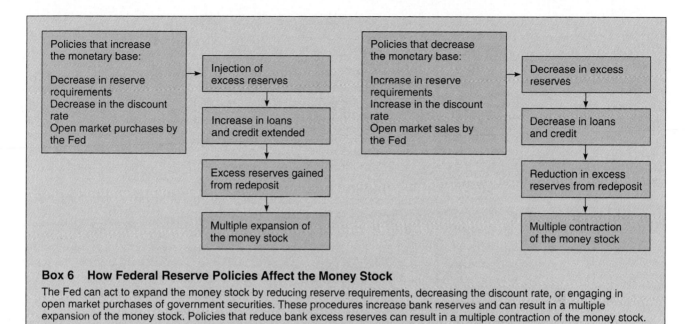

Box 6   How Federal Reserve Policies Affect the Money Stock

The Fed can act to expand the money stock by reducing reserve requirements, decreasing the discount rate, or engaging in open market purchases of government securities. These procedures increase bank reserves and can result in a multiple expansion of the money stock. Policies that reduce bank excess reserves can result in a multiple contraction of the money stock.

daily with FOMC members to make sure their objectives are being achieved. If the objective on a given day is to increase bank reserves, the manager will purchase government securities from dealers who act as agents for the banks and the general public. If, instead, the objective is to decrease bank reserves, the manager will sell government securities.

Open market operations are the most flexible and direct tool available to the Fed to influence bank reserves and the money supply. For example, open market operations are more direct than discount policy. A reduction in the discount rate doesn't necessarily increase bank reserves. Banks may not respond to the lower discount rate by borrowing significantly more. Another advantage of open market operations is that they are easily reversed. If the manager of the trading desk overshoots the target for bank reserves on a given day by buying too many securities, the manager can easily correct the mistake the following day by selling a bit more than would have been offered otherwise.

The chart in Box 6 summarizes the policies used by the Fed to influence the monetary base and shows how the impact of those policies on excess reserves affects bank loans and the money creation process.

CONCEPT CHECK

- How can the Fed control the nation's monetary base? How does an increase in the monetary base increase the potential of the banking system to create money?

- On a given day the Fed purchases $50 billion worth of government securities and sells $20 billion worth of government securities. What is likely to happen to bank excess reserves as a result?

- Why is an increase in open market sales likely to be a more effective way of decreasing the monetary base than an increase in the discount rate?

SECURITIES PRICES, INTEREST RATES, AND THE MONETARY BASE

One question that may have crossed your mind is: How does the Fed get banks and the public to readily buy or sell securities so that the monetary base and bank reserve targets can be met? The answer lies in the price adjustments that allow securities markets, like all markets, to equilibrate. In fact, much of the trading that takes place is in short-term securities of the U.S. government that don't yield explicit interest. The return earned on these short-term assets depends on the difference between their purchase price and the price at which they can be redeemed when they mature. (A financial asset *matures* when its principal, or face value, is repaid by the borrower.)

Almost all open market transactions of the Fed are trades of Treasury bills. *Treasury bills* are short-term obligations of the U.S. government, with maturities of three months to one year, that are sold at auction without a stated rate of interest. If you buy a $10,000 one-year Treasury bill for $9,500 and hold it until it matures, you can redeem it for $10,000. Your effective interest is represented by the $500 *discount* you received from the face value when you bought the bill. In this case the effective annual interest rate would be 5.3 percent = ($500/$9,500)(100%).

When Treasury bill prices decline, their effective interest yield increases. For example, if you could buy a $10,000 one-year Treasury bill for $9,000, your annual interest would be the $1,000 discount from the face value of the bill. The annual interest rate on the bill would now be 11.1 percent = ($1,000/$9,000)(100%). A decrease in the auction price for Treasury bills therefore implies an increase in their effective interest yield. Similarly, an increase in the price of a security implies a decrease in its effective yield.

A similar relationship exists between securities prices and effective interest rates for Treasury notes and bonds with fixed yields. A *coupon bond* yields a certain stated percentage interest rate based on its face value. This interest rate is called the "coupon yield." For example, a bond with a $1,000 face value and a 10 percent coupon yield would pay $100 in interest over the year. If market prices of previously issued bonds decrease, the bonds sell at a *discount*. In addition to the coupon yield, the purchaser of a previously issued bond that sells at a discount will in effect earn additional interest when the bond is cashed in at maturity because of the discount in the bond price. For example, if you buy a one-year $1,000 bond with a 10 percent coupon yield for $900, you'll earn $100 per year interest plus an additional $100 (which was the discount on the bond) when you cash it in for its face value of $1,000 at maturity. Your effective yield if you hold the bond until it matures will be 22 percent = ($200/$900)(100%).

If the market price of a bond goes up, its effective yield goes down. For example, if the market price of a $1,000 bond with a 10 percent coupon yield were $1,050, you'd earn $100 interest on the bond. However, you'd still receive only $1,000 when the bond matures. The extra $50 you pay for the bond over its face value is a *premium* that reduces your effective yield on the bond.

With this bit of insight into the relationship between securities prices and their effective interest yields, you can better understand the impact of open market transactions on interest rates and the equilibrium quantity of securities held by banks and the public. On any given day, a certain amount of government securities (measured in dollar value) is available to banks and the public as financial assets. The amount held by the Fed is *not* available to the general public and banks as financial assets. The Fed holds such a large amount of government securities that it can

Box 7   Open Market Sales and Securities Prices

Open market sales by the Fed increase the supply of available government securities and decrease securities prices.

influence the prices of these Treasury bills, bonds, and notes by selling or buying from its portfolio.

The graph in Box 7 shows the impact of the Fed's open market sales on the price of government securities. The sales by the Fed *increase* the supply of securities available for the public to hold. The increase in supply, other things being equal, lowers the prices. Therefore, the securities sell at a deeper discount than they did initially. In effect, this increases their yield and makes them more attractive assets for banks and the public to hold in their portfolios. Banks, securities dealers, and private investors are induced to buy the securities offered by the Fed because the price changes and yield changes caused by the increased supply serve to increase the quantity demanded. In Box 7 the supply curve for securities shifts outward and lowers the price of Treasury bonds, notes, and bills from P_1 on average to P_2 on average. The dollar value of quantity demanded increases accordingly from Q_1 to Q_2. The sales reduce the monetary base as banks and the public increase the quantity of securities they hold.

Similarly, open market purchases by the Fed reduce the supply of government securities available to banks and the public for their portfolios. The graph in Box 8 shows the impact of open market purchases. Once again, the initial equilibrium price and quantity are P_1 and Q_1, respectively. After open market purchases, the supply of government securities available to banks and the public decreases. This increases the price of the securities, which means the effective yield at maturity will fall. Government securities are now a less attractive financial asset to banks and the general public. The quantity demanded is therefore willingly reduced by the amount of the Fed's purchases. As the price of securities goes up to P_3 in Box 8, the quantity demanded declines to Q_3. As banks and the public willingly sell their securities to the Fed, the monetary base increases. Bank excess reserves also increase, allowing a potential multiple expansion of checkable deposits.

This analysis points out an inevitable impact of the Fed's open market operations. As government securities are bought and sold, the equilibrium interest rates earned

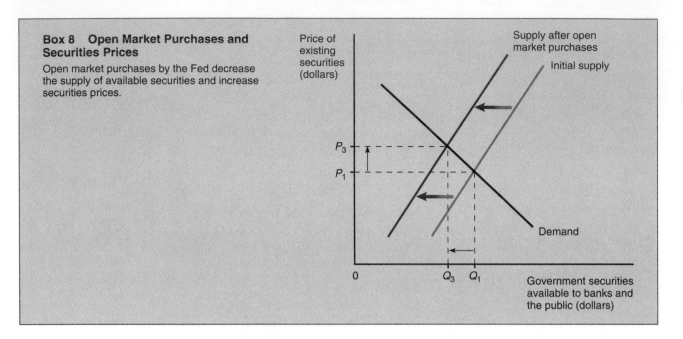

Box 8   Open Market Purchases and Securities Prices

Open market purchases by the Fed decrease the supply of available securities and increase securities prices.

on them change. Because these securities are substitutes for loans and other financial assets held by banks and the public, a change in their interest rates will affect the demand for and supply of all types of financial assets. In effect, the Fed influences the general level of interest rates in the economy when it conducts its open market operations. The Fed therefore influences the economy in two ways through open market operations:

1. It affects excess reserves and the monetary base available to banks and the public directly through its open market sales and purchases.

2. It affects the equilibrium amounts of money holdings, spending, and investment through its impact on interest rates.

Money Supply, Money Demand, and Equilibrium Interest Rates

The stock of money available on any given day must be willingly held by the public. The quantity of money demanded depends on the interest rate, the price level, real GDP, and other variables. In general, the lower the market rate of interest, the greater the quantity of money demanded. The higher the level of real GDP or the price level, the greater the demand for money. The graph in Box 9 depicts the demand for money as a downward-sloping function of the interest rate.

The money supply is a relationship between the quantity of money supplied in the form of currency and checkable deposits and the level of interest rates prevailing at a given point in time. An important influence on the money supply under the direct control of the Fed is the monetary base. One component of the monetary base, currency in circulation, is a part of the money stock. Bank reserves, the other component of the monetary base, are not part of the money stock. However, each dollar of bank reserves has the potential to support many times that amount of checkable deposits, depending on the willingness of banks to create checkable deposits by extending credit. Although the Fed has direct control over the monetary base, the banking system's willingness to lend out excess reserves is a major determinant of the quantity of checkable deposits supplied.

money supply a relationship between the quantity of money supplied in the form of currency and checkable deposits and the level of interest rates prevailing at a given point in time.

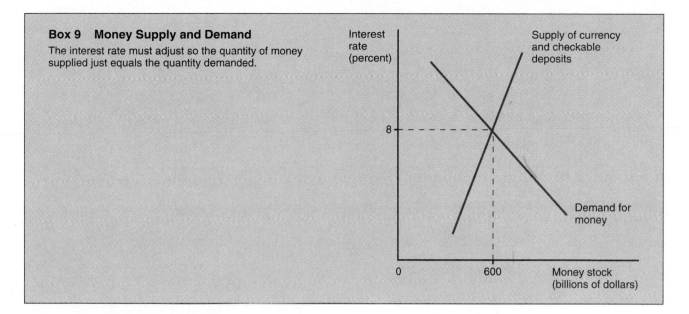

Box 9   Money Supply and Demand
The interest rate must adjust so the quantity of money supplied just equals the quantity demanded.

Interest rate (percent)

Supply of currency and checkable deposits

8

Demand for money

0   600   Money stock (billions of dollars)

The willingness of the banking system to create checkable deposits out of its available reserves is influenced by the prevailing level of interest rates. As was pointed out in the preceding chapter, banks desire to hold more excess reserves at low interest rates than at high interest rates. It follows that for any given available amount of bank reserves supplied by the Fed, the amount of checkable deposits made available by the banking system tends to increase as interest rates increase. This is because the profitability of making loans and extending credit in general tends to increase as interest rates rise. The total quantity of money supplied therefore tends to increase as market interest rates go up. The graph in Box 9 shows an upward-sloping money supply curve. The money supply curve shows the relationship between interest rates and the quantity of money supplied, given the monetary base and all the other influences on the willingness and ability of banks to extend credit.

In equilibrium, the interest rate must adjust so that the quantity of money demanded exactly equals the quantity supplied. The graph shows the demand for and supply of money balances. The equilibrium quantity of money balances is $600 billion at the equilibrium market interest rate (an average of all interest rates) of 8 percent. If the interest rate were higher than 8 percent, the quantity of money balances supplied would exceed the quantity demanded, and this would reduce interest rates. As interest rates fell, the quantity of money balances demanded would increase, while the quantity supplied by the banking system would decline. Similarly, if the interest rate were below 8 percent, the quantity of money balances demanded would exceed the quantity supplied and the interest rate would increase to 8 percent.

How the Fed Influences the Supply Curve of Money and the Equilibrium Interest Rate
The *equilibrium* quantity of money balances and the equilibrium interest rate level depend on the demand for and supply of money. The Fed can shift the money supply curve by influencing bank excess reserves, but it has no direct influence over the demand for money. Whenever the Fed engages in operations that increase bank

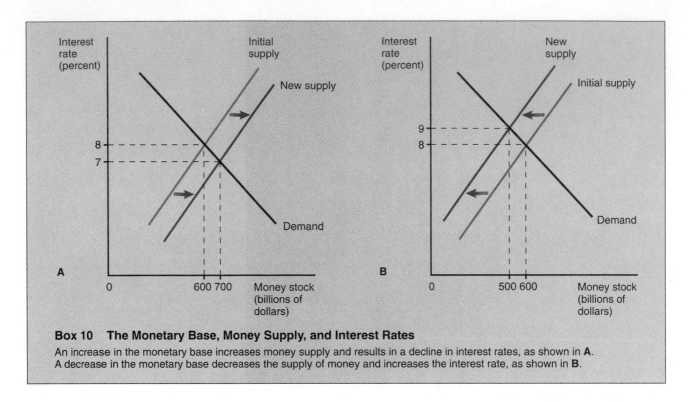

Box 10   The Monetary Base, Money Supply, and Interest Rates
An increase in the monetary base increases money supply and results in a decline in interest rates, as shown in **A**.
A decrease in the monetary base decreases the supply of money and increases the interest rate, as shown in **B**.

reserves or currency in circulation, it shifts the money supply curve to the right. As shown in graph **A** of Box 10, the increase in the money supply puts downward pressure on interest rates, which fall until the quantity of money demanded once again equals the quantity supplied. Similarly, open market operations by the Fed that decrease the monetary base tend to put upward pressure on interest rates (see graph **B**).

🌐 *the global economy*

International Operations of the Fed

The supply of and demand for the dollar in foreign exchange markets influence its price in terms of foreign currency. Changes in the price of the dollar affect the demand for U.S. exports and U.S. demand for imported goods, which in turn can influence real GDP and the price level.

Since the mid-1970s, when flexible foreign exchange rates became the norm, the Federal Reserve System has often intervened in foreign exchange markets to influence the price of the dollar. The Federal Open Market Committee of the Fed authorizes foreign currency purchases and sales, and a

special manager for foreign operations is employed to supervise these operations. When the Fed buys and sells dollars and other foreign currencies on foreign exchange markets, it often does so in conjunction with similar operations by foreign central banks. In these ways the Fed can affect the supply of and demand for dollars offered in foreign exchange and thus can control the price of the dollar to achieve certain policy objectives.

Suppose the price of the dollar increases sharply in terms of a foreign currency, such as the yen. This increases the prices of U.S. exports in terms of foreign currency (yen) and reduces the quantity of U.S. exports demanded. The higher price of the dollar therefore decreases aggregate demand for U.S. products. To avoid this, the FOMC may instruct its man-downward pressure on the dollar's price in terms of the yen. In this way the Fed can prevent the price of the dollar in terms of the yen from rising as much as it would otherwise.

Sometimes the Fed acts to prevent the price of the dollar from falling excessively. When the price of the dollar declines, this puts upward pressure on the prices of imported raw materials and imported final products, which contributes to inflation in the United States. When the Fed wants to avoid such declines in the price of the dollar, it buys dollars, using its holdings of deposits denominated in foreign currencies. When the Fed buys dollars, it increases the demand for U.S. currency, thus putting upward pressure on the price of the dollar in terms of foreign currency. This prevents the price of the dollar from falling excessively.

By intervening in the foreign exchange markets in this way, the Fed acts to stabilize the price of the dollar.

ager for foreign operations to sell dollars on the foreign exchange markets. The increase in the supply of dollars on the foreign exchange markets puts

---

■ The price of a $1,000 one year Treasury bill is $950. Calculate the annual return on the bill, assuming it is held for a full year.

■ How does the sale of government securities by the Fed affect their prices and yields?

■ Why does the quantity of money supplied by the banking system increase as market interest rates go up? How can the Fed shift the money supply curve?

CONCEPT CHECK
☐

THE POWER OF THE FED

In this chapter we've emphasized the mechanics of the Federal Reserve System's control of the monetary base and the money supply. The Fed's policies can affect both interest rates and the equilibrium money stock in ways that can influence real GDP and the price level in the economy. In the following chapter we analyze the impact of Fed actions that alter aggregate demand in the economy. To help you see how actions of the Fed affect the performance of the economy, we'll discuss the mechanism through which changes in interest rates and the equilibrium money stock affect aggregate demand curves.

SUMMARY

1. The Federal Reserve System, called *the Fed* for short, is the central banking system for the United States. The Fed consists of the Board of Governors of the Federal Reserve System and 12 regional Federal Reserve banks that perform central banking functions. The Federal Reserve banks are the ''bankers' banks'' that hold reserve deposits, issue currency, and provide check-clearing services for commercial banks and thrift institutions.

2. The Federal Reserve System operates as an independent authority that is not under the direct influence of the president or Congress. It earns income on government securities it holds as assets, and it does not receive any funding from Congress. The Fed also loans funds to banks.

3. The monetary base is the sum of currency in circulation and total bank reserves outstanding at any given time.

The monetary base consists of liabilities of the Federal Reserve System. The Fed can vary the monetary base by adjusting its liabilities and assets and by regulating banks to control reserve requirements.

4. By controlling required reserve ratios, the Fed can influence the maximum amount of checkable deposits that can be supported by any given amount of bank reserves. An increase in the required reserve ratio decreases excess reserves and can result in a chain reaction that reduces the money supply. Similarly, a decrease in the required reserve ratio increases the excess reserves available from a given amount of reserves and can result in an expansion of the money supply.

5. The discount rate is the interest rate the Fed charges banks that borrow funds from the Federal Reserve banks. As the lender of last resort, the Fed can create bank reserves through discount loans for banks in danger of failing so as to maintain confidence in the banks and discourage bank runs. By making it easy to borrow to increase reserves, a decrease in the discount rate tends to be an expansionary influence on the money supply.

6. Open market operations by the Fed represent the major means of influencing bank reserves and the money supply. Open market operations consist of daily sales and purchases of government securities by Federal Reserve banks. Sales of government securities by the Fed absorb bank excess reserves and decrease the banking system's potential to create money. Fed purchases of government securities increase bank excess reserves and increase the banking system's potential to create money.

7. When the Fed sells government securities, it puts downward pressure on securities prices by increasing the amount available to the public. The lower prices of government securities mean that their yield to maturity increases. The public is induced to hold the larger supply of securities because their lower prices and higher yields make them more attractive as assets. Similarly, when the Fed buys government securities, it decreases the amount available to the public. This puts upward pressure on the prices of securities and lowers their yields to maturity. In this case the public willingly holds a smaller quantity of securities because their higher prices and lower yields make them less attractive as assets.

8. The money supply curve for the economy tends to be upward sloping. As the general level of interest rates increases, the quantity of money supplied by banks increases. This is because banks find it more profitable to make loans when interest rates rise. Higher interest rates therefore increase the quantity of checkable deposits created by the banking system.

9. The equilibrium quantity of money balances and the equilibrium level of interest rates adjust to equate the quantity of money demanded with the quantity supplied. The Fed can shift the money supply curve outward by increasing the monetary base, thereby putting downward pressure on interest rates. Similarly, a decrease in the monetary base shifts the money supply curve inward, putting upward pressure on interest rates. Although the Fed can influence money supply, it has no direct control over money demand. Actual money supply and interest rates depend on the interaction of the demand for and supply of money.

KEY TERMS

Board of Governors of the Federal Reserve System *344*

regional Federal Reserve banks *344*

Federal Open Market Committee (FOMC) *345*

monetary base *347*

discount rate *347*

open market operations *347*

discount loans *349*

money supply *356*

CONCEPT REVIEW

1 Briefly describe the organization and functions of the Federal Reserve System.

2 What are the major liabilities of the Federal Reserve banks?

3 How can the Fed influence the nation's monetary base and interest rates?

4 What is the money supply?

PROBLEMS AND APPLICATIONS

1. In what sense is the Federal Reserve System independent of Congress and the president of the United States? How can the president influence the Fed's policies despite the fact that the president has no direct control over the central bank? **1**

2. The Fed increases its liabilities. Explain why this means that the monetary base will increase. How does the monetary base differ from the money stock? **2**

3. Suppose the Fed wishes to increase the money stock

by \$100 billion over the next three months. What techniques can it use to accomplish its objective? 🔳

4. On a certain day the Fed buys \$30 billion worth of government securities and sells \$20 billion worth. Show the changes in the Fed's and the banking system's balance sheets. What effects will the Fed's operations have on securities prices and interest rates that day? 🔳

5. Suppose on another day the Fed sells \$80 billion worth of government securities and buys \$30 billion worth. Show the changes in their balance sheets and the impact on securities prices and interest rates that day. 🔳

6. When the economy moves into a recession, bank demand for excess reserves increases. How can the Fed use open market operations to increase the money

supply under these circumstances? Use supply and demand analysis to show the impact of the Fed's policies, assuming the demand for money is given. 🔳

7. The Fed decreases the monetary base. Show the impact of the Fed's action on the supply of money in the economy and the likely impact of the action on the level of interest rates. 🔳

8. Under what circumstances will open market sales and purchases by the Fed have *no effect* on the level of interest rates in the economy? 🔳

9. Suppose the demand for money increases. How can the Fed act to prevent the market rate of interest from increasing? 🔳

10. Explain why Federal Reserve System open market operations can increase bank reserves but do not guarantee an increase in the money supply. 🔳

inside information

Beige, Blue, and Green Books: How Monetary Authorities in the United States Compile Information to Examine Stabilization Policy Options The Federal Open Market Committee (FOMC)—the policy arm of the nation's central bank, the Federal Reserve System—meets eight times each year in Washington to develop and implement monetary policy. The information it uses to formulate policy is contained in three pamphlets, each of which is identified by the color of its cover—beige, green, and blue. All but one of the books are so "strictly confidential" that their contents are not made available to the public until five years after they are written!

The *Beige Book* is the best known of the Fed's three pamphlets, because it is released to the public at the same time it is made available to the FOMC. It begins with an overall summary of economic activity in all Federal Reserve districts including a discussion of consumer spending, manufacturing activity, construction and real estate markets, agriculture, and credit conditions. This introduction is followed by a discussion of economic conditions in each district. If you want to find out how the economy is doing and how each region of the nation is faring relative to one another, your best bet is to examine a copy of the most recent *Beige Book*. Your library may have a copy, but if it does not you can obtain one by writing directly to the Board of Governors of the Federal Reserve System.

The *Green Book,* one of the strictly confidential pamphlets, gives a picture of the major forces shaping spending, credit, prices, and foreign exchange developments as they influence the U.S. economy. It comes in two parts, each with a bright green cover. Part 1 provides a summary of economic conditions and discusses the outlook for the future. It examines the spending components of real GDP and the projections for growth in real GDP and inflation. The projections are prepared by the staff of the Board of Governors of the Federal Reserve System. This part also reviews economic conditions and the outlook abroad. Part 2 contains more detail on recent economic developments and is loaded with data and charts.

The *Blue Book* is also strictly confidential. This book provides members of the FOMC with a look at monetary policy alternatives for the coming months. It discusses movements in monetary aggregates such as M1 and M2 along with movements in bank reserves and bank borrowing and interest rates. The *Blue Book* provides three alternative scenarios for monetary policy in the coming three-month period. The scenarios are based on alternative growth rates for money and credit, and the associated changes in short-term interest rates expected with each of these alternatives. The information in this book provides the basis for discussion at the FOMC meeting to choose the actual target growth rates for key policy variables and to gauge the effects of the policy on interest rates and economic activity.

part VI

Stabilizing the Economy

CONCEPTS

Stabilization Policies

Monetary Policy

Income Velocity of Circulation of Money

Equation of Exchange

Quantity Theory of Money and Monetarism

Fiscal Policy

Automatic Stabilizers

Federal Budget Deficit and the National Debt

The Crowding-Out Effect

Ricardian Equivalence

Phillips Curve

Rational Expectations

Claude Monet, *Impression, Sunrise* (after restoration), 1872.
Paris, Musee Marmottan/Art Resource, NY

16 chapter

Stabilization of the Economy through Monetary Policy

Remember that in earlier chapters we discussed the disruptive effects of cyclical unemployment and rampant inflation on the economy. Now that you understand some of the basic causes of unemployment and inflation, we can begin to examine policies designed to stabilize the economy.

By studying the macroeconomic effects of monetary policy, you can see how changes in financial markets caused by shifts in the money supply are transmitted to the rest of the economy. Daily shifts in the money supply result in frequent changes in equilibrium interest rates. You'll now see that, over longer periods, changes in market interest rates and the equilibrium quantity of money affect the willingness and ability of buyers to spend.

The shifts in aggregate demand that result from changes in monetary policy also affect the demand for money in ways that further influence financial market equilibrium. In other words, there's a complex relationship among money, financial markets, and product markets that we must understand to evaluate the ultimate impact of monetary policy.

☐ CONCEPT PREVIEW

After reading this chapter, you should be able to:

1. Discuss the mechanism through which monetary policy affects interest rates.

2. Show how an expansionary monetary policy shifts the economy's aggregate demand curve and affects macroeconomic equilibrium.

3. Show how a contractionary monetary policy shifts the economy's aggregate demand curve and affects macroeconomic equilibrium.

4. Discuss the quantity theory of money and the possible long-term effects of monetary policy on the price level.

5. Discuss the basic ideas and implications of monetarism for monetary policy.

6. Discuss monetary policy in the United States and some of the challenges the Fed faces in influencing interest rates in the modern global economy.

STABILIZATION AND MONETARY POLICY

Stabilization policies are the procedures undertaken by governing authorities to maintain full employment and a reasonably stable price level. The federal government often seeks to stabilize the economy by using its expenditure and taxing powers to influence macroeconomic equilibrium. Central banks also use their powers to stabilize the economy through their influence on the money supply and the level of interest rates. In this chapter we concentrate on the ways central banking authorities seek to stabilize the economy and the difficulties they encounter in doing so. We also discuss how the growth rate of the equilibrium money stock can affect real GDP and the price level over the long run and how central banks seek to avoid the specter of hyperinflation.

Monetary policy consists of actions taken by central banks, such as the Fed, to influence the money supply or interest rates in attempts to stabilize the economy. Remember that there's a normal tendency for profit-motivated banks to increase loans during periods of economic expansion, when interest rates are rising. The expansion of credit and the quantity of money supplied during periods of peak economic activity tends to increase aggregate demand just when it needs to be restrained to prevent inflation from heating up. Similarly, during economic downturns, when interest rates are falling, there's a normal tendency for banks to cut back on loans and increase their holdings of excess reserves. As banks create fewer dollars of checkable deposits, the resulting reduction in the availability of credit and slowdown in the growth of the money stock could decrease aggregate demand and turn an economic contraction into a recession. By influencing the money supply, the Fed attempts to stabilize aggregate demand in ways that smooth out the swings of the business cycle.

A growing economy requires a growing money supply. Over time monetary policy is set to ensure that the banking system has adequate growth in excess reserves so that the long-term upward trend in real GDP isn't held down by inadequate monetary growth. However, monetary policymakers must also take care to avoid excessive monetary growth, which can cause high and continued rates of inflation.

stabilization policies procedures undertaken by governing authorities to maintain full employment and a reasonably stable price level.

monetary policy actions taken by central banks to influence the money supply or interest rates in attempts to stabilize the economy.

MONEY AND SHORT-TERM MACROECONOMIC EQUILIBRIUM

Monetary policy affects the economy daily through its impact on investment spending, household spending, and international transactions. Economic stabilization is an art, not a science. No policymaker or economist has a flawless crystal ball that can foresee all the possible effects of a policy. Unexpected changes in an economy can frustrate the goals of the most carefully planned policies. The Federal Reserve System is one of two major forces acting to stabilize the U.S. economy. The other major force is the federal government itself, whose spending and taxing policies affect aggregate demand and, in some cases, attempt to influence aggregate supply over the long run.

Fiscal policy, which is the use of government spending and taxes to stabilize the economy, is the subject of the following chapter. In many ways your understanding of the effects of fiscal policy on the economy will be enhanced if you first master the impact of monetary policy on economic performance. Studying monetary policy will help you understand the role of money in the economy and will enable you to see how the goals of fiscal policy must be coordinated with those of monetary policy. You'll then be better able to understand some of the controversies you often read about in the newspapers regarding the choice of appropriate policies to even out the swings of the business cycle.

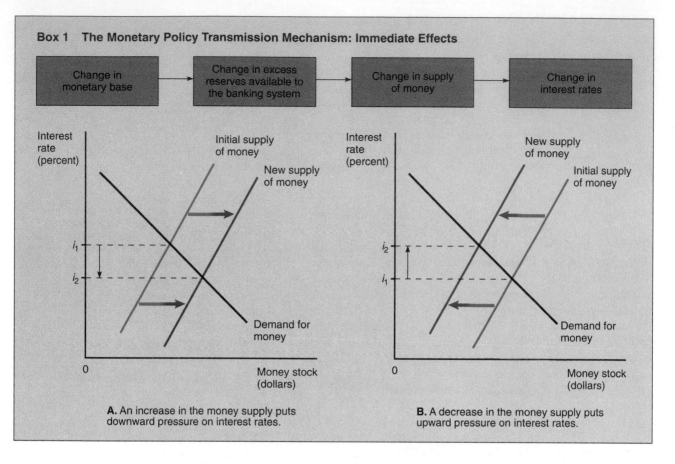

Box 1   The Monetary Policy Transmission Mechanism: Immediate Effects

A. An increase in the money supply puts downward pressure on interest rates.

B. A decrease in the money supply puts upward pressure on interest rates.

Our first step in understanding how monetary policy affects the economy is to examine the mechanism through which changes in the monetary base (currency and bank reserves) by the Fed influence financial markets and aggregate demand on a day-to-day basis.

Short-Term Impact of Monetary Policy

In the preceding chapter we showed how increases in excess reserves available to banks increase the capacity of the banking system to make loans. When the Fed supplies the banking system with new excess reserves, an expansion of the money supply results as banks use the new reserves to extend credit and thereby create new checkable deposits. The increased supply of money puts downward pressure on short-term interest rates and increases the quantity of credit demanded. The Fed also directly affects the level of short-term interest rates through the impact of its open market operations on securities prices. As interest rates fall, the opportunity cost of holding money falls and the public willingly holds an expanded money stock created through new loans.

The chart and graphs in Box 1 summarize the immediate effects on interest rates of a decision by the Fed to adjust the excess reserves available to depository institutions. As you can see, a decrease in the money supply causes interest rates to rise, while an increase in the money supply causes interest rates to fall.[1] When the

---

[1] Note that changes in money demand can also affect interest rates in the economy. An increase in money demand puts upward pressure on interest rates in much the same way as is done by a decrease in money supply. By the same token, a decrease in money demand puts downward pressure on interest rates.

Fed acts to increase the monetary base or its rate of growth by pumping excess reserves into the banking system, it is engaging in an expansionary monetary policy. When the Fed acts to decrease the monetary base or its rate of growth by decreasing the excess reserves available to depository institutions, it is said to be engaging in a contractionary monetary policy.

Interest Rates and Aggregate Demand

In studying the effects of monetary policies, we must investigate the relationship between changes in financial markets and changes in product markets. Our next step is therefore to show how changes in short-term interest rates caused by changes in the money supply affect aggregate demand.

When the Fed shifts the money supply, it influences nominal short-term interest rates. Spending decisions over the long term are influenced by real interest rates. The Fed must increase nominal interest rates relative to the inflation rate generally expected by the public if it wants to decrease aggregate demand over a longer period. Conversely, it must reduce nominal interest rates relative to the expected rate of inflation to increase aggregate demand.

Expected inflation is a subjective concept that the Fed can influence only indirectly. However, because spending decisions depend on the real interest rate, the Fed must make some estimate of expected inflation in formulating monetary policy. Its job is simplified if inflationary expectations are fixed or change very slowly, because then an increase in the nominal interest rate will also increase the real interest rate. Many economists argue that a goal of both monetary and fiscal policy for the long run should be the creation of an economic environment that contributes to very stable expectations of changes in the price level.

The component of aggregate demand that is likely to be most responsive to changes in real interest rates is investment purchases, including purchases of homes. Lower real interest rates encourage increased investment purchases, while higher real interest rates cause business firms to scale back their planned investment expenditures. Of course, some consumer expenditures are also sensitive to changes in real interest rates because such changes affect the monthly payments associated with installment purchases. Here, to simplify the analysis, we will concentrate on the impact of changes in real interest rates on investment purchases.

Graph **A** in Box 2 draws the demand curve for investment goods in the economy. When, through the transmission mechanism we just discussed, the Fed causes real interest rates to decline, the quantity of investment goods demanded increases. Other things being equal, the increase in investment purchases means the economy's aggregate purchases line will shift upward, as shown in graph **B**. An increase in aggregate purchases means the economy's aggregate demand curve will shift outward, as shown in graph **C**.

We can now begin to see how an expansionary monetary policy can affect macroeconomic equilibrium through shifts in aggregate demand. A decrease in interest rates caused by an expansionary monetary policy affects the investment component of aggregate demand. As aggregate demand increases, other things being equal, it puts upward pressure on real GDP and the price level. You can test your understanding of how monetary policy works to influence aggregate demand by working out the implications of a contractionary monetary policy for the economy. An increase in real interest rates resulting from a decrease in the money supply will decrease planned investment purchases. This will shift the economy's aggregate purchases line downward. A decrease in aggregate purchases at any given price level will shift the economy's aggregate demand curve inward, putting downward pressure on real GDP and the price level. The Fed can therefore act to restrain surging

expansionary monetary policy action by the Federal Reserve System to increase the monetary base or its rate of growth.

contractionary monetary policy action by the Federal Reserve System to decrease the monetary base or its rate of growth.

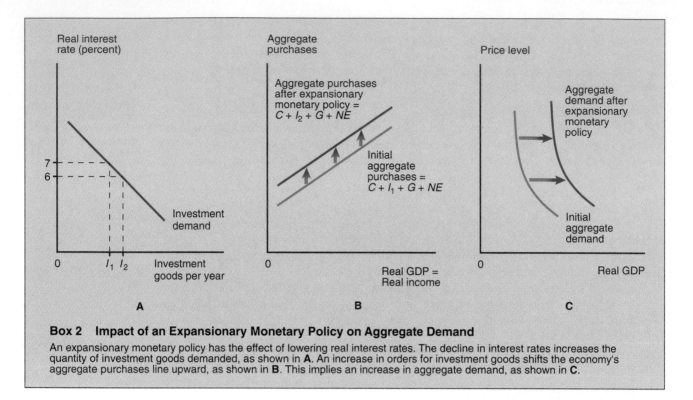

Box 2   Impact of an Expansionary Monetary Policy on Aggregate Demand

An expansionary monetary policy has the effect of lowering real interest rates. The decline in interest rates increases the quantity of investment goods demanded, as shown in **A**. An increase in orders for investment goods shifts the economy's aggregate purchases line upward, as shown in **B**. This implies an increase in aggregate demand, as shown in **C**.

aggregate demand in periods of expansion by pursuing policies to increase the level of real interest rates in the economy. Now let's see how the Fed's use of an expansionary monetary policy can help pull the economy out of a contraction or a recession.

Using an Expansionary Monetary Policy to Eliminate a Recessionary GDP Gap

When the economy is operating at an equilibrium level of real GDP that falls short of potential real GDP, a recessionary GDP gap will prevail. Under these circumstances, there will be cyclical unemployment. Policies designed to stimulate aggregate demand can help restore full employment.

Assume the economy is initially in equilibrium at a real GDP level of $4,700 billion and a price level of 100. Potential real GDP, at which full employment will be achieved, is $5,000 billion. There is therefore a $300 billion recessionary GDP gap. The current level of aggregate demand is insufficient to result in an equilibrium real GDP equal to the economy's potential real GDP of $5,000 billion.

If you were chairman of the Board of Governors of the Federal Reserve System, what would you do to eliminate the recessionary GDP gap and restore full employment? Well, if you followed the line of reasoning just given, you know that the Fed can act to lower real interest rates by engaging in an expansionary monetary policy. The decline in real interest rates will then increase planned investment and other interest-sensitive purchases, which represent an important component of aggregate demand. As a result, the aggregate demand curve will shift outward.

The impact of just such a policy on macroeconomic equilibrium for the economy is illustrated in Box 3. After an expansionary monetary policy has increased aggregate demand, equilibrium real GDP will increase from $4,700 billion to $5,000 billion,

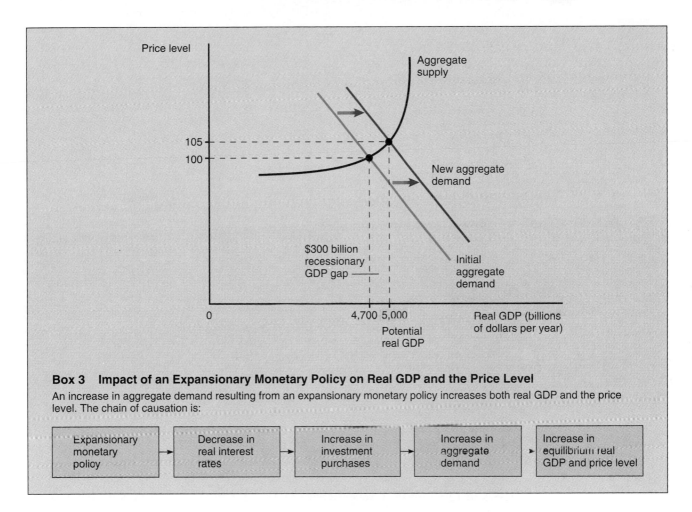

Box 3 Impact of an Expansionary Monetary Policy on Real GDP and the Price Level

An increase in aggregate demand resulting from an expansionary monetary policy increases both real GDP and the price level. The chain of causation is:

| Expansionary monetary policy | → | Decrease in real interest rates | → | Increase in investment purchases | → | Increase in aggregate demand | → | Increase in equilibrium real GDP and price level |

eliminating the recessionary GDP gap. By acting to decrease real interest rates through its influence on bank excess reserves and the money supply, the Fed can stimulate aggregate demand and increase equilibrium real GDP to potential real GDP after a recession hits. But the Fed's policies also increase the price level. In the graph the price level goes up from 100 to 105 after the expansionary monetary policy has shifted aggregate demand. There is therefore 5 percent inflation during the year as a result of the expansionary monetary policy. The Fed must take care not to decrease the level of interest rates too much in order to avoid initiating a process of inflation that can result from steady increases in aggregate demand. Too much growth in excess reserves for the banking system can result in shifts in money supply that can ultimately cause inflation to become a serious problem.

The risk of inflation from increases in aggregate demand depends on how close the economy is to full employment. If the economy is in a serious recession, it will be operating with considerable excess capacity and high cyclical unemployment. Under these circumstances, an expansionary monetary policy is likely to run little risk of starting an inflationary process because the economy will be operating in the flat portion of its aggregate supply curve. Increases in aggregate demand will therefore have little effect on the price level during a deep recession. The closer the economy is to full employment, however, the greater the risk that an expansionary policy

principles in practice

Business Brief: Monetary Policy, Real Interest Rates, and the Yield Curve

The most direct effect of the Fed's monetary policy is on bank reserves. A contractionary monetary policy, in which reserves become scarcer, increases the federal funds rate, the interest rate charged by one bank to another for short-term use of reserves. Conversely, under an expansionary monetary policy, the federal funds rate decreases as reserves become more abundant. As the federal funds rate changes, so will other short-term interest rates. However, competition in financial markets will lead to repercussions that will eventually affect long-term interest rates as well.

Interest rates on long-term loans or deposits depend both on short-term rates and on expectations about future interest rates and future inflation rates. For example, suppose you want to save some money over a two-year period. You can put your money into a one-year CD and then renew the certificate the following year at the going rate of interest; or you can put your money into a two-year CD and earn a certain interest rate over the two-year period.

Suppose the interest rate on the one-year CD is 8 percent, while the rate on the two-year certificate is 9 percent. Typically, in a period of relatively stable prices, longer-term securities yield more than shorter-

term securities because they are less liquid. Depositors and lenders usually want an extra premium for tying up their funds for longer periods of time. If the inflation rate is constant at 5 percent per year, in each of the two years of your CD you will earn a real rate of interest of 4 percent per year, the 9 percent nominal interest rate less the 5 percent rate of inflation. This rate is higher than the real interest rate of 3 percent you would earn on the one-year CD each year. If inflation and nominal interest rates are constant over the two-year period, your real interest rate each year on the one-year CD for each period would be the nominal rate of 8 percent less the 5 percent inflation rate, which is 3 percent.

Suppose you expect inflation to heat up next year. To slow it down, you think the Fed will engage in a contractionary monetary policy that will increase nominal interest rates. Under these circumstances, you may be better off putting your money into the one-year CD. With 5 percent inflation, this year you will earn a real interest rate of 3 percent. If the interest rate on the one-year CD goes up to 10 percent next year and inflation goes up to 6 percent, you will earn a real interest rate of 4 percent next year. Your real rate of return will average 3.5 percent for the two years. If you buy the two-year

designed to eliminate a recessionary GDP gap will start a process of demand-pull inflation.

How Effective Is Monetary Policy in Increasing Aggregate Demand?

Suppose you were a member of the Federal Open Market Committee. It would be nice to know exactly how much you would have to increase bank excess reserves in order to increase aggregate demand and eliminate a recessionary GDP gap. Unfortunately, monetary policy is not an exact science, and its effectiveness depends on how responsive both banks and investors are to changes in the monetary base and the level of real interest rates.

The effectiveness of an expansionary monetary policy in increasing aggregate demand depends on two factors:

1. The willingness of the banking system to create new checkable deposits by making loans using newly created excess reserves.

2. The responsiveness of investment and other credit-sensitive purchases to declines in interest rates.

Suppose the banking system *does* respond to an increase in excess reserves by making more loans. As this occurs, banks will create more checkable deposits for their customers and the supply of money will increase, putting downward pressure on interest rates. The effectiveness of an expansionary monetary policy in increasing aggregate demand will then hinge on the responsiveness of investment purchases to

CD, in the second year the return will be 9 percent less the 6 percent inflation rate, or 3 percent. Your average return will be 3.5 percent, the same as your return on the one-year CDs. Because you will not get more real interest to compensate for the loss of liquidity, the long-term CD becomes less attractive.

In general, when inflation or short-term nominal interest rates are expected to increase, short-term loans become more attractive than long-term loans. This will increase the supply of short-term credit and decrease the supply of long-term credit, pushing up long-term rates relative to short-term rates.

Given inflationary expectations, the Fed can influence long-term interest rates through the effect of its operations on short-term interest rates. As short-term interest rates rise and short-term credit becomes more attractive, the supply of long-term credit will decrease and long-term interest rates will rise as well (these effects will be reinforced by shifts in the demand for long-term and short-term credit as well as by borrowers who seek to minimize their real interest costs). In this way a contractionary monetary policy affects both short-term and long-term credit markets.

When inflation is expected to increase substantially, the "yield curve," which shows how nominal interest rates vary with the time to maturity of a loan, can flatten out. The curve labeled A in the illustration shows a normal upward-sloping yield curve that will prevail

when the inflation rate is expected to neither accelerate nor decelerate. The curve labeled B shows a flat yield curve, which indicates that long-term rates are not higher than short-term rates. When this is the case, the general feeling of the financial markets is that inflation is going to accelerate and short-term rates will soon rise. Curve C shows an inverted downward-sloping yield curve. This type of yield curve will prevail in the market if it is generally expected that inflation will soon decelerate and the Fed will be taking actions to lower the federal funds rate and other short-term rates.

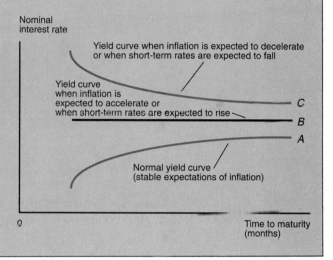

the change in interest rates. The more responsive investors are to declines in real interest rates, the greater the increase in investment purchases from any given decrease in real interest rates.

In periods of deep recession, the short-term business outlook may be so gloomy that banks may prefer to hold on to their excess reserves rather than extend credit. Under such circumstances, because of the high risk of default on bank loans, bank managers will hold liquid assets in the form of excess reserves. Therefore, the increase in excess reserves pumped into the banking system by the Fed will have little effect on the money supply because the banks will not use them to extend credit and thus create checkable deposits. There will be no increase in the equilibrium money stock. As a consequence, there will be little downward pressure on interest rates in the first place. If interest rates don't fall, investment purchases will not increase in response to the increase in the monetary base.

John Maynard Keynes was quite pessimistic about the effectiveness of monetary policy as a means of pulling an economy out of a deep recession. He argued that in a deep recession banks would be unwilling to extend credit through loans or bond purchases because of fear of default or fear of a fall in bond prices. Under such circumstances, the Fed would have a hard time shifting the money supply curve to the right to lower interest rates.

Even if the Fed were effective in increasing the equilibrium money stock in a deep recession, Keynes argued that its effect on the market rate of interest might be negligible. This is because during a deep recession money is likely to be a very attractive asset for households and businesses compared to stocks and bonds. After all, inflation rates are low during a recession (or even negative, as was the case during the Great Depression). There would be little risk of loss in the dollar's purchasing power. As people try to increase the quantity of money they hold during a recession, the Fed's attempt to lower interest rates is stifled. The increased money stock ends up being held as currency or checkable deposits. As a result, there is little increase in the supply of loanable funds. Therefore, there is little downward pressure on the level of interest rates.

Sometimes unusual factors limit the effectiveness of monetary policy in stimulating demand in the short run. During the recession of 1990–91, for example, the Fed acted to increase bank reserves, which resulted in a substantial decline in short-term interest rates. At the same time, however, many banks were forced to raise their standards for approving loans because new laws were then enacted to reduce the exposure of banks to loan defaults. Regulators were pressuring banks to reduce the riskiness of their portfolios so as to reduce the rate of bank failure. The result was a "credit crunch" that had a strong impact on small businesses trying to get loans approved for new ventures. Between 1990 and 1992, banks used increased reserves to acquire relatively riskless government securities and reduced the volume of loans in their portfolios. All these factors combined to reduce the ability of the Fed's expansionary monetary policy to increase commercial credit and investment spending.

Using a Contractionary Monetary Policy to Prevent the Economy from Overheating

3 Now let's turn the tables on you. As chairman of the Federal Reserve Board, suppose you're more worried about inflation than about unemployment. Suppose the current rate of unemployment is only 5.5 percent and you have good reason to believe the economy is in danger of overheating. Recall that an overheated economy is one that is temporarily operating beyond its potential because of excessive aggregate demand. You know that as the economy is approaching full employment, there is real danger that shifts in aggregate demand will trigger an inflationary process. You also know that demand-pull inflation at full employment can start a wage-price spiral. Demand-pull inflation can be followed by cost-push inflation as workers negotiate wage increases to keep up with anticipated inflation. As chairman of the Fed, you want to avoid such an inflationary scenario. You're likely to recommend that a contractionary monetary policy be pursued to prevent an inflationary process from beginning.

The graph in Box 4 shows an economy that is initially in equilibrium at point *E*, at which real GDP is at its potential level of $5,000 billion per year and the price level is 100. If aggregate demand increases still further, the economy will move to point *E'*, at which real GDP will increase to $5,500 billion and the price level will go up to 105. Because wages will tend to be fixed, at least in the short-run period of about one year, the increase in the price level will not be matched by increased wages over the year. In the following year, however, wages will start to increase as workers seek to keep up with inflation. The increase in wages will shift the aggregate supply curve inward. The economy will eventually move to point *E"* on its long-run aggregate supply curve, at which point real GDP returns to potential real GDP and the price level increases to 110.

To prevent inflationary gaps from occurring, the Fed will have to engage in a contractionary monetary policy as the economy approaches full employment. To do so, it will attempt to decrease the excess reserves available to depository institutions

principles in practice

Policy Perspective: Monetary Policy during the Great Depression

How the Fed Prevented the Banking System from Recovering and Allowed the Money Supply to Decline Much of what you know about the Great Depression of the 1930s may come from reminiscences of older relatives. Whether or not they personally endured the severe hardships and poverty that afflicted large numbers of Americans, the people who lived through those gloomy days can testify to the fear and pessimism engendered by the massive economic collapse.

How did the Federal Reserve System respond to this titanic challenge? To state the case tactfully, this was not the Fed's finest hour. Let's look at what happened and what the Fed did—and didn't—do about it.

Between 1929 and 1933, one out of every four workers in the labor force was unemployed. Real GDP fell by one third over this period, and the price level declined by 25 percent. Investment purchases by business firms were reduced to virtually nothing. The great stock market crash of 1929 wiped out the accumulated wealth of many shareholders after the market plunged to an 80 percent decline in value.

Because of bank failures between 1929 and 1933, the public held a high proportion of money in the form of currency rather than bank deposits. Bank failures were common because banks lacked the reserves needed to meet the demand for withdrawals of deposits. The series of bank failures increased the demand for currency, which, in turn, contributed to further bank runs and bank failures. The surviving banks naturally became very cautious in making loans because of their desire to hold liquid assets to meet depositor demands for currency. Banks held high proportions of their assets in excess reserves.

During this period the Fed allowed the money stock to decline. By not supplying the banking system with reserves to meet the demand for withdrawals, the Fed contributed to bank failures and to the unwillingness of bankers to extend loans. Ironically, during this time of acute economic distress, the Fed failed to fulfill its major function of ensuring the stability of the banking system. The Fed had the power to create bank reserves simply by making loans that would create bank deposits at the Fed. By allowing bank reserves to decline, the Fed contributed to the severity of the Depression and prolonged its duration.

The Fed also contributed to the stock market collapse by encouraging the expansion of credit in 1927. During that year the Fed had engaged in open market purchases that induced declines in interest rates and encouraged borrowing to speculate on stock prices. When the Fed raised its discount rate in 1929 and started to put the brakes on money supply growth, banks began to call in loans. In the fall of 1929, the stock market collapsed, in part because of the panic selling of stocks to obtain funds to pay off loans.

The decline in the money supply during the Depression contributed to deflation in the price level, but this was insufficient to get the economy's self-correcting mechanism to work. Aggregate production remained in equilibrium at a real GDP level well below the economy's potential.

The monetary policy pursued by the Fed during the early years of the Depression contributed to the severity of the economic decline. The Fed's unwillingness to supply the banking system with reserves undermined the system's integrity. As confidence in the banking system dissolved, the money stock contracted rapidly, contributing to further declines in aggregate demand that aggravated the already miserable economic picture.[*]

The major lesson learned during the Great Depression is that measures must be taken to stimulate aggregate demand when economic forces contribute to its decline.

[*] For an excellent historical analysis of the Fed's policies, see Sidney Ratner, James H. Soltow, and Richard Sylla, *The Evolution of the American Economy* (New York: Basic Books, 1979), chap. 22.

(or reduce their rate of growth) in order to put upward pressure on interest rates as the economy moves to full employment. Monetary policy will be effective in preventing an inflationary gap if it can keep the aggregate demand curve from shifting outward. If monetary policy achieves this objective, the economy will never reach an equilibrium at point E' and will avoid the bout of stagflation that would eventually decrease aggregate supply and result in an equilibrium at E''. In this way the Fed can prevent a wage-price spiral from occurring.

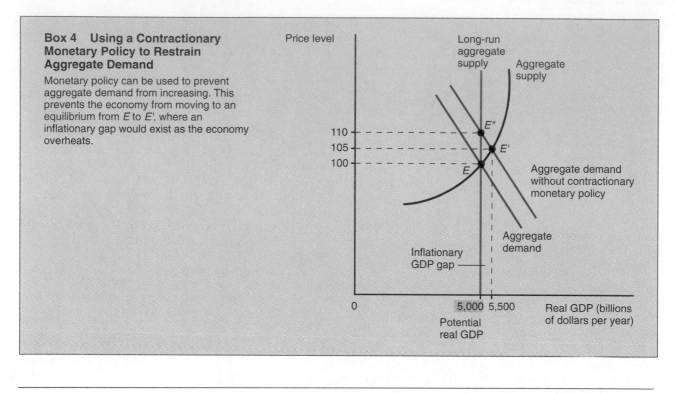

Box 4   Using a Contractionary Monetary Policy to Restrain Aggregate Demand

Monetary policy can be used to prevent aggregate demand from increasing. This prevents the economy from moving to an equilibrium from *E* to *E'*, where an inflationary gap would exist as the economy overheats.

CONCEPT CHECK

☐

- A decline in aggregate demand is expected during the year as a result of a gloomy outlook for consumer spending. How can monetary policy be used to offset the adverse effects on the economy of the decline in aggregate demand?

- What is the purpose of a contractionary monetary policy?

- What influences the effectiveness of monetary policy in achieving its objectives?

MONEY, REAL GDP, PRICES, AND MONETARY POLICY

Earlier in this chapter we pointed out that monetary policy is an art rather than a science. That may be putting it mildly if we consider the fact that there's great controversy about the way changes in monetary policy and changes in the money stock affect the economy. Economists agree that monetary policy has the potential to influence aggregate demand. However, they disagree about the mechanism through which monetary policy affects aggregate demand and macroeconomic equilibrium. In this section we'll concentrate on the relationship between money and prices in the economy over the long run, when wages and prices are likely to be more flexible than they are over shorter periods.

The major impact of the money supply on real GDP over a short period occurs through the transmission mechanism discussed earlier. Changes in the money supply affect interest rates, thereby affecting investment and other credit-sensitive purchases that, in turn, affect aggregate demand. The long-term impact on the economy of changes in the money supply depends on the relationship between growth in the money stock available, growth in potential real GDP, and shifts in the demand curve for money.

A long-term objective of monetary policy is to adjust the growth of the money stock to accommodate long-term growth in the transaction demand for money.

Remember that as GDP grows, so does the transaction demand for money (see the chapter entitled "The Functions of Money"). By doing this, central banks ensure a stock of money and a supply of credit that allow the economy to expand without excessive inflation or recession.

The Concept of Income Velocity of Circulation of Money

Take out a dollar bill from your wallet or purse, and look at it. Unless you've just gotten a nice, crisp, newly printed bill, it is likely to be dirty and worn. It's seen a bit of action. In fact, each dollar of the money stock, in either checkable deposits or currency, is used a number of times each year to make purchases of final products. Therefore, the dollar volume of the final transactions that can be supported by a given quantity of money, on average per day over the year, is a multiple of the available money stock.

The **income velocity of circulation of money** is the number of times per year, on average, a dollar of the money stock is spent on final products. Because nominal GDP also equals aggregate income in the nation, income velocity also measures the number of times per year, on average, a dollar of the money stock is paid out as income. For example, in 1991 nominal GDP, representing the market value of final products at current prices that year, was $5,677.5 billion. The average daily stock of currency and checkable deposits that year (M1) was $860 billion. The $860 billion money stock supported the nearly $6 trillion of aggregate income generated from the final production of goods and services that year. The income velocity of circulation, V, of money is computed from the following formula.

income velocity of circulation of money the number of times per year, on average, a dollar of the money stock is spent on final products or paid out as income.

$$\text{Income velocity of circulation} = V = \text{Nominal GDP/M1}$$

when M1 is the average daily stock of currency and checkable deposits held over the year.

In 1991 the velocity of circulation of money was therefore

$$\frac{\$5,677.5 \text{ billion}}{\$860 \text{ billion}} = 6.6$$

If velocity was about 6, the dirty old dollar in your wallet was involved in six transactions during the year to purchase final products. The dollar was received as income six times during the year. Perhaps it was used to buy a gallon of gas, and thus became part of the income of the gas station owner. Perhaps the gas station owner held it awhile but eventually spent it on a cup of coffee at the local drugstore, when it became income to the store owner. When a dollar of the money stock is not being used, someone is holding it either as a checkable deposit or as currency.

The Equation of Exchange

The **equation of exchange** is an identity that shows the relationship among nominal GDP, the money stock, and the income velocity of circulation of money. The equation of exchange is obtained directly from the definition of velocity. Velocity is

equation of exchange an identity that shows the relationship between nominal GDP, the money stock, and the income velocity of circulation of money.

$$V = \text{Nominal GDP/M1}$$

Multiply both sides of the formula for velocity by M1. This gives the following result:

$$(\text{M1})V = \text{Nominal GDP}$$

Nominal GDP can be expressed as the price level, P, multiplied by the quantity, Q, of final transactions, which is real GDP:

$$\text{Nominal GDP} = PQ = (\text{Price level}) (\text{Real GDP})$$

If you just remember that money is measured by M1, the symbol *M* can be used for money to make the equation a little less cluttered. This gives

$$MV = PQ$$

which is the equation of exchange. Note again that the relationship is an *identity*. The term *MV* represents total dollar expenditure on the nation's final products over the year. The term *PQ* represents total receipts from the sale of final products over the year. Because receipts always equal expenditures, the equation is an identity.

Using the Equation of Exchange to Understand Money's Role in the Economy

The preceding analysis of the impact of money on the economy emphasized how changes in money supply can affect interest rates and investment. These short-run effects of changes in the money supply shift aggregate demand, and they can increase or decrease real GDP when it diverges from its potential level in the short run.

Over longer periods, *provided velocity is more or less stable,* changes in the money supply will affect the price level. The classical quantity theory of money is a model of the long-run functioning of the economy, according to which changes in the money stock result in proportional changes in the price level over the long run. We first discussed the ideas of the classical economists in the chapter on using aggregate demand and supply analysis. You'll recall that they believed flexibility of wages and prices would ensure the equality of equilibrium real GDP and potential GDP. They also believed that temporary deviations from potential real GDP would eventually be followed by shifts in aggregate supply that returned the economy to equilibrium at full employment.

According to the classical quantity theory of money, the transmission mechanism through which changes in the money stock ultimately affect the economy differs from the mechanism previously discussed. In the short run, when wages and prices may be temporarily inflexible according to the classical economists, increases in the money supply can affect interest rates, investment, and real GDP. In the long run, however, potential real GDP will be equilibrium real GDP and changes in the money stock can affect only the price level. To see this, you can think of *Q* in the equation of exchange as real GDP, while *P* represents the price level. If money supply goes up while velocity is fixed, then nominal GDP, which is represented by *PQ*, must increase. However, because in the long run an increase in *M* does not affect real GDP, any increase in nominal GDP will be fully accounted for by increases in the price level, provided *V* is constant. If *V* is constant, then increases in the growth rate of *M* will increase the rate of inflation whenever the growth rate of the money stock exceeds the growth rate of real GDP.

For example, suppose the federal government declares that each dollar in checking accounts and each dollar of currency is now worth two dollars. The money stock will double. But if real GDP is equal to potential real GDP, the resulting increase in the dollar value of aggregate demand cannot result in more output. There may be a temporary overheating of the economy, but you know that real GDP cannot exceed its potential for long without causing decreases in aggregate supply. As you and your friends run out to spend your newly created dollars, prices are sure to rise if quantity supplied cannot increase. If velocity (*V*) is fixed and *Q* is also fixed at potential real GDP, the equation of exchange shows you that a doubling of the money stock will also double the price level in the economy!

In general, if the economy is already operating at its potential and *V* is constant, the price level will increase by the same proportion as the dollar amount of money in

classical quantity theory of money a model of the long-run functioning of the economy according to which changes in the money stock result in proportional changes in the price level over the long run.

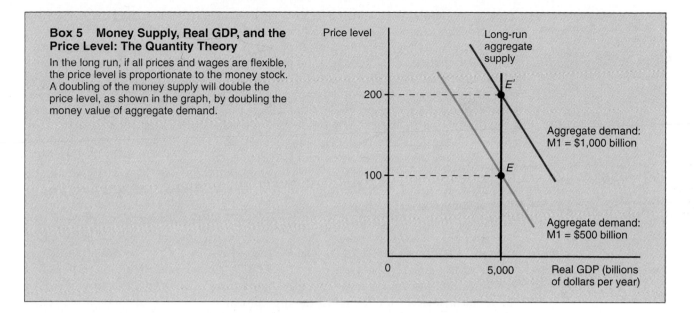

Box 5   Money Supply, Real GDP, and the Price Level: The Quantity Theory

In the long run, if all prices and wages are flexible, the price level is proportionate to the money stock. A doubling of the money supply will double the price level, as shown in the graph, by doubling the money value of aggregate demand.

circulation increases. The increase in the price level increases the demand for money and therefore induces people to hold the larger money stock because, given real GDP, an increase in the price level increases the transaction demand for money (see the chapter entitled "The Functions of Money"). If the price level doesn't change, some other variable, say a decrease in interest rates or an increase in real GDP, will have to change to induce people to willingly hold the available amount of money. The quantity theory of money, in its crudest form, does not consider changes in the interest rate. It also assumes that real GDP is in equilibrium at its full-employment level. Remember that the classical quantity theory of money was developed at a time when the classical economists believed the economy's self-correcting mechanism would work to keep the economy operating at close to full employment. Therefore, the price level must rise to induce the public to willingly hold the larger money stock.

The graph in Box 5 shows how the increase in aggregate demand caused by a doubling of the money stock will double the price level, assuming flexible prices and wages. The initial equilibrium is at point *E* along the vertical long-run aggregate supply curve. A doubling of the money supply will increase aggregate demand. The new aggregate demand curve will intersect the long-run aggregate supply curve at point *E'*. At that point real GDP remains at its full-employment level, *but the price level has also doubled.*

Keep in mind that this conclusion is true only if nothing else changes as the money supply and price level change. This ensures a stable money demand and a fixed income velocity of circulation of money.

Monetary Policy: Implications of the Classical Quantity Theory

If the classical quantity theory is correct, it has some important implications for monetary policy. Suppose the income velocity of circulation is constant. Also assume that over the long run wage and price flexibility ensure that real GDP does not differ from potential real GDP for long. In a growing economy, for which the assumptions of the classical quantity theory held, stable prices could be maintained if the money stock were allowed to grow at the same rate as potential real GDP. For example, suppose potential real GDP were to grow at an annual rate of 3 percent. In this case, other things being equal, the right side of the equation of exchange, PQ, would also increase by 3 percent annually. Now if V were constant, how much could the money stock increase to prevent the price level from going up? The answer would be 3 percent. What would happen if the money stock were allowed to increase more rapidly than 3 percent? For example, if the money stock were to grow at an annual rate of 10 percent, MV would also grow by 10 percent per year if V were constant. The right side of the equation would also have to grow by 10 percent per year. Because the growth rate of real GDP is dependent on such factors as technological progress and growth in labor productivity, its rate of growth would be unaffected by the growth rate of the money stock. It follows that the growth rate of the price level would increase to make up the difference between the growth rate of the money stock and the growth rate of potential real GDP.

Assuming velocity is constant, the classical quantity theory of money implies that over the long run rapid inflation can be caused by growth of the money stock in excess of the long-term growth rate of real GDP. This implies that monetary policy can keep inflation under control over the long run by making sure the growth rate of the money stock does not exceed the growth rate of real GDP over the long run.

However, the income velocity of circulation of money is not constant. In the United States velocity fell from about 3.5 in 1929 to slightly less than 2 in the mid-1940s. Beginning in 1945, it climbed steadily, reaching a high of 7 between 1982 and 1983. It declined between 1983 and 1984, and since 1985 it has fluctuated between 6 and 7.

The variability of velocity casts doubt on the simplest version of the quantity theory, which is based on the assumption of fixed velocity. But why does velocity increase and decrease over time? The answer lies in shifts of the demand curve for money in the economy.

The higher the income velocity of circulation, the faster the turnover of dollars as income. Higher velocity means money is being used more frequently to purchase final products and is spending less time as idle cash balances. In other words, given nominal GDP and the level of interest rates over the year, an increase in velocity means the money demand curve has shifted inward. A decrease in money demand is therefore indicative of an increase in the velocity of circulation of money. You can readily see this from the formula for velocity. Given nominal GDP, an increase in V means the quantity of money held on average per day over the year has declined, because V = Nominal GDP/M1. Other things being equal, this implies that the demand for money has declined.

Velocity varies as the demand for money varies. Any change in a nation's financial system that reduces the transaction costs of converting near money to money is likely to decrease the money stock demanded by the public. When such a change occurs, a smaller equilibrium money stock can support a given nominal GDP, and velocity will increase. Technological change in the payment mechanisms of an economy can increase velocity. For example, velocity will be increased by the introduction of a computerized network that allows instantaneous transfer of funds in savings accounts to funds in checkable deposits.

The sharp increase in velocity from 1950 to 1985 can be explained by the many financial innovations that occurred in the United States at that time. One such innovation was widespread use of credit cards, which allowed users to write one check in payment for several purchases made during a month. Many mutual fund accounts allowed easy transfer of investment balances into money market funds that had check-writing privileges. These innovations allowed the public to economize on the money it held.

The variability of velocity measured as GDP/M1 will increase with the variability of interest rates. Remember that interest rates are a major determinant of the demand for money balances. When interest rates rise, the opportunity cost of holding money also rises, and individuals economize on their money balances to take advantage of higher yields on such financial assets as money market mutual funds. A lower demand for money means that a lower dollar volume of M1 will be used to conduct transactions. Consequently, a decrease in the demand for money will be associated with an increase in velocity, while an increase in the demand for money will be associated with a decrease in velocity. When interest rates are highly variable, as was the case in the late 1980s, velocity will also be highly variable.

Movements in velocity became much more difficult to predict in the 1980s, when the long-term trend toward increasing velocity was apparently broken. There were highly variable interest rates over the period, leading to increased variability.

Monetarism

You may think the variability of velocity over time has rendered the quantity theory of money useless. However, many economists still believe the equation of exchange provides important insights into the way the economy functions and the way monetary policy can affect the price level over time.

Monetarism is a theory of long-term macroeconomic equilibrium, based on the equation of equation of exchange, according to which shifts in velocity are reasonably predictable. Monetarists argue that changes in the money stock are the predominant influence on *nominal* GDP and nominal income in a nation. They maintain that if predictions about changes in velocity are reasonably accurate, monetary policy can be used in the long run to control the rate of inflation. They believe after adjusting for changes in the rate of increase (or decrease) in velocity, careful control of the equilibrium money stock is necessary to stabilize the economy. If, after adjusting for changes in V, the money stock is not allowed to grow rapidly enough to accommodate the growth in real GDP, monetary policy could cause a recession. This is because if monetary growth is not fast enough, nominal GDP (which is PQ in the equation of exchange) cannot increase. For example, suppose the money stock were to grow by less than the growth in real GDP. If, after adjusting for changes in V, the growth of MV is less than the growth of PQ (which is nominal GDP), growth in nominal GDP will be held back by inadequate availability of money. Typically, except in a severe recession, the price level (P) does not fall to allow Q, which is real GDP, to continue growing under such circumstances. Businesses and households will not have enough money to meet their daily requirements for transactions. As they increase their demand for money, the credit supplied to financial markets will shrink and real GDP growth will fall and may even become negative. This implies that an economic contraction or recession can be precipitated by inadequate monetary growth.

On the other hand, if monetary growth, after adjusting for changes in V, is much faster than real GDP growth, nominal GDP will increase more rapidly than real GDP. Therefore, the rate of inflation will increase. The major conclusion of the monetarists is that over the long run the growth rate of the money stock is the major factor influencing the rate of inflation in the economy. They recommend concentrating on the long-term effects of monetary growth. They therefore focus on the impact of monetary growth on the price level. (See the Economic Thinkers box on Milton Friedman, America's preeminent monetarist.)

monetarism a theory of long-term macroeconomic equilibrium, based on the equation of exchange, according to which shifts in velocity are reasonably predictable.

economic thinkers

Milton Friedman

Milton Friedman, America's best-known monetarist and an apostle of libertarian economics, is a bold and outspoken defender of the free-market system. Because he is able to express complicated ideas in simple, often colorful language (such as using ice cream cone imagery in a letter to *The Wall Street Journal*), Friedman is popular with the media and is a well-known public figure.

Friedman is a respected economist who has attacked the foundations of Keynesian economics. He believes wholeheartedly that free markets can do almost anything and that they work best without government interference. According to him, the key to a healthy, stable economy is for the money supply to expand at a constant rate in accordance with growth in the economy's capacity to produce. Business fluctuations are caused by short-run, erratic changes in the money supply, including such major downturns as the Great Depression, which Friedman says would not have developed if the Federal Reserve had increased the money supply after the stock market crash of 1929.

He is a firm believer in laissez-faire capitalism and a diehard fan of Adam Smith. He has attempted to build on Smith's classic liberal philosophy and defends it eloquently. For his work, he has received nearly every significant honor the field of economics has to offer, including the Nobel Prize in 1976. *A Monetary History of the United States, Capitalism and Freedom,* and *Free to Choose* are among his best-known works.

Friedman taught at the University of Chicago for 30 years, where he eventually led the strongly free-market economists associated with that university. He retired in 1977 and currently works out of the Hoover Institute at Stanford University.

In an attempt to replace government influence with market solutions, Friedman has advocated the elimination of physician licensing, public schools, agricultural price supports, and food stamps. He has made major contributions to economic theory in the area of risk and insurance and by describing consumption patterns that are based on wealth, rather than current income alone.

Suppose the long-term trend of about 3 percent annual growth in real GDP continues. At what annual rate must the money stock grow to prevent excessive inflation? According to the equation of exchange,

$$MV = \text{(Price level)(Real GDP)}$$

If real GDP goes up by 3 percent per year, *MV* must increase by no more than 3 percent per year to prevent inflation over the long run. If *MV* increases by less than 3 percent per year, aggregate demand will grow less quickly than aggregate supply and there will be downward pressure on real GDP and the price level.

To prevent excessive inflation, a monetary growth management policy must also predict changes in *V* over the long run. For example, if velocity increases over time (as it did between 1950 and 1985), a 3 percent monetary growth rate will be inflationary because both the increase in velocity and the increase in the money supply will exert upward pressure on the price level over time. A strict rule governing the increase in the money supply can therefore result in inflation if *V* changes unexpectedly. On the other hand, if velocity declines (as it did between 1984 and 1987), a 3 percent growth rate of the money stock will be deflationary. Monetary growth will not provide enough new money to accommodate economic growth. This situation can cause a recession because interest rates will rise unless the price level is downwardly flexible.

Monetarists believe that shifts in velocity are fairly predictable and therefore recommend a rule that allows the money supply to increase within the range of 3 percent to 5 percent per year, depending on predicted changes in velocity.

- The money stock increases by 10 percent during the year. Assuming velocity is constant and real GDP is at its potential level, what is the long-run effect on the price level of the increase in the money stock?

- Why would you expect interest rates to rise during a period of expansion in the economy, other things being equal?

- How can an increase in the income velocity of circulation of money affect nominal GDP, assuming the money stock is fixed?

CONCEPT CHECK
☐

MONETARY POLICY IN THE UNITED STATES SINCE 1942

During the period 1942 to 1951, the Fed pursued policies to keep interest rates at low levels. The federal government had accumulated a tremendous debt as a result of bonds issued to finance the nation's participation in World War II. Up to 1951 the Fed enabled the government to keep its interest costs low by adjusting the money supply in response to shifts in money demand. 6

When the Fed engages in a policy of keeping interest rates low, it loses its ability to stabilize the economy. It loses the opportunity to influence aggregate demand in the short run through changes in interest rates, and it also gives up control of the money stock, because it must adjust the money supply to keep interest rates fixed.

Normally, the demand for money increases as the economy expands, because as real GDP increases or the price level rises, individuals demand higher transaction balances. The outward shift in the money demand curve during an economic expansion puts upward pressure on interest rates. To keep interest rates from rising, the Fed must increase the money supply. As shown in Box 6, the increase in the money supply keeps interest rates pegged at a target level, but the equilibrium money stock increases. The increase is likely to add to inflationary pressures just as the economy is nearing full employment. Thus, keeping interest rates at low levels means that the Fed runs the risk of contributing to inflation in the long run by increasing the money supply whenever the demand for money increases. It also loses its ability to stabilize the economy in the short run when it agrees to keep interest rates pegged.

Box 6 shows interest rates rising from 6 to 7 percent during an expansion as the demand for money increases. The rising interest rates dampen the expansion if money supply growth is not increased. By dampening the expansion, the rising interest rates help keep the economy from overheating. However, when the Fed increases the money supply in order to keep interest rates fixed (6 percent in Box 6), the risk of an overheated economy increases.

In 1951 the Treasury and the Fed reached a famous "accord" in which it was agreed that the Fed would have more discretion in influencing interest rates. Subsequently, the Fed sought to keep interest rates within certain bounds and carefully watched bank excess reserves and discount loans as indicators of the availability of loanable funds. Unfortunately, the Fed's stabilization record wasn't very good. When the economy was booming, it engaged in policies that tended to decrease interest rates. When the economy was slack, it engaged in policies that tended to increase interest rates. Rather than stabilizing the economy, the Fed's policies

Box 6   How an Increase in Money Supply Can Keep Interest Rates from Rising During an Expansion

As the economy expands, the demand for money increases, putting upward pressure on interest rates. The Fed can keep interest rates from rising to 7 percent by expanding the monetary base. As the monetary base increases, so does money supply, putting downward pressure on interest rates. In the graph, the Fed's policy keeps interest rates at 6 percent during the expansion but allows the money stock to grow from $500 billion to $600 billion.

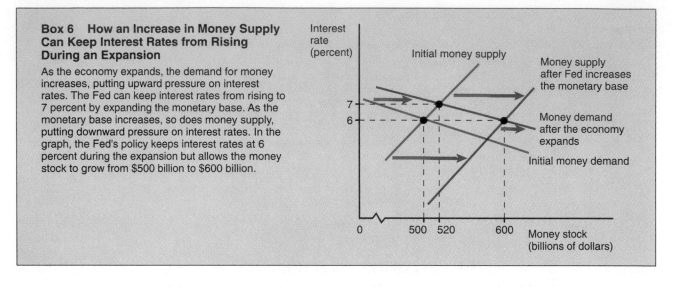

throughout much of the 1950s and 1960s contributed to the severity of cyclical ups and downs of real GDP!

In the 1970s the Fed began to choose monetary growth targets rather than interest rate targets. It sought to control the growth rates of M1 and M2 while keeping short-term interest rates from fluctuating too widely. During this period, whenever an increase in real GDP or the price level caused an increase in money demand, the Fed would react to the resulting upward pressure on interest rates by engaging in open market purchases of government securities. These purchases would increase securities prices, thereby decreasing interest rates. However, the open market purchases tended to increase the money supply, thus getting the Fed off its M1 target. The Fed would then react at the next Federal Open Market Committee meeting to decrease the monetary base. Whenever the Fed missed its target on short-term interest rates, it would increase the rate of monetary growth. This made it hard to control the money stock, which by 1973 was growing at 8 percent per year and putting upward pressure on inflation and nominal interest rates. In 1974 the sharp increase in the price of oil along with high interest rates contributed to a recession.

Between 1974 and 1979 the money supply tended to grow along with the price level during that inflationary period. In 1979, however, the Fed began to engage in policies that sharply slowed the growth rate of bank reserves and M1. Because money demand continued to grow over that period, this decision resulted in upward pressure on nominal interest rates. By the end of 1980, nominal interest rates in the economy were in double digits.

In 1981 the prime rate rose to nearly 20 percent. Given the prevailing inflation rate of 9 percent, the real interest rate paid on prime rate loans in 1981 was at the unprecedentedly high level of 11 percent! The increase in interest rates decreased investment spending sharply and, in 1982, contributed to the most severe recession the nation had experienced since the Great Depression. Apparently, the Fed had reduced the growth rate of M1 too sharply. The basic problem the Fed faced during this period was the familiar one of accurately predicting cyclical increases in money demand that put upward pressure on interest rates.

When the Fed applies the brakes to monetary growth in an expanding economy, interest rates soar. The soaring interest rates can cause a recession, as was the case in 1982. As the Fed restricted the rate of growth of the money stock in 1981, when

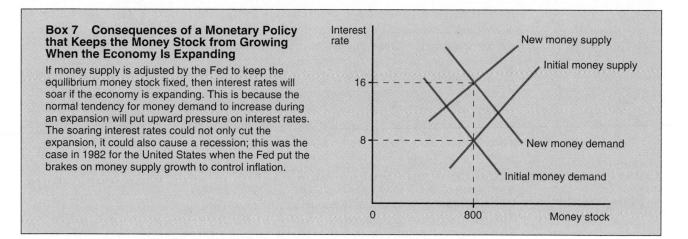

Box 7 Consequences of a Monetary Policy that Keeps the Money Stock from Growing When the Economy Is Expanding

If money supply is adjusted by the Fed to keep the equilibrium money stock fixed, then interest rates will soar if the economy is expanding. This is because the normal tendency for money demand to increase during an expansion will put upward pressure on interest rates. The soaring interest rates could not only cut the expansion, it could also cause a recession; this was the case in 1982 for the United States when the Fed put the brakes on money supply growth to control inflation.

money demand was still increasing due to a rising price level and still-increasing real GDP, interest rates increased to the double-digit level. This caused a recession, which, in turn, reduced money demand and eventually allowed interest rates to fall.

Box 7 shows the consequences of a monetary policy that adjusts money supply in order to keep the money stock from growing while the economy is expanding. As the economy expands, money demand increases, putting upward pressure on interest rates. If the Fed then reduces money supply to keep the equilibrium money stock from growing, further upward pressure is placed on interest rates. The higher interest rates reduce aggregate demand and can cause a recession.

This case illustrates the often unpleasant effects of pegging the money stock to low growth levels in periods of expansion. The decreased growth rate of the money stock controls inflation over the long run at the cost of risking a severe recession in the short run. However, the bitter resolve of the Fed to halt monetary growth is often necessary to reduce inflation over the long run at the expense of causing a contraction, or even a recession, over the short run.

Inflation was sharply reduced after the 1982 recession, and from 1983 through 1987 the Fed worried less about its effect on the economy. The Fed allowed M1 to grow to accommodate the increased demand for money in an expanding economy. In 1986 nominal interest rates fell sharply and inflation remained low. Throughout 1986 real interest rates remained quite high by historical standards. In 1986 the Fed engaged in policies that caused real interest rates to fall. By 1987, as the economy approached full employment, fears of inflation increased, and the Fed engaged in policies to increase real interest rates. That increase, combined with the falling international value of the dollar, contributed to a stock market collapse in October 1987.

The economy approached full employment in 1988 and operated at or near full employment in 1989 and 1990. From 1987 to early 1990, money supply growth was sharply curtailed, with M1 barely increasing in 1989. Interest rates increased substantially as money demand grew while the Fed chose to control the growth of monetary aggregates during a period when the economy was expanding. In July 1990, in part because of slow growth in the money supply, the U.S. economy fell into a recession.

Monetary Policy since 1990

The recession of 1990–91 and the sluggish recovery that followed was a trying period for U.S. monetary policy. Increases in bank reserves and declining short-term interest rates resulting from an expansionary monetary policy had little effect on aggregate demand. Long-term interest rates remained relatively high throughout 1992 because inflationary expectations remained high.

When the Fed acted to increase bank reserves in 1991 and 1992, short-term interest rates fell. There was a sharp reduction in the return to money market mutual funds and CDs, from around 6 percent to 3 percent and less. As a result, the public shifted assets out of CDs and money market mutual funds and into checking accounts. The public also placed more money in long-term assets whose yields were relatively high, such as Treasury bonds. Because of these shifts in asset demand, the growth rate of M2 fell below what the Fed intended to achieve. The increased demand for M1 assets reduced the income velocity of circulation of money, but M1 grew more rapidly than expected. The lagging growth of M2 and the reduced velocity of circulation of M1 made it difficult for the Fed to interpret the results of its policies and to stimulate the economy.

This was complicated by the "credit crunch" that we discussed earlier in this chapter. As banks were pressured to reduce the default risk of their loans and to raise the ratio of owner-supplied capital to assets, they responded by making fewer loans despite the fact that their excess reserves were increasing. They used the excess reserves to purchase government securities instead of using them to supply credit to businesses. Moreover, high business and household debt burdens inherited from the 1980s made it difficult for many to qualify for new loans and reduced the demand for such loans. The demand for real estate credit all but collapsed because of overbuilding in the 1980s.

For all these reasons, the lower short-term interest rates that resulted from the expansionary monetary policy of the late 1980s failed to generate the substantial increase in aggregate demand needed for a vigorous recovery. However, the lower interest rates did reduce debt burdens for many as refinancing of mortgages and corporate debt took place. By early 1993, reduced debt burdens, due in part to lower interest rates, were beginning to increase aggregate demand. As inflationary expectations were also reduced in 1993, a fall in long-term interest rates stimulated a more robust expansion.

🌐 *the global economy*

How U.S. Integration into the Modern Global Economy Has Affected Monetary Policy

The increased integration of the United States into the modern global economy has had an impact on the way the Fed conducts monetary policy. Policymakers at the Fed must now be concerned about the effects of changes in U.S. interest rates on the international value of the dollar. Changes in U.S. interest rates affect the demand for the dollar, which in turn affects its exchange rate relative to other currencies. The changes also affect the demand for U.S. exports and the U.S. demand for imported products. The United States can also be buffeted by changes in monetary policy in other nations. For example, in-creases in interest rates in Germany and other nations in the early 1990s decreased the supply of loanable funds in the United States, putting upward pressure on U.S. interest rates. It was more difficult for the Fed to lower interest rates in 1990 because larger increases in the money supply were necessary to reduce interest rates in the face of a decrease in the supply of loanable funds from abroad.

An expansionary monetary policy that puts downward pressure on real interest rates relative to those in other nations can cause the dollar to decline in value relative to other currencies. The lower interest rates induce foreign holders of dollars to sell those dollars so that they can buy relatively higher interest-yielding assets denominated in other currencies. The consequent increase in the supply of dollars on foreign exchange markets causes their value to fall.

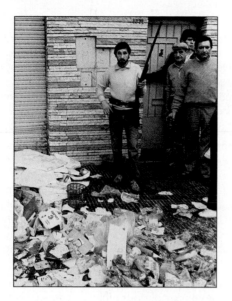

Sometimes the Fed keeps interest rates high in the United States to avoid causing the value of the dollar to fall.

The downward movement in the dollar must be accounted for in monetary policy. When the dollar declines in value, the prices of U.S. exports decrease in terms of foreign currency, thereby increasing the demand for U.S. goods abroad. At the same time, the declining dollar puts upward pressure on the prices of imported goods, inducing consumers to substitute U.S. goods for imported products. Both of these effects increase the net export component of real GDP. This expansionary influence on the economy is added to the increase in investment demand normally expected from an expansionary monetary policy. If these effects are not considered, the Fed can easily cause the economy to overheat, possibly starting an inflationary wage-price spiral.

Similarly, the Fed must take the international repercussions into account when it engages in a contractionary monetary policy. A contractionary monetary policy increases real interest rates in the United States relative to those abroad. Foreigners increase their demands for dollars because they now find investment in dollar assets more desirable. The foreign exchange rate of the dollar increases, which decreases the demand for U.S. exports and increases the U.S. demand for imports. Thus, the net export component of real GDP declines, adding to the contractionary effect of the decrease in investment purchases that results from the rise in real interest rates.

The Fed's policies can also be affected by policy changes abroad. In the 1980s America's huge balance of trade deficits put lots of dollars into the hands of foreigners and increased the supply of loanable funds offered by foreigners to U.S. financial markets. Because of the globalization of financial markets through satellite communications, when interest rates in Japan, Germany, or other foreign nations increase or decrease, there are rapid repercussions in U.S. financial markets. A small change in real interest rates abroad has an almost immediate effect on the supply of loanable funds at home. Such effects make it harder for the Fed to manipulate interest rates and may require larger shifts in the money stock to achieve a given change in interest rates. The larger shifts can destabilize the economy over the long run.

During the first quarter of 1990, for example, the Fed wanted to reduce U.S. interest rates to ease the contractionary monetary policy it had followed in 1989. However, interest rates refused to budge downward despite increases in the monetary base. The Fed's difficulty arose because, over the same period, interest rates were inching up in Tokyo because Japanese policymakers were engaged in a contractionary monetary policy and in Frankfurt because increased demands for funds resulted from the impending unification of East and West Germany. As the supply of loanable funds from foreign sources decreased, there was upward pressure on interest rates in the United States. The Fed was not powerless, but the decrease in the supply of loanable funds from foreigners made a *larger* increase in the money supply necessary to lower U.S. interest rates. This larger increase could have resulted in inflation later as its long-run effects were felt in the economy.

Similarly, a fall in interest rates abroad can increase the supply of loanable funds in the United States, putting downward pressure on interest rates just when the Fed may want to increase them. The Fed may then have to decrease the money supply more than it really wants to and run the risk of inducing a recession over the longer run.

At Federal Open Market Committee meetings, officials of the Fed now carefully listen to the report of their chief international economist before making key decisions. The increased dependence of the U.S. economy on events in foreign nations has also led many policymakers to seek closer international coordination of economic policy. To achieve this goal, the United States meets regularly with seven other advanced nations to achieve a reasonable coordination of macroeconomic policy.

SUMMARY

1. Monetary policy consists of actions taken by central banks to influence interest rates and the money supply in ways that affect aggregate demand.

2. An expansionary monetary policy consists of increases in the monetary base or its rate of growth, while a contractionary monetary policy consists of decreases in the monetary base or its rate of growth.

3. An expansionary monetary policy puts downward pressure on interest rates and encourages investment spending by business firms. The increase in aggregate purchases resulting from an expansionary monetary policy puts upward pressure on equilibrium real GDP. An expansionary monetary policy has the effect of shifting the economy's aggregate demand curve outward.

4. The effectiveness of an expansionary monetary policy in increasing aggregate demand depends on the banking system's willingness to extend credit with newly supplied excess reserves and on the responsiveness of investment spending to declines in interest rates.

5. A contractionary monetary policy can prevent an economy from overheating. By increasing interest rates, such a policy puts downward pressure on aggregate demand and aggregate purchases.

6. The income velocity of circulation of money, which is nominal GDP divided by the money stock, measures the number of times each dollar of the money stock is received as income during a year.

7. The equation of exchange is an identity that shows the relationship among nominal GDP, the money stock, and the income velocity of circulation of money. The classical quantity theory of money argues that in the long run money stock changes will affect the price level rather than real GDP, provided the income velocity of circulation of money is stable. According to the classical theory, in the long run the price level in an economy is proportional to the supply of money. In this view, a doubling of the money supply will eventually double the price level.

8. The income velocity of circulation of money has varied considerably in the United States since 1929. Between 1960 and 1985 the income velocity of circulation of money increased as financial innovations reduced the demand for money. Income velocity was very unstable in the 1980s.

9. Monetarism, a theory of long-term macroeconomic equilibrium based on the equation of exchange, assumes that shifts in the income velocity of circulation of money are reasonably predictable. Monetarists argue that although monetary policy influences aggregate demand, errors in its use prevented its objectives from being achieved in the past. To avoid destabilizing the economy through errors in monetary policy, monetarists advocate steady and predictable monetary growth each year.

10. Shifts in money demand affect interest rates. Money increases during periods of peak economic activity and decreases as nominal GDP declines. Financial innovations that decrease the transaction cost of converting near money into money also decrease the demand for money.

11. Shifts in money demand make it difficult for the Fed to control interest rates and the money supply simultaneously, because an increase in the money supply induced by the Fed increases aggregate demand. The increase in aggregate demand increases either real GDP or the price level, which, in turn, increases the demand for money. As the demand for money goes up, there is upward pressure on interest rates and an increase in the equilibrium quantity of money held. To control the money supply requires accurate forecasts of shifts in money demand induced by shifts in aggregate demand.

12. When the Fed tries to keep interest rates stable, it allows the money supply to adjust to accommodate shifts in money demand. When the Fed keeps the money supply fixed, shifts in aggregate demand that occur over the business cycle will result in fluctuations in interest rates.

KEY TERMS

stabilization policies *365*
monetary policy *365*

expansionary monetary policy *367*
contractionary monetary policy *367*

income velocity of circulation of money *375*
equation of exchange *375*

classical quantity theory of money *376*
monetarism *379*

CONCEPT REVIEW

1. Why will the federal funds rate go up if the Fed engages in open market sales of government securities?

2. How does an expansionary fiscal policy increase aggregate demand in the short run?

3. How can a contractionary monetary policy prevent the economy from overheating?

4. Write down the equation of exchange, and briefly sum-

marize the assumptions and implications of the classical quantity theory of money.

5 What is monetarism?

PROBLEMS AND APPLICATIONS

1. The current level of interest rates in the economy is about 8 percent. The Fed believes aggregate demand will decline during the year. How can the Fed counteract the expected decline in aggregate demand in a way that will prevent a recession? **1**, **2**

2. Inflation is currently 4 percent per year. The Fed believes an increase in aggregate demand will put upward pressure on the price level during the year. What actions should the Fed engage in to counteract the inflationary pressures in the economy? **1**, **3**

3. Show how an expansionary monetary policy influences the money supply and the market rate of interest. How are the effects of an expansionary monetary policy transmitted to the economy at large in a way that affects real GDP and the price level? Use aggregate supply and demand analysis to predict the impact of an expansionary monetary policy. **1**, **2**

4. Explain how a contractionary monetary policy will affect real interest rates and the quantity of investment goods demanded per year. Show how the contractionary monetary policy will affect macroeconomic equilibrium, assuming that the aggregate supply curve is stable. **3**

5. Suppose banks held excess reserves made available through Federal Reserve System open market purchases. Under these circumstances, how effective will monetary policy be in stimulating the economy? **2**

6. Suppose the demand curve for investment goods is a vertical line plotting investment purchases against the real rate of interest. Under these circumstances, how effective will monetary policy be in eliminating a recessionary GDP gap? **2**

7. The economy is currently at full employment. During the year the money stock is increased by 25 percent. Assuming the income velocity of circulation of money is constant during the year, what will be the impact on the price level? **4**

8. Suppose the Fed pursues a monetary policy that allows the money supply to grow at the same rate as the long-term growth rate of real GDP. During a five-year period for which this policy is pursued, the income velocity of circulation of money doubles from 2 to 4. What will happen to the price level over the five-year period? **4**, **5**

9. Explain why the demand for money will increase as the economy begins to pull out of a recession. Why will interest rates tend to rise as the economy moves into this expansionary phase of the business cycle? How can the Fed prevent the rise in interest rates from dampening the recovery from the recession? Why does keeping interest rates from rising mean the money supply must grow? **6**

10. Why are the long-term effects of monetary policy likely to differ from the short-term effects? Why can a policy designed to keep interest rates from fluctuating cause inflation in the long run? **4**, **6**

6 Explain why interest rates will soar if the Fed keeps the money stock fixed while the economy expands.

17 *chapter*

Stabilization of the Economy through Fiscal Policy

You don't have to be an economist to understand that the federal government has a tremendous impact on the U.S. economy. If you have a job, you know that through its tax policies the federal government affects disposable income, a key influence on consumer purchases. You also know that the federal government is a big spender, paying out more than $1 trillion annually, which is about one quarter of GDP. Retired workers rely on the federal government for their Social Security pensions, and defense contractors and their employees obtain much of their income from federal government purchases. Finally, federal tax and subsidy programs also affect incentives to save, invest, and work.

Government spending and tax policies affect aggregate demand, and the impact of government policies on incentives can affect aggregate supply over time. The federal government has legal responsibility under the Employment Act of 1946 and the Humphrey-Hawkins Act of 1978 to use its spending and taxing powers to help achieve full employment. The *Council of Economic Advisers* assists the president in recommending policies that maintain economic stability and pursue goals of full employment and low inflation.

In this chapter we'll examine the impact of the federal government budget on macroeconomic equilibrium. In the following chapter we'll zero in on the federal government budget deficit to analyze its impact in depth.

□ CONCEPT PREVIEW

After reading this chapter, you should be able to:

1. Explain how expansionary fiscal policies affect the economy and show how such policies can be used to eliminate recessionary GDP gaps.

2. Explain how contractionary fiscal policies affect the economy and show how such policies can help prevent inflation.

3. Show how automatic stabilizers moderate shifts in aggregate demand.

4. Explain how supply-side fiscal policies can affect the economy in the long run and assess the effectiveness of recent supply-side policies.

THE FEDERAL BUDGET AND ITS IMPACT ON THE ECONOMY

When there's a presidential election, one of the biggest issues is always the state of the economy. In the United States we expect the president to pursue policies that reduce cyclical unemployment, keep inflation under control, and ensure adequate economic growth. The president is inevitably blamed for poor performance of the economy and is quick to claim the credit when the economy performs well. Inflation, unemployment, and the rate of economic growth are political issues. Pressure groups and ordinary citizens expect the federal government to take measures to achieve full employment and stable prices.

The use of government spending and taxing for the specific purpose of stabilizing the economy is called fiscal policy. The short-term goals of fiscal policy are to prevent excessive unemployment and to control inflation. Over longer periods fiscal policy seeks to ensure adequate economic growth to permit improvements in the national standard of living. You've already seen how monetary policy seeks to help control the cyclical ups and downs of the economy by influencing aggregate demand. Now you'll learn how fiscal policy can be used to stabilize the economy.

fiscal policy the use of government spending and taxing for the specific purpose of stabilizing the economy.

The spending and taxing activities of the federal government are influenced by many political considerations, not just those relating to stabilization. Our first step in understanding fiscal policy in the United States is to review the process through which federal government spending and taxes are approved annually.

The Federal Budget

The government budget is a plan for spending funds and for raising revenues through taxation, fees, and other means, and for borrowing funds if necessary. During the budgetary process politicians, citizens, and government officials propose, debate, and make decisions that affect government spending, taxing, and borrowing.

government budget a plan for spending funds and for raising revenues through taxation, fees, and other means, and for borrowing funds if necessary.

The budget sets the spending and revenue plan for the federal government's *fiscal year*, which runs from October 1 to September 30. When government revenues raised from taxation and means other than borrowing exactly cover government expenditures during the fiscal year, the budget is said to be *balanced*.

Government spending often exceeds government revenues. A *budget deficit* is the annual excess of government spending over government revenues. When the budget is in deficit, the federal government must borrow funds by issuing government securities that are sold in credit markets, such as Treasury bills, notes, and bonds. The federal government budget in the United States has been in deficit every year since 1970.

A *budget surplus* prevails when government revenues exceed government expenditures during the year. When the federal government runs a budget surplus, it can use the excess revenue to pay off some of its debt.

As you undoubtedly know from watching the nightly news, the deficit is a hotly debated political and economic issue. In the following chapter we'll sort out the arguments for and against budget deficits. Our goal in this chapter is to examine the general effects of government spending and taxes on macroeconomic equilibrium in order to understand how the government budget can be used to stabilize the economy.

How the Federal Government Budget Affects Aggregate Demand:
A Quick Review

As you know, government purchases represent a major component of aggregate demand. Nearly 1 of every 10 dollars spent on the purchase of goods and services in the United States is spent by the federal government. The federal government also makes direct transfer payments to members of households and to state and local governments. These payments, which include welfare benefits, Social Security pensions, veterans' benefits, interest payments to holders of government securities, and grants to state and local governments, constitute sources of income to recipients. Government purchases and transfer payments, other things being equal, add to aggregate demand by increasing disposable income in the United States.

To finance its purchases of goods and services and the payments it makes to individuals and organizations each year, the federal government collects funds through taxation, which accounts for the bulk of federal government revenues. Taxes paid reduce the ability of households and business firms to purchase goods and services for their private use and therefore tend to reduce aggregate demand.

The overall effect of the federal budget on aggregate demand depends on the expansionary effect of government purchases or other payments and on the contractionary effect of taxes. When there is a budget deficit, the federal government adds more to aggregate demand than it takes away, because it will spend more on purchases and transfer payments than it raises from taxes. A budget deficit therefore indicates that the government is putting upward pressure on aggregate demand. The government can use this upward pressure to offset cyclical declines in investment or net export demand, thus employing fiscal policy to prevent the economy from falling into a recession.

The government can *decrease* aggregate demand by running a budget *surplus*. In such cases the government collects more in taxes than it spends. Just as you save when you spend less than your income, the government can save by running a budget surplus. When the federal government spends less than it collects in revenues, it adds less to aggregate demand than it takes away. A budget surplus is therefore a contractionary influence on the economy that can be used to offset surges in consumption and investment demand that might cause inflation.

Government borrowing to finance a budget deficit can affect equilibrium in credit markets in ways that indirectly influence aggregate demand. Increased demand for credit by the government can put upward pressure on interest rates. The higher real interest rates can decrease investment purchases. Similarly, when the government runs a budget surplus, its decreased demand for credit can put downward pressure on interest rates. In the following chapter we'll examine the impact of the federal budget deficit on financial markets.

CONCEPT CHECK

□

- What is fiscal policy?
- How does fiscal policy influence aggregate demand in the economy?

- When does a budget deficit prevail?

USING FISCAL POLICY TO INFLUENCE AGGREGATE DEMAND

expansionary fiscal policy a policy under which the government acts to increase aggregate demand by increasing spending or decreasing taxes, or both.

An **expansionary fiscal policy** is one under which the government acts to *increase* aggregate demand by adjusting its budget during the year. It can do this by increasing its purchases of goods and services, by increasing transfer payments to individuals and organizations, or by decreasing taxes. Of course, the government can choose to increase aggregate demand by decreasing taxes *and* increasing spending.

Expansionary fiscal policy can be used to increase equilibrium real GDP and to reduce the cyclical unemployment that prevails when the economy is in a recession. This was the remedy proposed by Keynes for an economy in deep recession. Keynes believed that because the outlook for increased sales would be gloomy in a deep recession, banks would be cautious about making loans and investors would be unresponsive to reductions in interest rates. Keynes's solution was for the government to increase its spending when others would not. To eliminate a recessionary GDP gap, the government would allow its budget balance to shift to a deficit. The resulting stimulus to aggregate demand would then increase aggregate purchases, and as aggregate production increased, unemployment would be reduced. Once the economy was on course again, the government could reduce spending and let the budget return to balance.

To restrain aggregate demand, the government can engage in a **contractionary fiscal policy** that will decrease government spending or increase taxes, or both. A contractionary fiscal policy can be used to put downward pressure on the price level, thereby combating the inflation in periods when the economy is overheating.

contractionary fiscal policy a policy under which the government acts to restrain aggregate demand by decreasing government spending or increasing taxes, or both.

How an Increase in Government Purchases Can Help Pull an Economy Out of a Recession

Let's begin our analysis of fiscal policy by examining how an increase in government purchases can increase aggregate demand and eliminate a substantial recessionary GDP gap. In Box 1 the economy is in equilibrium at a level of real GDP equal to $4,000 billion. Potential real GDP is assumed to be $5,000 billion. The economy is therefore experiencing a $1,000 billion recessionary GDP gap. It's also assumed that the economy is currently stagnating in a severe recession, so that it's operating along the flat portion of its aggregate supply curve. Through the use of fiscal policy, the government can increase aggregate demand without heating up inflation during the year.

Remember from our analysis of the multiplier that less than $1 of autonomous spending, such as government purchases, is required to increase real GDP by $1 (see the chapter on Keynesian analysis of aggregate purchases). Suppose the marginal respending rate in the economy is 0.5. The marginal respending rate is less than 1 because a portion of the increased annual income generated from an initial round of autonomous purchases is used to buy imported goods and to pay taxes. Some is saved. When the marginal respending rate is 0.5, the multiplier for any initial injection of new spending into the economy is

$$\text{Multiplier} = 1/(1 - \text{Marginal respending rate})$$
$$= 1/(1 - 0.5) = 1/0.5$$
$$= 2$$

Each dollar of government purchases that is initiated at the beginning of the year will therefore ultimately increase real GDP and real income in the nation by $2 as it is spent and respent.

Assuming nothing else changes, G, an increase in government purchases generating $500 billion in additional business receipts at the beginning of the year, can eliminate the recessionary gap because the total increase in spending resulting from G will be

$$\text{Increase in real GDP} = (\text{Increase in } G) (\text{Multiplier})$$
$$= (\$500 \text{ billion})(2)$$
$$= \$1,000 \text{ billion}$$

The graphs in Box 1 show how the expansionary fiscal policy will affect the macroeconomic equilibrium for an economy in a recession. As shown in graph **A**, the economy is initially in equilibrium at point E, where aggregate purchases just equal

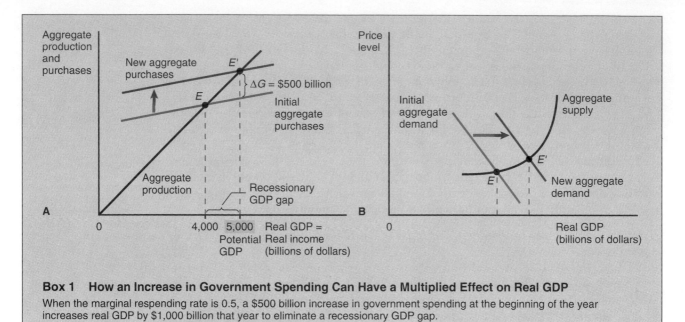

Box 1   How an Increase in Government Spending Can Have a Multiplied Effect on Real GDP

When the marginal responding rate is 0.5, a $500 billion increase in government spending at the beginning of the year increases real GDP by $1,000 billion that year to eliminate a recessionary GDP gap.

aggregate production at the current price level (see the chapter on Keynesian analysis of aggregate purchases for discussion of this graph). Other things being equal, an injection of $500 billion of new government purchases shifts the aggregate purchases line upward and results in a new equilibrium at point E'. At that point real GDP increases to $5,000 billion as the recessionary GDP gap is closed.

Graph **B** shows that the increase in government purchases shifts the aggregate demand curve outward. It also shows that the expansionary policy has little impact on the price level when the economy is operating in the relatively flat portion of its aggregate supply curve, as is likely to be the case in an economy experiencing a deep recession. Increases in aggregate demand that result from an expansionary fiscal policy are therefore unlikely to contribute to an inflationary process for an economy experiencing a deep recession.

Using Tax Cuts or Government Transfers to Stimulate a Sluggish Economy

A sluggish economy can also be stimulated through a tax cut or an increase in government transfer payments. However, the impact of these measures on aggregate demand is less direct than the impact of an increase in government purchases. Remember that *net taxes* are the difference between government tax revenues and government transfers. In effect, transfers can be viewed as negative taxes. To engage in an expansionary fiscal policy, the government reduces net taxes by decreasing taxes or increasing transfers. In doing so, the government increases disposable income, which results in increased consumer purchases.

It's easy to show that the expansionary effect of a reduction in net taxes is less than that of an equivalent dollar increase in government purchases. When the government makes purchases of $500 billion, it directly increases business receipts by that amount at the initial stage of the spending increase. However, when the government puts $500 billion into the pockets of individuals through a reduction in net taxes (either through an increase in government transfers such as Social Security or welfare payments or through a lump-sum refund of taxes to all taxpayers), purchases of U.S. final products will not go up by that amount at the initial stage. Some of the increased disposable income that results from the cut in net taxes will be spent on imported goods, and some will be saved. For example, suppose the marginal propensity to save is 0.2 and the marginal propensity to import is 0.1. This means that 30 percent of the dollar value of the $500 billion tax cut, or $150 billion, will not be directly spent on U.S. final products. The initial increase in the purchases of U.S. final products that results from the tax cut will therefore be only $350 billion. The multiplier process thus begins with a $350 billion injection of new spending rather than a $500 billion injection, as was the case when government purchases increased by $500 billion. The $350 billion initial increase in purchases will then be spent and respent in the course of the multiplier process. Some of the extra income generated in this process will be used to make purchases in the United States, but some will be saved, some will be used to purchase imported items, and some will be used to pay taxes on the extra income. Assuming a multiplier of 2 for the economy, this means the $500 billion tax cut will result in a $700 billion increase in real GDP ($350 billion $\times$ 2 = $700 billion).[1]

We can conclude that an increase in government purchases is more expansionary for the economy than a decrease in net taxes of an equal amount. Other things being equal, increasing transfer payments or reducing taxes is less stimulating to the economy than increasing government purchases.

The expansionary effect of a tax cut can also be less than that of an increase in government purchases because households may treat the extra income differently from the way they treat extra income earned. If the tax cut is viewed as only temporary, the proportion saved is likely to be higher for a dollar of reduced taxes than for a dollar of extra earnings.

However, tax cuts have been used with some success to help pull the economy out of recessions. Tax cuts were proposed by the Kennedy administration in the early 1960s to help pull the economy out of a serious recession. In 1964 Congress reduced average personal income taxes by 18 percent. This reduction was widely credited with spurring an increase in consumer purchases that lifted the economy out of the recession. However, in 1975, when President Ford persuaded Congress to reduce income taxes to help increase aggregate demand during a recession, much of the tax cut was apparently used to increase saving and aggregate demand did not increase substantially.

In 1981 a tax cut designed to increase aggregate supply rather than aggregate demand was proposed by President Reagan and enacted by Congress. In the short run, however, the effect of the Reagan tax cut was to increase the federal budget deficit. The resulting increase in aggregate demand helped pull the economy out of the recession of 1982.

Equal Increases of Government Purchases and Net Taxes Are Expansionary

The analysis of the two preceding sections can be used to reach a surprising conclusion: An equal increase in government purchases and net taxes has an expansionary effect on the economy. A $500 billion injection of government purchases

---

[1] We have to mention one more complication here. Tax cuts are sometimes a refund of taxes with no change in marginal tax rates, as is assumed in this example of a lump-sum tax refund. At other times, however, the marginal tax rate may be lowered when taxes are cut, as was the case under the Tax Reform Act of 1986. When the marginal tax rate is lowered, the multiplier is increased. Review the Appendix to the chapter entitled "Keynesian Analysis of Aggregate Purchases" to see how the multiplier is related to the marginal tax rate.

results in a $1,000 billion increase in real GDP, other things being equal, when the multiplier is 2 for an initial injection of new spending into the economy.

A $500 billion *increase* in net taxes to cover the increased government purchases would result in a multiplied *decrease* in private expenditures because it decreases disposable income. However, the initial reduction in private spending on U.S. goods and services resulting from a $500 billion increase in taxes would be less than $500 billion. This is because some of the $500 billion collected in taxes would have been saved or used to purchase imported goods. Using the same marginal propensities to save and import as in the previous example, a $500 billion increase in net taxes will decrease purchases of U.S. goods by only $350 billion. The remaining $150 billion of the tax increase would have been spent on imports or saved and thus would not have added to aggregate demand. The initial tax-induced reduction in spending on U.S.-produced goods and services of $350 billion will then result in a $700 billion reduction in real GDP, assuming a multiplier of 2. Notice that after the multiplier process has been played out, the reduction in real GDP attributable to the increase in net taxes is *less than* the $1,000 billion increase in real GDP attributable to the increase in government purchases. As a result of this increase in government purchases, which is fully covered by the increase in net taxes, there is upward pressure on aggregate demand. The increase in equilibrium real GDP is the multiplier effect of the purchases ($1,000 billion) less the multiplier effect of the taxes ($-$700 billion), or $300 billion.

Because the expansionary effect of each dollar of government purchases exceeds the contractionary effect of each dollar of taxes used to finance the purchases, the net effect on the economy of an equal increase in government purchases and net taxes is expansionary. An increase in government spending that is exactly covered by an increase in taxes will increase real GDP. It follows that increased spending adds to aggregate demand even when that spending doesn't increase the government deficit! Beware, then, of politicians who say that increased government spending won't add to inflationary pressures when that spending is fully financed by taxes. Fiscal policies may be expansionary even if they don't increase the deficit.

The Effects of Fiscal Policy on the Price Level

Any expansionary influence on aggregate demand resulting from fiscal policy will increase both the price level and real GDP as the economy moves toward its potential real GDP. The increase in the price level will dampen private spending over the year, and the multiplier effect on the economy will be correspondingly less. The graph in Box 2 shows how the increase in the price level chokes off some private purchases. The economy is initially in equilibrium at point *E,* at which real GDP is $4,500 billion and the price level is 100. The full-employment level of real GDP is $5,000 billion, implying that there is a $500 billion recessionary GDP gap. Fiscal policy is used to shift the aggregate demand curve outward. If the multiplier is 2, a $250 billion increase in government purchases is sufficient to increase real GDP by $500 billion. If there were no increase in the price level, the resulting outward shift of the aggregate demand curve would be sufficient to eliminate the recessionary GDP gap. However, because the price level rises from 100 to 105 as a result of the increase in aggregate demand, the economy achieves a new equilibrium at point *E'*. At the new equilibrium, the price level is 105 and real GDP is only $4,900 billion. The higher prices choke off $100 billion in private purchases. In this case *more than* $250 billion in government purchases is required to increase real GDP by $500 billion.

The multiplier will be less than that implied by the formulas in previous chapters when the price level is responsive to changes in aggregate demand. In addition, there

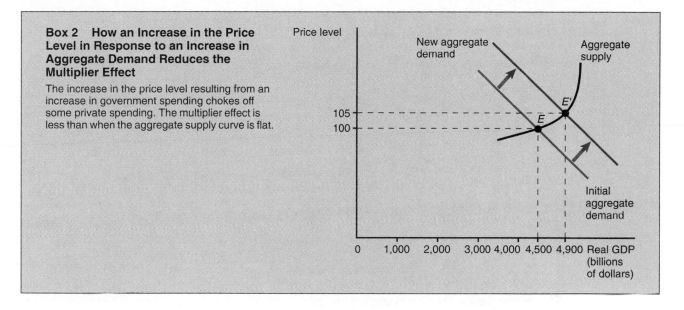

Box 2   How an Increase in the Price Level in Response to an Increase in Aggregate Demand Reduces the Multiplier Effect

The increase in the price level resulting from an increase in government spending chokes off some private spending. The multiplier effect is less than when the aggregate supply curve is flat.

is more risk that fiscal policy will overheat the economy when the economy is already close to its potential real GDP. Fiscal policy must therefore be used with care to avoid starting an inflationary spiral when only a modest gap exists between potential and actual GDP.

The government spending and borrowing required for an expansionary fiscal policy can also affect the level of interest rates in the economy. In the next chapter we'll discuss this possibility and its consequences for private spending.

Contractionary Fiscal Policy

Contractionary fiscal policy seeks to restrain aggregate demand by either decreasing government purchases or increasing net taxes. By restraining aggregate demand, a contractionary fiscal policy can help reduce inflation. Such a policy results in a reduction of the federal budget deficit or a movement toward a budget surplus.

The graph in Box 3 shows how a contractionary fiscal policy can help eliminate an inflationary gap or help prevent an economy from overheating. The economy is initially in equilibrium at point *E*, at which the price level if 100 and real GDP is at its potential level of $5,000 billion. If the aggregate demand curve shifts outward due to a stock market boom that boosts household wealth, the economy can reach equilibrium at point *E'*, at which real GDP will increase to $5,500 billion and the price level will go up to 110. If the economy is beginning to overheat in this way, a contractionary fiscal policy can offset the increase in aggregate demand. For example, if the Council of Economic Advisers projects that investment will increase during the year, it may expect a $500 billion inflationary GDP gap like the one shown in Box 3. A reduction in government purchases or an increase in net taxes can offset the expected increase in aggregate demand. Such a contractionary fiscal policy can keep the economy at point *E* and prevent it from moving to point *E'*. If nothing is done to prevent the economy from moving to *E'*, the result may be an inflationary wage-price spiral that eventually moves the economy to point *E''*, at which GDP has again fallen to $5,000 billion and the price level has risen to 115. In other words, fiscal policy can prevent a wage-price spiral from beginning.

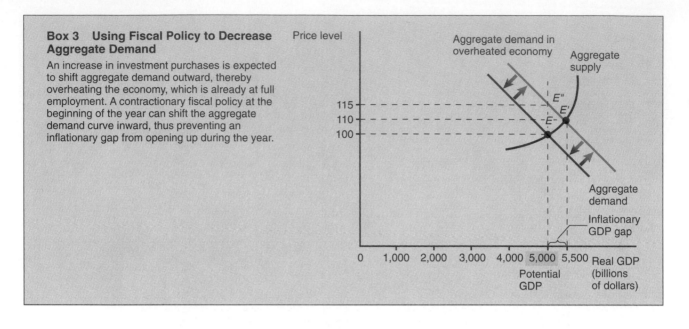

Box 3   Using Fiscal Policy to Decrease Aggregate Demand

An increase in investment purchases is expected to shift aggregate demand outward, thereby overheating the economy, which is already at full employment. A contractionary fiscal policy at the beginning of the year can shift the aggregate demand curve inward, thus preventing an inflationary gap from opening up during the year.

Problems in Effectively Implementing Fiscal Policy

Fiscal policy is based on forecasts of shifts in aggregate demand. Unfortunately, such forecasts are often inaccurate. Moreover, the thin line corresponding to potential real GDP is difficult to see in practice. A tax cut or government purchases increase designed to pull the economy out of a recession can easily overshoot the mark and overheat the economy! Stabilization policy is far from being an exact science.

Contractionary fiscal policy often runs into political problems. During the budgetary process, elected representatives oppose cuts in government spending that are likely to reduce their constituents' benefits. Every legislator wants budget cuts to reduce income in someone else's district! For this reason it's difficult to gain approval for cuts in government purchases and increases in net taxes. On the other hand, expansionary fiscal policies are quite popular. Increases in government purchases and reductions in net taxes provide direct benefits to politicians and their constituents.

The fact that the government budget has been almost consistently in deficit during both the ups and the downs of the business cycle since 1970 appears to support the idea that there is an expansionary bias to fiscal policy. There is also a temptation for politicians in power to engage in expansionary fiscal policies just prior to major elections, because the party in power is more likely to be reelected during economic upturns than during downturns! In any event, it's clear that in many cases fiscal policy takes a backseat to political maneuvering.

Another problem in implementing fiscal policy has to do with its effects on expectations. If participants in credit markets believe that an increase in the government budget deficit will substantially increase inflation, they will revise their expectations about inflation, which will put upward pressure on equilibrium long-term interest rates. As this occurs, the quantity of funds demanded for private investment will decline and the fiscal stimulus of the budget will be offset by a decline in investment spending. In effect, increased government purchases financed by borrowing could simply displace private spending without providing any stimulus to the economy. We will discuss this complication in the next chapter when we look at the budget deficit's effect on the economy in greater detail.

Over the years fiscal policy has had both its successes and its failures. The tax cut of 1964 increased aggregate demand at just the right time and encouraged economic growth. However, during the period 1965 to 1967, when government purchases for the Vietnam conflict were increasing, no tax increase was enacted. Despite a tax increase in 1968, the expansionary fiscal policy pursued by the Johnson administration at that time contributed to a period of inflation when the economy overheated in the late 1960s and early 1970s.

Lags in Fiscal Policy Implementation and Effects on Real GDP

Wouldn't it be nice if fiscal policy could be used as a precision tool to keep the economy always at full employment with inflation under control? Unfortunately, any stabilization policy, monetary or fiscal, is difficult to implement flawlessly. There are often problems in timing. For example, as just pointed out, it's hard to determine exactly when an economy is slipping into a recession or beginning to overheat. As a result, there's often a *recognition lag* between the time the economy begins to move away from full employment and the realization by policymakers that such a movement is actually occurring. Remember from our analysis of leading indicators that economic forecasts are anything but infallible! Economists did a poor job of forecasting the major recessions in the 1970s and 1980s.

There's also an *administrative lag* in implementing a fiscal policy change. Sometimes it takes a year or longer for a major tax cut to be enacted. The tax cut of 1964 was actually three years in the making! Sometimes such lags are so long that the economy's own self-correcting mechanism begins to work before fiscal policy gets a chance to exert an impact.

Finally, there's an *operational lag* between the time a change is made in government purchases or net taxes and the time it takes for equilibrium real GDP to change. The multiplier process is not instantaneous. It takes awhile for increases or decreases in disposable income resulting from fiscal policy to have an effect on private spending.

Just as monetary policy has its critics (see the preceding chapter), so too does fiscal policy. Many critics argue that because of its expansionary bias and the lags in its implementation and operation, the use of fiscal policy to stabilize the economy often does more harm than good.

- Explain why a decrease in net taxes is less expansionary for the economy than an equal increase in government purchases.
- Suppose the multiplier is 3. What will happen to equilibrium real GDP as the result of a $200 billion tax cut, assuming that the marginal propensity to save is 0.2 and the marginal propensity to import is 0.1?
- Why is the multiplier effect of fiscal policy reduced when the aggregate supply curve is upward sloping?

CONCEPT CHECK

☐

AUTOMATIC STABILIZERS AND CYCLICAL INFLUENCES ON THE BUDGET DEFICIT

The ups and downs of the economy have an automatic effect on certain government expenditures and revenues. For example, when real GDP falls below its potential value, unemployment increases, thereby increasing government expenditures for unemployment insurance. Also, as real GDP declines, federal tax collections decline, because most taxes used by the federal government are collected from labor earnings and earnings from the use of capital or loanable funds. Our earlier discussion concentrated on *discretionary* fiscal policy, which represents deliberate changes in government purchases and net taxes for the purpose of stabilizing the economy. We now turn our attention to the effects of *nondiscretionary* fiscal policy, which consists of changes in government spending and revenues that result automatically as the economy fluctuates.

The magnitude of the budget deficit or surplus is influenced by the inevitable fluctuations of the economy. Budget deficits or surpluses are not under the direct control of policymakers, at least in the short run. Cyclical fluctuations in real GDP and the price level must therefore be accounted for if the government budget deficit is to be predicted accurately.

Automatic Stabilizers

automatic stabilizers features of the federal budget that automatically adjust net taxes to stabilize aggregate demand as the economy expands and contracts.

Automatic stabilizers are features of the federal budget that automatically adjust net taxes to stabilize aggregate demand as the economy expands and contracts. When the economy begins to contract, these stabilizers increase transfer payments and reduce tax collections in order to stimulate aggregate demand. When the economy begins to expand, the automatic stabilizers increase tax collections and reduce transfer payments in order to constrain growth in aggregate demand.

A key automatic stabilizer is the federal income tax. As the economy expands, income tax collections rise as income earned increases. Given government purchases, the increased tax collections prevent aggregate purchases from increasing in proportion to the increase in earnings. In a sense, the income tax acts as a damper on private spending as real GDP and real income increase. It slows the growth of aggregate demand and controls upward pressure on the price level when the economy is expanding. This can help slow inflation if the funds are not spent by government but instead are used to reduce the government budget deficit.

Government tax receipts are also quite responsive to changes in business conditions, in part because marginal tax rates increase with income. As national income increases, more people are pushed into higher tax brackets. Therefore, the increase in taxes collected is greater proportionately than the increase in income. Similarly, when a recession causes real GDP and national income to decline, the decrease in taxes is greater proportionately than the decline in real GDP, because more people are pushed into lower tax brackets. Their tax bills decline proportionately more than their income does. Corporate profits taxes are particularly sensitive to shifts in the business cycle. Corporate profits typically plummet during a recession, as do receipts from the corporate income tax. The decline in tax collections during an economic contraction prevents aggregate demand from decreasing excessively.

Also included in the automatic stabilizers are programs that increase transfer payments to individuals when the economy contracts and decrease such payments when the economy expands. These increases and decreases don't require acts of Congress or changes in administration policies, because most transfers are part of *entitlement* programs that mandate government payments to individuals who meet certain eligibility standards. Because eligibility is based mainly on income and joblessness, government expenditures for transfer programs naturally increase during economic contractions, when unemployment increases and income declines.

Government purchases of goods and services tend to be quite stable over the business cycle. The variation in government expenditures over the business cycle results from changes in transfer payments under entitlement programs. The major entitlement programs that serve as automatic stabilizers are:

1. *Unemployment insurance.* Expenditures for this program increase during recessions, when there are more unemployed workers and longer periods of unemployment. During expansions, as unemployment rates decline, unemployment insurance payments also decline.

2. *Cash assistance welfare programs.* When a recession hits, more people become eligible for programs of cash assistance such as Aid to Families with Dependent Children and Supplemental Security Income. Although such programs are designed primarily for people outside the labor force, many of the eligible people manage to find at least part-time work when the economy is healthy. During contractions and recessions, more eligible people must rely on welfare programs for their full support, so cash assistance to the poor increases. During expansions, more eligible people manage to find at least some work and payments decline.

3. *In-kind assistance programs.* These programs include food stamps, medical care, and housing assistance for people with annual incomes below certain threshold levels. As a contraction or recession hits, many workers lose their jobs or suffer reductions in earnings, thus becoming eligible for in-kind assistance programs. Government payments under these programs increase during contractions, thus bolstering aggregate demand, and decline during expansions, putting a damper on aggregate demand.

4. *Social Security pension payments.* During a contraction or a recession, more elderly workers retire and fewer Social Security recipients continue to work. Therefore, government expenditures for pension payments increase. During an expansion, some people forgo part of their pensions to work, which reduces Social Security payments.

In periods when national income declines, all of the transfer programs tend to maintain aggregate demand by automatically increasing payments as the number of eligible people increases. This increases the consumption component of real GDP, which would otherwise decline as earnings fell. During expansions, the transfer programs increase net taxes by reducing transfers as the number of people entitled to benefits declines.

Gauging the Impact of Fiscal Policy

The automatic stabilizers influence the size of the federal budget deficit. Obviously, when aggregate demand declines and the economy is in a downturn, tax receipts fall. However, because of the transfer programs discussed in the preceding section, federal government expenditures tend to increase. Both the decrease in tax revenues and the increase in expenditures contribute to an increase in the budget deficit during recessions. During boom periods, tax revenues increase and transfer payments decline, contributing to a decrease in the budget deficit or to a budget surplus.

To eliminate the cyclical effects of automatic stabilizers on the budget deficit, economists compute the cyclically adjusted **high-employment deficit (or surplus),** the budget deficit (or surplus) that would prevail if the natural rate of unemployment were achieved.

high-employment deficit (or surplus) the budget deficit (or surplus) that would prevail if the natural rate of unemployment were achieved.

The high-employment budget indicates the relationship between government spending and taxes for a given level of government purchases that would prevail if the economy achieved full employment. Receipts and expenditures for the high-employment budget are typically based on an unemployment rate of 5 percent to

Box 4   Cyclical Effects on the Federal Budget and the High-Employment Deficit

Net taxes tend to increase as real GDP is higher during a given year. The federal budget tends to be thrown into deficit when real GDP is well below its potential during a year because the increase in transfer payments and reduction in taxes reduce government revenues. Government purchases, however, tend to be fixed during the year. Here, the high-employment deficit is $150 billion when real GDP is $5,000 billion.

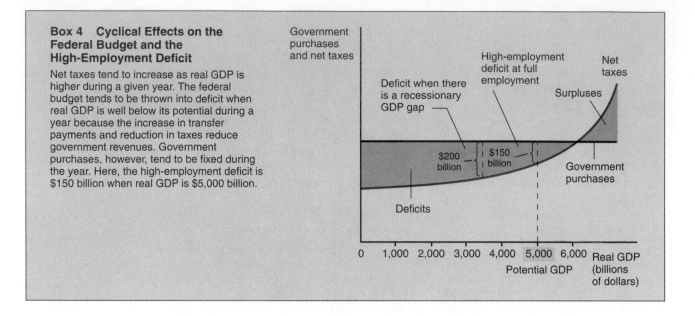

6 percent. The high-employment budget is designed to show how much stimulus to aggregate demand the federal government is providing to the economy by setting net taxes equal to the amount that would be observed at full employment.

The graph in Box 4 shows how the federal budget deficit can vary with real GDP for the year. The line showing net taxes is upward sloping. As real GDP increases, so do net taxes. The slope of the curve increases as real GDP goes up, because more people are pushed into tax brackets with higher marginal tax rates. Net taxes also rise with real GDP because government transfer payments are higher at lower levels of national income than they are at higher levels. Remember that net taxes are taxes paid less transfers received. Government purchases are drawn as a horizontal line because they are authorized at the beginning of the year and, unlike net taxes, are not subject to cyclical fluctuations.

When government expenditures exceed tax revenues for the year, a budget deficit prevails. When tax revenues exactly equal government expenditures, the budget is in balance. When revenues exceed expenditures, there is a surplus. The graph in Box 4 shows that the lower the level of real GDP realized for the year, the higher the budget deficit. Conversely, the higher the level of real GDP, the lower the deficit. At some level of real GDP the budget will be in balance, and increases in national income beyond that level will result in a surplus.

Suppose potential real GDP is $5,000 billion. At this high-employment level of real GDP, the deficit is $150 billion. However, if real GDP during the year is less than $5,000 billion, the deficit will be greater because net tax collections will be less. The graph in Box 4 shows that if equilibrium real GDP is only $3,500 billion, the deficit will be $200 billion.

The actual high-employment deficit depends on government purchases and tax rates for the year. For example, if government purchases were lower or tax rates were higher, the net taxes curve and the government purchases line might intersect at the point corresponding to potential real GDP. This implies that the budget would be in balance at the higher employment level. If policymakers want to expand the economy, they must choose a fiscal policy that increases the high-employment deficit. Such a policy would either shift the tax revenue line downward or shift the government purchases line upward. The actual budget deficit (or surplus) in a given year depends both on the high-employment deficit (or surplus) and on the cyclical impact of the automatic stabilizers.

The high-employment budget has been in deficit almost continuously since 1960, indicating that expansionary fiscal policy has been more prevalent than contractionary fiscal policy. The high-employment budget deficit averaged close to 2 percent of GDP from 1960 to 1980 and was approaching 5 percent of GDP in the mid-1980s.

Forecasting the federal budget deficit for any given year is more an art than a science! For example, in 1982, a recession year, the Reagan administration projected that outlays for fiscal year 1983 would be $757 billion, while revenues would be $666 billion, resulting in a budget deficit of $91 billion. However, the president's economists did a poor job of forecasting the intensity of the recession. Unemployment in 1983 turned out to be much higher than expected, and the growth rate of real GDP was −2.9 percent that year instead of the +3 percent projected by the administration! This was complicated by the fact that in enacting the president's proposed budget, Congress cut expenditures less than the president wished. Congress also enacted a larger tax cut than the president requested. As a result, the actual federal budget deficit in 1983 turned out to be a whopping $195 billion, which was over $100 billion more than the amount projected!

In 1992 the Congressional Budget Office estimated that based on a natural rate of unemployment of 5.5 percent, the high-employment deficit was $201.5 billion, while the actual budget deficit that year was nearly $300 billion!

- What are automatic stabilizers?
- Explain why a budget approved by Congress will run a higher deficit during the year if a recession prevails than it would otherwise.

- What is the purpose of calculating a high-employment budget deficit?

CONCEPT CHECK

☐

🌐 *the global economy*

Fiscal Policy and the Balance of International Trade

The economy is like a complex computer. A change in one bit of information cascades through it and is processed by thousands of decision makers who act as the system's "chips." A fiscal policy that generates a deficit can have a pronounced effect on the nation's balance of trade with foreign nations, depending on how interest rates, the international value of the dollar, and other prices respond to information on the deficit.

Let's examine some basic macroeconomic identities for the economy to show how the budget deficit is related to the balance of international trade.

The basic identity between aggregate expenditure and aggregate income can be expressed as

$$C + I + G + (E - M) = C + S + T$$

Aggregate expenditure = Aggregate income

Net exports, which are measured as $(E - M)$, roughly equal the U.S. balance of trade deficit when imports exceed exports. *Gross domestic purchases* $(C + I + G)$ represent all spending by U.S. households, businesses, and governments on final products, *including* imported products (which are included in the C, I, and G components of GDP).

Gross domestic purchases differs from aggregate purchases of domestic final products (GDP) because it does not include the export sales of U.S. firms, but it does include spending on imports. When domestic spending exceeds aggregate income, domestic spending must also exceed GDP, which is equal to aggregate income.

Because GDP is the amount of final products we

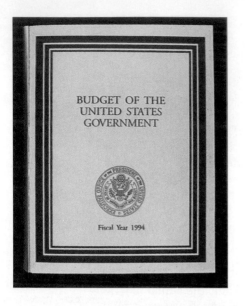

produce, it follows that we must import more than we export when we end up spending more than we produce. Therefore, when gross domestic purchases exceed aggregate income, the difference is the balance of trade deficit. This can easily be seen by rearranging terms in the previous identity. Simply move aggregate income $(C + S + T)$ to the left side of the equation by subtracting it from both sides and then subtract $(E - M)$ from both sides, which gives

$$(C + I + G) - (C + S + T) = (M - E)$$

$$\underset{\substack{\text{Gross} \\ \text{domestic} \\ \text{purchases}}}{} - \underset{\substack{\text{Aggregate} \\ \text{income}}}{} = \underset{\substack{\text{Balance} \\ \text{of trade} \\ \text{deficit}}}{}$$

We can also show that a balance of trade deficit implies that national saving is insufficient to fund gross private domestic investment and that the difference between investment and national saving is made up by a net inflow of foreign saving into the United States. Simply reduce the previous equation. Because consumption appears as a term in both gross domestic purchases and aggregate income, when we subtract income from spending, consumption disappears and we get the following:

$$I + G - S - T = (M - E)$$

Now simply rearrange terms by taking everything except investment over to the right side:

$$I = (T - G) + S + (M - E)$$

The term $(T - G)$ is the difference between net taxes and government purchases. This represents the budget deficit of the government sector when government purchases exceed net taxes. The term S is business and household saving. The sum of the government budget deficit and business and household saving is national saving. When we spend more than we earn, national saving is insufficient to finance gross private domestic investment and we must borrow from foreigners to make up the difference. The term $(M - E)$ is the balance of trade deficit, which, as we have shown in the chapter entitled "Gross Domestic Product and the Performance of the National Economy," must also equal the net inflow of foreign saving in the United States over U.S. saving abroad:

$$\text{Investment} = \underset{\substack{\text{Government} \\ \text{budget} \\ \text{deficit}}}{} + \underset{\substack{\text{Private} \\ \text{saving}}}{} + \underset{\substack{\text{Balance} \\ \text{of trade} \\ \text{deficit}}}{}$$

Because the sum of the government budget deficit and private saving is national saving and because the balance of trade deficit must equal the net inflow of foreign saving into the United States, we can rewrite the identity as follows:

$$\underset{\substack{\text{Domestic} \\ \text{investment}}}{} = \underset{\substack{\text{National} \\ \text{saving}}}{} + \underset{\substack{\text{Net inflow} \\ \text{of foreign} \\ \text{saving}}}{}$$

When fiscal policy increases the government budget deficit in a given year, it contributes to an increase in gross domestic purchases. However, the deficit contributes to a reduction in national saving. Unless there is a corresponding increase in domestic investment or private saving, the net inflow of foreign saving must increase.

The process of adjustment works through changes in interest rates and foreign exchange rates. In the 1980s a combination of high interest rates and a high international value of the dollar combined to increase foreign saving in the United States as the balance of trade deficit increased in response to the high dollar. In the early 1990s short-term interest rates fell in the United States, and so did the international value of the dollar, which contributed to a reduction in the balance of trade deficit and a corresponding decline in the net inflow of foreign saving. In this case the government budget deficit was financed by a combination of a decline in domestic investment and a modest increase in private saving in response to relatively high long-term interest rates.

SUPPLY-SIDE FISCAL POLICIES

Steady and predictable growth in aggregate demand gives business firms an economic environment that fosters investment purchases. Over the long run, however, economic growth depends on growth in aggregate supply. Policies that encourage saving, investment, and increased labor-force participation can increase the economic growth rate in a nation over the long run. Government policies can influence incentives to save, work, and invest by affecting the *net return* to these activities. For example, investment can be subsidized, as it has been in the United States, through credits that reduce the tax bills of businesses investing in new structures and equipment. Government can also affect the net return to these activities through changes in marginal tax rates. Workers, savers, and investors respond to the *after-tax* return they receive. When marginal tax rates on labor, interest, or investment income decline, the after-tax return of working, saving, or investing goes up, providing an incentive to undertake more of the activity.

Supply-side fiscal policies seek to influence long-run growth in real GDP through government subsidies and tax reductions. By increasing investment and work effort, these policies aim to shift the aggregate supply curve for the economy outward at a faster rate than would otherwise be the case. The effectiveness of the policies depends on the responsiveness of workers, savers, and investors to increases in the net returns to work, saving, and investment over the long run. The supply-siders maintain that cuts in marginal tax rates—the tax rates on extra income—will increase both work effort and investment in the long run. They contend that this will increase aggregate supply in the long run, thereby contributing to higher real GDP and lower price levels.

supply-side fiscal policies policies that seek to influence long-run growth in real GDP through government subsidies and tax reductions.

How Supply-Side Fiscal Policies Can Influence Labor Markets

Let's first consider programs designed to increase work effort. The rationale for these programs is that when people decide whether to enter the labor force and how many hours to work, they look at the *net after-tax wages* they can earn. The higher the marginal tax rate, the lower the after-tax wage for additional work.

The graph in Box 5 illustrates supply and demand in the labor market. Initially, the market equilibrium wage is $10 per hour, and L hours of labor per year are supplied at that wage. If the marginal tax rate on labor income is currently 20 percent, the net after-tax marginal return to additional work is only $8. This is equal to the gross wage less the marginal tax of 20 percent on extra hourly earnings, or $2.

The labor supply curve can shift when tax rates are changed. Suppose the marginal tax rate applied to labor income is reduced to 15 percent. At the current equilibrium wage, the marginal net after-tax return to additional labor hours will go up to $8.50 (the $10 gross wage paid by employers less the $1.50 tax per hour of work resulting from the 15 percent marginal tax rate). The higher net marginal return to work resulting from the tax cut can attract more workers into the labor force and encourage existing workers to work more hours per year. As a result, the labor supply curve will shift outward and there will be downward pressure on wage rates. In Box 5, as a result of the tax-induced shift in the labor supply, the market wage falls to $9.75 and the equilibrium number of hours worked increases to L'. The new equilibrium after-tax net wage is 85 percent of the gross wage, or $8.29.

The effectiveness of the tax cut depends on the increase in labor hours that it causes. If the policy results in more work per year, labor will become more abundant and labor costs will fall, thereby stimulating production in the economy and encouraging growth.

Box 5   How Supply-Side Fiscal Policies Seek to Influence Labor Markets

Supply-side policies seek to shift the labor supply curve outward. By lowering tax rates, the policies increase the net after-tax return to work. If labor supply increases as a result, the market equilibrium wage paid by employers will fall, encouraging them to use more labor hours per year and increase national output.

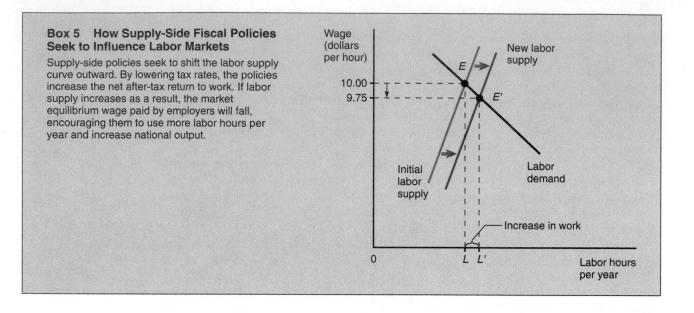

The responsiveness of labor supply to tax cuts can only be estimated. Workers can choose to pocket the increase in net wages and not work any extra hours at all. In fact, estimates suggest that for a large portion of the labor force, wage increases in the past have had little effect on hours worked. Because tax cuts operate mainly through increases in net wages, this suggests that the response to modest tax cuts will be little, if any, increase in work effort. Thus, there is quite a bit of pessimism about the long-run impact of supply-side tax cuts. However, some have disputed this view, arguing that in the past the federal income tax discouraged work effort. For example, an estimate by Jerry Hausman suggests that, on average, married males have worked 8 percent less because of income taxes than they would have otherwise. Hausman's results also suggest that for married women, a 10 percent increase in the net wage resulting from a cut in marginal tax rates would result, on average, in a 9 percent to 10 percent increase in hours worked per year.[2] These estimates are based on past experience.

The Impact of Supply-Side Incentives to Save
A reduction in the marginal tax rate for interest income has the same effect in principle as a reduction for labor income. Assuming that savers respond to the net after-tax marginal return to saving, a decrease in the marginal tax rate will increase the supply of saving. This will cause the curve for the supply of loanable funds for the economy to shift outward, as illustrated in Box 6.

Suppose the initial market rate of interest is 8 percent, the gross rate paid by debtors. If savers who supply loanable funds are subject to a 30 percent marginal tax rate, they will earn only 5.6 percent net interest after tax because their net return will be only 70 percent of the interest earned. The marginal tax rate on interest income is typically higher on average than that on labor income because those who earn interest income are generally in higher tax brackets. If the marginal tax rate on

---

[2] Jerry A. Hausman, "Labor Supply," in *How Taxes Affect Economic Behavior,* ed. Henry J. Aaron and Joseph J. Pechman (Washington, D.C.: Brookings Institution, 1981).

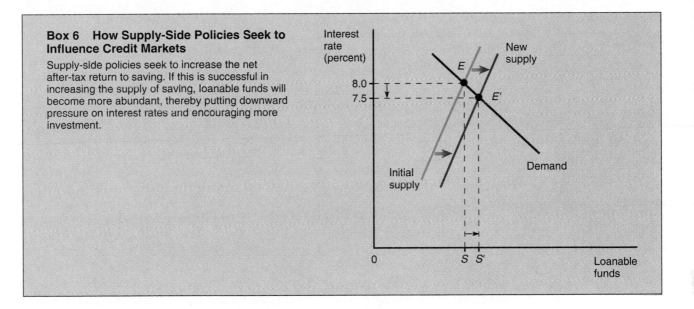

Box 6   How Supply-Side Policies Seek to Influence Credit Markets

Supply-side policies seek to increase the net after-tax return to saving. If this is successful in increasing the supply of saving, loanable funds will become more abundant, thereby putting downward pressure on interest rates and encouraging more investment.

interest income were reduced to 20 percent, the supply curve for loanable funds would shift outward, because the decrease in the marginal tax rate would raise the after-tax marginal net return to saving from 5.6 percent to 6.4 percent. The higher net return to saving provides an incentive to save more. As the supply of loanable funds curve shifts outward, the market rate of interest falls to 7.5 percent. After the new equilibrium is achieved, the quantity of annual savings supplied as loanable funds to financial markets increases from S to S' dollars per year and the net after-tax marginal return to saving is 80 percent of the gross interest rate of 7.5 percent, which is 6 percent. At the lower market equilibrium gross interest rate, investment will be encouraged, which will contribute to increased economic growth.

As is the case for reductions in the tax on labor increase, the effectiveness of the tax cut in reducing market interest rates and increasing saving depends on the responsiveness of savers to changes in the after-tax interest they can earn on additional saving. Once again, no one knows how responsive savers will actually be to tax cuts. A number of empirical studies show that saver response to changes in interest rates has been virtually nil in the United States.[3] Other studies find that saving is modestly responsive to changes in interest rates.

Under the Reagan administration, a number of supply-side policies sought to encourage personal saving. Two of these policies were:

1. *A reduction in the top marginal tax rate applied to income from saving.* The top marginal tax rate applied to nonlabor income was reduced from 70 percent in 1980 to only 28 percent for most taxpayers in 1988. (Some taxpayers, however, were subject to a marginal tax rate as high as 33 percent.)

2. *Special tax treatment of savings placed in individual retirement accounts.* Some taxpayers were able to significantly reduce their taxes by placing some of their savings in special retirement accounts that allowed them to defer taxes on the

---

[3] Irwin Friend and Joel Hasbrouck, "Savings and After-Tax Rates of Return," *Review of Economics and Statistics* 65 (November 1983), pp. 537–43.

amounts saved, provided they withdrew no income from the accounts until they retired. Critics of this tax break have argued that it merely results in a shuffling of saving from one account to another without increasing the actual amounts saved per year.

Tax Breaks That Subsidize Investment

A final type of supply-side policy involves tax breaks that directly subsidize business investment. These consist of investment tax credits for new equipment and structures and for research and development. **Accelerated depreciation allowances** are generous deductions from pretax business income that are allowed when firms acquire new equipment or new structures. These allowances permit firms to recover the cost of capital equipment on their tax accounts much more rapidly than the equipment actually wears out. The more rapid the depreciation allowed for tax purposes, the greater the immediate tax benefit from new investment. For example, suppose a firm subject to a 50 percent marginal tax rate buys a machine that costs $1 million and will last 10 years. If the firm is allowed to deduct $1/10$ of the cost of the machine each year ($100,000 per year) for 10 years, the tax benefit of buying the machine will be $50,000 per year. However, if the firm is allowed to deduct one fifth of the cost of the machine ($200,000 per year) for five years, it will enjoy a tax saving of $100,000 per year for five years. The quicker depreciation enables the firm to get the tax benefit from the machine sooner, providing more incentive to invest. Similarly, an investment tax credit of, say, 10 percent can be deducted from the firm's tax liability as a way of subsidizing investment.

> **accelerated depreciation allowances** generous deductions from pretax business income that are allowed when firms acquire new equipment or new structures.

The *marginal tax benefit* of investment is the annual reduction in taxes from each dollar of additional investment. The graph in Box 7 shows how investment demand can be affected by the marginal tax benefit of investment. Normally, a firm invests each year up to the point at which the marginal return to the investment falls to equal the real rate of interest. When investment is subsidized through tax credits or accelerated depreciation, the marginal tax benefit of the investment is added to its marginal return to obtain the full benefit to the firm. The full marginal return to the investment is now

Marginal return to the investment + Marginal tax benefit of the investment

where the marginal tax benefit is the reduction in tax due per year resulting from investing one extra dollar expressed as a percentage of that dollar. When the marginal tax benefit is added to the marginal return to investment, the investment demand curve shifts outward, as shown in Box 7. Given the market interest rate, i, this results in an increase in annual investment from I to I'.

As with all of the other supply-side policies we've discussed, the effectiveness of this policy in encouraging investment and therefore promoting economic growth depends on how responsive investment is to changes in the tax law. In a deep recession, when the business outlook is gloomy, it's unlikely that added tax benefits for investment will have much effect. There's some evidence, however, that over the long run, when the ups and downs of the business cycle average out, subsidies to investment can increase the quantity of new investment goods demanded.[4]

The Short-Run and Long-Run Impact of Supply-Side Policies

The idea behind supply-side tax cuts and subsidies is to shift the aggregate supply curve outward over time. However, it may be a considerable amount of time before

---

[4] See William R. Hosek and Frank Zahn, "Real Rates of Return and Aggregate Investment," *Southern Economic Journal* 51, no. 1 (July 1984), pp. 157–65.

An Assessment of Their Impact The supply-side approach hit Washington like a storm with the election of Ronald Reagan in 1980. It moved quickly from a slogan to actual policy as President Reagan pushed through the Economic Recovery Tax Act of 1981 (ERTA). This act featured a substantial tax reduction. However, unlike demand-side tax cuts, the ERTA tax reduction was designed to increase aggregate supply. There was a 25 percent across-the-board reduction in income tax rates. ERTA concentrated on reducing *marginal* tax rates, which determine the *extra* taxes that taxpayers must pay on additional dollars of income earned during the year. ERTA's master stroke was a reduction, from 70 percent to 50 percent, in the top marginal tax rate applied to nonlabor income. Finally, there were various incentives designed to increase saving and investment. These included the development of individual retirement accounts (IRAs) that allowed savers to deduct from their taxable income a limited amount of their saving for retirement. Accelerated depreciation rules for business investment reduced tax bills for firms investing in new machinery, vehicles, and structures.

In addition to ERTA, the Reagan supply-side policies, dubbed "Reaganomics," included reductions in spending for Social Security and welfare programs believed to have had adverse effects on work incentives and the reallocation of federal spending to finance a large increase in military expenditures.

Some supply-siders made extravagant claims for the impact of their policies on the economy. Among these claims were:

1. The ERTA tax cut would increase tax revenue because it would encourage increased work and investment that would increase equilibrium real GDP.
2. The budget deficit would not increase substantially as a result of the tax cut. Even if there were an increase in the deficit, its inflationary effects would be offset by an increase in saving resulting in part from the tax cut.
3. The supply-side effect of increasing real GDP would put downward pressure on the price level and reduce inflation at the same time real GDP increased.

Many economists regarded these claims as excessive.* However, the economy managed to recover from a serious recession in 1982. Inflation was reduced sharply, and unemployment, although remaining at fairly high levels after the recession, seemed to be less of a problem. The Reagan administration claimed credit for the recovery, and voters affirmed their confidence in the president and his economic policies with an overwhelming landslide reelection in 1984.

How much of the reduction in inflation and the increase in real GDP can be attributed to the supply-side policies? First, let's look at the results in the first half of the 1980s:

1. Actual growth between 1981 and 1985 was 10.9 percent, well below the 19.1 percent predicted by Reagan economists.
2. The economy did recover from the recession of 1982, but many economists attribute this recovery to the increase in the money supply and other policies implemented by the Federal Reserve.
3. There did not appear to be any significant increase in work effort as a result of the reduction in marginal tax rates.
4. There was little appreciable increase in saving.
5. Federal tax revenues did not increase as a result of the reduction in marginal tax rates. However, they did not decrease as much as many non-supply-siders expected, indicating that the disincentive effects of high marginal tax rates are not negligible. Reductions in tax revenues and increases in federal spending combined to increase the federal budget deficit to over $200 billion by 1986.

Critics of the supply-side policies of the early 1980s contend that these policies did little to shift the aggregate supply curve. These critics argue that the ERTA tax cut provided an increase in aggregate demand between 1982 and 1984 that pulled the economy out of the recession.† They point out that the supply-side policies coincided with other important changes that stimulated the economy, such as declining interest rates and declining oil prices. Prices of imported goods also fell during the early 1980s, which contributed to lower inflation.

The budget deficit did not fall, as many supply-siders had hoped it would. Instead, it increased to record levels. Many economists argued that the large budget deficit kept interest rates at high levels throughout the early 1980s. High interest rates were blamed by many for the reduced investment and increased imports of recent years.

In short, the report card on the supply-side policies of the early 1980s is mixed. There was no significant short-run increase in aggregate supply or economic growth as a result of the supply-side policies.

---

* See Martin Feldstein, "Supply-Side Economics: Old Truths and New Claims," *American Economic Review* 76, no. 2 (May 1986), pp. 26–30.
† See Lawrence Chimerine and Richard M. Young, "Economic Surprises and Messages of the 1980s," *American Economic Review* 76, no. 2 (May 1986), pp. 31–36.

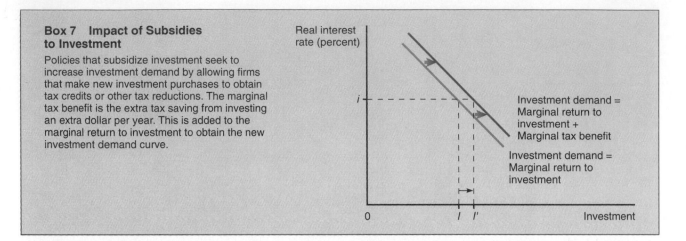

Box 7   Impact of Subsidies to Investment

Policies that subsidize investment seek to increase investment demand by allowing firms that make new investment purchases to obtain tax credits or other tax reductions. The marginal tax benefit is the extra tax saving from investing an extra dollar per year. This is added to the marginal return to investment to obtain the new investment demand curve.

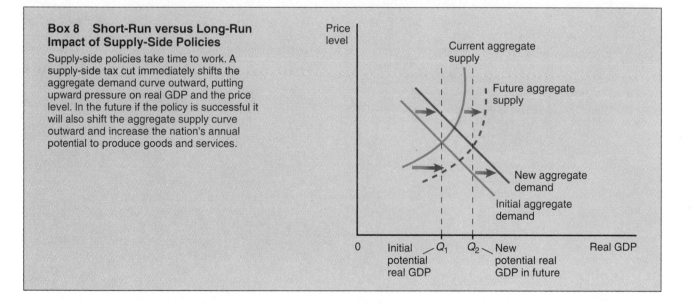

Box 8   Short-Run versus Long-Run Impact of Supply-Side Policies

Supply-side policies take time to work. A supply-side tax cut immediately shifts the aggregate demand curve outward, putting upward pressure on real GDP and the price level. In the future if the policy is successful it will also shift the aggregate supply curve outward and increase the nation's annual potential to produce goods and services.

the supply curve actually starts moving. Although increases in work effort can shift the aggregate supply curve outward immediately, it takes a number of years before any increased investment adds significantly to the existing capital stock. As a result, it takes awhile for supply-side policies to generate an increase in productive capacity for the economy. Meanwhile, unless the tax cuts are balanced with increases in other taxes or reductions in government spending, they will contribute to an increase in aggregate demand.

The graph in Box 8 shows the short-run impact of a supply-side tax cut that is not balanced by increases in other taxes or by a reduction in government spending, similar to the case for the tax cut enacted in 1981. Because the effect of the Economic Recovery Tax Act of 1981 (ERTA) was to increase the federal deficit substantially, it shifted the aggregate demand curve outward. At the time this turned out to be a fine demand-side fiscal policy because the economy was in the depths of a severe recession! As a result, the tax cut contributed to an economic recovery toward the end of 1983. However, the shift in aggregate supply, even after a five-year

principles in practice

Clintonomics

A New Administration Brings a Change in Fiscal Policy
When American voters put Bill Clinton in the White House, the vote was interpreted by the new Democratic president as a mandate for change. Among the most fundamental changes instituted by the new administration in 1993 was a new direction for fiscal policy.

A fundamental thrust of the new fiscal policy was a new set of budgetary proposals designed to cut the projected federal budget deficit nearly in half by fiscal year 1997. Clinton proposed to do this mainly by a combination of policies designed to control or redirect government spending and raise new revenue. The Clinton plan included a major new tax on energy consumption that would hit most Americans and increased marginal tax rates on those Americans and corporations with the highest incomes.

The Clinton plan also included proposals to "fine-tune" the economy, an approach that had been shunned by Clinton's Republican predecessors. Clinton was disturbed about the slow rate of job growth since the end of the 1990–91 recession and proposed a $30 billion short-term stimulus package for the economy that comprised increased government spending on bridges and roads and a new investment tax credit designed to increase business investment purchases. The short-term stimulus package was, however, rejected by Congress in 1993. Clinton also proposed $160 billion in new spending for transportation, technology development, housing, and community development over the four years of his administration. These outlays, along with a decline in defense spending, would mean a fundamental redirection of federal purchases toward investment in physical and human capital.

Clinton's new fiscal policy was intended to increase investment and future economic growth through deficit reduction, more government spending on investments, and stimulation of private investment spending. If all went as Clinton hoped it would, reduction in the federal deficit would free funds for private investment and put downward pressure on long-term interest rates, thereby adding further incentive for private sector investment.

There were both demand-side and supply-side aspects to Clinton's plan. The demand-side aspects were the new spending incentives and a slight increase in the deficit from its previously projected levels for fiscal year 1993. The supply-side aspects included the longer-term deficit reduction program.

The new plan pleased those who liked increased spending on social programs such as Head Start. However, many economists were critical of the heavy tax increases on corporations and upper-income Americans and worried about the impact of these tax increases on work and saving incentives. Jumps in marginal tax rates that amounted to as much as 37 percent on persons with relatively high incomes had the potential to derail the Clinton plan for both cutting the deficit and increasing the long-term rate of economic growth. Possible unfavorable supply-side effects on work and saving incentives resulting from the tax increases could make the deficit bigger by slowing income growth below the rates projected.

The new fiscal policy emphasizes higher taxes to reduce the deficit and attempts to redirect federal spending away from defense and toward investment in physical and human capital. It remains to be seen whether that policy will work. Ideally, the new fiscal policy will spur the recovery from the last recession, keep inflation in check, and get the economy on a path to higher future growth. Only time will tell whether the new prescriptions of "Clintonomics" are the right ones for the U.S. economy.

---

period, appeared to be slight. ERTA didn't significantly contribute to an increase in saving and investment, and there was no marked increase in work effort. The inflationary tendency was muted in the early 1980s because of the severe recession that prevailed in 1981 and 1982.

The graph in Box 8 shows the impact of a supply-side tax cut that increases the budget deficit. The increase in the deficit shifts the aggregate demand curve outward, contributing to a higher price level and a higher level of real GDP. Although the aggregate supply curve and potential real GDP can also shift outward, the magnitude of this shift is likely to be small over a five-year period. As a result, the overall impact of the tax cut and the resulting increase in the deficit is upward pressure on the price level and increases in real GDP. If the economy is close to full employment,

insights on issues

Will the U.S. Economy Grow without High Inflation and Unemployment?
Talking with Lawrence Lindsey and Allan H. Meltzer

Lawrence Lindsey is a governor of the Federal Reserve System. He was born in Peekskill, New York, in 1954. He earned his undergraduate degree from Bowdoin College and his master's and Ph.D. from Harvard. He has served as a special assistant to the president for policy development. Born in Boston in 1928, Allan Meltzer received his undergraduate degree from Duke and his master's and Ph.D. from UCLA. He is a professor of economics at Carnegie-Mellon University and a visiting scholar at the American Enterprise Institute. He also has been an acting member of the Council of Economic Advisers. His most recent book is titled *Political Economy*.

What is the outlook for economic growth, unemployment, and inflation in the U.S. economy over the next 10 years?
Governor Lindsey: The outlook really depends on the kind of policies we pursue. In the last decade, public policy has focused on making our economy run more efficiently, with lower inflation, lower rates of taxation, and a careful look at the costs and benefits of regulation. As a result, inflation remained low and the natural rate of unemployment was reduced from about 6.5 to 5.5 percent. While no policy can repeal the business cycle, continuing these policy themes could help us achieve a decade of low inflation (under 3 percent), sustainable but moderate economic growth (3 percent), and an unemployment rate that averages 6 percent or less.

Professor Meltzer: On many occasions, the U.S. economy has shown that it can grow without inflation. Over long periods of time, the economy grows about 2.5 percent per year. That is the best quick estimate an economist can make. I do not believe we will return to the relatively high inflation of the 1970s, but we will not maintain price stability (defined as inflation between 0 and 2 percent to allow for bias in most price indexes).

Is fiscal policy an effective way to fine-tune the economy to achieve economic growth with low inflation and low unemployment?
Governor Lindsey: Fiscal policy is not currently well-adapted to fine-tuning the economy. Because there are long lags between when economic events occur and when the fiscal system responds, fiscal policies often take effect at the wrong time in the business cycle. The focus of fiscal policy should be long-

---

the resulting increase in aggregate demand can result in an inflationary GDP gap that overheats the economy and contributes to an inflationary spiral.

Over the long run, say 10 years, further outward shifts in aggregate supply can exert downward pressure on the price level along with upward pressure on real GDP. However, it's unlikely that supply-side policies will result in a significant increase in potential real GDP in the short run. The notion that supply-side tax cuts can increase federal tax revenue is now discredited. The downward pressure of tax cuts on tax revenues doesn't appear likely to be offset by the upward pressure that increases in national income exert on tax collections.

CONCEPT CHECK
☐

- The marginal tax rate on labor income is reduced from 20 percent to 10 percent. What effect will this have on the incentive to work?

- How can policies that reduce the marginal tax rate on interest income serve to reduce the level of interest rates in the economy?

- How can supply-side policies encourage investment?

term. Taxes should be gathered as efficiently as possible to minimize their adverse effects on economic growth. Spending programs should strive to benefit the economy to at least as great an extent as the cost of extracting revenue to pay for those programs.

Professor Meltzer: Experience in many countries has shown that policymakers and their economic advisers cannot fine-tune an economy successfully. The best forecasters, government or private, cannot distinguish between a boom and a recession one year, or even one quarter, ahead.

What should be the goals of monetary policy?

Governor Lindsey: The primary goal should be to assure a rate of nominal GDP growth consistent with long-term real economic growth and low inflation.

Professor Meltzer: The main goal should be domestic price stability. If other major countries adopt this goal, the United States will enjoy increased stability of nominal exchange rates as a byproduct. This will be of lasting benefit to us and to other countries that choose to tie their currencies to ours. They will be able to import price stability and keep a fixed exchange rate, creating what economists call a public good for third countries.

Is there a tradeoff between inflation and unemployment?

Governor Lindsey: There may be a short-run tradeoff, but in the longer run there is no tradeoff. That is, temporarily lower unemployment can be purchased only at the price of permanently higher inflation. Furthermore, high rates of inflation may reduce long-term economic growth by raising the effective tax rates on saving and investing and by discouraging long-term planning. Although these may not affect the rate of unemployment, they do mean that high inflation might actually lower real wages and living standards in the long term.

Professor Meltzer: The evidence shows that there is a short-term tradeoff between inflation and unemployment, but it is not stable in magnitude or timing. There is no long-term tradeoff.

What can we do to increase economic growth for the future?

Governor Lindsey: Government policies should adhere to the equivalent of the Hippocratic oath: Above all, do no harm. Government should make sure each dollar it spends produces at least as much economic benefit as it would have if left in the private sector. It should raise revenue in the least distorting way possible. And monetary authorities should allow enough liquidity for sustained nominal GDP growth consistent with low inflation.

Professor Meltzer: Build human and physical capital. Remove the bias in the system toward consumption so that saving will increase. We should reduce features of the tax and regulatory system that discourage investment in human and physical capital. We need to limit the share of output or GDP spent by government and reduce regulation.

SUMMARY

1. Fiscal policy is the use of government spending and taxing for the specific purpose of stabilizing the economy and encouraging economic growth.

2. The federal government budget represents a plan for spending funds and for raising revenues through taxation, fees, borrowing, and other means.

3. A budget deficit is the annual excess of government spending over government revenues raised by taxes and other means. When a deficit prevails, the federal government must borrow funds through issuance of Treasury bills, notes, and bonds to meet expenses not covered by tax revenues. A budget surplus prevails when government revenues exceed government expenditures during the year.

4. The overall influence of the federal budget on aggregate demand depends on the expansionary effect of government purchases and other payments and the contractionary effect of taxes. When there is a budget deficit, the federal government adds more to aggregate demand than it takes away.

5. An expansionary fiscal policy is one for which the government increases aggregate demand by adjusting its budget during the year. To increase aggregate demand, the government increases spending or decreases taxes. A contractionary fiscal policy restrains aggregate demand through a decrease in government spending or an increase in taxes.

6. When an economy is in deep recession, increased aggregate demand will not put upward pressure on the price level. Under these circumstances, an expansionary fiscal policy can be used to eliminate a recessionary GDP gap with little risk of inflation.

7. A sluggish economy can be stimulated by decreases in net taxes or increases in government spending. A dol-

lar of government spending is more stimulating to the economy than a dollar cut in net taxes because a portion of the tax cut will be saved or spent on imports. Thus, the economy can be stimulated without increasing the budget deficit when government spending increases are fully covered by increases in net taxes.

8. When the economy is experiencing only a mild recession, an increase in aggregate demand through an expansionary fiscal policy is likely to increase the price level. The increase in the price level chokes off some of the multiplier effect. Multipliers for fiscal policy are therefore lower when increases in aggregate demand cause the price level to increase.

9. A contractionary fiscal policy decreases aggregate demand and results in a multiplied decline in real GDP. Contractionary fiscal policies often meet the political opposition of legislators who seek to avoid cuts in government spending or increases in net taxes that would adversely affect their constituents. For this reason expansionary fiscal policies are more likely to be pursued than contractionary fiscal policies.

10. The cyclical ups and downs of the economy affect government tax collections and government expenditures for transfers. Declines in real GDP reduce federal net tax collections as tax revenues go down and transfer payments go up. The opposite holds for the impact of increases in real GDP on the federal budget.

11. Automatic stabilizers are government revenue and expenditure programs that automatically adjust aggregate demand to changes in the level of real GDP.

12. Because of the impact of automatic stabilizers, the federal budget deficit tends to increase during recessions and economic downturns. The cyclically adjusted high-employment deficit gives the budget deficit (or surplus) at some selected level of high employment. The high-employment budget can be used to measure the impact of the federal budget on aggregate demand after adjusting for cyclical influences on the budget deficit.

13. The principles of fiscal policy are to run a high-employment deficit to stimulate a sluggish economy and to reduce the high-employment deficit or run a high-employment surplus to contract an overheated economy.

14. Fiscal policies that encourage saving, investment, and increased labor-force participation can increase a nation's rate of economic growth over the long run. Supply-side fiscal policies seek to influence long-run economic growth in real GDP through government subsidies and tax reductions. The effectiveness of supply-side policies depends on the responsiveness of workers, savers, and investors to increases in the net returns to work, saving, and investment.

15. Supply-side policies that lower taxes to encourage increased work in the long run can increase aggregate demand in the short run and thus put upward pressure on real GDP and the price level.

KEY TERMS

fiscal policy *389*
government budget *389*
expansionary fiscal policy *390*
contractionary fiscal policy *391*
automatic stabilizers *398*
high-employment deficit (or surplus) *399*
supply-side fiscal policies *403*
accelerated depreciation allowances *406*

CONCEPT REVIEW

1 How can the federal government engage in an expansionary fiscal policy?

2 What should the federal government do to its budget if it wants to prevent the economy from overheating?

3 Give some examples of automatic stabilizers in the federal budget.

4 Give some examples of supply-side fiscal policies.

PROBLEMS AND APPLICATIONS

1. Real GDP has declined during the past quarter, and the forecast is for a continued decline in real GDP because of a gloomy business outlook. Business investment is expected to plummet next year. As chairman of the President's Council of Economic Advisers, what fiscal policy would you recommend for the coming year? **1**

2. Estimates indicate that of each $1 increase in national income, 60 cents is spent on domestic products, 20 cents is used to pay taxes, 10 cents is spent on imported goods, and 10 cents is saved. The economy is currently in a deep recession, with a $1,000 billion recessionary GDP gap and 15 percent unemployment. How much of an increase in government purchases for

the year will be sufficient to pull the economy out of the recession and achieve full employment? **1**

3. If the marginal respending rate is 0.6, calculate the impact on real GDP of a $1 billion reduction in net taxes. How much of a tax cut will get the economy out of the recession with the $1,000 billion recessionary GDP gap discussed in Problem 2? **1**

4. The economy is currently experiencing an $800 billion recessionary GDP gap. A proposal is made to increase transfer payments in order to stimulate aggregate demand. If the marginal respending rate is 0.5, how much must transfers be increased to eliminate the recessionary GDP gap? Use a graph to show the impact on the economy, assuming that the economy operates in the flat portion of its aggregate supply curve up to full employment. **1**

5. Suppose the aggregate supply curve for an economy experiencing a $500 billion recessionary GDP gap is upward sloping. Use graphic analysis to show that if the marginal respending rate is 0.5, elimination of the GDP gap requires that government purchases increase by more than $250 billion per year. **1**

6. Suppose the price level is downwardly inflexible during the year. If the marginal respending rate is 0.5, calculate the tax increase or the decrease in govern-

ment purchases necessary to eliminate a $1,500 billion inflationary GDP gap. **2**

7. The president's advisers propose a budget designed to result in a deficit of $60 billion for the year. In their estimate the advisers assume that the unemployment rate for the year will average 7 percent. Explain why the estimate will fall short of the actual deficit if the unemployment rate each month during the year averages 9 percent instead of 7 percent. **3**

8. A law is passed requiring that the federal budget be in balance every year. Why would this law prevent the automatic stabilizers from operating and thus be likely to destabilize the economy? **3**

9. Suppose a law abolishes taxes on interest income accruing to saving in all forms. Use graphic analysis to show the possible effects of this law on the supply of loanable funds in credit markets and on the equilibrium market rate of interest. Show the impact of the law on investment. **4**

10. The Tax Reform Act of 1986 eliminated the investment tax credit and reduced the tax benefit of accelerated depreciation allowances. Forecast the impact of these changes on investment demand and market interest rates. **4**

18 chapter

The Federal Budget Deficit and the National Debt

You've read about it in the newspaper and heard about it on TV. Cartoonists depict it as a ghoulish monster. What is it? It's the budget deficit of the federal government. Why all the concern about the fact that the federal government hasn't been able to balance its budget in recent years? What effects do the deficit and the growth in the national debt have on you and your future well-being?

In this chapter we will examine how the federal deficit and the national debt affect the economy. As you'll see, by borrowing to finance its deficits, the federal government can affect interest rates, future tax rates, the price level, and private investment. The deficit can also contribute to adverse indirect effects on the U.S. balance of trade with other nations. However, the effects of the deficit on the economy are quite complex and often misunderstood. Our goal in this chapter is to clarify the issues regarding the impact of the deficit and the national debt on our national economic performance and our national well-being. We will also discuss the consequences of reducing the deficit and of running a federal budget surplus in future years.

☐ CONCEPT PREVIEW

After reading this chapter, you should be able to:

1. Discuss the federal budget deficit, how it is financed, and how its possible impact on interest rates can influence private investment, economic growth, international trade, and macroeconomic equilibrium.

2. Discuss the impact of the national debt on the well-being of current and future generations.

3. Discuss some of the problems involved in measuring the federal budget deficit.

4. Discuss the concept of Ricardian equivalence of tax and deficit finance.

THE FEDERAL BUDGET BALANCE BETWEEN REVENUES AND EXPENDITURES

As we pointed out in the preceding chapter, a *federal budget deficit* prevails whenever federal government outlays in a given year exceed receipts (or revenues). In fiscal year 1992 the federal budget deficit amounted to $290 billion. In that year the federal government borrowed one of every five dollars it spent.

The federal budget has been in deficit every year since 1970. A consequence of this chronic condition is a growing national debt. For eight years the Reagan administration, which was ideologically opposed to the concept of a budget deficit, ran the largest deficits in history! The federal budget deficit grew from $73.8 billion in 1980 to $221.2 billion in 1986. In 1992 the debt of the federal government amounted to more than $4 trillion. Interest payments on the national debt represents 15 percent of annual federal government expenditures.

Concern about the inability of the federal government to balance its budget led to passage of the Balanced Budget and Emergency Deficit Control Act of 1985. Revised in 1987 and commonly called the Gramm-Rudman-Hollings Act, this legislation placed limits on the federal budget deficit and stipulated annual reductions in the deficit with the goal of eliminating it in 1993. In 1990, when it became clear that the Gramm-Rudman-Hollings target of a balanced budget in 1993 would not be met, Congress enacted new legislation designed to prevent the deficit from growing still larger. The Budget Enforcement Act of 1990 added new enforcement mechanisms to the budget process in an effort to put some caps on federal spending. Despite these laws, the deficit continued to grow.

The table and graph in Box 1 show federal receipts, outlays, and the deficit or surplus for each fiscal year from 1950 to 1992. For the period shown, the budget has achieved a surplus in only five years. A federal budget surplus is achieved when federal outlays are less than receipts for the fiscal year.

As you saw from our analysis of fiscal policy in the preceding chapter, federal budget deficits add to aggregate demand and are expansionary influences on the economy. They are desirable during economic downturns to stabilize the economy. They are undesirable during inflationary periods because the boost they give to aggregate demand puts upward pressure on the price level.

Up until the 1930s it was viewed as prudent fiscal practice to balance the federal budget each year. However, an annually balanced federal budget rules out any chance for the automatic stabilizers to do their jobs. Balancing the budget can cause the economy to suffer destabilization by decreasing aggregate demand when consumption, investment, and net exports are declining. For example, if the economy experiences a recession, the federal government's net tax receipts will naturally fall. Transfers paid out will increase because payments for welfare, Social Security, and unemployment insurance benefits typically go up during a recession. The decline in income will reduce income tax collections. If the budget is to be consistently in balance, government purchases will also have to decline during a recession to accommodate the decline in tax revenues and the increase in transfer payments.

Similarly, an annually balanced budget prevents the federal government from constraining aggregate demand by running a surplus during periods when the economy is overheated. During a boom period, tax collections naturally rise and transfer payments decline. As a result, net taxes increase during a boom period. If the government were to spend all of the increase, it would add to the already booming aggregate demand thus aggravate the upward pressure on the price level.

An annually balanced budget therefore contributes to decreases in aggregate demand during downturns and to increases in aggregate demand during upturns.

Box 1   Federal Receipts, Outlays, and Budget Deficit or Surplus, 1950–1992 (Billions of Dollars)

Fiscal year or period	Total			Fiscal year or period	Total		
	Receipts	Outlays	Surplus or deficit (−)		Receipts	Outlays	Surplus or deficit (−)
1950	39.4	42.6	−3.1	1970	192.8	195.6	−2.8
1951	51.6	45.5	6.1	1971	187.1	210.2	−23.0
1952	66.2	67.7	−1.5	1972	207.3	230.7	−23.4
1953	69.6	76.1	−6.5	1973	230.8	245.7	−14.9
1954	69.7	70.9	−1.2	1974	263.2	269.4	−6.1
1955	65.5	68.4	−3.0	1975	279.1	332.3	−53.2
1956	74.6	70.6	3.9	1976	298.1	371.8	−73.7
1957	80.0	76.6	3.4	1977	355.6	409.2	−53.6
1958	79.6	82.4	−2.8	1978	399.6	458.7	−59.2
1959	79.2	92.1	−12.8	1979	463.3	503.5	−40.2
1960	92.5	92.2	0.3	1980	517.1	590.9	−73.8
1961	94.4	97.7	−3.3	1981	599.3	678.2	−78.9
1962	99.7	106.8	−7.1	1982	617.8	745.7	−127.9
1963	106.6	111.3	−4.8	1983	600.6	808.3	−207.8
1964	112.6	118.5	−5.9	1984	666.5	851.8	−185.3
1965	116.8	118.2	−1.4	1985	734.1	946.3	−212.3
1966	130.8	134.5	−3.7	1986	769.1	990.3	−221.2
1967	148.8	157.5	−8.6	1987	854.1	1,004.6	−149.7
1968	153.0	178.1	−25.2	1988	909.0	1,064.0	−155.1
1969	186.9	183.6	3.2	1989	990.7	1,143.2	−152.5
				1990	1,031.3	1,252.7	−221.4
				1991	1,054.3	1,323.8	−269.5
				1992	1,091.6	1,381.8	−290.2

SOURCE: *Economic Report of the President*, 1993.

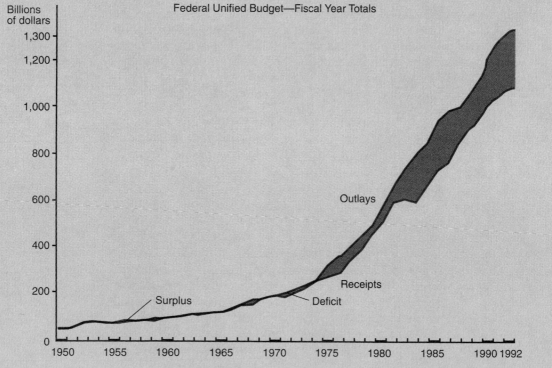

Federal Unified Budget—Fiscal Year Totals

Preventing the budget from ever being in deficit will clearly prolong recessions and may also contribute to their severity.

The recent concern about the imbalance in the federal budget is related to deficits rather than surpluses. Over the past 25 years, on average, the federal budget has been an expansionary influence on the economy. The concern is that political pressures lead to the use of borrowing as a means of financing popular government programs. The borrowing of funds to finance current programs means that the taxes to pay for these programs are postponed to the future.

Financing Deficits: Money Creation versus Borrowing from the Public

You know what happens when you want to spend more than you earn—you have to borrow the difference. The federal government must also borrow when it runs a deficit. The deficit must be *financed,* which means that somehow the government must obtain the funds to meet its expenditures when its receipts fall short of those expenditures. However, the federal government has a little trick up its sleeve that serves as an alternative to borrowing. It can engage in policies that create new money to pay its bills! At the extreme the federal government has the power to simply *print* new currency to pay its bills.

Financing a deficit by money creation is more expansionary than borrowing from the public. The resulting increase in the money supply is likely to increase the price level over the long run.

The federal government is unlikely to actually print new currency if it chooses to finance a deficit by money creation because, like most households and business firms, it pays for most of its expenses by check. *Monetization of the federal deficit* occurs whenever the Federal Reserve expands the monetary base to finance the deficit. The Fed is prohibited by law from buying new issues of government securities directly from the U.S. Treasury. However, it can still monetize the debt (as central banks in other nations have done) by increasing its purchases of already existing government securities through open market operations. When the Fed does this, it increases the monetary base in the same way it does when it engages in any other open market purchase (see the chapters on the Federal Reserve System and monetary policy). Full monetization of the deficit occurs when the Fed increases its purchases of government securities in an amount equal to the deficit, thereby expanding the money supply while the federal government is running a deficit. Because this policy increases bank excess reserves, it's also likely to result in a multiple expansion of checkable deposits.

Monetizing the federal deficit carries a double punch for aggregate demand. First, the deficit contributes to an increase in aggregate demand because it allows an increase in government purchases without a corresponding increase in taxes. Second, monetizating the deficit contributes to an increase in the money supply, which results in downward pressure on the level of interest rates and upward pressure on the equilibrium money stock. The decrease in interest rates and consequent increase in private investment purchase then add further to aggregate demand. Monetizing the deficit is therefore likely to result in upward pressure on the price level unless the economy is in a deep recession.

Because of the inflationary effects of financing a deficit by money creation, the Fed is careful not to monetize the deficit. The federal government borrows by issuing Treasury bills, notes, and bonds. When it borrows from the public, it must compete for available loanable funds with households, business firms, and state or local governments. An increase in borrowing by the federal government to cover a deficit adds to the demand for loanable funds and puts upward pressure on interest rates.

Under these circumstances, the Federal Reserve does not intervene to increase its purchase of government securities and therefore does not increase the money supply to finance the deficit.

The effect of borrowing from the public is less expansionary than the effect of directly monetizing the deficit. When the public purchases government securities, a portion of loanable funds available from saving is allocated to make loans to the federal government. When the federal government borrows in this way, there is no increase in bank reserves and no consequent expansion of the money supply. However, the impact on aggregate demand is more expansionary than it would be if taxes instead of borrowing were used to finance the deficit. Borrowing does not reduce disposable income, while taxation does. In effect, borrowing to cover a federal budget deficit postpones the payment of taxes to the future. It also causes the federal government to pay interest on its debt to the people who acquire government securities.

The graph in Box 2 shows the impact on macroeconomic equilibrium of three possible means of financing government expenditures. Suppose federal government expenditures are $1,000 billion per year. If these expenditures are fully financed by tax revenues, the economy is in equilibrium at point E_1, where the price level is 100 and real GDP is $5,000 billion. If, instead, the government runs a $200 billion deficit and borrows that sum from the public, the aggregate demand curve shifts farther outward and the economy achieves equilibrium at a price level of 105 and real GDP of $5,500 billion. If the Fed monetizes the $200 billion deficit, the aggregate demand curve shifts outward still farther and the economy is in equilibrium at a price level of 110 and real GDP of $6,000 billion for the year. The conclusion is straightforward: Deficit financing is more expansionary than tax financing, but a monetized deficit is the most expansionary of all!

The Crowding-Out Effect

To understand the impact on interest rates of borrowing to cover the deficit, we must examine the impact of deficits on credit markets. The graph in Box 3 shows the credit market for the economy. The demand curve for loanable funds by private borrowers intersects the supply curve for loanable funds at an interest rate of 8 percent. At that interest rate, the amount of loanable funds borrowed during the year to finance consumer durables and business investment would be $900 billion. In other words, if there were no borrowing by the federal government during the year, the market rate of interest would be 8 percent and the equilibrium volume of credit would be $900 billion.

Now suppose the federal government borrows $200 billion from the public to cover its deficit. This represents a substantial increase in the demand for loanable funds. As a result, the demand curve shifts outward and puts upward pressure on the level of interest rates in the economy. The new market equilibrium occurs at an interest rate level of 9 percent for the economy, and the equilibrium volume of credit extended at that interest rate is $1,000 billion. The government's borrowing to finance the deficit has therefore resulted in an increase in the market rate of interest and a consequent increase in the quantity of loanable funds supplied. This analysis assumes that as the government borrows, nothing else changes that might shift the demand or supply curves for loanable funds.

You should notice that the net increase in credit extended through the market is only $100 billion. However, the government borrows $200 billion. Where does the extra $100 billion in funds come from? To find out, go to the curve of the private demand for credit. At the new equilibrium interest rate of 9 percent, the quantity of

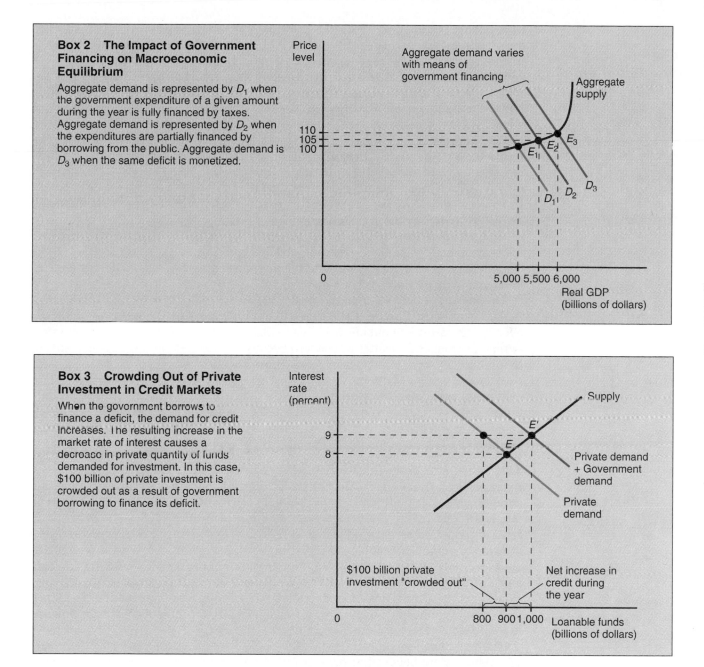

Box 2   The Impact of Government Financing on Macroeconomic Equilibrium

Aggregate demand is represented by D_1 when the government expenditure of a given amount during the year is fully financed by taxes. Aggregate demand is represented by D_2 when the expenditures are partially financed by borrowing from the public. Aggregate demand is D_3 when the same deficit is monetized.

Box 3   Crowding Out of Private Investment in Credit Markets

When the government borrows to finance a deficit, the demand for credit increases. The resulting increase in the market rate of interest causes a decrease in private quantity of funds demanded for investment. In this case, $100 billion of private investment is crowded out as a result of government borrowing to finance its deficit.

loanable funds demanded for private investment falls from $900 billion to $800 billion for the year. In other words, the higher interest rate causes private investors to revise their plans and cut back their investment for the year by $100 billion. The **crowding-out effect** is the reduction in private investment purchases caused by the higher interest rates that result from government borrowing. In this case the crowding-out effect is a reduction in private spending of $100 billion for the year.

The extent of the crowding-out effect depends on the responsiveness of interest rates to the increased government demand for loanable funds and on the reaction of private investors to the higher interest rates. If investment demand is unresponsive

crowding-out effect
the reduction in private investment purchases caused by the higher interest rates that result from government borrowing.

to a change in interest rates, the crowding-out effect will be quite small. The crowding-out effect also depends on how responsive the quantity of loanable funds is to increases in the demand for credit. If the economy is in a deep recession, a substantial amount of excess reserves is likely to be available to the banking system. Under these circumstances, extra borrowing by the government may put little upward pressure on interest rates because the supply of loanable funds curve will be quite flat.

We can conclude that the crowding-out effect is less pronounced during a deep recession than it is when the economy is operating close to its potential. In fact, increased government spending during a deep recession may improve the business outlook thereby encouraging more investment!

The crowding-out effect dampens the expansionary impact of the federal budget deficit by reducing the private component of aggregate demand. The cutback in private spending then acts to reduce the multiplier effect of an increase in government spending. This implies that the upward pressure on the price level resulting from deficits in an economy close to full employment will be moderated as government spending displaces private investment.

The impact of deficits on interest rates has been a subject of empirical investigation by economists. Some studies have found little impact, which suggests that, on average, the crowding-out effect is small.[1] However, even if the crowding-out effect is small, it remains a matter of concern because a reduction in business investment that continues over a number of years can have serious long-term consequences. Less business investment means that workers will not have as much or as modern equipment with which to work, a situation that will adversely affect their productivity. Thus, if the crowding-out effect causes a decline in investment, the result could be a decrease in the rate of improvement of living standards as worker productivity growth slows down the increase in real GDP per person.

The Deficit and Long-Term Interest Rates in the Early 1990s

In the early 1990s the chronic federal deficit appeared to be having adverse effects on inflationary expectations, which in turn kept long-term interest rates high. Despite legislation enacted in the 1980s and in 1990 to deal with the deficit, it continued to grow at a rate greater than projected. In 1992, partly as a result of the recession and growing government health care expenditures, it ballooned to 5 percent of GDP. In 1991 and 1992, investors continued to be fearful that the deficit would remain large and difficult to reduce and that it would contribute to an increase in inflation. Consequently, a high "inflation premium" caused long-term interest rates to remain very high even though monetary policy had pushed short-term interest rates down to low levels that had not been seen in nearly 50 years.

The high long-term interest rates necessary to compensate lenders for their fears of inflation were believed to have crowded out private investment. The long-term debt that the government had issued to finance its deficit competed directly with corporate borrowing. Corporate investment stagnated as long-term interest rates increased. In addition, banks found the high long-term rates on government securities a very attractive alternative to business loans. A shift of bank portfolios away from business loans and toward government securities contributed to a "credit crunch" that made it difficult to fund new business. Moreover, the capacity of banks

---

[1] See Laurence H. Meyer, ed., *The Economic Consequences of Government Deficits* (Boston: Kluwer-Nijoff Publishing, 1983).

to lend was reduced as depositors reduced their holdings of time deposits and shifted their assets into more lucrative long-term government bonds.

The sensitivity of long-term interest rates to the inflationary effect of increasing the federal deficit is another factor that should be considered before increasing the size of the deficit in an attempt to stimulate a sluggish economy.

 the global economy

Deficits and the Price of the Dollar

Another detrimental effect of the federal budget deficit on the economy may result from the impact high interest rates have on the foreign exchange rate of the dollar. High real interest rates in the United States relative to those abroad increase the demand for U.S. dollars by foreigners who acquire them to purchase U.S. government securities and other U.S. financial assets. The increased demand for the dollar indirectly caused by the budget deficit can put upward pressure on the price of the dollar in terms of foreign currencies. As the price of the dollar goes up in terms of Japanese yen, German marks, and other foreign currencies, the prices of our exports in foreign markets go up as well. At the same time, a high-priced dollar makes imports cheaper to Americans. The net effect of a rise in the price of the dollar is adverse to the U.S. balance of trade because a high-priced dollar discourages exports and encourages imports. A decline in net exports is a contractionary influence on

the economy that hits certain industries harder than others.

There was concern in the early 1980s that high real interest rates in the United States were also contributing to a higher international value of the dollar. At that time foreigners were bidding up the price of the dollar in terms of foreign currency so as to make investments in the United States. As this occurred, the price of U.S. exports in terms of foreign currencies soared and the balance of trade, and therefore net exports, became negative. Despite a sharp reduction in the international value of the dollar in 1987, the balance of trade deficit remained negative. The federal budget deficit can therefore indirectly prolong a balance of trade deficit if it keeps interest rates in the United States higher than interest rates in foreign nations. (See the Global Economy feature in the preceding chapter.)

The federal budget deficit can also adversely affect the U.S. balance of trade by contributing to an increase in disposable income in the United States. This occurs because of the deficit's expansionary effect on real GDP and because deficit financing allows lower tax rates. When the deficit results in higher disposable income, it increases purchases of imports, because such purchases tend to vary with disposable income. The greater level of import purchases made possible by deficit financing in turn contributes to a balance of trade deficits.

To the extent that there is crowding out of private investment, the deficit can also make U.S. industries less competitive in foreign markets. Government borrowing absorbs savings that U.S. industries could otherwise channel into new investments in technological advances and other cost-saving advances. As a result, unit costs of production in the United States will become higher relative to the unit costs of foreign competitors who make such investments. Ultimately, this indirect effect of the deficit is the most harmful to the international competitiveness of U.S. industries. Private investment is the key to advances in productivity that allow lower costs of production. When the budget deficit curbs private investment by keeping real interest rates high, eliminating the U.S. trade deficit becomes harder. However, if the budget deficit is used to finance government programs that enhance productivity (such as government programs to develop new technologies), the negative impact of reduced private investment on productivity could be offset by the positive impact of the government programs.

CONCEPT CHECK
□

- How can the federal budget deficit be monetized?
- Why is the impact of the deficit less expansionary when the deficit is financed by borrowing from the public rather than expanding the money supply?
- What is the crowding-out effect? How can the budget deficit prolong the U.S. balance of trade deficit?

THE NATIONAL DEBT

You may not lose sleep over it yourself, but lots of politicians and other people in the United States worry about the national debt. In this section we show how government deficits add to the national debt and examine the consequences of an increased national debt for you and the economy.

national debt the dollar amount that the federal government owes its creditors at a given time.

The national debt is the dollar amount that the federal government owes its creditors at a given time. It is the cumulative legacy of previous government deficits, and it increases each year that the federal budget is in deficit. When the budget is in surplus, the federal government can reduce the sum of the debt by not renewing government securities that mature. It can also use the surplus to pay off some debt before it matures. In these ways the government can reduce its demand for credit and put downward pressure on interest rates when a surplus prevails.

As of early 1992, the national debt amounted to $4 trillion. Three quarters of that debt was held by the public, and the remainder was held by the Federal Reserve banks and government agencies. The portion of the national debt held by the Fed and government agencies is debt that the government owes to itself rather than to creditors. Interest paid on this portion of the debt usually returns to the Treasury, thereby increasing government revenues. Similarly, when the debt held by the Fed and government agencies matures, the government itself obtains the funds. Only the

net federal debt the portion of the national debt owed to debtors other than the Federal Reserve and government agencies.

net federal debt, the portion of the national debt owed to debtors other than the Fed and the government agencies, represents credit extended to the federal government by the public.

The graph in Box 4 shows the national debt held by the public from 1950 up to 1992. Notice how that volume of debt began to skyrocket in 1975. Despite the increase in the dollar value of the debt since 1975, the national debt as a percentage of GDP has actually declined since 1950 (when it amounted to 89 percent of GDP) because much of the debt issued to finance government purchases during World War II was retired after 1950. Since 1980, however, the national debt has risen from 33 percent to nearly 50 percent of GDP.

The rise in the national debt as a percentage of GDP since 1980 reflects the sharp increase in the federal budget deficits that have occurred since that year. During the Reagan administration, tax rates were reduced significantly, but government spending was not. As a result, the deficit skyrocketed, contributing to the upward trend in the national debt as a percentage of GDP.

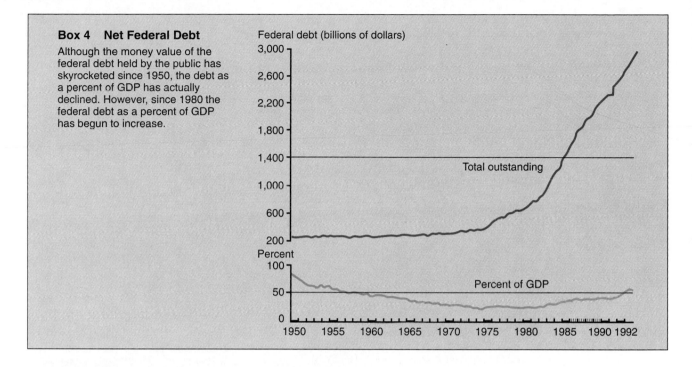

Box 4   Net Federal Debt

Although the money value of the federal debt held by the public has skyrocketed since 1950, the debt as a percent of GDP has actually declined. However, since 1980 the federal debt as a percent of GDP has begun to increase.

Who Are the Nation's Creditors?

The nation's creditors are the individuals and organizations that hold the net federal debt. When taxes are used to pay off the debt, what really happens is that some people suffer a decrease in income, while those who hold government bonds enjoy an increase in income. In other words, retirement of the debt and payment of interest on the debt transfer income among citizens. However, some of the debt is held by foreigners. (In 1992, for example, about 18 percent of the national debt owned by the public was held by foreigners.) When interest payments are made to foreign holders, a portion of the aggregate income earned in the United States is used to pay the nation's foreign creditors. This could become a contractionary influence on the U.S. economy if the foreign holders don't use their interest earnings to purchase U.S. goods and services.

The bulk of the national debt is the internal debt, the portion of the debt the nation owes to its own citizens. The rest is the external debt, the portion that the nation owes to citizens of other nations. The internal debt is very different from private debt. Payment of interest and principal on the debt doesn't drain income from the nation. As pointed out earlier, payment of interest on the debt redistributes income among U.S. citizens and therefore doesn't directly decrease aggregate demand. However, as the portion of the debt held by foreigners increases, more and more interest is paid out each year to foreign citizens. Payment of interest on the external debt could exert some downward pressure on aggregate demand, contributing to a possible future contraction of the economy.

The table in Box 5 shows the ownership pattern of the net federal debt in September 1992. As you can see, individuals, commercial banks, and state and local governments were the major creditors of the federal government. The portion of the debt held by foreigners depends on interest rates in the United States compared to interest rates in foreign countries. In June 1980, when interest rates in the United States were very high relative to those abroad, a whopping 22 percent of the net

internal debt the portion of the national debt owed to the nation's own citizens.

external debt the portion of the national debt owed to citizens of other nations.

principles in practice

The Impact of Deposit Insurance Claims on the Budget Deficit

The estimates of the costs of bailing out insolvent savings and loan associations are mind-boggling. Over the 1990s, as much as $500 billion of federal spending could be allocated to meet the deposit liabilities of failed thrift institutions. And the federal government could spend more if the FDIC, the agency that insures commercial bank deposits, becomes insolvent due to an increase in the failures of U.S. banks.

Federal spending for deposit insurance claims adds to the budget deficit. These claims result from the fact that government insurance of bank deposits, unlike private insurance, is backed by the taxing power of the federal government. When the claims against federal deposit insurance agencies exceed the assets of those agencies, the federal government must either raise taxes or borrow to meet the obligations of the agencies. In effect, federal deposit insurance promotes stability of the banking system by transferring to taxpayers at large losses that depositors would otherwise incur.

However, federal borrowing to bail out failed banks differs fundamentally from borrowing to finance government spending programs. It merely trades federal debt for a debt that already exists. Such borrowing is unlikely to add to aggregate demand or to increase the demand for loanable funds. For this reason, spending to meet the federal government's deposit insurance liabilities is unlikely to add to inflationary pressures in the economy or to put upward pressure on interest rates.

To understand the economic effect of federal spending and borrowing to bail out financial institutions we need to examine how the funds used for these purposes will be spent.* If the funds are used to pay off depositors at insolvent thrift institutions, the depositors will be no better off after receiving them because the income of the depositors will not increase as a result of receiving them. Therefore, aggregate demand will not increase. If the funds are used to induce investors to acquire the assets of failed thrift institutions, the investors will not be made better off, because the funds merely represent payment for debt the investors must assume when they acquire the insolvent institutions.

It is unlikely that interest rates will rise or that private investment will be "crowded out" because of federal borrowing to pay the debts of insolvent S&Ls. Depositors of failed S&Ls who receive payments from the federal government will redeposit the payments in other banks, assuming that no changes will reduce their saving rates or their desire to hold money. As other banks acquire deposits, they will use them to make loans that maintain the supply of credit. The increased amount of credit supplied is exactly offset by the increased credit demanded by the federal government.

For example, suppose the federal government shuts down a thrift institution with $200 million in deposits and only $150 million in assets, mainly in the form of mortgages. The depositors of the thrift institution will redeposit the $200 million they receive from the federal government in other banks, providing those banks with the wherewithal to make nearly $200 million in new loans. The federal government will sell the $150 million in mortgages (which will absorb part of the funds deposited elsewhere) and will borrow the additional $50 million from credit markets through the sale of new government securities. The $200 million in funds deposited in other banks will increase the total availability of credit so as to finance the acquisition of the failed thrift institution's assets and the new government borrowing to cover the difference between the liabilities and assets of the failed institution without putting upward pressure on interest rates.

While federal borrowing to finance deposit insurance claims increases neither aggregate demand nor interest rates, it does affect you as a taxpayer. You will have to pay higher taxes to pay off the new debt. Those higher taxes will allow you and other bank depositors to rest assured that you will not lose any of the funds you have on deposit at thrift institutions or commercial banks. In effect, federal deposit insurance has forced us to trade higher taxes for a stable banking system and for the guarantee that we will not bear any risk when we deposit funds in U.S. banks.

* See Martin Feldstein, "FSLIC Funding Belongs Off-Budget," *The Wall Street Journal*, March 1, 1989. The analysis in this section is based on the discussion in Feldstein's article.

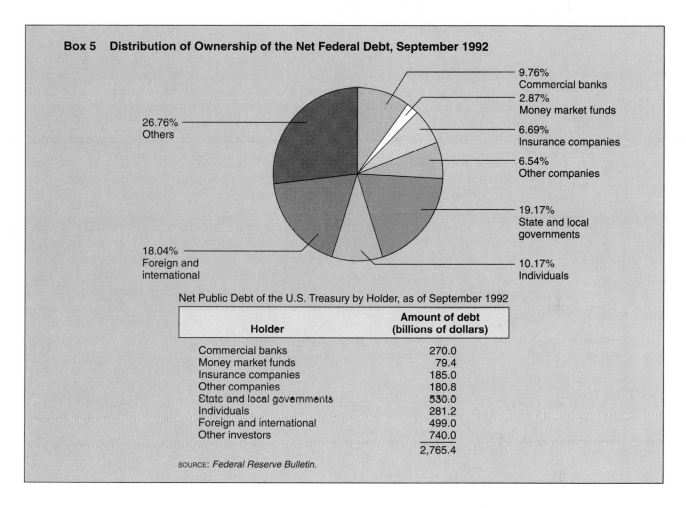

Box 5   Distribution of Ownership of the Net Federal Debt, September 1992

9.76% Commercial banks

2.87% Money market funds

6.69% Insurance companies

6.54% Other companies

19.17% State and local governments

10.17% Individuals

18.04% Foreign and international

26.76% Others

Net Public Debt of the U.S. Treasury by Holder, as of September 1992

Holder	Amount of debt (billions of dollars)
Commercial banks	270.0
Money market funds	79.4
Insurance companies	185.0
Other companies	180.8
State and local governments	530.0
Individuals	281.2
Foreign and international	499.0
Other investors	740.0
	2,765.4

SOURCE: *Federal Reserve Bulletin.*

federal debt was held by foreigners. In late 1986, when interest rates in the United States were relatively low, only 16 percent of the net federal debt was held by foreigners.

Burden of the Debt

Will the federal government go bankrupt if it continues to run deficits? There's no need to worry about this, because the federal government has a few tricks up its sleeve that are unavailable to a private debtor. First of all, the federal government can pay the interest on its debt from tax revenues. Second, at the extreme, the government can print money to pay off its debt. The risk of default on the debt is therefore virtually nil. Of course, the government can always roll its debt over by issuing new securities to pay off the ones that mature. However, this involves continued upward pressure on interest rates in credit markets.

Two major burdens result from a larger national debt:

1. *A larger portion of the taxes paid by future generations will be used to pay interest on the debt instead of providing government goods and services.* Interest on the national debt currently accounts for about 15 percent on federal government expenditures. This means that currently 15 cents of each dollar in taxes is used to provide interest payments to holders of the debt instead of such services as roads, defense, and education. If there is no substantial decline in interest rates and the debt continues to grow because of additional deficits, the portion of taxes allocated to interest instead of goods and services will increase.

2. *If the crowding-out effect is substantial, a growing national debt will decrease private investment and reduce the growth rate of private capital stock.* This will decrease economic growth. As the growth rate of worker productivity declines because of a decrease in the growth rate of capital, the growth in GDP per capita will also decline. Therefore, a growing national debt will retard the growth rate of potential real GDP and result in a lower standard of living for future generations.

The burden of the national debt can be offset, however, if taxpayers increase saving in order to pay the higher taxes they expect in the future as a result of the debt. If taxpayers save more in anticipation of the future burden of taxation, the supply of loanable funds will increase. This will put downward pressure on interest rates and offset some of the crowding-out effect. Similarly, if the deficit actually makes real GDP higher than it would be otherwise by making cyclical downturns less likely, it will also contribute to higher savings.

Finally, the burden of the debt can be offset by increased benefits to future generations from government services. The nation may have fewer factories and machine tools, but it may have more and better roads, better schools, and other government projects that increase worker productivity. This outcome is particularly likely if the federal government uses its borrowings to finance long-lasting projects such as roads, dams, and parks. If that is done, higher interest payments and decreased growth of the private capital stock will be balanced by future benefits from government investments.

CONCEPT CHECK
□

- How is the national debt related to the federal budget deficit?

- What is the distinction between external and internal debt?

- In what sense is the national debt a burden, and in what ways can that burden be offset?

MEASURING THE DEFICIT AND ITS IMPACT

▣ The size of the budget deficit provides citizens with information regarding both the state of federal government finances and the impact of the budget on aggregate demand. Interpreting the impact of the deficit on the economy is quite difficult because the magnitude is influenced by cyclical fluctuations in the economy and by some peculiarities in government accounting techniques. In this section we discuss some of the problems involved in interpreting the meaning of the deficit and in measuring the impact on the economy.

High Employment versus the Actual Deficit

As was pointed out in the preceding chapter, the actual budget deficit or surplus in any given year is influenced by the effects of the automatic stabilizers. When the economy is operating below its potential, the deficit naturally rises. To adjust for the cyclical effects of the automatic stabilizers, the high-employment budget deficit or surplus can be computed. The resulting figure can be used to show whether the federal budget will add to or detract from aggregate demand if the economy is operating at its potential, other things being equal.

For example, in 1991, a recession year, the actual budget deficit was $269.5 billion. In that year the high-employment deficit excluding deposit insurance was only $179.8 billion. The extra $89.7 billion in deficit spending for the year resulted from the cyclical effect of the automatic stabilizers on net taxes and outlays for deposit insurance claims. The recession reduced tax collections, and increased transfer payments above the level that would have prevailed if the economy had achieved a 6 percent unemployment rate.

Remember, when the economy is operating below its potential, a high-employment deficit provides a stimulus that boosts aggregate demand and thus pulls up real GDP.

Other Influences on the Size of the Deficit

The size of the deficit (or surplus) in any given year depends not only on the level of employment, taxes, and federal spending but also on the rate of economic growth. The greater the rate of economic growth as measured by the annual percentage change in real GDP, the greater the rate of increase in tax revenues for the year. Federal tax collections are quite sensitive to changes in the growth of both personal and corporate income. Given the tax rates, the greater the growth of income, the greater the growth of the federal government's tax revenues. A higher rate of economic growth is often associated with declining unemployment, which reduces outlays for federal unemployment insurance and federal aid to the poor, further reducing the deficit. When the economy is growing, tax collections tend to increase faster than the rate of inflation.

The sensitivity of federal revenues and outlays to the rate of economic growth complicates budget planning for the federal government. Each year the President's Council of Economic Advisers, the Office of Management and Budget, and the Treasury make assumptions about economic growth during the year and provide analysis in the budget to account for changes in economic conditions. If they overestimate economic growth, as they sometimes do, the actual deficit will exceed the forecast deficit.

The size of the budget deficit, measured in current dollars, is also sensitive to inflation and the level of interest rates in the economy. Other things being equal, inflation tends to increase federal receipts more than federal outlays. As a result, an increase in the rate of inflation tends to reduce the nominal size of the deficit. Other things being equal, increases in interest rates increase the size of the federal deficit because federal outlays for interest payments on the national debt go up. In 1990, for example, the Bush administration's economists underestimated the level of interest rates for the economy while correctly estimating the rate of inflation, which was fairly stable. The higher-than-forecast interest rates added substantially to federal outlays and resulted in the need for additional funds to meet the deficit targets for the year.

Sometimes inflation *and* interest rates move together. Higher inflation can result in expectations of higher future inflation, pushing up nominal interest rates as lenders reduce the supply of loanable funds. When both inflation and interest rates rise together, the unfavorable effects on the higher interest rates on the deficit are offset by the favorable effects of the higher rate of inflation.

Which Deficit?

Measurement of the federal government's budget deficit is complicated by the fact that some receipts and expenditures of the federal government operate through trust funds that are officially "off budget." The two main government operations treated in this way are Social Security and the U.S. Postal Service. In recent years the Social Security trust funds have run a substantial surplus (in 1992 it was $50 billion, while the U.S. Postal Service has run a small deficit (in 1992 it lost $0.6 billion). Even though trust funds are budgeted for separately, their revenues and expenditures have an effect on the federal government's overall borrowing demands on the credit markets. When the Social Security trust funds run a surplus, the surplus is lent to the Treasury and reduces the Treasury's demands on the credit markets.

The *unified budget deficit* is the difference between all federal government expenditures and all federal government revenues, be they ''on budget'' or ''off budget.'' The unified budget deficit is the best measure of the amount of the funds that the federal government must borrow in any given year. However, from the point of view of measuring the long-term impact of the deficit on the economy, the unified budget deficit has some shortcomings. The net economic effect of the budget depends entirely on the negative saving or *new debt* it generates. In recent years, some of the federal government's borrowing has been done to cover the losses of failed savings and loan associations and commercial banks. Such borrowing merely assumes old debt (see the Principles in Practice feature on deposit insurance) and reflects past obligations of the government that should have been included in past deficits but were not.

The *NIPA budget deficit* is the official measure of the federal deficit in the National Income and Product Accounts. *The NIPA budget deficit does not include any transactions that finance preexisting debts, such as outlays for deposit insurance*. The NIPA budget is the best measure of the net new debt (negative saving) that results from the federal budget deficit. For this reason the NIPA budget deficit is most often used to gauge the long-term impact of changes in the budget deficit.

Contingent Claims, Inflation, and the Growth of the Deficit Burden

Included in the federal budget are outlays for claims paid under various government-sponsored insurance programs. Among the most well known of these programs is deposit insurance for savings and loan associations, commercial banks, and other depository institutions. The federal government also runs insurance programs for pension funds and for natural disasters such as floods. Ideally, an account for the present value of future payouts under these insurance programs should be established in the federal budget. Each year funds should be set aside for expected future claims on the insurance programs and charged off as an expenditure. Unfortunately, current federal budgeting procedures do not make such charges and payouts on the insurance funds are charged only as they are actually made. Because of the failure to budget for contingent claims against the insurance funds, current deficits appear to be smaller than they really are and future deficits appear to be larger. A better budgeting system would use actuarial methods to forecast future payouts under federal insurance programs and budget for those payouts today rather than tomorrow. This system would allow taxpayers to see the true costs of these programs instead of being shocked by large future claims, as was the case with deposit insurance.

While the failure to include contingent claims results in an underestimation of the current budget deficit, the failure to account for the effects of inflation results in an overestimation of the deficit burden. Inflation is great for debtors. When a borrower makes a loan of an interest rate that isn't fully adjusted for future inflation, the borrower can pay off the loan in dollars worth less than those borrowed. Obviously, the federal government, a debtor that owes more than $3 trillion to the public, can gain substantially from inflation. Inflation reduces the value of the national debt and can be thought of as a tax on those who hold that debt. For example, the 5 percent inflation that prevailed in 1990 reduced the value of the national debt by a whopping

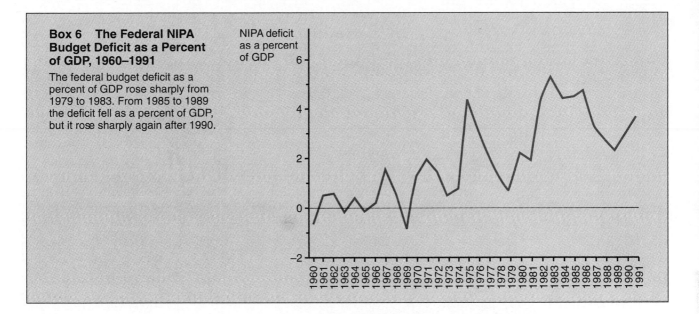

Box 6   The Federal NIPA Budget Deficit as a Percent of GDP, 1960–1991

The federal budget deficit as a percent of GDP rose sharply from 1979 to 1983. From 1985 to 1989 the deficit fell as a percent of GDP, but it rose sharply again after 1990.

$100 billion. Some economists therefore recommend the deficit be adjusted for inflation each year and this *real deficit* be used to gauge the stimulative effect of the deficit.

An alternative to adjusting the deficit for inflation is simply to gauge its burden relative to gross domestic product. Because both the deficit and nominal GDP rise with inflation, the deficit as a percentage of GDP shows how much of a burden federal borrowing is *relative to* our aggregate income.

The graph in Box 6 shows how the NIPA budget deficit has varied as a percentage of GDP since 1960. Despite the cyclical ups and downs reflecting the effect of the automatic stabilizers on the budget, there is a clear upward trend in the graph over the period shown. This indicates that the negative saving of the federal government has grown as a share of the nation's income since 1960. Other things being equal, the growth of this share contributes to a slowdown in economic growth, which in turn contributes to declines in future living standards.

DO DEFICITS MATTER? RICARDIAN EQUIVALENCE AND THE IMPACT OF FEDERAL DEFICITS ON REAL INTEREST RATES

The effects of a budget deficit on the economy depend crucially on the impact the deficit has on national saving and real interest rates. According to some economists, since taxpayers know government will have to raise taxes in the future to pay back the funds (and the interest on those funds) it is borrowing today, they will begin saving now to pay their higher future tax bills. Increased government borrowing is therefore offset by a cut in household consumption as taxpayers increase their saving.

David Ricardo (1772–1832), a famous English classical economist, was the first to argue that increased government borrowing results in increased saving by forward-looking taxpayers. **Ricardian equivalence** prevails when an increase in government borrowing to finance a deficit causes a sufficient increase in private saving to keep the real interest rate fixed. Ricardian equivalence implies that the way an increase in government purchases is financed is irrelevant. According to this view, the level of

Ricardian equivalence a situation that prevails when an increase in government borrowing to finance a deficit causes a sufficient increase in private saving to keep the real interest rate fixed.

principles in practice

The Social Security Trust Fund Surplus and the Federal Budget Deficit

Sweeping changes in the way the Social Security system finances its pensions were enacted by Congress in 1977 and 1983. As a result, the payroll taxes paid by almost all workers in the United States have risen dramatically. In fact, many workers now pay more in payroll taxes to finance Social Security than they pay in income taxes.

The payroll tax collections and taxes levied on the Social Security pensions of certain upper-income taxpayers are used to purchase special government securities issued by the U.S. Treasury. These securities make up two Social Security trust funds, one for old-age and survivors insurance and the other for disability insurance. When the payroll tax and other Social Security tax collections exceed the payout rate, the Social Security trust funds increase. The extra money purchases more special Treasury securities. The trust funds also grow from the interest paid by the Treasury to the funds.

In the 1970s and 1980s the Social Security system was on a "pay-as-you-go" basis. Payroll taxes levied on current workers were used immediately to pay the pensions of retirees. In the 1970s the Social Security trust funds balance was a mere 15 percent of annual pensions paid. By 1990 the Social Security trust funds balance had risen to more than half of the pension benefits paid.

As the year 2000 approaches, the trust funds will grow steadily because payroll tax receipts will exceed pension benefits paid. The funds will continue to grow and earn interest until the year 2025. Thereafter, their Treasury securities will have to be cashed in to pay pensions because of a growing proportion of retirees in the population. At that time the Treasury will have to repay, with interest, the special government securities held by the Social Security trust funds. This repayment could require income and other tax increases if annual pension payments exceed payroll tax and other tax receipts earmarked for Social Security at that time.

What does all this business about the Social Security trust funds have to do with the budget deficit? The answer is, "A whole lot." Because any surplus in the trust funds is, in effect, loaned to the Treasury, the surplus in the trust funds account reduces the overall federal budget deficit. Because of the concern that the funds might be used to finance other government expenditures (or increased Social Security pension benefits), the Budget Enforcement Act of 1990 established new rules that dedicate the Social Security trust funds surpluses through 1995 to reducing the overall federal budget deficit.

Increases in future income are necessary to prevent higher future tax rates to pay future pensions. The new budget rules represent an attempt to make sure that the trust funds surplus will add to national saving rather than help finance current federal spending programs. If we save more today, we will have more income in the future and future tax rates will not have to be increased to generate sufficient funds to pay Social Security pensions at that time.

government purchases can affect aggregate demand, but the way government finances those purchases has no effect on the economy. Ricardian equivalence and the irrelevance of the deficit have been advanced in recent years by the American economist Robert Barro.

We can illustrate Ricardian equivalence with a simple diagram similar to the one we used to illustrate the crowding-out concept earlier in this chapter. When the government increases its demand for loanable funds to cover a deficit, the total demand for loanable funds in the economy increases, putting upward pressure on real interest rates. The higher real interest rates crowd out some private investment and adversely affect future generations by reducing the rate of capital accumulation. However, when forward-looking households realize that their future taxes will increase as a result of the increase in the deficit, they begin saving to pay the higher taxes and the supply of loanable funds increases. If they increase their saving exactly enough to pay back the funds borrowed by government, the supply curve will shift just enough to keep real interest rates constant, as illustrated in Box 7. As a result of the forward-looking behavior of taxpayers, there is no increase in real interest rates and no crowding out of private investment. Therefore, saving and investment do not fall as a result of the deficit.

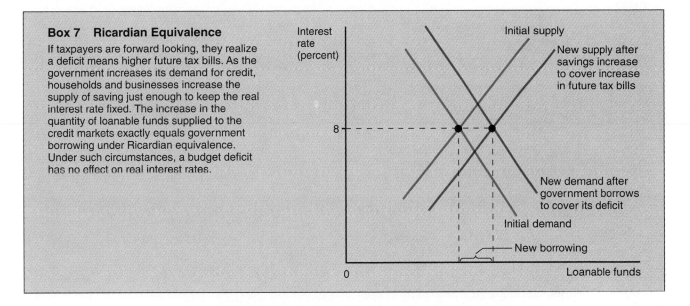

Box 7   Ricardian Equivalence

If taxpayers are forward looking, they realize a deficit means higher future tax bills. As the government increases its demand for credit, households and businesses increase the supply of saving just enough to keep the real interest rate fixed. The increase in the quantity of loanable funds supplied to the credit markets exactly equals government borrowing under Ricardian equivalence. Under such circumstances, a budget deficit has no effect on real interest rates.

Ricardian equivalence is among the most controversial ideas in modern economics. If, in fact, people behave in the forward-looking manner, the implication is that we should not worry about the size of the federal deficit. While the deficit by itself decreases national saving, the proponents of Ricardian equivalence argue that it also causes a reaction exactly offsetting its negative effect on saving.

Ricardian equivalence implies that people take future taxes into account not only for themselves but also for future generations. This is because government borrowing for a chronic deficit like the one the United States has experienced since 1970 can rarely be paid off within the lifetime of current taxpayers. Many economists find it difficult to believe that U.S. households are forward looking enough to save in this way.

There is conflicting evidence on the effect of deficits on interest rates and saving. A number of empirical studies have shown that real interest rates are primarily affected by the level of government purchases. After adjustment for the effect of increases in government purchases on aggregate demand, variation in the deficit has had little effect on real interest rates in recent years. Other empirical studies suggest that there has been some increase in private saving over and above what occurred as a result of the deficit. However, this research also indicates that the increase in saving has not been sufficient to offset the increase in government borrowing. This research implies that government borrowing has caused consumption and aggregate demand to increase and has put upward pressure on interest rates.

Should the Federal Government Run a Surplus?

Even if the budget deficit has caused private saving to increase because households are forward looking, private saving in the United States remains abysmally low by international standards. For this reason many economists and politicians have advocated quick elimination of the federal deficit so as to make the funds it currently absorbs available for private investment. Some economists argue that as we approach the 21st century, the federal government should make a positive contribution to the national saving rate by running a budget surplus. By running a surplus, the government could reduce the net federal debt and put downward pressure on real interest rates. Unless a decrease in the federal deficit causes private saving to decline

insights on issues

Why Worry about the Federal Budget Deficit? Talking with Robert Eisner

Robert Eisner has taught economics at Northwestern University since 1952. He is a past president of the American Economic Association and a fellow of the Econometric Society and the American Academy of Arts and Sciences. He was born in New York City and earned his Ph.D. from Johns Hopkins. His book *How Real Is the Federal Deficit?* is published by the Free Press.

What are the costs of a large chronic federal budget deficit? Costs of the deficit are greatly exaggerated and are based on myth, dogma, and irrelevant or inaccurate assumptions. A too-large deficit would be one that created so much aggregate demand at full employment as to be inflationary. Federal Reserve efforts to curtail inflation would then raise interest rates and crowd out investment. If the deficit were financing public investment, one might still have more total investment even

with a deficit that was "too large." When cutting the deficit means cutting public investment, it may not be a wise goal. The deficit as it is now measured fails to distinguish between current and capital or investment expenditures.

Is there a burden of the federal debt? The debt is a burden only if it discourages public or private investment, leaving the future with less capital. In fact, because the economy generally has had slack and less than full employment, deficits and debt have brought about not only more consumption but also more investment and saving. Deficit and debt have thus brought more saving, not less, and have crowded in investment, not crowded it out.

What can be done to reduce the budget deficit? The one beneficial way to reduce the deficit so that the debt grows only in proportion to income is to bring the economy back to full employment and a high growth path. This can be bone by a combination of easing the money supply and stimulating investment, especially public investment and investment in people, education, training, research, and new technology.

Deficit reduction by tax increases or cuts in spending kills

jobs. If the government spends less, the government buys less, and that means fewer jobs for those producing what the government buys. If taxes are raised (or benefits cut), the public has less purchasing power. That means fewer jobs for those who produce what all of us buy. Lower unemployment and faster economic growth are the one sure way to reduce the deficit.

Should the federal government run a budget surplus after the year 2000? The federal government should not run a budget surplus. This would mean reducing the debt, but in a growing economy everything grows. Private debt, both household and business, grows. Most American families do not balance their budgets; they borrow to buy houses and finance their children's education. Private business keeps borrowing (and thus running "deficits") to finance its investment in new plant and equipment.

Similarly, worthwhile government investment financed by borrowing will create jobs now and raise productivity and our standard of living in the future. Increasing debt generally goes with increasing capital as borrowing finances investment. So it should also be for the federal government.

(as Ricardian equivalence would imply), a decline in the federal deficit will increase national saving.

By reducing the nation's saving rate, the deficit has the long-run potential to decrease future American living standards, because a low supply of savings contributes to higher real interest rates. Higher real interest rates imply lower rates of investment that reduce the growth rate of labor productivity. Finally, all this translates into a reduced growth rate for real GDP, which will contribute to a lower growth of future per capita income in the United States. In the 1980s large inflows of foreign saving contributed to increased supplies of savings in the United States and helped finance our investment. However, we cannot continually rely on foreign savings to finance our spending spree.

One compelling argument for running a budget surplus to increase the national saving rate is that the proportion of retired persons in the population will inevitably increase in the first half of the 21st century. As this occurs, the Social Security trust funds will go into deficit. Additional tax revenue will eventually be required to pay for the pensions of the large portion of the population expected to be on Social Security at that time. Unless real GDP increases more rapidly than the 2 percent per year anticipated in the near future, this could mean increasing tax rates to generate the revenue necessary to pay the pensions. The increased investment made possible by increasing our saving through a budget surplus would help increase the future growth rate and make it possible to generate tax revenue without sharply increasing tax rates after the year 2025.

CONCEPT CHECK □

- How can a federal budget deficit contribute to higher interest rates?
- What is the basic idea behind *Ricardian equivalence* between a deficit and tax financing of government outlays?
- Explain how the federal budget deficit affects the national saving rate and future living standards?

SUMMARY

1. A federal budget deficit prevails whenever outlays in a given year exceed its receipts. When the budget is consistently in deficit, the national debt increases

2. The federal budget can be financed by the creation of new money or by borrowing from the public. Whenever the Federal Reserve increases the money supply to help the federal government over a deficit, the deficit is said to be *monetized*. Monetizing the deficit adds to aggregate demand directly as the government spends the newly created funds and indirectly as an increase in bank reserves allows expansion of the money supply.

3. The federal budget deficit is usually financed by borrowing from the public. If that is done, the increase in government purchases that are financed by the deficit is paid for by an allocation of saving to purchase government securities. There is no increase in bank reserves. However, borrowing is more expansionary than tax financing because disposable income is not reduced. In effect, borrowing to finance a federal budget deficit postpones the burden of taxation to the future.

4. When the government borrows in credit markets to finance a deficit, it puts upward pressure on interest rates by increasing the demand for loanable funds. The higher interest rates result in a crowding out of investment and a decline in the quantity of loanable funds demanded for investment purposes. The federal budget deficit therefore results in a crowding out of private investment as it causes real interest rates to go up. The extent of the crowding-out effect depends on the responsiveness of investment demand to changes in interest rates.

5. Upward pressure on interest rates resulting from the deficit can have adverse effects on the U.S. balance of trade. High interest rates induce foreigners to hold dollars as savings in the United States rather than using them to purchase U.S. goods. This prevents the price of the dollar from falling in terms of foreign currencies, thus making U.S. exports more expensive to foreigners and imports cheaper to U.S. buyers. In addition, the deficit contributes to higher disposable income, which also increases the demand for imports.

6. The national debt is the dollar amount that the federal government owes its creditors at a given time. The creditors are those who hold government securities and receive interest payments from the government.

7. The net federal debt is the portion of the national debt owed to those other than the Federal Reserve or government agencies.

8. The bulk of the national debt is an internal debt because it is owed to U.S. citizens. When interest is paid on the debt, income is redistributed from taxpayers to debt holders. However, a portion of the national debt is owed to foreigners who have purchased U.S. government securities. When interest is paid on this external debt, income is transferred from U.S. taxpayers to foreigners.

9. The burden of the national debt is the sacrifice U.S. citizens in the aggregate will have to make to repay it. Because the bulk of the debt is owed to U.S. citizens, repayment will make people who receive interest payments better off while making those who pay taxes worse off.

10. Another burden of the national debt is the sacrifices of future government services as more tax revenues are allocated to paying interest on the debt instead of providing government programs. In addition, if the crowding-out effect of deficit financing is strong, a growing national debt will cause the growth rate of private capital stock to decrease. This can make U.S. workers less productive and can contribute to lower income and higher U.S. unit costs of production relative to foreign competitors.

11. The burden of the national debt can be offset if deficits result in higher saving. Higher saving would put downward pressure on interest rates and offset the crowding-out effect. The burden of the debt can also be offset if the government invests in roads, dams, and other long-lasting projects that increase worker productivity.

12. The federal budget deficit is influenced by the cyclical ups and downs of the economy.

13. Inflation erodes the real value of the national debt and allows the government to pay off its debt in dollars that have less purchasing power than those it borrowed.

14. Deficits can induce forward-looking taxpayers to increase their saving to pay future taxes. Ricardian equivalence between deficit and tax financing of government outlays prevails when an increase in government borrowing to finance a deficit causes a sufficient increase in private saving to keep the real interest rate fixed.

15. A federal budget deficit decreases the national saving rate because it represents negative saving. Federal borrowing absorbs loanable funds that would otherwise finance private investment.

KEY TERMS

crowding-out effect *419*   net federal debt *422*   external debt *423*   Ricardian equivalence *429*
national debt *422*   internal debt *423*

CONCEPT REVIEW

1 Briefly discuss the possible impact of the federal budget deficit on the economy and how that impact can vary with the way the deficit is financed.

2 How can the national debt burden future generations?

3 What is the best measure of the federal budget deficit's impact on debt?

4 Explain why Ricardian equivalence implies that an increase in the federal budget deficit will not increase real interest rates.

PROBLEMS AND APPLICATIONS

1. Suppose a new law is passed that requires the federal government to run a surplus each year until the national debt has been paid off. Explain why such a policy would be likely to destabilize the economy and contribute to recessions when the private components of aggregate demand decrease. **1**, **3**

2. Suppose the federal government runs a chronic deficit of $200 billion per year and finances that deficit by selling new government securities directly to the Federal Reserve System. Show how, other things being equal, either currency in circulation or bank reserves will increase as a result of this means of financing the deficit. Why would the impact on the economy of this means of financing the deficit be the same as if the government merely printed money to pay its expenses? Why would the impact on the economy be inflationary in the long run? **1**

3. Suppose the federal deficit is financed by borrowing funds from the general public. Track the impact of such borrowing on interest rates, private saving, and private investment. Under what circumstances will government borrowing reduce private investment? **1**

4. Suppose taxpayers increase the supply of savings as a direct result of the government deficit. Show how, if the increase in the supply of savings is large enough, borrowing to finance the deficit will not affect interest rates and will not crowd out private investment. **4**

5. Why is financing government expenditures by borrowing more expansionary than tax financing? **1**

6. Suppose both the supply of savings and investment demand are completely unresponsive to changes in the market rate of interest. What will be the impact of a

federal budget deficit on consumption, investment, and aggregate demand? What impact will the deficit have on the price level and real GDP if the economy is in a deep recession, so that the economy is operating in the flat portion of its aggregate supply curve? **1**

7. How can a large deficit prolong a nation's international balance of trade deficit? **1**

8. Suppose that over the years the portion of the net federal debt owned by foreigners increases from 5 percent to 30 percent of the amount outstanding. What is the implication of this change for the future burden of repaying the debt? **2**

9. Suppose all of the net federal debt is internal debt. In what sense does repayment of such a debt involve a redistribution of income? Is there a burden of the debt on future generations in this case? In what ways can the burden of the debt on future generations be offset? **2**

10. What is the impact of inflation on the burden of repaying the debt and on taxpayers? **1** , **2**

career profile

Nancy Shepherdson "Studying economics gives you flexibility and prepares you mentally for many different fields," says Nancy Shepherdson, owner of The Write Word, a successful small business. The company handles a variety of writing and training projects. Shepherdson specializes in translating technical subjects into language audiences can understand, and she attributes this skill to the analytical tools derived from her economics training.

Shepherdson started out at the University of Illinois with a major in Asian studies. "I was interested in less developed countries, and it seemed clear that economics was intimately involved in their fates," she explains. "So I took one econ class and was fortunate to have the most entertaining professor of my college career, Prof. Gottheil. He really made the subject live for us, and I wound up with a double major."

She went on to get her master's in economics at the University of Michigan. "I didn't go on for a Ph.D. because by that time I'd discovered that economists had sometimes done more harm than good by trying to impose their theories on the real world."

After a stint as an analyst for the state of Michigan, Shepherdson started at First Illinois Bank as assistant to the business development officer in the financial and trust services division. When her boss left, she was promoted. "I had the latitude to create my own job," she says, "I added marketing support and boosted sales by 25 percent." She also wrote newsletters and brochures aimed at clients who had at least $100,000 in investable assets. "Strangely, those customers didn't think of themselves as well off," she recalls. "They pinched every penny. My experience at the bank led me to formulate a little economic theory of my own: You can't get rich if you like to spend money."

While at the bank, Shepherdson attended Northwestern's Kellogg Graduate School of Business part-time, completing her MBA in 1986. One week after receiving her MBA Shepherdson quit her job to found The Write Word.

Armed with the knowledge that more than half of all small businesses fail, Shepherdson prepared for the worst, with enough savings to live on for a year in case The Write Word flopped. But her precautions were not needed; she turned a profit the first year and increased revenues every year since. "My mother is floored that I make more money now than when I was working for someone else," she observes.

Shepherdson says that small businesses like hers help stabilize the economy. "Large companies tend to overreact to economic downturns," she explains. "But if they've been supplementing their staff with freelancers to handle short-term projects, they don't have to let any full-time employees go, and they've saved on overhead all along. Until the economy picks up again, they hire independent contractors and tailor the staff to the amount of work available."

Somehow there's always enough work for a self-employed writer, even in a recession. "I have the best job security in the world," she declares. "I may not get free health insurance or paid holidays, but I never have to worry about getting laid off. I spread the risk among a number of different clients, so even if one folds or relocates, I still have enough work."

In her writing career, Shepherdson has continued to emphasize finance and marketing, although to a lesser extent than in the past. Recently, she has branched out into the travel writing, celebrity profiles, and writing for kids—a far cry from economics. But many of the clients who hire her to train their employees in business writing are financial institutions. And the World Bank has even sent her to sub-Saharan Africa to cover an international conference on structural adjustment. "I originally wanted to be an itinerant economist," Shepherdson says, "and the World Bank project gave me a taste of what that would have been like. I'm happy to have the background, but I'm also happy to be a writer."

19 chapter

Issues in Stabilization Policy
Inflation versus Unemployment and Rational Expectations

It seems that in modern economies it's often difficult, at least in the short run, to simultaneously reduce inflation and reduce unemployment. While grappling with the short-run trade-off between inflation and unemployment, policymakers must also consider the long-run impact of stabilization policies on economic growth and aggregate supply. But policies such as subsidies and tax breaks that seek to increase the nation's productive potential over the long run can overheat the economy in the short run by increasing aggregate demand.

In this chapter we consider the historical trade-off between inflation and unemployment. We also examine the effect of stabilization policies and expectations about inflation on the decisions of the participants in the economy. Remember that expectations regarding future prices and incomes are an important determinant of the demand for and supply of goods and services. Here we examine how such expectations are formed and we consider the possible effects of changes in such expectations on nominal wages, aggregate supply, and macroeconomic equilibrium. We also review issues in stabilization policy and contrast the positions of various schools of economic thought.

☐ CONCEPT PREVIEW

After reading this chapter, you should be able to:

1. Discuss the historical trade-off between inflation and unemployment in modern economies through the use of the Phillips curve.

2. Show how shifts in aggregate supply can affect the trade-off between the goals of reducing inflation and reducing unemployment.

3. Understand how rational expectations of changes in the price level can affect the behavior of workers and investors and influence macroeconomic equilibrium.

4. Understand some of the difficulties of implementing stabilization policies and compare the views of major schools of economic thought on such policies.

THE PHILLIPS CURVE: INFLATION VERSUS UNEMPLOYMENT

Throughout the world the 1970s were greeted as the "Age of Aquarius," as popu-   ▣
larized in the musical *Hair*. When the 1980s rolled in, it appeared as though this
decade would be characterized as the "age of inflation." Inflation in the United
States in 1986 was running at an annual rate of 13.5 percent, and the nation was
plagued by double-digit inflation from 1979 through 1981. Inflation was even worse in
the nations of Western Europe. In the early 1980s inflation in both Italy and the
United Kingdom was galloping at 20 percent annual rates. Then in 1982 a recession
hit as monetary authorities around the world engaged in policies to combat inflation.
Inflation declined to 4 percent in the United States in 1982, and similar dramatic
decreases in the rate of inflation were experienced in Western European nations. But
unemployment rates soared to double digits in the United States, and the economies
of Western Europe also suffered from recessions as inflation came down. Inflation
has fallen since 1990, but unemployment rates have moved upward, and throughout
1992 and 1993 they were at levels in the range of 7 percent.

As you might expect from your familiarity with aggregate demand and aggregate
supply analysis, declines in aggregate demand that cause recessions also moderate
inflation if aggregate supply is more or less stable. To see this, just shift an aggregate
demand curve to the left (as we have done many times now), assuming a stable
aggregate curve, and note how this results in downward pressure on prices but also
decreases real GDP. We would expect that when inflation is primarily of the "demand-pull" type, reducing inflation by decreasing aggregate demand can also decrease equilibrium real GDP. The decrease in real GDP contributes to increased
cyclical unemployment. In other words, reducing inflation by policies that cause
aggregate demand to decline can also increase cyclical unemployment.

The trade-off between inflation and unemployment implied by a model of demand-
pull inflation has been well documented for certain historical periods. In the late
1950s A. W. Phillips, a British statistician, conducted research to examine the
historical relationship between the unemployment rule and the rate of change in
wages.[1] Phillips used data for the United Kingdom over the period 1861 to 1957. He
plotted the annual rate of change in wages on the vertical axis of a graph and the
annual unemployment rate on the horizontal axis. He then made a remarkable
discovery. A curve sketched through the resulting scatter of points corresponding to
the coordinates of the points seemed to fit the data very well. The curve traced out a
negative relationship between unemployment and the rate of change in wages. When
unemployment increased, the rate of change in wages tended to decrease. As you
can see in Box 1, the curve also showed that as unemployment fell below 5 percent
or so, further decreases in the unemployment rate then seemed to be associated with
faster increases in the rate of change in money wages. On the other hand, when the
unemployment rate was very high, say over 6 percent, further increases in unemployment did not tend to reduce the rate of change in wages very much. In fact,
wages actually fell in some of the years from 1861 through 1957. In other words, the
rate of change in wages was negative over certain periods.

The relationship between annual wage changes and the unemployment rate is in
accord with aggregate supply and demand analysis. When the unemployment rate
falls to 5 percent, the economy is likely to produce its potential level of real output.
Increases in aggregate demand at that point are likely to overheat the economy,
thereby causing rapid inflation and rapid increases in money wages over the year. On

---

[1] A. W. Phillips, "The Relationship between the Unemployment Rate and the Rate of Change in Money Wage Rates in the United Kingdom, 1861–1957," *Economica* 25 (November 1958), pp. 283–599.

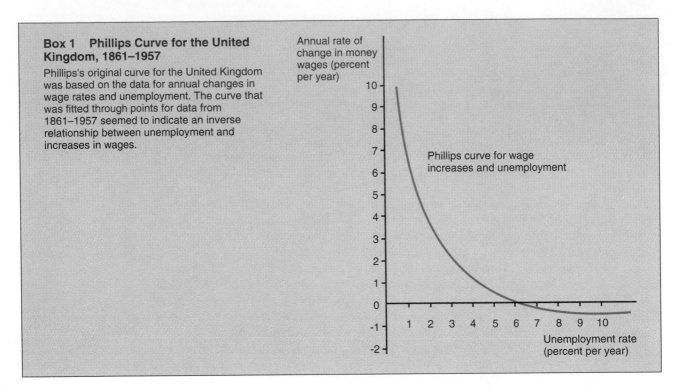

Box 1   Phillips Curve for the United Kingdom, 1861–1957

Phillips's original curve for the United Kingdom was based on the data for annual changes in wage rates and unemployment. The curve that was fitted through points for data from 1861–1957 seemed to indicate an inverse relationship between unemployment and increases in wages.

the other hand, when there is slack in the economy and unemployment rates are high, increases in aggregate demand result in more output and increased employment with little upward pressure on wages and prices. The curve in Box 1 is therefore consistent with a model of an economy in which aggregate demand fluctuates, while the aggregate supply curve is fairly stable.

Phillips's work tended to support a widely held hypothesis among economists that shifts in aggregate demand were mainly responsible for changes in equilibrium real GDP and the price level. Therefore, economists were quick to adapt his work to U.S. data. However, they made one change: Instead of plotting the annual rate of change in money wages on the vertical axis, they plotted the annual rate of increase in the price level, which measures inflation. This curve, showing the hypothesized inverse relationship between unemployment and inflation, is called a **Phillips curve** in honor of A. W. Phillips. The graph shown in Box 2 appears to confirm that there was indeed a negative historical relationship between inflation and unemployment in the United States between 1960 and 1969.

Phillips curve a curve showing the hypothesized inverse relationship between annual unemployment and annual inflation in a nation.

Using the Phillips Curve

In the 1960s and the early 1970s, economists believed that the Phillips curve accurately represented the trade-off between unemployment and inflation. It was taken for granted that unemployment could be reduced at the expense of higher inflation. Policymakers therefore believed that recessionary GDP gaps could easily be eliminated with expansionary fiscal or monetary policies. Real GDP would quickly increase in the short run, and in the long run the price level would increase as the increase in aggregate demand resulted in an inflationary process.

In fact, these trade-offs did seem to be confirmed by the data for the 1960s, as you can see in Box 2. During the turbulent 1970s, however, something seemed to go wrong with the standard Phillips curve.

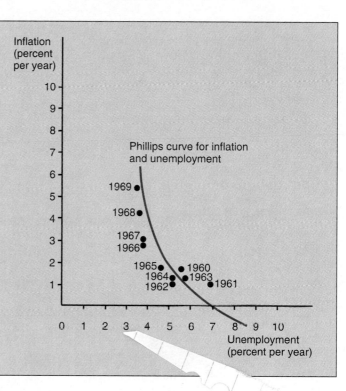

Box 2   Phillips Curve for the United States, 1960–1969

Data for the United States on unemployment and inflation seemed to trace out a negative relationship indicated by this Phillips curve. When unemployment was below 7 percent per year, inflation tended to be positive. The lower the unemployment rate, the higher the inflation rate in any given year.

Supply-Side Shocks and the Phillips Curve for the 1970s

Remember that the idea underlying the Phillips curve is that short-run fluctuations in aggregate demand are mainly responsible for changes in macroeconomic equilibrium. The theory behind the curve assumes that the short-run aggregate supply curve for the economy tends to shift outward at a regular and predictable pace. The theory also neglects the role played by inflationary expectations.

During the 1970s there was a series of supply-side shocks such as the unexpected increase in the prices of petroleum products in 1973. There was also a series of crop failures in the early 1970s that pushed agricultural prices upward. These shocks sharply increased the price level and contributed to a period of stagflation.

In the 1970s, at least in the short run, the aggregate supply curve shifted *inward* more than the aggregate demand curve shifted *outward!* When this happens, you can expect the price level to rise and real GDP to fall. This scenario is shown in Box 3. With a growing labor force, a fall in equilibrium real GDP means that jobs become scarcer relative to the number of job seekers. Both unemployment and the price level go up! This was the stagflation that dominated the U.S. economy in the 1970s. Steady decreases in aggregate supply swamped the effects of increasing aggregate demand, and an increase in inflation was accompanied by *increased* rather than decreased unemployment.

Between 1978 and 1980 the unemployment rate in the United States increased from a bit less than 6 percent of the work force to more than 7 percent. At the same time, the inflation rate increased from slightly more than 8 percent per year to *more than 13 percent per year.*

The graph in Box 4 plots points corresponding to U.S. annual inflation and annual unemployment from 1970 to 1980. Compare the pattern traced by the points in Box 4 with that shown in Box 2. The points don't trace out a clearly distinguishable pattern

Box 3 Stagflation and Macroeconomic Equilibrium

Stagflation exists when annual decreases in aggregate supply are stronger than annual increases in aggregate demand. In the graph, the equilibrium price level rises while equilibrium real GDP falls as the equilibrium point moves from E_1 to E_2.

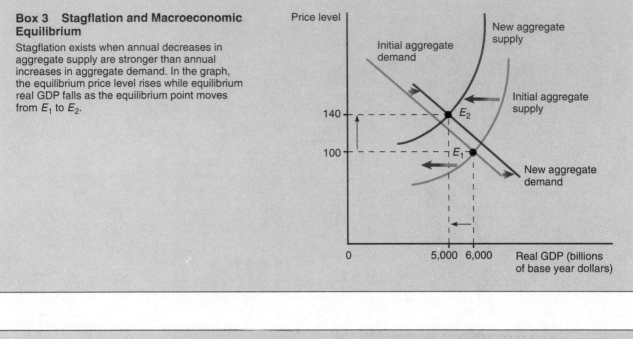

Box 4 Inflation and Unemployment in the United States, 1970–1980

Data on unemployment and inflation from 1970 through 1980 do not fit the pattern of the Phillips curve. The graph shows actual inflation and unemployment rates for the period and connects the points with arrows.

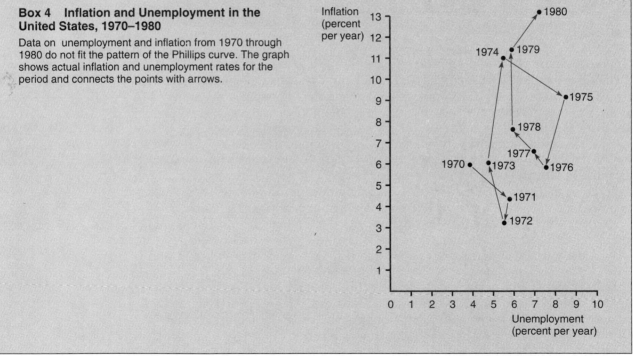

through which a neat Phillips curve can be drawn. Instead, they are dispersed widely on the graph. For data after 1973, there are many cases of jumps in *both* inflation and unemployment in the same year. For example, both inflation and unemployment increased in 1974. Although inflation declined in 1976, there was only a slight decrease in unemployment that year. In 1980 unemployment and inflation again shot up together.

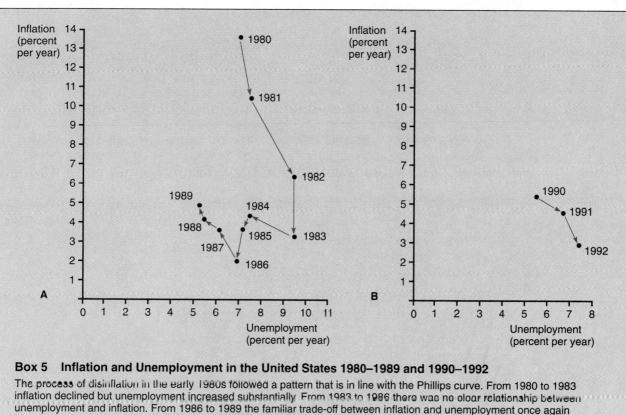

Box 5   Inflation and Unemployment in the United States 1980–1989 and 1990–1992

The process of disinflation in the early 1980s followed a pattern that is in line with the Phillips curve. From 1980 to 1983 inflation declined but unemployment increased substantially. From 1983 to 1986 there was no clear relationship between unemployment and inflation. From 1986 to 1989 the familiar trade-off between inflation and unemployment once again appeared. In the early 1990s inflation declined but unemployment increased.

The Phillips Curve in the 1980s and 1990s

Between 1980 and 1982 a familiar pattern reasserted itself as a recession hit. The unemployment rate started to increase, but the inflation rate dropped. In fact, in 1982, a recession year, the inflation rate declined dramatically from 13.5 percent in 1980 to 6.1 percent. However, the unemployment rate increased to about 10 percent in 1982 as a result of a contractionary monetary policy that raised interest rates. In the mid-1980s inflation remained fairly low (between 3 percent and 4 percent per year), but unemployment, which fell below 8 percent in 1983, remained between 7 percent and 8 percent per year. Then, by the end of 1987, the unemployment rate fell below 6 percent, but the inflation rate inched up to the range of 4 percent per year. By 1989 the unemployment rate was down to 5.2 percent, but inflation was nearly 5 percent.

Disinflation is a sharp reduction in the annual rate of inflation. When disinflation occurs, the price level continues to rise, but its rate of increase is sharply reduced. Disinflation was successfully achieved between 1980 and 1982. However, the policies that achieved disinflation also increased unemployment. Apparently, the relatively high unemployment rate was one consequence of the policies that achieved a relatively low inflation rate in the mid-1980s.

Graph **A** in Box 5 shows the relationship between inflation and unemployment in the 1980s. Between 1980 and 1983 the familiar pattern of the original Phillips curve appears to be traced out as the process of disinflation increased unemployment

disinflation a sharp reduction in the annual rate of inflation.

substantially. The inflation rate was reduced from 1984 to 1986, but there was also a reduction in the unemployment rate.

Between 1986 and 1989 the apparent trade-off between unemployment and inflation reappeared. As the economy approached full employment in the late 1980s, inflation began to heat up. This led many economists to believe that fluctuations in aggregate demand were again dominating fluctuations in aggregate supply and that the Phillips curve trade-off between unemployment and inflation would again be a factor in the choice of stabilization policies.

Between 1990 and 1992 inflation fell from 5.3 percent to 2.9 percent, but the unemployment rate rose from 5.5 percent to 7.4 percent. Once again, an upward-sloping Phillips curve could be traced out, as shown in graph **B** of Box 5.

CONCEPT CHECK

☐

- ■ What does the Phillips curve show?
- ■ What is the underlying macroeconomic theory that explains the shape of the Phillips curve?

- ■ Do the data for inflation and unemployment in the United States during the 1970s trace out the relationship implied by the Phillips curve?

THE THEORY OF RATIONAL EXPECTATIONS AND THE TRADE-OFF BETWEEN INFLATION AND UNEMPLOYMENT

No one has a crystal ball for accurately foreseeing the future. For this reason, many economic decisions are made on the basis of some guess or expectation about what the future will hold. In considering macroeconomic equilibrium and the trade-off between inflation and unemployment, some economists have formulated theories that give heavy weight to the role of expectations in economic decisions. These theories are quite controversial. In this section we examine the formation of expectations about the future and the possible effects of changing expectations on aggregate supply and inflation. We also examine how shifts in expectations can cause shifts of the Phillips curve and therefore shifts in the trade-off between unemployment and inflation.

How Are Expectations Formed?

In forming expectations, people use the information available to them along with some notion about the functioning of the sector of the economy in which they operate. They use past data on prices, and they also consider likely changes in the pattern of prices.

On the basis of past values of an economic variable, some people make educated guesses about the future behavior of the variable. If the guesses prove incorrect, these people will use their mistakes to improve their forecasts. In adjusting their expectations when they discover a mistake, these people are using *adaptive expectations*. For example, suppose you want to forecast next year's price level. If you form your expectations adaptively, you will collect data on recent price levels and use these data to make an educated guess. If you find that the current price level is lower than the level you expected, you may lower your estimate of the future price level. If the price level is higher than you expected, you may raise your estimate of the future price level. You constantly adjust your expectations according to the errors of your previous forecasts. Note, however, that because it takes time for you to recognize your mistakes, adaptive expectations imply a relatively sluggish adjustment of expectations when there is a change in the course of economic variables. It is quite likely that for a time you will systematically under- or overpredict the price level.

Some economists argue that the process by which expectations are formed is more complex than is suggested by the idea of adaptive expectations. These economists argue that in predicting the future course of an economic variable it is rational for people to use *all* available information—not just the past behavior of that variable. Incorrect forecasts can prove costly, so it pays to minimize the size of possible error by utilizing any relevant economic models and data. Because it is "rational" for people making economic forecasts to use all of the relevant data available to them at costs they consider reasonable, expectations formed in this manner are called *rational expectations*. More formally, rational expectations are the use by individuals of all available information, including any relevant economic models, in their forecasts of economic variables.

To illustrate the difference between adaptive and rational expectations, suppose you are about to lend money to a friend for a year and you need to estimate next year's inflation rate so that you can charge an appropriate nominal rate of interest. If you form your expectations *adaptively,* you will look at past rates of inflation, putting more emphasis on the recent past. For example, if the inflation rate has been 5 percent per year for the past four years, *adaptive expectations* will lead you to forecast an inflation rate of 5 percent. In contrast, if you form your expectations *rationally,* you will examine potential changes in Fed policy, the prospective federal budget deficit or surplus, the possibility of a supply-side shock, and any other relevant economic information. In addition, you will use all of this information in a simple model, like the models presented in previous chapters, to generate an inflation forecast. By using all of this information, you are quite likely to generate a better forecast, that is, one subject to smaller error.

This is not to say that you must have a Ph.D. in economics or statistics to form rational expectations. It simply means you have enough experience to understand the factors influencing the prices of the goods or services you buy or sell. You may have had some contact with business managers or farmers who plan their activities by guessing what future prices will be. Although these people may lack formal education, they are often quite sophisticated in understanding the operation of the markets in which they sell their goods. They are often well aware that interest rates and government policies affecting interest rates will influence their profit opportunities.

Forecasting the future of the economy is a common activity of economists. However, the forecasts of economists are not always correct. You might read *The Wall Street Journal* or *Time* magazine to follow economists' forecasts. Every major daily newspaper has a business section containing information about possible changes in real GDP and prices. You sort out all of the information available to you and form your own expectations.

Large corporations are more sophisticated in their information gatherings. In addition to making use of their own economists and statisticians, they may hire consultants to help them predict the future. They may use sophisticated economic forecasting models or simulation studies. Neither you nor the large corporations will necessarily make the correct forecasts all the time. The theory of rational expectations argues that expectations are based on some underlying notion, right or wrong, about the way the economy functions. The theory also assumes that people revise their expectations when new information becomes available.

The theory of rational expectations does not imply that people always perfectly anticipate the future. Their predictions about the levels of economic variables will sometimes prove correct, and sometimes incorrect. But since rationally formed

rational expectations the use by individuals of all available information, including any relevant economic models, in their forecasts of economic variables.

expectations exploit all available information and use all relevant economic models, forecasts of economic variables using such expectations will not be systematically high or low. Put another way, people's best guesses about the future course of important economic variables will vary from the actual path of such variables in a random manner.

How Changes in Rational Expectations Can Affect the Aggregate Supply Curve

Expectations of future inflation are important because they exert a strong influence on the nominal wage level at the beginning of the year. Changes in expectations can shift labor supply, which, in turn, can affect equilibrium nominal wages in labor markets. For example, if workers expect inflation to rise, all other things being equal, labor supply will decrease, thereby increasing equilibrium nominal wages for the year. The resulting increase in unit labor costs will shift the economy's aggregate supply curve inward, putting upward pressure on the price level and downward pressure on real GDP.

We can easily show the implications of the theory of rational expectations for aggregate supply and macroeconomic equilibrium. Suppose the AFL–CIO wants to forecast next year's inflation rate so it can bargain for a new contract wage. Rationally formed expectations will not just look at past inflation rates. Rather, they will be based on all available information and on any relevant economic models. Suppose the AFL–CIO's staff economists project that a change in either fiscal or monetary policy will increase aggregate demand during the year. If labor unions anticipate that the increased aggregate demand will cause inflation to heat up, they will hold out for higher increases in nominal wages during the year to prevent their real wages from declining. When a policy to increase aggregate demand causes rational expectations to change in this way, the increase in aggregate demand is accompanied by a decrease in aggregate supply as nominal wages increase. This effect is illustrated in Box 6. As the aggregate demand curve shifts outward and rational expectations of inflation increase, the aggregate supply curve shifts inward because nominal wages and other input prices will rise in anticipation of the increased inflation. As a consequence, the increase in aggregate demand and the resulting decrease in aggregate supply set up an inflationary process that causes the price level to rise. *There is no change in equilibrium real GDP,* because product prices must rise more rapidly than input prices to provide producers with the incentive (which is increased profit) to produce more. When nominal wages and other input prices increase along with output prices, producers cannot profit by supplying more output.

The conclusion of the theory of rational expectations is that policies shifting the aggregate demand curve are unlikely to have much effect on real GDP, and therefore on the unemployment rate, if they also result in widespread changes in rational expectations of inflation. Instead, policies that shift aggregate demand will also shift aggregate supply. As shown in Box 6, this implies that the price level will rise but that there will be no change in equilibrium real GDP.

The critics of the theory of rational expectations argue that it assumes workers and managers to be much better informed than they actually are about changes in policy and the way the economy operates. Therefore, many economists are skeptical of the theory's contention that stabilization policies are anticipated in a way that prevents them from changing real GDP. These economists believe that expectations of inflation are formed *adaptively* and thus don't change rapidly when economic policies change.

One implication of the theory of rational expectations is that the economy has a very good self-correcting mechanism that operates through shifts in aggregate supply

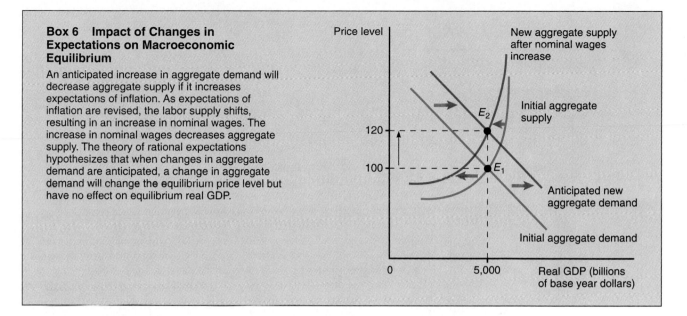

Box 6 Impact of Changes in Expectations on Macroeconomic Equilibrium

An anticipated increase in aggregate demand will decrease aggregate supply if it increases expectations of inflation. As expectations of inflation are revised, the labor supply shifts, resulting in an increase in nominal wages. The increase in nominal wages decreases aggregate supply. The theory of rational expectations hypothesizes that when changes in aggregate demand are anticipated, a change in aggregate demand will change the equilibrium price level but have no effect on equilibrium real GDP.

generated by changes in rational expectations about inflation. This implies that once full employment is attained, any deviations from full employment will set up a process that soon returns the economy to equilibrium at potential real GDP. According to the theory of rational expectations, deviations from full employment will be random and temporary. For example, the theory holds that if there is an inflationary GDP gap, the resulting inflation will cause rational expectations to set up a process that quickly decreases aggregate supply as nominal wages increase. This results in downward pressure on real GDP and upward pressure on the price level until full employment is restored. Similarly, if there is a recessionary GDP gap, there will be rapid downward pressure on the price level, resulting in downward revisions in rational expectations of inflation that increase aggregate supply. The increase swiftly moves the economy back to full employment. The implications of the theory of rational expectations are exactly the same as those for the classical model of macroeconomic equilibrium we first discussed in the chapter on the forces of aggregate supply and demand. Hence adherents of the theory of rational expectations are often called *new classical economists.* University of Chicago economist Robert Lucas is generally credited with adapting the theory of rational expectations to macroeconomic thought (see Economic Thinkers box).

Inflationary Expectations and the Phillips Curve

The Phillips curve is based in part on the assumption that people don't formulate expectations about inflation that influence their behavior. But as we've just seen, inflationary expectations can be an important influence on economic decisions and aggregate supply. If economic fluctuations are, in fact, attributable in part to shifts in aggregate supply caused by changes in rational expectations, then a change in inflationary expectations can shift the entire Phillips curve.

Suppose the Phillips curve would normally intersect the horizontal axis at the level of unemployment corresponding to the natural rate of unemployment when, by and large, the inflation rate is not expected to be greater than it was in the preceding year. If unemployment were lower than its natural rate, the economy would be overheated, and therefore upward pressure on the price level would cause inflation.

economic thinkers

Robert Lucas

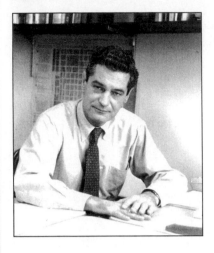

Although he was not the original author, Robert Lucas is generally credited with introducing the theory of rational expectations to macroeconomic thought. John Muth, another economist, developed the concept in the early 1960s to analyze commodities markets. Lucas took the idea and adapted it for all of macroeconomics, a revolutionary breakthrough that completely altered how economists model people's expectations of future events.

Lucas uses rational expectations to show that the proper role for government policy is not the active interventionism called for by Keynesians to counteract the business cycle. He shows that people can anticipate these actions, given their knowledge of policy, past experience, and expectations about the future. When people act on this anticipation, the effects of government policy are nullified. Lucas concludes that government policy should follow strict guidelines, since discretionary policy has no effect.

Needless to say, these ideas raised controversy, and Lucas was initially considered to be on the fringe of economic thought. However, as more economists have introduced rational expectations theory into their analysis, the method has become generally accepted, even if Lucas's conclusions have not.

Lucas earned his Ph.D. in economics in 1964 from the University of Chicago. There he received training in Keynesian analysis. By the late 1960s Keynesian economists were struggling to develop policies to reduce unemployment, and Lucas was disillusioned with their view of the economy. He wrote *Econometric Testing of the Natural Rate Hypothesis,* which was published in 1972 and is considered a landmark piece, and he has written numerous other articles using rational expectations analysis since that time. The work attracted many followers because of the high rates of inflation and unemployment that were occurring simultaneously at that time, for which Keynesian analysis offered no real solution.

If unemployment were higher than its natural rate, there would be downward pressure on the price level. In the graph in Box 7, the initial Phillips curve intersects the horizontal axis at a level of unemployment corresponding to 5 percent. There would be inflation if unemployment were lower than its natural rate of unemployment, and there would be deflation—a drop in the price level—if unemployment were higher than its natural rate. A Phillips curve that intersects the horizontal axis at the natural rate of unemployment represents the curve for an economy in which inflationary expectations are stable and zero inflation is expected at full employment.

Now suppose that expectations of future inflation are revised upward and that, as a result, the aggregate supply curve for the economy shifts to the left. When this occurs, achievement of the natural rate of unemployment is unlikely to be associated with zero inflation. Even if the economy does achieve full employment, inflation will exist as a result of the precautions workers and other input suppliers take in negotiating contracts to increase wages and other input prices. As input prices rise, so do output prices! In effect, according to this theory of macroeconomic equilibrium and inflation, the *anticipation* of inflation actually *causes* inflation. As a result of increased inflationary expectations, the Phillips curve shifts upward, as shown in Box 7.

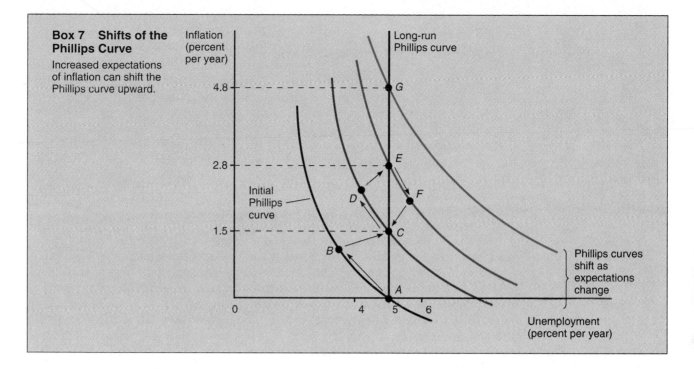

Box 7   Shifts of the Phillips Curve

Increased expectations of inflation can shift the Phillips curve upward.

The idea of a shifting Phillips curve can explain how attempts to reduce unemployment below the natural rate of unemployment can themselves initiate a process of cost-push inflation. The **accelerationist hypothesis** argues that attempts by policymakers to reduce unemployment below the natural rate can succeed only in the short run. The hypothesis maintains that aggregate demand policies seeking to reduce unemployment will have little effect on unemployment in the long run but will contribute to increased inflation. For example, suppose the natural rate of unemployment is 5 percent and policymakers mistakenly believe it is only 4 percent. As a result, they pursue monetary or fiscal policies to reduce the unemployment rate to 4 percent. In doing so, they move along the Phillips curve that intersects the horizontal axis at 5 percent unemployment in Box 7 from point *A* to point *B*. Reducing unemployment to 4 percent opens up an inflationary gap as the economy overheats. Workers find that inflation is greater than expected and that their real wages will decline. According to the accelerationist hypothesis, they will negotiate higher nominal wages in the following year.

The consequent inward shifts in aggregate supply set up a process that results in inflation even if the economy attains full employment. The cost-push inflation induced by inward shifts of the aggregate supply curve moves the Phillips curve upward. Eventually, the economy will eliminate the inflationary gap as real GDP declines and the price level rises, but the upward shift of the Phillips curve means that a higher rate of inflation will be associated with the full-employment level of real GDP. The economy will then be at point *C*. If policymakers then again try to reduce unemployment to 4 percent, the process will begin again as the economy moves to point *D* and then to point *E*, where the natural rate of unemployment is once again achieved. The policymakers will succeed in lowering unemployment below its natural rate only temporarily. If they persist in trying to lower unemployment below its natural rate, they will set up an inflationary process as inflationary expectations are

accelerationist hypothesis the theory arguing that attempts by policymakers to reduce unemployment below the natural rate can succeed only in the short run.

continually revised. Each time the economy reattains long-run equilibrium at the natural rate of unemployment, the inflation rate will accelerate.

It follows that when inflation is expected to increase, the Phillips curve will shift upward. A reduction in inflationary expectations shifts the curve downward. According to the theory of rational expectations, the culprit in shifting the Phillips curve is shifts in aggregate supply. As aggregate supply shifts and affects the price level, people revise their expectations of inflation and negotiate contracts for input services at the beginning of the year based in part on these revised expectations.

The implication of this analysis is that when inflationary expectations increase, the rate of inflation associated with any given rate of unemployment is higher. Policies that increase inflationary expectations can therefore aggravate the trade-off between inflation and unemployment.

The Long-Run Phillips Curve

The Phillips curve can also shift down. For example, suppose the natural rate of unemployment is actually 5 percent and that policymakers mistakenly believe it to be 6 percent. When 5 percent unemployment is achieved, policymakers may mistakenly believe that the economy is overheated and engage in contractionary monetary or fiscal policy. Look back at the curves in Box 7. Suppose the economy is currently at point *E*, at which full employment prevails, and the rate of inflation is 2.8 percent. If the policymakers believe the economy is overheated, they will engage in contractionary policies to increase the actual unemployment rate above the natural rate of unemployment in the short run. The contractionary policies will move the economy from point *E* to point *F*, where the unemployment rate increases to 6 percent. Because the 6 percent unemployment rate exceeds the natural rate of unemployment, there is now a recessionary gap in the economy. The gap puts downward pressure on prices and results in a downward revision of inflationary expectations that causes aggregate supply to increase. The Phillips curve then shifts *down*. Eventually, the economy reaches an equilibrium at point *C*, where the actual unemployment rate is again equal to the natural rate of unemployment.

The economy can be in equilibrium only temporarily at an unemployment rate that exceeds the natural rate of unemployment. Policies that push the actual unemployment rate above the natural rate of unemployment eventually result in reequilibration of the economy at full employment but also reduce the equilibrium inflation rate. Monetary authorities often use this method of *decelerating* the inflation rate. By causing an economic contraction and even a recession (as was done in 1982 by the Fed), monetary authorities can reduce inflationary expectations and shift the economy's Phillips curve down. The cost is a temporary increase in the rate of unemployment rate over the natural rate. The gain is a permanent reduction in the economy's equilibrium inflation rate.

long-run Phillips curve
a curve that shows the unemployment rate that prevails for the economy in the long run.

The economy's **long-run Phillips curve** shows the unemployment rate that prevails for the economy in the long run. It is a vertical line that intersects the horizontal axis of the graph in Box 7 at the natural rate of unemployment. It shows that full employment is consistent with varying rates of inflation, depending on the effect of economic policies on inflationary expectations. Therefore, there is a trade-off between inflation and unemployment in the short run only. In the long run, expansionary or contractionary policies have no effect on the unemployment rate. In the long run, expansionary monetary and fiscal policies increase inflationary expectations and the economy's equilibrium inflation rate. Contractionary monetary and fiscal policies also have no effect on the unemployment rate in the long run, but they decrease inflationary expectations and the economy's equilibrium inflation rate. The long-run Phillips curve is based on the assumption that the economy has a very good self-correcting mechanism. This curve will shift only if the natural rate of unemployment changes.

▪ How are rational expectations formed, and why are they often inaccurate?	▪ How can rational expectations of the effects of stabilization policies prevent those policies from achieving their goals?	**CONCEPT CHECK** ☐
▪ How can expectations of inflation during the year by workers and other input suppliers shift the Phillips curve for the economy?		

ISSUES AND OPTIONS IN STABILIZATION POLICY

Diagnosing the Causes of Cyclical Fluctuations in the Economy: Demand-Side Management

Perhaps the biggest problem faced by policymakers is to distinguish supply-side shocks from demand-side shocks. For example, suppose the natural rate of unemployment increases because more younger workers, who tend to quit jobs more often than older workers, are entering the labor force. Policymakers confuse this with an increase in unemployment caused by a decline in aggregate demand. If they pursue expansionary policies to reduce unemployment, they will be shooting for an impossible goal. Although they may achieve temporary reductions in unemployment, in the long run the price level and inflationary expectations are likely to increase sharply as the economy eventually returns to the higher natural rate of unemployment.

In 1989 many economists believed that the natural rate of unemployment was declining. However, some policymakers at the Fed apparently believed that the economy was overheating and therefore engaged in a contractionary monetary policy. If they had been wrong and the decline in the unemployment rate in 1989 reflected a decline in the natural rate of unemployment, their policy would have induced a recession. The recession would have then resulted in some disinflation as inflationary expectations were revised. The temporary increase in the unemployment rate would have therefore reduced the economy's equilibrium inflation rate, which was then equal to 4.8 percent. Luckily, the Fed's policy worked very nicely in 1989. The unemployment rate remained low and inflation remained steady. By mid-1990, however, unemployment started to increase as the Fed's contractionary monetary policy contributed to the start of a recession.

Development of an active countercyclical stabilization policy requires predicting shifts in consumer demand, investment demand, and money demand. Government spending, tax reductions, or changes in the money supply can be used to offset changes in private demand so as to minimize the amount of time for which equilibrium GDP differs from potential GDP. *The first problem of stabilization policy is therefore to predict changes in aggregate demand.*

To deal with this problem, policymakers typically use economic indicators that show where the economy is headed. The U.S. Department of Commerce publishes an index of leading indicators that is used to gauge the future state of aggregate demand. Included in the index are the number of housing starts, the length of the workweek, stock prices, the money supply, changes in business inventories, and new orders for goods, materials, and investment. The theory is that these variables will begin to turn down before real GDP falls. However, the index is not perfect. It typically declines before a recession, but sometimes no recession follows its decline.

The second problem is to quickly implement policies that counteract changes in private demand. The quick implementation of fiscal policies is particularly difficult to achieve. Government spending and taxes are political issues. Except for the automatic stabilizers, changes in government purchases and net taxes must come through the time-consuming budgetary process of presidential submission, congressional debate, and congressional approval. It often takes bureaucrats time to spend money that has been appropriated. Appropriated funds for particular projects, such as military procurement, are often not spent until the next fiscal year. These lags often result in fiscal policies that accomplish too much too late.

There are also lags in monetary policy, even though monetary policy is generally more flexible than fiscal policy. It takes time to collect data and analyze its implications. When the Fed finally does decide on a countercyclical policy, it takes time for a change in the money supply to change the behavior of consumers and investors.

The third problem is to predict the impact of changes in the money supply or the government deficit on real GDP and the price level. As you've seen in this chapter, changes in aggregate demand caused by economic policies may cause changes in rational expectations of inflation. Therefore, economic policies that affect aggregate demand through shifts in the money supply, government purchases, or net taxes can also shift aggregate supply. This makes it more difficult to predict the ultimate effect of a change in economic policy on real GDP and the price level.

The reaction to stabilization policies is likely to depend on whether the policies are anticipated or unanticipated. The extent to which people plan for the future also influences the effectiveness of such policies. For example, the expansionary effects of increases in budget deficits can be offset if people increase their saving to pay the higher future taxes implied by the increases.

The Stabilization Policy Debate

Critics of stabilization policies argue that although the intentions of such policies are good, the policymakers often make mistakes that end up destabilizing the economy. Among the harshest critics of stabilization policies is Nobel prize–winning economist Milton Friedman.[2]

Friedman argues that in the past policy mistakes have destabilized the economy. He points out that the Great Depression of the 1930s was made more severe by bad policies. In the early 1930s the Fed actually decreased the money supply. This contractionary policy decreased aggregate demand at a time when the economy needed stimulation of aggregate demand. In the late 1930s the Fed increased the reserve requirements of banks, which contracted an economy that needed to expand (see the Principles in Practice and Economic Thinkers boxes in the chapter on stabilizing the economy through monetary policy).

policy rule a preannounced government rule that informs the public of future economic stabilization policies.

Friedman argues that the solution to imperfect stabilization policies is a **policy rule,** a preannounced government rule that informs the public of future economic stabilization policies. The goal of this would be to incorporate stable expectations of government responses to shocks in the economy into the choices of businesses, consumers, and investors. For example, Friedman recommends that the money supply be increased at a steady rate of, say, 3 percent to 5 percent per year. This

---

[2] Milton Friedman, *A Program for Monetary Stability* (New York: Fordham University Press, 1960).

recommendation is based on Friedman's belief that much of the cyclical instability in the economy is caused by sharp swings in the money supply.

Policy rules would be incorporated into the ideas that people use in formulating their expectation. Anticipated policies would therefore affect current decisions. The impact of government policy on private choices would be more predictable under strict policy rules than under erratic policy decisions.

Proponents of flexible stabilization policies counter Friedman by arguing that discretion in adjusting policies, although admittedly not a perfect solution, has stabilized the economy. As evidence, Friedman's opponents point out that because of increased federal government activity to stabilize the economy, economic fluctuations in the United States have been much less severe since the end of World War II than they were during the prior period.

A Comparison of Views: The Classical School, Keynesians, Monetarists, and New Classical Economists

The controversy between the monetarists, the new classical economists, and the Keynesian economists still rages in the field of economics. The Keynesians, whose views on the functioning of the economy are rooted in the theories of John Maynard Keynes, believe that the economy remains unstable and lacks a reliable self-correcting mechanism to cure recessions. They believe the key to keeping the economy at full employment is a countercyclical fiscal policy because in the event of a severe recession the economy would be unresponsive to an expansionary monetary policy and could stagnate at a level of real GDP well below potential real GDP. Modern proponents of the Keynesian theory include James Tobin of Yale University. The monetarists and the new classical economists have more confidence in the ability of the economy to automatically adjust to economic fluctuations without the help of policymakers. Both the monetarists and the new classical economists have much in common with the classical school of thought in macroeconomics. Recall that the classical economists believed the self-correcting mechanism of the economy would restore it to macroeconomic equilibrium at full employment when equilibrium real GDP temporarily fluctuated above or below potential real GDP.

Keynesians have supported incomes policies and wage-price guidelines to control the effects of wage-price spirals. Remember that although Keynes believed that nominal wages and prices were inflexible in the downward direction, they were very flexible and responsive in the upward direction once the economy overheated. To control the pricing process, Keynesians have often advocated direct controls over the price-setting powers of firms.

The monetarists, whose views are represented by Milton Friedman, believe that in the long run the quantity of money is the major influence on aggregate demand. Monetarists believe the economy is basically very stable and its self-correcting mechanism will return it to full employment when a recession hits. They also believe the quantity of money in circulation must be closely monitored to prevent it from growing faster than the long-term growth rate of potential real GDP after adjustment for changes in the velocity of circulation of money. For the reasons discussed above, monetarists favor a policy rule to expand the money supply at a steady and predictable rate each year in order to stabilize both the economy and expectations.

Monetarists believe that fiscal policy has little or no power to stabilize the economy. According to them, the multiplier for fiscal policy is very low because an increase in government purchases causes a nearly equal reduction in private purchases. Monetarists believe investment spending is highly responsive to the real interest rate. When government spending increases, so do the price level and

Box 8   Stabilization Policy: A Summary of the Views of the Major Schools of Thought in Macroeconomics

The Classical Economists

Basic Assumptions

1. The economy is basically stable with equilibrium real GDP equal to potential real GDP on average over the long run.
2. Flexible wages and prices.
3. Say's Law: Supply creates own demand.
4. The quantity theory of money: In the long run, the price level is proportional to the money stock.
5. Households are forward looking.

Adjustment Mechanism for the Economy: Self-Correction

The economy has a self-correction mechanism. When aggregate demand fluctuates so that equilibrium real GDP is less than potential real GDP and unemployment exceeds that natural rate of unemployment there would be downward pressure on wages and prices. As nominal wages fall, the aggregate supply curve shifts out until macroeconomic equilibrium is reattained at full employment. The process is reversed when aggregate demand increases so as to overheat the economy. In an overheated economy, nominal wages would rise until equilibrium real GDP fell to potential real GDP and the price level rose.

Policy Implications

1. Because the economy is viewed as having a good self-correction mechanism through flexibility of nominal wages and other prices, there is no need for discretionary changes in monetary and fiscal policy to adjust for shifts in aggregate demand that temporarily cause equilibrium real GDP to vary from potential real GDP.
2. Monetary policy should limit the rate of growth of the money stock to the rate of growth of potential real GDP. If the money stock were to grow faster than the rate of growth of real GDP there would be inflation. Inflation is caused only by excessive growth in the money stock.
3. It makes no difference how government purchases are financed: tax finance and deficit finance are equivalent and an increase in the deficit has no effect on real interest rates or capital accumulation (Ricardian equivalence).
4. Fiscal policy cannot increase real GDP in the long run—it merely changes the mix of government and private purchases.

The Keynesians

Basic Assumptions

1. Nominal wages and other prices are inflexible in the downward direction.
2. The economy is unstable subject to unpredictable shifts in aggregate demand.
3. In a deep recession, real interest rates are unresponsive to changes in money supply because increases in the money stock or excess reserves will be held rather than used to make loans when the risk of business failure and default on bonds is great. Changes in the real interest rate do not increase investment in deep recession because there is little demand for new capital and much of the existing stock of capital is idle.
4. There is a large multiplier effect for changes in government spending and changes in tax rates.

Adjustment Mechanism for the Economy: Discretionary Manipulation of Aggregate Demand

The economy is prone to periodic recessions from declines in aggregate demand. Once a macroeconomic equilibrium at a level of real GDP below potential real GDP is achieved, the economy will stagnate in equilibrium there unless expansionary fiscal policy is used to increase aggregate demand. Inflation can be kept under control with either a contractionary fiscal or monetary policy.

Policy Implications

1. Fiscal policy should be used to manage aggregate demand.
2. Monetary policy is useful in the long run to keep inflation under control; however, in a deep recession, monetary policy becomes useless because increases in the money stock do not lower interest rates and do not increase investment.

The Monetarists

Basic Assumptions

1. The velocity of circulation of money is reasonably stable or varies in a predictable manner. This implies that the quantity of money demanded is not very responsive to changes in interest rates.
2. Investment purchases are sensitive to changes in the real interest rate in the short run.
3. The economy can be unstable in the short run but in the long run tends to achieve potential real GDP through its own self-correction mechanism.
4. Short-run effects of monetary policy operate through changes in real interest rates but the long-run effects operate through changes in the money stock.
5. Inflation is a monetary phenomenon and is caused by excessive monetary growth relative to the growth in potential real GDP and money demand.
6. Nominal GDP depends on the money stock after adjustment for any possible changes in velocity.

Adjustment Mechanism for the Economy: Self-Correction in the Short Run, Control of the Money Stock to Maintain Price Attainability, and Economic Growth in the Long Run

Economy has a good self-correction mechanism in the long run but can be unstable in the short run. Discretionary stablization policies are more likely to cause recessions and inflation than are policies that provide clear and predictable rules for monetary growth and fiscal policy.

Policy Implications

1. Fiscal policy primarily affects the mix between private and government use of resources and expansionary fiscal policy can lead to inflation when accommodated by monetary authorities with increased money growth.
2. High marginal tax rates can reduce potential real GDP by harming incentives to work and save.
3. The growth of the stock of money is the most important influence on nominal GDP in the long run.
4. To stabilize the economy, policies should be based on clear and credible rules that will reduce uncertainty in the economy.
5. The rate of growth of the money stock over the long run should equal the rate of growth of potential real GDP after adjustment for possible shifts in the velocity of circulation of money.
6. Long-term growth in potential real GDP should be encouraged by keeping marginal tax rates low and controlling the rate of growth of government programs that decrease incentives to work and save.

The New Classical Economists: Rational Expectationists and Supply-Siders

Basic Assumptions

1. Rational expectations: Households and businesses make forecasts about the future and the effects of changes in economic policies based on the information available to them and some basic idea about how the economy operates.
2. Aggregate supply is responsive to changes in expectations about inflation.
3. Changes in stabilization policy are anticipated by households and businesses who respond by adjusting their expectations of inflation.
4. Incentives to produce, work, and save are affected by government policies that influence marginal tax rates and subsidize households and businesses.

Adjustment Mechanism for the Economy: Self-Correction

Self-correction based on shifts in aggregate supply caused by changes in expectations of inflation. Once potential real GDP is attained it can be maintained but the price level can be affected by economic policies that shift aggregate demand.

Policy Implications

1. Expansionary policies tend to raise the price level.
2. Attempts by stabilization to expand the economy beyond potential real GDP will raise inflationary expectations, the price level, and nominal interest rates.
3. Fiscal policy will mainly affect the mix between private and government use of resources in the short run.
4. In the long run, high marginal tax rates and government policies that adversely affect incentive to work will lower the rate of growth of potential real GDP.
5. Fiscal policies that encourage saving and work effort can improve future living standards.
6. Clear and credible policies that keep monetary growth close to the rate of growth of potential real GDP can prevent inflation.

nominal interest rates as aggregate demand increases. As real interest rates increase, there is a large reduction in investment purchases. In effect, monetarists believe that both real interest rates and private purchases are highly responsive to changes in government spending or a reduction in tax rates, rendering fiscal policy very ineffective. The views of the monetarists contrast sharply with those of the Keynesians when it comes to prescribing a remedy for a recession. Monetarists argue that an expansionary fiscal policy is ineffective in pulling the economy out of a recession.

Monetarists believe the prime objective of monetary policy is to provide a stable and credible economic environment to foster the growth of the economy. This means making sure that the supply of money and credit grows sufficiently to allow actual real GDP to remain fairly close to potential real GDP. At the same time, monetarists argue that great care must be taken to keep the growth rate of the money stock from becoming greater than the growth rate of potential real GDP after adjusting for changes in the demand for money (and therefore the velocity of its circulation).

Monetarists argue that inflation is primarily a monetary phenomenon—that the only way to keep inflation from getting out of hand is to control the growth of the money stock. They believe that incomes policies and wage-price controls merely distort the operation of markets and lead to an inefficient allocation of resources without getting at the underlying cause of inflation—excessive growth of the money stock.

Finally, the new classical economists, such as Robert Lucas, attach great importance to the role of expectations in influencing macroeconomic equilibrium. Their views have been discussed at length in this chapter. Economists like Lucas have views similar to the classical economists and the monetarists in the sense that they believe the economy is inherently stable and has a reliable self-correcting mechanism. In many ways the views of the new classical economists are similar to the monetarists. The new classical economists believe that policies designed to stabilize the economy often end up destabilizing it. They believe that expansionary fiscal policy is powerless to increase real GDP in the long run because it tends to increase inflationary expectations. The higher inflation expectations induce shifts in aggregate supply that cause real GDP to fall and the price level to rise. Many of the new classical economists propose clear and well-announced policy rules to stabilize the economy and support supply-side policies designed to increase the growth rate of potential real GDP. These economists believe that credible and predictable policies reduce economic uncertainty and promote efficient use of resources.

There is much to be learned from the insights of all the major schools of macroeconomic thought, and each of these schools has contributed to our understanding of the way the economy works. A large majority of economists now believe that both monetary and fiscal policies have powerful effects on the economy, that stabilization policies are likely to affect interest rates and foreign exchange rates and to influence the incentives of both households and businesses to make purchases, and that policies encouraging the long-term growth of potential real GDP are likely to raise the future living standards of households.

Economic advisers to Presidents Reagan and Bush in the 1980s and early 1990s advocated that fiscal and monetary policies have clearly stated and credible long-term goals. A major stated goal of fiscal policy in the 1990s has been the elimination of the chronic federal budget deficits that have been the rule since 1970. Keeping the inflation rate within reasonable bounds has been a major goal of monetary policy. There is a strong consensus that stabilization policies should promote noninflationary economic growth even though there are honest differences of opinion about how to achieve that goal.

Box 8 provides a convenient summary of the major schools of thought in the field of macroeconomics. It presents the ideas of the classical economists first as a benchmark to compare the ideas of the Keynesians, the monetarists, and the new classical economists.

SUMMARY

1. The Phillips curve shows a hypothesized inverse relationship between annual unemployment and annual inflation in a nation. The Phillips curve is based on the assumption that shifts in aggregate demand are mainly responsible for changes in equilibrium real GDP and the price level.

2. When the economy's aggregate supply curve shifts inward, the resulting stagflation causes both unemployment and inflation to increase during the year. The stagflation of the 1970s meant that the data on inflation and unemployment for those years poorly fit the relationship implied by the Phillips curve.

3. The process of disinflation in the United States in the early 1980s showed that the Phillips curve relationship remains relevant. During that period the inflation rate was reduced at the expense of sharp increases in the unemployment rate.

4. Expectations of future changes in the economy are important influences on the current decisions of business firms and households.

5. Adaptive expectations are those in which people look at the past performance of an economic variable to be forecast. Under adaptive expectations, people who overestimate the inflation rate in the current year will lower their estimate of the inflation rate in the following year.

6. Rational expectations differ from adaptive expectations in that they are based on more information and on an idea about the process through which prices are determined in the economy. Although rational expec-

tations are not always correct, they differ from actual magnitudes only by random amounts.

7. A change in rational expectations of future inflation can shift the Phillips curve because it results in a shift of the economy's aggregate supply curve. Expectations of increased inflation result in decreases in labor supply that put upward pressure on nominal wages. This tends to increase the inflation rate for each possible level of real GDP and unemployment during a given year.

8. Rational expectations of the effects of economic policies that seek to shift aggregate demand can frustrate the goals of those policies by causing simultaneous shifts in aggregate supply.

9. If stabilization policies are to achieve their objectives, they must be based on accurate forecasts of shifts in aggregate demand. Such policies must be quickly implemented to offset destabilizing shifts in aggregate demand.

10. Critics of stabilization policies argue that although the intentions of the policymakers are good, the policymakers often make mistakes that end up destabilizing the economy.

11. A policy rule is a preannounced government rule that informs the public of future economic stabilization policies. The use of a policy rule would enable the public to fully anticipate such policies and thus could avoid destabilizing shifts in expectations that cause the aggregate supply curve to shift.

KEY TERMS

Phillips curve *438*

disinflation *441*

rational expectations *443*

accelerationist hypothesis *447*

long-run Phillips curve *448*

policy rule *450*

CONCEPT REVIEW

1 What is a Phillips curve?

2 Explain how supply-side shocks affect the trade-off between unemployment and inflation and what implications such shocks have for the Phillips curve.

3 How do changes in rational expectations of inflation affect the aggregate supply curve?

4 Discuss the controversies regarding stabilization policy.

PROBLEMS AND APPLICATIONS

1. An economy is currently operating at 6 percent unemployment. An increase in aggregate demand during the year is anticipated, while the economy's aggregate supply curve is expected to be stable. Why is the Phillips curve for this economy likely to be downward sloping for the year? **[1]**

2. Under what circumstances does the relationship implied by the Phillips curve suggest that the price level will fall when unemployment increases? **[1]**

3. Suppose the annual rate of inflation is 15 percent and the unemployment rate is 4 percent. Monetary authorities decide to sharply cut back the growth rate of the money supply during the year and possibly to even reduce the available money stock. Assuming that the policies of the monetary authorities are not anticipated by the public, show how the resulting process of disinflation will affect the economy. Draw the likely Phillips curve for the economy. **[2]**, **[3]**

4. Show how an increase in expected inflation by workers who rationally expect a sharp increase in aggregate demand during the year can shift the aggregate supply curve. Explain why the theory of rational expectations implies a self-correcting mechanism for the economy similar to that implied by the classical model of macroeconomic equilibrium. **[2]**, **[3]**

5. How do expectations of future prices affect economic decisions? Think about how your expectations of future changes in the economy affect your own choices. After completing your economics course, how will you form your own expectations of the future? How do rational expectations differ from adaptive expectations? **[3]**

6. Why are rational expectations often different from actual outcomes? **[3]**

7. During the year, sharp increases in food and housing prices result in decreases in the supply of agricultural products and lumber. The price increases reduce the real wages of workers. Show how rational expectations of further inflation can shift the Phillips curve for the economy upward. **[2]**, **[3]**

8. What can shift the Phillips curve for the economy downward? **[2]**

9. Explain how increases in the money supply could start a wage-price spiral even though the economy is not at full employment. **[2]**, **[3]**

10. Outline some of the difficulties involved in choosing and implementing a successful stabilization policy for the economy. Why do critics of stabilization policies favor a strict policy rule? **[4]**

part VII

International Economic Issues

CONCEPTS

Absolute and Comparative Advantage

Real Terms of Trade

Consumption Possibilities Curve

Tariffs and Import Quotas

Less Developed Country

Socialism and the Centrally Planned Command Economy

Foreign Exchange Rates and Markets

Currency Appreciation and Depreciation

International Balance of Payments

Economic Systems

Diego Rivera, *Dream of a Sunday Afternoon in the Alameda*, detail, 1947–48. Alameda, Mexico/Art Resource, NY

20 chapter

International Trade and Economic Development

If you are like most Americans, you enjoy the benefits of consuming products that cannot be easily produced in the United States, such as bananas and other tropical fruits. You may also own an automobile, a VCR, or a compact disc player produced abroad. International trade not only permits you to obtain products unavailable domestically, it also permits you to purchase some items at lower prices than would be possible otherwise. The modern global economy requires that domestic businesses compete in international markets. To compete effectively in the global economy, U.S. businesses often must stay on the cutting edge of technology to allow productivity to grow and keep costs down.

In this chapter we will examine the process of international trade and show how mutual gains are possible to trading partners. You will see how international trade contributes to your well-being by allowing an international division of labor and specialized production. We will also explain why some groups seek protection against foreign competition, and examine who gains and who loses as a result of tariffs and import quotas to restrict international trade.

We will also broaden our international perspective on economic issues by examining the process of economic development. To do so, we will first discuss some ideas of the classical economists and Karl Marx on the industrialization process. We will analyze alternative economic systems, including socialism and centrally planned economies. We will examine how former communist nations are now struggling to improve their living standards through a painful process of transition from central planning to private enterprise and free markets. Finally, we will discuss some unique economic problems of less developed nations whose citizens have very low incomes, as well as ways of speeding economic development in those nations.

☐ CONCEPT PREVIEW

After reading this chapter, you should be able to:

1. Understand the underlying basis for international trade, the principle of comparative advantage, and the gains in well-being possible from free trade with foreign nations.

2. Show how productivity changes in specific industries can affect their comparative advantage in international trade.

3. Discuss protectionism and analyze the impact on the economy of tariffs, import quotas, and other trade restrictions.

4. Understand the ideas of the classical economists and Karl Marx on economic development and how those ideas gave rise to centrally planned economies whose systems are now being restructured.

5. Discuss some unique economic problems of less developed nations and the causes of low per capita income and slow economic growth in those nations.

INTERNATIONAL TRADE

In 1992, the total dollar value of U.S. merchandise exports amounted to over $400 billion. Exports helped drive the U.S. economy toward full employment in the late 1980s and provided a livelihood for hundreds of thousands of workers. In 1991 the United States imported nearly $500 billion of merchandise from foreign lands, allowing U.S. businesses and households to enjoy and use materials, supplies, and goods produced abroad. As you will see, international trade is a two-way street—not only because it involves exchanges of goods among nations but also because it allows mutual gains to the trading partners.

The Basis for International Trade

One basis for international trade is that through international trade goods can be obtained that are unavailable or too costly to produce domestically. Another basis for international trade lies in the fact that both human and natural resources vary among nations. For example, the Swiss are noted for their traditional skills in making watches and producing fine chocolate candies. The Italians have long been known for the high quality of their leather goods. The United States is well endowed with timber and coal.

Early in this book we discussed the advantages of specialization and the division of labor. Specialization is the use of labor and other resources in a nation to produce the goods and services for which those resources are best suited. Many Japanese workers specialize in the production of automobiles and electronic goods, while many U.S. workers excel in the production of aircraft. The larger output possible from specialization often results in economies of scale that lower production costs still further. International trade is firmly rooted in the gains that are possible from specialization as well as the gains that can be obtained by acquiring locally unavailable natural resources.

specialization the use of labor and other resources in a nation to produce the goods and services for which those resources are best adapted.

When nations specialize in the production of certain items, their output of those items exceeds the amounts demanded in domestic markets at current prices. The firms can then sell the surplus goods in foreign markets. The foreign currency obtained from these export sales can be used to buy the products of other nations. For example, Italy specializes in the production of wine. By exporting wine, it can gain foreign currency to purchase petroleum products, which it requires as an input into production but does not produce domestically in sufficient quantities. Similarly, the United States specializes in the production of wheat, which it exports to Italy in exchange for Italian lire that can be used to purchase Italian wines. China and Russia have sought to encourage tourism as a means of earning foreign currency to purchase goods offered for sale by Western nations.

We Americans are fortunate in that we live in a nation well endowed with both natural resources and a skilled labor force. Our nation's vast and diverse productive capacity means we are less dependent on international trade for such basic resources as fuel, food, and fiber than are other nations. Such nations as Japan and Israel rely heavily on imports of basic natural resources. These nations are under pressure to export goods and services to earn the foreign exchange necessary to finance such imports.

International trade is often opposed by groups that seek to insulate themselves from what they regard as unfair foreign competition. Many people argue that foreign competition is unfair because cheap foreign goods are produced with cheap labor and are heavily subsidized by foreign governments that are under pressure to earn dollars from international trade. Although there are long-run mutual gains from international

principles in practice

U.S. Trade

What We Export and Import In 1991 the United States exported $422 billion worth of products and imported $488 billion worth of products. The pie charts give information on the broad distribution of U.S. merchandise imports and exports in 1991. Major U.S. exports include machinery, transport equipment, chemicals, and other items purchased as intermediate products or investment goods by foreigners. In 1991, 9 percent of U.S. exports consisted of agricultural products. The top manufactured export of the U.S. economy in 1991 was aircraft, which accounted for $35 billion, or 7 percent, of the nation's export revenue that year. Computer equipment generated another $16 billion of export revenue. Other major U.S. exports in 1991 were valves, motor cars, and

motor vehicle parts. The value of U.S. food and live animal exports was $30 billion in 1991. The large volume of these products suggests that U.S. businesses enjoy a comparative advantage with regard to them.

In 1991, nearly 10 percent of the value of U.S. imports was accounted for by purchases of foreign motor cars and other vehicles. In that year, over $45 billion worth of foreign vehicles was exported to the United States. In 1991 crude oil and other petroleum products accounted for about 7 percent of the value of U.S. imports. Other major U.S. imports in 1991 included computers, automotive parts, telecommunication equipment, footwear, and apparel.

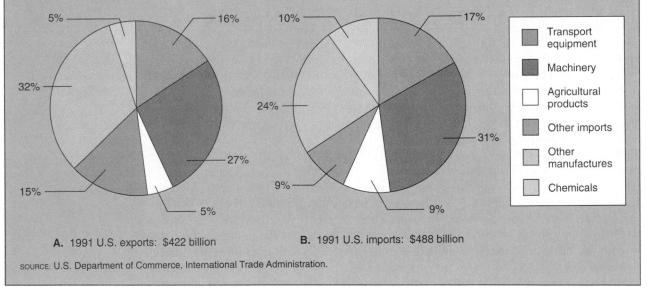

A. 1991 U.S. exports: $422 billion

B. 1991 U.S. imports: $488 billion

Legend:
- Transport equipment
- Machinery
- Agricultural products
- Other imports
- Other manufactures
- Chemicals

SOURCE: U.S. Department of Commerce, International Trade Administration.

---

trade, it's clear that in the short run particular groups, such as workers with specialized skills or owners of specialized equipment, can be harmed by increased imports.

The Principle of Comparative Advantage

mutual gains from international trade on average, citizens in all trading nations gain from exchanging goods in international markets.

There are **mutual gains from international trade,** which means that, on average, citizens in all trading nations gain from exchanging goods in international markets. A simplified example can be used to illustrate the underlying basis for international trade. Suppose two nations both have the capability of producing bananas and wheat. Both nations have the same quantity of natural resources, labor, and capital. The table in Box 1 shows the production possibilities in the two nations when they devote all of their resources to producing either bananas or wheat.

Nation A can produce 20 tons of wheat *or* 20 tons of bananas per year if it specializes in one item or the other. Nation B can produce 5 tons of wheat *or* 10 tons

---

Box 1   Production Possibilities for Two Nations

Nation A (annual output)	Nation B (annual output)
20 tons of wheat and no bananas or 20 tons of bananas and no wheat	5 tons of wheat and no bananas or 10 tons of bananas and no wheat

Oppportunity cost	Nation A	Nation B
Each ton of wheat costs	1 ton of bananas	2 tons of bananas
Each ton of bananas costs	1 ton of wheat	0.5 ton of wheat

---

of bananas per year by specializing in one item or the other. Notice that with the same resources nation A can produce more wheat when it specializes in that good than can nation B. Similarly, nation A can produce more bananas when it specializes in production of that item than can nation B. With the same resources nation A can therefore produce more than nation B no matter how it specializes.

A nation has an absolute advantage over other nations in the production of an item if it can produce more of the item over a certain period with a *given* amount of resources than the other nations can. Nation A has an absolute advantage in the production of wheat over nation B in this example because, with the same resources, nation A can produce more wheat by specializing in wheat production than can nation B. In this example nation A *also* has the absolute advantage in the production of bananas because with the same resources as are available in nation B, it can produce more bananas than can nation B.

Another way of interpreting nation A's absolute advantage over nation B in both wheat and banana production is to point out that in nation A each unit of either wheat or bananas can be produced with less input than is needed to produce it in nation B. For example, suppose that the only inputs used to produce wheat are land and labor. Suppose both nation A and nation B have 2,000 labor hours available per year and the same amount of land. When nation A specializes in wheat production, it can produce 20 tons per year with its 2,000 labor hours. The *labor cost* per ton will be

$$\frac{2{,}000 \text{ labor hours}}{20 \text{ tons}} = \frac{100 \text{ labor hours}}{\text{per ton of wheat}}$$

The labor cost per ton of wheat in nation B when nation B specializes in wheat production will be

$$\frac{2{,}000 \text{ labor hours}}{5 \text{ tons}} = \frac{400 \text{ labor hours}}{\text{per ton of wheat}}$$

Given the same quantity of land in both nations, wheat is four times as expensive in terms of labor required per ton in nation B as it is in nation A.

Similarly, just by looking at labor cost, you can see that nation A's absolute advantage over nation B in banana production means it can produce bananas with fewer labor hours per ton than can nation B. The labor cost per ton of bananas in nation A is

$$\frac{2{,}000 \text{ labor hours}}{20 \text{ tons}} = \frac{100 \text{ labor hours}}{\text{per ton of bananas}}$$

absolute advantage the advantage a nation has over other nations in the production of an item if it can produce more of the item over a certain period with a given amount of resources than the other nations can.

In nation B the labor cost per ton of bananas is

$$\frac{2{,}000 \text{ labor hours}}{10 \text{ tons}} = \frac{200 \text{ labor hours}}{\text{per ton of bananas}}$$

Bananas therefore cost twice as much in terms of labor input per ton in nation B compared to nation A.

We can show that nation A's absolute advantage over nation B in both items means that each ton requires less land in A than it does in B. *In general, when a nation has an absolute advantage, it can produce the specific item with fewer inputs per unit than other nations.*

Despite the fact that nation A has an absolute advantage over nation B, we can easily demonstrate that the citizens of nation A can gain by specializing in one of the goods and then trading with nation B to obtain the other. This remarkable conclusion stems from the fact that the gains possible from trade are determined by the opportunity cost of each unit of one good in terms of the other good rather than by the input cost. To see this, begin by calculating the *opportunity cost per unit* of each of the goods in each nation. To simplify the analysis, suppose that each ton of each good involves the sacrifice of a constant amount of the other good in each nation.

Because nation A can produce either 20 tons of wheat or 20 tons of bananas, it will give up the opportunity to produce 20 tons of bananas if it chooses to specialize in the production of wheat. The *opportunity cost* of each ton of wheat is the sacrifice of the bananas associated with the production of each extra ton of wheat. Assuming constant costs per ton of wheat, the opportunity cost of each ton of wheat in nation A is 1 ton of bananas.

A similar calculation can be performed for nation B. Because nation B can produce either 5 tons of wheat or 10 tons of bananas, it follows that it gives up 2 tons of bananas for each extra ton of wheat, assuming constant costs. The opportunity cost of producing a ton of wheat is therefore 2 tons of bananas for nation B.

The opportunity cost of bananas for each of the two nations is calculated in the same way. The table in Box 1 shows that the opportunity cost of bananas is 1 ton of wheat in nation A and $\frac{1}{2}$ ton of wheat in nation B, assuming constant costs.

The graphs in Box 2 show the production possibilities curves for these two goods in each of the two nations. The curves have been drawn under the assumption that in each nation there is a constant rate at which bananas are sacrificed for more wheat as resources are allocated from banana production to wheat production. This implies *constant opportunity costs per unit,* meaning that the opportunity cost of each unit of one of the goods in terms of the other is constant, as was assumed in the calculation of Box 1. The main point of the analysis also holds for the case of increasing costs, but the argument for that case is considerably more complicated. Note that the slope of each production possibilities curve represents the opportunity cost of bananas in terms of wheat multiplied by -1. The slope of the production possibilities curve for nation A is -1, which means each extra ton of bananas produced per year involves the sacrifice of 1 ton of wheat per year. The slope of the production possibilities curve for nation B is -0.5, which means each extra ton of bananas produced per year involves the sacrifice of $\frac{1}{2}$ ton of wheat per year.

comparative advantage
the advantage that a nation has over a trading partner in the production of an item if it produces that item at lower opportunity cost per unit than its partner does.

A nation has a comparative advantage over a trading partner in the production of an item if it produces that item at lower opportunity cost per unit than its partner does. The gains possible from international trade stem from the decrease in opportunity cost per unit of output that is possible when nations specialize in goods in whose production they enjoy a comparative advantage. By specializing, a nation uses its resources to produce items for which it enjoys a comparative advantage. It

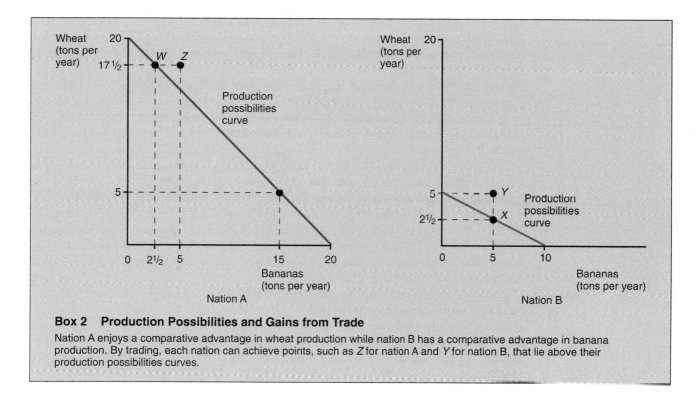

Box 2   Production Possibilities and Gains from Trade

Nation A enjoys a comparative advantage in wheat production while nation B has a comparative advantage in banana production. By trading, each nation can achieve points, such as Z for nation A and Y for nation B, that lie above their production possibilities curves.

then exports some of its annual output in exchange for other goods that can be obtained at lower opportunity costs per unit when they are produced by other nations.

Despite its absolute advantage in both goods, nation A is *relatively more efficient in the production of wheat only compared to nation B*. Nation A gives up only 1 ton of bananas for each ton of wheat, while nation B must give up 2 tons of bananas for each ton of wheat. Nation A, however, is *relatively less efficient in the production of bananas compared to nation B* because it must give up a ton of wheat for each ton of bananas if it produces bananas, while nation B has to give up only $\frac{1}{2}$ ton of wheat.

Gains from Specialization and Trade

It's easy to show how both nation A and nation B can gain from specializing in the good for which they enjoy a comparative advantage and then trading to enjoy other goods. Suppose nation B uses all of its resources to produce bananas in a given year. By doing so, it will produce 10 tons of bananas per year. Now suppose it offers 5 tons of its production to nation A. What is the maximum amount of wheat that nation A will trade for the 5 tons of bananas? It would cost nation A 5 tons of wheat to produce 5 tons of bananas. If the traders of nation B were skillful enough to extract a bargain like that, they would have 5 tons of bananas to enjoy and 5 tons of wheat. If nation B produced 5 tons of bananas and engaged in no trade, the best it could do, given its production possibilities curve, would be to enjoy $2\frac{1}{2}$ tons of wheat. This would correspond to point X on its production possibilities curve in Box 2. By specializing in banana production and trading with nation A, the traders of nation B can enjoy as much as 5 tons of wheat! International trade therefore gives a nation's citizens the potential to achieve points that lie above their production possibilities curve, such as point Y in Box 2. Of course, the citizens of nation B would be able to achieve this as long a they received anything more than 2½ tons of wheat for their 5 tons of bananas. If nation A were to trade anything less than 5 tons of wheat for the 5 tons of bananas offered by nation B, the citizens of nation A would also be able to achieve points above their production possibilities curve. *International trade opens up the possibility of gains in world efficiency from resources by allowing mutual gains that would not be possible if each nation attempted to remain self-sufficient.*

It's easy to show how nation A can gain by specializing in wheat. Suppose nation A produced 17½ tons of wheat per year. The graph in Box 2 shows that without trade it could enjoy at most only 2½ tons of bananas per year. However, if nation A specialized in wheat production, it would be able to produce 20 tons per year. It could offer 2½ of these 20 tons to nation B in exchange for bananas. What is the maximum amount of bananas nation B would give up, without being made worse off, to obtain 2½ tons of wheat? Nation B would have to sacrifice as much as 5 tons of bananas to produce that much wheat by itself. This is the maximum amount of bananas it would be willing to exchange for 2½ tons of wheat. If it did give up 5 tons of bananas for 2½ tons of wheat, it would be no worse off. However, if traders for nation A could strike such a clever bargain, nation A would be able to consume 17½ tons of wheat per year and 5 tons of bananas. This would allow nation A to move *beyond* its own production possibilities curve from point *W* to point *Z*. Of course, if nation B gave up anything less than 5 tons of bananas for the wheat, it would gain as well. As you can see, specialization according to comparative advantage allows mutual gains from trade that enable each trading nation to move beyond its own production possibilities curve.

Free international trade allows citizens in trading nations to enjoy consumption possibilities that extend beyond their own production possibilities. Although the simple example we used to illustrate this point is quite abstract, it has great relevance to the world we live in. For example, Japan enjoys a comparative advantage in 35-mm cameras, while the United States enjoys a comparative advantage in aircraft. U.S. workers can gain by specializing in the production of aircraft and other items in which the United States enjoys a comparative advantage. If U.S. aircraft are traded for Japanese cameras, the aggregate output of both these goods can increase. American citizens can enjoy more cameras (because they cost less when purchased from Japan) for any given output of aircraft than would be possible without international trade. At the same time, Japanese citizens can enjoy more aircraft (because they cost less when purchased from the United States) for any given output of cameras.

The Mercantilist Fallacy

International trade benefits all trading nations. What one nation gains in the aggregate from trade is not lost by its trading partner in the aggregate. This point was misunderstood by 17th- and 18th-century advocates of *mercantilism,* a doctrine arguing that nations could increase their power by encouraging exports and discouraging imports. In the 18th and early 19th centuries, gold and silver were used as international currency to settle foreign debts. Nations that consistently ran a balance of trade surplus would require nations with a balance of trade deficit to settle the difference in gold and silver. Nations that exported more than they imported thereby accumulated gold and silver in their national treasuries. The mercantilists mistakenly believed that nations losing gold and silver were made worse off by international trade.

What they didn't understand was that a nation's well-being is not measured by gold, silver, or other commodities in storage. Instead, its well-being depends on the goods and services its citizens can purchase with their available incomes. International trade allows citizens in the aggregate to expand their consumption possibilities beyond their domestic production possibilities. The gains from trade consist of the expansion of consumption possibilities. A nation pursuing policies that encouraged exports but discouraged imports in order to gain gold, silver, or other commodities to hold in storage simply gained purchasing power for the future. If such policies artificially restricted imports, the nation's citizens were deprived of the opportunity to enjoy imported goods that other nations could produce at lower opportunity costs.

Terms of Trade

Trade enables consumers in each nation to gain by obtaining certain goods at lower opportunity cost than would be possible if the goods were domestically produced. To gain from trade, nation B would have to obtain wheat from nation A at any price *below* its opportunity cost of 2 tons of bananas for each ton of wheat. Similarly, to gain from trade, nation A would have to obtain bananas from nation B at a price *below* its opportunity cost of 1 ton of wheat per ton of bananas.

In actuality, prices for goods are determined by world demand and supply. The **real terms of trade** are the actual market exchange rate of one good for another in international trade. Incentive to trade exists if the real terms of trade are below a nation's opportunity cost per unit of producing a good domestically. The greater the difference between the real terms of trade and the nation's opportunity cost of producing each extra unit of the good it wants to import, the more the nation gains from trade. For example, nation B is better off if the terms of trade allow it to get 1 ton of wheat for $1\frac{1}{2}$ tons of bananas than it is if it has to give up 2 tons of bananas for each ton of wheat. However, nation A is better off if the terms of trade are 2 tons instead of $1\frac{1}{2}$ tons of bananas for a ton of wheat. *When the terms of trade for a pair of goods improve for a nation specializing in one of the goods, they deteriorate for its trading partner specializing in the other good.* However, as long as the terms of trade are less than each nation's opportunity cost of producing each unit, *both nations gain from engaging in specialization and trade.*

Suppose the agreed-upon terms of trade are $1\frac{1}{2}$ tons of bananas for each ton of wheat. It's now easy to show how each nation's *consumption possibilities* are extended beyond its *production possibilities* by international exchange of goods at the agreed-upon terms of trade. Note that the agreed-upon terms of trade can also be expressed as $\frac{2}{3}$ ton of wheat for each ton of bananas. For example, if nation A specializes in wheat production and trades its entire annual output of 20 tons of bananas, it will receive 30 tons of bananas in exchange by trading with nation B, which specializes in banana production. By specializing, nation A can consume a maximum of 30 tons of bananas instead of 20 tons. A **consumption possibilities curve** shows the combinations of two goods a nation can consume, given its resources, technology, and international trade. The graph in Box 3 shows nation A's consumption possibilities curve when it can trade wheat at the rate of $\frac{2}{3}$ ton for each ton of bananas. The consumption possibilities curve is not as steep as the production possibilities curve, because less wheat must be given up for each ton of bananas in trade than in production. In fact, as shown in Box 4, at the agreed-upon terms of trade, the cost of a ton of bananas to the residents of nation A has fallen from 1 ton of wheat to $\frac{2}{3}$ ton of wheat. Thus, bananas are a better buy as imports than as domestic products.

The shaded area in the graph in Box 3 represents the combinations of wheat and bananas that nation A can enjoy when trade is possible at the agreed-upon terms but cannot be enjoyed if nation A tries to be self-sufficient in bananas and wheat.

real terms of trade the actual market exchange rate of one good for another in international trade.

consumption possibilities curve a curve showing the combinations of two goods that a nation can consume, given its resources, technology, and international trade.

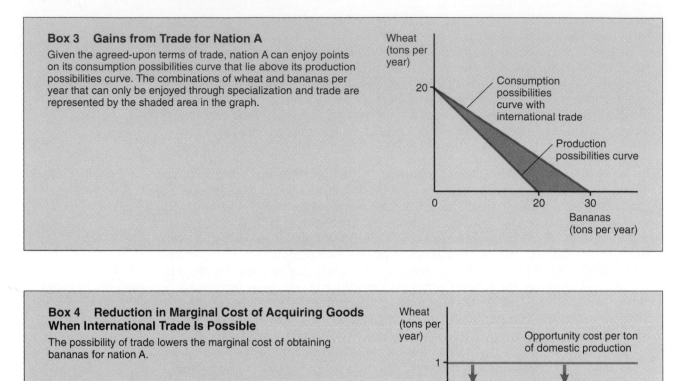

Box 3   Gains from Trade for Nation A

Given the agreed-upon terms of trade, nation A can enjoy points on its consumption possibilities curve that lie above its production possibilities curve. The combinations of wheat and bananas per year that can only be enjoyed through specialization and trade are represented by the shaded area in the graph.

Box 4   Reduction in Marginal Cost of Acquiring Goods When International Trade Is Possible

The possibility of trade lowers the marginal cost of obtaining bananas for nation A.

International trade allows consumers of nation A to consume more of *both* wheat and bananas.

Similarly, the graph in Box 5 shows how trade shifts nation B's consumption possibilities above its production possibilities. For example, by specializing in banana production and selling its entire annual crop of 10 tons on international markets, nation B can consume $6\frac{2}{3}$ tons of wheat per year. If, instead, it allocates all of its own resources to wheat production, the most it can consume is 5 tons of wheat. The slope of nation B's consumption possibilities curve is steeper than the slope of its production possibilities curve because, as shown in Box 6, international trade decreases its opportunity cost of enjoying a ton of wheat from 2 tons of bananas to only $1\frac{1}{2}$ tons of bananas. The shaded area in the graph in Box 5 shows the combinations of wheat and bananas attainable through trade that would not be attainable if nation B attempted to be self-sufficient in wheat and bananas.

As a result of international trade, citizens in both nation A and nation B have the opportunity to enjoy points on their consumption possibilities curves rather than their production possibilities curves. Given their resource availability, citizens in all nations will enjoy more goods and services when they trade. This is not to say that all people will be better off. As you'll see shortly, international trade can make some people worse off, especially in the short run.

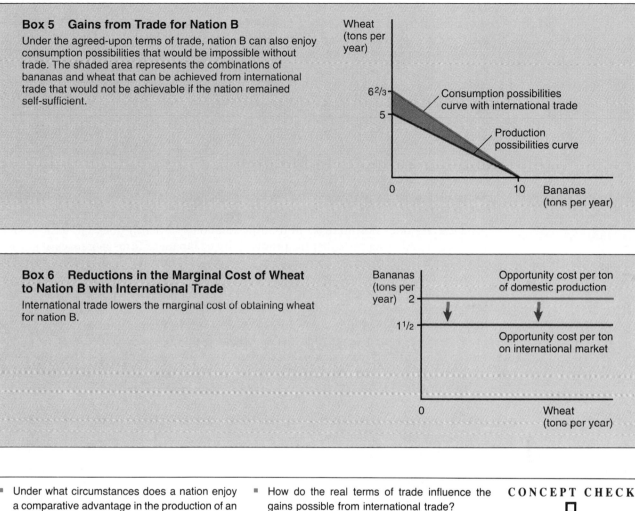

Box 5   Gains from Trade for Nation B

Under the agreed-upon terms of trade, nation B can also enjoy consumption possibilities that would be impossible without trade. The shaded area represents the combinations of bananas and wheat that can be achieved from international trade that would not be achievable if the nation remained self-sufficient.

Box 6   Reductions in the Marginal Cost of Wheat to Nation B with International Trade

International trade lowers the marginal cost of obtaining wheat for nation B.

- Under what circumstances does a nation enjoy a comparative advantage in the production of an item?
- Explain how a nation can have an absolute advantage in auto production yet fail to enjoy a comparative advantage in auto production.

- How do the real terms of trade influence the gains possible from international trade?

CONCEPT CHECK

PRODUCTIVITY AND TRADE

The comparative advantage enjoyed by producers of particular goods in a nation can be eroded over time if their productivity growth lags behind that of competing foreign producers. Throughout the 1970s, large U.S. steel firms operated in aging plants. Their productivity growth lagged behind that of Japanese firms whose plants were more modern. As a result, they failed to compete successfully with Japanese firms in international and domestic markets.

Because productivity increased faster in the Japanese steel industry than in the U.S. steel industry, the opportunity cost of U.S. steel rose relative to the opportunity cost of Japanese steel. U.S. steel became less attractive in international markets because Japanese producers were able to sell steel at prices lower than U.S. producers while still covering their opportunity costs.

How to Lose Comparative Advantage in International Markets

In examining the trade process, it's useful to trace out the implications of lagging productivity growth. We can use the analysis of comparative advantage to show how lagging productivity can affect the competitiveness of the U.S. steel industry compared to that of the Japanese steel industry in international markets.

The graphs in Box 7 show hypothetical production possibilities curves for food and steel in the United States and Japan, assuming constant opportunity costs. The initial production possibilities curve for the United States has a slope of -1, indicating that the opportunity cost of each ton of steel is 1 ton of food. The initial Japanese production possibilities curve has a slope of -2, indicating that the opportunity cost of each ton of steel is 2 tons of food.

Initially, the United States enjoys a comparative advantage in steel production because, measured in terms of food forgone, its opportunity cost of each ton of steel is one half that of Japan. Suppose, however, that, over time in both nations, productivity does not increase in food production but that it does increase in steel production. Also suppose that the productivity of Japanese firms increases at a faster rate than do U.S. firms. The production possibilities curve will swivel outward and become flatter as productivity growth increases. In Box 7 such growth shifts the U.S. production possibilities curve until it intersects the horizontal axis at 12 tons per day. However, steel productivity growth is much more pronounced in Japan, so its production possibilities curve now intersects the horizontal axis at 10 tons per day instead of $2\frac{1}{2}$ tons. Notice that the Japanese production possibilities curve is now flatter than the U.S. production possibilities curve. *The opportunity cost of a ton of steel in Japan has fallen below that in the United States.*

The graphs in Box 8 show that Japan's amazing growth in productivity has reduced the opportunity cost of a ton of steel in that country from 2 tons of food per day to only $\frac{1}{2}$ ton. Meanwhile, the low growth of productivity in the United States has merely reduced the opportunity cost of a ton of steel from 1 ton of food per day to 0.83 ton. *As a result of lagging productivity growth, the United States, in this example, has lost its comparative advantage in steel production.* Japan can now produce steel at a lower opportunity cost than the United States.

This example teaches an important lesson: An industry that lags behind the times in technology or equipment will lose its comparative advantage in international markets. Fortunately, productivity in many U.S. steel mills has improved dramatically since the 1980s. Many U.S. steel producers now appear to be gaining a comparative advantage in steel production. As a consequence, U.S. steel exports and domestic sales have increased in the 1990s.

Implications of Lagging Productivity Growth

Each nation enjoys a comparative advantage in some products relative to its trading partners. Although the lag in productivity growth in the United States in the 1980s contributed to a loss of comparative advantage in some products, the United States retains a comparative advantage in many other products and is gaining a comparative advantage in still other products as the pattern of productivity growth changes. Moreover, the United States is likely to gain a comparative advantage in the new products it develops.

Since 1985 U.S. manufacturers have been closing obsolete plants and applying improved technology and management techniques that promise to result in future productivity gains. Since 1985 productivity growth in U.S. manufacturing has approached 3 percent per year. In addition, U.S. research in new technologies, such as

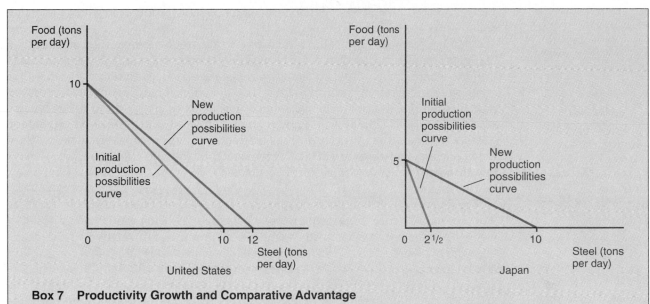

Box 7   Productivity Growth and Comparative Advantage

Faster productivity growth in the steel industry in Japan compared to the United States can result in the loss of the comparative advantage in steel production for U.S. firms.

Box 8   Impact of Differences in Productivity Growth on Comparative Advantage

Increased productivity growth causes the opportunity cost per ton of steel (in terms of food) in Japan to fall below the opportunity cost of steel (in terms of food) in the United States.

superconductivity, may lead to the development of new products in which the nation will enjoy a comparative advantage.

What are the implications for U.S. workers of a loss of comparative advantage in particular export markets? Obviously, workers in such industries as steel and electronics, where comparative advantage has been eroded, will be harmed more than other workers. Keep in mind, however, that all nations enjoy a comparative advantage in some goods. For example, notice that in the example from the preceding section the United States will enjoy a comparative advantage in food production relative to Japan when it loses its comparative advantage in steel production. When the opportunity cost of a ton of steel in terms of food in the United States rises above that in Japan, the opportunity cost of a ton of food in terms of steel must fall below that in Japan.

The impact of this adjustment process, however, is bitter medicine for U.S. workers in industries where comparative advantage is being eroded. As a result of lagging productivity gains, their wages will necessarily fall relative to the wages enjoyed by workers in competing nations. For industries in which comparative advantage has been lost, some workers with specialized skills and other owners of specialized inputs will suffer permanent reductions in income. Some of these workers must find employment in other industries. In recent years the U.S. steel and electronics industries have undergone such disruptions. Similar disruptions have occurred in the textile industry, whose lagging productivity growth has caused the United States to lose comparative advantage in international markets.

A key to keeping productivity growth high is adequate investment in new equipment and plants and the development of new products. Business investment in the United States has lagged in recent years, and many economists believe this is the chief cause of the nation's decline in manufacturing productivity.

We can get a rough idea about the areas in which the United States has a comparative advantage by looking at the balance of trade in recent years. In the 1970s and 1980s the United States consistently exported more chemicals, aircraft, and agricultural products than it imported. During the 1970s and early 1980s the United States was a net exporter of semiconductors, computers, and copiers. By 1983, however, the balance of trade in these areas had shifted, and the United States now imports more of these items than it exports. Thus, we have probably lost our comparative advantage in major portions of the high-tech market. Similarly, in the mid-1970s the United States became a net importer of machine tools, which indicated a loss of comparative advantage for these products.

Throughout the 1970s and 1980s the United States consistently imported more automobiles, consumer electronic products, steel, and textile products than it exported, which suggests that we do not have a comparative advantage in the production of these products.

PROTECTIONISM VERSUS FREE TRADE

3 As noted earlier, declines in a nation's comparative advantage caused by declines in its productivity growth inevitably disrupt particular industries. Workers with specialized skills lose their jobs, and owners of other specialized inputs also suffer reductions in income. Some of these workers and owners seek protection from foreign competition, because their incomes will be higher if they obtain such protection.

Arguments in Favor of Protecting Domestic Industries from Foreign Competition

The arguments in favor of free trade have been covered in the analysis of comparative advantage. Free trade expands a nation's consumption possibilities beyond its production possibilities. It allows higher standards of living by increasing real incomes from available resources. This implies lower prices for goods and services. In this section we look at the arguments *against* free trade and in favor of protecting domestic industries.

1. *National security*. Many people believe that self-sufficiency is necessary for reasons of national security. According to this argument, relatively inefficient domestic industries producing strategically important materials and commodities should not be allowed to go out of business because of foreign competition. A good domestic mix of industries, particularly for food, fiber, steel, and petroleum products, ensures that the United States will not be overly dependent on foreign sources of supply. This will assure stable supplies of these basic goods in the event of an international crisis. The inevitable cost of such protectionism is higher prices for American consumers.

2. *Reducing structural unemployment*. Transaction costs are associated with adjustment to a new industrial mix. For example, you may support protection of the U.S. automobile industry because you think that in the long run the United States will be able to produce cars more cheaply than Japan. When the industry is protected in the short run, structural unemployment is reduced. In the long run consumers won't pay higher prices for cars because a new investment program will result in higher productivity gains and lower prices.

3. *Protecting infant industries*. Protection of a newly established or "infant" industry from foreign competition allows the new industry to expand to the point at which it can enjoy economies of scale. In this case consumers pay higher prices as a result of protection in the short run but hope to enjoy lower prices as the new industry achieves productivity gains in the long run. The problem with this argument is that it's difficult to identify an infant industry that will achieve such gains. In addition, protected infant industries often fail to mature to the point where they can be competitive precisely because of the inimical effects of the absence of competition.

4. *Protecting U.S. industries against subsidized foreign producers*. Some governments subsidize exporting firms to enable them to sell their goods at lower prices in foreign markets. These lower prices are not the result of more efficient production in the exporting country. Because such subsidies cause American industries to go out of business, they give foreign suppliers more control over U.S. market prices in the long run. When a foreign government reduces or eliminates such a subsidy, the price of the imported good rises. Supporters of U.S. protection against such policies argue that there are gains from not letting subsidized goods temporarily disrupt U.S. industries. The chief gain is the reduction in the transaction costs associated with setting up and ceasing operations as foreign subsidies come and go. Another gain is a reduction in the risk that foreign suppliers will acquire monopoly power.

The gains from protecting U.S. industries must always be weighed against the costs to American consumers in terms of higher prices and reduced real incomes. Remember that the gains from international trade are increased consumption possibilities. These gains are mutually enjoyed by all trading partners. The purpose of international trade is not to maximize the differences between exports and imports! Even nations with huge balance of trade deficits, as has been the case for the United States since the 1980s, gain from international trade because such trade expands consumption possibilities. The consumption possibilities gained from international trade raise the standard of living of Americans in the aggregate. Most of the arguments against international trade stem from the *redistribution* of income that results when some firms fail because of foreign competition.

The "Cheap Labor" Fallacy

One common argument in favor of protectionism is that American workers should be insulated against competition from "cheap foreign labor." For example, U.S. textile workers complain that textiles produced in nations using inexpensive labor are sold in the United States for very low prices, thereby reducing sales of domestic textiles. These workers contend that it's unfair for nations that use cheap labor to cause them to lose their jobs. A strong implication of this argument is that foreign firms exploit their workers by underpaying them.

There are a number of weaknesses in this argument. First, foreign workers, particularly in less developed nations, are typically less productive than American workers because they usually work with less capital equipment and less modern technology. These workers are therefore not necessarily "underpaid." Their low wages are attributable to low productivity. Second, the argument ignores the basis for gains from foreign trade, which come from a nation's comparative advantage in producing particular items. The source of that advantage could be relatively abundant labor! An abundant supply of labor capable of producing textiles lowers the cost of producing textiles in terms of other goods. Naturally, an abundant labor supply means cheap labor. The cheap labor argument simply tries to use the reason for a nation's comparative advantage as an excuse not to benefit from that nation's low marginal costs and prices! It sidesteps the main issues involved in the arguments for or against free foreign trade. The basis for gains from international trade is comparative advantage rather than absolute advantage.

Instruments of Protectionism: Tariffs

tariff a tax on imported goods.

Those who favor protecting domestic industries against foreign competition often support a **tariff,** a tax on imported goods, as a means of making imported goods less attractive to domestic consumers. Simple supply and demand analysis shows us how a tariff works.

Assume that in the absence of tariffs imported cars sell at an average price of $10,000 in the United States. At that price 3 million imported cars per year are sold. The graph in Box 9 shows that the initial market equilibrium for foreign cars corresponds to point E_1, at which the demand and initial supply curves for foreign cars intersect. If a tariff is placed on foreign cars sold in the United States, the cost of selling foreign cars in the United States increases. Suppose the tariff is $1,000 per car. The marginal cost of selling an imported car increases from its initial level by $1,000. The supply curve shifts upward by $1,000, reflecting the increase in cost. The new market equilibrium corresponds to point E_2, at which the new supply curve just intersects the demand curve.

The tariff has the following effects on the market for foreign cars:

1. The price of foreign cars increases. In the graph in Box 9, the price goes up from $10,000 to $10,800. The extent of the price increase depends on the price elasticities of demand and supply for foreign cars. Other things being equal, the more inelastic the demand for foreign cars, the greater the price increase.

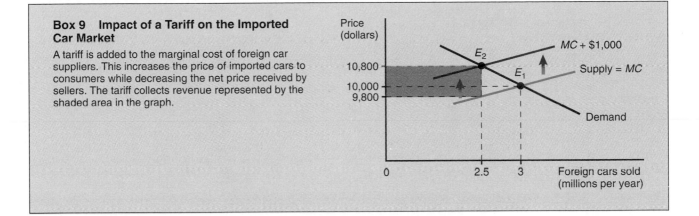

Box 9   Impact of a Tariff on the Imported Car Market

A tariff is added to the marginal cost of foreign car suppliers. This increases the price of imported cars to consumers while decreasing the net price received by sellers. The tariff collects revenue represented by the shaded area in the graph.

2. The price *received* by foreign sellers of cars *declines* from its previous level. In Box 9 the price received by foreign sellers for each car sold is the $10,800 paid by buyers *less* the $1,000 tariff per car. The sellers' net price after payment of the tariff is only $9,800, which is $200 less per car than they enjoyed before the tariff was imposed. Foreign producers therefore don't benefit from the increase in the market price of their cars caused by the tariff. In fact, the profitability of selling cars in the U.S. market declines after the tariff is imposed. The impact of the price decline on foreign sellers depends on the price elasticities of demand and supply for foreign cars. In general, both foreign manufacturers and their U.S. dealers suffer a reduction in income as a result of the tariff.

3. As a result of the price increase, the annual quantity of foreign cars demanded decreases. In Box 9, the annual quantity of foreign cars sold declines from 3 million to 2.5 million cars per year as a result of the tariff. The more elastic the demand for foreign cars, the greater the reduction in annual sales of foreign cars as a result of the tariff.

4. The tariff collects revenue that can be used to reduce reliance on other taxes, to increase government spending, or to reduce federal budget deficits and debt. In this case the annual revenue collected from the tariff is $1,000 multiplied by the 2.5 million cars sold, which is $2.5 billion. Note that the greater the reduction in sales of foreign goods as a result of the tariff, the less revenue the tariff collects. In effect, tariffs that do a good job of protecting domestic producers from foreign competition are poor revenue producers because they cause sharp reductions in imports.

How does a tariff benefit domestic producers? The graph in Box 10 shows the demand for and supply of domestic cars. Assume that before the imposition of the tariff the average price of domestic cars is $10,000 and that domestic cars are perfect substitutes for foreign cars. Of course, this is a simplification because quality differences among different makers of cars often lead buyers to prefer the cars of one producer, foreign or domestic, over those of other producers. Differences in quality allow the prices of various car models to differ. However, the basic impact of a tariff on domestic producers can be shown even though quality differences are ignored.

The increase in the price of foreign cars resulting from a tariff *increases the demand for domestic cars* because domestic cars become a more attractive buy after the tariff has been imposed. However, the increase in demand increases the price of U.S. cars. In fact, if foreign and domestic cars are *perfect* substitutes, the price of U.S. cars must go up to exactly $10,800. In Box 10 the effect of the tariff is to shift

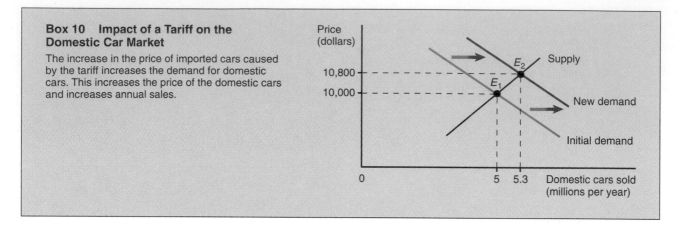

Box 10   Impact of a Tariff on the Domestic Car Market

The increase in the price of imported cars caused by the tariff increases the demand for domestic cars. This increases the price of the domestic cars and increases annual sales.

the market equilibrium for domestic cars from point E_1 to E_2. Annual sales increase from 5 million to 5.3 million cars. The impact of the tariff on the market for domestic cars can be summarized as follows:

1. The price of domestic cars increases, and the annual quantity of domestic cars sold goes up. However, because of the general increase that the tariff causes in the price of cars, there is a decline in the aggregate (foreign plus domestic) annual quantity of cars sold. This makes consumers worse off.

2. In the short run the profits of domestic car manufacturers increase. Workers with specialized skills and owners of specialized inputs also benefit from the tariff as wages and the prices received for specialized inputs increase in response to the increase in demand. In general, prices remain higher than they would have been in the absence of a tariff.

In short, tariffs tend to increase the prices of both domestic and foreign goods. This redistributes income to domestic producers and owners of specialized inputs used in domestic production. A tariff causes foreign producers to suffer a decrease in sales and domestic consumers to suffer a decrease in real income. Government gains the revenue that the tariff collects.

Instruments of Protectionism: Import Quotas

import quota a limit on the quantity of foreign goods that can be sold in a nation's domestic markets.

An **import quota** is a limit on the quantity of foreign goods that can be sold in a nation's domestic markets. *Voluntary export restraints (VERs)* are a way of establishing import quotas through informal negotiation between two governments. In the early 1980s a VER establishing import quotas on Japanese cars was negotiated between the United States and Japan. The import quotas were used from 1981 to 1984 to protect U.S. car producers. There have also been import quotas on certain textiles, and special interests in a variety of industries continually seek to use their political influence to protect their interests with import quotas. Import quotas can protect domestic industries just as tariffs do, but they don't generate revenue that can be used to reduce government reliance on taxes.

Supply and demand analysis can be used to show the impact of import quotas. Suppose, as before, in the absence of restrictions on international trade the price of foreign cars averages $10,000 and 3 million foreign cars per year are sold at that price. The initial equilibrium is at point *E* in the graph in Box 11. Now suppose a strict import quota of 2.5 million foreign cars per year is imposed. No matter what the price of foreign cars or the willingness of foreign producers to sell in domestic

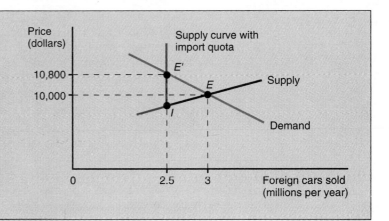

Box 11   Impact of an Import Quota on Foreign Car Sales

An import quota limits the number of new foreign cars that can be sold per year in the United States. This increases the market price of the cars. Sellers of foreign cars lose 500,000 sales per year, but this is offset by a gain in revenue from the higher price. This corresponds to point E', where the demand curve intersects the vertical portion of the supply curve after the quota is imposed.

markets, no more than 2.5 million foreign cars will be permitted to enter U.S. markets each year. In effect, the quota truncates the foreign supply curve at point I, as shown in Box 11, which corresponds to 2.5 million cars per year. The quantity supplied cannot increase beyond the quota limit. The upward-sloping supply curve beyond point I is no longer relevant to the domestic market. Instead, the supply curve is vertical beginning at point I. The supply of foreign cars is therefore perfectly inelastic after 2.5 million cars per year had been imported.

Given the new supply curve, the new market equilibrium corresponds to point E'. At that point the price of foreign cars increases to $10,800 per year. This is the point at which the demand curve intersects the vertical portion of the new supply curve. At that price the quantity demanded falls from 3 million to 2.5 million cars per year. *If the import quota is established at the quantity that results from the $1,000 tariff, the impact of the quota on the price of foreign cars is exactly the same as the impact of the tariff.* An import quota can therefore protect domestic producers in the same way that a tariff can. As a result of the import quota, the demand for domestic cars increases, just as it did with the tariff, as shown in Box 9. Domestic producers gain, and owners of specialized inputs used in domestic production also gain.

However, there are important differences between a tariff and an import quota:

1. Unlike a tariff, an import quota does not raise any revenue for government authorities.

2. An import quota raises the market price paid by consumers of foreign goods but does not reduce the net price received by foreign sellers. Foreign sellers and their U.S. dealers therefore gain revenue as a result of a quota because they receive higher prices per car. However, this gain is offset by the reduction in revenue as sales decline by 500,000 cars per year. If the demand for a foreign good is very inelastic, the increase in revenue from the price increase can offset the decline in revenue from the sales decline. *If the demand for a foreign good is very inelastic, then foreign sellers and their U.S. dealers may actually be better off with a quota than they will be under free trade!*

The Problem of Retaliation

Playing with tariffs is a bit like starting a war. Foreign governments whose citizens are harmed by tariffs or quotas may very well retaliate against the United States by placing tariffs or quotas on U.S. exports to their nations. They may also try to counter the effects of U.S. trade restrictions by subsidizing domestic producers. By reducing the costs of selling in the United States, such subsidies can be effective in increasing supply and thus counteracting the effects of tariffs. However, the subsidies will not have any effect on supply if import quotas are used, because import quotas limit the quantity that can be sold in U.S. markets.

The problem of retaliation must be considered by policymakers when tariffs and import quotas are used. Gains from tariffs and other trade restrictions in some industries may be offset by losses in other industries when foreign governments retaliate.

CONCEPT CHECK
□

- Suppose the domestic shoe industry finds that its sales decline because imported shoes are cheaper. What can the industry do to regain its sales?

- How do tariffs and quotas protect domestic producers?

- How do tariffs, quotas, and other instruments of protectionism affect domestic consumers?

---

 the global economy

Removing Barriers to Free Trade

NAFTA, Regional Trading Blocks, and GATT In 1992 the United States, Canada, and Mexico announced a comprehensive plan to improve freedom of trade across North America. The North American Free Trade Agreement (NAFTA) was lauded by many businesses but viewed skeptically by many labor groups, which feared that it would result in a loss of U.S. jobs. NAFTA was designed to reduce tariffs on thousands of products; open Mexico's banking, insurance, and securities industries to more foreign competition; and create a panel to resolve international environment disputes. It also contained provisions to prevent European companies from bypassing American tariffs by shipping goods through Mexico.

Although the industrial mix of the three parties to NAFTA will change in response to freer trade offered by NAFTA, broad benefits will result from NAFTA through price reductions on many products. Changes in international investment rules will make it easier for U.S. and Canadian firms to set up businesses in Mexico. Such businesses will be subject to environmental protection and rules relating to worker health and safety. Duties on farm products and cars exported from Canada and the United States to Mexico will be phased out. Reductions in U.S. tariffs on apparel are likely to sharply increase U.S. apparel imports from Mexico that will probably displace current apparel imports from the Far East but may also eventually reduce employment in the U.S. apparel industry.

NAFTA, when (or if) approved by Congress, will establish a new world trading bloc. Trading blocs have also been established in Southeast Asia, Northern Europe, and South America. Former communist nations in Eastern Europe and the Balkans have realigned themselves by entering into trade agreements with Western nations. Within free-trade areas such as that established by NAFTA, virtually all barriers to trade among nations are eliminated. A *customs union* such as the European Community (EC), a major trading bloc consisting of 12 European nations, not only eliminates internal barriers to trade among member nations but also establishes common tariffs on imports from nonmember nations. Under NAFTA, foreign sellers could ship their exports to a low tariff member of the pact and then hope that those products could be reshipped—duty free—to another member. NAFTA has rules to limit the incentive for such transshipment of imports. Over time NAFTA is likely to establish common tariffs for such products as computers and to become more like a customs union.

Both regional free-trade pacts and customs unions could become multinational forms of protectionism that confine international trade to insulated blocs and restrict exports from nonmember nations. Some economists fear that regional trading blocs will undermine the broader General Agreement on Trade and Tariffs (GATT), which is designed to promote worldwide trade.

The General Agreement on Trade and Tariffs (GATT) was drafted in Geneva, Switzerland, in 1947 and signed by 23 nations, including the United States. It went into effect in 1948. Since 1948 membership in the GATT system has grown to 96 nations that account for about 80 percent of world trade.

GATT is a uniform system of rules for the conduct of international trade by which all member nations abide. A major function of GATT is trade liberalization, which it accomplishes through periodic negotiations among members to lower tariffs. GATT has sponsored seven "rounds" of tariff reductions. The inaugural round occurred as a result of negotiations in Geneva in 1947. The most recent round, "the Uruguay Round," was launched in 1986. Each round of tariff reductions is accomplished through long and sometimes excruciatingly painful negotiations that address a number of specific areas. As a result of GATT tariff reduction, the average tariff rate on dutiable imports coming into the United States fell from a level of nearly 30 percent just after World War II to a current level of less than 4 percent.

Despite the work of GATT, many barriers to international trade remain. Some observers argue that protectionism may even have increased in the 1970s through nontariff barriers to international trade, which are often hidden from view. Major forms of nontariff barriers to free international trade include:

1. Import quotas and other import policies that restrict free entry of imported goods and services.

2. Standards, testing, labeling, and certification requirements that make it difficult for foreign products to enter foreign markets.

3. "Buy National" government procurement policies that prevent foreign suppliers from bidding for government contracts.

4. Export subsidies. Subsidies that lower the price of a nation's exports, often below unit costs of production, make it difficult for other nations to compete in international markets in which the subsidies prevail. This problem is particularly severe in agricultural markets.

5. Lack of intellectual property protection. Inadequate patent, copyright, and trademark protection in some nations leads to "pirating" of products and ideas without compensation to their creators. Such inadequacy reduces exports of intellectual properties from the nations in which they were created.

6. Services barriers. Such barriers include restrictions on the international flow of data and on international data processing.

7. Investment barriers. These make it difficult for one nation to acquire stocks or build facilities in another nation.

The GATT talks continue, and in 1992 the United States was negotiating to have European subsidies to farm products reduced, to break up European telephone monopolies so as to allow more trade in international telephone services, and to gain more access to financial markets in such nations as Korea, Japan, and India. Perhaps the most difficult stumbling block to GATT trade liberalization in recent years has been the elimination of agricultural subsidies. Heavy agricultural subsidies, such as those often used in Europe, result in large surpluses that are dumped on world markets and push world prices down to artificial levels that distort the allocation of resources and harm low-cost producers. Because of subsidies in developed nations, farmers in less developed nations with a comparative advantage in agricultural production are often harmed because even at their low costs of production they cannot compete with the low prices resulting from subsidies.

Ideally, new regional trade pacts such as NAFTA should not prevent GATT from continuing to improve free trade.

ECONOMIC DEVELOPMENT

4️⃣ As nations develop economically, they generally increase the amount of their industrial and commercial activity and reduce the share of the resources they devote to agriculture. The process of economic development involves the creation of new physical and human capital and increases in the per capita income and productivity of workers. Nations in the initial stages of industrialization typically have to devote much of their labor and other resources to providing food and other basic resources to a population that lives at levels close to bare subsistence. Such nations lack capital, and their work force is typically poorly educated and without skills. The low productivity of workers means they have low incomes. Such nations must often rely on raw materials exports to gain the foreign exchange that will enable them to purchase or create the capital needed to improve their living standards. As we will see, international trade and economic development are closely related. But first let's take a historical view of the process of economic development and how economic theories have influenced the economic systems that nations use to organize their productive resources.

The Ideas of the Classical Economists

The process of economic development has been analyzed extensively by economists over the past 200 years. The classical economists, many of whose ideas are embodied in the work of David Ricardo and Thomas Malthus, painted a bleak picture of the economic development process. Thomas Malthus believed that population would grow faster than the resources needed to provide economic well-being. Ricardo formulated the "iron law of wages," according to which wages would at best rise only temporarily above levels that provided bare subsistence to workers. Drawing on the ideas of Malthus, Ricardo hypothesized that if wages increased above the subsistence level, the improved health of the working class would cause population to increase. This increase would increase the supply of labor, which would put downward pressure on wages until they returned to equilibrium at the subsistence level.

In the early days of industrialization, in the 19th century, the theories of the classical economists appear to have been borne out. Workers in the early capitalist system of Great Britain were often paid wages that barely allowed them to survive. Conditions in factories were abominable, and wages seemed to be in perpetual equilibrium at subsistence levels. Industrialization seemed to involve perpetual conflict between a small class of capitalists who controlled the means of production and masses of workers who lived in conditions of abject poverty. The ideas of the classical economists and the conditions of the workers gave rise to the work of Karl Marx (1818–83) whose classic book *Das Kapital*, first published in 1867, emphasized conflict between economic classes (see Economic Thinkers box) and became the basis for an ideology that still has a profound worldwide influence.

The Ideas of Karl Marx

labor theory of value a principle maintaining that only labor can produce something worth paying for.

surplus value the difference between a worker's subsistence wage and the value of the worker's production over a period.

Much of Marx's work was based on the labor theory of value, which maintained that only labor could produce something worth paying for. Capitalists treated labor like any other commodity and paid wages that just allowed labor to survive. However, because workers produced more than the value of the resources necessary for their survival (the subsistence wage), capitalists were able to lay claim to a surplus value from the labor used in production. Surplus value was defined by Marx as the difference between the worker's subsistence wage and the value of the worker's production over a period. Surplus value was the source of capitalist profit, which, in

Marx's view, was obtained by exploiting workers. Marx regarded capitalists as completely unproductive. He believed that the capital equipment with which they provided their workers merely represented value created by other workers who were exploited by other capitalists. In his analysis, surplus value was represented by the sum of earnings paid out in the form of interest, rent, and profit that were actually generated by the productivity of labor.

Marx argued that the capitalist system he observed in his lifetime would not survive. He believed that increases in demand for goods associated with population growth would encourage capital accumulation but that competition among capitalists would keep profits from increasing. Despite capitalists' attempts to continually exploit workers, Marx believed that profit would decline in the long run as more capital was used in place of labor. (Remember that in Marx's view all profits were derived from the exploitation of workers. Less employment meant less profits.)

Marx viewed capitalists, who owned the factories and other capital equipment, as a class separate and distinct from workers, who owned virtually nothing. He regarded capitalists as parasites who exploited workers by paying them less than the value of their production. He saw capitalists as attempting to increase their profits by investing in better technology and equipment, and he believed that workers would not gain from such capital accumulation because their wages would remain close to the subsistence level. In fact, many would lose their jobs as capital was substituted for labor in production. Marx expected a vast "reserve army of the unemployed" to spring into existence, aggravating the labor supply problem and putting further downward pressure on wages. A deficiency in aggregate demand would eventually result from unemployment, and Marx expected this to cause the collapse of capitalism. As the size of the work force declined because of increased use of capital, a decline in profits would contribute to the collapse of the capitalist system. Eventually, the working class would revolt and establish a system in which capitalists no longer existed and exploitation would cease.

Why Were Marx's Predictions Wrong?

In a nutshell, Marx's predictions about wages proved to be wrong because labor market conditions in most capitalist nations did not develop as he expected. Although competition among firms does tend to push economic profits *in a given industry* down to zero in the long run, new profit opportunities keep arising with changes in demand and technology. Entrepreneurs who respond to changes in supply and demand can earn profits by creating new products and processes. There is still conflict between workers and capitalists, as can be seen by occasional disputes between unions and employers. However, there is no doubt that *both* workers and their employees have gained from the tremendous growth in productivity associated with capital accumulation.

Simple analysis of labor market changes over time will show you why wages have risen well above the subsistence level in most nations. Suppose that wages were close to subsistence at the beginning of the Industrial Revolution. Over time population growth increased the supply of workers, which put downward pressure on wages. However, increased capital accumulation increased the productivity of workers. When productivity increased, employers were willing to pay higher wages because each worker added more to employer revenue. A firm that didn't raise wages when productivity increased was likely to lose workers to competing firms that could pay higher wages and still increase profits by hiring away the first firm's most productive workers. Competition among firms for labor services tended to bid up wages because additional profits could be made by hiring more workers when

economic thinkers

Karl Marx

During his lifetime Karl Marx alienated as many people with his stubbornness and intolerance as he attracted with his brilliance and dynamic personality. His lifelong friend, Friedrich Engels, a fellow revolutionary, was his collaborator, compatriate, and benefactor. Marx was the epitome of the German scholar—meticulous, deep thinking, and a painstaking perfectionist.

In works like the *Communist Manifesto* and *Das Kapital,* Marx advocated defending the oppressed. He forged a concept of class conflict that became the center of his theories of economic and political development. He emphasized the importance of economic conflict as the source of class conflict and social change. According to his theories, the division of society's wealth among economic classes inevitably caused conflict between those classes. Capitalism would destroy itself because of the conflict between workers and capitalists over the division of wealth and income. He worked with revolutionary groups until the end of his life, preparing for the day when capitalism would collapse.

Despite financial assistance from Engels, who led a double life of capitalist and communist revolutionary, Marx and his family lived in extreme poverty in London, where they fled after being expelled from Germany, France, and Belgium. Marx worked on *Das Kapital* day after day at the British Museum and occasionally wrote articles for the New York *Tribune.*

Even though he was never financially rewarded, this driven economist, sociologist, historian, and philosopher changed the history of the world with his views of economic conflict. His ideas spurred social progress in early capitalistic economies and ultimately resulted in drastic changes in the social systems under which much of the world's population lives.

their productivity increased. The resulting increase in demand for workers put upward pressure on wages.

It's apparent that, on average, the increase in the demand for labor outstripped the increase in supply. Population growth in industrial nations turned out to be much slower than many 19th-century economists predicted. The rate of increase in worker productivity was also greater than predicted. As shown in the graphs in Box 12, shifts in the demand for and supply of labor have pushed wages well above subsistence for the average factory worker since the 1850s.

Marx's prediction of a huge reserve army of the unemployed simply didn't materialize. Technological advances increased the incomes of workers in modern capitalist economies and helped provide markets for the goods that these economies produced. Although the business cycle still exists and there are inevitable ups and downs, the lot of workers, on average, has improved vastly since the turn of the century. Of course, labor unions have provided a voice for workers and contributed to higher wages in capitalist systems, but less than 15 percent of the labor force in the United States currently belongs to unions. The main factors keeping wages high are competition among employers for workers and technological change and investment that contribute to increased labor productivity.

Finally, advances in social policy, evidenced by increased government transfer programs and social insurance, have helped alleviate poverty and improve working conditions. Much of the growth of government in the United States, particularly in

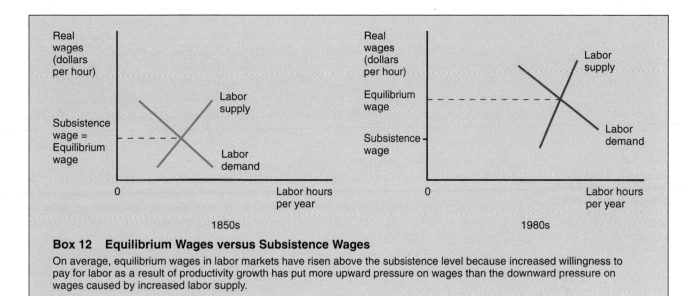

Box 12   Equilibrium Wages versus Subsistence Wages

On average, equilibrium wages in labor markets have risen above the subsistence level because increased willingness to pay for labor as a result of productivity growth has put more upward pressure on wages than the downward pressure on wages caused by increased labor supply.

the 1970s, can be attributed to policies designed to ensure retired workers minimum standards of living through more generous Social Security pensions. Welfare programs provide support for the nonworking poor. Government intervention in the marketplace to pursue social goals and provide services that profit-motivated firms lack the incentive to make available has prevented the social unrest that Marx expected to lead to revolution.

This is not to suggest that the modern mixed economy works perfectly. Poverty and low wages for unskilled workers remain as social problems in the United States. In spite of this nation's many advantages, a distressingly large percentage of the U.S. population is still classified as living in poverty. There is also concern about the monopoly power exercised by firms in certain sectors of the economy. However, the widespread misery and the vast gap between the well-being of the entire class of workers and a small minority of capitalists that were envisioned by Marx have failed to materialize. Extensive social programs administered by governments and improved productivity of workers have lifted average living standards well above the subsistence level for the vast majority of workers.

Socialism versus Capitalism
Although Marx's predictions proved wrong, they spawned change and revolutions throughout the world that eventually resulted in governmental actions in many nations to correct some of the shortcomings of the capitalist system. The threat of revolution and social unrest induced politicians to support social reform. In Germany during the late 1800s the first system of social insurance was enacted with the support of Chancellor Bismarck. Other nations passed legislation to improve working conditions in factories and alleviate poverty.

However, Marxism also resulted in the establishment of ways of organizing economic activity in Russia that evolved into a political and economic system that dominated much of the world in the latter half of the 20th century. The Union of Soviet Socialist Republics came into existence with the Bolshevik Revolution of 1917. Although czarist Russia was less industrialized than such nations as Great

Britain and the United States, industrialization had already begun at the time of the revolution. The communist leadership of the Soviet Union implemented an economic system in which the government owned virtually all of the land and capital and the private pursuit of profit in free markets was shunned. Although the Soviet Union did transform itself into a major economic power, fundamental problems in its system eventually led to its collapse, in 1991. To understand the process of transition that the former Soviet Union and other former communist nations are undergoing, we must first briefly examine how their economic system operated.

Socialism and the Command Economy

An **economic system** is an accepted way of organizing production, establishing rights to ownership and use of productive resources, and governing economic transactions in a society. The evaluation of alternative economic systems is often closely tied to political and moral views. Opinions regarding human rights often influence our ideas about the desirability of one economic system compared to another.

The two basic alternative economic systems are capitalism and socialism. *Capitalism* is generally associated with private ownership of economic resources, free enterprise, and exchange of goods and services in markets. **Socialism** is usually associated with government ownership of productive resources and with central planning to determine prices and resource use.

The system that prevailed in the former Soviet Union and the former communist nations of Eastern Europe was called a **command economy** because under that system central planning authorities determined resource allocation, production goals, and prices. A command economy differs from a market economy in two important ways.

1. *In a command economy the state owns productive resources, including natural resources, land, factories, financial institutions, retail stores, and the bulk of the housing stock.* Government enterprise and government ownership of resources are the rule rather than the exception in a command economy.

An *enterprise* was the basic productive unit in the former Soviet command economy, analogous to a business firm in a capitalist nation. Each enterprise was run by a professional manager, but it had to fill state orders for output handed down to it by an official ministry.

In a command economy, the government and its many enterprises pay wages to their employees, but freedom of choice on jobs and occupations is less extensive than in democratic nations.

2. *In a command economy, authoritarian methods are used to determine resource use and prices.* A **centrally planned economy** is one in which politically appointed committees plan production by setting target outputs for factory and enterprise managers and in general manage the economy to achieve political objectives.

Transition from a Command Economy to a Free-Market Economy

The republics of the former Soviet Union and the formerly communist nations of Eastern Europe are now engaged in a historical transformation of their economies from a system of central planning under socialism to a system of free enterprise in markets. The republics of the former Soviet Union functioned for more than 70 years under a system in which private enterprise and production for profit did not exist in any major form. Throughout much of its history, the government of the former

economic system an accepted way of organizing production, establishing rights to ownership and use of productive resources, and governing economic transactions in a society.

socialism an economic system usually associated with government ownership of productive resources and with central planning to determine prices and resource use.

command economy an economy in which resource allocation decisions are determined largely by the central planning authorities who set production goals.

centrally planned economy an economy in which politically appointed committees plan production and manage the economy to achieve political objectives.

Soviet Union emphasized defense-related production and heavy industry in its central plans.

Although consumer products were often subsidized, so that workers whose low wages were controlled by the state could afford them, supplies of such basics as bread were often inadequate relative to the amounts demanded at the low prices charged for them. The result was ever-present shortages and waiting lists for such key products as cars and apartments. The low prices also led to waste. Farmers often fed the cheap subsidized bread to hogs instead of buying feed grain, because the price of the bread was less than the value of the grain than went into it! The citizens of communist nations on average had lower living standards than the citizens of other industrial nations because relatively few resources were devoted to the production of consumer products. The system also provided little in the way of incentives to economize on the use of resources. Environmental and natural resources were overexploited in the former Soviet Union, and wasteful production methods were the rule rather than the exception. High technology was used in defense but it was rarely applied to consumer-related industries.

When the central planning system collapsed, in the late 1980s and early 1990s in Eastern Europe and in 1991 in the former Soviet Union, the leaders of the former Soviet republics and other former communist nations were faced with an enormous resource reallocation problem. They had to deal with economies in which formerly state-owned factories and farms would eventually be sold (or given away) to private interests (privatized) and operated for a profit. In 1992 the Russian government issued privatization vouchers to all Russian citizens that could be used to buy shares in state-owned factories or sold to others for cash payments. The idea was to allow citizens to obtain means of purchasing some of the state-owned capital. Like citizens in capitalist countries who bought shares in successful companies, those who bought shares in profitable companies could eventually get rich. Private ownership and competition would eventually result in a price system that directed resource use toward the satisfaction of market demands.

However, because the command economy overallocated resources to heavy industries and defense industries, many of these industries would have to be shut down, causing unemployment. Many inefficiently run factories whose operations could not be made profitable would also have to be shut down in the move to a market economy. To avoid very high unemployment and the social chaos that could result from it, the leaders of the former Soviet republics and other former communist nations often chose to keep inefficient or defense-related plants open. But, since often no one wanted to buy the products of these plants, their operation pumped the purchasing power of their workers' money into the economy without balancing that purchasing power with salable output. This resulted in inflation, which eroded the purchasing power of retired workers and others on relatively fixed incomes.

In short, the transition to free markets promised to be a very rocky road, with high unemployment, high inflation, or both in the former Soviet republics. In Russia in 1992, production declined, unemployment rates soared, and hyperinflation was rearing its ugly head. However, the uncomfortable transition seemed to be the only way to restructure the former communist economies so as to allow the price system to improve future living standards. The risk remained that the pain of a very long transition would cause a political backlash. By 1992, however, so much of the apparatus of the old Soviet command economy had unraveled that a return to socialism seemed to be only a remote possibility.

principles in practice

Transition from Central Planning to Free Markets in Russia, Poland, and China

Nations whose economies have been dominated by central planning are choosing diverse ways of moving to a free-market system. Each of these nations has its unique institutions and its unique problems. Perhaps the most difficult task is faced by the Russians and other peoples of the former Soviet Union because they have had little experience with free markets in the 20th century. Let's take a look at progress in the transition to free markets as of the early 1990s for three nations: Russia, China, and Poland.

Russia The key to improving living standards in Russia and other republics of the former Soviet Union is privatization of profitable state-owned enterprises and the establishment of conditions conducive to free enterprise and free markets. The citizens of the former Soviet republics grew up under a system that viewed profit as a dirty word, and many of these citizens still distrust capitalism and are resentful of prosperous farmers and other budding capitalists who succeed by innovating in free markets. As of 1992, much of the capital and factories in Russia were still owned by government authorities and much of the labor force was still allocated according to a central plan. As of 1992, the economy of Russia had a long way to go before it could call itself a free-market economy.

Although some foreign firms have been investing in Russia, doing business in that country remains difficult because of materials shortages, corruption, and the legacy of a slow-moving bureaucracy that is accustomed to

regulating all economic activity. In 1992 President Yeltsin launched a bold new plan to encourage Russian citizens to become "capitalists" and to speed the privatization of government-owned enterprises. Each of Russia's 148 million citizens was issued a "privatization voucher" that gave each of them the right to buy a share in a state-owned factory. Almost immediately after their issuance, a secondary market in these vouchers sprang up. Skeptical Russians who did not want to invest in former Soviet factories or who needed rubles to survive sold their vouchers to middlemen who either held them as an investment or sold them in formal markets similar to capitalistic stock markets. As the vouchers were acquired by more sophisticated investors, they were used to buy shares in state enterprises that showed promise of becoming profitable private companies.

The face value of each of the privatization vouchers was initially set at 10,000 rubles, which was about $24 based on the exchange rate prevailing as of late 1992. Some skeptical citizens sold their vouchers for as little a 3,000 rubles. As of late 1992, the value of the vouchers on secondary markets ranged between 7,000 and 8,000 rubles and many investors were hopeful that their value would skyrocket as privatization proceeded.

China Although China remains a communist nation with only limited political rights for its citizens, in the past few years it has made major strides in granting economic liberties and transforming itself into a free-market economy. By virtue of its size and population,

Less Developed Countries

[5] There is great disparity in levels of per capita output among nations. Real per capita output is a measure of real output per person in a nation. It is calculated by dividing a nation's real GDP by the nation's population. Output per capita in the United States and other industrial nations generally ranges well over $10,000. In less developed countries (LDCs), however, real GDP per capita is generally much less than $1,000 per year. In fact, in some very poor nations in Africa and Asia, output per capita is less than $200 per year! The incredible disparity in levels of average well-being among nations, measured by output per capita, is a source of great concern to many caring people. The problem is all the more serious because about 75 percent of the world's population lives in LDCs. Unfortunately, there is no simple way to raise living standards in less developed countries. The problems of these nations must be looked at within the context of international trade and economic relations.

real per capita output
a measure of output per person in a nation; calculated by dividing real GDP by population.

less developed country (LDC) a country whose real GDP per capita is generally much less than $1,000 a year.

Causes of Low per Capita Output in Less Developed Countries

The problems of each particular nation with low per capita income are unique. In general, large portions of the populations of LDCs are engaged in agricultural

China could soon be the largest economy in the world as measured by its GDP. When per capita incomes rise rapidly in a nation with as many people as China, the results are startling. If China reached the per capita income level that currently prevails in Taiwan, its GDP would be larger than the combined total of all the industrial nations in the world.

GDP has been growing rapidly in China in part because it has unleashed the profit motive. As of 1992, central planning accounted for only 6 percent of China's industrial production and state-owned companies were producing less than one third of China's total output. Private enterprise has been spreading rapidly in Chinese agriculture and many Chinese industries. China has a well-educated labor force, and many Chinese workers have become entrepreneurs. The Malthusian specter of uncontrolled population growth no longer haunts China. China's tough family planning policies have sharply curtailed population growth. One dark spot for the future is the possibility of political instability as the older leaders die off.

Poland In 1992 Polish butcher shops were well stocked with sausages and hams. This was in stark contrast to the situation in the 1980s, when shortages of food products and bare shelves in stores were the rule. Poland's GDP rose in 1992 after having fallen for the first three years of its "cold-turkey" transition to a market economy.*

The turnaround in Poland is all the more startling because Poland had one of the worst-performing economies in Eastern Europe in the 1980s and because it was suffering from hyperinflation in 1989. Although inflation and unemployment remain problems in Poland, the Polish experience is now being used as a model showing how living standards can be improved by quick dismantling of a centrally planned economy. As of 1992, the private sector employed 60 percent of Poland's workers.

Rapid privatization of state-run enterprises is credited with awakening the entrepreneurial spirit in many of Poland's 39 million citizens. Average wages have increased nearly tenfold as worker productivity has increased and inefficient former state-owned enterprises have been closed down. Poles are now gobbling up new cars, home appliances, and other consumer goods that were unavailable in Poland at any price five years ago. The economy has been transformed from one that relied on heavy industry to a more diverse one with a better mix of financial, commercial, and manufacturing. Foreign trade with the West has increased, and Poland has run a balance of trade surplus since 1990.

Among the policies credited with helping achieve the Polish economic miracle are:

1. Balancing the federal budget and reducing consumer and worker subsidies.

2. Allowing prices to be determined by supply and demand and decreasing government regulations while opening Polish markets to imports and encouraging market competition.

3. Making the Polish currency (the zloty) fully convertible into foreign currencies.

4. Privatizing state-run enterprises.

* See John Daniszewski, "Poland Recovering after Economic Shock," *News and Observer*, Raleigh, North Carolina, December 6, 1992.

pursuits and use older methods of farming. Despite the high input of labor in agriculture, many of these nations barely produce enough food to feed their populations. Life expectancy is low, living conditions are often miserable, and people have a standard of material well-being that barely allows them to survive. In most LDCs, however, population growth is much higher than it is in industrialized nations.

A number of basic causes of relatively low per capita output can be identified:

1. *Low rates of saving and capital accumulation.* The key to economic growth is the accumulation of capital such as roads, structures, bridges, equipment, and vehicles. The accumulation of capital requires saving. Less developed countries are so poor that their saving is close to zero. To obtain capital, these nations must often borrow from more industrialized nations. Per capita incomes are low in LDCs because workers have little capital equipment to work with. As a result, their productivity is low and their output per capita is low. This prevents them from saving, a vicious circle that can often be broken only by assistance from other nations. Such assistance can come from foreign governments or from direct investment by private corporations. For example, if a U.S. tire manufacturer builds its

own plant in an African nation, capital will flow into that nation and contribute to higher incomes.

2. *Poorly skilled and educated workers*. Human capital is as important as physical capital for the productivity of workers. In less developed countries, workers are often illiterate and have little training. Low productivity is caused by a lack of human capital as well as a lack of physical capital.

3. *Lagging technological know-how*. Production methods in less developed nations are often old-fashioned. The use of dated technology is related to a lack of capital and a poorly informed and trained work force. The problem is particularly acute in agriculture, where the use of more modern cultivation methods can result in enormous productivity gains that would free labor for use in industrial activities and generate an exportable surplus of food.

4. *High population growth and unemployment*. Medical advances in many poor nations have reduced the death rate while the birthrate remains high. This contributes to a rate of population growth that is often as much as 10 times the rate in typical industrialized nations. The average age of the population tends to be low in poor nations, which contributes to a higher rate of natural unemployment. Much of the unemployment in less developed nations is disguised in the sense that the marginal product of many workers is close to zero. Traditional practices provide many people with work of little social value. For example, many government jobs could be eliminated without making anyone worse off except the workers who lose their salaries. Similarly, on many farms four workers do the job of one worker. Spreading work out over more workers than necessary disguises the fact that many workers have zero marginal products.

5. *Political instability and government policies that discourage production*. Many LDCs are in the throes of social upheaval. Political insurgency and guerrilla warfare are common in many nations of Africa, Asia, and Central and South America. Governments are often corrupt, and international aid payments often enrich a few at the expense of many. Governments sometimes pursue policies that are helpful in the short run but slow long-run development.

Price control policies may keep food prices and prices of other basic goods low, but they inevitably destroy farmers' incentives to produce and innovate. Governments of LDCs often support their own currency with price controls that overvalue the currency relative to the equilibrium value in international markets. This decreases the demand for a nation's exports and makes its imports appear to be cheap, which discourages local businesspeople and farmers from innovating to increase productivity.

International Trade and Less Developed Countries

Less developed countries are often dependent on trade with foreign nations to obtain the capital and technical know-how that they need to increase productivity and living standards. Paying for foreign capital in foreign currency is impossible unless the less developed countries export more. Increased exports of either agricultural or industrial products from these countries are likely to affect world prices and possibly make workers in industrialized nations worse off. Competition from less developed countries will increase if their economies begin to take off. At the same time, growing per capita incomes in these countries will provide broader markets for the products of the United States and other industrialized nations. There is great risk, however, that short-sighted protectionist policies in the advanced nations will prevent export growth in the poorer nations.

The United States and other advanced nations often make gifts of direct aid and technical assistance to less developed countries. The *World Bank,* an international organization of over 140 nations, provides loans at reduced interest rates to help developing nations acquire capital. Such gifts and loans can help these nations acquire the capital that will enable them to increase their per capita output.

- What assumptions underlie Marx's theory of economic development?

- In what ways does a socialist command economy differ from a capitalist free-market economy?

- What are some difficulties less developed countries must overcome to improve the living standards of their citizens?

CONCEPT CHECK
☐

---

economic thinkers

David Ricardo

A cool head for business and astute judgment earned David Ricardo a fortune estimated at $2 million, an unbelievable sum for the early 19th century. Economics began for him as a hobby. He had little formal training, but when he retired from business in 1814 he began to pursue his interest in the invisible laws working behind the scenes in the market.

Instead of focusing on the details of the business world he knew so well, Ricardo created an abstraction of it, stripping it of everything unnecessary in order to study the mechanisms underlying its everyday life. Although perhaps his greatest contribution to the science of economics, this powerful analytical tool—modeling—was certainly not his only legacy. His 1817 book, *Principles of Political Economy and Taxation*, surveyed the field to that date and set the stage for economic debate for half a century.

In his exposition of the principle of comparative advantage as it relates to international trade, Ricardo used a clearcut illustration involving the production of wine and cloth in Portugal and England (similar to the example of bananas and wheat used in this chapter). Also set forth in his influential *Principles* is Ricardo's theory of economic growth, in which he posited that the economy ultimately would reach a "steady state" and cease to grow. At this point, Ricardo believed, the wage rate would decline to the subsistence level. Although drawing markedly different inferences, socialist philosopher Karl Marx was profoundly influenced by Ricardo's theory of economic growth.

Ricardo was born in England in 1772, the son of a Jewish immigrant. He went to work for his father at the age of 14 and started in business for himself at 22. He converted to Quakerism to marry the girl he loved, and when he retired he purchased a country estate and a seat in Parliament.

Ricardo earned his fortune mainly through securities and real estate investments. A strong supporter of freedom of speech and an opponent of government corruption and religious persecution, which were nonpopular stances at the time, Ricardo nonetheless enjoyed tremendous popularity and was frequently called on to speak at the House of Commons.

insights on issues

How Successfully Will U.S. Industries Face the Challenge of Competing in the Global Economy? Talking with Rachel McCulloch

A professor of economics at Brandeis University, Rachel McCulloch has written many articles on international trade, investment, and technology transfer. She is a research associate of the National Bureau of Economic Research and a member of the Advisory Committee of the Institute for International Economics. Professor McCulloch holds degrees from the University of Pennsylvania and the University of Chicago.

How important is international trade to the U.S. economy? One standard way to measure trade is to look at a country's merchandise exports, imports, or their sum as a share of GDP. By this measure, trade is less important for the United States than for most economies, especially small ones. Even though the relative importance of U.S. exports has more than doubled since 1960, exports are still below 8 percent of GDP. (Trade-oriented small economies like Hong Kong and Singapore have ratios well above 100 percent. But for Japan, usually regarded as a super-exporter, the ratio is less than 10 percent.)

However, these numbers can be misleading. In an economy open to foreign competition, even producers serving only the domestic market must meet an international standard of quality and price. Also, the standard measure looks only at merchandise trade (tangible goods like wheat and computers), but U.S. output is increasingly dominated by services. Finally, aggregate indices hide the much larger (or smaller) impact on particular industries. Foreign markets are overwhelmingly important for some sectors.

Even though U.S. trade is small as a share of GDP, the United States is still number one worldwide in absolute volume of trade. Because U.S. trade is so important to other countries, U.S. officials are often tempted to bend trade policy to serve foreign policy goals, as with trade boycotts and preferential arrangements.

What factors affect the competitiveness of U.S. industries? A U.S. firm's ability to compete with foreign producers depends on the combined impact of many economic factors. The most important are dollar costs of labor, capital, and other inputs; productivity (which reflects both technology and the organization of production); product characteristics; seller reputation, service facilities, and warranties; exchange rates; and tariffs, quotas, and other trade policies. Even "domestic" policies (antitrust, environmental, health care) can be important.

Competitiveness is always relative. As firms abroad improve products or adopt advanced manufacturing techniques, and as foreign nations upgrade education and infrastructure, U.S. producers will lose competitiveness unless they do likewise.

SUMMARY

1. International trade stems from differences among nations in endowments of resources, skills, and technical know-how. International trade offers citizens of a nation the opportunity to specialize in the production of certain goods and to exchange them for other goods produced in foreign nations.

2. Mutual gains are possible from international trade.

3. A nation has an absolute advantage over other nations in the production of an item if it can produce more of the item over a certain period with a given amount of resources.

4. A nation has a comparative advantage in the production of a particular good if its opportunity cost per unit is lower than that of its trading partners. Even nations that enjoy an absolute advantage in the production of all goods can gain from trade. A nation can gain from international trade by specializing in the production of goods in which it enjoys a comparative advantage and trading domestic surpluses of those goods for goods that other nations can produce at a comparative advantage.

What are the links among productivity growth, job growth, and international trade? All else being equal, higher productivity at home means increased competitiveness abroad. If productivity grows at the same pace abroad, international competitiveness won't be affected. But the higher productivity will still mean more jobs and higher earnings, both at home and abroad. Think of trade as a superior technology that allows more output from a given amount of inputs.

Many people see exports as a source of additional jobs and imports as taking away jobs. This is true only in a very limited sense. Changing the level of trade in a given industry may increase the number of U.S. jobs in that industry, but any increase is likely to be offset by job losses in other sectors. Manipulating trade to increase employment at home is called "beggar-your-neighbor" trade policy, but it can beggar even the country that tries it (as it did during the worldwide depression of the 1930s).

Is U.S. manufacturing losing ground in international markets? U.S. manufacturing overall did lose ground in the mid-1980s, when a very strong dollar priced U.S. goods out of global markets. A lower international value for the dollar has helped U.S. firms rebuild market share in many industries. In 1992 the United States was the world's top exporter, and manufactured goods accounted for more than 90 percent of the value of its exports.

However, aggregates hide important differences across sectors. Since World War II, the United States (like other industrial countries) has steadily lost competitiveness in some "mature" industries, especially apparel and footwear, where labor-abundant, less-developed nations can produce quality products at lower cost. In high technology, the United States remains an active exporter.

How do trading blocs affect the pattern of international trade? Trading blocs and other preferential arrangements have three effects. First is trade creation, the substitution of imports for inefficient domestic production. The second, related effect is increased market size. This brings advantages from large-scale production as well as efficiency benefits from competition among more firms. But the third effect, trade diversion, may reduce global efficiency and even participants' gains. Discriminatory trade arrangements may lead to substitution of member imports for lower-cost goods from outside the group. Caribbean nations worry that Mexican goods will replace their exports to the United States in a North American Free Trade Area.

Some fear that blocs will raise the barriers faced by nonmembers (e.g., Fortress Europe), but trade both within the European Community and with nonmembers has increased. And regional trade negotiations let nations resolve policy conflicts too complicated to address in a forum as large and diverse as the GATT.

What role should governments play in international trade? Although in theory free trade is not usually optimal, experience teaches that in pluralistic political systems, activist trade policy tends to serve special interests, not the national interest.

Governments can help by keeping markets open, including their own. U.S. protection often reflects concern about workers displaced by competing imports, even though jobs "saved" in this way come at great expense to the nation.

5. Through international trade, citizens of a nation can obtain goods in which they do not enjoy a comparative advantage at prices that are below the opportunity costs per unit of producing those goods domestically. This allows consumption possibilities that would not be available if the nation were self-sufficient in the production of all goods.

6. The real terms of trade represent the actual market exchange rate of one good for another in international trade. For there to be incentive to trade, the terms of trade for a good must be less than the opportunity cost per unit of producing that good domestically.

7. Changes in productivity growth among trading nations can alter the pattern of comparative advantage. When a nation's productivity growth lags behind that of its international competitors, its cost of production per unit will rise relative to that of its competitors. In the long run this can cause it to lose its comparative advantage in the production of the good.

8. When lagging productivity growth causes a domestic industry to lose its comparative advantage in international markets, the income of input suppliers and workers in that industry will decline.

9. Loss of income in industries suffering from foreign competition often leads to demands for protection from foreign competition. Arguments in favor of protectionism include self-sufficiency in industries producing materials necessary for national defense, reduction in structural unemployment, protection of industries just getting started, and protection of domestic sellers from unfair competition by subsidized foreign sellers.

10. The ''cheap labor'' fallacy turns the basis for gaining from trade into an argument against trade. A nation with cheap labor may have low labor costs per unit of a good, which give it a comparative advantage in the good precisely because labor is cheap. The productivity of workers in foreign nations who are paid low wages is often lower than U.S. workers.

11. A tariff is a tax on imported goods. Tariffs raise the prices paid for the foreign goods on which they are levied and reduce the net prices received by foreign sellers of those goods. As a result of the increase in the prices paid by consumers, the quantity of foreign goods demanded tends to decline. A tariff raises government revenue and makes foreign goods more expensive relative to their domestically produced substitutes.

12. An import quota is a limit on the quantity of foreign goods that can be sold in a nation's domestic markets. Like tariffs, quotas seek to protect domestic producers from foreign competition. Quotas act to limit supply, thereby raising the prices of the goods produced by the industries they protect. However, quotas, unlike tariffs, do not raise revenue for government authorities.

13. An economic system is an accepted way of organizing production, establishing rights to the ownership and use of productive resources, and governing economic transactions in a society.

14. Opinions regarding human rights often influence our ideas about the desirability of one economic system compared to another.

15. *Capitalism* is an economic system associated with private ownership of economic resources, free enterprise, and exchange of goods and services in markets. *Socialism* is an economic system associated with government ownership of productive resources.

16. Karl Marx was a 19th-century economist and philosopher who emphasized conflict between economic classes and the notion that workers are exploited by capitalists. Much of his argument was based on the labor theory of value, which maintains that only labor can produce something worth paying for.

17. Marx believed that capitalists would pay workers only a subsistence wage. Marx's theory predicted the eventual collapse of the capitalist system because of substitution of capital for labor, increased unemployment, and declining profits.

18. Marx did not consider the possibility that increased worker productivity would increase the wages willingly paid by employers above the subsistence level. He also did not consider the possibility that profit opportunities would arise in new industries as profit levels fell to zero in existing industries.

19. In a command economy, productive resources are usually owned by the government, which regulates all economic activity through a central plan. In such an economic system, prices are determined by planning boards and do not reflect the free play of supply and demand in markets. In a command economy, the profit motive does not provide signals that govern the allocation of resources. The command economies that prevailed in the former Soviet Union, Eastern Europe, and China throughout much of the 20th century typically emphasized military goods and services and heavy industry and did little to satisfy consumer demands. These economies were plagued with inefficient resource use and slow growth in living standards. Most of the former command economies are now undergoing a painful transition in which government-owned enterprises are being privatized and free markets are being established.

20. A less developed country is one whose real GDP per capita is generally much less than $1,000 per year. In such countries, large portions of the population are typically involved in agriculture and labor productivity is low. Because of widespread poverty, saving and capital accumulation are also low. High population growth often makes it difficult for increases in real GDP to outstrip annual population increases and thus to improve average living standards. Many less developed countries rely heavily on international trade to obtain capital equipment and technical know-how. These countries typically export raw materials or agricultural commodities.

KEY TERMS

specialization *459*

mutual gains from
international trade *460*

absolute advantage *461*

comparative
advantage *462*

real terms of trade *465*

consumption possibilities
curve *466*

tariff *472*

import quota *474*

labor theory of value *478*

surplus value *478*

economic system *482*

socialism *482*

command economy *482*

centrally planned
economy *482*

real per capita output *484*

less developed country
(LDC) *484*

CONCEPT REVIEW

1 Explain why international trade allows economies to achieve points that lie above their production possibilities curves.

2 How is a nation's comparative advantage in a product affected by productivity changes in the industry making that product?

3 What are the instruments of protectionism, and how do they affect prices?

4 Why were Marx's predictions about the collapse of capitalist economies wrong?

5 What are some characteristics of less developed countries?

PROBLEMS AND APPLICATIONS

1. Suppose two nations are capable of producing clothing outfits and food. Nation A can produce 200 outfits per year or 10 tons of food. Nation B, which has an identical resource endowment, can produce 180 outfits per year or 5 tons of food. Assuming that constant costs prevail, plot the production possibilities curve for each of these nations. Which nation has the absolute advantage in the production of clothing? Which nation has the absolute advantage in the production of food? **1**

2. Plot the opportunity cost per unit of clothing and the opportunity cost per unit of food for each of the two nations based on the data in Problem 1. Which nation has the comparative advantage in food production? Which nation has the comparative advantage in clothing production? **1**

3. Derive the consumption possibilities curve that would exist for each nation if the real terms of trade were 30 clothing outfits for each ton of food. Under what circumstances would changes in productivity result in no gains possible from international trade in this example? **1**, **2**

4. The decline in U.S. manufacturing jobs as a result of import competition has been particularly sharp since the mid-1970s in automobiles, steel, textiles, and shoes. Suppose you are asked to head a commission to improve the international competitiveness of these industries. What measures would you recommend to help these industries regain their comparative advantages? **2**

5. Why would an isolationist trade policy banning international trade result in a sharp decline in the standard of living of U.S. citizens? **3**

6. Firms in the domestic shoe industry argue in favor of shoe import quotas. They point out that such quotas will not increase the costs of selling foreign-made shoes in the United States and therefore will not increase the prices of these shoes. Do you agree with their argument? **3**

7. Suppose you are a Korean exporter of shoes. The U.S. Congress is considering the imposition of either a tariff or a quota on your shoes. Assuming that under either of the two proposals you will sell the same quantity of shoes in the United States, why would you prefer the quota to the tariff? **3**

8. Why does the labor theory of value imply that profit can be obtained only by exploiting workers? **4**

9. Why did Karl Marx's theory of economic development in capitalist economies imply that profit would fall as capital was substituted for labor? In your answer, be sure to explain how Marx thought profit was related to the concept of surplus value. **4**

10. If you were an adviser to a less developed country, what policies would you propose to raise per capita income in that country? **5**

21 chapter

The Economics of Foreign Exchange and the Balance of International Trade

By now you're well aware of the growing importance of international trade in the U.S. economy. If you follow the news reports, you can't help being aware of the ups and downs of the price of the dollar in terms of foreign currencies. The price of a unit of a nation's currency in terms of units of foreign currencies is an important determinant of the prices of its exports in foreign markets and of the prices you must pay for such imported products as Japanese cameras and German automobiles.

Our goal in this chapter is to provide you with a basis for understanding the causes and impact of fluctuations in foreign exchange rates on the performance of the U.S. economy. As you've already learned, when the United States imports more goods than it exports, the result is a balance of trade deficit. Such a deficit implies negative net exports, which, other things being equal, is a contractionary influence on the U.S. economy and spells trouble for those American industries that face foreign competition. In this chapter we'll examine the measurement and the consequences of balance of trade deficits and the financial aspects of international trade.

☐ CONCEPT PREVIEW

After reading this chapter, you should be able to:

1. Understand how international transactions between the United States and the rest of the world involve the exchange of dollars for units of foreign currencies.

2. Use supply and demand analysis to show how exchange rates of one currency into another are established in foreign exchange markets and explain the causes of currency appreciation and depreciation.

3. Discuss the evolution of the current international monetary system and understand how a U.S. balance of trade deficit in a given year implies an increase in net foreign acquisition of U.S. financial and other assets in that year.

INTERNATIONAL TRADE TRANSACTIONS

If you've ever taken a trip to a foreign country, you know you must purchase foreign currency to pay your expenses while in that country. All your bills, even those you pay by credit card, will be in terms of that country's currency: French francs, Italian lire, Japanese yen. The credit card bills you receive when you return home will be converted into dollars based on the prevailing exchange rate at the time. You'll pay in dollars, but the credit card company will have its bank pay the bills in the foreign currency.

The price of one nation's monetary unit in terms of the monetary unit of another nation is called its **foreign exchange rate.** The foreign exchange rate of the French franc in dollars is the number of dollars necessary to buy each French franc. For example, suppose the foreign exchange rate of French francs in dollars is 10 cents per franc. This means that if you exchange $100, you'll receive 1,000 French francs in return. You can then use your francs to purchase French goods and services while visiting France. Similarly, French tourists visiting the United States will have to purchase dollars to meet their expenses while in this country. To do so, they'll go to an American bank or foreign exchange dealer, where they'll sell their francs for dollars. The foreign exchange rate of the dollar for francs is the price of the dollar in francs. If it takes 10 cents to buy each franc, it follows that the foreign exchange rate for dollars is 10 francs per dollar. The foreign exchange rate of the dollar is the inverse of the foreign exchange rate of the franc:

> **foreign exchange rate**
> the price of one nation's monetary unit in terms of the monetary unit of another nation.

$$\text{Exchange rate of the dollar} = 1/\text{Exchange rate of the franc}$$

$$10 \text{ francs per dollar} = 1 \text{ franc}/(\$0.10 \text{ per franc})$$

An American tourist can figure out the equivalent number of dollars necessary to buy an item priced in francs by multiplying the price of the item in francs by the exchange rate:

$$\text{Dollar price} = (\text{Price in French francs})(\text{Exchange rate of francs})$$

If a hotel room costs 1,500 French francs per night and the dollar exchange rate is 10 cents per franc, the price of the room in dollars is

$$(1,500 \text{ French francs})(\$0.10 \text{ per French franc}) = \$150$$

However, if the dollar exchange rate of the French franc were 18 cents, as was the case in mid-February 1993, the cost of the room would be $1,500($0.18) = $270! When the dollar exchange rate of the French franc goes up, so do the dollar prices of items priced in francs.

Similarly, a French tourist would use the exchange rate of dollars expressed in francs to figure out the price of a hotel room in the United States in francs:

$$\text{Price in French francs} = (\text{Dollar price})(\text{Exchange rate of the dollar})$$

If the room costs $200 and the exchange rate is 10 French francs per dollar, the price of the room in francs will be

$$(\$200)(10 \text{ francs per dollar}) = 2,000 \text{ French francs}$$

If, instead, the exchange rate of the dollar were only 5 francs per dollar, then the price of the hotel room would be only 1,000 French francs. Thus, a decrease in the exchange rate of the dollar makes goods priced in dollars cheaper to people with French francs.

International Transfers of Bank Deposits Resulting from International Transactions

As is true for most transactions *within* the United States, most *international* transactions involve transfers of deposits among banks. In the case of international transactions, however, the bank deposits are denominated in a variety of monetary units, such as dollars, francs, marks, and pesos. The foreign exchange market is a market in which buyers and sellers of bank deposits denominated in the monetary units of many nations exchange their monies. Only a small fraction of daily transactions in foreign exchange markets involve trading of actual currency. When you buy francs in the form of paper currency or coins while visiting France, you engage in a retail transaction with a foreign exchange dealer, usually a bank. The retail price you pay for the francs in terms of dollars is naturally higher than the wholesale price representing the rate the dealer must pay to exchange francs for dollars or dollars for francs. When banks and other dealers trade currencies, each of their transactions is in millions of dollars. The foreign exchange market is highly competitive. Hundreds of banks and other dealers maintain contact by telephone and electronic devices to exchange *bank deposits* denominated in one currency for bank deposits denominated in another currency.

How Foreign Trade Is Carried Out: An Export Transaction

Suppose an American grain dealer arranges to sell 10,000 bushels of grain to a French miller. If the price of the grain is $4 per bushel, the total transaction is $40,000. Naturally, the American grain dealer will want to be paid in dollars rather than francs, while the French miller will want to pay in francs.

Suppose the exchange rate is 10 francs to the dollar. To finance the transaction, the French miller can write a check for 400,000 French francs, the equivalent of $40,000. The miller will send the check directly to the U.S. grain dealer, who will present it to a U.S. bank for conversion into dollars. The miller can also purchase a bank draft (a check drawn on a bank) made out to the grain dealer in U.S. dollars, a more common option. The miller will pay a French bank a small fee for the draft. In assisting the miller in the international trade transaction, the French bank loses deposits of 400,000 francs. Where do these francs go? They go to a U.S. bank or another foreign exchange dealer that obtains the 400,000 francs in exchange for $40,000.

Assume that the francs are sold to a U.S. bank. This bank then holds the francs as a deposit in a French bank in which it has an account, called a *correspondent bank*, or in its French branch (if it has one) for future use or sale. As long as the French francs are held in a French bank after the sale of the grain, there is no reduction in the French money stock. A U.S. bank acquires deposits in a French bank that can be invested in French assets or used to buy French goods and services. The deposits of the grain exporter are increased by $40,000 at its bank when the exporter deposits the draft from the French bank. The $40,000 draft will be written against the French bank's account in a U.S. correspondent bank. As a result of the export transaction, U.S. banks obtain assets of 400,000 francs, which are held in foreign banks, and liabilities of $40,000. The table in Box 1 summarizes the immediate financial implications of the grain export transaction.

How Foreign Trade Is Carried Out: An Import Transaction

Suppose a U.S. distributing company imports 20,000 videocassette recorders from a producer in Japan. The wholesale price of the VCRs is 12,500 Japanese yen per unit.

Box 1   Changes in Assets and Liabilities of U.S. and French Banks as a Result of Export of U.S. Grain to France

Banks	Assets	Liabilities
French banks	No change	–400,000 French francs deposited in account of grain importer
		+400,000 French francs deposited in U.S. banks
U.S. banks	+400,000 French francs deposited in French banks	+$40,000 deposited in grain exporter's account

Box 2   Changes in Assets and Liabilities of U.S. and Japanese Banks as a Result of a U.S. Import Transaction

Banks	Assets	Liabilities
Japanese banks	+$2 million deposited in U.S. banks	+250 million Japanese yen deposit of VCR exporter
U.S. banks	No change	–$2 million deposit of U.S. importer
		+$2 million deposit of Japanese banks

If the exchange rate of the yen is $0.008 per yen, the dollar price of a VCR is

$$\text{Dollar price} = (12{,}500 \text{ yen})(\$0.008 \text{ per yen}) = \$100$$

The total cost of the 20,000 VCRs in dollars is $2 million, which is equivalent to 250 million Japanese yen at the current exchange rate of $0.008 per yen. Note that at this exchange rate it will take 125 yen to purchase each dollar. The exchange rate of the dollar in this example is therefore 125 yen per dollar.

The mechanics of the transaction are similar to those we discussed for the export of grain from the United States to France. In this case, however, the U.S. distributor goes to the local bank to arrange the exchange of dollars into yen to pay for the purchase of imported goods. The distributor writes a check for $2 million (plus a small fee to the bank) in exchange for a bank draft for 250 million yen made out to the Japanese exporter. The account of the distributor is debited by $2 million as a result of the purchase. The $2 million ends up in the hands of a Japanese bank or other foreign exchange dealer that purchases the dollars in exchange for 250 million yen. The yen could be supplied by any U.S. bank holding deposits denominated in yen at a Japanese bank. The account of the Japanese exporter ends up with 250 million more yen. As long as the Japanese bank or other dealer purchasing the dollars for yen keeps those dollars on deposit at an American correspondent bank, there is no reduction in the U.S. money stock. The dollars held in accounts of this kind can be used to purchase U.S. financial assets, such as corporate bonds or government securities, or held to finance future import transactions in which dollars will be sold for foreign currency. The table in Box 2 summarizes the immediate impact of the import transaction on assets and liabilities in U.S. and Japanese banks.

CONCEPT CHECK
□

- It takes 1,500 Italian lire to purchase a U.S. dollar. How much U.S. money is necessary to purchase a bottle of Italian wine that sells for 8,000 lire?

- Explain why an export of corn to Italy will result

in U.S. banks gaining deposits of lire in Italian banks?

- Why will Italian banks gain deposits of dollars in U.S. banks when U.S. firms import wine from Italy?

FOREIGN EXCHANGE MARKETS

Whenever a foreign firm or individual purchases U.S. goods or services, a supply of foreign currency to be exchanged for dollars is created. Similarly, whenever a U.S. firm or citizen wishes to purchase foreign goods or services, a demand for foreign currency is created. Because of the many banks and other dealers buying and selling bank deposits and other funds denominated in various currencies, the market for foreign exchange of any money is quite competitive. Foreign exchange is the money of one nation held by citizens of another nation as either currency or bank deposits.

foreign exchange the money of one nation held by citizens of another nation as either currency or bank deposits.

Keep in mind that foreign exchange must be willingly held either as deposits in bank accounts or as assets denominated in foreign monetary units. Foreigners holding dollars must either keep them as idle balances in their U.S. correspondent banks or lend them out to U.S. firms or governments. They make such loans by purchasing the debt instruments of governments, banks, or households. The foreign holders of dollars can also use them to make direct investments in the United States by purchasing U.S. assets such as real estate or corporate stocks.

The demand for U.S. dollars as foreign exchange depends on foreign demand for U.S. goods and services and on the willingness of foreigners to hold their dollars as deposits (or cash) for future use or to invest the dollars in U.S. real and financial assets. The supply of dollars to foreigners depends on the willingness of U.S. households, firms, and governments to exchange their dollars for foreign currency. This, in turn, depends on U.S. demand for foreign goods and services as well as the willingness of U.S. citizens and governments to use dollars to acquire financial and real assets denominated in foreign monetary units.

There are really many foreign exchange markets—one for each possible pair of currencies. Of course, the market of dollars for marks is the same as the market of marks for dollars, because once the equilibrium exchange rate of dollars for marks is established, so is the equilibrium exchange rate of marks for dollars. For example, suppose the equilibrium dollar price of German marks is 50 cents per mark. The equilibrium exchange rate of marks for dollars must therefore be 2 marks per dollar. If this were not the case, what would happen? If a dollar cost only 1 mark, while the mark cost 50 cents, you could make some quick profits as a foreign exchange dealer. You could buy 2 marks for $1, then turn around and sell each of those marks for $1, thus making a quick $1 profit on your $1 purchase! Profit opportunities like this exist whenever there are discrepancies in the exchange rate of dollars into a currency and of that currency into dollars. Because firms specializing in foreign exchange transactions are quick to seize opportunities to earn profit when such exchange rate discrepancies crop up, the discrepancies are quickly eliminated. In the preceding example, the demand for marks would increase, pushing up the price of the mark in terms of dollars, and the supply of dollars offered in exchange for marks would increase, putting downward pressure on the price of the dollar in terms of marks. The exchange rates of the mark and the dollar would adjust until profits could no longer be made by buying marks and then quickly selling them for dollars.

Box 3   Equilibrium in the Foreign Exchange Market of Marks for Dollars

The equilibrium exchange price is 2 marks per dollar. If the price were 1.5 marks per dollar, there would be a shortage of dollars available for marks in the foreign exchange market. This would put upward pressure on the exchange rate. If the exchange rate were 3 marks per dollar, there would be a surplus of dollars in exchange for marks. This would put downward pressure on the exchange rate.

Equilibrium Exchange Rates

As with any good or service, the price (exchange rate) of a nation's currency in terms of any foreign currency depends on the market demand for and supply of the nation's currency. The graph in Box 3 shows the demand and supply curves for dollars based on the exchange rate of marks for dollars, which represents the price of a dollar in terms of marks.

The demand for dollars by the people and businesses that hold marks depends on the desires of those people and businesses to use dollars to purchase U.S. goods and services and to invest in U.S. financial and physical assets. Other things being equal, the lower the price of a dollar in terms of marks, the lower the cost of purchasing U.S. items for holders of marks. To see this, suppose the current price of a personal computer manufactured in the United States is $2,000. If the current exchange rate is 2 marks per dollar, that computer will cost a German citizen 4,000 marks. However, if the exchange rate were only 1 mark per dollar, the same computer would cost a German citizen only 2,000 marks. Naturally, the lower the price of the dollar in foreign currency, the lower the price of U.S. goods, services, and assets (denominated in dollars) in terms of that currency and the greater the demand for these items by holders of the currency. This increase in demand increases the quantity of dollars demanded by holders of the foreign currency. The demand curve for dollars is therefore downward sloping.

The supply of dollars offered in exchange for a foreign currency, such as the German mark, depends on the willingness of dollar holders to purchase marks. The supply of dollars for marks depends on the desires of U.S. citizens to purchase German goods and services and to invest in German assets. Other things being equal, an increase in the exchange rate of dollars in terms of marks is likely to increase the quantity of dollars supplied in exchange for marks. To see why this is so, suppose the price of a new BMW available as a U.S. import is 50,000 marks. If the exchange rate is 2 marks per dollar, the dollar equivalent of the marks necessary to purchase the car is $25,000. How much will the car cost someone paying in dollars if the exchange rate increases to 2.5 marks per dollar? To find out, simply multiply the 50,000 marks by the 1/2.5 dollars necessary to buy each mark. The price in dollars is now only $20,000. Naturally, the BMW, as well as other German goods, is now more attractive to holders of dollars because its price in terms of dollars is lower. A higher exchange rate increases the quantity of dollars supplied to foreign exchange markets because it increases U.S. demand for imports. The supply curve of dollars for a foreign currency therefore slopes upward.

In Box 3 the equilibrium price of the dollar is 2 marks per dollar. At that price the number of dollars demanded per day by holders of marks exactly equals the number of dollars supplied per day by holders of dollars in exchange for marks. If the equilibrium price were 3 marks per dollar, the quantity of dollars supplied for marks would exceed the quantity demanded. The resulting surplus of dollars offered for marks would put downward pressure on the exchange rate of marks for dollars. If the price of the dollar were 1.5 marks, the quantity of dollars demanded by holders of marks would exceed the quantity of dollars supplied for marks by holders of dollars. The resulting shortage of dollars would put upward pressure on the exchange rate of marks per dollar.

Actual equilibrium exchange rates change in response to shifts in the demand for and supply of dollars for foreign currencies. In fact, foreign exchange rates are quite volatile. They move up and down almost daily. The fluctuations of foreign exchange rates make international transactions a bit risky. For example, suppose a U.S. car dealer contracts to import 20 BMWs, each at a price of 40,000 German marks. If the current exchange rate is 2 marks per dollar, the dealer expects the cars to cost $20,000 each, for a total outlay of $400,000. The dealer will pay for the cars on delivery, which is expected in about three months. If over the three months the exchange rate falls to 1.5 marks per dollar, each BMW will cost the dealer $26,666 and the dealer's total outlay for the 20 cars will be $533,333! Of course, if the price of the dollar in terms of the mark were to rise, the cost in terms of dollars would fall. If 4 marks were necessary to purchase each dollar, the price per BMW would be only $10,000. As you can see, fluctuating exchange rates add risk to international transactions.[1]

The table in Box 4 shows the exchange rates of various foreign currencies per dollar as of mid-July 1986 and February 1993. The table also shows the exchange rates of dollars for foreign currencies—the number of dollars necessary to purchase a unit of a foreign currency. It's a good idea to compare these exchange rates with the ones prevailing today. To do so, turn to the financial section of any major newspaper, where exchange rates for the dollar are reported daily.

The Determinants of Foreign Exchange Rates

Remember that the demand for dollars by foreigners is generated by the desire and ability of foreigners to buy U.S. goods and services and to acquire real and financial assets denominated in dollars. These are the factors that determine the supply of dollars in foreign exchange markets.

The foreign exchange rate of the dollar is likely to change in response to change in a variety of economic conditions that change the demand for or supply of dollars in foreign exchange markets. Six major influences on the demand for and supply of dollars are foreign demand for U.S. exports, U.S. demand for imports, real interest rates in the United States relative to those in foreign nations, the profitability of direct investments in U.S. businesses and real estate relative to the profitability of similar investments abroad, expectations of the dollar's future price in terms of foreign currencies, and the U.S. price level relative to price levels in foreign nations.

---

[1] Some of this risk can be controlled by engaging in forward transactions in foreign exchange markets. To do so, traders purchase marks at a fixed price for delivery one to three months in the future.

Box 4   Foreign Exchange

Country	U.S. dollars per unit of foreign currency	Foreign currency per U.S. dollar
July 11, 1986		
Britain	1.5015 U.S. dollars per British pound	0.666 British pound per U.S. dollar
Canada	0.7257 U.S. dollar per Canadian dollar	1.378 Canadian dollars per U.S. dollar
France	0.1420 U.S. dollar per French franc	7.0445 French francs per U.S. dollar
Italy	0.000665 U.S. dollar per Italian lira	1,500 Italian lire per U.S. dolllar
Japan	0.006186 U.S. dollar per Japanese yen	161.65 Japanese yen per U.S. dollar
Germany	0.4554 U.S. dollar per German mark	2.196 German marks per U.S. dollar
February 19, 1993		
Britain	1.4540 U.S. dollars per British pound	0.6878 British pound per U.S. dollar
Canada	0.7954 U.S. dollar per Canadian dollar	1.2572 Canadian dollars per U.S. dollar
France	0.1804 U.S. dollar per French franc	5.5420 French francs per U.S. dollar
Italy	0.000638 U.S. dollar per Italian lira	1,568.50 Italian lire per U.S. dollar
Japan	0.0008428 U.S. dollar per Japanese yen	118.65 Japanese yen per U.S. dollar
Germany	0.6109 U.S. dollar per German mark	1.6370 German marks per U.S. dollar

Foreign Demand for U.S. Exports   If British importers sharply increase their demand for U.S. grain without decreasing their demand for other U.S. products, British demand for U.S. dollars will go up. British citizens' entire demand curve for dollars will shift outward. Other things being equal, an increase in British demand for U.S. exports tends to put upward pressure on the exchange rate of the dollar in terms of British pounds.

An increase in foreign demand for U.S. exports can result from increases in real income in foreign nations. Remember that income is a major determinant of import demand (see the chapter on the components of aggregate demand). As income in a foreign nation increases, the annual dollar volume of imports from the United States tends to increase. An increase in real income in foreign nations therefore tends to put upward pressure on the exchange rate of the dollar. A decrease in income in foreign nations tends to decrease the demand for U.S. dollars and to put downward pressure on the price of the dollar. From 1985 to 1993, lagging income and high unemployment rates in many foreign nations were responsible for slack demand for U.S. dollars, which put downward pressure on the price of the dollar in terms of foreign currencies.

Similarly, changes in tastes can affect the demand of foreigners for U.S. goods. If U.S. goods become more fashionable, the demand of foreigners for U.S. dollars will increase, putting upward pressure on the price of the dollar.

The graph in Box 5 shows how an increase in German citizens' demand for dollars resulting from an increase in German demand for U.S. exports causes an increase in the exchange rate of the dollar. If the growth rate of real income in Germany exceeds that in the United States, the result is likely to be upward pressure on the exchange rate of the dollar, as shown in Box 5.

U.S. Demand for Imports   An increase in U.S. demand for imports will increase the supply of dollars offered in foreign exchange markets. For example, if the U.S. demand for BMWs and Mercedes-Benzes increases along with the U.S. demand for other German products, the result will be an increase in the supply of dollars in foreign exchange markets. This will decrease the exchange rate of the dollar. The graph in Box 6 shows how an increase in the supply of dollars reduces the price of the dollar in terms of marks.

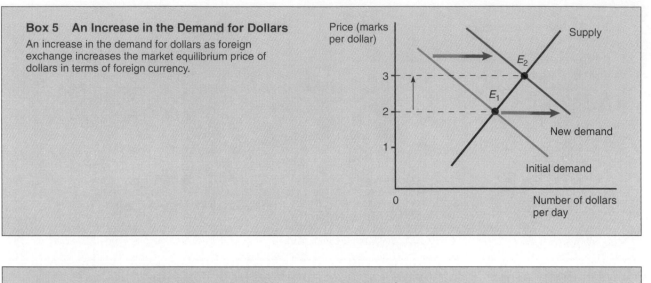

Box 5   An Increase in the Demand for Dollars
An increase in the demand for dollars as foreign exchange increases the market equilibrium price of dollars in terms of foreign currency.

Box 6   An Increase in the Supply of Dollars
An increase in the supply of dollars as foreign exchange decreases the market equilibrium price of dollars in terms of foreign currency.

A major factor influencing the U.S. demand for imports is real income in the United States. An increase in aggregate real income tends to increase the U.S. demand for imports. As this occurs, the supply of dollars offered in foreign exchange markets increases, putting downward pressure on the price of the dollar. Similarly, a decrease in aggregate real income in the United States tends to decrease the U.S. demand for imports. As the supply of dollars declines, there is upward pressure on exchange rates.

Real Interest Rates in the United States Relative to Those in Foreign Nations The willingness of foreigners to hold dollar assets in the United States depends on the interest rates that can be earned on assets denominated in dollars. The higher U.S. real interest rates are relative to real interest rates in foreign nations, the greater the demand of foreigners to hold dollar financial assets and, other things being equal, the higher the exchange rate of the dollar.

High real interest rates in the United States in the early 1980s contributed to strong demand by foreigners for dollars and caused the exchange rate of the dollar to soar. In 1985 and 1986, when U.S. interest rates fell relative to those in foreign nations, the exchange rate of the dollar against such key currencies as the mark and the yen plummeted. Note that such changes in the demand for dollars can be caused either by a change in U.S. real interest rates or by changes in foreign real interest rates. In 1992 and 1993 U.S. real interest rates were low relative to those in Germany and the dollar fell in value relative to the mark.

Higher real interest rates in the United States relative to those in foreign nations will decrease the supply of dollars offered on foreign exchange markets, because given higher real U.S. interest rates, U.S. investors will be less interested in selling dollars to make loans to foreign governments and to buy the securities of foreign businesses. This will tend to put upward pressure on the exchange rate as the supply curve of dollars shifts to the left.

The Profitability of Direct Investments in U.S. Businesses and Real Estate Relative to the Profitability of Similar Investments in Foreign Nations Foreigners also demand dollars to purchase U.S. corporate stock, U.S. real estate, and other U.S. assets. As the profitability of U.S. assets rises relative to that of assets in foreign nations, the demand for dollars to make such investments increases, putting upward pressure on exchange rates. At the same time, the supply of dollars to make direct investments in foreign nations decreases. This too puts upward pressure on the exchange rate of the dollar.

Expectations of the Dollar's Future Price in Terms of Foreign Currencies The demand for and supply of a given currency depends in part on expectations of future changes in exchange rates. Expectations of a higher future price for the U.S. dollar will increase the current demand for dollars, putting upward pressure on the current exchange rate. Expectations of a decrease in the price of the dollar in terms of foreign currency will decrease the current demand for dollars and put downward pressure on the current exchange rate.

If the exchange rate of the dollar is expected to rise, the supply of dollars will tend to decrease. U.S. importers will delay their purchases from foreign nations until the exchange rate increases, because an increase in the price of the dollar in terms of a foreign currency signifies a decrease in the price of the foreign currency in terms of the dollar. The decrease in the supply of dollars will put upward pressure on the exchange rate. Imports will become cheaper as the exchange rate of the dollar rises.

The U.S. Price Level Relative to Price Levels in Foreign Nations If the prices of U.S. goods go up by 10 percent relative to the prices of competing goods supplied by foreign producers and the exchange rate is unchanged, it follows that the effective prices of U.S. goods in foreign currency will also be 10 percent higher. This will decrease the quantity of U.S. goods demanded by foreign buyers, which, in turn, will decrease the demand for dollars. The result will tend to be a reduction in the exchange rate. Further, an increase in the U.S. price level relative to that in foreign nations will make foreign goods cheaper relative to U.S. goods, other things being equal. The increase in import demand will increase the supply of dollars offered on foreign exchange markets, putting further downward pressure on the exchange rate of the dollar. Similarly, a fall in U.S. prices relative to foreign prices will increase the demand for U.S. exports and thus increase the price of the dollar in terms of foreign currencies.

Appreciation and Depreciation of Currencies

As was just pointed out, exchange rates change frequently under the current system of international exchange. Currency appreciation occurs when there is an increase in the number of units of one nation's currency that must be given up to purchase each unit of another nation's currency. For example, the dollar appreciates relative to the

currency appreciation a situation that occurs when there is an increase in the number of units of one nation's currency that must be given up to purchase each unit of another nation's currency.

German mark if the equilibrium price (the exchange rate) of the dollar increases in terms of the mark. If the equilibrium price of a dollar goes up from 2 marks to 3 marks, the dollar has appreciated relative to the mark. Similarly, currency depreciation occurs when there is a decrease in the number of units of one nation's currency that must be given up to purchase each unit of another nation's currency. The data in Box 4 show that the dollar depreciated against the mark between July 1986 and February 1993, when its exchange rate fell from 2.196 marks per dollar to only 1.637 marks per dollar.

currency depreciation a situation that occurs when there is a decrease in the number of units of one nation's currency that must be given up to purchase each unit of another nation's currency.

When the dollar appreciates in terms of the mark, it follows that the mark depreciates in terms of the dollar. It takes more marks to purchase a dollar, and fewer dollars are needed to purchase a mark. Similarly, when the dollar depreciates in terms of the mark, the mark appreciates in terms of the dollar. Between July 1986 and February 1993 the mark appreciated from 0.4554 to 0.6109 mark per dollar.

Note that when the U.S. dollar appreciates, other things being unchanged, goods and services produced in the United States become more expensive in terms of foreign currencies. This tends to decrease the foreign demand for U.S. goods and services and to decrease U.S. net exports and real GDP. Similarly, because foreign currencies depreciate when the U.S. dollar appreciates, foreign goods and services become cheaper in terms of the U.S. dollar when the U.S. dollar appreciates, inducing U.S. citizens to spend more dollars on them. This also decreases aggregate demand for U.S. goods.

The appreciation or depreciation of a currency in a free market results from shifts in either the demand for or supply of the currency. Forecasting changes in foreign exchange rates thus requires an understanding of the forces underlying foreigners' demand for dollars and for assets denominated in dollars. It also requires an understanding of the forces influencing the supply of dollars offered in exchange for foreign currencies.

The Principle of Purchasing Power Parity

purchasing power parity a principle stating that the exchange rate between any two currencies tends to adjust to reflect changes in the price levels in the two nations.

The principle of purchasing power parity of one nation's money for another's states that the exchange rate between any two currencies tends to adjust to reflect changes in the price levels in the two nations. The logic behind purchasing power parity is that similar goods produced in different nations should sell for the same price when exchange rates and transaction costs are taken into consideration. Using this logic, a rise in the U.S. price level tends to result in a depreciation of the dollar in terms of foreign currency. Similarly, a decline in the U.S. price level tends to result in an appreciation of the dollar in terms of foreign currency. If purchasing power parity held precisely, whenever the U.S. price level rose 10 percent relative to, say, the German price level, the price of the dollar in terms of the mark would fall by *exactly* 10 percent.

Purchasing power parity holds only if foreign exchange markets are free. However, as you'll soon see, central banks and other governing authorities often intervene in foreign exchange markets. For example, the Federal Reserve System may buy dollars in international markets, thereby increasing demand for the dollar and preventing the price of the dollar from falling in terms of foreign currencies. Similarly, governments often control exchange rates to keep the prices of imports low to their citizens. Moreover, even when foreign exchange markets are free, there is often a lag between changes in the price levels and changes in foreign exchange rates between these nations.

the global economy

The ECU

The European Community Struggles to Create a New Currency If all goes well with the plan it's going to be just a matter of time before French francs, German marks, Italian lire, and other European currencies become as extinct as the dodo bird! As part of its plans to facilitate commerce and financial integration among the 12 members of the European Community (EC), the EC administration hopes to create a new monetary unit that will become the currency of all the EC member nations.

The Maastricht Treaty of 1991 specifies that by the year 2000 a new European currency, to be called the "Ecu," will be the medium of exchange in the European Community. A single currency for the 12 EC nations will greatly facilitate financial and commercial transactions among them by eliminating the risk of exchange rate fluctuations and reducing the transaction costs of exchanging currencies. The EC nations will be much more like a "United States of Europe" if they operate with a single currency. A single currency will also imply a single central bank and a single monetary policy for the 12 EC nations, and this could contribute to lower interest rates by eliminating the risk of devaluation of individual currencies and the risk of divergent and erratic national inflation.

As a prerequisite to monetary integration, the EC nations are currently operating under a system of pegged exchange rates in which most of their currencies are tied to the German mark. This means that a fixed exchange rate between the German mark and each of the 11 other currencies is established by mutual agreement and not allowed to fluctuate. However, if the inflation rate or interest rate of any one nation gets out of line with the rate that prevailed at the time of the initial agreement, shifts in the demand for or supply of its currency could cause the pegged rate to become a disequilibrium rate.

In fact, in 1992 interest rates soared in Germany after the reunification of West Germany and East Germany caused inflationary pressures. In the United Kingdom, where interest rates had been lowered to stimulate an economy in recession, further lowering of interest rates to further stimulate the sluggish economy could not be made without causing a flurry of sales of British pounds to buy German marks. The selling of British pounds, Italian lire, and Spanish pesos required the central banks in the United Kingdom, Italy, and Spain to intervene in the foreign exchange markets by borrowing marks and buying their own currencies. To gain the freedom to lower interest rates and encourage export demand, the United Kingdom and other nations in recession such as Italy, Portugal, and Spain were forced to devalue their currencies relative to the German mark in 1992.

Ultimately, a single ECU currency will require that inflation rates and interest rates be the same in all European nations. The Maastricht treaty specifies that current inflation rates and interest rate levels in all EC countries be equalized as the year 2000 approaches. In recent years, nations with high inflation have often had to devalue their currencies relative to the German mark.

The Maastricht treaty specifies standards that an EC nation must meet in order to join the European Monetary Union and use the Ecu as its national currency. It must have an inflation rate that is no more than 1.5 percentage points above the average inflation rate of the three EC nations with lowest inflation. The interest rate on its long-term government bonds must be no more than 2 percent higher than those of the same three nations. Its budget deficit must be no greater than 3 percent of its GDP, its government debt must not exceed 60 percent of its GDP, and its currency must not have been revalued in the pegged arrangement for at least two years. As of 1992, only three EC nations (Denmark, France, and Luxembourg) met these standards. It is going to take a lot of policy changes to reduce inflation and budget deficits in the other EC nations. A political backlash against the austere requirements for membership in the European Monetary Union could prevent the Ecu from emerging as a common currency in the EC nations.

NOMINAL AND REAL EXCHANGE RATES

nominal exchange rate the price of a unit of one nation's currency in terms of a unit of a foreign currency.

real exchange rate the sacrifice of goods and services that buyers must make when they use their own nation's currency to purchase a unit of the currency of another nation.

The **nominal exchange rate** of a currency is the price of a unit of that currency in terms of a unit of a foreign currency. The **real exchange rate** of a currency is the sacrifice of goods and services that buyers must make when they use their own nation's currency to purchase a unit of the currency of another nation. For example, the real exchange rate of a dollar to an Italian person is the sacrifice of Italian goods and services that the person makes when using Italian lire to buy a dollar.

An increase in the real exchange rate of the dollar occurs when the price of the dollar in terms of lire increases after adjustment for differences in the inflation rates of the United States and Italy. When the real exchange rate of the dollar increases, foreigners give up more purchasing power for each dollar's worth of U.S. goods they buy. On the other hand, when the real exchange rate of the dollar increases, U.S. buyers sacrifice fewer goods and services for any given purchase of foreign goods denominated in a foreign currency. For example, the purchase of 400,000 lire worth of Italian goods involves less of a sacrifice for U.S. buyers when the real exchange rate of the dollar rises in terms of the lira. When the exchange rate of the dollar appreciates in terms of the lira, the exchange rate of the lira in terms of the dollar must fall. Thus, changes in real exchange rates affect the demand for U.S. exports in foreign markets and the U.S. demand for imports by changing the prices of imports and exports after adjustment for inflation.

The Real Exchange Rate of the Dollar, 1973–1990

The real exchange rate of the dollar is usually estimated by the level of U.S. consumer prices in relation to an average of consumer prices in other nations. Consumer prices in other nations are weighted by the trade shares of these nations and adjusted by the dollar exchange rates of their currencies. The graph in Box 7 shows an index (1973 = 100) of the real exchange rate of the U.S. dollar against the currencies of 10 major industrialized nations from 1973 to 1990. Most of the movement is a result of changes in nominal exchange rates. As you can see, the real exchange rate increased sharply from 1980 to 1985 and then fell between 1985 and 1987. In 1988 the real exchange rate increased again as interest rates increased. It then declined in 1989 and 1990.

Despite the decline in the value of the dollar in 1985, the prices of imports did not increase substantially at first. *Empirical evidence suggests that import prices lag up to two years in their response to changes in exchange rates*. Evidence indicates that the profit per unit of output increased for foreign suppliers to U.S. markets between 1980 and 1984, when the dollar appreciated. When the dollar began to depreciate, many foreign sellers apparently chose to get along with less profit per unit rather than raise prices significantly.[2] In addition, many foreign currencies were tied to the dollar, and the dollar did not depreciate substantially against them. Over the period in the 1980s during which the dollar depreciated against the yen and the mark, it actually appreciated against the Korean won, thereby making Korean goods less expensive to U.S. buyers!

---

[2] See *Economic Report of the President, 1987* (Washington, D.C.: U.S. Government Printing Office, 1987), p. 116.

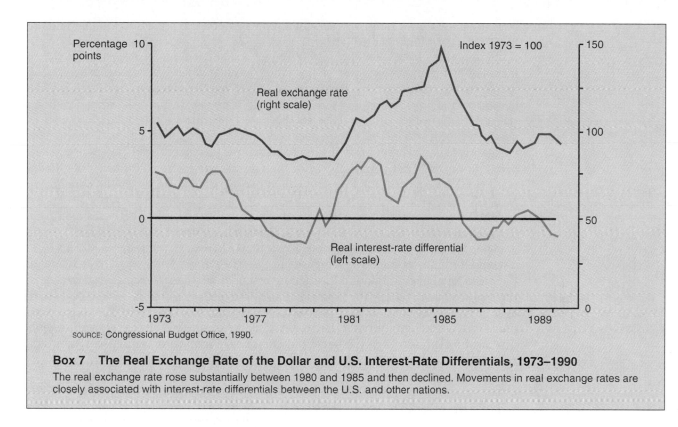

Box 7   The Real Exchange Rate of the Dollar and U.S. Interest-Rate Differentials, 1973–1990

The real exchange rate rose substantially between 1980 and 1985 and then declined. Movements in real exchange rates are closely associated with interest-rate differentials between the U.S. and other nations.

Why did the dollar appreciate considerably in the early 1980s, and why did it decline between 1985 and 1987? Like most prices, the price of the dollar responds to changes in influences on its demand and supply. A key factor that has influenced the price of the dollar in recent years has been real interest rates in the United States relative to those in foreign nations. The high real interest rates that prevailed from 1981 to 1985 increased the demand for dollars that foreigners could use to make investments in U.S. real and financial assets. Large budget deficits and Federal Reserve policies to reduce the rate of inflation contributed to high real interest rates in the early 1980s. Not surprisingly, policies that sharply lowered real interest rates in 1985 and 1986 resulted in marked depreciation of the dollar on international markets.

The graph in Box 7 also shows the real interest-rate differential measured by the difference between U.S. real long-term interest rates and a weighted average of foreign real long-term interest rates. When the interest-rate differential between the United States and foreign nations increases, it becomes more attractive to hold the dollar. As the demand for the dollar increases, so too does the real exchange rate. As you can see from the graph in Box 7, movements in the interest-rate differential between the United States and other nations are followed by similar movements in the real exchange rate of the dollar.

In 1988, when short-term real interest rates began to rise again as the Fed instituted a contractionary monetary policy, the dollar began another upward climb. Moreover, a booming U.S. economy in 1988 and early 1989 also contributed to increased import demand, putting additional upward pressure on the price of the dollar. By late 1989, as short-term interest rates fell somewhat and the U.S. economy began to slow down, there was downward pressure on the price of the dollar and the real exchange rate began to fall.

As you know from your study of aggregate demand–aggregate supply analysis, an increase in the exchange rate of the dollar reduces aggregate demand because it increases the prices of our exports while decreasing the prices of our imports. The decrease in aggregate demand puts downward pressure on both the price level and real GDP. However, an increase in the exchange rate of the dollar also causes aggregate supply to increase by reducing the prices of imported inputs. The increase in aggregate supply puts downward pressure on the price level but puts upward pressure on real GDP. An increase in the real exchange rate therefore puts downward pressure on the price level but can either increase or decrease the equilibrium level of real GDP.

Similarly, a decrease in the real exchange rate of the dollar increases aggregate demand and decreases aggregate supply. Aggregate demand increases when the real exchange rate falls, because the demand for U.S. exports increases, while U.S. demand for imports falls. The increase in aggregate demand puts upward pressure on the price level and on real GDP. Aggregate supply decreases because a decrease in the real exchange rate of the dollar increases the prices of imports. The decrease in aggregate supply puts upward pressure on the price level but also puts downward pressure on equilibrium real GDP. Thus, a decrease in the real exchange rate puts upward pressure on the price level but can either increase or decrease equilibrium real GDP.

CONCEPT CHECK

☐

- What could cause the foreign exchange rate of the dollar to increase?

- In early 1987 the price of the dollar in terms of yen plummeted. What could have caused the decline in the yen price of dollars?

- How can an increase in the real exchange rate of the dollar against foreign currencies influence macroeconomic equilibrium in the United States?

INTERNATIONAL PAYMENTS AND THE INTERNATIONAL MONETARY SYSTEM

3 You've just seen how fluctuations in foreign exchange rates can affect the economy. The current international monetary system allows exchange rates to be influenced by market forces. However, governments and central banks also influence exchange rates as they intervene in foreign exchange markets in attempts to control the macroeconomic effects of exchange rate fluctuations on their economies.

We're now ready to discuss the evolution of the current international monetary system. Flexible foreign exchange rates have been the exception rather than the rule throughout much of the past century. This section gives you a quick tour of the way the international monetary system has changed since 1900.

gold standard an international monetary system that required currencies to be convertible into gold at a fixed price.

The Gold Standard   For much of the time prior to the 1930s, the international monetary system was based on a gold standard, under which currencies were required to be convertible into gold at fixed prices. Convertibility into gold resulted in fixed exchange rates as long as nations kept the value of their currencies constant in terms of gold. Until the beginning of World War I, for example, the U.S. dollar was worth $1/20$ ounce of gold, while the British pound was worth $1/4$ ounce of gold.

Therefore, it took $5 to buy a British pound because $5 was necessary to buy $5/20 = $ $1/4$ ounce of gold.

It's easy to see how the system worked. Suppose the price of a case of Scotch was 100 British pounds. At the fixed exchange rate it would take $500 to purchase the case. Suppose, however, the British pound appreciated, so that it took $6 to buy each British pound. Under the gold standard, no one would buy pounds for dollars at any exchange rate significantly higher than $5, because each pound could be bought just as easily for $1/4$ ounce of gold. Transferring the $1/4$ ounce of gold to British ownership would cost only $5 plus a modest fee. Under the gold standard, currencies could fluctuate only within narrow bands that depended on the costs of transferring gold ownership between nations.

There were important consequences of international changes in gold ownership. Each nation used gold as an international reserve that constituted its monetary base. When a nation lost gold, its money supply usually decreased because of the resulting decline in its bank reserves. The decrease in the money supply tended to reduce that nation's price level in the long run. Similarly, when a nation gained gold, its money supply usually increased, which tended to increase its price level in the long run. *Under the gold standard, changes in relative price levels among nations caused by gold flows tended to keep currencies from appreciating or depreciating in the long run.*

Under the gold standard, few nations played the game strictly according to the rules. Nations hesitated to let their price levels fall for fear that because of inflexible wages, reductions in the money supply would cause short-run unemployment and recessions. To avoid changes in their price levels, nations commonly changed the official quantity of gold that could be exchanged for their currency. By devaluing their currency in terms of gold, they allowed it to officially depreciate. For example, if the pound were devalued so that it was worth only $1/8$ ounce of gold, it would take only $2.50 to purchase each pound. Such a devaluation would stimulate the demand for British exports without the need for a fall in the British price level through an outflow of gold.

The Bretton Woods System   In 1944, representatives of the United States and other industrial nations met at Bretton Woods, New Hampshire, to develop a new international monetary system. Like the international monetary system based on the gold standard, this system was characterized by fixed exchange rates. *However, the Bretton Woods system tied the value of foreign currencies, not to gold, but to the U.S. dollar!* The United States had accumulated a great deal of foreign exchange and gold and was in a strong financial position compared to that of most European nations, many of which had been shattered by World War II. The dollar was directly convertible into gold by foreign nations and their central banks at the fixed price of $35 per ounce. Central banks agreed to intervene in foreign exchange markets to buy or sell currencies whenever the currency of their nation appreciated or depreciated. Few of the nations that entered into the Bretton Woods system had any gold; instead, most of them held dollars as their international reserves. Of course, such purchases and sales of currencies would alter the money supply within nations just as gold flows did under the gold standard. On the other hand, under the Bretton Woods system the United States was responsible for buying and selling gold so as to keep its price at $35 per ounce.

The system allowed nations to *devalue* (officially depreciate) or *revalue* (officially appreciate) their currency in terms of dollars. Nations would devalue or revalue their

Bretton Woods system an international monetary system developed in 1944 and based on fixed exchange rates, with the value of foreign currencies tied to the U.S. dollar.

currencies on occasion to affect net exports in ways designed to stabilize their economies.

The Bretton Woods agreement also established the International Monetary Fund (IMF), which set rules for the international monetary system to make loans to nations that lacked international reserves of dollars.

Dissatisfaction with the Bretton Woods system developed in the 1960s. Nations whose currencies were undervalued relative to the equilibrium exchange rate in terms of dollars were unwilling to allow the international price of their currencies to rise because the resulting decline in net exports would have decreased aggregate demand in those nations. Another problem was that under the Bretton Woods rules the United States could not devalue its currency to stimulate net exports. In 1971 the United States suspended convertibility of the dollar into gold, and by 1973 the United States and other nations in the Bretton Woods system abandoned fixed exchange rates in favor of a system of flexible or *floating* rates determined in part by market forces.

The Current System   The current international monetary system allows free-market determination of exchange rates, but it also allows central banks to buy and sell currencies to stabilize exchange rates. In effect, the current system is a managed float in which central banks affect the supply of and demand for currencies in ways that influence equilibrium in foreign exchange markets. Under the current system, central banks frequently buy their own nation's currency on international foreign exchange markets to keep it from depreciating. They often resist currency depreciation because it makes imported goods, such as those from the United States, more expensive for the citizens. However, when central banks buy their own nation's currency, they lose reserves of foreign currencies, such as dollars. The loss of reserves by debtor nations is a matter for concern. When nations such as Mexico lose their dollar reserves, the only way they can acquire more dollars is by running a balance of trade surplus with the United States. Nations that combine a loss in dollar reserves with a decline in net exports run the risk of defaulting on their international loans. This reduces the profitability of U.S. banks that hold those loans as assets.

The current international monetary system has a paper substitute for gold called a special drawing right (SDR). SDRs are created by the International Monetary Fund and distributed to member nations for use as *international reserves* with which to make international payments. SDRs fulfill the role that gold played in settling international debts when a nation lacked the foreign exchange to do so. Gold is now completely demonetized because no major currency is convertible into it. Gold can be bought and sold on the free market like any other good.

THE INTERNATIONAL BALANCE OF PAYMENTS AND BALANCE OF TRADE AND FOREIGN SAVING IN THE UNITED STATES

When the United States runs a balance of trade deficit, foreign saving in the United States must increase. We can now examine the financial relations between the United States and the rest of the world to show that the balance of trade deficit is equal to the net increase in foreign saving in the United States over any given period.

A nation's international balance of payments is a statement showing the net exchange of that nation's currency for foreign currencies from *all transactions* between that nation and foreign nations in a given year. For example, the U.S. balance of payments statement shows the number of dollars supplied for *all* foreign transactions and the number of dollars demanded by *all* foreign nations. *The actual number of dollars purchased by foreigners must always equal the actual number of*

International Monetary Fund (IMF) established under the Bretton Woods agreement, set rules for the international monetary system to make loans to nations that lacked international reserves of dollars.

managed float the current international monetary system, under which central banks affect supply of and demand for currencies in ways that influence equilibrium in foreign exchange markets.

special drawing right (SDR) a paper substitute for gold created by the International Monetary Fund and distributed to member nations for use as international reserves.

balance of payments a statement showing the net exchange of a nation's currency for foreign currencies from all transactions between that nation and foreign nations in a given year.

Box 8   U.S. International Balance of Payments, 1991 (billions of dollars)

	Amount‡
Current account	
1. Merchandise exports	+416.0
2. Merchandise imports	−489.4
3. Balance of trade = Merchandise exports — Merchandise imports	− 73.4
4. Net investment income	+ 16.4
5. Net military transactions	− 5.4
6. Net travel and transportation receipts	+ 17.1
7. Other services	+ 33.7
8. Balance on goods and services	− 11.7
9. Remittances, pensions, and other transfers	+ 8.0
10. Balance on current account*	− 3.7
Capital account	
11. Foreign assets in U.S.	+ 67.0
12. U.S. government assets abroad	+ 3.4
13. U.S. private assets abroad	− 71.4
14. U.S. official reserve assets†	+ 5.8
15. Statistical discrepancy	− 1.1
16. Capital account balance	+ 3.7

*Excludes military.

†Consists of gold, SDRs, convertible currencies, and U.S. reserve position in IMF.

‡Totals may not add because of rounding.

SOURCE: *Economic Report of the President,* 1993.

dollars sold over the year. The international transaction reported in the U.S. balance of payments accounts include exports and imports of goods, transactions for foreign services (including expenditures of dollars abroad by U.S. travelers), purchases of foreign shipping and insurance services, and transactions involving the exchange of financial and other assets.

The Current Account

The table in Box 8 shows the U.S. balance of payments accounts for 1991. The *current account* summarizes the transactions involving international exchange of goods and services purchased during the year and miscellaneous transactions, including unilateral transfers and military transactions. A plus sign indicates that the transaction earned U.S. sellers the equivalent amount of dollars in foreign exchange. A minus sign indicates a transaction in which the dollar equivalent in foreign exchange was supplied by U.S. buyers to foreigners. Lines 1 and 2 of the table show the dollar value of exports and imports of merchandise in 1991. These figures indicate transactions for merchandise only, not for services. Line 3 shows the **balance of trade,** which is the difference between the dollar value of the merchandise exported by U.S. firms and U.S. imports of foreign merchandise.

The balance of trade gets considerable attention in the press because of its impact on industrial employment in the United States. In 1991, exports of merchandise by U.S. firms didn't earn enough money to balance U.S. imports of merchandise. The balance of trade deficit in that year was $73.4 billion. In 1975, on the other hand, the dollar value of U.S. exports exceeded the dollar value of U.S. imports—the United States had a balance of trade surplus of nearly $9 billion.

balance of trade the difference between the value of merchandise exported by a nation's firms and the nation's imports of foreign merchandise.

principles in practice

The Current Account Deficit

Why Worry about It? OK, the U.S. imports more than it exports—what's the big deal? Why do we worry about the current account deficit? Should we engage in policies that reduce current income or even cause a recession for the sake of eliminating the deficit? Or will the deficit eventually turn around and become a surplus without any government intervention?

The current account deficit increased between 1982 and 1987 primarily because of a decline in U.S. saving. The United States simply went on a consumption binge, increasing the demand for all products, including imported products. This increase in aggregate expenditures over aggregate domestic production contributed to the current account deficit. From 1987 to 1990, U.S. saving increased somewhat and was accompanied by a reduction in the current account deficit of 30 percent from its mid-1987 peak. Therefore, one way to reduce the current account deficit is to increase our saving rate. If we reduce the federal budget deficit—a major negative component of national saving—the current account trade deficit could easily become a surplus.

Another cause of the current account deficit is currency appreciation. From 1982 to 1985, the U.S. dollar appreciated by an amazing 60 percent. The current account deficit ballooned as imports became cheaper and the prices of U.S. exports soared in foreign markets. The sharp upward swings in foreign exchange rates caused U.S. firms to lose market share in both domestic and international markets.

A policy that contributes to reasonably stable exchange rates can prevent sharp swings in the current account deficit or surplus. Exchange rates tend to fluctuate with changes in interest rates. Thus, erratic monetary policies that cause interest rates to fluctuate widely will also cause fluctuations in exchange rates.

A current account deficit usually implies negative net exports. A negative net export component of aggregate demand means that the international sector of the economy is an overall contractionary influence on equilibrium real GDP. High negative net exports can therefore contribute to an economic downturn and even a recession.

Income and employment from the sale of certain domestic goods and services decline as a result of foreign competition. As this occurs, there are inevitably pressures for protectionist trade policies, including tariffs and import quotas, that can lead to inefficient resource use over the long run. Domestic protectionism can spill over into the global economy if other nations retaliate.

Monetary policy is unlikely to improve the current account balance because it is a double-edged sword whose use simultaneously encourages and discourages net exports. For example, if the Fed were to engage in a contractionary monetary policy to reduce aggregate demand, import demand would decline. The rise in real interest rates would increase the demand for the dollar, which, in turn, would increase its real exchange rate. The increase in the real exchange rate of the dollar would decrease export demand and increase import demand. The improvement in the current account balance due to the decline in import demand would therefore be offset by the exchange rate effects of the contractionary monetary policy.

Some nations engage in "austerity programs" to improve their current account deficits. Monetary authorities engineer massive declines in aggregate demand to offset the exchange rate effects of higher interest rates. The result is often a recession. Many economists regard austerity programs as a cure much worse than the disease.

Finally, monetary authorities sometimes intervene in foreign exchange markets to reduce the foreign exchange rate of their currency. As the exchange rate falls, exports increase and imports decline, contributing to an improvement in the current account balance. If carried on for a long period, however, such exchange rate policies distort resource allocation and reduce efficiency of production by making imported inputs and outputs seem more expensive than they really are. Artificially low exchange rates also subsidize exports, causing a nation's export industries to grow more than they otherwise would.

The problem with most policies designed specifically to improve a nation's current account deficit is that they have undesirable side effects. Austerity measures and contractionary monetary policy can cause a recession and, in general, reduce living standards in the nation. Over the long run, exchange rate intervention distorts resource use. The only lasting cure for a current account deficit is programs designed to increase national saving. Such programs may involve lower current living standards, but they will raise future living standards.

In 1991 the U.S. current account deficit declined substantially because that year a recession in the United States reduced the U.S. demand for imports.

Because international trade transactions also involve the receipt and payment of interest and investment income during the year and the exchange of services, the balance of trade provides an incomplete picture of the net current inflow and outflow of payments. For example, as shown on line 4 of the table, net investment income in 1991 from international transactions was $16.4 billion, the amount by which receipts from U.S. investment abroad exceeded payments to foreign investors in the United States. Lines 5, 6, and 7 of the table show other service transactions, including travel and transportation. The *balance of goods and services* on line 8 indicates that when international transactions for services are added to those for merchandise, Americans supplied $11.7 billion more to foreigners than foreigners supplied in the dollar equivalent of foreign currency to the United States. Payments for pensions, remittances, and other unilateral transfers of funds, such as gifts and foreign aid, shown on line 9, amounted to $8 billion in 1991.

The **balance on current account of the balance of payments,** shown on line 10, which includes transactions involving services, investment income, and transfers, is roughly equal to U.S. net exports as measured by the National Income and Product Accounts.[3] In 1991 the United States had a deficit on current account of $3.7 billion. That year Americans supplied foreigners with that many more dollars than foreigners supplied to the United States in foreign exchange for American goods and services and as interest or investment income.

balance on current account of the balance of payments measures U.S. net exports for the year, including transactions involving services, investment income, and transfers.

The graph in Box 9 shows the U.S. merchandise trade balance (balance of trade) and the current account balance from 1950 to 1991. The balance of trade has been in deficit every year since 1975. Except for a short period in the late 1970s and the early 1980s, the current account has also been consistently in deficit since 1975.

The Capital Account

The balance on current account represents the relationship between current earnings of dollars from international trade and current payments of U.S. dollars to acquire foreign exchange to settle payments to foreigners. When the current account is in deficit, as it was in 1991, the United States has to pay more dollars out in international transactions than it earns from international transactions during the year. In 1991 the United States had to borrow and sell assets to finance the deficit on current account.

The increase in foreign assets in the United States, shown on line 11 in Box 8, represents borrowing from foreigners to balance the current account deficit. This represents *foreign saving in the United States.* Lines 12 through 14 represent purchases and sales of assets by individuals, the U.S. government, and the Federal Reserve System.

When the data gathered for the capital account don't exactly match, there is a *statistical discrepancy,* shown on line 15. The statistical discrepancy in 1991 was $1.1 billion. This sum represents foreign payments of dollars in the United States that the data gatherers estimated existed but could not track down by source. For example, a portion of the $1.1 billion obtained in this way may have resulted from smuggling and other illegal transactions involving exports of U.S. goods and services.

Line 16 of the table in Box 8 shows the capital account balance, which is +$3.7 billion. *The capital account balance is a surplus that is exactly equal to the deficit on*

---

[3] Because of slightly different accounting techniques, the balance on current account is not exactly equal to net exports.

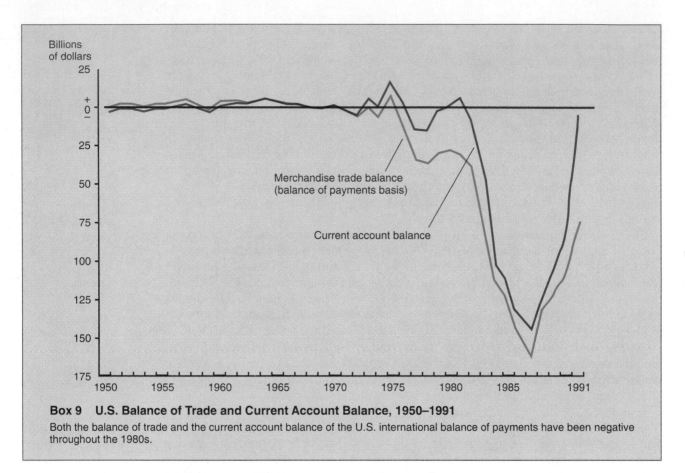

Billions of dollars

Box 9   U.S. Balance of Trade and Current Account Balance, 1950–1991

Both the balance of trade and the current account balance of the U.S. international balance of payments have been negative throughout the 1980s.

the balance on current account. Whenever the current account is in deficit, there must be a net increase in the real and financial assets held by foreigners over the foreign assets acquired by Americans during the year. You learned this earlier in the circular flow analysis in the chapter on the GDP. *Whenever net exports are negative, net foreign saving in the United States increases by an amount equal to the excess of imports over exports.* Similarly, if net exports were positive, the balance on the current account would be a surplus, which a net increase in U.S. saving abroad would offset. As was pointed out earlier in this chapter, foreign saving in the United States increases the supply of loanable funds in U.S. credit markets, thereby putting downward pressure on real interest rates in the United States.

The way the capital account is related to the current account points out an important long-term implication of chronic deficits on the current account. A deficit on the current account implies that the United States must borrow from foreigners or sell foreign assets. As this occurs, the United States in the aggregate becomes more indebted to foreigners or reduces its holdings of foreign assets. The deficits on the current account since 1975 has resulted in a sharp increase in foreign ownership of U.S. assets. In the future foreigners will earn more U.S. interest and investment income each year, which, in turn, will force the United States to export more or import less to avoid a deficit on the current account. Similarly, by reducing its holdings of assets abroad, the United States will have less income from abroad to offset import purchases.

- How did the gold standard work as an international monetary system?
- If the balance on the current account of the U.S. balance of payments is −$140 billion, what is the balance on the capital account?
- How will foreign saving in the United States be affected if the United States runs a balance of trade surplus? What effect will the balance of trade surplus have on real interest rates in the United States?

SUMMARY

1. A nation's foreign exchange rate is the price of its monetary unit in terms of the monetary unit of another nation. Buyers and sellers of bank deposits denominated in the monetary units of many nations exchange their monies in the foreign exchange market.

2. For U.S. sellers an export transaction requires that foreign buyers purchase dollars by writing checks on their own bank accounts denominated in their nation's currency. When paid, exporters gain dollars and U.S. banks gain deposits in foreign banks denominated in foreign currencies. Import transactions by U.S. buyers result in payments in foreign currencies to foreign suppliers and in the acquisition of dollar deposits in the United States by foreign banks as dollars are used to purchase foreign currencies from foreign banks.

3. *Foreign exchange* is the money of one nation held by citizens of another nation as either currency or as bank deposits.

4. The number of dollars demanded as foreign exchange tends to increase as the price of the dollar declines in terms of foreign currencies. As the price of the dollar declines, U.S. goods become cheaper in terms of foreign currencies.

5. The demand for dollars as foreign exchange is likely to increase in response to an increase in foreign demand for U.S. exports, an increase in real income rates in the United States relative to those in foreign nations, expectations of a future increase in the price of dollars in terms of foreign currencies, or a decrease in the U.S. price level relative to price levels in foreign nations.

6. The number of dollars supplied in exchange for foreign currencies depends on the demand of U.S. citizens for foreign goods, services, and assets. An increase in the price of the dollar in terms of foreign currencies increases the number of dollars supplied to foreigners because it makes foreign goods cheaper to U.S. buyers.

7. The supply curve of dollars offered in exchange for foreign currency can shift in response to any change that increases the demand of dollar holders for U.S. goods and services or U.S. assets.

8. Currency appreciation occurs when there is an increase in the number of units of one nation's currency that must be given up to purchase each unit of another nation's currency. Currency depreciation occurs when there is a decrease in the number of units of one nation's currency that must be given up to purchase each unit of another nation's currency.

9. The principle of purchasing power parity of one nation's currency for another's states that the exchange rate between the currencies of any two nations tends to adjust to reflect changes in the price levels in the two nations.

10. The real exchange rate of a nation's currency is the sacrifice of goods and services that buyers must make when they use their own nation's currency to purchase a unit of another nation's currency.

11. A change in the real exchange rate of the dollar can shift both aggregate supply and aggregate demand. An increase in the real exchange rate of the dollar will decrease inflationary pressures in the U.S. economy. The effect of the higher dollar on equilibrium real GDP depends on both the demand-side and supply-side effects. A higher dollar decreases aggregate demand by reducing net exports, but it also increases aggregate supply by reducing the prices of imports.

12. The gold standard was an international monetary system under which currencies required to be convertible into gold at fixed prices. The gold standard limited the range of variation in exchange rates because it was cheaper to pay in gold than in foreign currency when the exchange rate rose above certain levels. Under the gold standard, nations tied their money supply to gold inflow and outflow. As a result, price levels eventually went up and down as nations gained or lost gold.

13. The Bretton Woods system tied the value of foreign currencies in the U.S. dollar, which was convertible into gold at the rate of $35 per ounce. The system collapsed in 1973, when a system of flexible exchange rates was adopted. Currently, exchange rates are influenced by the forces of supply and demand, but central banks frequently intervene in the market to affect supply and demand.

14. An international balance of payments is a statement showing the net exchange of a nation's currency for foreign currencies from all transactions between that nation and foreign nations in a given year.

15. The balance of trade is the difference between the value of merchandise exports and the value of merchandise imports. A balance of trade deficit exists when merchandise imports exceed merchandise exports for the year, while a balance of trade surplus exists when merchandise exports exceed merchandise imports for the year.

16. The balance on current account of the balance of payments measures U.S. net exports for the year, including transactions involving services, investment income, and transfers. A deficit on current account puts downward pressure on aggregate demand.

17. The capital account of the international balance of payments shows transactions involving physical and financial assets for the year. A deficit on the current account must always be offset by an equal surplus on the capital account.

KEY TERMS

foreign exchange rate *493*
foreign exchange market *494*
foreign exchange *496*
currency appreciation *501*
currency depreciation *502*

purchasing power parity *502*
nominal exchange rate *504*
real exchange rate *504*
gold standard *506*
Bretton Woods system *507*

International Monetary Fund (IMF) *508*
managed float *508*
special drawing right (SDR) *508*

balance of payments *508*
balance of trade *509*
balance on current account of the balance of payments *511*

CONCEPT REVIEW

1 If it takes 5 French francs to purchase a dollar, how many dollars will you need to pay for a hotel room in Paris that costs 520 francs?

2 What can cause the dollar to depreciate on foreign exchange markets?

3 Briefly describe how the current international monetary system functions.

PROBLEMS AND APPLICATIONS

1. Suppose you export $300,000 of lumber to a builder in Italy. The current exchange rate is 1,500 lire to the dollar. Show the effect of your transaction on the balance sheets of U.S. and Italian banks. **1**

2. As a U.S. auto dealer, you import 200 BMWs from Germany during the year. The total dollar volume of your import transaction is $3 million. The current exchange rate is 2 German marks per U.S. dollar. Show the impact of your import transaction on the balance sheets of U.S. and German banks. **1**

3. Suppose the dollar depreciates on international markets so that it is worth only 1.5 marks. Each BMW that cost 30,000 marks last year still costs the same in terms of marks this year. Calculate last year's and this year's cost of a BMW in terms of dollars. Assuming that as an auto dealer you pay an average of 30,000 marks per BMW and that you import 200 BMWs this year, calculate the cost of your annual order using the new exchange rate. **1**, **2**

4. The U.S. dollar can be purchased for 1.4 Canadian dollars. How many U.S. dollars are necessary to purchase a Canadian dollar? **1**, **2**

5. The current price of the dollar in terms of the Japanese yen is 140 yen per dollar. Suppose real interest rates increase in Japan but fall in the United States. Use supply and demand analysis to show how the change in relative interest rates is likely to affect the exchange rate of the dollar in terms of yen. **2**

6. Suppose the price level in Japan increases relative to that in the United States. What impact is this likely to have on the exchange rate of the dollar in terms of yen? **2**

7. Suppose U.S. firms mount a successful advertising campaign that increases the Japanese demand for U.S. goods. Assuming that nothing else changes, predict the effect on the price of the dollar in terms of the yen. **2**

8. The current account balance of the U.S. international balance of payments is − $150 billion. What effect have international transactions had on aggregate demand in the United States for the year? What is the capital account balance of the U.S. international balance of payments for the year? **3**

9. Explain why a U.S. surplus on the current account of the international balance of payments implies that U.S. ownership of foreign assets must increase. Why does a deficit on the current account imply that foreign ownership of U.S. assets must increase? ▣

10. In 1987 the real exchange rate of the dollar depreciated sharply against the Japanese yen and the German mark. However, there was little improvement in the U.S. international balance of trade. Explain why the fall of the dollar in 1987 had little short-run impact on the balance of trade deficit. ▣ , ▣

career profile

Brian Gendreau The same subject that was almost Brian Gendreau's downfall in high school has become a mainstay of his job, as well as a hobby.

Gendreau, a vice president at Morgan Guaranty Trust Co., used to be poor in math because he saw no point to it. But when he decided to major in economics, he realized how useful math would be to him. As Brian puts it, "I needed a better tool kit. The analytical tools of higher math are so strong they let you see connections and consequences that would otherwise be invisible," he explains. "And as a hobby, it beats working crossword puzzles. In fact, it provides the same kind of intellectual satisfaction as playing chess."

The son of a Foreign Service Officer, Gendreau spent much of his childhood in Latin America. In college, he planned to major in philosophy because he had normative questions about the world: Why are people poor? Is the state ever justified in limiting personal liberty? Should we redistribute wealth? His freshman year at Northwestern University, Gendreau had the good fortune to be taught by Jonathan Hughes, author of *The Vital Few,* a study of such key figures in American history as William Penn and Andrew Carnegie. He became more interested in theory and in the power of the market to allocate resources effectively—as well as the problems that occur when markets fail—and that led him to economics.

By the time he had received his Ph.D. in business economics from the Wharton School of the University of Pennsylvania, Gendreau says, "Education had made me into a skeptic. When politicians of any stripe began describing their wish lists for new programs, my first reaction was, 'Who's going to pay for it?' and 'Is there a less expensive way of doing the same thing?' Economists are trained to think in terms of trade-offs, and I began to realize that the pros and cons often even out at the margin. People are continuously balancing opportunities against costs."

Following stints at the Federal Reserve and Morgan in which he covered banking markets, Gendreau jumped at the chance to head up a team within Morgan's economic research department that focuses on "emerging markets"—the new term for developing countries in Asia, Latin America, Eastern Europe, and Africa. Gendreau now is often called on to provide instant analyses of events in the emerging market countries. The process begins at an 8:30 meeting every morning when he and other economists brief J. P. Morgan traders and salespeople, and continues throughout the day as news stories hit the wire services. "It's hard to do because you have to tell the traders something they don't already know, and they are in constant communication with the markets. So we have to go one step farther; we have to put the event in context and tell them what is likely to happen next."

Not surprisingly, Gendreau's job involves lots of travel. "In the first three months of 1992 alone I was in Miami, Washington, Sao Paulo, Hong Kong, Shanghai, and Beijing. To be sure, many of the trips I take are to interesting and exotic places; but waiting in airport queues, living out of a suitcase, and trying to remember what time zone I'm in gets old after a while." Another drawback is long hours: 70-hour workweeks are common, and Gendreau once worked nearly a year without a single weekend off. "Working that much is disorienting," he says, "but it's by no means unique to my company. Wall Street is full of aggressive people willing to work long hours to beat the competition."

The plus side of his job is the opportunity to write for an audience of market participants and policymakers who listen to what his firm has to say. A big part of Gendreau's job is supervising the production of two publications, a weekly and a quarterly, dedicated to the emerging market economies. He coordinates the efforts of 10 economists, some stationed in places as far away as Hong Kong, London, and Singapore, to make sure the publications are readable and informative and meet the deadlines. "We communicate and exchange drafts through a global electronic mail system. Four years ago we couldn't do what we do today; the technology didn't exist. Now we routinely edit our publication one week in London and the next in New York."

Gendreau says that an ability to communicate, especially in writing, is as important to his job as is knowledge of economics. "If people can't understand what you are trying to tell them, you've failed regardless of how good your ideas may be."

A appendix

Elasticity of Supply and Demand

Suppose you're the owner of a popular pizzeria. You're considering raising the price of your double-cheese deluxe by $1—but how will your customers react? You know that, according to the law of demand, when a good's price rises, quantity demanded generally falls. But what you really need to know is the *extent* to which the quantity demanded of your deluxe pizzas will fall if you boost the price by $1.

To forecast the effect of price changes on their revenues, businesses need a measure of buyer sensitivity to changes in price called the *elasticity of demand*. In this chapter we'll look at the conceptual problems involved in measuring elasticity of demand along points on the demand curve for a good. We'll also develop measures of demand sensitivity to changes in such important demand determinants as consumer income and prices of substitutes and complements. Knowledge of demand sensitivity to income and the prices of related goods helps businesses market their products and manage resource use. For example, a retailer of casual clothing who knows the sensitivity of demand for jackets to fluctuations in consumer income can manage her inventory to avoid running short of jackets or incurring high costs for storing and financing stocks of the jackets.

Elasticity of supply is a measure of the sensitivity of *supply* to changes in prices. As you'll learn, knowledge of the supply elasticity of products is very useful in forecasting the impact of policies designed to influence quantities supplied by sellers in markets. You'll also learn how knowledge of elasticity of both supply and demand is crucial in forecasting the impact of taxes and changes in tax rates on prices and government tax collections.

☐ CONCEPT PREVIEW

After reading this chapter, you should be able to:

1. Explain the uses of the concept of price elasticity of demand and show how it can be calculated for points on a given demand curve.

2. Use information on price elasticity of demand to forecast changes in total expenditure on an item and total revenue from its sale when its price changes.

3. Explain how to use other elasticity measures, including the income elasticity of demand, the cross-elasticity of demand, and the price elasticity of supply.

4. Show how the price elasticities of supply and demand are relevant to explaining the impact of taxes on market prices of goods and services.

PRICE ELASTICITY OF DEMAND

Price elasticity of demand is a number representing the percentage change in quantity demanded resulting from each 1 percent change in the price of a good. This number is used to gauge the sensitivity of quantity demanded of a good to percentage changes in the price of that good. Price elasticity of demand is a *measure* of the responsiveness of quantity demanded to price changes along a given demand curve.

Price elasticity is calculated by dividing the percentage change in quantity demanded of a good by the percentage change in price that caused it, other things being equal:

$$\text{Price elasticity of demand} = \frac{\%\ \text{change in quantity demanded}}{\%\ \text{change in price}}$$

For example, suppose the price of cars went up by 1 percent this year and the resulting decline in cars purchased was 2 percent. The price elasticity of demand would be

$$\frac{-2\%}{1\%} = -2$$

Note that price elasticity of demand is a number without units of measurement because it's obtained by dividing two percentage changes. Also note that price elasticity of demand is a negative number. This is because an increase in price will generally result in a decrease in quantity demanded, other things being equal. Therefore, if the percentage change in price is positive, the percentage change in quantity demanded will be negative, as shown in the calculation just presented. Similarly, if price were to decline, the percentage change in price would be negative and the percentage change in quantity demanded would be positive. For example, suppose the price of gasoline declines by 2 percent and the annual increase in gasoline sales attributable to this price decline is also 2 percent. The price elasticity of demand for that price decline would therefore be

$$\frac{2\%}{-2\%} = -1$$

How to Use Price Elasticity of Demand to Make Market Forecasts

You've just learned how to calculate price elasticity of demand from percentage changes in quantities demanded that result from certain percentage changes in price. Suppose instead you have a good estimate of the price elasticity of demand for the product you sell. Now you can work backward and use the concept of elasticity to make predictions of changes in quantity demanded in response to price changes.

For example, imagine you run a car dealership. Last year you sold 10,000 cars. This year you know that the price of each car you sell will go up by 10 percent. You know the law of demand implies that, other things unchanged, you'll sell fewer cars this year; but the law gives no hint of *how many* fewer you'll sell. You can now see the relevance of the concept of price elasticity of demand. You know from past experience that the price elasticity of demand for the cars you sell is -2. Because you know the percentage change in price and the price elasticity of demand for your product, you can easily calculate the percentage change in quantity demanded:

$$\frac{\%\ \text{change in quantity demanded}}{10\%} = -2$$

Therefore,

$$\% \text{ change in quantity demanded} = -20\%$$

You therefore expect a 20 percent reduction in sales as a result of the price increase. This means you can expect to sell only 8,000 cars instead of 10,000 this year, assuming that your estimate of price elasticity of demand is accurate and that nothing else changes that might affect car sales. You can use this estimate of reduced sales volume to cut back on your orders for cars from the manufacturer and avoid tying up your funds in a large inventory of unsold cars.

You can also use price elasticity of demand to formulate pricing strategies if you own a firm that can control its prices. For example, suppose you manage a stereo store and you want to increase your annual quantity of rack systems sold by 20 percent. You estimate that the price elasticity of demand for your rack systems is −4. One obvious way to increase the quantities you sell is to lower prices. Other things being equal, how much must you cut prices to increase sales by 20 percent? The answer is easy because you know the price elasticity of demand for your rack systems and you know the percentage increase in quantity demanded. To calculate the necessary percentage reduction in price, simply use the formula for price elasticity of demand:

$$\frac{20\%}{\% \text{ change in price}} = -4$$

Therefore,

$$\% \text{ change in price} = -5\%$$

In this case you'd need to reduce prices by 5 percent to achieve your desired increase in rack system sales volume.

Categorizing Price Elasticity of Demand as Elastic or Inelastic

In categorizing demand as more or less elastic, it's convenient to *ignore the minus sign* in front of the number measuring the elasticity of demand. The larger the number after the minus sign, the more elastic the demand. In other words, the larger the *absolute value* of the price elasticity of demand, the more elastic the demand. For example, if the elasticity of demand for cars is −2, while the elasticity of demand for bread is −0.5, the demand for cars is more elastic than the demand for bread.

elastic demand prevails if the price elasticity of demand for a good exceeds 1, ignoring the minus sign.

An **elastic demand** prevails if a good's price elasticity of demand turns out to exceed 1, ignoring the minus sign. For example, if the price elasticity of demand for fur coats were −5, the demand for fur coats would be elastic. If the price elasticity of demand for sweatshirts were −2, their demand would also be elastic. However, note that the demand for fur coats would be more elastic than the corresponding demand for sweatshirts. If demand is elastic, the percentage change in quantity demanded caused by a price increase will exceed the percentage change in the price (ignoring the direction of change).

inelastic demand prevails if the price elasticity of demand for a good is equal to or greater than 0 but less than 1, ignoring the minus sign.

A good has an **inelastic demand** if its price elasticity of demand is equal to or greater than 0 but less than 1, ignoring the minus sign. The smaller the number after the minus sign, the more inelastic the demand for the good. For example, demand for milk would be categorized as inelastic if its price elasticity of demand were −0.8 because 0.8 is less than 1. If the price elasticity of demand of aspirin were −0.5, its demand would be considered more inelastic than the demand for milk because 0.5 is less than 0.8. Ignoring the direction of change, the percentage change in quantity demanded will be less than the percentage change in price that caused it when

---

Box 1   Price Elasticity of Demand as a Gauge of Demand Responsiveness

Demand response	% change in quantity demanded relative to % change in price (ignoring direction of change)	Value of elasticity of demand (ignoring minus sign)
Inelastic	% change in quantity demanded is *less than* % change in price	Equal to or greater than 0 but less than 1
Unit elastic	% change in quantity demanded *equals* % change in price	1
Elastic	% change in quantity demanded is *greater than* % change in price	Greater than 1

---

demand is inelastic. If the price elasticity of demand for a good were 0, this would imply that consumers wouldn't respond at all to price changes and demand would be considered *perfectly* inelastic.

Finally, a good has a unit elastic demand if its price elasticity of demand is exactly equal to 1 when the minus sign is ignored. If demand for a good is unit elastic, the percentage change in its quantity demanded caused by a price change will equal the percentage change in price, again ignoring the direction of change. For example, if each 1 percent increase in the price of milk resulted in a 1 percent decline in the quantity demanded, demand for milk would be unit elastic.

Box 1 summarizes the range of variation for price elasticity of demand and the various ways of categorizing the demand for a product according to its price elasticity. Remember, the larger the number after the minus sign, the more elastic the demand.

> **unit elastic demand** prevails if the price elasticity of demand for a good is exactly equal to 1 when the minus sign is ignored.

Determinants of Price Elasticity of Demand

A number of factors can influence the price elasticity of demand for an item. These factors include:

1. *The availability of substitutes.* Remember that a substitute for a good is one that serves the same general purpose. In general, the more and better substitutes that exist for an item, the more elastic its demand. For example, it's quite likely that diabetics' demand for insulin is extremely inelastic because insulin has few, if any, substitutes. However, the demand for a particular car brand is likely to be very elastic because many substitute brands are available in the market.

2. *Time.* In general, demand tends to become more elastic with *time* because we find more substitutes for goods over longer periods. Over longer periods we also have more time to adjust our consumption patterns in response to price changes, which also contributes to a more elastic demand. For example, within a period of a month or two there may be little that we as drivers can do to react to an increase in gas prices. However, over several years we can seek out more fuel-efficient cars and buy them to replace our older gas guzzlers. We can also move closer to work. Also, over a period of several years more substitutes are developed for goods whose prices go up. For example, a sharp permanent increase in the price of gas might lead to the development of substitute fuels.

3. *The proportion of income consumers spend on the good.* As consumers, we tend to spend high proportions of our income on housing and cars. A 10 percent increase in the prices of these goods is likely to reduce substantially our ability to

buy them and to result in sharp percentage declines in quantities demanded. The demand for goods on which we spend large percentages of our income is likely to be quite elastic. On the other hand, a 10 percent increase in the price of pencils will have little effect on the purchasing power of our income and is unlikely to result in sharp percentage declines in quantities demanded. Of course, there are exceptions to this rule. We might spend only a small portion of our income on oysters, but the demand for oysters might be elastic because oysters are considered dispensable luxuries. In general, other things being equal, the smaller the percentage of income spent on a good, the less elastic the demand unless the good is considered a dispensable luxury.

Calculating Price Elasticity of Demand from Two Points on a Demand Curve

We can use the concept of price elasticity of demand together with the demand curve to reach some interesting conclusions. The graph in Box 2 shows a downward-sloping linear demand curve for granola bars. Suppose the equilibrium price of granola bars is currently $1 and 20,000 bars are sold at that price each week. This corresponds to point A on the demand curve. Now suppose, as a result of a decrease in the supply, the price of granola bars increases to $1.10 and the quantity demanded falls to 15,000 per week as the equilibrium moves from point A to point B on the demand curve. To calculate the price elasticity of demand for the data, we follow these steps:

  1. Calculate the change in price (ΔP) and the change in quantity demanded (ΔQ). In this case the change in price is $\Delta P = 10$ cents and the resulting change in quantity demanded is $\Delta Q = -5,000$.

  2. Calculate the *percentage change* in price caused by the decrease in supply. Here a slight problem occurs when the change in price or quantity demanded is substantial. The 10-cent increase in price is 10 percent of the initial price (P_1) of $1 but is only 9.1 percent of the *new price* (P_2) of $1.10. To see this, divide the 10-cent change in price by the new price. This will give you the following result: $0.10/$1.10 = 0.091. To convert this to a percentage, multiply the result by 100 percent, which gives you 9.1 percent.

Because you'll get a different percentage change depending on whether you use the initial or new market price to make your calculation, economists often use the *average* of the initial and new prices to calculate a compromise percentage change. In this case the average price will be ($1.00 + $1.10)/2, which equals $1.05. The percentage change in price can therefore be calculated as ($0.10/$1.05)(100%) = 9.5%.

In symbolic terms, the percentage change in price can be written as

$$\left[\frac{\Delta P}{\frac{1}{2}(P_1 + P_2)} \right] 100\%$$

where P_1 is the initial price and P_2 is the new price.

  3. Calculate the percentage change in quantity demanded caused by the price increase. Here the change in quantity demanded is $-5,000$ granola bars per week. This is equal to 25 percent of the initial quantity demanded (Q_1) of 20,000 bars and 33 percent of the *new* quantity demanded (Q_2) of 15,000 bars after the price increase. To resolve the ambiguity, once again calculate the percentage change on the basis of the average of the initial and new quantities demanded. The average quantity demanded is (20,000 + 15,000)/2 = 17,500 granola bars per week. The percentage change in quantity demanded will therefore be ($-5,000/17,500$)(100%) = -28.6%.

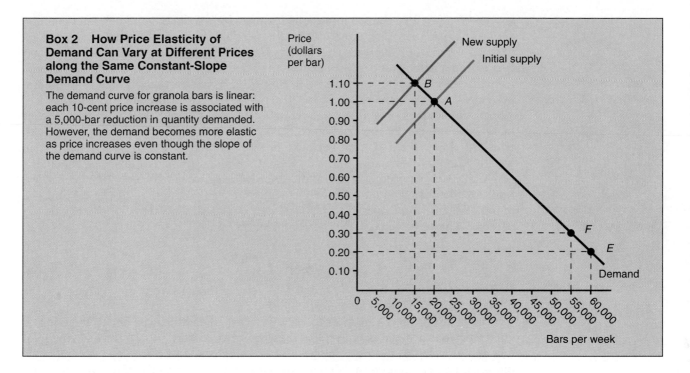

Box 2   How Price Elasticity of Demand Can Vary at Different Prices along the Same Constant-Slope Demand Curve

The demand curve for granola bars is linear: each 10-cent price increase is associated with a 5,000-bar reduction in quantity demanded. However, the demand becomes more elastic as price increases even though the slope of the demand curve is constant.

In symbols, the percentage change in quantity demanded is

$$\left[\frac{\Delta Q}{\frac{1}{2}(Q_1 + Q_2)}\right] 100\%$$

where Q_1 is the initial quantity demanded and Q_2 is the new quantity demanded.

4. Divide the percentage change in quantity demanded by the percentage change in price to get the price elasticity of demand:

$$\text{Price elasticity of demand} = \frac{-28.6\%}{9.5\%} = -3.01$$

Because the number after the minus sign exceeds 1, the demand for granola bars can be categorized as *elastic*.

The formula for calculating the price elasticity of demand between two points on a demand curve can be written as

$$\text{Price elasticity of demand} = \frac{\Delta Q/(Q_1 + Q_2)}{\Delta P/(P_1 + P_2)}$$

which is obtained simply by dividing the expression for the percentage change in quantity demanded just shown by the expression for the percentage change in price.

How Price Elasticity Can Vary along a Demand Curve

From the calculation you just made, can you conclude that the price elasticity of demand for granola bars will *always* be -3.01 no matter what the price? The answer is *no*. In fact, we can easily show that the price elasticity of demand varies continuously at different points on a downward-sloping linear demand curve. To see why this is so, suppose the initial price of granola bars was 20 cents instead of $1. Of course, at a price that much lower, the quantity of granola bars demanded would be substantially higher. The graph in Box 2 shows that the quantity demanded is 60,000 bars per week when the price is 20 cents. This corresponds to point *E* on the demand curve drawn in the graph. Now suppose the price of granola bars goes up by 10 cents as before. The percentage increase in this case, based on the average of the initial price of 20 cents and the new price of 30 cents, is 40 percent. Because the downward-sloping demand curve is *linear*, the reduction in quantity demanded for each 10-cent increase in price is the same a before: 5,000 bars. A linear demand curve is one with constant slope: Each 10-cent increase in price results in a 5,000-bar reduction in weekly quantity demanded, no matter what the initial price and quantity demanded (see Chapter 1 Supplement). After the price increases from 20 cents to 30 cents, we find that the change in quantity demanded expressed as a percentage of the average of initial quantity demanded (60,000) and new quantity demanded (55,000) equals -9 percent. The price elasticity of demand is therefore

$$\frac{-9\%}{40\%} = -0.23$$

Because the number after the minus sign is less than 1, we'd now categorize the demand for granola bars as *inelastic*.

   If you use elasticity estimates to make forecasts, heed this warning: If the demand curve for your product is linear, like the one drawn in Box 2, then price elasticity of demand will change as price changes. When using past data based on previous price changes, be very careful to calculate the *current* price elasticity of demand for your product. *Assuming that the demand curve for your product is linear (or almost linear) like the one in Box 2, the demand for your product will tend to be more elastic at higher prices than at lower prices.* We can also state this proposition in a slightly different way: The greater the quantity demanded along a given linear demand curve, the more inelastic the demand in response to further price declines.

   We can apply this proposition directly to the marketing of products. When a new product is introduced at a relatively high price, demand is likely to be quite elastic. This means sellers can expect consumers to be quite responsive to price declines for a new product. For example, when the personal computer was introduced in the early 1980s, increases in supply resulted in small percentage declines in price but much larger percentage increases in quantity demanded. By the late 1980s the market became saturated with computers, meaning that the quantity sold per year was quite large as prices fell drastically in response to increased supply. In 1987 sellers found that further price declines resulted in only modest percentage increases in quantity demanded and that demand had become much more inelastic than it had been.

   Here's a simple way to understand why price elasticity along a linear demand curve changes as price changes: When the initial price is low rather than high, a 10-cent change in price is a higher percentage of the average of the initial and final prices. Also, when the initial price is low, the quantity demanded will be high. Along a linear demand curve, each given change in price will result in the same change in quantity demanded. So, even though the quantity demanded is high at low prices, each 10-cent increase in price will still result in a 5,000-bar reduction in the weekly quantity of granola bars demanded. Naturally, the 5,000-bar change in quantity demanded is a smaller percentage of the average of the initial and final quantities demanded at low prices (when quantity demanded is high) than at high prices (when quantity demanded is lower). As price increases over time in 10-cent increments along a linear demand curve, therefore, the percentage change in price decreases, while the percentage change in quantity demanded tends to increase. Price elasticity of demand will move further away from zero as price increases along a linear demand curve, meaning that demand becomes more elastic. (See the graph in Box 2.)

In summary:

1. Even though a linear demand curve has constant slope, its elasticity varies from point to point. The slope of the demand curve in Box 2 can be expressed as −$0.10/5,000 granola bars because each 10-cent change in price is associated with a 5,000-bar change (in the opposite direction) in quantity demanded. This number can be expressed only as a ratio of dollars to granola bars and is therefore a cumbersome measure of responsiveness that varies with units of measurement. The price elasticity of demand is, however, a negative number with no units of measurement.

2. Along a downward-sloping linear demand curve, demand is very elastic at high prices but becomes less elastic as price declines. Demand becomes inelastic at relatively low prices, and it approaches zero as prices get lower and lower.

3. Don't judge the price elasticity of demand at points on different demand curves by looking at their slopes. To calculate price elasticity of demand for points on each demand curve, you need to calculate percentage changes in prices and quantities demanded. These percentage changes will vary with the actual price and quantity demanded.[1]

Perfectly Inelastic and Perfectly Elastic Demand Curves

Suppose the price elasticity of demand for a good were *always* zero, no matter what the price. What would its demand curve look like? If the price elasticity of demand is zero, the percentage change in quantity of the good demanded will always be zero, no matter what the price or how much the price changes. For this to be the case, the quantity demanded of the good would have to be completely insensitive to changes in price. A demand curve that corresponds to such a situation is drawn in graph **A** in Box 3. This demand curve is a vertical line, indicating that if the price changes, there's no change in quantity demanded. The percentage change in quantity demanded along this demand curve is therefore zero, and the price elasticity at all points is 0/Percentage change in price = 0.

It's doubtful that any good has a perfectly inelastic demand curve. For this to be the case, the good would have to have virtually no substitutes or it would have to be a good on which consumers spend only minute fractions of their income. In most cases we'd expect the demand curve for a good to have at least some downward slope. Diabetics' demand curve for insulin might be close to a vertical line because insulin has few, if any, substitutes. However, higher prices for insulin could induce diabetics to watch their diet more carefully and to pursue other measures that might affect the frequency with which they take insulin.

---

[1] When the price change is very small, there will be little difference between the initial and final prices and quantities. For points on a demand curve, the formula for price elasticity of demand can be written as

$$\frac{(\Delta Q/Q)\ 100\%}{(\Delta P/P)\ 100\%} = \frac{(\Delta Q/Q)}{(\Delta P/P)} = \frac{P}{Q}\frac{\Delta Q}{\Delta P}$$

for any given P or Q. As Q approaches zero, price elasticity of demand approaches an infinitely large negative number. As P approaches zero, price elasticity of demand also approaches zero.

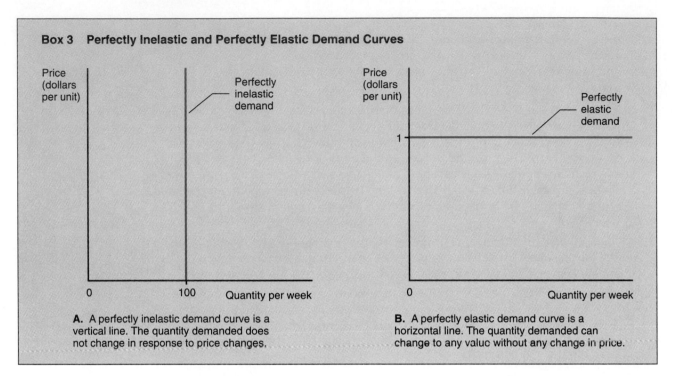

Box 3   Perfectly Inelastic and Perfectly Elastic Demand Curves

A. A perfectly inelastic demand curve is a vertical line. The quantity demanded does not change in response to price changes.

B. A perfectly elastic demand curve is a horizontal line. The quantity demanded can change to any value without any change in price.

In Box 3, graph **B** illustrates a demand curve that can be regarded as infinitely elastic at all prices. This demand curve is flat. You can think of such a demand curve as one that is approached when a downward-sloping demand curve becomes so flat that it can't be distinguished from a horizontal line. An almost flat downward-sloping demand curve implies that the most minute change in the price of a good will result in an infinite change in the quantity demanded. You can also understand why the demand curve shown in graph **B** is considered perfectly elastic by reasoning that along the curve no change in price is necessary to change quantity demanded.

An infinitely elastic demand curve would prevail for a product that has a great many perfect substitutes. In fact, such a demand curve can be regarded as existing for a particular seller in a competitive market. For example, suppose you're one of a million sellers of eggs in the egg market. Because eggs are a standardized product, buyers will view your eggs as a perfect substitute for those of any other seller. You could sell all the eggs you wanted at the market price of $1 per dozen, and the demand curve for *your* eggs would be perfectly elastic, like the one shown in **B** in Box 3.

CONCEPT CHECK
☐

- How is price elasticity of demand calculated? If the price elasticity of demand for ice cream is equal to −0.8, calculate the effect of a 10 percent decrease in the price of ice cream on the quantity demanded.

- Under what conditions is demand for a good categorized as elastic? When would it be in-

elastic? Relate your answer to percentage changes in price and quantities demanded.

- The slope of the demand curve for cassette tapes is −2 at all points. Will the price elasticity of cassette tapes also be constant at all points?

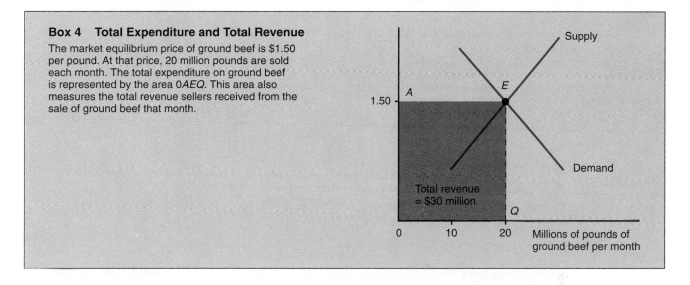

Box 4   Total Expenditure and Total Revenue
The market equilibrium price of ground beef is $1.50 per pound. At that price, 20 million pounds are sold each month. The total expenditure on ground beef is represented by the area 0*AEQ*. This area also measures the total revenue sellers received from the sale of ground beef that month.

USING PRICE ELASTICITY OF DEMAND TO FORECAST CHANGES IN TOTAL EXPENDITURE AND TOTAL REVENUE WHEN PRICES CHANGE

Total Expenditure and Total Revenue

In 1991 Apple Computer, Inc. slashed the prices on its Macintosh computers by as much as 50 percent on some models. The market response to the price cuts was phenomenal—by the end of the year, Apple reported an 85 percent jump in the sale of its Macs and the company's revenues had soared. The price elasticity of demand for Macintosh computers was even more elastic than the company's managers had estimated. Apple continued to cut prices in 1992, and by the end of that year revenues had again increased, contributing to higher profits for the company.

Price elasticity of demand is a vital factor when businesspeople estimate the **total revenue** they can expect to make. All sellers are interested in the amounts consumers will spend on an item because consumer expenditure is an important determinant of their profits. Expenditures by consumers represent the total revenue sellers take in from selling their products.

Total expenditure by consumers over any given period is the number of units of a product purchased over that period, Q, multiplied by the price of the product, P:

$$\text{Total expenditure} = PQ = \text{Total revenue}$$

This equation shows that PQ, price times quantity, over any period equals *both* the total expenditure on that product by consumers *and* the total revenue sellers receive from selling the product.

For example, if the price of ground beef averaged $1.50 per pound and 20 million pounds were sold last month, total expenditure on ground beef was $30 million. This sum also equals the total revenue received that month by sellers in the market.

Box 4 shows the demand for and supply of ground beef assuming a $1.50 per pound equilibrium price and an equilibrium quantity of 20 million pounds per month. Consumers' total expenditure can be represented as the rectangular area 0*AEQ* on the graph. The width of this rectangle is the $1.50 price per pound represented by the

2

total revenue the dollars earned by sellers of a product; the amount sold over a period multiplied by the price (PQ).

total expenditure over any given period, the number of units of a product purchased over that period multiplied by the price of the product (PQ); equals sellers' total revenue.

Box 5   Impact of an Increase in Price on Expenditure and Revenue

An increase in price caused by a decrease in supply tends to increase revenue. However, the decrease in quantity demanded caused by the increase in price tends to decrease revenue and expenditure on the good.

distance $0A$ on the vertical axis. The length of the rectangle is the 20 million pounds sold per month, represented by the distance $0Q$ on the horizontal axis. Multiplying the length by the width gives the rectangle $0AEQ$, which represents $30 million per month. This area represents both the total expenditure by consumers and the total revenue of sellers.

Predicting Changes in Total Expenditure and Revenue in Response to Price Increases

Suppose there's a decrease in the supply of ground beef. Box 5 shows how such a decrease in supply affects the price of ground beef and the quantity demanded. As a result of the decrease in supply, the market equilibrium price of ground beef increases from $1.50 per pound to a new price, P_2. The increase in price causes the quantity demanded per month to decline to Q_2. What effect will the increase in price have on consumer expenditure on ground beef and on the total revenue of sellers?

There's no clear-cut answer to this question. The increase in the price of ground beef acts to increase total consumer expenditure by increasing the P component of PQ. However, the law of demand indicates that as price goes up, the quantity of ground beef demanded will go down. The Q component of PQ thus will decrease whenever price goes up. There are therefore two forces that influence PQ when price goes up, and they act in opposite directions. If we know the price elasticity of demand for ground beef, however, we can forecast the change in PQ. This is because we can use price elasticity of demand to predict the relative magnitudes of the upward and downward forces influencing expenditure and revenue. Thus, sellers can use price elasticity of demand to predict changes in their total revenue when prices change.

Suppose the demand for ground beef is *inelastic*. This means the percentage reduction in quantity demanded caused by the price increase will be *smaller* (ignoring the direction of change) than the percentage increase in price that caused it. Under such circumstances, the *upward* influence on the price increase on revenue is stronger than the *depressing* effect of the reduction in quantity demanded on revenue. For example, if a 10 percent price increase results in only a 5 percent decline in quantity demanded, as would be the case if the elasticity of demand for ground beef were -0.5, total revenue will *increase* as a result of the price increase. *An inelastic demand therefore implies that total revenue and total expenditure on a good will increase when price rises.*

In the graph in Box 5, the gain in revenue as a result of the price increase is represented by the area *ABFH*. This represents the increase in revenue from the Q_2 pounds of ground beef sold at the higher price. The loss of revenue from the reduction in quantity demanded is represented by the area *GHEQ*. This represents revenue that sellers would have enjoyed by selling more units had the price remained at \$1.50 per pound. *When demand is inelastic, the gain in revenue from the price increase will exceed the loss in revenue from the decline in sales volume.* At the extreme, suppose the price elasticity of demand for a good were 0. This implies that an increase in price would have no effect on the quantity demanded. If this were the case, the total revenue taken in by sellers would increase by the percentage increase in price.

Now suppose demand were *elastic*. This implies that the percentage reduction in quantity demanded (ignoring the direction of change) would exceed the percentage increase in price that caused it. In this case the upward pressure on revenue caused by the price increase would be more than offset by the downward pressure on revenue resulting from the reduction in quantity demanded. As a consequence, total revenue, and therefore total expenditure, would decline. For example, if the demand for ground beef were equal to -1.50, indicating an elastic demand, sellers could expect the price increase to adversely affect their revenue.

Finally, if the demand for a product is unit elastic, any given percentage change in price will result in an equal but opposite percentage change in quantity demanded. The net effect would be no change in total revenue, because the upward force on revenue would be exactly offset by the downward force. For example, estimates of the demand for housing indicate that its price elasticity is about -1. This implies that consumers tend to spend constant amounts on housing irrespective of its price.

Price Decreases, Total Expenditures, and Total Revenue

When price falls, it exerts downward pressure on total expenditure that can be offset by increases in quantity demanded. The net effect on revenue or expenditure of a price decrease depends on the relationship between the percentage decrease in price and the percentage increase in quantity demanded. Why would a decrease in price have a favorable effect on the total revenue from sale of a good whose demand is elastic, but an unfavorable effect on the total revenue from sale of a good with inelastic demand? Elastic demand implies that the percentage increase in quantity demanded is greater than the percentage decrease in price that caused it. The downward pressure on total revenue caused by the price decline would therefore be more than offset by the upward pressure on total revenue resulting from the increase in quantity demanded.

Similarly, a decrease in the price of ground beef would decrease sellers' total revenue if the demand for ground beef were inelastic. For example, assuming the price elasticity of demand for ground beef is -0.5, a 10 percent decline in the price of ground beef would result in only a 5 percent increase in the quantity demanded by consumers. The 5 percent increase in purchases wouldn't offset the 10 percent decline in price, and *PQ* would decline.

Of course, if demand is unit elastic, a decrease in price will have no effect on either total revenue or total expenditure. This is because the downward pressure of the price decline would be exactly offset by the upward pressure of the increase in quantity demanded as price fell.

principles in practice

Managerial Methods: How to Maximize Revenue

Pricing Theater Tickets during Off-Peak Hours Suppose you manage a movie theater and want to maximize profits for midweek screenings. Demand is slack during midweek, and it's likely to take a very low price to fill the theater. You know that once you open the theater and screen a movie, your costs are independent of the number of admissions you sell. Under these circumstances, you can maximize your profit from the sale of tickets when you maximize revenue from admissions.

Assuming the demand curve for admissions to your midweek screenings is linear, it's easy to apply the analysis in this chapter to choose the price that maximizes revenue. Graph **A** shows the demand curve for midweek screenings. Along the linear demand curve, each 1-cent reduction in ticket prices results in the sale of two more tickets. The theater's capacity is 600 persons.

The demand curve indicates that if you choose a ticket price of $3, the number of admissions demanded would be 200. Total revenue would be $600 for the evening (the $3 ticket price multiplied by the 200 admissions). Because $3 is a relatively high price, demand for theater admissions is elastic at that price. This means that if you were to lower the price, your total revenue would increase. You can verify this by choosing a lower price, such as $2.50, and remembering that each 1-cent reduction in price results in two more admissions. It follows that if price were $2.50, the number of admissions demanded would increase by 100, to 300, and your total revenue would be $750 per screening.

Total revenue will continue to increase as long as demand remains elastic and will begin to decline just at the point at which price is reduced to make demand

inelastic. For example, if you reduced the price to $2 per admission, the number of admissions demanded would be 400 and your total revenue would be $800 for the evening. At a price of $2, demand is unit elastic, because if price were reduced an additional 1 cent, to $1.99, admissions would increase to 402 and total revenue would decline to $799.98. If the price were reduced to $1.50, the quantity demanded would go up to 500, but total revenue would decline still further, to $750, because demand would be inelastic. Graph **B** shows how total revenue varies with the number of admissions when the demand curve shown in graph **A** prevails.

Also note from the table and graph **A** that you could fill up the theater if you charged $1 for admission. At that price you'd fill all of your 600 seats for each screening, but your total revenue would be only $600! To maximize revenue, you'd therefore choose to price your tickets at $2 and be content with filling only two thirds of your seating capacity but enjoying $800 revenue for the evening.

The point of this example is that if a business wants to maximize revenue, it must choose the price at which demand just becomes inelastic. This is the price for which demand is unit elastic.

Demand and Total Revenue per Midweek Screening

Price (dollars)	Number of admissions demanded	Total revenue	Price elasticity of demand
3.00	200	600	Elastic
2.50	300	750	Elastic
2.00	400	800	Unit elastic
1.50	500	750	Inelastic
1.00	600	600	Inelastic

Box 6   Price Elasticity of Demand and Total Revenue or Expenditure

Price elasticity	Implication (ignoring direction of change)	Change in $P \cdot Q$ for price decrease	Change in $P \cdot Q$ for price increase
Elastic	% change in quantity demanded exceeds % change in price	+	−
Unitary	% change in quantity demanded equals % change in price	0	0
Inelastic	% change in quantity demanded is less than % change in price	−	+

Box 6 summarizes the relationship between price elasticity of demand and total revenue or expenditure.

OTHER DEMAND ELASTICITY MEASURES

In addition to price elasticity of demand, income elasticity of demand and cross-elasticity of demand provide useful information. Income elasticity of demand is a number that measures the sensitivity of consumer purchases to given percentage changes in income. Cross-elasticity of demand is a number used to measure the sensitivity of consumer purchases of one good to percentage changes in the price of a substitute or complementary good.

income elasticity of demand a number that measures the sensitivity of consumer purchases to each 1 percent change in income.

cross-elasticity of demand a number used to measure the sensitivity of consumer purchases of one good to each 1 percent change in the price of a substitute or complementary good.

Income Elasticity of Demand

Income elasticity of demand measures the percentage change in the number of units of a good consumers demand, other things being equal, resulting from each 1 percent change in income. We calculate income elasticity by dividing the percentage change in the quantity of a good purchased by a corresponding percentage change in income, assuming that only income and no other demand determinant changes:[2]

$$\text{Income elasticity of demand} = \frac{\% \text{ change in number of units consumers demand}}{\% \text{ change in income}}$$

For example, an income elasticity of 3 for foreign travel means that a 1 percent increase in income will result in a 3 percent increase in consumer trips overseas.

Income elasticity of demand for a good may be positive or negative. A positive income elasticity implies that increases in income (other things being equal) are associated with increases in the quantity of a good purchased. Goods that have positive income elasticity of demand are called normal goods. The quantity of such goods that consumers demand is positively associated with consumer income. A good whose income elasticity is greater than 1 is sometimes called a "luxury good." Foreign travel in fact has an estimated elasticity of about 3, indicating that it can be considered a luxury good. Goods with income elasticities between 0 and 1 are considered necessities.

A negative income elasticity of demand implies an inverse relationship between income and the amounts of a good purchased. Goods with negative income elasticities are those that consumers will eventually stop buying as their incomes in-

normal goods goods that have positive income elasticity of demand

[2] For small changes in income, the income elasticity of demand is $\frac{\Delta Q/Q}{\Delta I/I}$, where Q is the initial quantity consumers demand and I is the initial income.

principles in practice

Empirical Estimates of Demand Elasticities

The key to understanding market demand for products often lies in estimating the relevant elasticities of demand. Firms and governments are well aware of this and spend large sums of money each year to estimate these elasticities for products. Economists regularly estimate demand elasticities as part of their research. The three tables in this box show estimated demand elasticities for various goods and services. Table A shows both short-run and long-run estimated price elasticities. For most goods, demand is more elastic with respect to price over longer periods of time than over the short run. Over longer periods consumers have more time to find substitutes for goods whose prices increase. In addition, more substitutes are developed and made available by sellers in the long run.

For the items in Table A, all the estimated short-run elasticities (except for china, glassware, and tableware; intercity rail travel; household natural gas use; and automobiles and parts) indicate inelastic demand because the values of the estimated elasticities are between 0 and −1. The short-run price elasticity of demand for household electricity use is nearly 0. Demand is quite elastic for most products in the long run.

Table B presents empirical estimates of income elasticities for various goods and services. Estimated income elasticities for automobiles, foreign travel by U.S. citizens, and household appliances are quite high (greater than 1) and positive. These are goods whose demands

A. Estimated Price Elasticities of Demand

Item	Short run	Long run
Stationery	−0.47	−0.56
Jewelry and watches	−0.41	−0.67
Tires and tubes	−0.86	−1.19
Gasoline	−0.4*	−1.5†
Foreign travel by U.S. residents	−0.14	−1.77
Housing	−0.3	−1.88
Household electricity use	−0.13	−1.89
Tobacco products	−0.46	−1.89
Household natural gas use‡	−1.4	−2.1
Automobiles and parts	−1.87	−2.24
China, glassware, tableware	−1.54	−2.55
Toilet articles and preparations	−0.20	−3.04
Intercity rail travel	−1.4	−3.19
Movies	−0.87	−3.67
Radio and TV repair	−0.47	−3.84

NOTE: Except where otherwise indicated, data are from Hendrik S. Houthakker and Lester D. Taylor, *Consumer Demand in the United States: Analyses and Projections* (Cambridge, Mass.: Harvard University Press, 1970).

* Robert Archibald and Robert Gillingham, "An Analysis of the Short-Run Consumer Demand for Gasoline Using Household Survey Data," *Review of Economics and Statistics* 62 (November 1980), pp. 622–28.

† J. M. Griffin, *Energy Conservation in the OECD, 1980–2000* (Cambridge, Mass.: Ballinger, 1979).

‡ G. R. Lakshmanan and William Anderson, "Residential Energy Demand in the United States," *Regional Science and Urban Economics* 10 (August 1980), pp. 371–86.

---

inferior goods goods that have negative income elasticity of demand.

crease. For example, if income elasticity of demand for bus travel is negative, bus travel can be expected to decline as income increases. Goods that have negative income elasticity of demand are called inferior goods. These are goods we tend to consume less of as our income increases. You'd expect such goods as poor cuts of meat, secondhand clothing, and used cars to have negative income elasticity of demand.

Using market data, we can estimate income elasticity of demand to get an indication of the sensitivity of consumer purchases of an item to fluctuations in consumer income. For current and potential sellers, income elasticity of demand is an extremely important number. For example, if you believe Americans will become more affluent in the future, you'll probably want to market products with income elasticities greater than 1—luxury items like yachts, Rolls-Royces, and world tours.

The income elasticity of food, on the other hand, is usually estimated to be less than 1. This means that the percentage increase in the demand for food is likely to be less than the percentage increase in income over time. Thus, if you're a dairy farmer, you can expect the demand for your milk to grow less quickly than the nation's income grows.

are quite responsive to changes in income and increase when income goes up.

Both short-run and long-run estimates of income elasticities are presented in Table B. In most cases, as

B. Estimated Income Elasticities of Demand

Item	Short run	Long run
Potatoes*	N.A.	−0.81
Pork†	0.27	0.18
Beef†	0.51	0.45
Furniture	2.6	0.53
China, glassware, tableware	0.47	0.77
Dental services	0.38	1.00
Chicken†	0.49	1.06
Automobiles	5.5	1.07
Spectator sports	0.46	1.07
Physician services	0.28	1.15
Clothing	0.95	1.17
Gasoline and oil	0.55	1.36
Household appliances	2.72	1.40
Shoes	0.9	1.5
Jewelry and watches	1.0	1.6
Owner-occupied housing	0.07	2.45
Foreign travel by U.S. citizens	0.24	3.09
Toilet articles and preparations	0.25	3.74

NOTE: Unless otherwise indicated, data are from Hendrik C. Houthakker and Lester D. Taylor, *Consumer Demand in the United States: Analyses and Projections* (Cambridge, Mass.: Harvard University Press, 1970).

⁽ᵒ⁾ Dale M. Heien, "The Structure of Food Demand: Interrelatedness and Duality," *American Journal of Agricultural Economics* 64, no. 2 (May 1982), pp. 213–21.

† M. K. Wohlgenant and W. F. Hahn, "Dynamic Adjustment in Monthly Consumer Demand for Meats," *American Journal of Agricultural Economics* 64, no. 3 (August 1982), pp. 553–57.

we'd expect, long-run elasticity exceeds short-run elasticity. Notable exceptions are household appliances, furniture, and automobiles. These are durable goods. Consumers don't always replace them as their incomes increase. Note that the income elasticity of demand for potatoes is negative, indicating that consumers tend to reduce purchases of potatoes as their incomes increase.

Table C presents some estimated long-run cross-elasticities. The estimates indicate that consumers regard margarine and butter, pork and beef, and natural gas and electricity as substitutes for each other. The estimated cross-elasticities for these goods are positive.

C. Estimated Cross-Elasticities of Demand

Item	Estimate
Natural gas with respect to price of electricity	0.8*
Margarine with respect to price of butter	1.53†
Pork with respect to price of beef	0.40†
Chicken with respect to price of pork	0.29†

* G. R. Lakshmanan and William Anderson, "Residential Energy Demand in the United States," *Regional Science and Urban Economics* 10 (August 1980), pp. 371–86.

† Dale M. Heien, "The Structure of Food Demand: Interrelatedness and Duality," *American Journal of Agricultural Economics* 64, no. 2 (May 1982), pp. 213–21.

Cross-Elasticity of Demand

Another useful price elasticity concept is cross-elasticity of demand, which measures the sensitivity of purchases of one good to changes in the price of *another good*. For example, the cross-elasticity of demand for beef with respect to the price of pork would measure the percentage change in purchases of beef resulting from a 1 percent change in the *price of pork*, other things being equal. The formula for the cross-elasticity of demand between the demand for good X and the price of some other good, Y, is:[3]

$$\text{Cross-elasticity of demand} = \frac{\% \text{ change in the number of units of } X \text{ consumers demand}}{\% \text{ change in the price of } Y}$$

Cross-elasticity of demand may be positive or negative. A positive cross-elasticity of demand implies that the two goods are substitutes. Whenever the price of one good changes, other things being equal, the demand for the other moves in the same

---

[3] The cross-elasticity of demand for small changes in the price of good Y is $\frac{\Delta Q_X / Q_X}{\Delta P_Y / P_Y}$ where Q_X is the number of units of X consumers demand and P_Y is the price of good Y.

direction. This means that a price increase for one of the goods leads to an increase in the amounts purchased of the other. For example, one estimate of the cross-elasticity of demand between chicken and the price of pork is 0.299.[4] Since this is a positive cross-elasticity, it indicates that consumers treat these two meats as substitutes. In general, the greater the substitutability between two goods, the higher the value of their cross-elasticities of demand. A zero cross-elasticity of demand means that the consumption of one good is independent of the price of the other.

The cross-elasticity of demand between two competing brands, such as Coke and Pepsi, is likely to be quite high. The same is probably true for any two brands of 19-inch televisions. However, the cross-elasticity of demand for unrelated goods, such as ice cream and typewriters, is likely to be 0.

Goods that are complements have a negative cross-elasticity of demand. Coffee and nondairy creamer are complements. An increase in the price of coffee is likely to decrease the demand for nondairy creamer. We'd therefore expect the cross-elasticity of demand between nondairy creamer and the price of coffee to be negative.

Estimates of the cross-elasticity of demand for a product are important for business planning. For example, suppose a sharp increase in natural gas prices is expected. This is likely to increase demand for electricity because the two are regarded as substitutes for heating, cooking, and other uses. Electric companies can plan to meet the increased demand for their product if they know its cross-elasticity with respect to the price of natural gas. For example, if the cross-elasticity of demand for electricity with respect to the price of natural gas is 0.8, then a 20 percent increase in the price of natural gas can be expected to result in a 16 percent increase in the number of kilowatt-hours that consumers demand per year.

CONCEPT CHECK
◻

- If the price elasticity of demand for shirts is −2, what will happen to expenditure on shirts and shirt sellers' total revenue if the market price of shirts rises? What will happen if the market price falls?

- Explain how furniture sales would fluctuate with income if the income elasticity of demand

for furniture were 5. How would sales of potatoes fluctuate with income if the income elasticity of demand for potatoes were −0.5?

- The cross-elasticity of demand for wine with respect to beer is 2. What conclusions would you draw from this?

PRICE ELASTICITY OF SUPPLY

price elasticity of supply a number that indicates the percentage change in quantity supplied resulting from each 1 percent change in the price of a good, other things being equal.

The concept of **price elasticity of supply** is similar to the concept of price elasticity of demand. The price elasticity of supply is a number used to measure the sensitivity of changes in quantity supplied to given percentage changes in the price of a good, other things being equal. Price elasticity of supply indicates the percentage change in quantity supplied resulting from each 1 percent change in price. It can be calculated by dividing the percentage change in quantity supplied by the percentage change in price that caused it, given all other supply determinants:[5]

$$\text{Price elasticity of supply} = \frac{\%\ \text{change in quantity supplied}}{\%\ \text{change in price}}$$

---

[4] See Dale M. Heien, "The Structure of Food Demand: Interrelatedness and Duality," *American Journal of Agricultural Economics* 64, no. 2 (May 1982), pp. 213–21.

[5] For small changes in price, the price elasticity of supply can be expressed as $\frac{\Delta Q_S/Q_S}{\Delta P/P} = \frac{P\Delta Q_S}{Q_S\Delta P}$ where Q_S is quantity supplied.

Box 7 Price Elasticity of Supply as a Gauge of Supply Responsiveness

Supply response	% change in quantity supplied relative to % change in quantity demanded	Value of elasticity of supply
Inelastic	% change in quantity supplied is *less than* % change in price	Equal to or greater than 0 but less than 1
Unit elastic	% change in quantity supplied *equals* % change in price	1
Elastic	% change in quantity supplied is *greater than* % change in price	Greater than 1

For example, if a 10 percent increase in price results in a 20 percent increase in quantity supplied, the price elasticity of supply would be

$$\frac{20\%}{10\%} = 2$$

Since supply curves generally slope upward, supply elasticity tends to be positive. An increase in price tends to generate an increase in quantity supplied, while a decrease in price tends to generate a decrease in quantity supplied. In the equation for price elasticity of supply, the signs of the numerator and the denominator are the same. The ratio therefore has a positive sign.

As with demand, be sure you remember that the slope of a supply curve is an unreliable measure of its elasticity. The price elasticity of supply is related to but isn't the same as the slope of the supply curve.[6]

The price elasticity of supply ranges from 0 to infinity. An elastic supply prevails when the price elasticity of supply is greater than 1. If the price elasticity of supply is equal to or greater than 0 but less than 1, an inelastic supply prevails. Finally, when the price elasticity of supply is just equal to 1, a unit elastic **supply** prevails. Box 7 summarizes the relationship between percentage changes in price and quantity supplied for various cases. The greater the price elasticity of supply of an item, the more responsive, or elastic, is the quantity supplied to given percentage price changes.

Determinants of Price Elasticity of Supply

In general, a good's price elasticity of supply depends on the extent to which costs per unit rise as sellers increase output. If unit costs of production rise only slightly as output expands, small percentage increases in price will result in large percentage increases in quantity supplied. Under such circumstances, supply will be very elastic because small increases in price will allow sellers the possibility of large additional gains.

When the price of an item increases. not only do existing firms tend to produce more, but additional firms are attracted to production of the item. However, it often takes a considerable amount of time for new firms to start producing an item. For this reason, supply tends to become more elastic over time, as the lure of profits attracts more sellers.

For example, rising petroleum prices in the 1970s led to new exploration and development of previously unprofitable sources of oil. Over time the quantity of

elastic supply prevails when the price elasticity of supply is greater than 1.

inelastic supply prevails when the price elasticity of supply is equal to or greater than 0 but less than 1.

unit elastic supply prevails when the price elasticity of supply is just equal to 1.

---

[6] For an analysis of the relationship between price elasticity of supply and the slope of the supply curve, see David N. Hyman, *Modern Microeconomics: Analysis and Applications*, 3rd ed. (Homewood, Ill.: Richard D. Irwin, 1993), chap. 9.

petroleum products supplied increased substantially. After the sharp increase in the price of crude oil in 1973, oil reserves from the North Sea, Alaska, and Mexico were slowly developed. High oil prices slowly, but surely and massively, resulted in a response by suppliers.[7] However, an immediate response was impossible because of the time required to develop new petroleum resources. The time necessary to gear up and make new supplies available varies from industry to industry. This variation in response time is an important determinant of variations in the price elasticity of supply among industries.

The supply of housing also tends to become more elastic over time. For example, suppose rent controls like those described in Chapter 4 reduce market rents to 20 percent lower than they would be without the controls. Over a short period the rental housing supply is likely to be quite inelastic, say 0.7. We can easily calculate the reduction in rental housing in the short run caused by the 20 percent reduction in market rents:

$$0.7 = \frac{\% \text{ change in quantity supplied}}{-20\%}$$

$$\% \text{ change in quantity supplied} = -14\%$$

Let's assume that over 10 years the price elasticity of supply of rental housing is higher, say equal to 2. In this case the percentage reduction in the quantity of rental housing supplied ultimately resulting from the 20 percent decline in rents will be

$$2 = \frac{\% \text{ change in quantity supplied}}{-20\%}$$

$$\% \text{ change in quantity supplied} = -40\%$$

Landlords' reaction to rent controls will therefore intensify as time goes by. This implies that the shortage resulting from rent controls will become more acute over time.

Perfectly Inelastic and Perfectly Elastic Supply

When supply is fixed, sellers have no opportunity to vary the quantity they can offer. A perfectly inelastic supply curve for a good is a vertical line above a certain minimum price necessary to induce sellers to make the good available for sale. No matter what the percentage change in price above this minimum price, the percentage change in quantity supplied is always 0. Price elasticity of supply is always 0 along such a curve. Note that the supply curve doesn't hit the horizontal axis. This is because sellers require a minimum price before they'll make the item available for sale in a market. The supply of land in the United States is close to perfectly inelastic. No matter how much the price of land changes, there's unlikely to be any appreciable change in the total amount of usable land in the country.

The elasticities of supply of many goods are likely to be close to zero for very short periods. For example, the supply of fresh fish on a given day after the fishing fleet has brought in its catch will be perfectly inelastic. It takes time to catch more. Over time the supply of fish will be more elastic as higher prices induce fishers to catch more. As you can see in graph **A** in Box 8, when supply is perfectly inelastic, an increase in demand results in an increase in market price but has no effect on quantity supplied. However, if the price were below P_0, fishers wouldn't go out fishing and quantity supplied would be zero.

---

[7] See Arlon R. Tussing, "An OPEC Obituary," *Public Interest* 70 (Winter 1983), p. 12.

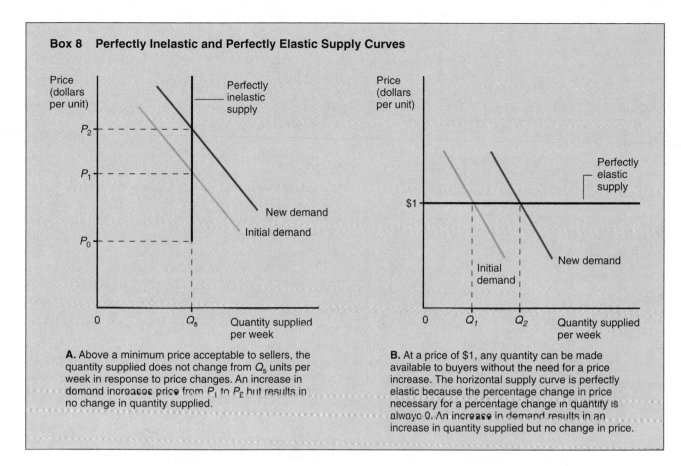

Box 8   Perfectly Inelastic and Perfectly Elastic Supply Curves

A. Above a minimum price acceptable to sellers, the quantity supplied does not change from Q_s units per week in response to price changes. An increase in demand increases price from P_1 to P_2 but results in no change in quantity supplied.

B. At a price of $1, any quantity can be made available to buyers without the need for a price increase. The horizontal supply curve is perfectly elastic because the percentage change in price necessary for a percentage change in quantity is always 0. An increase in demand results in an increase in quantity supplied but no change in price.

A perfectly elastic supply curve is a horizontal line such as that in graph **B** in Box 8. Price elasticity of supply is infinite on this line. You can think of such a supply curve as meaning that the slightest change in price would result in an infinite change in quantity supplied. The horizontal line also means that any change in demand results in a change in quantity supplied, but no change in price is necessary to induce sellers to supply more.

In effect, the supply curve of cheeseburgers to you in a McDonald's is probably shaped like the one drawn in graph **B.** You can buy all the cheeseburgers you want at the established price without causing the price to go up. In effect, to any particular buyer in a competitive market, the supply curve of a good will be perfectly elastic.

Another example of perfectly elastic supply would be an industry where over a long period the prices of inputs necessary to produce output don't increase as output increases. This means that no price increases would be required to increase quantities supplied because costs per unit of the good wouldn't increase as more was made available. There's evidence that the supply of new residential construction is nearly infinitely elastic over the long run.[8] Other things being equal, this implies that any increases in the price of new construction per square foot over short periods will eventually be balanced by future price declines. Over a long period an increase in

---

[8] James R. Follain, Jr., "The Price Elasticity of the Long-Run Supply of New Housing Construction," *Land Economics* (May 1979), pp. 190–99.

import quotas restrictions on the quantity of foreign goods that can be sold in a nation.

demand results in an increase in quantity supplied but no increase in market price. Temporary price increases tend to attract new firms into the construction industry. The resulting increase in supply acts to decrease price over a longer period.

the global economy

Import Quotas

How They Affect Supplies Import quotas are restrictions on the quantity of foreign goods that can be sold in a nation. Such quotas are often used to protect domestic industries from foreign competition. (See The Global Economy feature in Chapter 1, "Protectionism: Who Gains and Who Loses?") People who support import quotas argue that they merely limit quantities and do not necessarily raise prices for consumers. Using a bit of supply and demand analysis along with the concept of price elasticity of supply will convince you that import quotas are likely to result in price increases both for imports and for the domestic goods that are substituted for the imports!

For example, suppose a limit is placed on the number of Japanese cars that can be imported into the United States. Such an import quota was in effect during 1983 as part of a "voluntary export restraint" agreement negotiated by the U.S. and Japanese governments. The quota, set at 1.85 million cars for 1983, was designed to protect the U.S. auto industry

that year and to encourage U.S. producers to invest in new facilities.

The effect of an import quota is to make the supply of the imported good perfectly inelastic after a certain number of units have been sold. The supply curve for imported Japanese cars in the United States in 1983 is shown in Box 9. The curve is upward sloping up to point *A* and becomes vertical after point *A*. Point *A* corresponds to the import limit of 1.85 million cars.

The effect of a quota on the price of imported Japanese cars depends on the level of demand. If the demand curve intersects the supply at or below point *A*, the quota will neither reduce the quantity of cars purchased nor raise the price of the cars. If, however, demand is stronger so that it intersects the supply curve at a point like *B*, the price of Japanese cars would rise as a result of the quota but sales would remain fixed at the quota of 1.85 million units. In 1983 there was a surge in the demand for Japanese cars because consumer incomes were rising as the U.S. economy pulled out of a severe recession. As illustrated in the graph, the impact of the quota with the higher level of demand was to increase the price of Japanese cars by $1,000.

It has been estimated that quotas on Japanese car imports had the effect of raising the price of these cars by about $1,000 on average.[9] As illustrated in the graph, the $1,000 price increase also added $1.85 billion in revenue, represented by the shaded rectangle, to producers of imported cars and their dealers. Although quotas limit sales of imports, they add to the revenues of foreign suppliers by raising the price at which they can sell their products. For that reason Japanese car manufacturers don't complain too much about quotas!

What effect do quotas have on domestic producers? Because quotas tend to increase the price of foreign substitutes for domestic products, they tend to increase demand for domestic products. In the early 1980s, import quotas on Japanese cars contributed to an increase in demand for domestic cars that

[9] Robert W. Crandall, "Import Quotas and the Automobile Industry: The Cost of Protectionism," *Brookings Review* 2, no. 4 (Summer 1984), pp. 8–16.

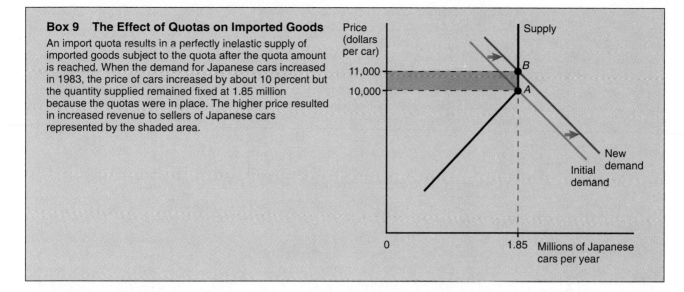

Box 9   The Effect of Quotas on Imported Goods

An import quota results in a perfectly inelastic supply of imported goods subject to the quota after the quota amount is reached. When the demand for Japanese cars increased in 1983, the price of cars increased by about 10 percent but the quantity supplied remained fixed at 1.85 million because the quotas were in place. The higher price resulted in increased revenue to sellers of Japanese cars represented by the shaded area.

acted to raise their price by an estimated $370 per unit on average. The higher price increased the quantity of domestic cars supplied and therefore helped the U.S. automobile industry.

But what was the cost of this gain in U.S. production? The total increase in the cost of buying both domestic and imported cars resulting from the quotas in the early 1980s came to over $4 billion. This cost was incurred to save an estimated 26,000 jobs in the U.S. auto industry. The total cost of the jobs saved when the quotas were in effect amounted to over $150,000 per worker per year, which was a lot more than the annual salaries earned by those workers![10] Do you think the benefits were worth the costs?

Quotas can also result in shortages if prices don't rise quickly in markets and if domestic producers can't respond quickly to increased demands for their products. For example, U.S. quotas on steel imports during the late 1980s contributed to shortages of unfinished steel. These shortages induced domestic users to import more expensive finished-steel products to meet their demands because the finished products were not subject to quotas.[11] In the United States, import quotas also contribute to higher prices for many textile products and agricultural commodities. These measures preserve jobs in U.S. industries at the cost of higher prices for consumers.

- What is measured by the price elasticity of supply? List some of the influences on the price elasticity of supply.

- Other things being unchanged, an increase in demand for a good increases its market price but has no effect on quantity supplied. What is the price elasticity of supply?

- Under what circumstances is the price elasticity of supply infinite?

CONCEPT CHECK
☐

TAX SHIFTING

The concepts of price elasticity of demand and supply are relevant to the analysis of taxes levied on sellers of such goods as gasoline, cigarettes, and alcoholic beverages. Even though these taxes are collected from sellers, buyers are often made worse off by them because they can result in shifts in supply that cause prices to rise. Tax shifting occurs when a tax levied on sellers of a good causes the market price of the good to increase. Under certain circumstances, the price of a good can increase by

④

tax shifting occurs when a tax levied on sellers of a good causes the market price of the good to increase.

---

[10] Ibid., p. 16.

[11] *Economic Report of the President, 1989* (Washington, D.C.: U.S. Government Printing Office, 1989), pp. 169–70.

exactly enough to cover the tax levied on each unit of the good. If we know the price elasticities of demand and supply of a taxed good, we can forecast the impact of the tax on the good's market price.

To find out how a tax affects market price, we need to analyze its impact on supply and demand conditions. Assume the government collects from sellers a 10-cent tax per gallon of gasoline. *From the sellers' standpoint, this means that the cost of each gallon of gasoline sold will go up exactly 10 cents*. The effect of the tax is exactly the same as the effect of having the price of an input used to produce gasoline go up 10 cents. The minimum price that sellers will accept for each gallon of gas will be increased by the amount of the tax. The supply curve for gasoline will therefore shift upward 10 cents for each quantity of gasoline sold. In effect, the tax causes a decrease in the supply of gasoline by reducing the gain obtained from selling each gallon.

Full Shifting

The graphs in Box 10 show two cases in which a supply decrease caused by the gasoline tax will cause the market price per gallon to increase by the *full amount* of the tax. In **A**, gas demand is perfectly inelastic. Here, as the supply decreases, buyers don't respond by decreasing the quantity demanded. The quantity demanded is 1 million gallons per month before and after the tax. The initial price is $1 per gallon. After the tax shifts the supply curve upward by 10 cents for any quantity, the price increases by exactly the amount of the tax per unit. The tax will collect $100,000 per month in this case, which equals the 10-cent per gallon tax multiplied by the 1 million gallons sold each month. The tax revenue is represented by the shaded area in **A**. *In effect, consumers pay the entire tax in the form of a 10-cent increase in the price of gasoline*. After the tax has been imposed, the market price buyers pay increases to $1.10. After paying the tax of 10 cents per gallon, sellers receive a net price of $1 per gallon, which is exactly the price they received before the tax was imposed. *When the demand for gasoline is perfectly inelastic, a tax collected from gas sellers is fully shifted to gas buyers as the gas price rises to cover the tax per unit*.

Sellers would also succeed in shifting the entire tax per unit to buyers if the *supply of gasoline* were perfectly elastic. In **B** in Box 10, the gas supply is assumed to be a horizontal line, implying a perfectly elastic supply. As before, the tax would shift the supply curve upward by 10 cents per gallon. In this case, however, the demand curve is assumed to be downward sloping, as is normally the case. As a result, the monthly quantity demanded declines from 1 million gallons to 750,000 gallons. However, the new supply curve intersects the demand curve at a price exactly 10 cents higher than the initial price of $1. At any price lower than that, sellers would be unable to cover their costs and would reduce production until price increased.

When the supply of gasoline is perfectly elastic at the $1 per gallon price before the tax has been imposed, sellers will be unwilling to make gas available at any price below $1 per gallon. The market price must rise to $1.10 per gallon for sellers to receive a net price of $1 per gallon after paying the 10-cent per gallon tax. Here, as in the first case, the price of gas goes up by the full amount of the tax per gallon. In this case, however, quantity demanded does decline; as a result, the tax collects only $75,000 per month, which is represented by the shaded area in **B** in Box 10. Nonetheless, the tax collected from sellers is still fully paid by buyers because the gas price increases by just enough to cover the tax. In general, if a good's supply is infinitely elastic, sellers can shift any tax collected from them to buyers by reducing the amount they supply until price increases by the full amount of the tax.

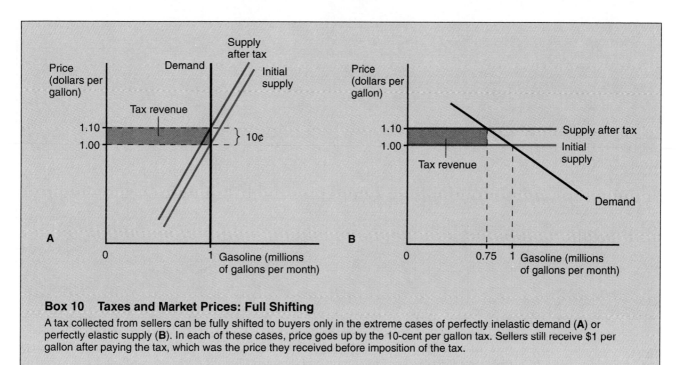

Box 10   Taxes and Market Prices: Full Shifting

A tax collected from sellers can be fully shifted to buyers only in the extreme cases of perfectly inelastic demand (**A**) or perfectly elastic supply (**B**). In each of these cases, price goes up by the 10-cent per gallon tax. Sellers still receive $1 per gallon after paying the tax, which was the price they received before imposition of the tax.

Partial Shifting

In reality, it's highly improbable that the price elasticity of demand for a good will be zero. Although the price elasticity of supply can be close to infinity over long periods, this too is highly improbable over short periods. Suppose, then, that neither the price elasticity of demand nor the price elasticity of supply takes on the extreme values of zero or infinity. In this case we can easily show that the tax will be *shared* by the buyers and sellers of the good. The case is illustrated in Box 11. The initial market equilibrium is at point *E*, which corresponds to a market price of $1 per gallon and monthly sales of 1 million gallons. As before, the tax shifts the supply curve up by 10 cents per gallon. The new market equilibrium corresponds to point *E'*, at which the market price paid by sellers increases to $1.04 and the quantity demanded declines to 850,000 gallons per month. After sellers pay the 10-cent per gallon tax, the net price they receive is $1.04 − $0.10 = $0.94. Total tax revenue collected is $85,000 per month, which is equal to the 10-cent per gallon tax multiplied by the 850,000 gallons sold per month. In effect, sellers pay 6 cents of the 10-cent per gallon tax because the price they receive per gallon falls from $1 to 94 cents after the tax has been imposed. The remaining 4 cents is shifted to buyers as a 4-cent per gallon increase in the market price.

What would happen if sellers tried to shift the full 10-cent per gallon tax to buyers by increasing price to $1.10? To find out, go to the graph in Box 11 and follow the dashed line from the price axis at $1.10 to the demand curve and the supply curve that prevail after the tax has been imposed. Note that the quantity demanded at that price would be only 630,000 gallons per month, while the quantity supplied would be 1 million gallons per month. There would therefore be a gas surplus that would push the market price down until it reached $1.04 per gallon.

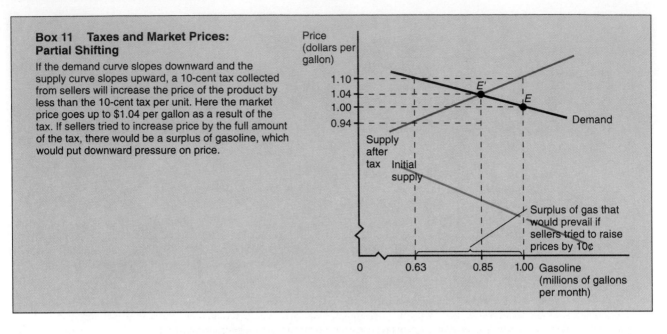

Box 11   Taxes and Market Prices: Partial Shifting

If the demand curve slopes downward and the supply curve slopes upward, a 10-cent tax collected from sellers will increase the price of the product by less than the 10-cent tax per unit. Here the market price goes up to $1.04 per gallon as a result of the tax. If sellers tried to increase price by the full amount of the tax, there would be a surplus of gasoline, which would put downward pressure on price.

The conclusion of this analysis is straightforward: *Sellers in competitive markets are subject to the laws of supply and demand when it comes to shifting taxes. Only in the unlikely case when demand is perfectly inelastic or when supply is perfectly elastic will sellers succeed in raising the price by the full amount of the tax.*

SUMMARY

1. Price elasticity of demand, a number that gauges the sensitivity of quantity demanded of a good to each 1 percent change in its price, is calculated by dividing the percentage change in quantity demanded by the percentage change in price that caused it.

2. Price elasticity of demand can range from 0 to an infinitely large negative number. Demand for a good is inelastic if the number indicating its price elasticity is less than 1, ignoring the minus sign. Demand for a good is unit elastic if the number indicating its price elasticity is exactly equal to 1, ignoring the minus sign. Demand for a good is elastic if the number indicating its price elasticity exceeds 1, ignoring the minus sign.

3. The price elasticity of demand for a good is influenced by the availability of substitutes for it, the proportion of their income consumers spend on it, and time.

4. Price elasticity of demand cannot be easily gauged from the slope of demand curves. For example, a downward-sloping demand curve with constant slope at all points will become more elastic as price increases.

5. A perfectly inelastic demand curve is a vertical line, while a perfectly elastic demand curve is a horizontal line.

6. The way consumers' total expenditure and sellers' total revenue change as price changes can be forecast if the price elasticity of demand for the good is known. If demand is elastic, price increases will decrease total revenue. If demand is inelastic, price increases will increase total revenue.

7. Income elasticity of demand gauges the sensitivity of demand for a good to changes in consumer income. Cross-elasticity of demand measures the sensitivity of demand for a good to changes in the prices of related goods.

8. Price elasticity of supply measures the sensitivity of changes in quantity supplied to each 1 percent change in the price of a good. It is calculated by dividing the percentage change in quantity supplied of a good by the percentage change in price that caused it.

9. When price elasticity of supply is greater than 1, supply is elastic. When the number is equal to or greater than 0 but less than 1, supply is inelastic. When the number is 1, supply is unit elastic.

10. A perfectly inelastic supply curve is a vertical line, while a perfectly elastic supply curve is a horizontal line.

KEY TERMS

price elasticity of demand *517*

elastic demand *518*

inelastic demand *518*

unit elastic demand *519*

total revenue *525*

total expenditure *525*

income elasticity of demand *529*

cross-elasticity of demand *529*

normal goods *529*

inferior goods *530*

price elasticity of supply *532*

elastic supply *533*

inelastic supply *533*

unit elastic supply *533*

import quotas *536*

tax shifting *537*

CONCEPT REVIEW

1 How is the price elasticity of demand for a product calculated? Under what circumstances is the demand for a product categorized as "elastic" or "inelastic"?

2 Why is information on the price elasticity of demand for a product required to forecast the effect of an increase in the price of the product on the total revenue earned by business firms selling it?

3 List some possible uses of each of the following concepts: income elasticity of demand, cross-elasticity of demand, and price elasticity of supply.

4 Under what circumstances would a tax collected from sellers of a product be shifted entirely to buyers in the form of a price increase? Why are excise taxes likely to be shared by buyers and sellers of the taxed product?

PROBLEMS AND APPLICATIONS

1. The price elasticity of demand for furniture you sell is estimated to be −3. What will be the effect on the quantity you sell if you lower your prices by 10 percent next month? What will happen to the total revenue you take in next month as a result of the price cut? **1**, **2**

2. The price elasticity of demand for brussels sprouts is estimated to be −0.5. Government authorities want to increase brussels sprouts consumption by 15 percent. By what percentage must the price to consumers fall to achieve this objective? What will happen to total consumer expenditure on brussels sprouts as a result of the price cut? **1**, **2**

3. The price of a package of Reese's Peanut Butter Cups rises from $1 to $1.25. As a result, the weekly quantity of Reese's demanded falls from 10,000 to 9,000 packages. Calculate the price elasticity of demand using the average of the initial and new prices and quantities as the basis for figuring the percentage changes. **1**

4. Suppose that for each 25-cent increase in the price of Reese's Peanut Butter Cups, the demand curve is such that the quantity demanded falls by 1,000 packages per week. Plot the demand curve for Reese's on a set of axes. Show that demand for Reese's becomes more elastic as price increases. **1**

5. Suppose Susan decides she'll spend $30 per month on Taco Supremes no matter what the price. Assuming she sticks to her decision, show that her demand for Taco Supremes is unit elastic at all possible prices. **1**, **2**

6. Draw the demand curve for a good that has a unit elastic demand at all possible prices. **1**

7. The supply of pencils decreases, but there's no change in the quantity demanded. Draw the demand curve for pencils, and comment on its price elasticity. What will happen to total expenditure on pencils as the price of pencils increases? **1**, **2**

8. The income elasticity of demand for furniture is 3. A recession reduces consumer income by 10 percent. What will happen to furniture sales? Explain why the demand for soap will be much less responsive to a reduction in income than the demand for furniture if the income elasticity of demand for soap is only 0.2. **3**

9. The cross-elasticity of demand for bacon with respect to the price of eggs is −2. What does this tell you about the way consumers perceive the relationship between bacon and eggs? **3**

10. The price elasticity of demand for cigarettes is −1.2. The price elasticity of supply for cigarettes is estimated to be 1. Will a 15-cent tax per pack of cigarettes increase the price of cigarettes by 15 cents per pack? **4**

glossary

a

absolute advantage the advantage a nation has over other nations in the production of an item if it can produce more of the item over a certain period with a given amount of resources than the other nations can.

accelerated depreciation allowances generous deductions from pretax business income that are allowed when firms acquire new equipment or new structures.

accelerationist hypothesis the theory arguing that attempts by policymakers to reduce unemployment below the natural rate can succeed only in the short run.

accounting cost measures the explicit costs of operating a business—those that result from purchases of input services.

acreage control programs programs that provide cash payments to farmers who agree to take some of their land out of production for certain crops.

aggregate demand a relationship between aggregate quantity demanded and the economy's price level.

aggregate demand curve a graph that shows how the amount of aggregate domestic production demanded, measured by real GNP, will vary with the price level.

aggregate expenditure the sum of consumption expenditures, investment expenditures, government purchases, and net exports during the year. Equivalent to GDP.

aggregate household debt the purchasing power of the sums of money outstanding that households have borrowed and are currently obligated to repay.

aggregate household wealth the purchasing power of all assets owned by households.

aggregate purchases the market value of final goods and services that will be purchased at any given level of income.

aggregate quantity demanded the amount of final products that buyers are willing and able to purchase at a given price level.

aggregate quantity supplied the quantity of final products that will be supplied by producers at a given price level.

aggregate real income the nominal (money) income of a nation, adjusted for inflation. Equivalent to real GDP.

aggregates broad totals of economic variables such as production, consumption, and investment.

aggregate supply a relationship between the price level and aggregate quantity supplied.

aggregate supply curve a graph showing how aggregate quantity supplied varies with the price level, other things being equal.

allocative efficiency a condition achieved when resources are allocated in ways allowing the maximum possible net benefit for their use.

antitrust statutes laws to prevent "unfair" business practices that give rise to monopoly power.

automatic stabilizers features of the federal budget that automatically adjust net taxes to stabilize aggregate demand as the economy expands and contracts.

autonomous consumption the portion of annual consumer purchases that is independent of, and not affected by, current disposable income.

autonomous purchases purchases such as investment or autonomous consumption that cause the economy's aggregate purchases line to shift.

average cost total cost divided by the number of units of output produced over a given period. Also called *average total cost* or *unit cost*.

average fixed cost fixed cost divided by the number of units of output produced over a given period.

average input cost the price of an input.

average product (of an input) the total output produced over a given period divided by the number of units of that input used.

average revenue total revenue per unit of a good sold.

average tax rate the amount of taxes paid divided by the dollar value of the item taxed.

average variable cost variable cost divided by the number of units of output produced over a given period.

b

backward-bending labor supply curve a curve implying that the substitution effect on a worker's labor services outweighs the income effect only at relatively low wages.

balance of payments a statement showing the net exchange of a nation's currency for foreign currencies from all transactions between that nation and foreign nations in a given year.

balance of trade the difference between the value of merchandise exported by a nation's firms and the nation's imports of foreign merchandise.

balance on current account of the balance of payments measures U.S. net exports for the year, including transactions involving services, investment income, and transfers.

bank a commercial bank or thrift institution that offers checkable deposits.

bar graph a graph that shows the value of a *Y* variable as the height of a bar for each corresponding value of the *X* variable.

barrier to entry a constraint that prevents additional sellers from entering a monopoly firm's market.

barter the process of exchanging goods (or services) for goods (or services).

behavioral assumption an assumption that establishes the motivation of persons for the purpose of understanding cause-and-effect relationships among economic variables.

bilateral monopoly a situation that exists when only one buyer and one seller trade input (or output) services in a market.

black market a market in which sellers sell goods to buyers for more than the legal prices.

Board of Governors of the Federal Reserve System the governing body that supervises the operation of the nation's banking system and acts as an authority to regulate the money supply. The Board consists of seven governors, each appointed by the president to serve a 14-year term.

bonds securities issued by corporations and governments representing the promise to make periodic payments of interest and repay borrowed funds at a certain time.

Bretton Woods system an international monetary system developed in 1944 and based on fixed exchange rates, with the value of foreign currencies tied to the U.S. dollar.

budget constraint as defined by a consumer's income and its purchasing power, indicates that income must equal expenditure.

budget deficit the amount by which government expenditures exceed government revenues in a given year.

budget surplus an excess of government revenues over government expenditures in a given year.

business cycle the term used to describe the fluctuations in aggregate production as measured by the ups and downs of real GDP.

business firm an organization under one management set up for the purpose of earning profits for its owners by making one or more items available for sale in markets.

C

capital the equipment, tools, structures, machinery, vehicles, materials, and skills created to help produce goods and services.

capitalism an economic system characterized by private ownership of economic resources and freedom of enterprise in which owners of factories and other capital hire workers to produce goods and services.

cartel a group of firms acting together to coordinate output decisions and control prices as if they were a single monopoly.

centrally planned economy an economy in which politically appointed committees plan production and manage the economy to achieve political objectives.

ceteris paribus a Latin phrase meaning "other things being equal." Used to acknowledge that influences other than the one whose effect is being analyzed must be controlled in testing a hypothesis.

change in aggregate demand a change in the amount of a nation's final products that will be purchased caused by something other than a change in the price level.

change in aggregate supply a change in the amount of national production resulting from something other than a change in the price level.

change in demand a change in the relationship between the price of a good and the quantity demanded caused by a change in something other than the price of the good.

change in input demand a change in the relationship between the quantity of an input demanded and its price caused by a change in a determinant of input demand other than price.

change in money demand a change, caused by a change in economic conditions, in the relationship between the level of interest rates and the stock of money demanded in the economy.

change in quantity demanded a change in the amount of a good buyers are willing and able to buy in response to a change in the price of the good.

change in quantity supplied a change in the amount of a good sellers are willing to sell in response to a change in the price of the good.

change in relative price an increase or decrease in the price of a good relative to the average change in the prices of all goods.

change in supply a change in the relationship between the price of a good and the quantity supplied in response to a change in a supply determinant other than the price of the good.

checkable deposits money deposited in bank accounts that can be used to write checks accepted to pay debts or that can easily be converted to currency.

check clearing the process of transferring Federal Reserve deposits among banks as checks are paid.

classical model of macroeconomic equilibrium a theory implying that excessive unemployment and unused productive capacity would set up forces that would eventually increase real GDP and eliminate the cyclical unemployment of workers.

classical quantity theory of money a model of the long-run functioning of the economy according to which changes in the money stock result in proportional changes in the price level over the long run.

closed shop a union arrangement with an employer that permits hiring only union members.

Coase theorem a principle stating that governments can help internalize externalities by establishing rights to use resources and by encouraging the trading of those rights.

collateral an asset a borrower pledges to a lender in case of default.

collective bargaining the process of negotiating for wages and improvements in working conditions between a labor union and employers.

command economy an economy in which resource allocation decisions are determined largely by the central planning authorities who set production goals.

commercial banks firms that acquire funds by accepting checkable deposits and savings deposits from households and business firms and use these funds to make loans to businesses and individuals.

commodity money an item that serves the functions of money but also has intrinsic value as a marketable item in addition to its value as the medium of exchange.

common property resources natural resources (such as the ocean and the atmosphere) whose use is not priced because property rights have not been established for them.

comparative advantage the advantage that a nation has over a trading partner in the production of an item if it produces that item at lower opportunity cost per unit than its partner does.

compensating wage differential a difference in money wages necessary to make total compensation for similar jobs equal when nonpecuniary wages are not equal to zero.

competitive firm one that sells its product in a perfectly competitive market in which it is a price taker.

competitive input market a market in which neither individual buyers nor individual sellers can influence the prices of input services.

complements goods whose use together enhances the satisfaction a consumer obtains from each.

conglomerate a firm operating plants that produce many different kinds of goods and services.

conglomerate merger a merger of firms selling goods in unrelated markets.

constant-costs industry one for which input prices are unaffected by the quantity of a good produced or the number of firms in the industry.

constant returns to scale prevail when economies of scale no longer exist and when average costs do not increase as a result of diseconomies of scale in the long run.

consumer equilibrium attained when a consumer purchases goods over a period until the marginal utility per dollar is the same for all goods consumed.

consumer price index (CPI) the price index most commonly used to measure the impact of changes in prices on households. The index is based on a standard market basket of goods and services purchased by a typical urban family.

consumer surplus the difference between the total benefit of a given quantity purchased by a consumer and the expenditure necessary to purchase that quantity.

consumption function a relationship between aggregate consumer purchases and disposable income in a certain year given all other influences of consumption.

consumption possibilities curve a curve showing the combinations of two goods that a nation can consume, given its resources, technology, and international trade.

contestable market a market in which entry of sellers is easy and exit is not very costly.

continuous variable a variable that can realistically and meaningfully take on minute fractions of values.

contraction a downturn from peak economic activity in the business cycle during which real GDP declines from its previous value.

contractionary fiscal policy a policy under which the government acts to restrain aggregate demand by decreasing spending or increasing taxes, or both.

contractionary monetary policy action by the Federal Reserve System to decrease the monetary base or its rate of growth.

coordinates a pair of numbers that correspond to values for variables X and Y when plotted on a set of axes.

corporation a business legally established under state laws that grant it an identity separate from its owners.

corrective subsidy an amount paid to consumers or producers of a good equal to the marginal external benefit of the good.

corrective tax a tax levied on polluters to simulate a charge equal to the marginal external cost of their actions.

cost-push inflation inflation caused by continual decreases in aggregate supply.

craft union an organization of workers in a particular skilled job, such as plumbers, electricians, carpenters, or musicians.

credit the use of loanable funds supplied by lenders to borrowers who agree to pay back the borrowed funds according to an agreed-upon schedule.

credit unions depository institutions whose depositors belong to a particular organization. Credit unions make loans only to their members.

cross-elasticity of demand a number used to measure the sensitivity of consumer purchases of one good to each 1 percent change in price of a substitute or complementary good.

crowding-out effect the reduction in private investment purchases caused by higher interest rates that result from government borrowing.

currency appreciation a situation that occurs when there is an increase in the number of units of one nation's currency that must be given up to purchase each unit of another nation's currency.

currency depreciation a situation that occurs when there is a decrease in the number of units of one nation's currency that must be given up to purchase each unit of another nation's currency.

curve   a straight or curved line drawn to connect points plotted on a set of axes.

cyclical unemployment   the amount of unemployment resulting from declines in real GDP during periods of contraction or recession, or in any period when the economy fails to operate at its potential.

d

default   nonrepayment of the principal and interest on a loan.

deflation   the rate of downward movement in the price level for an aggregate of goods and services.

demand   a relationship between the price of an item and the quantity demanded.

demand curve   a graph that shows how quantity demanded varies with the price of a good.

demand for money   the relationship between the sums of money people willingly hold and the level of interest rates in the economy, given all the other influences on the desirability of holding money instead of other assets.

demand-pull inflation   inflation caused by increases in aggregate demand.

demand schedule   a table that shows how an item's quantity demanded would vary with price, other things being equal.

depletable resource   a resource for which a given amount of known reserves is available at any point in time.

depository institutions   institutions that make loans and offer checkable deposit and time deposit accounts for use by households and business firms.

depreciation   an estimate of the value of capital goods that wear out or become obsolete during the year. Also called *consumption of fixed capital*.

derived demand   the demand for an input that is derived from the demand for the product that the input is used to produce.

diminishing marginal rates of substitution   the marginal rates of substitu-

tion of good X for Y will tend to decline as more X is substituted for Y along any consumer's indifference curve.

discounted present value   the current value of funds to be received in future periods.

discount loans   bank borrowings from the Federal Reserve System; also called *advances*.

discount rate   the interest rate Federal Reserve banks charge member banks for loans.

discouraged worker   a worker who leaves the labor force (stops actively seeking a job) after unsuccessfully searching for a job for a certain period.

discrete variable   a variable that cannot vary by fractions of units.

diseconomies of scale   increases in average costs of operation resulting from problems in managing large-scale enterprises. Also called *decreasing returns to scale*.

disinflation   a sharp reduction in the annual rate of inflation.

disposable income   the income individuals have to spend or save after payment of taxes.

dividend   the portion of a corporation's profit paid to its stockholders.

division of labor   the breakdown of a larger process into particular tasks performed by workers who specialize in those tasks.

dominant strategy   the strategy for which a player is getting the highest possible payoff, regardless of what the rival players are doing.

e

economic cost   the monetary value of all inputs used in a particular activity or enterprise over a given period.

economic growth   the expansion of production possibilities that results from increased availability and increased productivity of economic resources. Expansion in production measured by the annual percentage increase in a nation's level of real GDP.

economic model   a simplified way of

expressing how some sector of the economy functions. Contains assumptions that establish relationships among economic variables.

economic profit   the difference between total revenue and the cost of all inputs used by a firm over a given period.

economic rents   earnings that exceed the opportunity cost of an activity.

economic resources   the inputs used in the process of production.

economics   the study of the use of limited productive resources in a society to satisfy the unlimited desires of its members.

economic system   an accepted way of organizing production, establishing rights to ownership and use of productive resources, and governing economic transactions in a society.

economies of scale   reductions in unit costs resulting from increased size of operations. Also called *increasing returns to scale* or *economies of mass production*.

economy   the mechanism through which the use of labor, land, structures, vehicles, equipment, and natural resources is organized to satisfy the desires of those who live in a society.

elastic demand   prevails if the price elasticity of demand for a good exceeds 1, ignoring the minus sign.

elastic supply   prevails when the price elasticity of supply is greater than 1.

emissions charges   prices established for the right to emit each unit of a pollutant.

emissions standards   limits established by government on the annual amounts and kinds of pollutants that can be emitted into the air or water by producers or users of certain products.

entrepreneurship   the talent to develop products and processes and to organize production of goods and services.

entry-limit price   the price set by firms in a market that is low enough to prevent new entrants from entering the market as sellers.

equation of exchange   an identity that shows the relationship between nominal GDP, the money stock, and the income velocity of circulation of money.

equilibrium   the situation that prevails when economic forces balance so that economic variables neither increase nor decrease.

equimarginal principle   states that to maximize utility, a consumer must equalize the marginal utility per dollar spent on each good.

equity   the difference between the value of the assets and debt of a corporation or an individual.

excess burden   the loss in net benefits from resource use caused by the distortion in choices resulting from a tax.

excess capacity   the difference between the output corresponding to minimum possible average cost and the output produced by the monopolistically competitive firm in the long run.

excess reserves   the difference between total reserves and required reserves of a bank held against deposits.

expansion   an upturn of economic activity between a trough and a peak during which real GDP increases.

expansionary fiscal policy   a policy under which the government acts to increase aggregate demand by increasing spending or decreasing taxes, or both.

expansionary monetary policy   action taken by the Federal Reserve System to increase the monetary base or its rate of growth.

external debt   the portion of the national debt owed to citizens of other nations.

externalities   costs or benefits of market transactions that are not reflected in the prices buyers and sellers use to make their decisions.

f

federal funds   reserves loaned out on a short-term basis by one bank to another.

federal funds rate   the interest rate charged for the loan of reserves from one bank to another.

Federal Open Market Committee   an arm of the Federal Reserve System; affects the amount of excess reserves available to banks by instructing the Federal Reserve Bank of New York to buy or sell government securities on the open market.

federal system of government   numerous levels of government, each with its own powers, provide services and regulate private affairs.

fiat money   money that is accepted as a medium of exchange because of government decree rather than because of its intrinsic value as a commodity.

final products   goods and services sold to final users and not used as materials, parts, or services to be incorporated in the value of other items that are to be resold.

financial intermediaries   firms that specialize in borrowing funds from savers and lending those funds to investors and others.

fiscal policy   the use of government spending and taxing for the specific purpose of stabilizing the economy.

fixed costs   costs that do not vary as a firm varies its output. Also called *overhead costs*.

fixed input   an input whose quantity cannot be changed over the short run.

foreign exchange   the money of one nation held by citizens of another nation as either currency or bank deposits.

foreign exchange market   a market in which buyers and sellers of bank deposits denominated in the monetary units of many nations exchange their funds.

foreign exchange rate   the price of one nation's monetary unit in terms of the monetary unit of another nation.

fractional reserve banking   a process in which a banking system creates checkable deposits by making loans in some multiple of the reserves it actually has on hand to pay withdrawals.

fractional reserve ratio   the ratio of

actual cash reserves to total receipts for deposits.

fractional reserve ratio   the ratio of actual cash reserves to total receipts for deposits.

free markets   the situation that exists when there are no restrictions that prevent buyers or sellers from entering or exiting a market.

free rider   a person who seeks to enjoy the benefits of a public good without contributing to its costs.

frictional unemployment   the usual amount of unemployment resulting from people who have left jobs that did not work out and are searching for new employment, or people who are either entering or reentering the labor force to search for a job.

full employment   the situation that occurs when the actual rate of unemployment is no more than the natural rate of unemployment.

g

GDP deflator   the ratio of nominal GDP to real GDP (multiplied by 100); an index of the average of the prices used to deflate nominal GDP.

gold standard   an international monetary system that required that currencies be convertible into gold at a fixed price.

government budget   a plan for spending funds and for raising revenues through taxation, fees, and other means, and borrowing funds if necessary.

government failure   a situation that exists when voters approve programs for which marginal costs exceed marginal benefits.

government purchases of goods and services   expenditure on final products of business firms and all input costs, including labor costs, incurred by all levels of government in the United States.

government securities   interest-bearing debts of the federal government in the form of Treasury bills, Treasury notes, and Treasury bonds.

government   transfers   payments

made directly to certain people or organizations that do not provide a good or service in return at that time. Such payments are usually financed by taxes.

gross domestic product (GDP) the market value of the final goods and services produced by workers and other resources located within the borders of a nation over a period of one year.

gross national product (GNP) the market value of final output produced annually by all labor and property supplied by a nation's households, no matter where those resources are employed. Measures the aggregate income of a nation's households.

gross private domestic investment expenditure by business firms on new machinery and equipment (producer durables), the value of new residential and nonresidential construction, and the change in business inventories during the year.

b

high-employment deficit (or surplus) the budget deficit (or surplus) that would prevail if the natural rate of unemployment were achieved.

horizontal merger a situation that occurs when competing sellers in the same market form a single firm.

human capital the skills and qualifications of workers that stem from education and training.

hyperinflation inflation at very high rates of usually 200 percent or more prevailing for at least one year.

i

imperfect competition exists when more than one seller competes for sales with other sellers of competitive products, each of which has some control over price.

implicit costs the costs of nonpurchased inputs, to which a cash value must be imputed because the inputs are not purchased in a market transaction.

import quotas a limit on the quantity of foreign goods that can be sold in a nation's domestic markets.

income effect a change in consumption of a good *only* as a result of the variation in the purchasing power of money income caused by a price change.

income effect of a wage change the change in hours worked stemming from the change in income caused by the wage change.

income elasticity of demand a number that measures the sensitivity of consumer purchases to each 1 percent change in income.

income velocity of circulation of money the number of times per year, on average, a dollar of the money stock is spent on final purchases or paid out as income.

increasing-costs industry one for which the prices of at least some of the inputs increase as a direct result of the industry's expansion.

indifference curve a graph of various market baskets that provide a consumer with equal utility.

indifference curve analysis a technique for explaining how choices between two alternatives are made.

indifference map a way of drawing indifference curves to describe a consumer's preferences.

indirect business taxes taxes levied on sales of final products by business firms that increase the costs of these firms and are therefore reflected in the market value of goods and services sold.

induced consumption the portion of annual consumer purchases in a given year that responds to changes in current disposable income.

industrial union a union that represents all workers in a particular industry, regardless of their craft or skills.

industry a group of firms selling a similar product in a market.

inelastic demand prevails if the price elasticity of demand for a good is equal to or greater than 0 but less than 1, ignoring the minus sign.

inelastic supply prevails when the

price elasticity of supply is equal to or greater than 0 but less than 1.

inferior goods goods that have negative income elasticity of demand.

inflation the rate of upward movement in the price level for an aggregate of goods and services.

inflationary GDP gap the difference between equilibrium real GDP and potential real GDP when the economy is overheated.

injection (of spending) a purchase made by business firms, governments, or foreign buyers that increases the flow of income in a nation.

input market a market used to trade the services of productive resources for income payments.

inputs the labor, capital, land, natural resources, and entrepreneurship that are combined to produce products and services.

interest the price for the use of funds, usually expressed as a percentage per dollar of funds borrowed.

intermediate products products produced by business firms for resale by other firms or for use as materials or services that will be included in the value of resold goods.

internal debt the portion of the national debt owed to the nation's own citizens.

internalization of an externality a situation that occurs when the marginal cost or marginal benefit of a good has been adjusted so that market sale of the good results in the efficient output.

internal labor market exists within a firm when it fills positions by using its own employees, rather than hiring new employees, to fill all but the lowest-level jobs.

intersection the point at which two curves drawn on the same set of axes cross.

investment the process of replenishing or adding to capital stock.

isocost line gives all combinations of labor and capital that are of equal total cost.

isoquant a curve showing all combinations of variable inputs that can be used to produce a given quantity of output.

isoquant map shows the combinations of labor and capital that can be used to produce several possible output levels.

k

Keynesian model of macroeconomic equilibrium a model assuming that because of rigid nominal wages the economy can be in equilibrium at less than full employment.

l

labor the physical and mental efforts of human beings in the production of goods and services.

labor force the number of people over the age of 16 who are either employed or actively seeking a job.

labor supply curve a curve that shows a relationship between a worker's hourly wages and labor hours supplied for work over a given period.

labor theory of value a principle maintaining that only labor can produce something worth paying for.

labor union an organization formed to represent the interests of workers in bargaining with employers for contracts concerning wages, fringe benefits, and working conditions.

law of demand the principle stating that in general, other things being equal, the lower the price of a good, the greater the quantity of that good buyers will purchase over a given period.

law of diminishing marginal returns states that the extra production obtained from increases in a variable input will eventually decline as more of the variable input is used together with the fixed inputs.

law of diminishing marginal utility states that the marginal utility of any item tends to decline as more is consumed over any given period.

law of increasing costs a principle stating that the opportunity cost of each additional unit of output of a

good over a period increases as more of that good is produced.

law of supply the principle stating that in general, other things being equal, the higher the price of a good, the greater the quantity of that good sellers are willing and able to make available over a given period.

layoff the temporary suspension of employment without pay for a period of seven consecutive days or more.

leakage (of spending) a portion of income that is not used to purchase domestically produced goods during the year.

less developed country (LDC) a country whose real GDP per capita is generally much less than \$1,000 a year.

limited liability a legal provision that protects the owners of a corporation (its stockholders) by limiting their liability for debts of the corporation to no more than the amount invested in the firm.

long run a period of production that gives managers adequate time to vary *all* the inputs used to produce a good.

long-run aggregate supply curve (LRAS) a curve showing the relationship between the aggregate quantity supplied and the price level that would be observed if nominal wages and other money prices were flexible enough to allow the classical self-correcting mechanism to work.

long-run competitive equilibrium a condition that exists in an industry when there is no tendency for firms to enter or leave the industry or to expand or contract the scale of their operations.

long-run cost the minimum cost of producing any given output when all inputs are variable.

long-run industry supply curve a relationship between price and quantity supplied for points where the industry is in long-run competitive equilibrium.

long-run Phillips curve a curve that shows the unemployment rate that prevails for the economy in the long run.

Lorenz curve a plotting of data showing the percentage of income en-

joyed by each percentage of households ranked according to their incomes.

m

M1 a measure of the money stock that includes only currency and account balances commonly used to pay for goods and services; the sum of currency, traveler's checks, and checkable deposits.

M2 a measure of money including M1 and liquid assets that cannot be used directly as a medium of exchange but can be easily converted into checkable deposits or other components of M1. The sum of M1 and certain near monies.

M3 the sum of M2 and large-denomination (\$100,000 and more) certificates of deposit and other large-denomination liquid assets.

macroeconomic equilibrium a situation that occurs when the aggregate quantity demanded equals the aggregate quantity supplied.

macroeconomics a branch of economic analysis that considers the overall performance of the economy with respect to total national production and consumption, average prices, and employment levels.

managed float the current international monetary system, under which central banks affect supply of and demand for currencies in ways that influence equilibrium in foreign exchange markets.

manager a person who coordinates decisions within a firm.

marginal analysis a method economists use to study decision making; involves a systematic comparison of the benefits and costs of actions.

marginal benefit the dollar value placed on the satisfaction obtained from another unit of an item.

marginal benefit of work the extra income received from extra work, including any nonmonetary satisfaction obtained from a job.

marginal cost the sacrifice made to obtain an additional unit of an item.

marginal cost of work the value of extra leisure time given up to work.

marginal external benefit the extra benefit that accrues to third parties when a positive externality is present.

marginal external cost the extra cost imposed on third parties when a negative externality is present.

marginal input cost the extra cost associated with using one more unit of an input; the change in total input cost associated with a change in input services hired.

marginal product (of an input) the increase in output from one more unit of an input when the quantity of all other inputs is unchanged.

marginal profit the change in profit from selling an additional unit of a good, representing the difference between the marginal revenue from that unit and its marginal cost.

marginal propensity to consume the fraction of each additional dollar of annual disposable income that is allocated to consumer purchases.

marginal propensity to import the fraction of each extra dollar of income used to purchase imported products.

marginal propensity to save the fraction of each additional dollar of annual disposable income that is saved.

marginal rate of substitution the quantity of one good a consumer would give up to obtain one more unit of another good while being neither better off nor worse off by the trade.

marginal rate of technical substitution of labor for capital a measure of the amount of capital each unit of labor can replace without increasing or decreasing production.

marginal respending rate the extra purchases that result from each extra dollar of income.

marginal return on investment the percentage rate of return on investment of additional sums used to acquire more capital.

marginal revenue the extra revenue obtained from selling an additional unit of a good.

marginal revenue product (of an input) the change in total revenue that results when one more unit of an input is obtained.

marginal tax rate the extra tax paid on extra income or the extra dollar value of any other taxed item.

marginal utility the extra satisfaction received over a given period by consuming one extra unit of a good.

market an arrangement through which buyers and sellers meet or communicate in order to trade goods or services.

market basket a combination of goods and services.

market demand curve shows the relationship between a product's price and the total quantity demanded by *all* consumers willing and able to purchase the product at each price, other things being equal.

market demand for an input the sum of the quantities demanded by all industries and other employers using that input at any given price.

market equilibrium the situation attained when the price of a good adjusts so that the quantity buyers are willing and able to buy at that price is just equal to the quantity sellers are willing and able to supply.

market failure failure of the price system to achieve allocative efficiency; results when choices by buyers or sellers in unregulated markets result in an inefficient outcome.

market supply curve gives the sum of the quantities supplied by all firms producing a product at each possible price over a given period.

market supply of an input a relationship between the price of an input and the quantity of the input supplied for employment in all industries and other uses.

means test a standard establishing the fact that people in the groups eligible for welfare payments have incomes and property below the minimally acceptable amounts.

median voter given an odd number of voters, the voter whose most-preferred outcome is the median of all the most-preferred outcomes.

median voter rule a principle stating that when the marginal benefit of a pure public good declines for each vo-

ter as more of the good is made available, the political equilibrium under majority rule always corresponds to the median most-preferred outcome when there is an odd number of voters.

microeconomics a branch of economic analysis that concentrates on the choices made by individual participants in the economy. Also called *price theory*.

mixed economy an economy in which governments as well as business firms provide goods and services.

monetarism a theory of long-term macroeconomic equilibrium, based on the equation of exchange, according to which shifts in velocity are reasonably predictable.

monetary base the sum of currency in circulation and total bank reserves outstanding at any given time.

monetary policy actions taken by central banks to influence the money supply or interest rates in attempts to stabilize the economy.

money anything that is generally accepted as payment in exchange for goods or services. Money also serves as a standard of value, a standard of deferred payment, and a store of value.

money demand curve a curve that shows a relationship between the level of interest rates in the economy and the stock of money demanded at a given point in time.

money supply a relationship between the quantity of money supplied in the form of currency and checkable deposits and the level of interest rates prevailing at a given point in time.

monopolistic competition a condition that exists when many sellers compete to sell a differentiated product in a market into which the entry of new sellers is possible.

monopoly power the ability of a firm to influence the price of its product by making more or less of the product available to buyers.

monopsony a situation that exists when there is a single buyer with no rivals in an input market.

monopsony power the ability of a

single buyer to influence the price of an input service it purchases.

most-preferred political outcome   that alternative for which the marginal benefit just equals the tax a voter would pay if the voter were able to purchase the good or service in a market at a price equal to the assigned tax per unit.

multiplier   a number that indicates how many dollars of increase in real GDP results from each dollar of new autonomous purchases.

multiproduct firm   a firm that produces several different items for sale in markets.

mutual gains from international trade on average, citizens in all trading nations gain from exchanging goods in international markets.

mutual savings banks   depository institutions operating in some states that are similar to savings and loan associations in that they primarily attract savings deposits and in the past specialized in making mortgage loans.

n

Nash equilibrium   an equilibrium in which each of the players is getting the highest possible payoff no matter what strategy the other player chooses.

national debt   the dollar amount that the federal government owes its creditors at a given time.

national income   the NIPA measure of annual household and business earnings from the use of productive resources.

National Income and Product Accounts (NIPA)   the official system of accounting used to measure the flows of income and expenditures in the United States.

national saving   the sum of household saving, business saving, and saving by the government sector.

natural monopoly   a situation in which a firm emerges as the single seller in a market because of cost or technological advantages that lower the average cost of production.

natural rate of unemployment   the percentage of the labor force that can

normally be expected to be unemployed for reasons other than cyclical fluctuations in real GDP.

Natural resources   land used as sites for structures, ports, and other facilities; natural materials used in production; characteristics of an area that affect production, such as climate and environmental quality.

near monies   assets that are easily converted to money because they can be liquidated at low cost and little risk of loss.

negative externality   a cost, not reflected in a price, that is associated with the use of resources. Also called *external cost*.

negative income tax   government payments to people whose income falls below certain levels.

negative (inverse) relationship   the connection between variables that is depicted by a downward-sloping curve on a set of axes; indicates that variable *Y* decreases whenever variable *X* increases.

net benefit   the total benefit of the quantity of a good purchased less the dollar sacrifice necessary to purchase that quantity.

net exports   any excess of expenditure on exports over imports.

net federal debt   the portion of the national debt owed to debtors other than the Federal Reserve and government agencies.

net national product (NNP)   GNP less capital consumption allowances.

net private domestic investment gross private domestic investment less depreciation.

net taxes   the difference between taxes and transfer payments.

nominal exchange rate   the price of a unit of one nation's currency in terms of a unit of a foreign currency.

nominal GNP   the market value of a nation's final output based on current prices for the goods and services produced during the year.

nominal income   the actual number of dollars of income received over a year.

nominal interest rate   the annual per-

centage amount of money that is earned on a sum loaned or deposited in a bank.

nominal wages   hourly payments to workers in current dollars.

nonpecuniary wages   the nonmonetary aspects of a job that must be added to or subtracted from money wages to obtain total compensation per hour of work.

nonprice rationing   devices that distribute available goods and services on a basis other than willingness to pay.

nonscarce (or free) good   a good for which the quantity demanded does not exceed the quantity supplied at zero price.

nonwage money income   includes pensions, welfare payments and subsidies, interest, dividends, allowances, and any other type of income that is available independent of work.

normal goods   goods that have positive income elasticity of demand.

normal profit   that portion of a firm's cost that is not included in accounting cost. A measure of the implicit costs of owner-supplied resources in a firm over a given period.

normative analysis   a way to evaluate the desirability of alternative outcomes according to underlying value judgments about what is good or bad.

O

oligopoly   a market structure in which a few sellers dominate the sales of a product and entry of new sellers is difficult or impossible.

open economy   an economy linked to the rest of the world through international trade.

open market operations   the Federal Reserve System's purchases and sales of government securities conducted by the Federal Open Market Committee.

opportunity cost   the cost of choosing to use resources for one purpose measured by the sacrifice of the next best alternative for using those resources.

origin   on a set of axes, the point

designated by 0, at which variables X and Y both take on the value of zero.

overheated economy   an economy in which the actual unemployment rate is less than the natural rate of unemployment.

p

paradox of value   people are willing to give up zero or very small amounts of money to obtain certain items that provide them great total benefit.

parity   the idea that the prices of agricultural commodities must rise as fast as the prices of goods and services on which farmers spend their income.

parity price ratio   the ratio of average price for goods sold by farmers to average prices for goods on which farmers spend their income.

partnership   a business owned by two or more persons, each of whom receives a portion of any profits.

payoff matrix   matrix that shows the gain or loss from each possible strategy for each possible reaction by the rival player of the game.

perfectly competitive market   exists when (1) there are many sellers in the market; (2) the products sold in the market are homogeneous; (3) each firm has a very small market share of total sales; (4) no seller regards competing sellers as a threat to its market share; (5) information is freely available on prices; (6) sellers have freedom of entry and exit.

personal consumption expenditures household and individual purchases of both durable and nondurable goods and services.

personal income   the NIPA measure of annual income available to households.

personal saving   the portion of household income that is not used to make purchases or pay taxes.

Phillips curve   a curve showing the hypothesized inverse relationship between annual unemployment and annual inflation in a nation.

planned investment purchases   purchases of new or replacement residential and nonresidential structures,

producer durable equipment, and additions to inventories that business firms intentionally make during the year.

plant   a physical structure or location at which a firm's owners or employees conduct business.

point of diminishing returns   corresponds to the level of use of a variable input at which its marginal product begins to decline.

policy rule   a preannounced government rule that informs the public of future economic stabilization policies.

political equilibrium   an agreement on the quantity of a public good to be supplied through government, given the rule for making the public choice and given the taxes per unit of the public good for each voter.

pollution   waste in the air, in water, or on land that reduces the value of those resources in alternative uses.

pollution right   a government-issued certificate allowing a firm to emit a specified quantity of polluting wastes.

positive analysis   a way to look at the economy that seeks to forecast the impact of changes in economic policies or conditions on observable items such as production, sales, prices, and personal incomes, then tries to determine who gains and who loses as a result of the changes.

positive (direct) relationship   the connection between variables that is depicted by an upward-sloping curve on a set of axes; indicates that variable Y increases whenever variable X increases.

positive externality   a benefit, not reflected in a price, that is associated with the use of resources. Also called *external benefit*.

potential real GDP   the level of real GDP that would prevail if the economy achieves the natural rate of unemployment over a period of one year.

poverty income threshold   the income level below which a person or family is classified as being poor.

preferences   individual likes and dislikes.

price ceiling   a maximum price that can legally be charged for a good or service.

price discrimination   the practice of selling a certain product of given quality and cost per unit at different prices to different buyers.

price elasticity of demand   a number representing the percentage change in quantity demanded of a good resulting from each 1 percent change in the price of the good.

price elasticity of supply   a number that indicates the percentage change in quantity supplied resulting from each 1 percent change in the price of a good, other things being equal.

price floor   a minimum price established by law.

price index   a number used to measure the price level. The value of the index is set at 100 in the base year or period.

price leader   one dominant firm in an industry that sets its price to maximize its own profits, after which other firms follow its lead by setting exactly the same price.

price level   an indicator of how high or low prices are in a given year compared to prices in a certain base period.

price system   a mechanism by which resource use in a market economy is guided by prices.

price war   a bout of continual price cutting by rival firms in a market: one of many possible consequences of oligopolistic rivalry.

prime rate   the interest rate a bank charges its most creditworthy customers for short-term loans of less than one year.

private goods   goods whose benefits are rival in consumption and for which exclusion of those who refuse to pay is relatively easy.

product efficiency   the condition attained when the maximum possible output of any one good is produced given the output of other goods.

product group   represents several closely related, but not identical, items that serve the same general purpose for consumers.

production the process of using the services of labor and capital together with other inputs (such as land, materials, and fuels) to make goods and services available.

production function describes the relationship between any combination of input services and the maximum attainable output from that combination.

production possibilities curve a curve that shows feasible combinations of two goods (or broad classes of goods) that can be produced with available resources and current technology.

productivity a measure of output per unit of input.

profit the difference between the revenue a firm takes in over any given period and the costs incurred in operating the firm over the same period.

progressive tax a tax for which the fraction of income used to pay it increases as income increases.

proportional tax a tax for which the percentage of income paid in taxes is the same no matter what the taxpayer's income.

public choices choices made by voting.

public goods goods that are consumed equally by everyone, whether they pay or not.

purchasing power of a dollar a measure of how much a dollar can buy.

purchasing power parity a principle stating that the exchange rate between any two currencies tends to adjust to reflect changes in the price levels in the two nations.

pure inflation a condition that occurs when the prices of all goods rise by the same percentage over the year.

pure monopoly a condition that occurs when there is a single seller of a product that has no close substitutes.

pure monopsony a situation that exists when a single firm buys the entire market supply of an input that has few, if any, alternative employment opportunities.

pure public good a good that provides benefits to all members of a community as soon as it is made available to any one person.

q

quantity demanded the amount of an item that buyers are willing and able to purchase over a period at a certain price, given all other influences on their decision to buy.

quantity supplied the quantity of a good sellers are willing and able to make available in the market over a given period at a certain price, other things being equal.

r

rational behavior ways of acting that seek to gain by undertaking actions for which the extra benefit exceeds the associated extra cost.

rational expectations the use by individuals of all available information, including any relevant economic models, in their forecasts of economic variables.

real exchange rate the sacrifice of goods and services that buyers must make when they use their own nation's currency to purchase a unit of the currency of another nation.

real GDP a measure of the value of a nation's final products obtained by using market prices prevailing for products during a certain base or reference year.

real income the purchasing power of nominal income.

real interest rate the actual annual percentage change in the purchasing power of interest income earned on a sum of money that is loaned out.

real marginal return to investment an estimate of the percentage of each dollar invested that will be returned to a firm as additional revenue per year (adjusted for the effects of changes in the price level).

real per capita output a measure of output per person in a nation; calculated by dividing real GDP by population.

real terms of trade the actual market

exchange rate of one good for another in international trade.

real wages nominal wages deflated to adjust for changes in the purchasing power of a dollar since a certain base period.

recession exists when the decline in real GDP measured at an annual rate occurs for two consecutive three-month reporting periods.

recessionary GDP gap the difference between the equilibrium level of real GDP and potential real GDP when the economy is operating at less than full employment.

recovery the term used to describe an expansion in economic activity after a trough if the expansion follows a period of contraction severe enough to be classified as a recession.

regional Federal Reserve banks banks that perform central banking functions for banks within each of 12 Federal Reserve districts.

regressive tax a tax for which the fraction of income used to pay it decreases as income increases.

renewable resource a natural resource that can be restocked in time, such as fish, timber, and wildlife.

rent seeking the process by which people compete to obtain government favors that increase the economic rents they can earn.

required reserve ratio the minimum percentage of deposits that a bank must hold in reserves to comply with regulatory requirements.

required reserves the dollar value of currency and deposits in Federal Reserve banks that a bank must hold to meet current regulations.

reserve multiplier the maximum amount of new money stock that can be created from each dollar increase in the excess reserves available to the banking system.

reserves the balances that a modern U.S. bank keeps on deposit with the Federal Reserve bank in its district or as currency in its vault.

retained earnings the portion of corporate profits not paid out as dividends.

Ricardian equivalence a situation that prevails when an increase in government borrowing to finance a deficit causes a sufficient increase in private saving to keep the real interest rate fixed.

risk a measure of the variation between actual outcomes and expected outcomes.

risk averse a term that describes an investor who, given equal expected returns, chooses an investment with lower risk.

rule of reason the principle holding that acts beyond normal business practice unduly restraining competition for the purpose of excluding rivals can be used to infer intent to monopolize an industry.

S

saving the amount of income not consumed in a given year.

savings and loan associations depository institutions that acquire funds chiefly by attracting savings deposits and have in the past specialized in making mortgage loans.

scarcity the imbalance between our desires and the means of satisfying those desires.

screening a process in which an employer limits the number of applicants for a job to those the employer believes are most likely to succeed in the job.

secondary reserves government securities held by banks.

selling costs all costs incurred by a firm to influence the sales of its product.

shirking behavior by workers that prevents a firm from achieving the maximum possible marginal product of labor over a given period.

shortage the situation that exists in a market when the quantity demanded of a good exceeds the quantity supplied over a given period.

short run a period of production during which some inputs cannot be varied.

short-run supply curve the portion of

a competitive firm's marginal cost curve above the minimum point of its average variable cost curve.

shutdown point the point a firm reaches when price has fallen to a level below that which just allows the firm to cover its minimum possible average variable cost.

signals indicators displayed by job applicants and used by prospective employers to predict the future satisfaction and productivity of an applicant.

simple majority rule a means of enacting a proposal if it is approved by one more than half the voters casting ballots in an election.

single-product firm a firm that produces only one type of item for sale.

slope the measurement of the rate at which the Y variable, on the vertical axis, rises or falls along a curve as the X variable, on the horizontal axis, increases.

social cost of monopoly a measure of the loss in potential net benefits that results from monopoly control of price and supply.

socialism an economic system usually associated with government ownership of productive resources and with central planning to determine prices and resource use.

social regulation the use of government power to intervene in markets to reduce the risk of accidents and disease, and to achieve other social goals such as equality of opportunity.

sole proprietorship a business owned by one person.

special drawing right (SDR) a paper substitute for gold created by the International Monetary Fund and distributed to member nations for use as international reserves.

special-interest group an organization seeking to induce government to increase spending or take other actions that benefit particular people.

specialization the use of labor and other resources in a nation to produce the goods and services for which those resources are best adapted.

stabilization policies procedures un-

dertaken by governing authorities to maintain full employment and a reasonably stable price level.

staffing the process of recruiting and hiring workers to perform the various tasks required to produce goods and services.

stagflation term coined to describe an economy in which real GDP stagnates at a given level or actually declines from one period to the next while inflation ensues at relatively high rates.

structural unemployment unemployment resulting from permanent shifts in the pattern of demand for goods and services or changes in technology.

substitutes goods that serve a purpose similar to that of a given item.

substitution effect a change in consumption of a good only as a result of a change in its price relative to the prices of other goods.

substitution effect of a wage change the change in hours worked resulting only from a change in the opportunity cost of an hour of leisure.

supply a relationship between the price of an item and the quantity supplied.

supply and demand analysis a theory that explains how prices are established in markets through competition among buyers and sellers, and how those prices affect quantities traded.

supply curve a graph that shows how quantity supplied varies with the price of a good.

supply schedule a table that shows how the quantity supplied of a good is related to the price.

supply-side fiscal policies policies that seek to influence long-run growth in real GDP through government subsidies and tax reductions.

supply-side shock a sudden and unexpected change of the aggregate supply curve.

surplus the condition that exists in a market when the quantity supplied of a good exceeds the quantity demanded over a given period.

surplus value the difference between a worker's subsistence wage and the value of the worker's production over a period.

t

tangency   a point at which two curves just touch each other but do not intersect.

target price   a price level that guarantees sellers of agricultural commodities a minimum price per unit of output.

tariff   a tax on imported goods.

tax credit   a reduction in the tax liability of a person or corporation making certain purchases or engaging in certain activities.

taxes   compulsory payments associated with income, consumption, or wealth that individuals and corporations are required to make each year to governments.

tax expenditures   the losses in revenue to the federal government that result from tax breaks granted to individuals and corporations.

tax preference   an exemption, deduction, or exclusion from income or other taxable items in computing tax liability.

tax shifting   occurs when a tax levied on sellers of a good causes the market price of the good to increase.

technology   the knowledge of how to produce goods and services.

theory   a framework that helps us understand relationships between cause and effect; a simplification of actual relationships.

theory of games   a framework for analyzing the behavior of individuals or organizations with conflicting interests.

time deposits   interest-bearing accounts at commercial banks and thrift institutions for which the bank can legally request a 30-day notice before paying out the funds.

times series data   data that show the fluctuations in a variable over time.

total benefit   the maximum sum of money a consumer would give up to obtain a certain quantity of a good.

total cost   the sum of the value of *all* inputs used to produce goods over any given period; the sum of fixed costs and variable costs.

total expenditure   over any given period, the number of units of a product purchased over that period multiplied by the price of the product (PQ); equals sellers' total revenue.

total product curve   describes how output varies in the short run as more of any one input is used together with fixed amounts of other inputs under current technology.

total product of a variable input   the amount of output produced over any given period when that input is used along with other fixed inputs.

total revenue   the dollars earned by sellers of a product; the amount sold over a period multiplied by the price (PQ).

total saving in the United States   the sum of national saving and net foreign saving in the United States.

total utility   the total satisfaction enjoyed from consuming any given quantity of a good.

total value added in a nation   the difference between the market value of *all* products of business firms and the market value of all intermediate products. Equivalent of GDP.

transaction demand for money   the sum of money people want to hold per day as a convenience in paying their bills.

transfer payments   payments for which no good or service is currently received in return and that therefore do not represent expenditures for the purchase of final products.

u

unemployed person   a person over the age of 16 who is available for work

and has actively sought employment during the previous four weeks.

unemployment rate   the ratio of the number of people classified as unemployed to the total labor force.

unit elastic demand   prevails if the price elasticity of demand for a good is exactly equal to 1, when the minus sign is ignored.

unit elastic supply   prevails when elasticity of supply is just equal to 1.

utility   the satisfaction consumers receive from items they acquire, activities they engage in, or services they use.

v

value added   the extra worth that a business firm adds to intermediate products; measured by the difference between the market value of a firm's sales and the market value of intermediate products purchased.

variable   a quantity or dollar amount that can have more than one value.

variable costs   costs that change with output; the costs of variable inputs.

variable input   an input whose quantity can be changed.

vertical integration   a term used to describe a firm that owns plants used in various stages of its production.

vertical merger   a merger of a firm with its suppliers.

w

wage-price spiral   a situation that exists when higher product prices result in higher wages, which in turn increase prices still further through a decrease in aggregate supply.

wages   the prices paid for labor services.

welfare programs   government programs that assist the poor in the United States who are unable to work.

photo credits

about the author

Page v   Jim Mahaffer.

chapter 1

Page 14   © Anthony Edgeworth/The Stock Markct.
Page 18   Stock Montage.

chapter 2

Page 52   © James L. Shaffer.
Page 53   © Peter Breck/The Stock Market.

chapter 3

Page 60   Stock Montage.
Page 77   © Ed Bock/The Stock Market.

chapter 4

Page 99   © J. Messerschmidt/The Stock Market.
Page 101   © Jeff Greenberg/Photo Researchers, Inc.

chapter 5

Page 120   © Simon Nathan/The Stock Market.
Page 123   © Mike Greenlar/The Image Works.

chapter 6

Page 150   © Michael Siluk.

chapter 8

Page 192   © Lauren Goodsmith/The Image Works.

chapter 9

Page 219   © J. Pickerell/The Image Works.

chapter 10

Page 236   © Stephen Kresge.

chapter 11

Page 276   © Zefa-Streichan/The Stock Market.

chapter 12

Page 283   © Gerald Zanetti/The Stock Market.

chapter 13

Page 307   Ramsey and Muspratt Archives.
Page 324   © James L. Shaffer.

chapter 14

Page 341   UPI/Bettmann.
Page 345   © R. Stott/The Image Works.

chapter 15

Page 359   © John Gillmoure/The Stock Market.
Page 363   © Bob Daemmerich/The Image Works.

chapter 16

Page 378   Reuters/Bettmann.
Page 383   Michael Siluk.

chapter 17

Page 393   © James L. Shaffer.
Page 398   Reuters/Bettmann.

chapter 18

Page 416   © Michael A. Keller/The Stock Market.

chapter 20

Page 447   Reuters/Bettmann.

chapter 22

Page 477   Courtesy of Gary Becker.
Page 488   © Farrcll Grchan/Photo Researchers, Inc.

chapter 23

Page 499   © Tony Savino/The Image Works.
Page 501   © Bruce Brander/Photo Researchers, Inc.

chapter 24

Page 538   © Palmer/Kane/The Stock Market.
Page 540   © Anthony Edgeworth/The Stock Market.

chapter 25

Page 561   UPI/Bettmann.

chapter 26

Page 581   © Patti McConville/The Image Bank.

chapter 27

Page 606   © Palmer/Kane/The Stock Market.

chapter 28

Page 614   Stock Montage.

chapter 29

Page 642   © Eunice Harris/Photo Researchers, Inc.

chapter 30

Page 660   The Bettmann Archive.
Page 669   © Mark E. Gibson/The Stock Market.

chapter 31

Page 700   © George Disario/The Stock Market.

chapter 32

Page 722   © Andy Levin/Photo Researchers, Inc.
Page 724   © James L. Shaffer.

chapter 33

Page 743   © Paul Barton/The Stock Market.

chapter 34

Page 764   UPI/Bettmann.
Page 769   Reuters/Bettmann.

chapter 35

Page 786   © James L. Shaffer.
Page 794   Wide World Photos, Inc.

chapter 36

Page 805   Reuters/Bettmann.
Page 816   AP/Wide World Photos, Inc.

chapter 37

Page 830   © Patricia Evans.

chapter 38

Page 860   © Richard R. Hansen/Photo Researchers, Inc.
Page 864   Stock Montage.
Page 871   Stock Montage.
Page 872   © David Grossman/Photo Researchers, Inc.

chapter 39

Page 887   Reuters/Bettmann.

index

a

Absolute advantage, 461
Accelerationist hypothesis, 447–448
Adaptive expectations, 826
Aggregate demand, 203–208
  changes in, 205
  changes in exchange rates and, 239
  derivation of, 288–289
  influences on, 205
  interest rates and, 366–368
Aggregate demand curve, 203–208
  derivation of, 288–289
Aggregate expenditure, 142
Aggregate household debt, 250
Aggregate household wealth, 249
Aggregate purchases, 264–265, 269,
  292–296
  algebraic analysis of, 297–298
  macroeconomic equilibrium and,
  269–275
Aggregate quantity demanded, 203
Aggregate quantity supplied, 208
Aggregate real income, 142
Aggregate supply, 208–214
  changes in, 211–214
  changes in exchange rates and, 239
Aggregate supply curve, 208–214
  long-run, 228–229
  segments of, 21
Aggregates, 131
Agricultural price supports, 97–98
Allen, William R., 19n
Anderson, William, 530n
Anticipated inflation, 195
Archibald, Robert, 530n
Arrow, Kenneth J., 154
Aschauer, David Alan, 141n
ATS accounts, 305
Automatic stabilizers, 397–399
Autonomous consumption, 251
Autonomous purchases, 277
Axes, plotting points on, 26–27
  set of, 26

b

Balance of international trade, fiscal
  policy and, 401
Balance of payments, 508–512
  balance on current account of, 511
  capital account of, 511
  current account, 509–511

Balance of trade, 509
  deficit, 591
Balanced Budget and Emergency Deficit
  Control Act of 1985, 415
Bank deposits, international transfer of,
  494–495
Bar graph, 30–31
Barro, Robert J., 170n, 430
Barter, 106
Behavioral assumption, 19–20
Beige book, 361
Bergson, Abram, 101
Berliner, Diane T., 15n
Black Market, 95
"Black Monday," 80
Blue Book, 361
Bluestone, Barry, 173n
Board of Governors of the Federal
  Reserve System, 344
Bonds, 303
Bretton Woods System, 509
Brock, James W., 115n, 197n
Bronau, Reuben, 138n
Brooke, James, 115n
Brown, Charles, 111n, 96n
Budget deficit, 389
  exchange rates and, 420–421
  finance of, 417–418
  monetization of, 417–418
Budget surplus, 389, 431–433
Budgeting, personal, 48–49
Bureau of economic analysis, and calcula-
  tion of GDP, 143
Business cycle, 161–162
  dating of, 164–165
Business saving, 528

c

Cannan, Edwin, 19n
Capital consumption allowances, 144
Capitalism, 104
  American, 105
Capitalists, 479–481
Carson, Carol, 139n
Centrally planned economy, 482
Ceteris paribus, 17
Change in aggregate demand, 205
  effects in the economy, 206–207
Change in aggregate supply, 211
  effect on the economy, 219–220
Changes in demand, 62–65

Changes in quantity demanded, 62
Changes in quantity supplied, 67–68
Changes in relative price, 62
Changes in supply, 68–70
  impact on market equilibrium, 74–76
Charges for environmental damage, 114
Cheap Labor Fallacy, 472
Checkable deposits, 304–305
Chimerine, Lawrence, 407n
China
  economic development in, 101
  economic reform in, 484–485
  Circular flow of income and expendi-
    ture, 106–107
  macroeconomic perspective on,
    149–154
Class conflict, 478–480
Classical model of macroeconomic
  equilibrium, 226–228
Classical School, 451–456
Clinton, President Bill, 409
Clintonomics, 409
Command economy, 482
  transition to free markets in, 482–483
Commercial banks, 304
Commercial paper, 349
Commodity money, 302
Communism, 99–100
  transition to free markets from,
    99–100, 101
Comparative advantage
  loss of, 468
  principle of, 52–53, 460–462
Compensation of employees, 143
Complements, 65
Concave curves, 29–30
Consumer Price Index (CPI), 184–185
  market basket for, 186
Consumer spending and contractions or
  recessions, 272–276
Consumption
  autonomous, 251
  changes in debt and, 254–255
  changes in wealth and, 254–255
  determinants of, 249–251
  disposable income and, 249–253
  expectations and, 255
  function, 249
  induced, 250
Consumption function, 249–256
  graphing of, 252
Consumption possibility curve, 465

Continuous variable, 30–31
Contraction, 161
  Keynesian analyses of, 272–276
Contractionary monetary policy, 372
  use of to prevent overheating of the
    economy, 372–373
Convex curves, 29–30
Coordinates, 27
Correspondent bank, 474
Cost-push inflation, 220
Council of Economic Advisers, 388
CPI; see Consumer Price Index
Crandall, Robert W., 536n
Credit, 90
  crunch, 221
  market, 90–92
  unions, 304
Cross-elasticity of demand, 143, 145–146
Crowding out effect, 418–419
Currency appreciation, 501
Currency depreciation, 502
Current account deficit, 510
Curve, 27
Cyclical unemployment, 169, 172–175

d

Daniszewski, John, 485n
Das Kapital, 478
Debt, aggregate household, 250
Decisions, three basic economic, 10
Defense spending, 123
Deflation, 184
Demand, 59–65
  aggregate, 203
  changes in, 62–65
  curve, 61
  elastic, 518
  inelastic, 518
  law of, 60
  for money, 308–312
  price elasticity of, 517–529
  schedule, 60
Demand curve
  for money, 310–311
Demand deposits, 315
Demand for money, 308–309
  changes in, 310–311
  and interest rates, 310
Demand-pull inflation, 218
Denison, Edward F., 177n, 179n
Depreciation, 140
Descriptive graph, 33
Direct relationship, 27
Discount loans, 349
Discount policy, 349
Discount rate, 347
Discouraged worker, 168
Discrete variable, 30
Disinflation, 441
Disposable income, 148

Division of labor, 46
Dollar, price of, 77–79
Double coincidence of wants, 106
Drunken driving, 13
Du Mouchel, William, 13n

e

Economic development, 478–487
  ideas of classical economists on, 478
  ideas of Karl Marx on, 478–479
Economic growth, 46–51, 175–180
  costs and benefits of, 179
  expanding production possibilities
    and, 47
  sources of, 175–180
Economic issues for the 21st century, 2–5
Economic policies, gains and losses from,
    13–14
Economic resources, 37
  rivalry, 104
  system, 478
Economics defined, 9
Economy
  defined, 9
  global, 1–2
  government and, 118–120
  overheated, 235–238
  underground, 138–143
Edison, Thomas, 105
Eisner, Robert, 432
Elasticity
  cross, 529, 531–532
  of demand, 517–532
  empirical estimates of, 530–531
  income, 529–530
  of supply, 532–536
Electronic Bulletin Board of U.S. Dept.
    of Commerce, 157
Elliott, Kimberly Ann, 15n
Employment and Earnings, 157
Entitlement programs, 398
Entrepreneurs, 104–105
Entrepreneurship, 37
Equation of exchange, 375–377
Equilibrium, 70
  consumer, 161
  macroeconomic, 216–224
  in a market, 70–72
Eurodollars, 316
Exchange, mutual gains from, 104
Exchange rates, 70, 104–106
  impact of changes in aggregate
    demand, 239
  impact of changes in aggregate supply,
    239
  macroeconomic equilibrium and,
    233–241
Expansion, 162
Expansionary monetary policy, 367
  use of, 363–370

Expectations
  adaptive, 442
  consumption and, 255
  formation of, 442–443
  rational, 442
Exports
  macroeconomic equilibrium and, 222
  United States, 121, 460
  U.S. economy and, 155–157
External debt, 424
Externalities
  defined, 113
  negative, 113
  positive, 113
  resource use and, 113–117

f

Federal Advisory Council, 345
Federal budget, 389
Federal budget deficit, 415–418
  contingent claims and, 428
  effect of savings and loan bailout on,
    423
  inflation and, 428
  influences on, 427
  measurement of, 426–429
  Social Security trust fund and, 430
Federal Open Market Committee
    (FOMC), 345–346, 361
Federal Reserve Act of 1913, 344
Federal reserve notes, 302–303
Federal Reserve System, 728–731
  international operations of, 358–359
  organization of, 344–345
Feldstein, Martin, 407n, 423n
Fiat money, 302
Final products, 131
Fiscal policy, 365, 389
  balance of international trade and,
    401–402
  Clinton's administration, 409
  contractionary, 391, 395–397
  effects on the price level, 395–397
  expansionary, 370–374
  gauging the impact of, 399–401
  implementation of, 396–397
  supply-side, 403–410
  use of, 389–397
Fiscal year, 369
Follain, James R., 535n
Foreign exchange, 496
Foreign exchange markets, 77–79, 494,
    496–502
  equilibrium in, 497–498
Foreign exchange rate, 495
  determinants of, 497–501
  nominal, 504
  real, 504–505
Foreign saving in United States, 511
Free good, 84

Free markets, 104
   transition to in former communist
      nations, 99–100, 101
Freedom of enterprise, 104
Frictional unemployment, 168
Friedman, Milton, 380, 450
Friend, Irwin, 405n
Full employment, 170
Functional relationship, 26–27

g

Gains from exchange, mutual, 104–105
GATT; *see* General Agreement on Trade
   and Tariffs
GDP deflator, 186–187
Gendreau, Brian, 518
General Agreement on Trade and Tariffs
   (GATT), 14, 477
Gillingham, Robert, 530n
Gilroy, Curtis, 111n, 96n
Global economy, U.S. industries and,
   488–489
Gold standard, 506
Goldsmith, Arthur, 88n
Government budget, 389
   and aggregate demand, 389–390
Government budget deficit, 155
Government purchases, 140–141, 261–262
   macroeconomic equilibrium and,
      283–284
Gramm-Rudman-Hollings Act, 415
Graphs
   as an aid to understanding economics,
      23
   bar, 30–31
   descriptive, 33
Gravelle, Jane, 55
Great Depression of the 1930s, 163–164
   causes of, 232–233
   monetary policy during, 373
Green Book, (Federal Reserve), 361
Greenspan, Alan, 349
Gresham, Thomas, 303
Gresham's Law, 303
Griffin, J. M., 530n
Gross domestic product, 131–145
   calculation of, 132, 135–136
   expenditure components of, 139–142
   income side of, 142–144
   as a measure of national well-being,
      138–139
   nominal, 134
   real, 134
Gross national product, 145–146
Gross private domestic investment, 180
Grossman, Michael, 13n

h

Harrison, Bennett, 173n
Hasbrouck, Joel, 405n

Hausman, Jerry A., 404n
Hawrylyshyn, Oli, 138n
Health care,
   spending on, 76–77, 123
Health insurance, 76–77
Heien, Dale M., 532n, 533n
Hickok, Susan, 15n
High-employment deficit (or surplus),
   399–400
Highway deaths, 13
Hinds, Michael de Courcy, 94n
Holtz-Eakin, Douglas, 123
Hosek, William R., 406n
Houthakker, Hendrik, S., 530n
Hufbauer, Gary Clyde, 15n
Humphrey-Hawkins Act of 1978, 388
Humphrey-Hawkins Bill, 366
Hyman, David N., 533n
Hyperinflation, 196
   in Argentina, 197

i

Import quotas, 14–15, 474–475, 536–537
Imports
   United States, 121, 516
   U.S. economy and, 155–157
Income elasticity of demand, 529–533
Income statement for the economy,
   144–145
Income velocity of circulation of money,
   375
Indirect business taxes, 144
Induced consumption, 251
Inflation, 11, 184
   anticipated, 195
   effect on saving and investment,
      196–197
   history of, 187–188
   measurement of, 185
   pure, 185
   redistribution of income and wealth
      and, 192–193
Inflationary GDP gap, 218–219, 235, 289
Infrastructure, 141
Injection (of spending), 151
Inputs
   improvements in quality of, 47–48
Interest, 90
   net, 144
Interest rates
   aggregate demand and, 366–368
   money supply and, 356–357
   nominal, 133–134
   real, 193–194
   securities prices and, 354–359
Intermediate products, 132
Internal debt, 424
International monetary system, 506–508
International Monetary Fund, 510
International reserve currency, 316

International trade, 120–122
   basis for, 459–460
   gains from, 51–53
   less developed countries and, 486–487
   productivity and, 487
   transactions, 493–495
   United States, 460
   of United States with the world, 121
International Trade Commission (ITC), 14
Intersections, 32
Inventory change, unintended, 215–216
Inverse relationship, 27
Investment, 50–51
   economic growth and, 178–179
   gross private domestic, 140
   income and, 261
   net private domestic, 140
   planned purchases, 257
   real marginal return to, 257
   shifts in demand for, 258
   tax breaks that subsidize, 406

j

Japan
   import quotas on cars from, 15
   U.S. automobile production and, 1

k

Kamm, Thomas, 197n
Kan-ban system, 45
Keynes, John Maynard, 226, 258, 276,
   371, 450
Keynesian analysis
   of contractions or recessions, 272–276
   of macroeconomic equilibrium, 272
Keynesian model of macroeconomic
   equilibrium, 231–232
Keynesians, 451–456
Kniesner, Thomas J., 88n
Kohen, Andrew, 111n, 96n
Kristof, Frank S., 94n
Kuznets, Simon, 131

l

Labor, 37
   division of, 46
Labor contracts, wage flexibility and, 232
Labor force, 167
Labor markets, 86–89
   operation of in United States, 88
Labor theory of value, 478
Lakshmanan, G. R., 530n
Law of increasing costs, 40–42
   the environment and, 42–43
   the peace dividend and, 42–43
Law of supply, 66
Lawrence, Robert Z., 14n
Layoff, 169
LDCs; *see* Less developed countries

Leading economic indicators, 164–165
Leakage (of spending), 151
Lender of last resort, 349
Leonard, John, 469n
Less developed countries, 484–487
    and international trade, 487
Lilien, David M., 17n
Lindsay, Lawrence, 410–411
Litan, Robert E., 14n, 154
Lucas, Robert, 446

m

M1, 326
M2, 306–307
M3, 307
Macroeconomic equilibrium, 214–224
    aggregate purchases and, 269–272
    classical model of, 226–227
    conditions for, 271–272
    exchange rates and, 238–241
    exports and, 222
    in a growing economy, 242–245
    international trade and, 282–285
    Keynesian analysis of, 239–240
    Keynesian model of, 231–238
    money and, 370–374
    the multiplier and, 278–279
Macroeconomics, 11–12
Malthus, Thomas R., 226
Managed float, 508
Marginal analysis, 16–25
Marginal benefit, 20
Marginal cost, 20
Marginal propensity
    to consume, 253
    to import, 284
    to save, 254
Marginal respending rate, 231–282
Market, 59
    black, 95
    equilibrium, 70–72
    for foreign exchange, 77–79
    for medical services, 76–77
    self-equilibrating, 72
Market equilibrium, 70
    graphic depiction of, 71
    impact of changes in demand on, 72–74
    impact of changes in supply on, 74–76
Markets
    for credit, 90–92
    free, 104
    for labor, 86–89
    property rights and, 115
    stock, 80–81
Marshall, Alfred, 60
Marx, Karl, 478–480
    ideas of, 478–479
McCulloch, Rachel, 488
Measurement, units of, 30–31
Medicaid, 76

Medicare, 76
Meltzer, Allan H., 410–411
Mercantilism, 464–465
Mercantilist fallacy, 464–465
Meulendyke, Ann-Marie, 352n, 495
Meyer, Laurence H., 428n
Microeconomics, 11
Mill, John Stuart, 610
Minimum wages, 95–97
Mixed economy, 104, 118–120
    circular flow in, 119
Model, economic, 17–18
Monetarism, 379–381
Monetarists, 451–456
Monetary base, Fed's influence of,
    319–353
Monetary policy, 365
    contractionary, 367
    effectiveness of, 370–372
    expansionary, 367
    during great depression, 373
    international considerations in, 384–385
    real interest rates and, 306–365
    short-term impact of, 365–366
    since 1990, 383–384
    in United States, since 1942, 381–385
Money, 106
    as an asset, 309
    checkable deposits as a form of,
        364–365
    commodity, 302
    comprehensive definition of, 302
    demand for, 308–312
    fiat, 302
    functions of, 301–302
    macroeconomic equilibrium and,
        370–374
    measuring stock of, 305–308
Money demand curve, 310–311
Money stock
    changes in, 312–313
    federal reserve policies and, 349–357
Money supply, 356
Money supply curve, Fed's influence on,
    356–358
Monthly Labor Review, 157
Multiplier, 277–282
    formula for, 289
    for globally integrated U.S. economy,
        283–286
    the respending process for, 277–278
Muth, John, 446
Mutual gains from international trade, 460
Mutual savings banks, 364

n

National debt, 444–446
    burden of, 425–426
National income, 146–147

National Income and Product Accounts
    (NIPA), 131
National saving, 151–154
Natural rate of unemployment, 169–170
    influences on, 171
Natural resources, 37
Near monies, 306
Negative relationship, 27
Net exports, 141, 262–264
    aggregate purchases and, 284–285
Net federal debt, 422–426
    ownership of, 428
Net foreign investment and the U.S.
    economy, 157
Net foreign saving in United States,
    150, 157
Net interest, 144
Net national product, 146
Net private domestic investment, 140
Net taxes, 150
New classical economists, 451–456
New products, marketing of, 85–86
NIPA; see National Income and Product
    Accounts
Nominal exchange rate, 504
Nominal income, 189
    deflation of, 189–190
Nominal interest rate, 193
Nominal wages, 191–192
Noninflationary growth, 243–245
Nonprice rationing, 93–94
Nonscarce good, 84
Normal good, 529
Normative analysis, 12–13
North American Free Trade Agreement
    (NAFTA), 476–477
NOW accounts, 304

o

Ogawa, Eijii, 45
Open economy, 118–120
Open market operations, 347
    effect on bank balance sheets, 348–352
    execution of, 352
    use of by the Fed, 349–353
Opportunity cost, 9, 36, 48–49
Origin, 26
Overheated economy, 170, 235–238

p

Passell, Peter, 43
Peace dividend, 42–43
Peak (of business cycle), 161
Pechman, Joseph A., 506
Personal consumption expenditures, 139
Personal income, 147–148
Personal saving, 150
    in United States, 259
Phillips, A. W., 437

Phillips curve, 437–449
    long-run, 449
    in 1980s and 1990s, 441–452
    shifts of, 447
    supply-side shocks and, 439–440
    use of, 438–440
Planned investment, recessions and, 273–275
Poland
    economic reform in, 485
    transition from central planning to free markets, 100
Policy rule, 450–451
Positive analysis, 12–13
    an example of, 13
Positive relationship, 27
Potential real GDP, 170–172
Price ceilings, 92–93
Price elasticity of demand
    calculating for two points as a demand curve, 520–521
    categorizing, 518–519
    determinants of, 519–520
    in total revenue and expenditure, 525–529
    perfectly elastic, 523–524
    perfectly inelastic, 523–524
    use for market forecasts, 515–516
    using to forecast changes in total revenue and expenditure, 525–529
    variation along a demand curve, 522–523
Price elasticity of supply, 532–536
    categorizing, 533
    determinants of, 533–534
    perfectly inelastic and elastic, 534–535
Price floors, 95–98
Price index, 184
Price instability
    distortions and cost of, 189–194
    performance of economy and, 194–197
Price system, 104
    defects in, 112–117
    how it works, 108–112
Price theory, 11
Production, 37
    present versus future, 50–51
Production possibilities curve, 38–40
    cleaner environment and, 42–43
    law of increasing costs and, 40–42
    peace dividend and, 42–43
Productive efficiency, 43–46
    the division of labor and, 46
Productivity, international trade and, 467–470
Property rights, 115
Protectionism, 14–15, 470–476
    arguments in favor of, 471
    costs of, 15
    instruments of, 472–475

Purchasing power of the dollar, 191–192
Purchasing power parity, principle of, 502

q

Quantity demanded, 59
    changes in, 62
Quantity supplied, 59
    changes in, 62
Quantity theory of money, 371–381
    classical, 372–373

r

Rational behavior, 19–20
Rational expectations, 442–449
    aggregate supply curve and, 444
    macroeconomic equilibrium and, 448–449
Ratner, Sidney, 373n
Reagan, Ronald, 407
Reaganomics, 407
Real exchange rate, 504–506
    of the dollar, 505
Real GDP, fluctuations in, 161–167
Real income, calculation of, 189–190
Real interest rate, 183
    ex ante, 193
    ex post, 193
    monetary policy and, 366–368
Real per capita output, 434
    in LDCs, 484–486
Real terms of trade, 521
Real wages, 191–192
Recession, 161–163
    Keynesian analysis of, 272–276
    of 1990–1991, 221
Recessionary GDP gap, 217–218
Recovery, 162
Regional Federal Reserve banks, 344–345
Relative price, 62
Rent control, 92–95
    in New York City, 94
Rental income, 144
Required reserves, Fed's control of, 347–348
Reserve army of the unemployed, 479
Resolution Trust Corporation, 423
Resources
    economic, 37
    growth of, 47
    use of in United States, 123
Ricardian equivalence, 429–431
Ricardo, David, 487
Rosen, Harvey S., 390n
Russia
    effect of movement to free markets in, 101
    foreign investment in, 101
    transition to free markets in, 484

s

Saffer, Henry, 13n
Saving
    by business, 144
    income and, 259
Say, J. B., 226, 230
Say's Law, 230
Scarcity, 36
    defined, 9
    trade-offs and, 53
Securities prices, 354–358
Shortages
    in centrally planned economies, 100
    nonprice rationing of, 93–94
Sicilia, David B., 105
Silver coins, 363
Slope, 28–30
Smith, Adam, 18–19, 226
Smith, Fred, 105
Smoot-Hawley Tariff Act of 1930, 15, 232
Sobel, Robert, 105
Social Security Trust fund, the federal budget deficit and, 430
Socialism, 478
    versus capitalism, 478–479
Soltow, James H., 373n
Soviet Union, 482–483
Special drawing right (SDR), 508
Specialization, 104–106, 459
    trade gains and, 463–464
Spengler, Joseph J., 19n
Stabilization policy, 365
    debates about, 450–454
    issues and options in, 449–451
Stagflation, 237, 440
Standards of living in United States, 154–155
Statistical Abstract of the United States, 25
Statistics economic, reliability of, 247
Stigler, George J., 230n
Stock market, 80–81
Structural unemployment, 168
Subsidies, to higher education, 116
Subsistence wage, 479–481
Substitutes, 64
Supply, 66–70
    aggregate, 208
    changes in, 68–70
    curve, 67
    law of, 66
    schedule, 66
Supply and demand analysis, 59
    mastering the art of, 79
Supply curve, 67
Supply-side fiscal policies, 403–410
    effect on credit markets, 405
    effect on labor markets, 403–408
    impact of, 407
    incentive to save and, 404–405

Supply-side fiscal policies—*Cont.*
  investment and, 406
Supply-side shocks, 237–238
  Phillips Curve and, 439–440
Surplus, 70
Surplus value, 478
Survey of Current Business, 157
Sylla, Richard, 373n

t

Tangencies, 32–33
Tariffs, 14–15, 472–474
  Smoot-Hawley, 15
Taussig, F. W., 15n
Tax cuts, 392–393
Taylor, Lester D., 530n
Technology, 37
  changes in supply and, 68
  improvements in, 49–50
Terms of trade, 465–466
  real, 465
Theory, 16
Time deposits, 306
Time series data, 33
Tobin, James, 450
Total expenditure, 525
Total revenue, 525
Total saving in United States, 153
Toyota Motor Corporation, 45

Trade-offs, and scarcity, 53
Trading blocks, 476–477
Transaction costs, 115
Transfer payments, 141
Trough (of business cycle), 162
Tussig, Arlon R., 537n

u

Underground economy, 138–139
Unemployed person, 168
Unemployment, 167–175
  costs of, 173
  cyclical, 169, 172–175
  frictional, 168
  natural rate of, 169–170
  structural, 168
  variation with business cycle, 173
Unemployment insurance, 252–253
Unemployment rate, 11, 162–165
Union shop, 459–460
Units, of measurement, 30

v

Value added, 132–133
  computation of, 134
  tax on, 139
  total in a nation, 133
Value added tax (VAT), 139

Variables
  continuous, 30–31
  discrete, 30
  economic, 16–17
  extreme values of, 29–30
VAT; *see* Value added tax
Velocity, of circulation of money, 375
  variability of, 378–379

w

Wage flexibility, in United States, 282
Wage-price spiral, 235–236
Wampum, 302
Wealth, aggregate household, 249
Wessels, Walter, 96n
Whilakker, John, 126
Williams, Allan F., 13n
Williams, Rhonda, 125

y

Yield curve, 361–362
Young, Richard M., 407n

z

Zador, Paul, 13n
Zahn, Frank, 406n